NEW ART OF CUBA

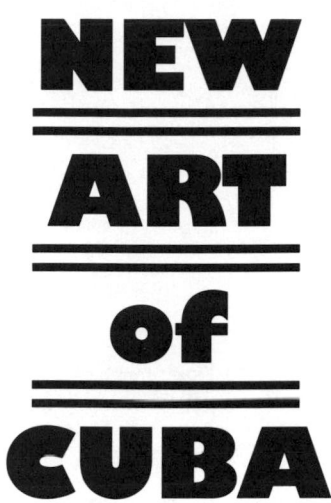

NEW ART of CUBA

LUIS CAMNITZER

UNIVERSITY OF TEXAS PRESS: AUSTIN

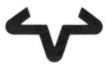

Requests for permission to reproduce material from this work should be sent to
Permissions, University of Texas Press, Box 7819, Austin, TX 78713-7819.

∞ The paper used in this publication meets the minimum requirements of
American National Standard for Informational Sciences—Permanence of Paper
for Printed Library Materials, ANSI Z39.48-1984.

Library of Congress Cataloging-in-Publication Data

Camnitzer, Luis, date
   New Art of Cuba / by Luis Camnitzer.— 1st ed.
       p.   cm.
   Includes bibliographical references and index.
   ISBN 0-292-71149-2
   ISBN 0-292-71161-1 (pbk.)
   1. Art, Cuban. 2. Art, Modern—20th century—Cuba. I. Title.
N6603.C26 1994
709'.7291'09048—dc20   92-43116

Design by Susan Gutnik

To Ana Mendieta

"Grandfather, what is power?"
"Power is to be able to act well in life
with what one knows and with what is at hand."
(Dialogue recorded by Orlando Fals Borda among the Indians
of the Mezquital Valley in Mexico)

"Arte o muerte, venceremos"
(Art or death, we shall overcome).
(Picket sign used by the Arte Calle group
in a performance in Havana, 1987)

CONTENTS

ILLUSTRATIONS **ix**

ACKNOWLEDGMENTS **xvii**

INTRODUCTION **xxi**

1 "VOLUMEN I" **1**

2 CUBAN INFLUENCES ON THE 1980S GENERATION **68**

3 ART WITHIN THE REVOLUTION **100**

4 ART EDUCATION IN CUBA **138**

5 THE GENERATIONS FOLLOWING "VOLUMEN I" **172**

6 THE INDIVIDUALS **201**

7 CUBAN ART AND POSTMODERNISM **298**

POSTSCRIPT **319**

SECOND POSTSCRIPT **325**

NOTES **329**

BIBLIOGRAPHY **367**

INDEX **387**

ILLUSTRATIONS

Anonymous, *Portrait of Che*   xxiii

Santería arrangement   xxiv

Hermanos Ameijeiras Hospital   xxvi

Opening of "Volumen I" exhibit, installation by Gustavo Pérez Monzón   2

Opening of "Volumen I" exhibit, installation by Leandro Soto   3

Opening of "Volumen I" exhibit, installation by José Manuel Fors   5

Opening of "Volumen I" exhibit, work of Juan Francisco Elso Padilla   6

Flavio Garciandía, *All You Need Is Love*   8

Tomás Sánchez, *Mella*   11

César Leal, *Pensar sin querer es soñar*   12

César Leal, *Retrato de familia*   13

Tomás Sánchez, *Laguna y mar*   13

Flavio Garciandía, *Catálogo de las malas formas*   19

Flavio Garciandía, *El lago de los cisnes*   20

Flavio Garciandía, *Pies de plomo*   21

Flavio Garciandía, *El síndrome de Marco Polo*   23

Flavio Garciandía, untitled installation, 1989   23

Rubén Torres Llorca, works at "Volumen I" exhibition   25

Rubén Torres Llorca, *El que nace para. . . . II*   26

Rubén Torres Llorca, *Te llevo bajo mi piel*   27

Rubén Torres Llorca, *La trampa*   28

Rubén Torres Llorca, *El rey que sabe . . .*   30

Leandro Soto finishing a piece   31

Leandro Soto, *Primero de enero*   32

Leandro Soto, *Kiko constructor*   33

Leandro Soto, *Tela Sagrada* (fragment)   34

Wifredo Lam, *El tercer mundo*   36

Manuel Mendive, *Che*   37

Manuel Mendive, performance at the Second Biennial of Havana   38

Santería arrangement   39

Palero arrangement   40

José Bedia, *Doce cuchillos*   42

José Bedia, untitled, 1982 (from the series "Crónicas americanas")   42

José Bedia, *Es el dueño del hierro*   43

José Bedia, *Sarabanda contra Siete Rayos*   43

José Bedia, *La comisión india . . .*   45

José Bedia, *¿Qué te han hecho Mama Kalunga?*   45

Ricardo Rodríguez Brey, page from *La estructura de los mitos*   47

Ricardo Rodríguez Brey, *La estructura de los mitos*   48

Ricardo Rodríguez Brey, *Un objeto inocente* (detail)   49

Juan Francisco Elso Padilla, untitled installation, 1981   51

Juan Francisco Elso Padilla, *Tierra, maíz, vida*   53

Juan Francisco Elso Padilla, *El monte*   54

Sacred Ahuehuete tree   55

Juan Francisco Elso Padilla, *Por América*   57

Juan Francisco Elso Padilla, *El rostro de Dios* (from *La transparencia de Dios*)   59

Rogelio López Marín (Gory), *Ayer*   61

Rogelio López Marín (Gory), *Es sólo agua en la lágrima de un extraño*   62

Rogelio López Marín (Gory), *Es sólo agua en la lágrima de un extraño*   63

Gustavo Pérez Monzón, untitled installation, 1981, in "Retrospectiva de artistas jóvenes"   65

Gustavo Pérez Monzón, work with children   65

Gustavo Pérez Monzón, *Tarot Cards*   66

Antonia Eiriz, *Mi compañera*   69

Santiago Armada (Chago), untitled drawing, 1963   70

Jesús de Armas, untitled silkscreen, 1989   71

Raúl Martínez, *26 de julio* 72

Raúl Martínez, *Martí y la estrella* 74

Raúl Martínez, untitled oil painting, ca. 1966 75

Anonymous, bust of Martí 75

Raúl Martínez, *Fenix* 77

Raúl Martínez, Mario García Joya (Mayito), and Antonia Eiriz, untitled installation, 1984, at the Venice Biennial 78

Mario García Joya (Mayito), *De nacionalidad a nación* 78

Pabellón Cuba (detail) 79

Light announcement 80

Cuban pavilion in the World's Fair of Montreal 80

Umberto Peña, *Buey desollado* 83

Umberto Peña, *Buey #8* 84

Umberto Peña, *Tú haces brrr con mi electricidad* 86

Umberto Peña, *Trapiz* 87

Umberto Peña, cover for *Revista de Casa de las Américas* 89

Anonymous, poster on the death of Ana Mendieta 92

Ana Mendieta, *Silueta Work in Mexico* 95

Ana Mendieta, *Anima* 96

Ana Mendieta, *Gunpowder Sculpture* 96

Ana Mendieta, *Escultura rupestre* 97

Víctor Manuel Garcia, *Gitana tropical* 102

Rafael Blanco, *Un novato en la otra vida* 103

Cover of *Revista de Avance* 104

Eduardo Abela, *El triunfo de la rumba* 105

Carlos Enríquez, *Nuevo ripalda* 106

Marcelo Pogolotti, *Paisaje cubano* 106

Roberto Diago, *Maternidad* 107

Raúl Martínez, *Lucía* 111

José Gómez Fresquet (Frémez), silkscreen from the series "Burgueses" 112

Guillermo Menéndez Madan, logotype for the literacy campaign 114

Exhibition of "Telarte VI" 115

Grupo Hexágono, Arte en la fábrica project 116

Eduardo Abela, *Guajiros* 134

Anonymous, *Martí Addressing the Tobacco Workers*   139
Constantino Arias, *Miss Universe*   140
Juan Bautista Vermay, *San Atanasio*   152
Wifredo Lam, *Eulalia Soliño*   154
Billboard for the "Salón de Mayo"   157
Performance by the Grupo de Teatro Escambray, ca. 1972   157
Cuadrodebate meeting   158
Cuadrodebate meeting   158
View of the Graduate Institute of Art (ISA)   160
Juana Borrero, *Pilluelos*   162
Grupo Hexágono, *Seis amigos visitan un paisaje*   174
Grupo Hexágono, *Arena y madera*   174
Arte Calle, performance, 1987   176
Billboard facing the U.S. Interests Office in Havana   176
Arte Calle, performance, 1987   180
Grupo Provisional, artist award, 1987   181
Arte Calle, mural painting (detail)   183
Grupo Puré, first exhibit, 1986   185
Ballester and Villazón, untitled acrylic painting, 1987   189
ABTV Team, "Che" project   189
Ponjuán and Rodríguez, *Samurai*   191
Nilo Castillo, *Picasso*   195
Arturo Cuenca, *Conocimiento*   203
Arturo Cuenca, *Conocimiento: objeto, análisis, síntesis*   204
Arturo Cuenca, *Estética de la moda* (detail)   205
Arturo Cuenca, untitled handpainted photograph, 1987–1988   206
Arturo Cuenca, *Ciencia e ideología*   207
José Franco, *Cobra y leopardos somos todos*   209
José Franco, *En el día natural*   210
José Franco, *Conversación 1910–1990*   210
Magdalena Campos, *Anticonceptivo*   212
Magdalena Campos, *La ofrenda de la propia sangre*   213
Magdalena Campos, *Todo es separado por el agua. . . .*   214
Magdalena Campos, *Hablando de árboles . . .*   214
Marta María Pérez Bravo, installation with shredded paper, 1983   216

Marta María Pérez Bravo, *Cascada*   216

Marta María Pérez Bravo, *No matar ni ver matar animales*   217

Marta María Pérez Bravo, *Prejuicios*   218

Amelia Peláez, *Naturaleza muerta con piña*   220

Antonio Eligio Fernández (Tonel), *Dos mojones*   223

Antonio Eligio Fernández (Tonel), *Cumbres del arte*   224

Antonio Eligio Fernández (Tonel), *El bloqueo*   225

Antonio Eligio Fernández (Tonel), *Marx (en sus cartas a Kugelmann)*   226

Tomás Esson, untitled tempera on cardboard, 1981–1982 (from the Portrait Series)   227

Tomás Esson, *Mi homenaje al Che*   228

Tomás Esson, *Vuelta de carnero*   229

Tomás Esson, *SPOULAKK*   230

Glexis Novoa, *Guamany*   232

Glexis Novoa, *Esta obra fue hecha en Cuba . . .*   233

Glexis Novoa, *Y de pronto resulta . . .*   234

Glexis Novoa, *Practical Stage*   235

Carlos Rodríguez Cárdenas, *Mi suerte está en el corazón*   237

Carlos Rodríguez Cárdenas, *Rectificar . . .*   238

Carlos Rodríguez Cárdenas, untitled watercolor, 1985   239

Carlos Rodríguez Cárdenas, *Filosofía popular* (detail)   240

Lázaro Saavedra, drawings from *Te estoy mirando*   242

Lázaro Saavedra, *Pintura rupestre que representa a un niño prodigio*   243

Lázaro Saavedra, *Caballero, no ven?*   243

Ciro Quintana, *Las maravillas del arte cubano* (fragment)   244

Ciro Quintana, *Made in Cuba* (detail)   246

Ciro Quintana, *Adiós a las armas*   247

Robaldo Rodríguez, untitled acrylic painting, 1988   248

Robaldo Rodríguez, untitled acrylic painting, 1988   249

Robaldo Rodríguez, portfolio of posters   250

ABTV Team, *Nosotros*   251

ABTV Team, *Homenaje a Hans Haacke* (the Yanes project)   253

Ponjuán and Rodríguez, untitled drawing, 1987   256

Ponjuán and Rodríguez, *No Smoking*   257

Ponjuán and Rodríguez, *Línea de fuego*   258

René Francisco Rodríguez, *Souvenir*   259

Eduardo Ponjuán, *Iluminación*   260

Alejandro Aguilera, *En el mar de América*   262

Alejandro Aguilera, *El tiempo histórico del símbolo* . . .   263

Alejandro Aguilera, *Mis zapatos de azulejos*   263

Alejandro Aguilera, *Treinta y tres flores para Camilo*   264

Gustavo Acosta, *Jovellanos* (from the series "Album Cuba, 1925")   265

Gustavo Acosta, *La capacidad de aguantar lo que caiga*   266

Gustavo Acosta, untitled acrylic, 1991   267

Humberto Castro, *La caída de Icaro*   268

Humberto Castro, *La caída de Icaro #2*   269

Humberto Castro, *Los lobos y el hombre*   269

Consuelo Castañeda, *La creación de la creación*   271

Consuelo Castañeda, untitled acrylic painting, 1984   272

Consuelo Castñeda, untitled acrylic painting, 1986   273

Segundo Planes, untitled drawing, 1986   274

Segundo Planes, untitled drawing and collage from the book *Jugando a ser loco*   275

Segundo Planes, untitled installation, 1988   276

Alexis Somoza, *El ilusionismo de la conciencia y su desorden*   278

Alexis Somoza, *Movimiento 26 de julio*   279

José Angel Toirac, untitled etching, 1987   280

José Angel Toirac and Tanya Angulo, labels for *Una cuadrícula, duplicado*   281

Dania del Sol, untitled installation, 1988   283

Dania del Sol, *Isomorfismo*   284

Dania del Sol, *Oposición naturaleza*   285

Ibrahim Miranda, untitled woodblock   286

Lázaro García, *Jesús y Magdalena*   287

Lázaro García, *Simbolismo abstracto*   288

Fernando Rodríguez/Fransisco de la Cal, *Che*   289

Nestor Arenas, *Cake (after Flavio Garciandía)*   290

Nestor Arenas, *La idea fija*   291

Luis Gómez, *El herrero, el artesano, el creador* (detail)   292

Luis Gómez, *Ya nada nos pertenece*   293

Alexis Leiva Machado (Kcho), *La peor de las trampas*   294

Eryk González Litvinov, setup for "Fosfenáutica"   295

Ana Albertina Delgado, *Nuevos oficios para Isabel, Lázara y Bertica*   296

Adriano Buergo, *Roto*   297

Adriano Buergo, *Roto se vende*   297

Jewish / *santería* jewelry   303

Ministry of Industry poster   304

Anonymous, fan in Havana home   306

José Angel Toirac, untitled pencil drawing on printed page, 1988   313

Constantino Arias, *Joyas y pieles*   315

Tania Bruguera, recreation of the work of Ana Mendieta   326

Angel Iñigo, sculpture at the Zoo, Guantanamo   356

Ramón Moya, *F.M.I.*   356

Eduardo Luis Rodríguez, house for a family doctor   363

Three balconies in the same building   364

ACKNOWLEDGMENTS

As stated in the Introduction, I consider this book the product of teamwork. Therefore, it is important for me to credit the people that contributed to this effort, and the first acknowledgment should be made to Sandra Levinson, director of the Center for Cuban Studies in New York City, who is the original culprit behind this enterprise. Sandra first approached me with the idea that I should write a book about the history of Cuban art, upon which I declared her insane and the idea was forgotten. After a trip to Cuba in 1987, I decided that, given the friendship I had with many of the Cuban artists of the 1980s, I could attempt something limited to that decade in a less amateurish manner than a full-blown history and without having to sacrifice my other interests and/or life. At least in regard to the latter part I was proven wrong, and this is the place where I should stereotypically—but meaningfully—thank my wife, Selby Hickey, and the children in my life: Miguel, Gabriel, Katie, and David. They made up for the gaps with extreme endurance and patience and with no apparent loss of love.

Sandra agreed to my proposal (basically insanity now had shifted over to me) and went over countless manuscripts and assisted me with advice, recollections, the Center's library, and padding my ego.

Since I had limited experience in writing, circumscribed to short essays and insulting university memos, Selby helped me move from a short-distance to a marathon runner by reprogramming my brain. In that sense she is as much to blame for this product as am I.

Rachel Weiss, director of Polarities, Inc., whose foundation sponsored the exhibit "The Nearest Edge of the World: Art in Cuba Now," was instrumental in translating my interpretation of the English language into a communication-specific tool. She not only holds the record number of readings of the manuscript, but she also had invaluable input based on insights gathered on her own trips to Cuba and her contact with the artists.

Shifra Goldman and Dore Ashton, both noted art historians with particular interest in Latin America, were my readers for the University of Texas Press and, as such, had important comments to make, which I tried to follow as closely as possible. Shifra, in particular, continued her support, poking her finger into as many weak points as she could spot, by means of her proverbial directness and tenacity.

Maricarmen Ramírez, curator of Latin American art at the Archer Huntington Gallery of the University of Texas at Austin volunteered to point out the pre-postmodernist distortions in my *Weltanschauung*. I tried to disguise them as well as I could.

All of this would have been meaningless if I had not had help in Cuba itself, and the more I advanced in the work the more friendliness and friendships became available as resources. Many of the names cited appear in the book, but I want here to acknowledge their help in matters not directly concerning their own work.

Gerardo Mosquera, the critic who has been involved most with the development of art in Cuba since the end of the 1970s (see the space he occupies in the bibliography) also is at the point of knowing the manuscript by heart. He is clearly the person most qualified to write this book, and I am still trying to puzzle together what conspiracy and whose purpose may it serve that I ended doing it instead of him. Gerardo, being a walking data bank, became my primary surrogate memory.

Flavio Garciandía, one of the most influential artists of the decade, had a similar role. He and Gerardo also were important in tying my feet to objectivity during those moments they saw me hovering excessively in the realms of utopia.

Marcia Leiseca, Beatriz Aulet, and Llilian Llanes were crucial with their advice, their interpretations, and their referrals. In the process they also cut me down to size.

Lucy Villegas, director of the Museo Nacional de Bellas Artes, opened the doors and cellars of her institution for me. Tonel, Rubén Torres Llorca, Tania Bruguera, Conchita Pedrosa Morgado, and Roberto Segre, all compulsive collectors of paper scraps, shared their treasures with unlimited generosity. Meanwhile, José Manuel Fors performed the miracle of unearthing negatives of unpublished photographs of the "Volumen I" exhibit, answering a casual wishful thought of mine. Another miracle was performed by José Veigas, who found the few existing photographs of the *Cuadrodebates*.

Unfortunately, there will be many names I will remember when it is too late, and I will feel awful about it. So far, I should randomly record Griselda Ramos, Rodolfo Gil Brotons, María Hayas (Marucha), José Franco, Pilar Fernández, and José Revellón in Cuba, and Magali Lara, Nina Menocal (both instrumental in gathering material located in Mexico), Hans Breder, Marifelis Pérez-Stable, Carolyn Etheridge, Mario Sagradini, Carlos Capelán, David Finkbeiner, César Paternosto, and Edward Hickey in the "free world." Future editions will fill in the absences. I also should take personal responsibility for all the translations (unless noted otherwise) from Spanish into English.

Luis Camnitzer
Great Neck, December 1991.

INTRODUCTION

The dedication of this book to Ana Mendieta means much more than paying dues to affection between friends. It was Ana who, on my first trip to Cuba in 1981, directed me to the artists who belong to the beginning of what I once called the Cuban Renaissance without worrying about the cultural dependency implied by the term. It is the subsequent friendship with many of these artists that in the final instance produced this book, not only because of the motivation but also because of their assistance in gathering data and providing ideas. Because of this, I consider this book the product of a team effort.

I was raised in Uruguay, made art and taught there, and made art and taught in the United States. The value of that repetition of activities in different parts of the map is that it helps identify and clarify issues of cultural dependence that are often invisible to those confined to only one place. It took me several years of being away, for example, to develop a sense of admiration for a bronze sculpture in Montevideo too closely inspired by the Venus de Milo, implying to the viewer that amputation is a sign of classic beauty. I also remember fondly a man who, in my childhood, would tell endlessly detailed stories about faraway places although, as I found out later, he had never left town. Only distance helped me see and feel the distortions and alienation operating on the periphery, which become part of culture and which condition one's thoughts and actions. Art in Cuba became interesting to me for the degrees of success and failure in addressing these distortions and alienation.

Artists in Cuba focus their work on their own country more than other Latin American artists, and in order to fully understand Cuban art, one must know the Cuban public and the Cuban sociocultural conditions to which the art is primarily addressed. But since Cuban artists are knowledgeable in the art game as it is played internationally, and since they play that game well, it is tempting to judge Cuban art by international standards. Doing this, one would neglect its role in national culture building, an issue not always visible but a factor in the minds of most of the artists discussed. It is because of this role in culture building, rather than for particular formal solutions, that Cuban art is interesting for Latin America as a model or as an alternative. This was a second important reason for why it caught my interest.

The Cuban process at large, since the Revolution, awoke strong expectations and a sense of curiosity at the same time that it strongly influenced the thoughts of my generation. This was true for the committed Left as much as for those like me who strongly distrusted any governmental structure. My generation had changed its views when, in 1954, the United States bombed Guatemala, overthrew its president, Jacobo Arbenz, and changed the destiny of that country. Coincidentally, this series of actions radicalized Che Guevara, who was in Guatemala at the time. We all felt the absurdity of the nation-state concept installed in Latin America by foreign imposition, and we longed for a way to erase our borderlines, to become a big country. When Latin America became one big police state about twenty years later, the dream nearly came true, though in a fashion very different from our original idea. Our conception had not been wrong, but it was suffused with the Esperanto syndrome. On its superficial merits, it seemed wonderful to have a common language, a common currency, a common government. We just had not counted on the possibility that the language some day might be English, the currency the dollar, and the government housed in the White House.

Both Simón Bolívar and José Martí had warned about this danger. Martí (1853–1895), Cuba's national hero, was particularly close to Uruguay since he had been its consul to the United States.[1] As Latin America deteriorated, Cuba became, more and more, a symbol of independence. The largest procession of cars in Uruguayan history until then was the one accompanying the Cuban ambassador to the airport in the early 1960s, when he had to leave Uruguay because of the OAS-forced break of diplomatic relations.

Travel to Cuba became extremely difficult, and it took me a long time to make my first visit. From Uruguay for many years it meant awkward detours via Czechoslovakia and dangerous harassment upon return. Later, residing in the United States, I felt even more intimidated, at least until the relative liberalization introduced by the Carter administration. By then, with military dictatorship widespread, a context was provided in which Cuba acquired still another distance and dimension. I felt envy.

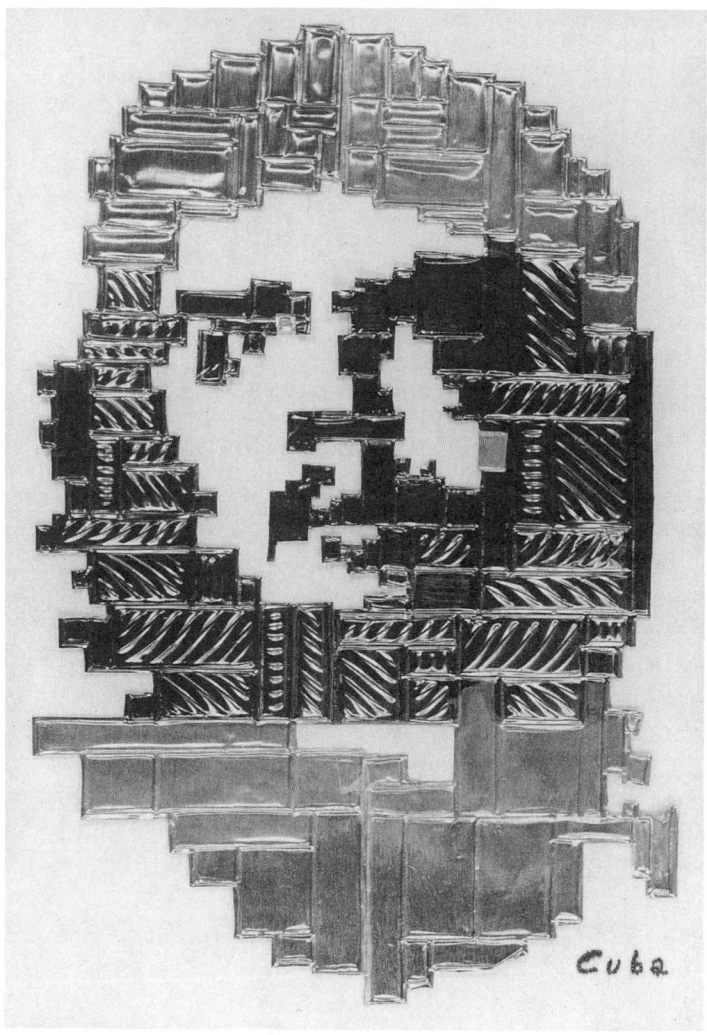

Anonymous, Portrait of Che, *ca. 1989, souvenir. Photo by Luis Camnitzer.*

I was both tempted and reluctant to enjoy the consequences of some-body else's revolution at a time when my own country was in an unre-solvable mess.

When I finally did go to Cuba, given this history where myth and misinformation had merged, I had developed my own brand of expec-tation and skepticism. I went to the "First Meeting of Latin American Intellectuals" in 1981. What I remember most about that trip is kitsch, recycling, and the new art generation.

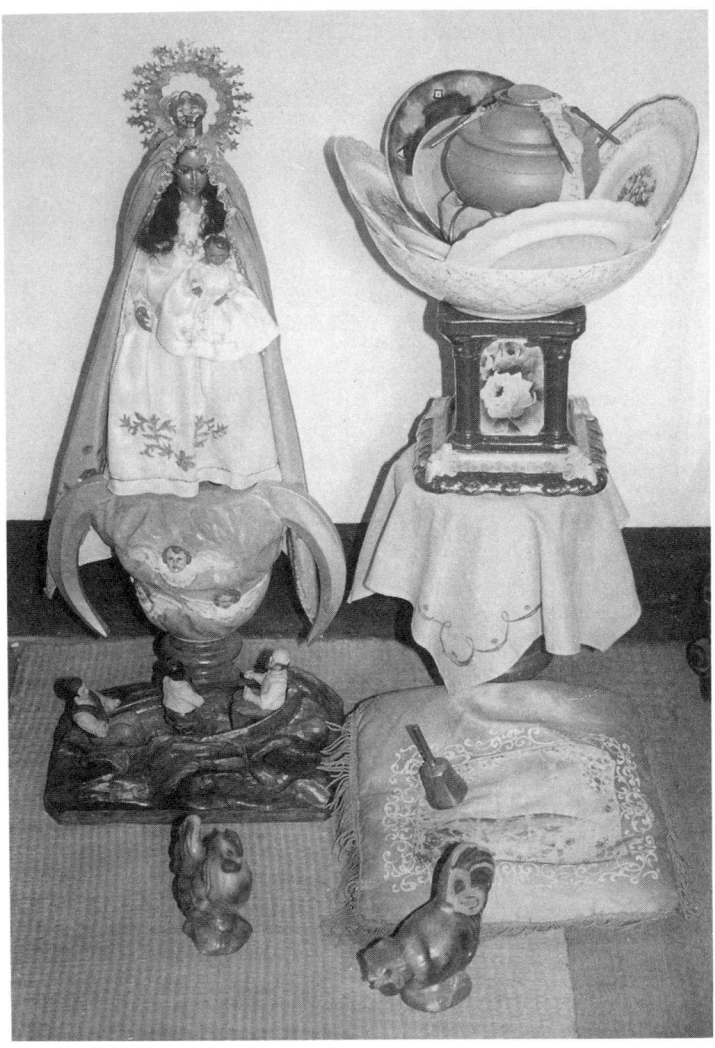

Santería *arrangement, Museo de Guanabacoa. Photo by Luis Camnitzer,*
1986.

Kitsch was omnipresent, partially because I was staying in the Hotel
Riviera. The hotel is a Meyer Lansky–North American Mafia monument
built in 1957, continually restored by the Cubans to maintain its original
look. As a synthesizing symbol, the hotel offers a staircase in the lobby
that stops halfway toward the ceiling with no apparent function beyond
being itself. It is still used today by just-married couples to pose for their
wedding pictures.

But kitsch is not only "made in the U.S.A."—it has also become an intrinsic part of Cuban culture as a byproduct of colonization, the "ersatz" both popularly accepted and generated as one of the responses to imposed culture. Despite the concern of the government for what some see as a debasement of culture, there has been no organized drive to eliminate kitsch. It has been syncretized in artifacts used in the Afro-Cuban rituals of *Santería*, appropriated and revitalized in some folk art and anonymous contributions, or used as an inspiration for high-culture products. It is also an occasional and accidental byproduct of recycling.

Recycling was present in everything from food to buildings. With admirable ingenuity, food remnants would be presented again in meals to follow rather than going to waste. At the other extreme, buildings in a pompous style inherited from the Batista regime were redesigned internally to serve more useful purposes. A building partially constructed under Batista to house the National Bank was finished under Castro as the biggest hospital in Havana, the "Hermanos Ameijeiras." This policy, while making economical sense, sacrifices the development of an official architectural language. New government buildings are variations of the international style nicely spiced with tropical vegetation and, mostly, respectful of the human scale. Fascist wedding-cake style buildings constructed in honor of Batista's glory are now used for socially useful functions such as hospitals. The symbolic communication of architecture becomes muddled, particularly for those future generations with no memory to be used as a corrective tool. The problem does not exist because of a lack of awareness but because of a scarcity of funds. It creates a critical situation that has been discussed by several Cuban architects.[2]

Between food and buildings I should mention the contributions of the ANIR (Asociación Nacional de Innovadores y Racionalizadores, or the National Association of Innovators and Rationalizers), a group designed to find alternative solutions for those technological products no longer available because of the U.S. blockade. When an institution needed hinges to build silkscreen drying racks, this group designed them by bending pieces of scrap aluminum that turn around nails. The whole printing industry was saved by ANIR, which was able to keep the presses functional by recreating missing and broken pieces. The paper industry was also reconstructed following this drive for a degree of self-sufficiency, and a process for paper-making was developed using an 80 percent bagasse (cane remnants from the sugar production) content.[3]

The new art generation was so impressive primarily because it was just that, a generation, formed by people educated after the Revolution, with no prerevolutionary memories.[4] Its members met regularly to discuss art-making problems in Cuba and their own work. A critic, Gerardo

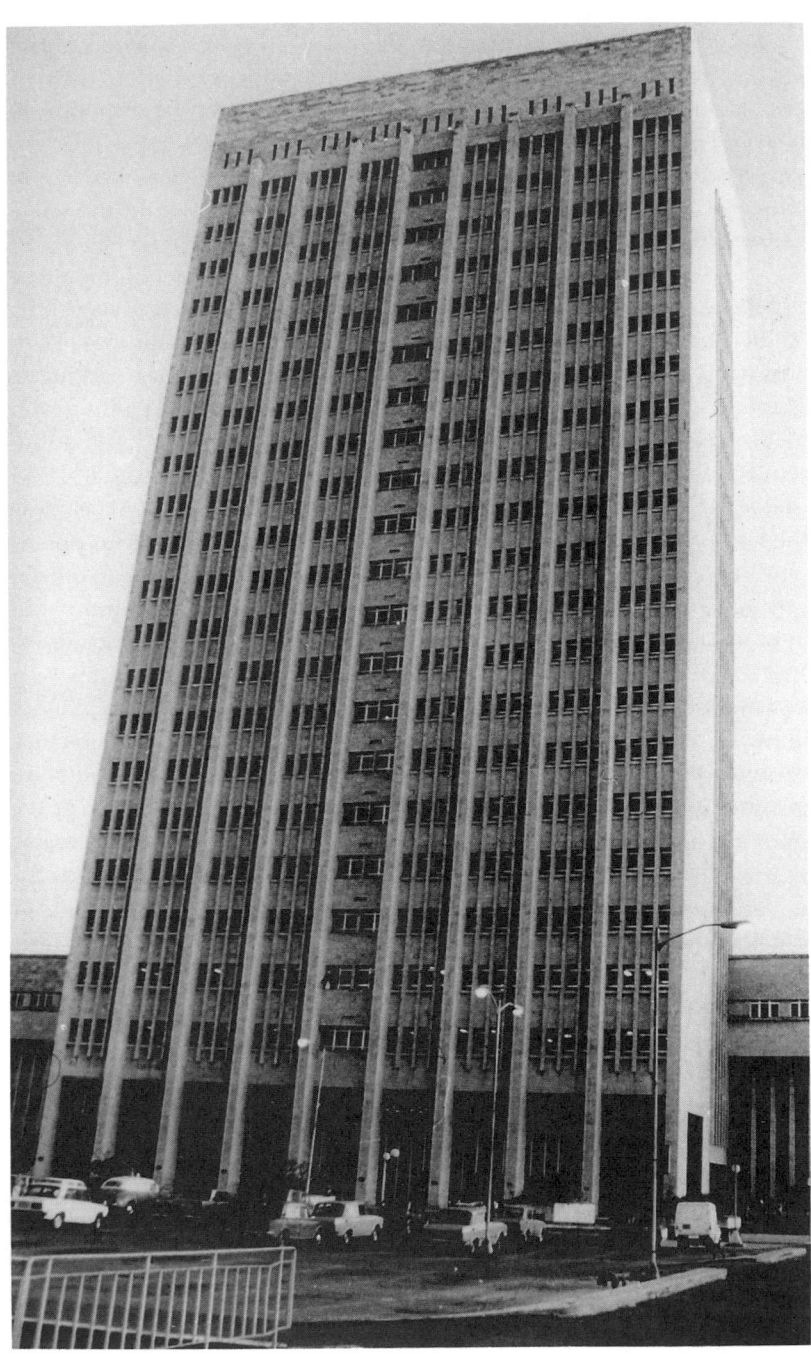

Hermanos Ameijeiras Hospital, Havana. Photo by Luis Camnitzer, 1991.

Mosquera, joined and provided them with a theoretical framework for their art. They were all under thirty, some still students, and well informed about both socialist and capitalist art and aesthetics. While sharing common concerns, they were developing distinct individual languages and showed a refreshing openness in their approaches. My ties with this group were strengthened in subsequent trips and later when three of the artists came to my college for a four-month artist-in-residence program.[5]

Going to Cuba under official auspices is like traveling through a smile. Generosity seems unlimited and friendship easy, profound, and lasting. As a result, first impressions are somewhat schematic, blending one's own prejudices with a conveyed aura of perfection. It took several trips for me to understand that Cuba is not a monolith. There is a constant interplay of alternative and sometimes opposing views on many issues. At least during the decade discussed here, what I often interpreted as representing a conservative art approach to some topics did not come from above in the form of governmental instructions but from the sides, from peer pressure. In the arts, there was the odd feeling that if any verticality in the power structure existed, it mostly operated from the bottom up. The complexity of the tendencies in the bottom level led to many contradictory results. The higher levels of the art bureaucracy during the 1980s, however enlightened and progressive in its intentions (meaning that I share most of them), often had to find middle grounds to accommodate these pluralistic tendencies.

The Cuban *proceso* is not neat. It is an "untidy revolution," where the ideological comb has not untangled all strands and where many issues seem to be overlooked or purposely left aside. Much of the power and seductiveness of the Cuban Revolution is based on this untidiness. The untidiness has acted as a protective shield even during the Revolution's more dogmatic moments, ensuring room for eccentricities and thus providing a fertile ground for the growth of this generation.

By and large, this generation has become dominant in Cuba today and represents the country in most international events. These are the artists who now are shaping the next generations and are beginning to be perceived by the younger artists as the new "establishment." Their art is not the only art being created, but in my view it is the most interesting art being made in Cuba today.[6] At the time of editing this text (early 1992), however, due to the economic conditions, many Cuban artists have moved out of Cuba. There are now fifty-seven artists in Mexico. Although they go back and forth to Cuba, the cultural momentum is bound to be affected.

By covering a period roughly from 1980 to 1990[7] I can refer to three generations of artists educated under the Revolution. The word *generation* does not refer precisely to the age of its members but to their place in the artistic development during this period. Above all, the manner in which the art was generated classifies these generations and puts them in sequence, rather than the direct appreciation of the work of the artists. The first group is the one I met in 1981. It achieved notoriety through a much-remembered exhibit, "Volumen I," in January 1981, which is now seen as an important formal break with previous Cuban art. A second group, closely attached to the first one, became known later and expanded its work. The third group is more properly a generation both in age and in interests. It started to exhibit in 1988 and defines itself clearly as separate from its predecessors and as a visual reflection of the present Cuban "rectification" process, a process that challenges a purely mechanical approach to economics and tries to bring in ethical and political motivation with renewed force. It is an artistically militant generation, intensely preoccupied with content and producing controversial work that raises some opposition in Cuba. With this generation, art is not subject to politics but is an active participant in politics.

My initial and convenient closing date for this book was 1988. I had chosen the Fourth Congress of the UNEAC (Union of Cuban Writers and Artists), which took place in January, as the final event. The UNEAC groups recognized cultural producers in Cuba and translates issues pertaining to rights and duties of artists and writers into law. Presently there are two thousand members in sections including music, writing, visual arts, performing arts, and film, radio, and television. Congresses are organized every five years to discuss major cultural policy issues. UNEAC membership has aged over the years. A great pressure was exerted during this last congress to open access for the newer generations, only a few of whose members have been allowed into the organization. Major speeches by Minister of Culture Armando Hart, Vice-President Carlos Rafael Rodríguez, and President Fidel Castro stressed the need for youth, the evils of dogmatic approaches, and the importance of freedom in form and content in the arts. In that sense, the congress was used to confirm most of the issues that were brought to the surface by the first generation of the 1980s. However, the nearly unrestricted openness signaled by the congress was subsequently subdued by controversies generated by exhibits of the younger generation in the following months. This new development was a consequence of a complex combination of factors that include some lack of tact on the side of the artists toward the quasi-religious atmosphere surrounding aspects of the Revolution. The artists produced work not completely rigorous in terms of the communication of content, sometimes accidentally expressing things that they did not believe in, and often focusing only on how artistically accomplished their work was from a formal point of view. The lower ranks of the art bureaucracy sometimes showed an excess of paternalism toward the public combined with a lack of artistic sophistication and an excess of dogmatic revolutionary zeal. Some of the events were exploited by pseudoartistic groups with a direct view toward international news services trying to imply an atmosphere parallel to that previously suffered by dissidents in the USSR.

The entanglement of these conditions and the crucial recognition that the artists are working *within* the Revolution and not against it, led the Ministry of Culture to organize a cycle of exhibitions in the Castillo de la Real Fuerza (Castle of the Royal Force), an old Spanish fortress in Havana, the construction of which was started in 1562. This program was created in order to allow these artists to express themselves publicly with more rigor, without a change of their political beliefs, and also to include explanatory and educational components. Their voice was to be heard in an unambiguous way, and an accurate debate of the issues was intended. This effort of the ministry was designed to stop a process of "self-censorship" that began in mid-1988 and that was threatening to echo a similar tendency in the late 1960s and early 1970s. The importance of these events led me to extend the span of the book beyond my initial plan. Some stunning exhibits took place; however, tensions did not subside and, if anything, increased. After less than a year the cycle was stopped.

As a nonhistorian I am particularly resentful of the constraints of historical narrative, of the distortions imposed by the need to fit events into a linear sequence of neatly circumscribed units. Chronology is often helpful, but I have the feeling of having to describe a bubbling surface; the bubbles coexist, some dominate for a moment, but no sequential order represents the process in its true essence. The frustration created by the incongruity between a preestablished design of the language and the complicated weaving of the subject matter is therefore a major component in this text. It makes me feel that I am about to touch things without being able to make contact with them.

My own generational deformations may prove another obstacle for any expected scholarly objectivity. I was formed in a set of contradictions, within a cultural tradition that celebrated art for its formal excellence and a political tradition that instinctively mistrusted any sign of authority and dogma. While writing this book I realized that both categories of my background contaminate each other. I often find myself hoping for a greater excellence in form in the political structure and more erasure of dogma and authority in art solutions. To compound the problem, this ideological seesaw often is inconsistent with my own taste in art. In many instances I found myself surprisingly doctrinaire in the realm of politics and, alternatively, excessively demanding or lenient in the realm of aesthetics. The new Cuban art generations operate on this same seesaw, but they often use a different rhythm, something I had to force myself to respect.

The difficulties are overridden by the interest inherent in many of the issues associated with contemporary Cuban art, especially in the context of the fragmentation and distortion of the information about Cuba that reaches the United States. The U.S. blockade isolates both countries from each other, not just Cuba from the United States. It therefore seems puzzling to an observer placed in the United States to see that artistic freedom is working well in a socialist system stereotyped as stymieing. The artists using this freedom not only break conventions but also soon after are placed in teaching positions from which they encourage the continuation of this process. The role of art education in Cuba is fundamental to this situation, initially because of the sheer length of the course of studies and more recently because of curricular reforms. Other issues pertain to the flow of information between the hegemonic mainstream and peripheral cultures. Art in Cuba was subject to unrestricted colonizing influences during the past, and it is from this unrejected past in combination with an informed present that the new Cuban art from this decade has emerged. And it points in a direction that I believe crucial as an example for the rest of Latin America.

NEW ART OF CUBA

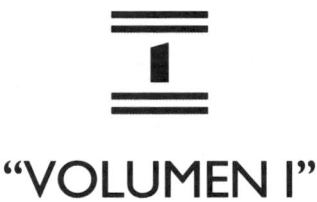

"VOLUMEN I"

Practically any writing elicited by contemporary Cuban art refers to an exhibition known as "Volumen I," which is seen as having set the tone for Cuban art thereafter. The myth surrounding the show is strong enough to have me treat the subject matter by first discussing the exhibit and then unraveling Cuban art from it.

The Exhibit and Its Repercussions

The "Volumen I" exhibit opened on January 14, 1981, in the Centro de Arte Internacional in Havana. The show has come to symbolize the emergence of the new art in Cuba for artists and critics alike. In that sense the exhibition had a historical impact in the Cuban arts of the twentieth century only paralleled by two previous events. The first was the "Exposición de Arte Nuevo," an exhibit sponsored by the *Revista de Avance* in 1927, which gave shape to modernism in Cuba. The second, with a more modest impact, was the appearance of Los Once, a group of painters and sculptors that introduced abstract expressionism in the 1950s (see Chap. 3).

In truth, "Volumen I" was neither the first nor the most radical of a series of exhibits by the artists of the 1980s generation.[1] Six artists of the group had already started planning an exhibit as far back as 1977. It was to be called "Six New Painters," and it included José Bedia, Juan Francisco Elso Padilla, José Manuel Fors, Gustavo Pérez Monzón, Ricardo Rodríguez Brey, and Rubén Torres Llorca. Originally the exhibit was conceived with ten artists,[2] but four of them separated from the group before the exhibit. The introduction to the catalogue was written by art critic Gerardo Mosquera (October 1977), and an appropriate exhibit

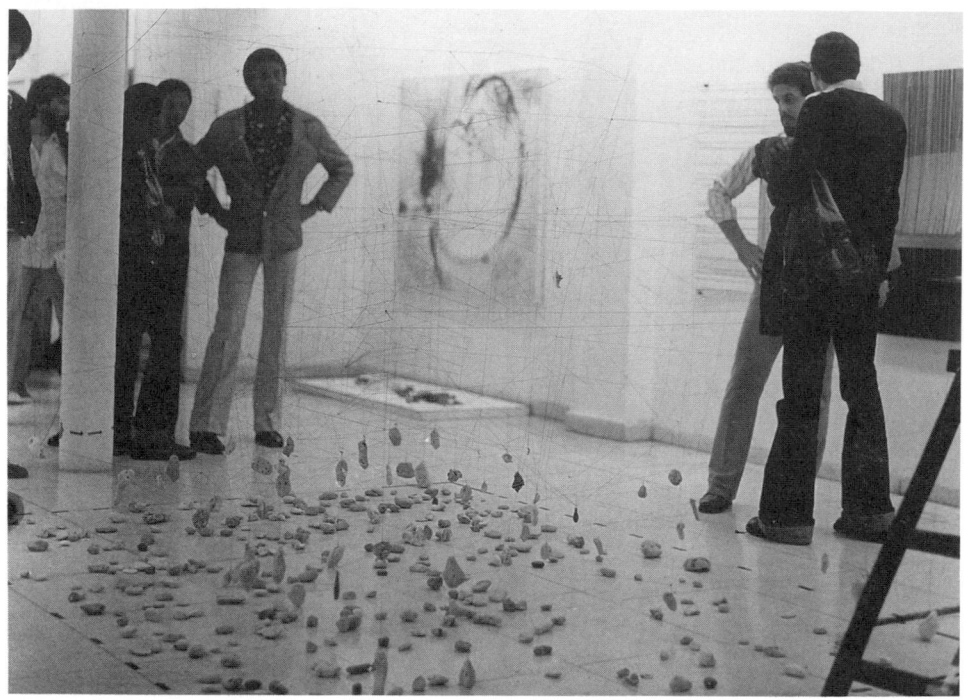

Opening of "Volumen I" exhibit, 1981. Installation by Gustavo Pérez Monzón. Photo by José M. Fors.

space was found for 1978. However, the show never took place. It was canceled by a functionary of the university that administered the assigned gallery because of "a general lack of quality . . . because the general impression of the show was negative; and because the work was a reflection of ugliness and unpleasantness in our reality."[3] It is understandable that work by such young artists could be rejected for lack of maturity. What is revealing in the statement is the invocation of the (in Cuba) outmoded Marxist-Leninist reflection theory in its narrowest and most sectarian interpretation to justify what probably was no more than a matter of personal taste.

With hindsight, many of the artists involved are now grateful for the cancellation. The work to be exhibited had not yet reached a peak, and the show probably would not have brought the consequences that the artists achieved later. After the cancellation, the artists worked on a second attempt, which was successful. In 1979, a semiprivate exhibition was arranged in Fors' house. The original six were expanded to eleven, including Flavio Garciandía, Rogelio López Marín (Gory), Carlos José Alfonso, Emilio Rodríguez, and Tomás Sánchez. Its title was "Pintura

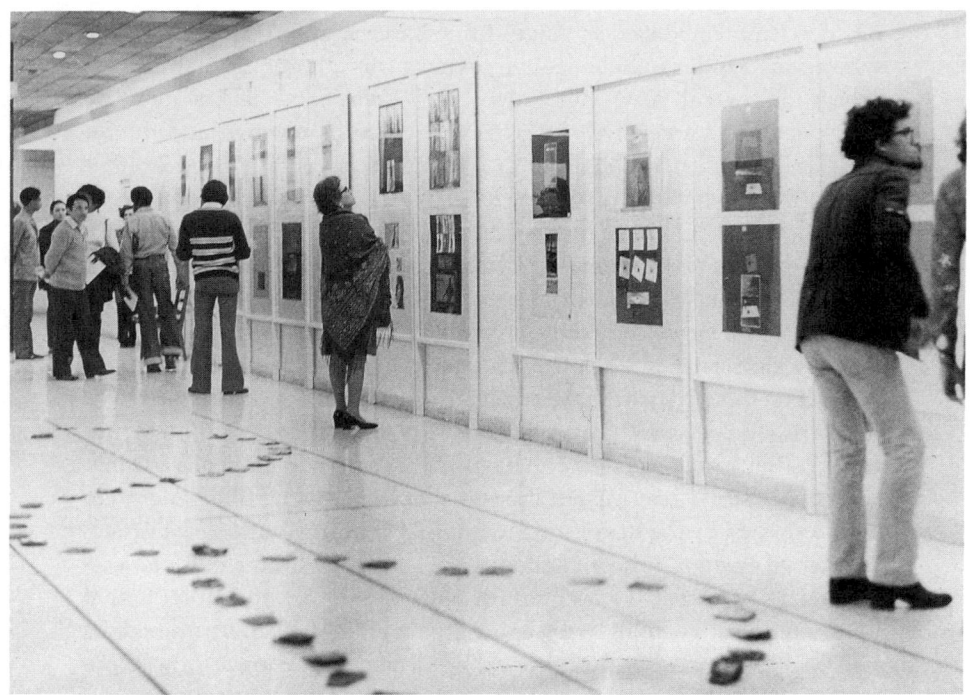

Opening of "Volumen I" exhibit, 1981. Installation by Leandro Soto. Photo by José M. Fors.

Fresca" (Fresh Paint). The title was used also for a second version of the exhibit, now with full ministerial support and with the addition of Leandro Soto, in an art gallery in Cienfuegos.

When "Volumen I" finally opened in Havana, it used that title as an indication of being the first of a series of "volumes" in a long story. Again the show comprised eleven artists: José Bedia (1959), Juan Francisco Elso Padilla (1956), José Manuel Fors (1956), Flavio Garciandía (1954), Israel León (1957), Rogelio López Marín (Gory) (1953), Gustavo Pérez Monzón (1956), Ricardo Rodríguez Brey (1956), Tomás Sánchez (1948), Leandro Soto (1956), and Rubén Torres Llorca (1957). The exhibit had an unprecedented eight thousand visitors in two weeks and engendered great controversy. It was probably the controversy that ensured its fame, rather than the actual work.

The exhibit had its prophet and its attacking devil. The prophet was Gerardo Mosquera (1945), who since 1977 has provided most of the written essays on the artists, both in catalogues and in the press. There have also been friendly and faithful writings by some other critics, notably Alejandro G. Alonso, but these had less of a theoretical impact. The opposition was symbolized by Angel Tomás, art critic of *El Caimán Barbudo*, who because of his initial negative reviews was ignored by many of the artists for several years subsequently. *El Caimán Barbudo*, a monthly newspaper, had a generally aggressive style in its reviews, and the review of "Volumen I," according to Tomás, was contaminated by that style beyond what was originally intended.[4] Looking back, Tomás concedes that he might have been excessively harsh, but he felt that at the time there was an exaggerated leniency in Cuban art. He was neither satisfied with the nationalist art nor with the photo-realism of the 1970s, and in that sense welcomed the "Volumen I" show aesthetically. But he feared a simplistic and disproportionate promotion, continuing a cycle of what he thought of as movements in which artists and critics acted as if no art had been produced before. At the time he did not think about the possibility of this generation having a certain right to break radically with the past. He had missed the fact that this was the first generation totally shaped by the Revolution, without any prerevolutionary burden. Tomás wrote then, "The exhibited work . . . promotes the cult of a creative activity primarily based on formalism and, therefore, a reduction of communicative signs with conceptual references to an immediate reality. . . . At the same time, the exhibit leans mainly toward the abandonment of our national identity, to fall into the false homogeneity of a cosmopolitan art which simulates the ignorance of geographic and ideological borders. This aesthetic attitude may imply the danger of taking routes designed by the 'avant-gardes' promoted and manipulated in the metropolis."[5] Tomás voiced with his statements the concerns of the generation of the 1970s, much preoccupied with a programmatic expression of nationality and identity, but he failed to acknowledge that this generation had internalized those problems and that it was ready to let those two factors be generated organically without the need of any explicit statement.[6]

In fact, the breaks "Volumen I" presented were not as radical as the controversy generated would suggest. Cuban art tradition had been connected with Western modernism since the famed and already mentioned "Exposición de Arte Nuevo" in 1927, a connection that had not been broken by the Revolution. Also, a closer look shows that "Volumen I" was more of a transitional exhibit fertilizing future changes than a total rupture. Tomás Sánchez, a painter in the hyperrealist tradition, had not seriously altered his style and was in the exhibit more for reasons of friendship than because of aesthetics. Older than the rest, he had been a printmaking teacher for most of the other participants. Garciandía, also coming from hyperrealism, was working on anamorphic distortions but keeping figuration intact. He projected photographs on slanted can-

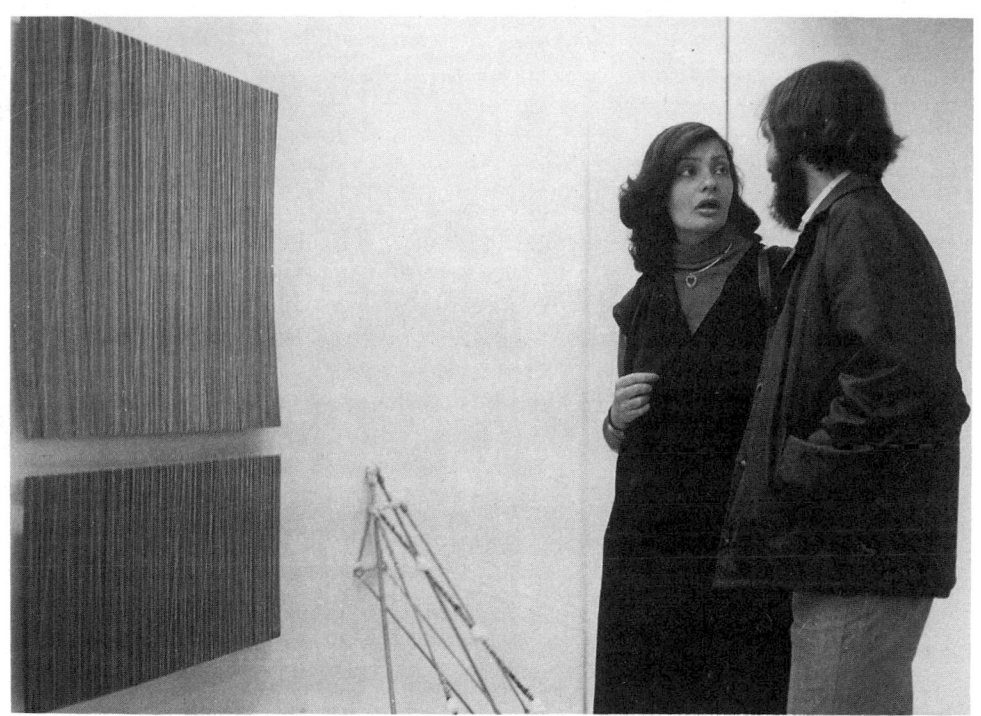

Opening of "Volumen I" exhibit, 1981. Installation by José Manuel Fors. Photo by José M. Fors.

vases, pushing them to the limits of recognition. Rogelio López Marín (Gory), still another hyperrealist (and a photographer), exhibited one of his paintings purposely unfinished and with the photograph that served as a model stuck on the canvas. With that, possibly unwittingly, he may have provided a symbol for an exact historical placement of the show—the gradual abandonment of photo-realism in favor of conceptual apertures.

The generation was defined more by a shared interest in experimentation than by age, level of studies, or aesthetic program. What gave importance to "Volumen I," much more than the work exhibited, was the fact that the exhibition became the starting point for a series of group shows, which brought together several combinations of the individuals in the group, and it began a process of increasingly radical ruptures with Cuban art traditions. It also fueled the break with an epic past, opened the way for self-referential issues about art that were absent during the 1970s, and dealt with the international art scene without a guilt complex. It is these changes that may have offended critic Tomás at the time.

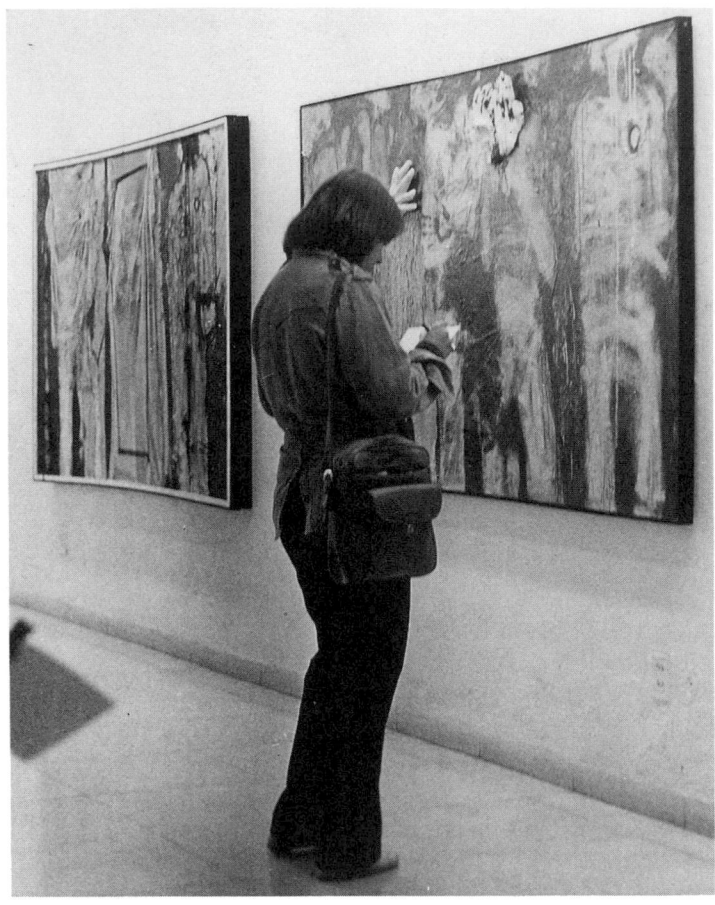

Opening of "Volumen I" exhibit, work of Juan Francisco Elso Padilla. Photo by José M. Fors.

"Volumen I" placed the artists on the Cuban cultural map but did not yet establish them. Although there were several exhibitions following, it took a generational confrontation in 1983 to set things on what these artists saw as the right track. On the occasion of a Meeting of Young Latin American Artists, organized by Casa de las Américas in October 1983, an intergenerational debate took place in front of a large audience dominated by art students. The public's endorsement of the positions espoused by the young artists finally closed the controversy.

"Volumen I" is important because it gave a profile to a new generation in a way that had not occurred in Cuba since the 1950s when Los

Once had organized. This new generation changed the perception of art in Cuba and the perception of Cuba in the international arena. Each time post–"Volumen I" art is shown outside Cuba, it does not elicit discussions about dogmatism and sectarianism but produces wonder about how a culture presumed to be dogmatic and sectarian by the information media can produce this degree of freedom of expression. This perception is not only attributable to the art itself but also to the way it was promoted on official levels, fusing freedom of creation with cultural policy.

The promotion effort, particularly by the Ministry of Culture, is not always seen kindly by groups and individuals espousing other aesthetics. Members of what will be discussed in this book as "the third generation" see the promotion as a symptom of entrenchment of those artists; critics such as Tomás consider it premature sainthood; and dogmatic sectors still see it as a sellout to cosmopolitanism. Higher ranks in a socialist country may possibly find themselves caught between two ideological extremes provided by local needs on one side and the need to function in international competition on the other. Placed on the borderline of both kinds of needs, and acting as a translation filter between both positions, the Ministry of Culture makes decisions for the sake of achieving a better understanding on the part of an international audience— decisions that can be seen as "deviations" by local "hardliners." With the development of a politically more active kind of art by the youngest artists in 1988 and with content gaining a special and controversial predominance, the Ministry's work has become even more delicate in its mediating role. The fragility of this mission has become increasingly apparent toward the end of the decade, when some high-ranking functionaries who sympathized with the "new" art resigned or were shifted to other jobs.[7] And 1990 seemed to be a year in which prominent young artists were exhibiting more in the international arena than in Cuba itself, thus simultaneously serving international acclaim and internal hardliners with less of a conflict.

The success of "Volumen I" was also the symptom of a new use, in Cuba, of planned strategy as an instrument in art affairs. The group started in a very organized way. Though there was a close friendship among Sánchez, López Marín (Gory), and Garciandía, they also provided credibility to the new and unknown other members. The group operated through a juried acceptance of new members, the jury being the group itself. Discussions dealt with the work in terms of consistency between theory and output. Exhibits, planned collectively, considered not only the individual piece but also its function in the total context of

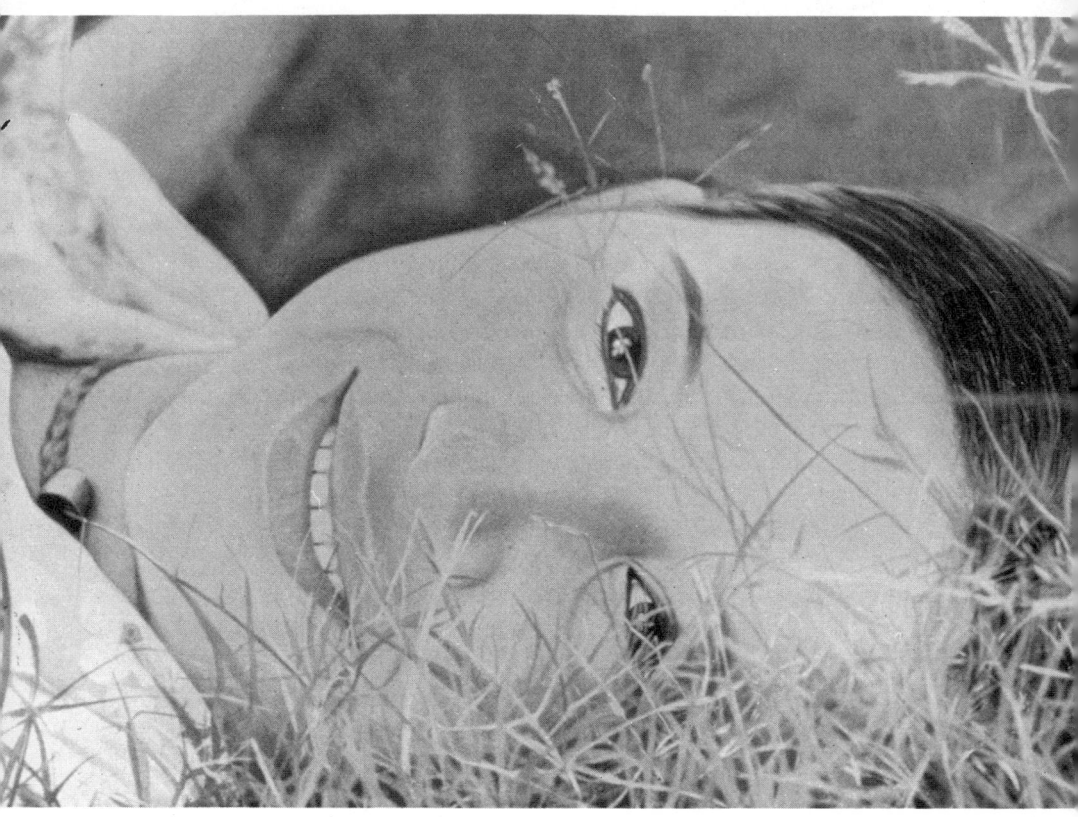

Flavio Garciandía, All You Need Is Love, *1975, oil on canvas, 96 × 116.5 cm. Museo Nacional de Bellas Artes, Havana.*

the show. Art literature considered relevant circulated among all the participants, and studio visits for collective criticism were frequent.

The Role of Realism as an Antecedent

Because of the traditional attribution of realist aesthetics to socialist regimes, it becomes important to analyze the function of realism in the Cuban development. Realism was indeed a strong formative element for most of the artists of the "Volumen I" group. Garciandía, for example, had received a major prize at age twenty-one, in 1976, for a painting (*All You Need Is Love*) that became emblematic for the Cuban photo-realist period, and most of the "Volumen I" artists had their work based on a solid realist platform. But realism in Cuba was not socialist realism in the old-fashioned Soviet sense. It was photo-realism, a label consciously used to define a Cuban brand of hyperrealism. It had sufficient strength and importance in Cuba to deserve a separate discussion here. In spite of its idiosyncratic nature, the movement was used by Western media to try to link Cuban with Soviet art as a proof of cultural dependency.

The aesthetic that was powerful between 1973 and 1979 was not a programmatic movement but rather the product of an aggregation of individuals.[8] The most acknowledged artists were César Leal, Aldo Menéndez, Nélida López, López Marín (Gory), and Garciandía. The stress on photo-realism had a vague ideological reason, possibly derived from the "testimonial" aesthetics developed in literature.

"Testimonial literature" was a category instituted by Casa de las Américas (a kind of ministry of culture for Latin American affairs) in the early 1970s for its literary competitions to accommodate diaries and reports about revolutionary processes. The category was not an arbitrary one but reflected instead an increasing production developed under the Revolution, which needed its own class to clarify standards not easily derived from other forms. The concept of "testimonial literature" covers material ranging from Martí's campaign diaries, through much of Che Guevara's writings, to established authors such as Miguel Barnet or non-writers who document events "without the aesthetic distance provided by the passage of time for settlement of experiences and thus avoiding a certain artistic paternalism toward people and events."[9] Beyond literature, the category influenced movie making (particularly the work of Santiago Alvarez), theatre, and song writing, where Carlos Puebla's work and some "protest songs"[10] are typical examples. Taken as an aesthetic, it constitutes a lively and functional alternative to socialist realism, effectively responding to some of the needs of the revolutionary process of the time. It developed into an idiosyncratic form of expression that directly conditioned the work of artists such as Leandro Soto and—in a more diffused and tongue-in-cheek form—the work of more recent artists, particularly exemplified by Carlos Rodríguez Cárdenas (see Chaps. 5 and 6).[11]

The term *photo-realism* was used to underline a direct documentary contact with reality as offered by the camera and its use as support for the artwork, ensuring some mass-appeal. Painter and photographer Raúl Martínez (see Chap. 2), one of the stronger influences on the "Volumen I" generation, employed this documentary attitude in his more schematic paintings, and the same thought process led to much of the stylized painting produced in those same years. While the presence of Soviet advisers in art schools may have had some technical influence, the movement was not generated by their aesthetic advice.[12]

Whatever Soviet artistic considerations that may have informed Cuba originated in post-Khrushchev aesthetic thinking, which opened the way to some experimentation even among the more dogmatic artists who were willing to follow the Soviet model. Artists such as Orlando Suárez and Carmelo González remained more comfortable under the flexible aegis of Mexican muralism or the art of Candido Portinari than under Stalinist models. If Soviet influence on Cuba was as great as its detractors claim, it can be said that Cuban intellectuals were lucky that the Revolution took place after the Twentieth Congress of the Soviet Communist Party in 1956. Cuban art remained relatively open, even during the most doctrinaire periods and in those times when the West felt that Cuba had a Soviet dependent culture. While some limits were set during the late 1960s and early 1970s (see Chaps. 2 and 3), as in the case of artists Umberto Peña and Antonia Eiriz, these restrictions were not based on a rigid aesthetic credo.

The influences on Cuban photo-realism were, in fact, multiple. There was some Soviet realism, though of the nineteenth-century variety more than socialist realism. Traditional European realism, Vermeer, Andrew Wyeth, an admiration for Hopper and Sheeler, and the information-theory elements that were then determining U.S. hyperrealism also had effects on Cuban art in this time. But above all, there was an interest in photography as a perceptual conditioner, at that time a typically Western consideration. As an example of eclecticism, Tomás Sánchez mentions as his great influences Wyeth's *Christina's World* and the work of Isaak Levitan (1860–1900) and Ivan Shishkin (1832–1898), both Russian realist painters.[13]

If there is a thought structure uniting the photo-realist period in Cuba, it is based on superficial humanism with some room for ideology. It is interesting that it was in the middle of the photo-realist period, and therefore unrelated to the origins of the movement, that the First Congress of the Cuban Communist Party (1975) expressed views on art and ideology that represented the art being produced. The artists in the movement had fed their ideas into the platform of the party. On art it was decided that there is a nexus between socialist art and reality. Art should apprehend the essences of this reality and define its aesthetic expression to this effect by means of the most appropriated formal structures. What matters is not the simple copy of reality but that the quality of life and knowledge lead, in art, to the "intimate truth of objective processes through the corresponding aesthetic languages." This position is

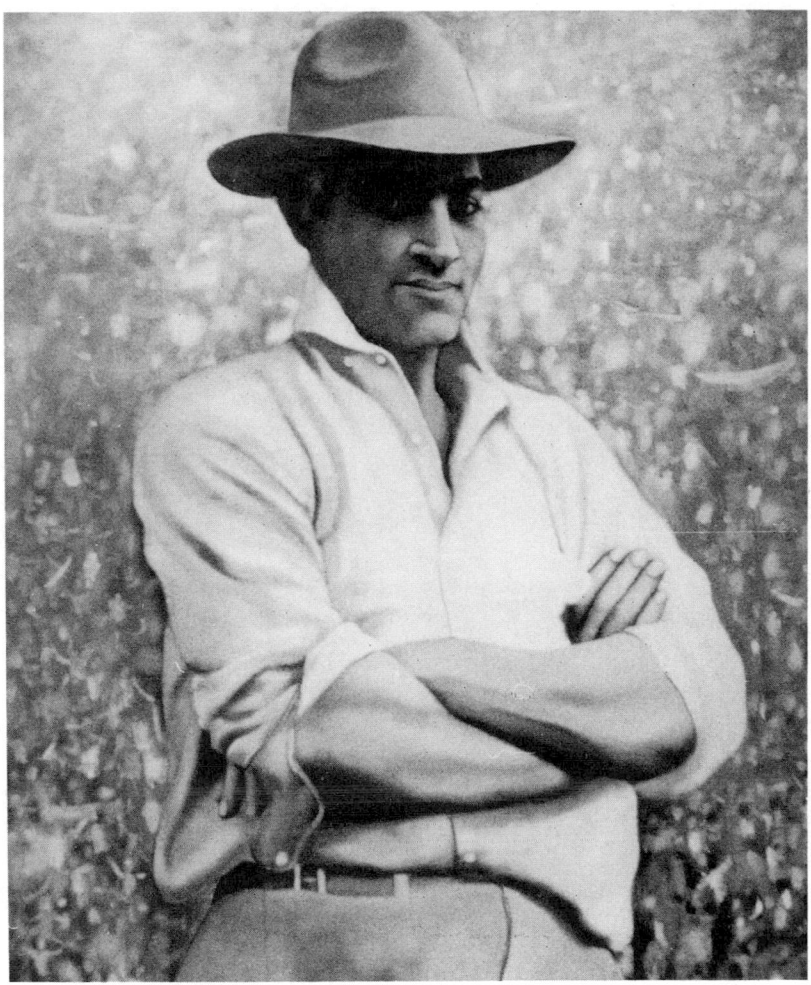

Tomás Sánchez, Mella, *1973, oil on canvas, 116.5 × 96 cm. Museo Nacional de Bellas Artes, Havana. Photo by Luis Camnitzer.*

totally removed from Soviet socialist realism and, if anything, it links up with the positions represented in the Soviet Union somewhat by Lenin and much by Lunacharsky during the early 1920s. On humanism, the same Congress sharply differentiated between "socialist humanism" and "bourgeois humanism," the first one representing the interests of the majority, the second conditioned by an interest in profit not conducive to promoting human values.[14]

So when Cuban artists worked in the realist manner, they were not in search of a frozen style in the Soviet vein. Instead, they incorporated

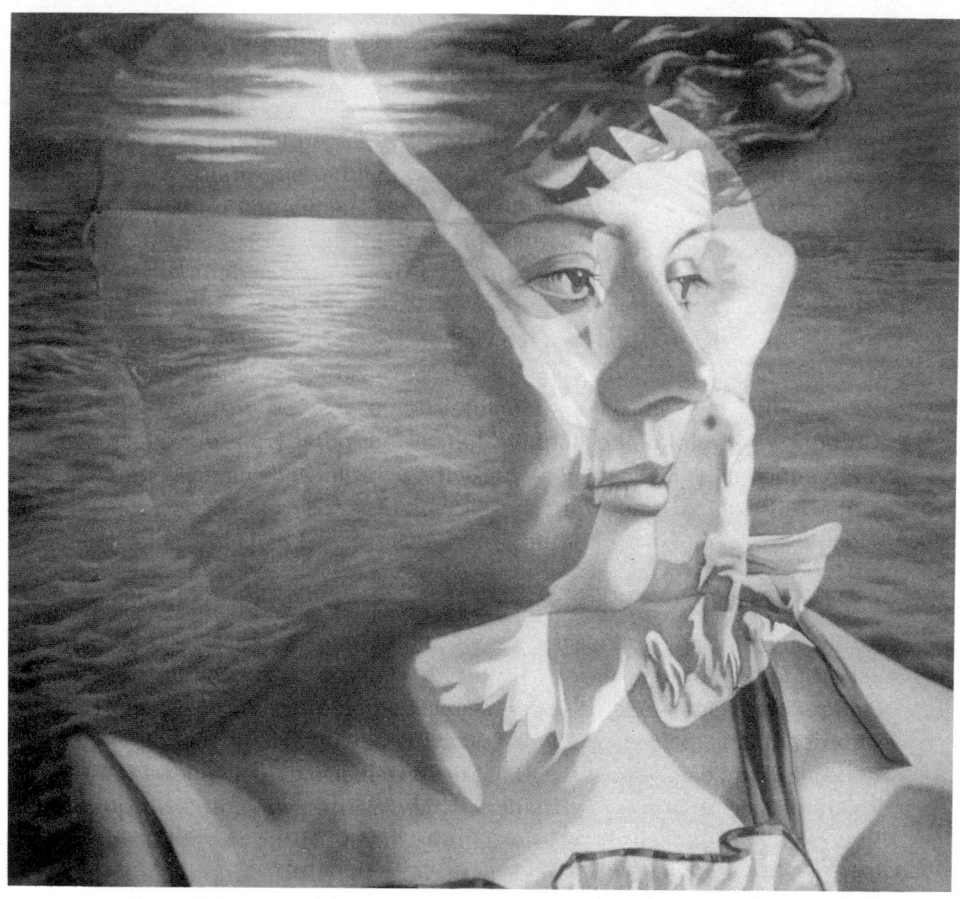

César Leal, Pensar sin querer es soñar (To Think without Wanting to Is to Dream), *1979, oil on canvas, 110.5 × 120 cm. Museo Nacional de Bellas Artes, Havana. Photo by Luis Camnitzer.*

"viewfinder composition," graphic layout aesthetics, documentary immediacy, and a feeling for the everyday atmosphere as it might be documented by a snapshot, while maintaining their individuality. Reality, of course, turned out to be predominantly positive and enjoyable, and, as an aesthetic speculation, the photo-realist period was not particularly interesting—but neither were its parallel manifestations in the rest of the world in spite of their success in New York.

What is interesting in the Cuban context is that this flexible realism served as a preparatory platform to launch the new art that followed. Very few artists remain in that aesthetic line. The work of more conservative artists, such as César Leal and Tomás Sánchez, evolved into other

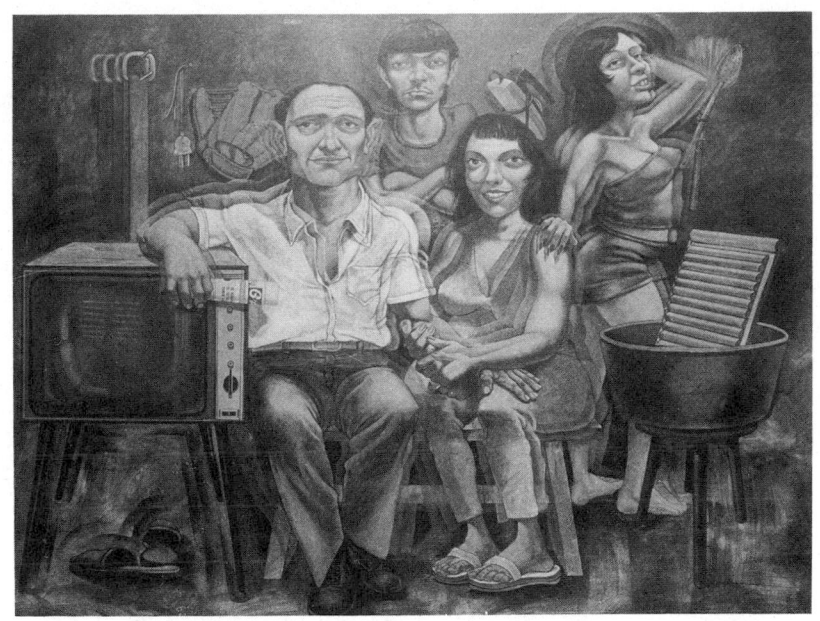

César Leal, Retrato de familia (Family Portrait), *1983, acrylic on canvas, 150 × 190 cm. Collection of the artist. Photo by Luis Camnitzer.*

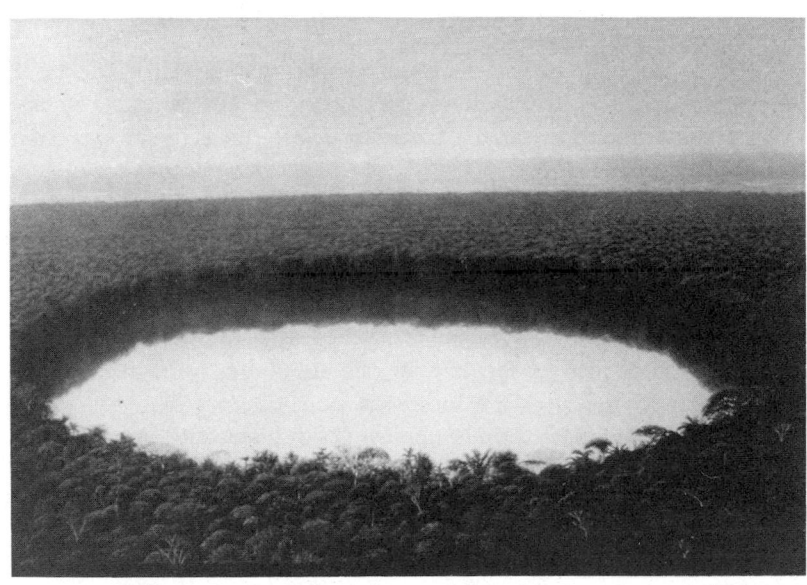

Tomás Sánchez, Laguna y mar (Lagoon and Sea), *1988, acrylic on canvas, 110 × 150 cm. Collection Ninart Centro de Cultura, Mexico.*

modes of paintings, even if they did not completely break with their past. César Leal developed a populist imagery—family and barroom scenes—with some visual solutions borrowed from Italian futurism (e.g., moving figures have repeated contours such as those used by Balla). His latest work has some coincidental connection with that of Chicano artist Luis Jiménez. Tomás Sánchez, in his later work, while continuing the focus on the Cuban landscape, takes some hints from Magritte to infuse it with a surreal mystical atmosphere.

Nevertheless, even during the peak of its period, photo-realism had produced a mixed public reaction, since it was considered closer to the North American trends than to "socially committed" art of the socialist countries. An absurd situation existed in which the public liked the images but not the aesthetic; the same functionary who would cancel the "Six New Painters" exhibit earlier had vetoed a photo-realist exhibit by Garciandía, Menéndez, Leal, and López Marín (Gory).

Garciandía sees himself as having been influenced more by the work of Chuck Close (as known from magazines) and places photo-realism squarely in the context of the international avant-garde. However, he concedes that there was a form of socialist realism involved in the work they were doing, not stemming from Soviet painting but from internalizing contemporary Soviet films.[15]

"Volumen I" and the Effect of Rupture

The flow of international visitors and art magazines into Cuba never stopped. Thus, even if sometimes delayed, there always was a knowledge of the development of the arts in the West. It was the awareness of the international avant-garde of the photo-realists that in part opened the path for "Volumen I." The exhibition forced the discussion of the raison d'être of Cuban art and the validity of the art produced until then and reaffirmed the right to look at what was being done outside of Cuba.

The intention of the artists was to find a Cuban answer to those movements, not to follow them. They expressed the wish to create an informed nationalist art rather than one stemming from isolationism. The tension created by the exhibit was labeled as a schematic one between internationalism and nationalism, both inside and outside Cuba. It also was branded by the Western media as a product of the conflict between Western modes of art and orthodox Communist Party aesthetics. Both interpretations seem inappropriate, leaving out the artists' more complex concerns in relation to Cuban culture. Most of the new artists were as much concerned with content as their predecessors had been or as they themselves had been in their previous work. Their search was for a better match between content and form, a match that was not always perfect.

Before "Volumen I," in 1980, members of the group had organized a series of performances in a private house under the title "Festival of the Short Piece." Bedia provided the poster, hitting on a drawing style that would become his trademark. Gustavo Pérez Monzón performed a piece called *Stella* as a pun on the North American painter's name and its frequency as a name given to girls in Cuba. A girl lying on the floor was covered with a fabric with a Stella-style design. The fabric, cut following the girl's outline, was taped to her. "Stella" then got up and left the room, facing the audience with the fabric. Ricardo Rodríguez Brey, in his piece *The Canadian Chicken,* had José Bedia chop a rubber chicken to bits with an ax. Torres Llorca performed *The American Film,* an improvised scene with cliché situations and unconnected dialogues dubbed into Spanish by an off-stage speaker. In *Alfatasgolfo,* by López Marín (Gory), two individuals tied themselves with ropes to their chairs and to each other while they repeated the word of the title and eventually tried to hop through a window. After the festival was over, the participants gave each other gold-painted objects as prizes. The event, though viewed by a small audience, became rapidly known in Havana. Some members of "Volumen I" believe that the rumors it propelled were instrumental in securing the exhibit.

"Volumen I" was followed by many exhibits of its members' works. During 1981 there were several more group shows, all with more radical approaches than the one considered as having been the path breaker. One of them, "Sano y sabroso" ("Healthy and Tasty"), in July of that year, took a gallery space and transformed it into a home, unknowingly reminiscent of the post-pop "Supermarket" show in New York's Bianchini Gallery in the 1960s. The exhibit also helped shape what would become the kitsch stream in Cuban art of the 1980s. Each artist took care of some part of the home: Rodríguez Brey made a bathroom; Elso produced a window; Garciandía's kitchen utensils referred to design in bad taste; Bedia did the bed sheets with a couple drawn on them; Torres Llorca constructed a television set.[16] Critic Angel Tomás titled his not-very-friendly review "Ni sano ni sabroso" ("Neither Healthy nor Tasty"). Because of its humorous intent, the exhibit was not really in line with the work of each artist and had less importance than other exhibits. It was also clearly an event where the products exhibited were not intended to last. Critical of this strategy, Tomás pointed out in his review that the ephemeral made sense as a statement against the commercialization of art in a capitalist society but not in a place where values for the social collective had to be developed.[17]

On the other hand, an earlier show, "Trece Artistas Jóvenes" ("Thirteen Young Artists"), which had taken place in March, and a later one, the "Retrospectiva de Jóvenes Artistas" ("Retrospective of Young Artists") in October 1981, fulfilled the potential opened by "Volumen I." "Trece Artistas Jóvenes" was an exhibit organized in honor of a prize received by Gerardo Mosquera for a book with the same title written in 1980, and the artists brought their work to an extreme. Rodríguez Brey, who two months earlier had shown work in which he made collages using abstract elements, animal illustrations, and geographical information, made an environmental piece with wool and branches. Bedia, who until then had worked on extremely realistic renderings of fictitious archeological sites mixed with purportedly found objects, built a wall installation using the artifacts and branches. Garciandía broke with his photo-realist residues and presented an installation based on pre-Columbian codicils formed by huge panels, some standing and some laid on the floor, with the claimed "information" partially hanging, glued, or loose on the floor. In his following show Garciandía changed again and started a *Catálogo de malas formas* (*Catalogue of Bad Forms*) (also an installation), a crucial development for his work to follow. Fors, who had mixed leftover materials on a surface and tied nylon string over them, with an insistence that gave the pieces a taste of op art, this time crossed the gallery with acrylic boxes containing leaves and soil. Pérez Monzón, on the surface borrowing from a constructivist and scientific tradition, had originally exhibited works reminiscent of the German Group Zero, with geometry and numbers on metallic paper. In this show he connected two big drawings filled with graphite-drawn circles—hanging on walls forming a corner—with an intricate and irrational mesh of strings that went into the corner as well. Elso Padilla, a relatively conservative neofigurative painter relying heavily on texture in a manner related to Dubuffet, also produced an installation in which instead of a painting he connected ceramic pieces with a pile of leaves on the floor.

While "Volumen I" broke the market, so to speak, "Trece Artistas Jóvenes" paved the aesthetic way for most of the artists. Not everybody pursued installations as a form of art from then on, but a majority seem to have undergone an aesthetic catharsis that helped focus with more clarity on the work to follow. After two years of intense collective showing, the artists were asked to do more and more one-person exhibits. What had started as an actual team became defined as a generation of powerful individuals, including another artist, Arturo Cuenca (1955). Cuenca, more connected with international conceptual tendencies, pursued his work independently from the other artists and will merit more comments in a later chapter because of his influence on the younger artists.

When Garciandía worked on his *Catalogue of Bad Forms,* he was also approaching issues of popular taste. At the other end of the age spectrum, when Glexis Novoa (an artist of the third generation—see Chaps. 5 and 6) uses abstract expressionism, it is a symbol for the "foreign," used as a background for something else. In that sense it can be said that most of Cuban art is "content" oriented, even that which in many cases may appear as formalist.

This tendency toward content, however vaguely it may be used in some cases, leads to issues to be identified among the "Volumen I" artists and those influenced by them. A rough organization can be provided by kitsch, Afro-Cubanism, and nationalism (and Americanism as an extension). The categories are not very precise when it comes to classifying the artists, as many deal with more than one of these either in the same work or in their development over the years.

An artist such as Torres Llorca, who was grouped easily with Garciandía and Soto for many years, has shifted in 1987 to a language that puts him closer to Elso Padilla and Bedia. Bedia, seriously interested in *Santería* and Afro-Cuban traditions, merges them with U.S. Native American traditions.

Other artists do not fit any category and deserve individual consideration, forming a fourth category by default. It is interesting that the primary interest of the "Volumen I" members only secondarily fits the category of nationalism, a rubric nearly fully occupied by members of the third generation. While looking for a national answer in the arts, their interest falls closer to kitsch and to Afro-Cuban issues. I will use these categories here to discuss "Volumen I" artists and again in Chapter 6 with the artists who followed them.

KITSCH

Kitsch has a powerful presence in Cuba. Kitsch is primarily a form of affectation used to overcome a cultural gap. Complexities are streamlined for effortless consumption by the culture wishing to overcome the gap. The characterization of kitsch is usually provided by another culture or by a distant party. In most of Latin America, there is at least a double-kitsch situation, one stemming from class differences, the other from colonialism. When its origins are in colonialism, kitsch can be subdivided again, since colonialism imports class-kitsch of its own and generates new kitsch through the definition of the picturesque.

Cuba covers all possibilities of kitsch, and the reasons for a certain fertility in this regard are not totally clear and are open to speculation. The native Indian population had disappeared very early—in 1511 there were an estimated 100,000 Indo-Cubans in Cuba; by 1555 it is believed that the population was down to 3,900 due to sickness and extermination.[18] With relative suddenness, Cuba was left without a strong tradition to fend off or enrich imports. This may explain why kitsch had an easy entrance and became such a strong cultural ingredient, lastly enhanced by the least enlightened tourist and mafia taste brought in from the United States.

Corny in English, *kitsch* in German and English, *cursi* in Spanish, all have clearly negative connotations and refer to cheap, sentimental, and superficial substitutes for true aesthetic phenomena, usually reflecting class differences. The word *corny* may have originated in an urban attempt to negate the assimilation efforts of new city dwellers coming from the peasantry. Chinese aristocrats referred to peasant paper cutouts used for hair ornaments as "the small skills of insect carving." The paper cutouts tried to imitate the gold, silver, jade, and ivory ornaments used in the hair of the Chinese upper classes.[19] In Cuba the word used is *picúo*,[20] which refers to the same class of products but recognizes some authenticity to them and has more tolerant and tender connotations.

Picúo is less directed to mass-produced commercial kitsch than to what is genuinely produced under its influence, such as bar decorations and carnival floats. All this determines that memories—prerevolutionary memory, childhood remembrances, romantic nostalgia—are all suffused with some *picúo* quality that can become a starting point for much of the Cuban work. *Picúo* applies to popular kitsch, not to bourgeois kitsch, and for the artists this becomes as much a part of Cuban identity as Afro-Cuban rituals.

A drawing by cartoonist Salcedo in the magazine *Revolución y Cultura* depicts an artist swan complaining in front of his work, "The things one has to listen to! I am the best portraitist in the pond, and they treat me like a miserable kitsch-maker."

Artists faced Cuban kitsch first as an aim for an educational task. Their mission was to eradicate it, and by presenting it in an art context the expected result was to shock the viewer into reason. While pursuing their noble intentions the artists involved discovered that the educational process had reversed and that they were learning from kitsch.[21] With extremely few exceptions, kitsch permeates most of the art of the decade within the tender interpretation of *picúo* and the acceptance of the vernacular.

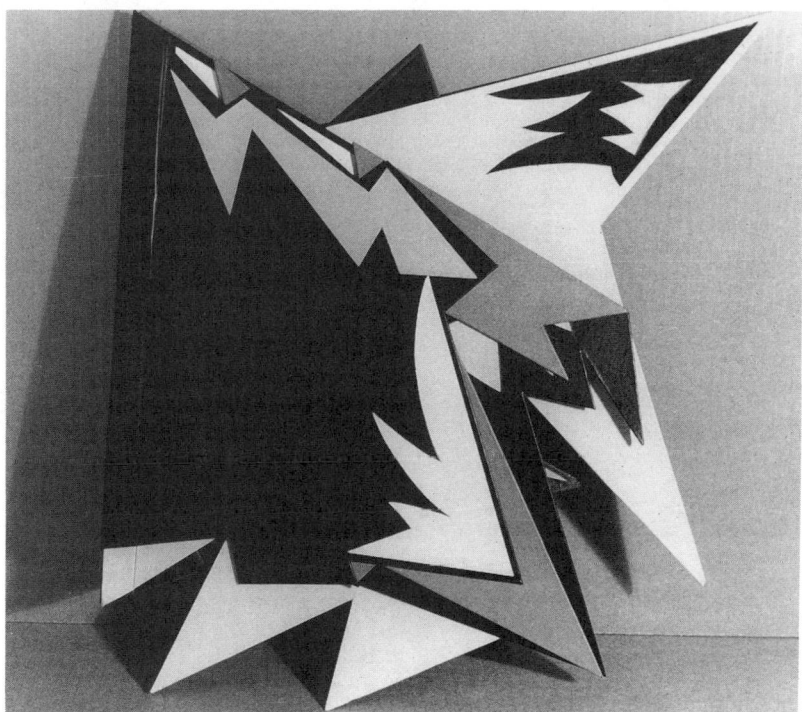

Flavio Garciandía, Catálogo de las malas formas (Catalogue of Bad Forms), *1982, cardboard, 48 × 48 × 48 cm. Private collection. Photo by Luis Camnitzer.*

Flavio Garciandía

After his many years of photo-realism, followed by a short influence by Matta, Garciandía worked with morphological issues, which got him interested in Frank Stella's work. In Stella's work he saw a link between high-culture products and kitsch (not unlike Martínez bridging Committee of Defense aesthetics with Warhol). "A lot of popular products in Cuba resemble pieces by Frank Stella. I documented some of those and passed them off as Stellas among my friends."[22] His work pursued the study of "bad forms," generating the related "catalogues" (essentially sculptures made out of paintings bound into books, with arbitrary shapes), which he exhibited in the Twelfth Biennial of Paris in 1982, and other works, which culminated with his entry for the First Biennial of Havana in 1984.

On the occasion of his exhibit "Vereda tropical" in 1982, he had clearly stated his guiding idea: "I am interested in expressing certain visual elements generated by the sudden inspiration of those who, alien

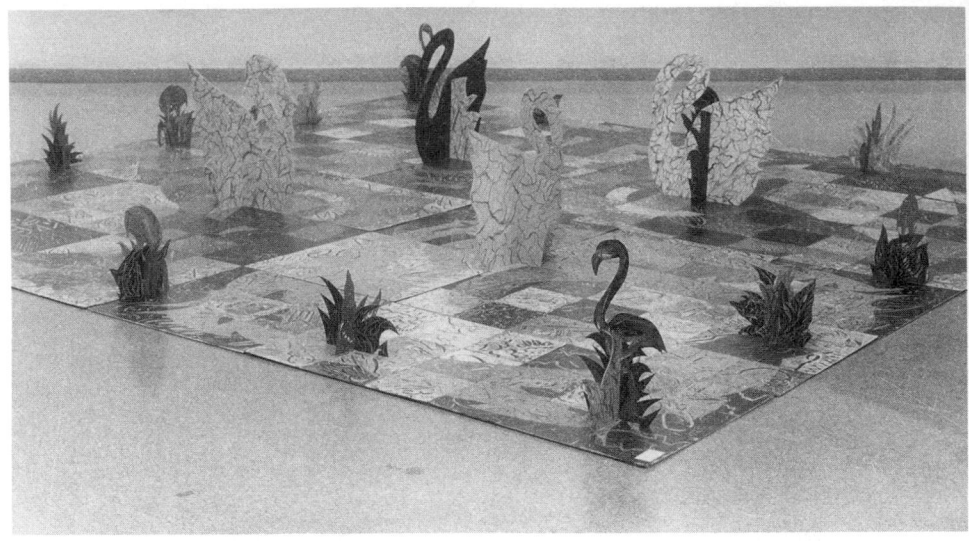

Flavio Garciandía, El lago de los cisnes (Swan Lake), *1983, acrylic on masonite, 300 × 300 cm. Collection of the artist. Photo by Luis Camnitzer.*

to the accepted graces of popular art and the most basic and traditional values of so called high art, have felt the need to manipulate shapes and colors."[23]

Swan Lake, one of the two installations Garciandía had at the First Biennial of Havana, was a major achievement in the pursuit of these issues. Originally an untitled piece, it was spontaneously christened by the public and the name subsequently adopted by the artist. A tiled floor made with painted squares of masonite, with a baroque wealth of images that deal with political symbols, weaponry, and painterly stereotypes, serves as a support for swans and palm trees sprinkled with glitter. The work is carefully set on the thin line that separates high art from low art and points to the conundrum stated by Gerardo Mosquera when he referred to Garciandía's work: "Why are these forms 'superior' when Flavio displays them in a gallery and 'inferior' in the hand of decorators or 'bad' TV set designers? . . . What would happen if Flavio worked 'inferior' forms not in the network of 'high' art but in that of mass culture where they are considered 'good'? . . . What would his work be: art or kitsch?"[24]

Garciandía answers Mosquera's question by saying, "I try to ensure that the work has different levels of reading and that all kinds of people find something to relate to. . . . I parody conceptualism, tautological statements, etc. I think that the work is accessible to the whole range,

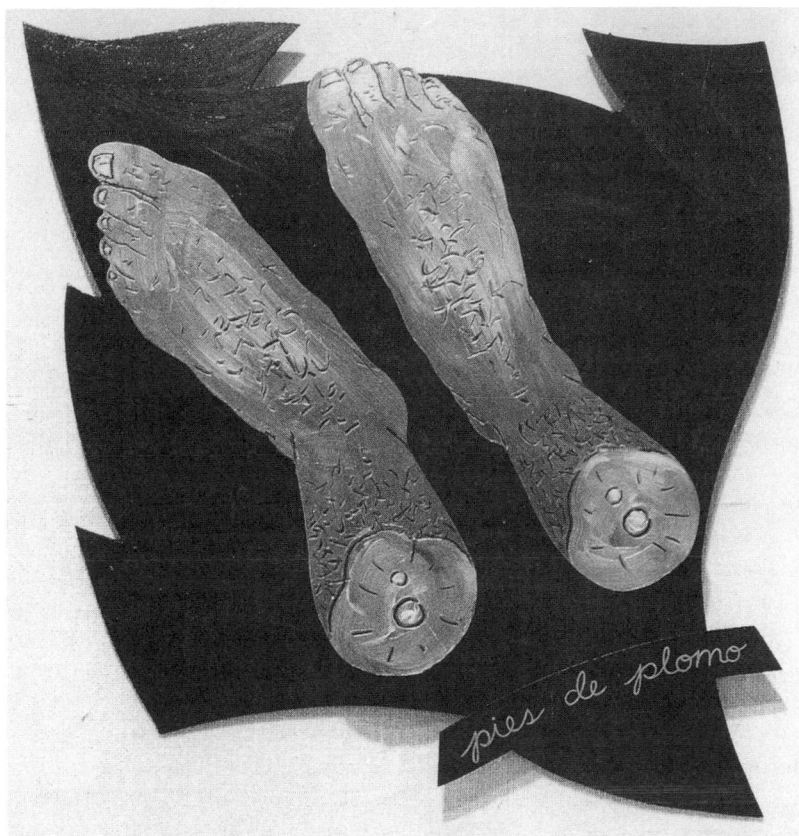

Flavio Garciandía, Pies de plomo (Leaden Feet), *1984, acrylic on masonite,
60 × 60 × 7 cm. Collection of the artist. Photo by Luis Camnitzer.*

from elite to the unprepared public. . . . The conflict is posed by the
choice of the channels of distribution."[25]

Swan Lake was followed by a series using Cuban proverbs. Executed
with the same materials, they illustrated the meaning of the text in the
most banal way possible. Half of the original proverb was written on the
image, and the viewer had to make up for the missing part. In these
pieces, Garciandía used fake marbling effects and cafeteria aesthetics as
well as painterly craft. Non-Cuban viewers, missing the connection with
a primary and very local humor, reacted mostly to the painterly surface
and thus single-mindedly internationalized the perception of his work.
Garciandía is not innocent of this misunderstanding. He is probably the
artist in Cuba most informed about contemporary art in the capitalist
mainstream.

His position is totally opposed to "naive" art-making (at least for himself) and is based on a belief that originality can only be correctly achieved as an aftermath of mastering all available information. During his stay in New York in 1985, Garciandía, passing by the entrance to a supermarket, introduced himself to artist Keith Haring whom he saw coming out with a bag. He had seen a photograph of Haring some years earlier in an American art magazine. While Cuban artists are well informed, Garciandía has carried this segment of knowledge to encyclopedic proportions and uses it as a point of departure to focus on Cuban culture. With an effort not to internalize the corresponding aesthetics, he uses his knowledge to maintain a critical distance from aesthetic phenomena and to implement their potentials in an unemotional fashion.

Many of Garciandía's works have an underlying rigor that places them much closer to constructivist art than to some of the postmodernist expressions to which they could be linked superficially. An example of this was another major installation in 1986 for the Second Biennial of Havana. The piece was called *The Marco Polo Syndrome* and borrowed from Chinese restaurant decoration. Two walls were covered with hangings, fans, and panels with a black-velvet look, bearing glitter drawings. Elpidio Valdés, a popular Cuban comics character, undertakes a mysterious voyage, full of wonder and unanswered questions. Each panel acts as a frame in a comics story, but there is no discernible story line, except for underlying musings about the meanings and uses of exoticism represented by Chinese elements. In spite of how all of this sounds, the way the images related in the installation had a dissective, analytical aura worthy of functionalist architecture.

In later work, Garciandía synthesizes both kitsch stereotypes and political symbols. Hammers and sickles blend in with penises, flamingos, and palm trees, outlined with glitter on flat black or red backgrounds or on surfaces imitating the effects of batik. In some ways, this work places him along the lines of many of the pursuits of the third generation. In a further development of this work, the symbols merge into compositions reminiscent of Delaunay and Tatlin. In these pieces, Garciandía purposefully appropriates elements from the repertoire of the early twentieth century avant-garde, trying to do so imitating the semi-ignorant manner in which Picasso appropriated elements from African objects.

With this new twist he tries to enrich the world of kitsch even further, coopting material that by cultural definition was supposed to be impervious to any contamination. But with these pieces and through an undoubtedly convoluted process, Garciandía is also engaging in a novel anticolonial battle where he uses the dynamic provided by the inertia of our traditional view of aesthetics as his weapon. Without changing the

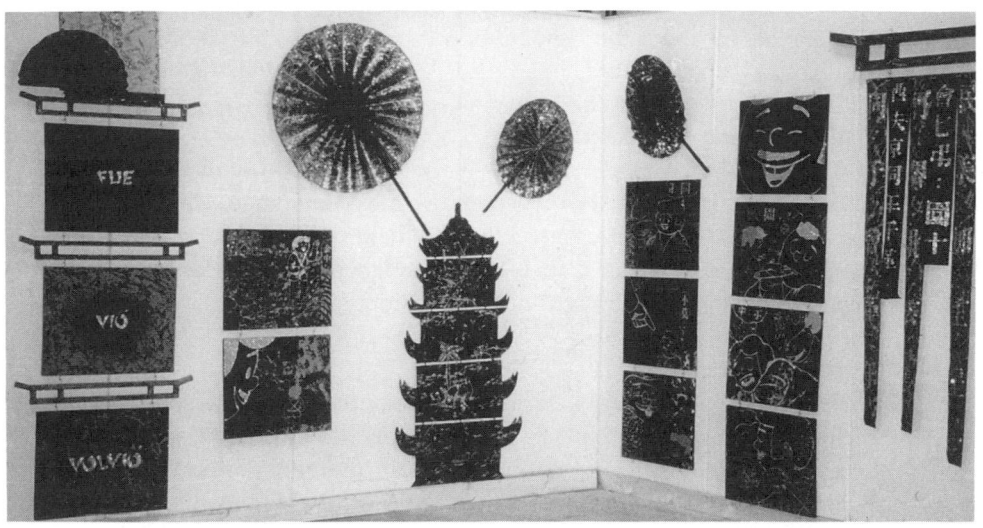

Flavio Garciandía, El síndrome de Marco Polo (The Syndrome of Marco Polo), *1986, installation in the Second Biennial of Havana. Collection of the artist. Photo by Luis Camnitzer.*

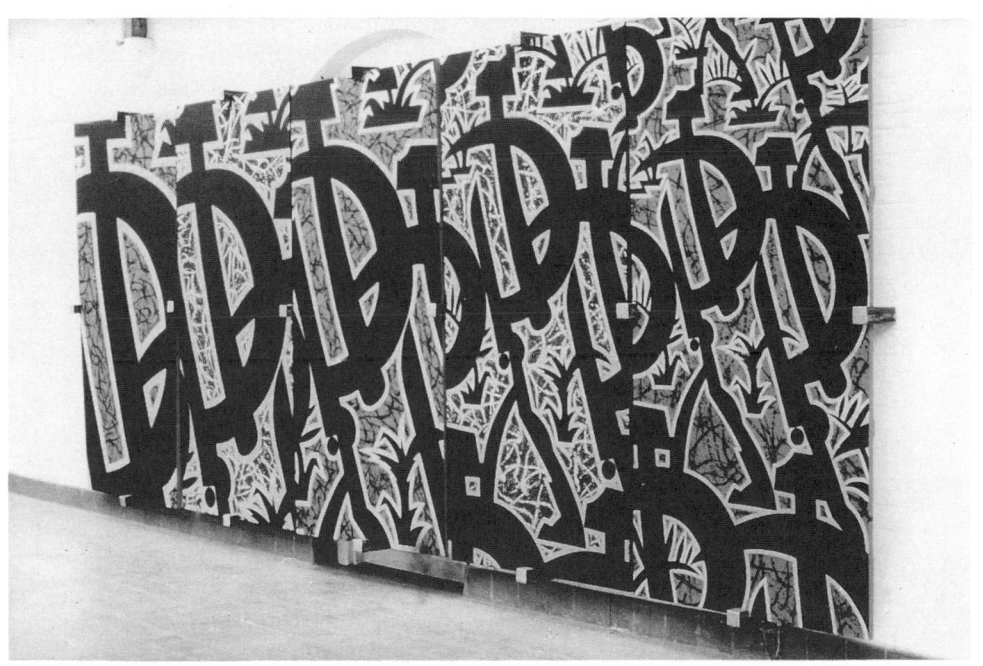

Flavio Garciandía, untitled. 1989. Installation in the Castillo de la Fuerza, Havana. Collection of the artist. Photo by Flavio Garciandía.

viewers' habits about the viewing of art, he leads them to perceive the absurdity of those habits. Garciandía is trying to ensure that both kitsch and high art, moving at their own speeds, meet so that a good and liberating collision can take place.

By the end of 1990, Garciandía's work was going through a phase of assembling past experiences into a more concise language. Maintaining the use of glitter and referring as much to hammer and sickles as to ancient caryatides hybridized with Matisse's dancing figures, he ventures into ever more rigidly thought-out compositions.

Rubén Torres Llorca

For many years Torres Llorca's work presumed to have a somewhat sociological character, dealing with mass-media aesthetics and their effect on Cuban taste. It was informed by international pop-art and "camp" attitudes and, as a consequence, seemed for many years to fit an internationalist aesthetic. But in fact this work was introspective and nostalgic. Sensitive to the influence of U.S. movies, television, and comics in his upbringing and the influence of his mother's seamstress trade, he tried to synthesize all these experiences in a quasi-therapeutic fashion.

Torres Llorca used pop-art devices in order to approach these issues with an appearance of objectivity; his use of irony allowed for a not-always-successful detachment. Typical work of this period was exhibited in his show "Cine del Hogar" ("Home Cinema") in 1983, based on a Cuban TV program that showed old Hollywood movies.

His work fluctuated back and forth between formalism and emotion. When a formalist, he tended to be excessively subject to aesthetic influences, and when emotional, the work would fall into the traps posed by illustration. The uneven trajectory of his work, which had been connected with the development of the new Cuban art since the cancelled "Six New Painters" in 1979, came to a peak in 1986 with his piece in the Second Biennial of Havana. A four-yard-long patchwork with the title *Te llevo bajo mi piel* (*I Carry You under My Skin*), the piece successfully summed up all his previous experiences and provided the ending point for the preceding period. Torres Llorca felt he had reached a dead end and proceeded to change his art radically.

Nevertheless, and despite the unevenness, like no one else in his generation he had explored vital aspects of Cuban culture and its internalized taste. The accepted value of blondness for cinematic deities, the status symbol of the refrigerator (placed at an angle against a corner in the living room), the import through cartoon dialogue bubbles of onomatopoeic sounds (in Spanish totally nonsensical) such as "bah,"

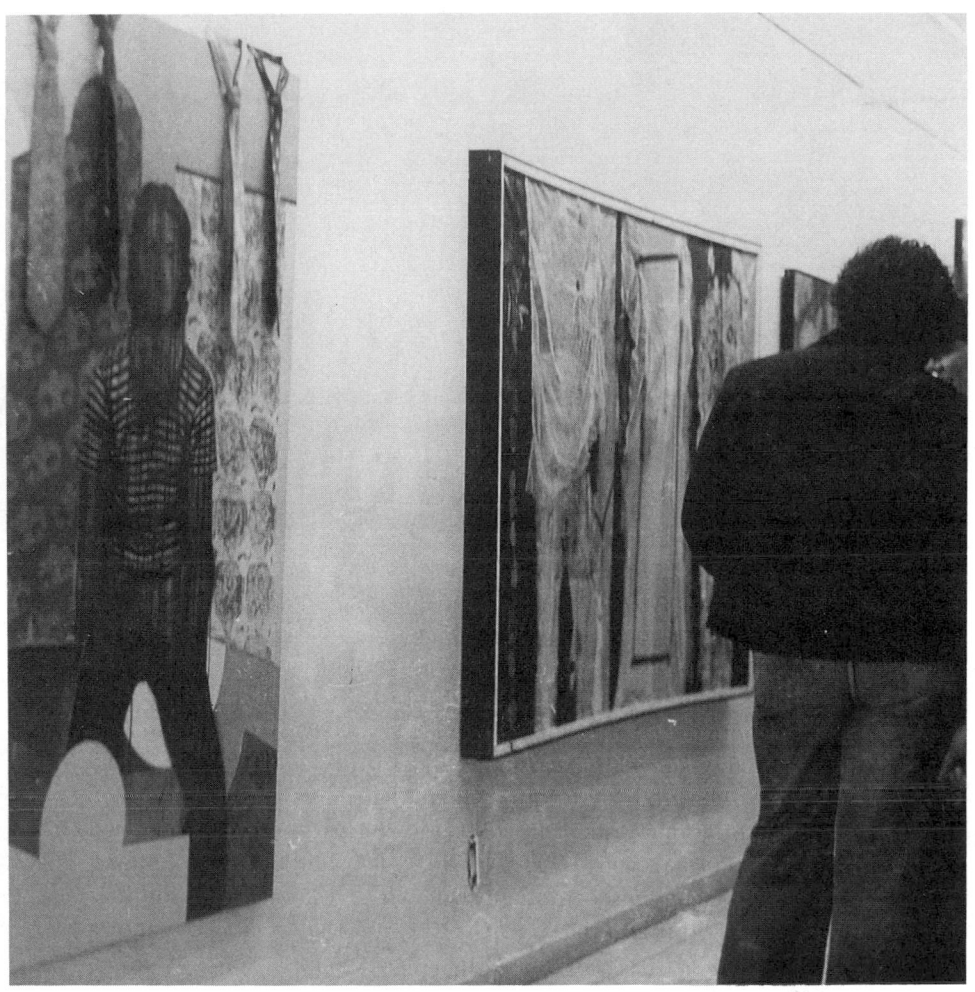

Rubén Torres Llorca, 1981. Works at "Volumen I" exhibit, Havana. Photo by José M. Fors.

"blam," and "hurrah," all became an imagery that denounced the colonial subversion of values. Pop-art resources were the overly obvious—but effective—tools to do this. In their obviousness they became one symptom more of what Torres Llorca wanted to express. He said, "Melodrama is completely mercenary, without ethics. It wants to please at any price. But there are resources within it that I think are redeemable. In a modest way, I am trying to get at these structures and elicit a critical reception. . . . Besides this, my work can be understood in many different ways, and above all as a personal mythology."[26]

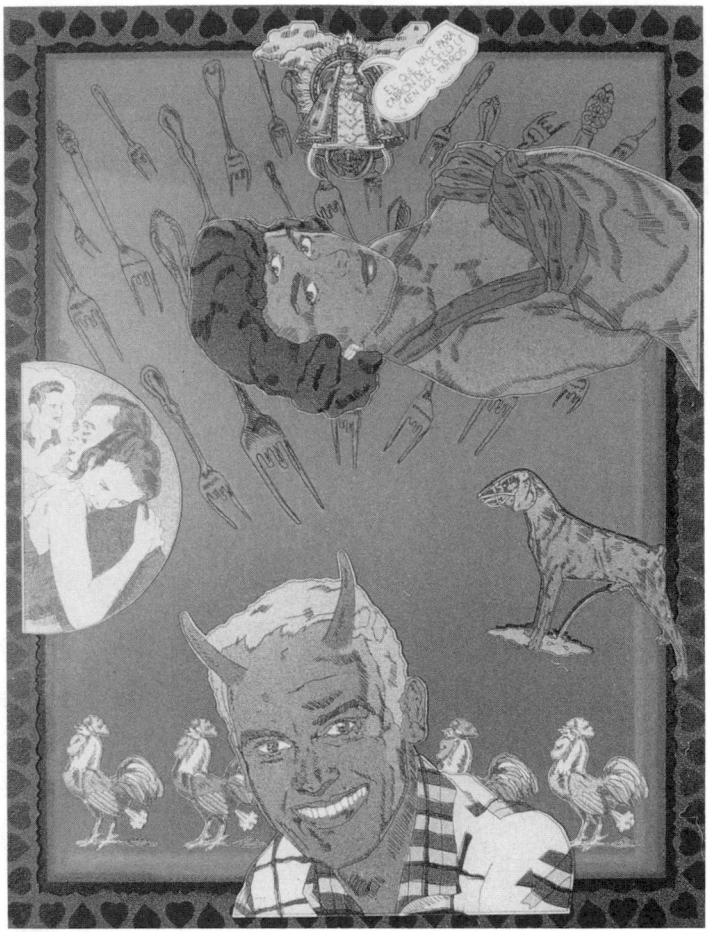

Rubén Torres Llorca, El que nace para. . . . II (He Who Is Born for . . . II), *1984–1986, mixed media on cardboard, 65 × 49 cm. Private collection. Photo by Luis Camnitzer.*

During the long process that culminated in the Second Biennial piece, Torres Llorca's main limitation may have been his baroqueness, which he had hinted at but never fully explored. Large and bearing unexplained ornamentation, the pieces focused on discrete situations, close-ups, and fragments of a reality too complex to be imagined or summed up by a detail. The Biennial piece was a breakthrough because it was his first epic piece. Based on advertising aesthetics and anatomical illustrations, it included mock romanticism and religious icons surrounded by a fake richness provided by the patterns of the fabric em-

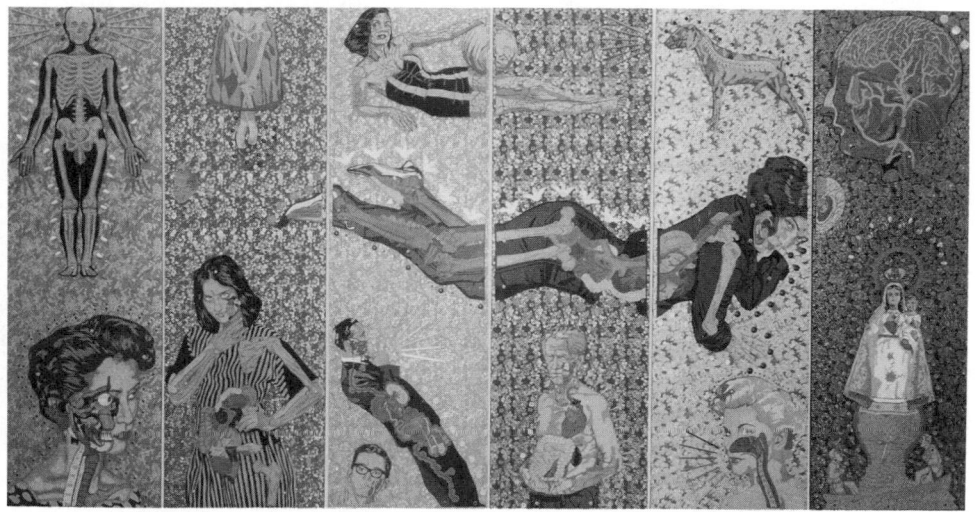

Rubén Torres Llorca, Te llevo bajo mi piel (I Carry You under My Skin),
*1985, mixed media, 215 × 400 cm. Collection of the artist. Photo by Luis
Camnitzer.*

ployed. The overall effect was that of a Max Ernst woodcut collage raised
to the proportions of public art.

Torres Llorca is, in his generation, closest to the younger artists. He
meets regularly with many of them to discuss both his and their work.
The result of these meetings has led to collective exhibitions, sometimes
designed as team work. This collaborative effort has had an effect on his
work. In "Estrictamente personal" ("Strictly Personal"), an exhibit at the
Fototeca in Havana in 1987, he grouped his work with originals and
photographic documentation about the art of twelve young artists. He
used his "strictly personal" criteria of selection for what essentially became another level of "patch work" for his own piece and for the museo-
graphic design of what became a group show.

The show was intended as a warning against the generational break,
and in the leaflet printed on occasion of the exhibit he stated, "It is paradoxical and sad that artists who suffered conservative attacks, once the
opportunity arrives, adopt decrepit positions faced with the new creators who are a product and the continuation of the ideas established by
them." In *Sombras nada más* (*No More than Shadows*) he constructed an
invented genealogical tree with distorted photographic portraits of his
friends in the shape of a multipaneled altar. Keeping the ornamental
elements of his previous work, symbols became more personal and, simultaneously, more loaded with religious evocations.

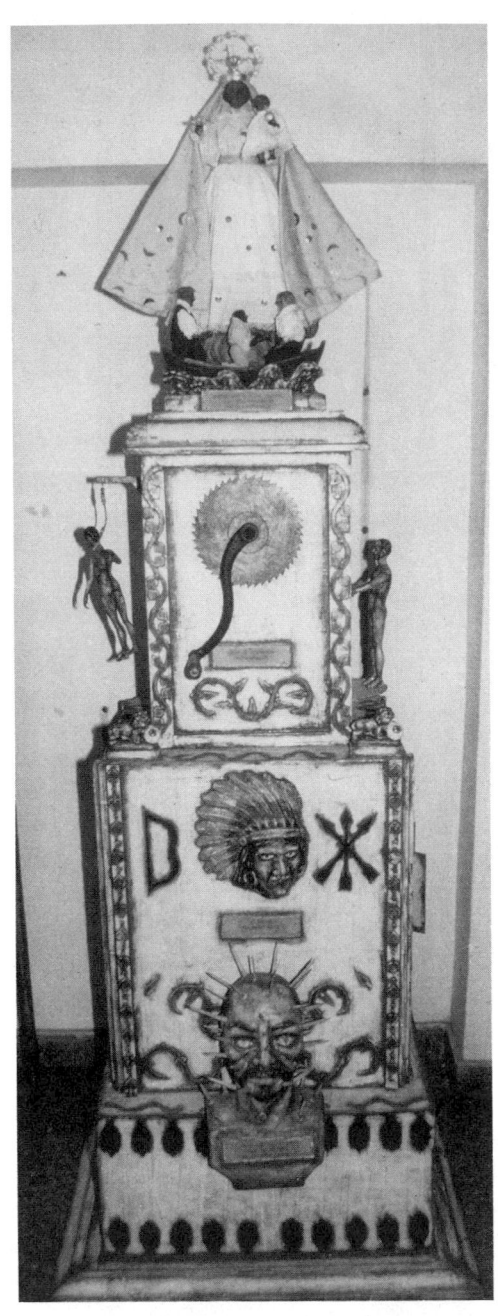

Rubén Torres Llorca, La trampa (The Trap), *1987, mixed media, 200 × 100 × 100 cm. Collection of the artist. Photo by Luis Camnitzer.*

A trip to Mexico in 1985 had widened his hitherto Cuba-oriented approach to a broader Latin Americanism, and Mexican religious art left its traces in his subsequent production. In his latest work, Torres Llorca has become more sculptural and has shifted his subject matter to cultural artifacts more connected with religious elements and less with mass-media aesthetics. With techniques derived from those used to make colonial-era church saints, he created environments held together with written phrases integrated in the pieces. A Cuban flag, once removed from a covered object, reveals two heads hatefully staring at each other attached to the lid of a box. Relief letters state, "With my enemy under the same roof." In another piece, a column holds up a bust with a heroic appearance while a red curtain in the back bears "What a problem if I lose my memory." The willed banality of Torres Llorca thus continues in his present work. The text is based on regurgitated everyday phrases while the image is reminiscent of icons that have lost their meaning over time but that still irradiate a sense of unexplained mystery. Together with the image, the text shifts from banality to drama, as if regaining the same power of assertion it might have had upon first utterance. Through these works kitsch appears to be no more than a transitional stage of banality suffered by images both visual and literary. Torres Llorca tries to bring back the prekitsch power to his postkitsch works without erasing history.

A later work, a 1989 exhibit done together with younger artist Lázaro Saavedra (see Chaps. 5 and 6) is based on the twenty-second century discovery of an exhibit produced in the twentieth century. In part reminiscent of the first generation (a glass-covered table is full of hand-colored photographs of the members of "Volumen I" with a text, "We are not anymore who we were"), the show deals with contemporary art problems illustrated with accumulations of sculptures constructed in a kitsch interpretation of Spanish colonial aesthetics. It is accompanied by photographs and didactic text explaining the objects to the future (in the show, "present") audience. Most of the pieces deal with idolatry, how individual ideals are betrayed by the followers, how there is an excessive respect for the foreign art stars, how personal ambitions come through in spite of one's wishes. Implicit points in the exhibit are that Cuba's art today inherits as much from previous art as it does from anthropology and the social sciences, and that art as a document is, when well done, better art than that concerned with formal issues. One of the pieces is dedicated to contemporary German artist Joseph Beuys; it is a Saint Joseph Beuys with offerings and their explanations: "Thank you for the computer," "Thank you for the trip," and so forth, attacking artists' venality. Titled "Una mirada retrospectiva" ("A Retrospective Look"), the

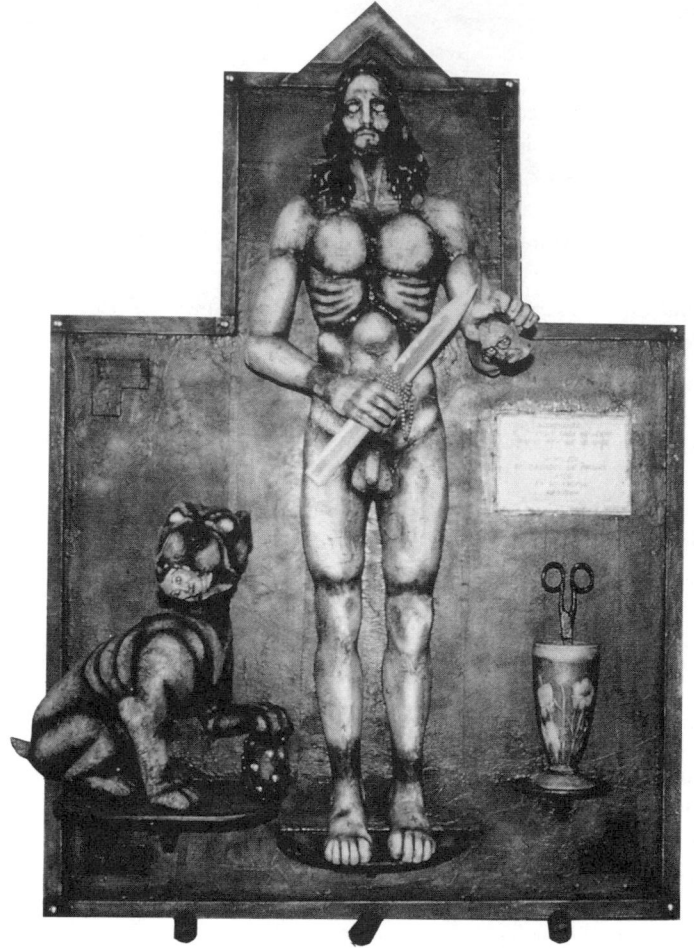

Rubén Torres Llorca, El rey que sabe no muere como el rey que no sabe
(The King Who Knows Doesn't Die Like the King Who Doesn't Know),
1988, mixed media. Collection of the artist. Photo by Luis Camnitzer.

introductory text to the brochure claims that the exhibit passed un-
noticed at the time but shared the effervescence of the art produced in
that moment. The work exhibited is dated imprecisely, as having been
made shortly after the first decantations of the products made by the
tribal group Arte Calle (see Chap. 5), a time when Cuban artistic prehis-
tory ended.

Torres Llorca worked for a while in Buenos Aires, Argentina, and is
now in Mexico, where he continues primarily with his altar-related
work. He finds himself "halfway between magic and psychology." As
Abdel Hernández writes, he appeals to subconscious cultural strata
through magic and to the patient for help in reconstructing traumas on
the conscious level.[27]

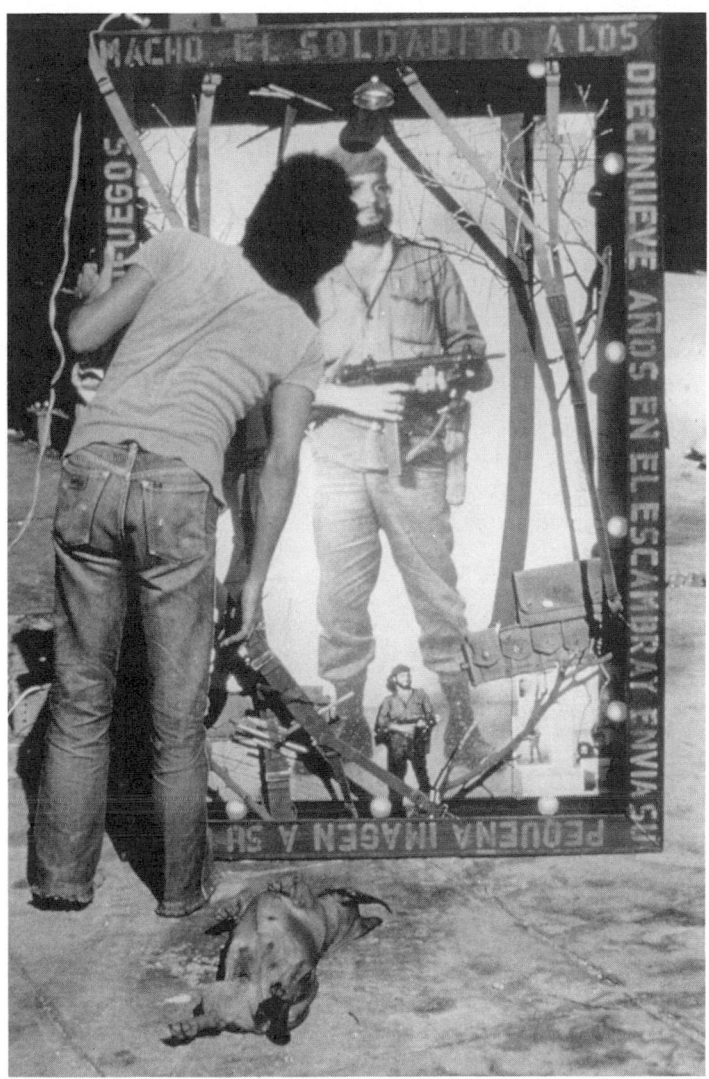

Leandro Soto finishing a piece, 1983.

Leandro Soto

Soto once wrote, "If I were a critic and—following the rules of the skill—had to marvel, I would say: 'I have seen a presentation where the style is within something named "Emotional Realism."'"[28] Except for this self-defined label, Soto's work over the years may not have any other common denominator.

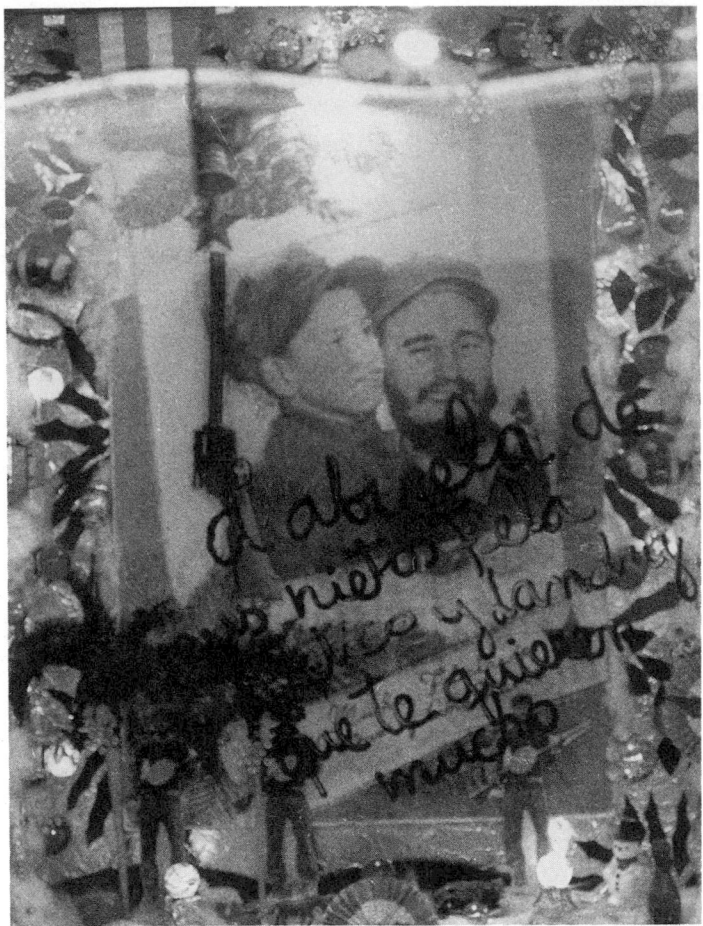

Leandro Soto, Primero de enero (January First), *1983, mixed media, 127 × 97 cm. Museo Nacional de Bellas Artes, Havana. Photo by Luis Camnitzer.*

Active in theatre, dance, and performances as well as in the plastic arts, his diversity of interests created a certain apparent disconnectedness of styles. He probably was Cuba's first performance artist, and parts of his early exhibits were built around the props and documentations for these performances.

In 1984, both in a one-man exhibit and in the First Biennial, things merged together most successfully in his work. Grouped under the title *Retablo familiar* (*Family Altar Piece*), the work of this period is primarily a series of showcaselike boxes filled with family memorabilia—photographs, postcards, toys, mantelpiece fetishes—set among lit light

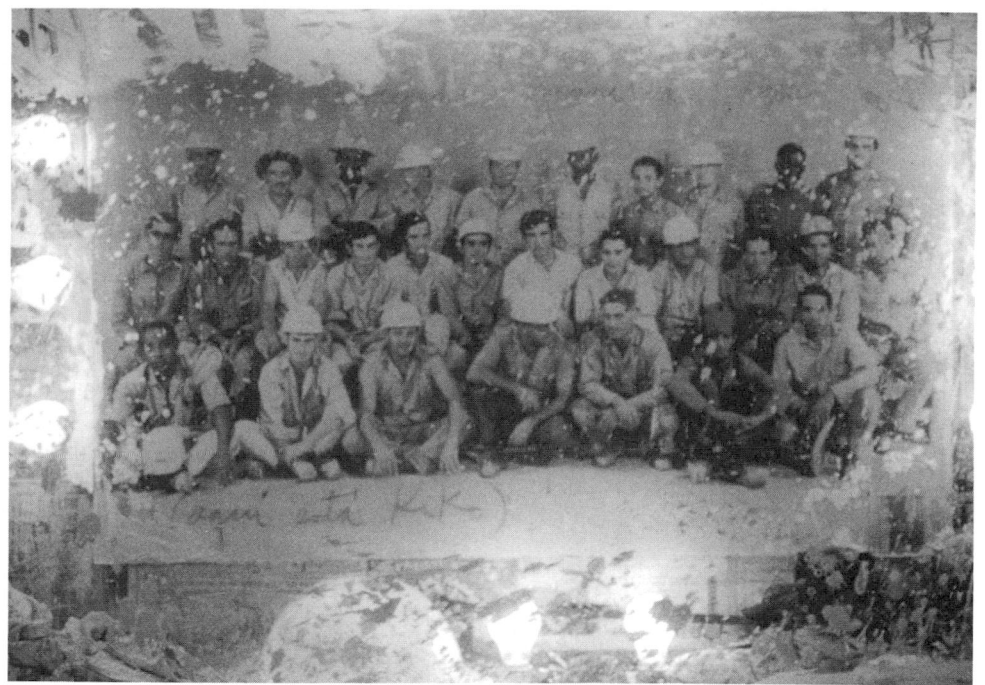

Leandro Soto, Kiko constructor (Kiko the Builder), *1983, mixed media, 97 × 127 cm. Collection of the artist. Photo by Luis Camnitzer.*

bulbs and accompanied by scribbles and words written on the glass. Describing them, I once excessively synthesized them as hybrids between Joseph Cornell and Robert Rauschenberg. The references are only valid as a superficial lead-in. Soto's showcases are to Cuban shop windows what Cornell's boxes are to Tiffany's windows. The parallel also clarifies the involvement of the public. Soto avoids the intimidation of preciousness and stays out of the arcane. His work has the mystery of memory. As with Rauschenberg in the 1960s, it is a popular memory in which banality is shamelessly included.

But more than shop windows, the boxes of Soto are altar pieces. While the aesthetics and aims of shop windows and altar pieces are by no means unrelated, in Soto's work the precision is important. The themes in his work are mostly of heroic nature, but he is not selling or promoting heroes. He is paying homage to his own heroes, the ones who came from his family and were his childhood supermen. His father, his uncle, like many others who anonymously helped create and defend the Revolution, become sacred through family romanticism and childhood projections of mysterious reverberations that act as secular halos.

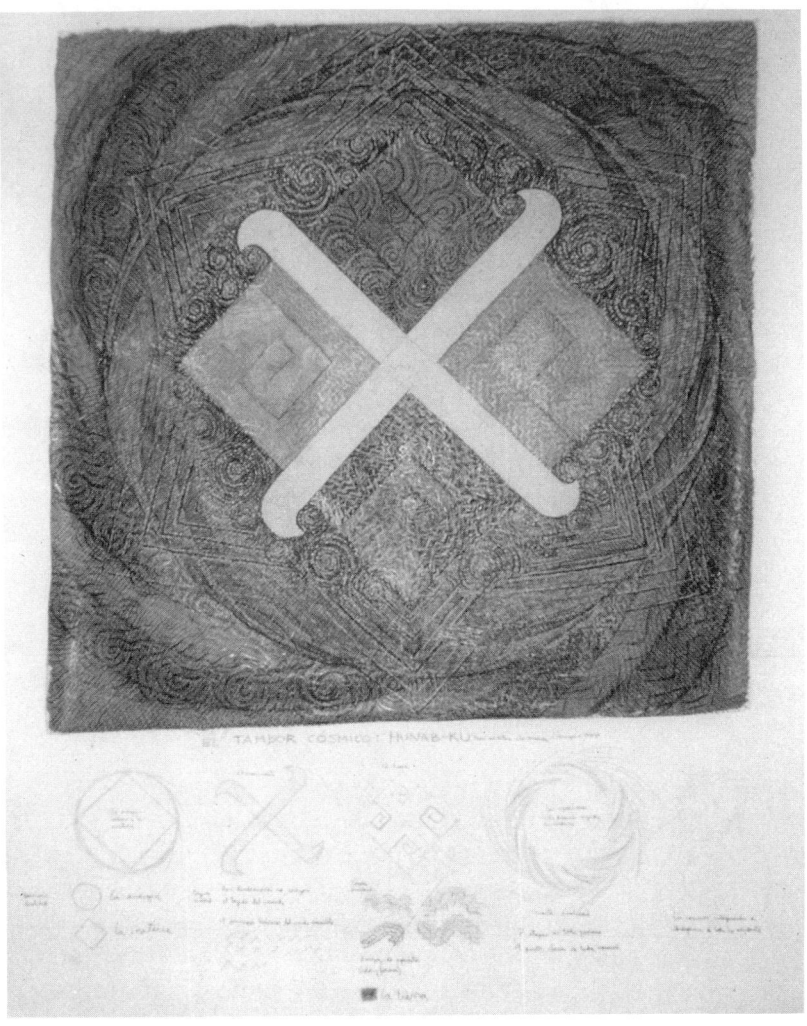

Leandro Soto, Tela Sagrada (Sacred Cloth), *fragment, 1989, mixed media. Collection of the artist. Photo by Luis Camnitzer.*

There is no detachment toward kitsch in the work of Soto. Kitsch is part of life and therefore an integral part of art. Historical reality is formed, according to him, by "every event, however quotidian, and every object, however ephemeral; [they] seem monuments of the unconscious flowing of days."[29] In this series of works, Soto connects with the "testimonial" period of Cuban art, updating the formal aspects without tampering with its essence. When a picture of Castro is included in a box, it creates the reverse of the dynamic inferred outside Cuba. It is not an homage to a superhero; it is rather a form of defining an extended family. Uncle, father, Fidel, all did the same. Soto himself and his friends all will do the same. There may be some sentimentality in the premise, but it is very much connected with reality, and "emotional realism" may be the best title for it.

In 1986, Soto started to break away from work dealing with the relatively distant past to start a series of pieces connected with a personal diary. With a more immediate and personally experienced memory on his mind, he drew cartoonish panels as pages (one series is called *The Book of the Fellowship Recipient*), gathering thoughts, personal aphorisms ("Ideas don't produce crises, crises produce ideas"), and experiences, thus removing himself from the kitsch experience.

In recent years Soto has worked in Mexico. His art production was interrupted when he went to work in a children's education program. Later he joined a native-Mexican music group through which he started a process of assimilation into their culture. Occasionally he still produces paintings, some of which he exhibited in the Third Biennial of Havana. Heavily inspired by pictographs and ornamental patterns, they seem a continuation of his personal diary and reflect his new mode of life.

AFRO-CUBANISM

Cuba's ethnographic and ethnocultural process is a complex product of the interaction of separatist racism and racial intermixing. Interracial relations were encouraged during the years of colonization starting as far back as 1503 when Isabel "the Catholic" encouraged miscegenation with a special decree and limited the access of white women to the colonies. By 1559 only 6.91 percent of the white population were women. Although Columbus already had brought black servants on his trip, the first official request to import black labor was in 1515, for twelve slaves to come from Hispaniola (now called Haiti and the Dominican Republic).

The rapid dwindling of the native population (Taino, Ciboney, and Guanahatabey Amerindians) through mistreatment and epidemics led to the rapidly increasing need for imported labor.[30] A request for three hundred more black slaves came in 1523, and by the middle of the sixteenth century there were one thousand slaves in Cuba. After 1762 sugar became Cuba's primary product. The semitropical climate was considered unfit for the work of white people, and the import of slaves accelerated rapidly; 300,000 slaves were imported between 1790 and 1820.[31] After the abolition of the trade in France in 1801 and in England in 1807, the import of slaves was illegal and difficult, so labor was imported from Asia.

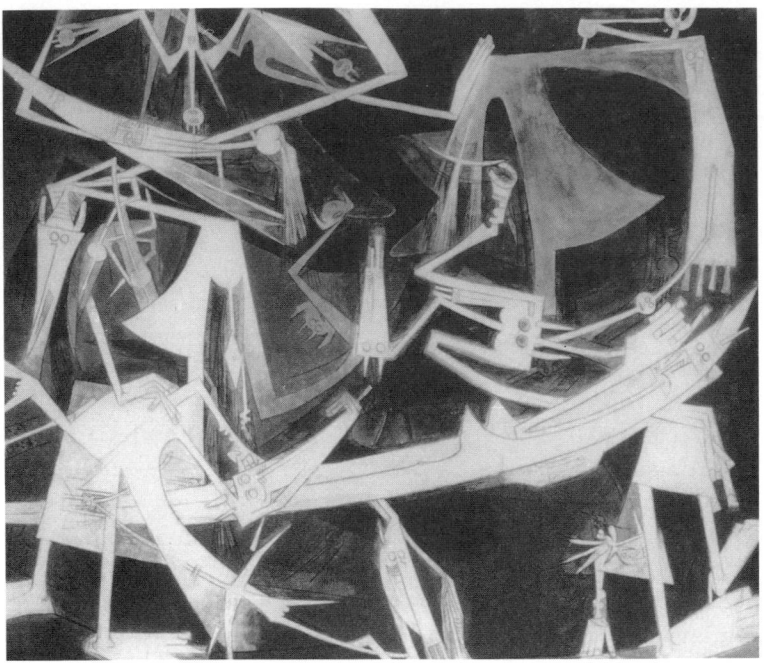

Wifredo Lam, El tercer mundo (Third World), *1965–1966, oil on canvas, 251 × 300 cm. Museo Nacional de Bellas Artes, Havana.*

Chinese workers were brought with a "contract" to work for eight years and with the condition that they must repay the expenses of their trip. The route of travel (via Manila, Acapulco, and Veracruz) avoided problems with the British. A thinly veiled slavery system thus brought 150,000 Chinese to Cuba. By 1861, there were 34,834 Chinese in Havana, of which only 57 were women.[32] Labor continued to be imported in the twentieth century. Between 1913 and 1924, 217,000 laborers from Haiti, Jamaica, and Puerto Rico went to Cuba to work for the sugar industry.[33]

Spaniards brought Catholicism to Cuba in different forms. There was the religion defined by the basic sacraments, but there were also subcults dedicated to the Virgin Mary, Christ, and the saints, including the custom of making ex-votos, little representations of parts of the body suffering ailments that, attached to the image of the appropriated saint, would lead to miraculous health.[34] This subdivision helped the process of syncretism with the original religions brought by the slaves.

Once the slave trade started, slaves had to be converted to Christianity on arrival in Cuba, a process that quickly deteriorated into a proforma ritual. A catechism book of the time was titled *Explanation of the*

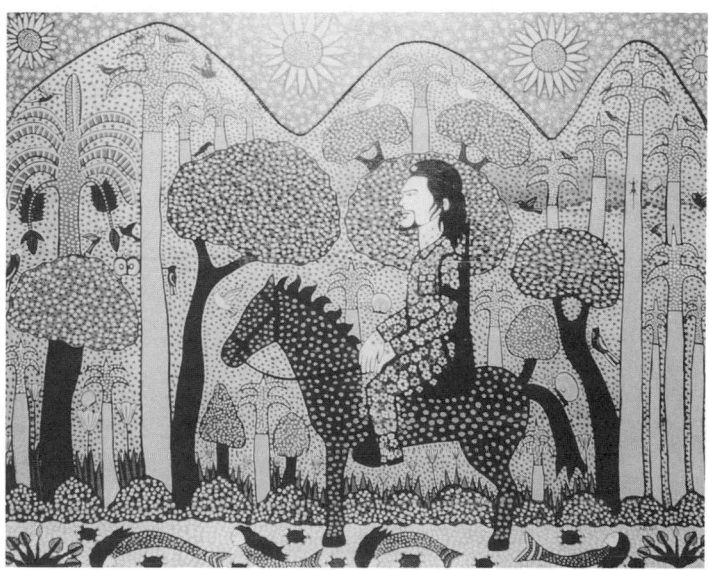

Manuel Mendive, Che 1967, enamel on wood, 120 × 140.5 cm. Museo Nacional de Bellas Artes, Havana. Photo by Luis Camnitzer.

Christian Doctrine Adapted to the Ability of the Bozal Black, a symbol of the paternalist attitude and the neglect of ideological rigor employed in the task.[35]

Manual activities were performed primarily by blacks, including for a long time the arts and crafts. Thus, much of the art destroyed by Bishop Espada y Landa in favor of divine order and neoclassic aesthetics (see Chap. 4, n. 37) was made by blacks.[36] The real impact of black artists on the Cuban mainstream had to wait until the appearance of Wifredo Lam (1902–1982). Lam was the son of a Chinese father and a mulatto mother. He grew up in an environment where *Santería* was part of everyday life. Antonica Wilson, a prestigious *Santera* (*Santería* priestess) of the time, was his godmother. Reality and beliefs were intertwined, and Lam remembered Tete, a neighbor whose house burned down to ashes and who escaped the fire by flying out through a window and landing in her native Africa.[37] As with many other Cuban artists, he was not himself a believer. *Santería* stood as a symbol of childhood magic and as a cultural background for his own individual definition. He used *Santería* mainly for his titles and as a starting point to develop a world of fantasy. On the other hand, *The Jungle* (1943), his most famous painting (presently decorating the lobby on the way to the coatroom of the Museum of Modern Art in New York), represents *orishas* (*Santería* deities) with great detail.[38]

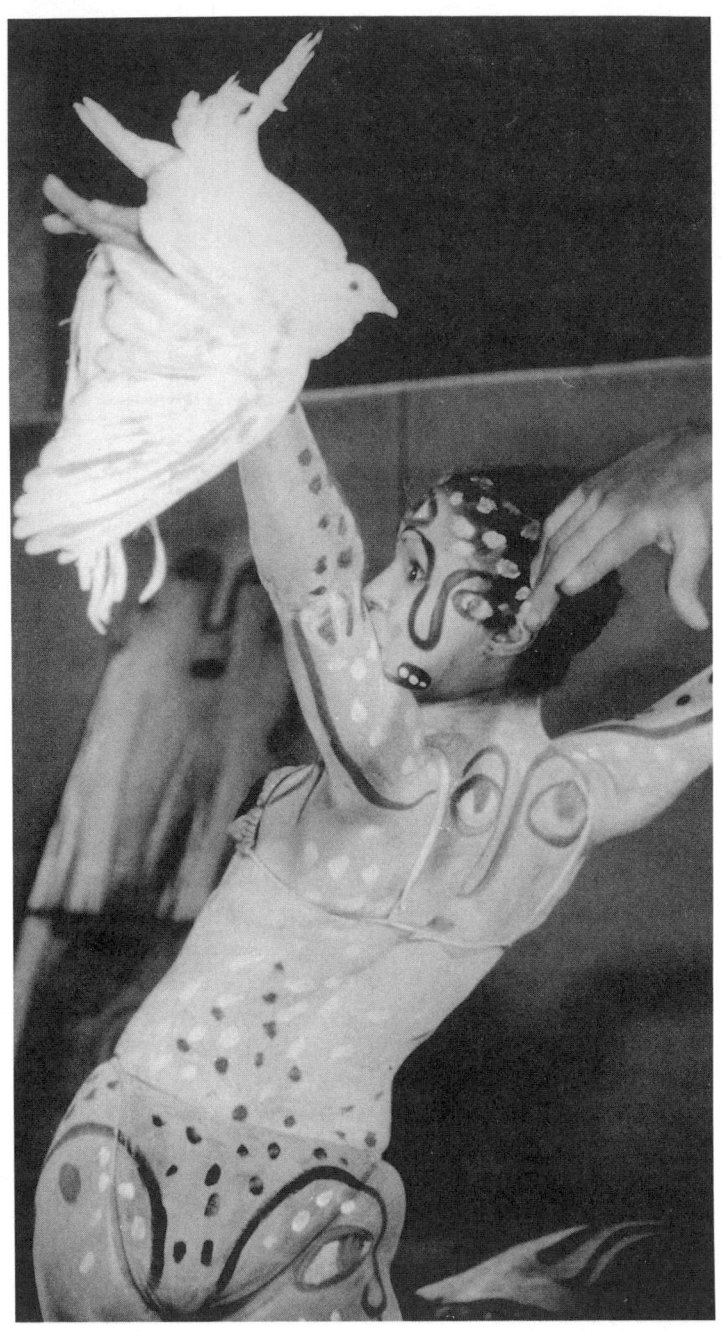

Manuel Mendive, performance at the Second Biennial of Havana, 1986. Photo by Luis Camnitzer.

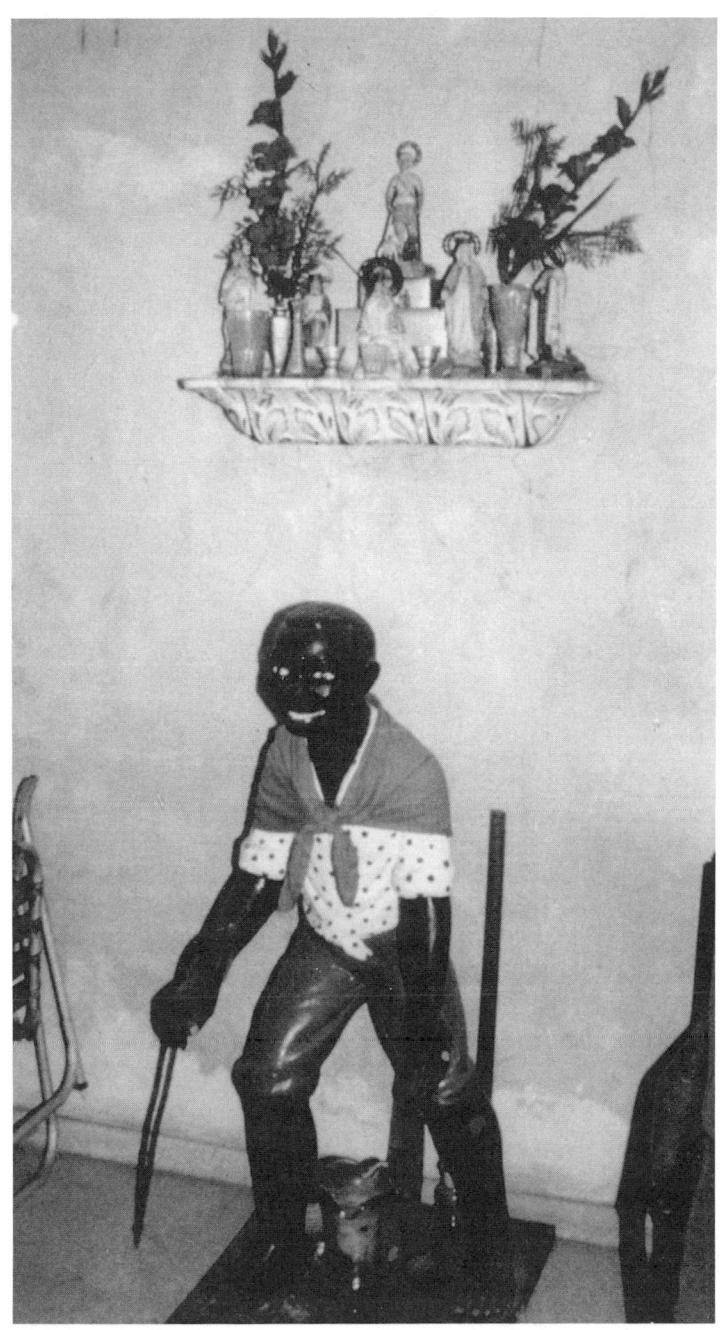

Santería *arrangement in a private home, Havana. Photo by Luis Camnitzer,*
1991.

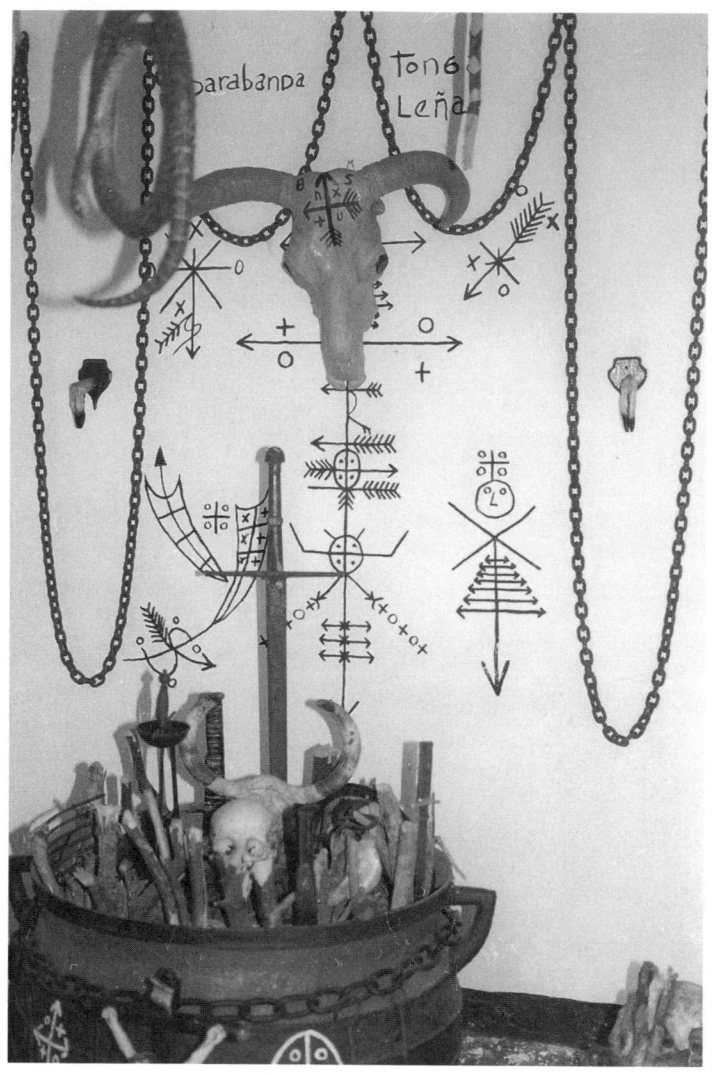

Palero *arrangement, Museo de Guanabacoa. Photo by Luis Camnitzer, 1986.*

Manuel Mendive (1944) continues the tradition in a more concrete fashion. Also a member of a practicing family, his art is more than an illustration of ritual motifs and is, particularly in his latest work, an extension of the ceremony. After a strong period in the 1960s during which he painted and carved deities on rough wooden planks, Mendive became excessively facile and decorative through the use of "naive" devices and some influence from Chagall.

While his paintings have not yet recovered from this sweetness, in 1986 he started to work on elaborate choreographies based on Yoruba rituals in which he painted the bodies of the dancers with his personal imagery. One of these performances merited a prize in the Second Biennial of Havana.

Santería (also referred to as *Regla de Ocha* or Ocha Rule) and *Palo Monte* (also known as *Regla de Conga* or Conga Rule) are the two main Afro-Cuban ritual systems having influence on the arts. Though there are many coincidences between both rituals, there seems to be a big difference in how the rituals are used. The initiation in *Santería* is considered a rite of purification and rebirth, connected with goodness. The initiation in *Palo* is a pact with death and the devil, connected with the possibility of performing evil.[39] Both rituals have followers among the artists of the 1980s, and some are more explicit about it than others, both in conversation and in how the beliefs are utilized in the work.

José Bedia

Bedia is a *Palero* (practitioner of *Palo Monte*). Erudite in Amerindian and African traditions, an indefatigable researcher of authentic popular art, and an avid collector of ceremonial artifacts, over the years his preferences landed in the *Palo Monte*. Although he is of Spanish ancestry and has no personal tradition to link him naturally to the ceremony, Bedia's studies and admiration have been so intense that it is no longer possible to draw the line to define his relation with the ceremony. It is not clear if he is a subject of the ritual or if the ceremony is the object of his analysis.

What matters is that Bedia is unable to visually define a Cuban essence without referring to the African tradition. (Fidel Castro once had referred to Cuba as a Latin-African country.) An overview of Bedia's work reflects his personal evolution in regard to these matters. His initial ethnographic interests were unfocused, more concerned with archeological research as a means of study. His work until 1981 represented realistically rendered fictitious archeological finds, validated through the attachment of fake objects with a credible look made by himself, and fragments of authentic pieces. Subsequently, he stopped his archeologist stance and became involved in the process. "It is no longer a question of hatchets or hoes dating back to such-and-such culture, but rather hatchet and hoes born of his artistic imagination and yet fit to be used the same way the primitive ones were used."[40]

An artistic precursor of what today is called "empirical anthropology," Bedia did not limit himself to the production of utensils but ventured into the production of symbology as well. In "The Persistence of Use," his one-man exhibit in March 1984, he explored his fascination

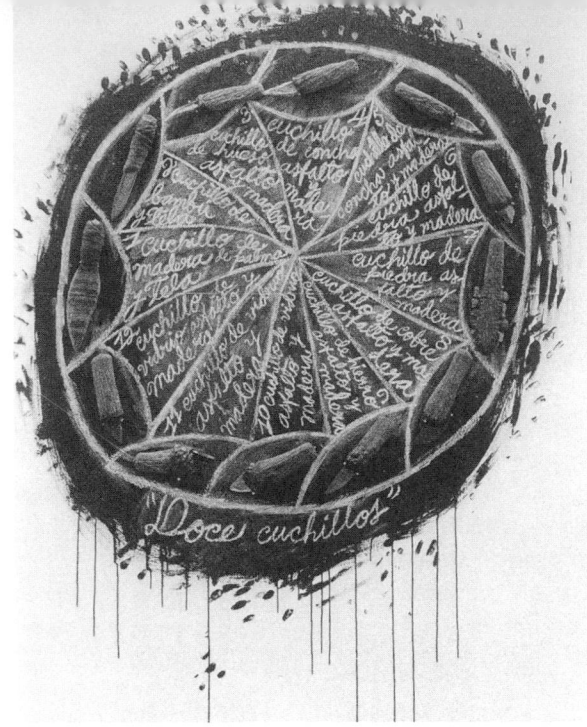

José Bedia, Doce cuchillos (Twelve Knives), *1983, mixed media on wall, 200 × 150 cm. Installation at the First Biennial of Havana. Photo by Luis Camnitzer.*

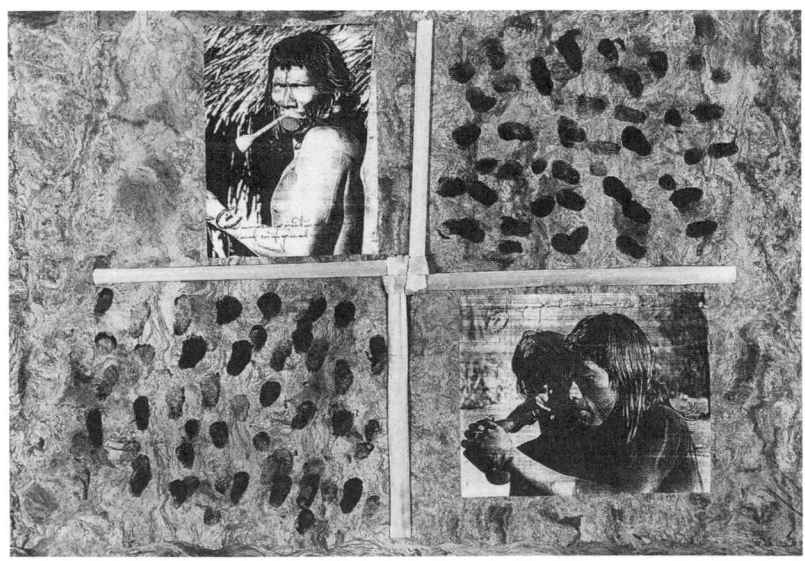

José Bedia, untitled, from the series "Crónicas americanas" (American Chronicles), 1982, mixed media amate paper. Collection of the Museo Nacional de Bellas Artes, Havana. Photo by Mario Díaz.

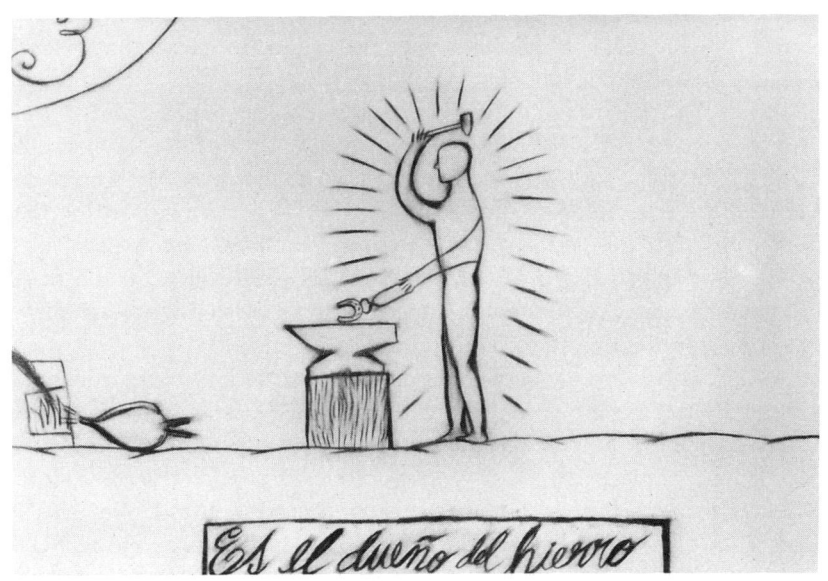

José Bedia, Es el dueño del hierro (He Is the Owner of Iron), *1984, pencil on paper, 56 × 76 cm. Collection of the artist. Photo by Luis Camnitzer.*

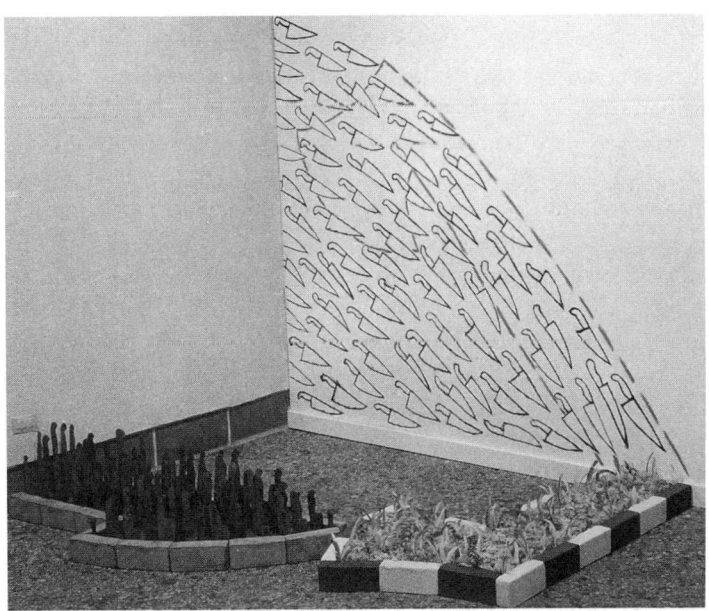

José Bedia, Sarabanda contra Siete Rayos, *1985. Installation at Amelie A. Wallace Gallery, State University of New York, Old Westbury, New York. Photo by Luis Camnitzer.*

with the constancy of function over the centuries. Two months later, in the First Biennial of Havana, he presented *Doce cuchillos* (*Twelve Knives*). A rough circular shape painted with dripping tar on the wall served as a blackboard holding knives made out of different materials and the manufacture explained in chalk-written words. The knives occupied the place of the numbers on a clock. In drawings starting that same year, Bedia illustrated *Palero* myths. In *Sarabanda contra Siete Rayos*, two *Palero* deities appear, and his drawing style borrows from the *firmas* (signatures), which are drawings specifically associated with each deity, used to start them in supernatural processes.

Although over the years Bedia has concentrated more rigorously on *Palero* elements, he has not neglected his other interests, and his work maintains a ceremonial eclecticism. The effigy of the North American Indian, particularly the Sioux with his plumage, available in dime stores in the form of kitschy plaster casts, is often used in Afro-Cuban rituals representing particular spiritual guides. But it is also a symptom of U.S. colonial influence. As Bedia himself noted, when a Latin American conjures the image of an Amerindian, it is not a Taino or an Inca who comes to mind; it is a Sioux.[41] Thus, there is a triple interest in this subject on Bedia's part—the ritual, the colonial symptom, and the culture itself—and North American Indians often appear in his work expanding the syncretism far beyond the Afro-Cuban tradition.[42]

In his generation, Bedia is probably the least interested in Western culture influences. While aware of the work of "shamanist" artists such as Beuys, he does not look for the enrichment of Western culture by means of "primitive" devices but aims at the continuation and revitalization of an old tradition. As Mosquera writes in the introduction of his catalogue to a 1987 exhibit of Bedia's work, "For the Third World it is not a matter of resuscitating precapitalist solutions, which correspond to the state when the internal evolution was interrupted by the Eurocentric expansion of capitalism. It is a matter of *making* Western art in [the Third World's] way and for [the Third World's] own benefit."[43]

From a less Western but a more truly international vantage point, much of the work of Beuys and other artists who produce "informed" primitivism can be classed as anthropological kitsch, which rarely goes beyond an affectation determined by the superficial appropriation of symptoms of presumed exoticism. The interest of Bedia's work, and that of others like him, is that it explores grounds for a new and more encompassing internationalism based on Third World values.

One of Bedia's most ambitious and successful pieces, his entry to the Biennial of São Paulo in 1987, bears the title *The Indian Commission and the African Commission against the Material World*. Third World symbols,

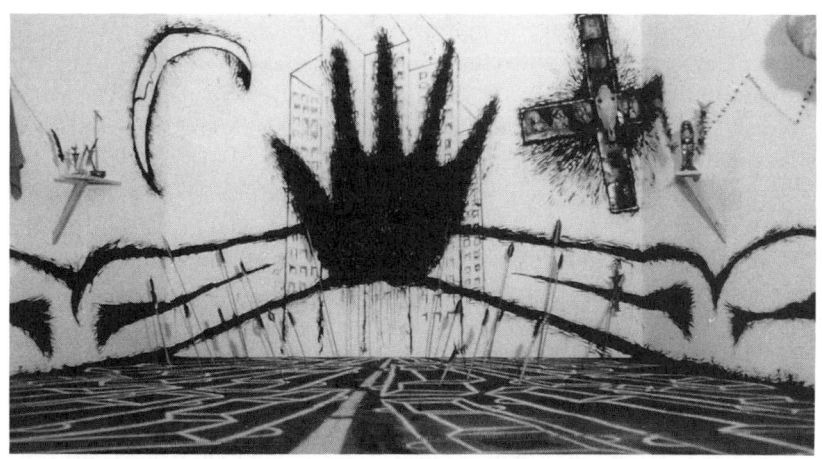

José Bedia, La comisión india y la comisión africana contra el mundo material (The Indian Commission and the African Commission against the Material World), *1987. Installation at the Biennial of Sao Paulo. Photo by José Bedia.*

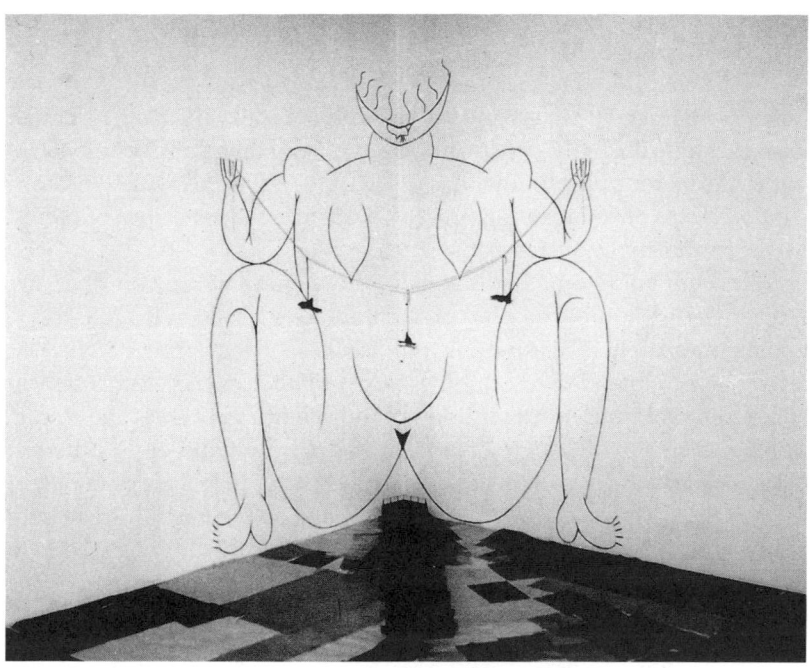

José Bedia, ¿Qué te han hecho Mama Kalunga? (Mama Kalunga, What Have They Done to You?), *1989. Installation at Castillo de la Fuerza, Havana. Photo by Luis Camnitzer.*

placed on a wall, rule over a platform that extends into the room and is covered by cars drawn with chalk. In the best expressway tradition, they get lost in the vanishing point of a forced perspective. The presence of diverse "primitive" symbols, through a magic spell, is destined to save the world against its own self-destruction.

The piece follows in the tradition of *Sarabanda contra Siete Rayos*, an installation Bedia had exhibited first during his stay at the College at Old Westbury in 1985. In these works, and in a manner he is still pursuing, he combines his powerful drawing with allegorical objects. Particularly the insights derived from *Sarabanda* led to *The Stroke of Time*, an installation in the Second Biennial of Havana, which earned him one of the prizes; his installation in the exhibition "Magiciens de la Terre" in 1989; his one-man show in the Third Biennial of Havana; and his *What Have They Done to You, Mama Kalunga?* installation in the 1990 Venice Biennial.

At this point Bedia has managed to codify his drawings into a rigid pictographic system, a quasi alphabet. Normally this would result in an array of formalistic recipes and artistic death. In Bedia's case it seems to have released him from a wasteful expressive struggle and freed him to deal with his startling visual and symbolic imaginativeness.

Ricardo Rodríguez Brey

Rodríguez Brey belongs to a family that traces its origins to what today is Nigeria. His ideas and art are influenced by the *Santería* ritual. Fascination with early nineteenth-century explorers and particularly with Alexander von Humboldt led Rodríguez Brey to work on more subtle aspects of colonization processes, such as the resistance of nature to imprisonment by systematic science.

Von Humboldt, who had intensive art training himself and had exhibited his art in the Academy of Berlin between 1786 and 1788, had a holistic approach to nature. He produced a "panorama of nature at large," which intended to combine the overall landscape with botanical and geological precision, merging art and science to present the results of his research.[44] Although Columbus had encountered eight different varieties of palm trees on his trips, eighteenth-century European depictions of the Latin American landscape insisted on the portraiture of date palms and were full of other stereotypes. Von Humboldt engaged fifty artists to use his sketches and instructions for the illustration of his books, and he encouraged them to take their own trips.

Von Humboldt visited Cuba in 1801 and stayed for about seven weeks. Rodríguez Brey considers him the second "discoverer" of Cuba after Columbus, and a far more sympathetic one (being a freethinker and opposed to slavery). While in Cuba, von Humboldt kept a diary that

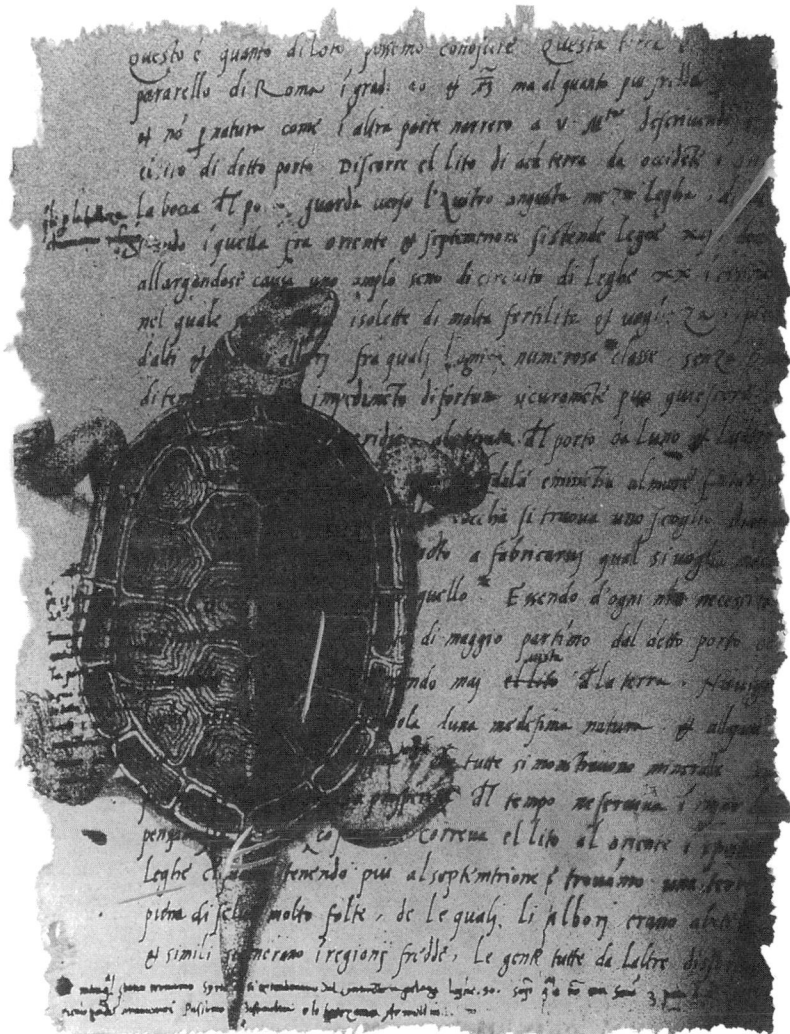

Ricardo Rodríguez Brey, page from La Estructura de los mitos *(The Structure of Myths), 1985, mixed media on paper, 24 × 20 cm. Private collection. Photo by Luis Camnitzer.*

was lost. It became Rodríguez Brey's self-assigned task to recreate this document. Using mimeograph stencils and photostats reproducing old writings and botanical and zoological drawings, he supplemented them with his own and with fake aging by means of the use of dyes. Bookworm marks were imitated by carefully cutting out their presumed path through the pages, and he frayed the brittle paper's edges with a rough file. The result was *La estructura de los mitos* (*The Structure of Myths*).

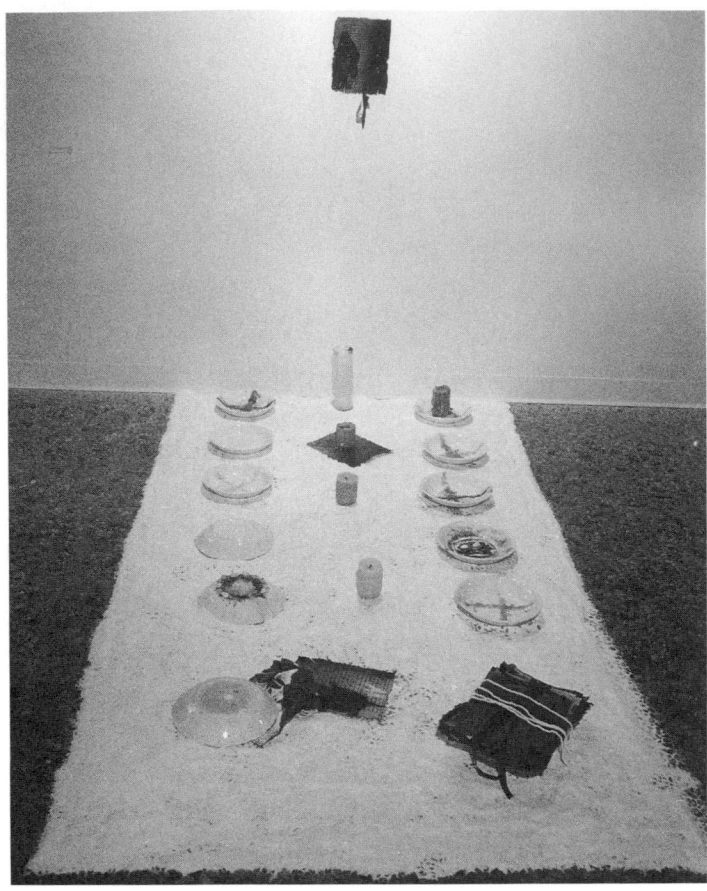

Ricardo Rodríguez Brey, La estructura de los mitos (The Structure of Myths), *1985. Installation at the Amelie A. Wallace Gallery, State University of New York, Old Westbury, New York. Collection of the artist. Photo by Luis Camnitzer.*

On the occasion of the "Kuba o.k." exhibition in Düsseldorf, Rodríguez Brey, who went to Germany, had the opportunity to inspect original diaries by von Humboldt. To his surprise and disappointment, the sheets of the originals were impeccably clean, without any trace of bookworm holes or signs of aging.

Initially Rodríguez Brey limited his pieces to expressing a gentle reluctance by an overwhelming tropic to be catalogued in the European way. "I was interested in [von Humboldt's] . . . effort to deal with Cuba on a scientific level while being confronted with a poetic reality. He would try to write down data in his diary such as what temperature he

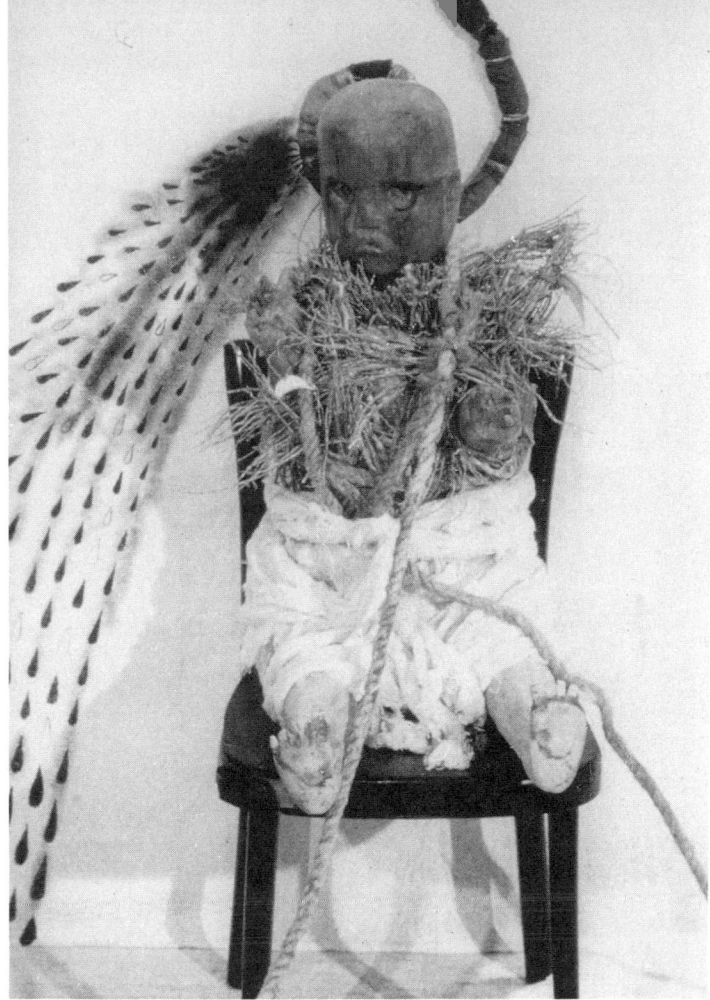

Ricardo Rodríguez Brey, Un objeto inocente (Innocent Object), *(detail), 1988, 200 × 600 cm. Installation at the Art Gallery of New South Wales. Collection of the artist. Photo by Charles Merewether.*

recorded on a given day, and then extemporaneously record how beautiful things are."[45] In time, however, the work expressed a Cuban takeover of the results.

The fictional diary became part of a *Santería* offering. In the installation *The Structure of Myths,* which Rodríguez Brey made in 1985 at the College at Old Westbury, rows of plates with candles and shells are placed on a bed of salt following the *Santería* ritual. The offering placed on one of the plates is a package of pages from the diary. Thus, *Santería* takes over.

In a subsequent exhibit of drawings at the Centro Wifredo Lam, "Sobre la tierra" (an ambiguous title that is both "About the Earth" and "On the Soil"), Rodríguez Brey worked on subjects related to Eleggua, the *Santería* god that opens and closes roads, but also on elements related to the *Palero* ritual. Images of rocks, plants, and cauldrons, the latter giving out fumes in magic shapes, have details repetitively annotated with the words designating them, creating both a poetic and an ornamental atmosphere. The deities are not represented but are presented through their everyday hidden appearance, only sometimes highlighted by the presence of vaguely ritual elements.

According to Rodríguez Brey, the rock does not allude directly to Eleggua but to the first steps that lead to the creation of myth as an answer to the individual's need to attach himself to beliefs to strengthen his spirit. "He is led to create gods and ascribes a system of values to the stone."[46]

Rodríguez Brey is now venturing more into sculpture. A close friend of Elso Padilla, he had stopped himself for many years from making sculpture, fearing that it might look like Elso Padilla's. This fear overcome, he is now carving his own objects, keeping a typical *Santería* ready-made attitude, using—as in the cult—everyday objects and loading them with meaning. Even when made by him, the objects follow *Santería* systems of bricolage (e.g., a ladder with spikes on the steps) and create what he calls a "mythical readymade" that combines elements from different cultural sources.

This process, initiated in 1989, led to his installation in the Third Biennial of Havana, a piece that did not seem yet completely resolved but that was impressive enough to have him invited to the 1992 Documenta exhibition in Kassel. Rodríguez Brey is presently also experimenting with what superficially appears to be traditional and somewhat decorative ways of painting. In reality he is trying to infuse the painterly process with *Santería* qualities, thus deriving power not from Western forms but from the Afro-Cuban ritual.

Juan Francisco Elso Padilla[47]

Sometime during March 1988, Cuban artist Juan Francisco Elso Padilla was diagnosed as having leukemia. Eight months later he was dead at the age of thirty-two. It was, in some ways, a more painful process for those of us who were left behind than for him. Elso's all-encompassing view of the world and of himself diminished the magnitude of his disappearance to the size of a small incident.

During his months of illness he wrote, "For me, art is a long personal process of apprehension of the world and of myself as part of the world. The processes and insights are more important than my work. They act as a nearly mystical learning experience and they shape my attitude to-

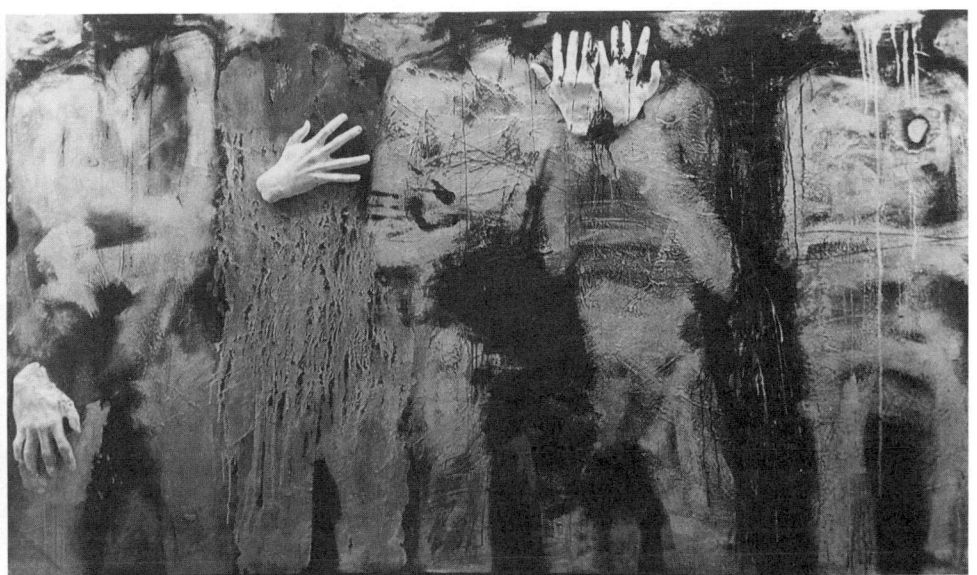

*Juan Francisco Elso Padilla, untitled, 1981. Installation at "Volumen I."
Photo by José M. Fors.*

wards life. . . . The whole of this experience is based on a Latin American spirituality which only now we are starting to project as a value system. . . . Cultural changes may come from this development and some of us may become its insignificant harbingers."[48]

The body of work that has become Elso's legacy is the product of one decade. Critics who saw it discerned a great promise, and hopeful expectations for the quality of the work to follow sharpened their criticism of the work already produced. Now, with that hope cruelly removed, that which was the foundation has taken the place of the building to be. But even before his retrospective exhibit in the Museo Carrillo Gil in Mexico City,[49] it was clear that Elso was not an "insignificant harbinger."

With a singular precision Elso embodied an odd mixture of secularity and mysticism, of magic and ethics, which ruled all his actions in art and in life. A continual back and forth from questions to answers, both phrased in a permanent dialogue within himself, formed the set of idiosyncratic parameters of his artistic activities. In a society other than Cuba this internal dialectic could have led to alienated individualism. Instead, Elso's lucidity, his nearly physical awareness of belonging to a complex social web, and his pantheistic view of the universe, transformed it into what indeed may be called a "Latin American spirituality."

Elso was drenched in spirituality without discarding the socialist ethic in which he grew up. This mixture, which he called a "dialectic mixture," defined him for himself as a Cuban. It also helped him transcend himself as a Latin American. And, in turn, this dialectic affected his use of scale. Using sculptural devices, Elso played on the viewer's space, always transmitting a certain fragility. José Martí, for him both a national and a universal symbol, was depicted smaller than human without any loss of power, eliciting both tenderness and awe—the awe inspired by the implicit mission. Elso wanted to represent "Martí and Bolívar brandishing the sky," which for him was roughly a political expression. But he also talked about "a mask of death capable of looking at the bearer and propitiating self-discovery, with the instruments of the creation of the world and other pieces representing the ethical foundation and mechanisms of the universe."[50]

Latin American suffering and hope was a fuel that Elso absorbed through his pores. While it gave him an unerring sense of direction, it was also a burden. Elso was a steady, but painfully slow, producer. Each twig, each lump of earth used in his art, "was" the universe. Somehow there were no means—everything was an end. There were infinite small ends that together added up to a large end. If there was to be a means, it could only be himself, in the most humble way conceivable. We now profoundly resent his slow and scarce production—he once said he would die as a ten-piece artist—and with the same ire we curse his death. But it is a selfish, consumerist anger, which denies all that Elso stood for.

Elso stood for the search for what he called a Latin American spirituality. For some, including myself, this is an intangible issue, an inexplicable one, and, perhaps, no more than the projection of a wish rather than a reality to be attained. For Elso, however, that search was *the* search for reality.

Like many of his colleagues, Elso was preoccupied with the dynamics of colonization and, in a parallel way, with *Santería*. But his main emphasis focused on a mythical America. He did not just address the reorganization of nature or, as in the case of other artists, the possibilities of rituals stemming from their origins. Using these elements he aimed at a new, continental mythology conscious of history. Both personally and aesthetically Elso was close to Ana Mendieta. Many of Ana's works seem to lean on Elso's work, but while Ana worked on an introspective study of the relation of tradition and uprootedness, Elso tried to transcend individuality to achieve a continentalism.

In the early 1980s Elso created a series of installations, primarily made out of ceramic elements but mixing natural elements with artificial

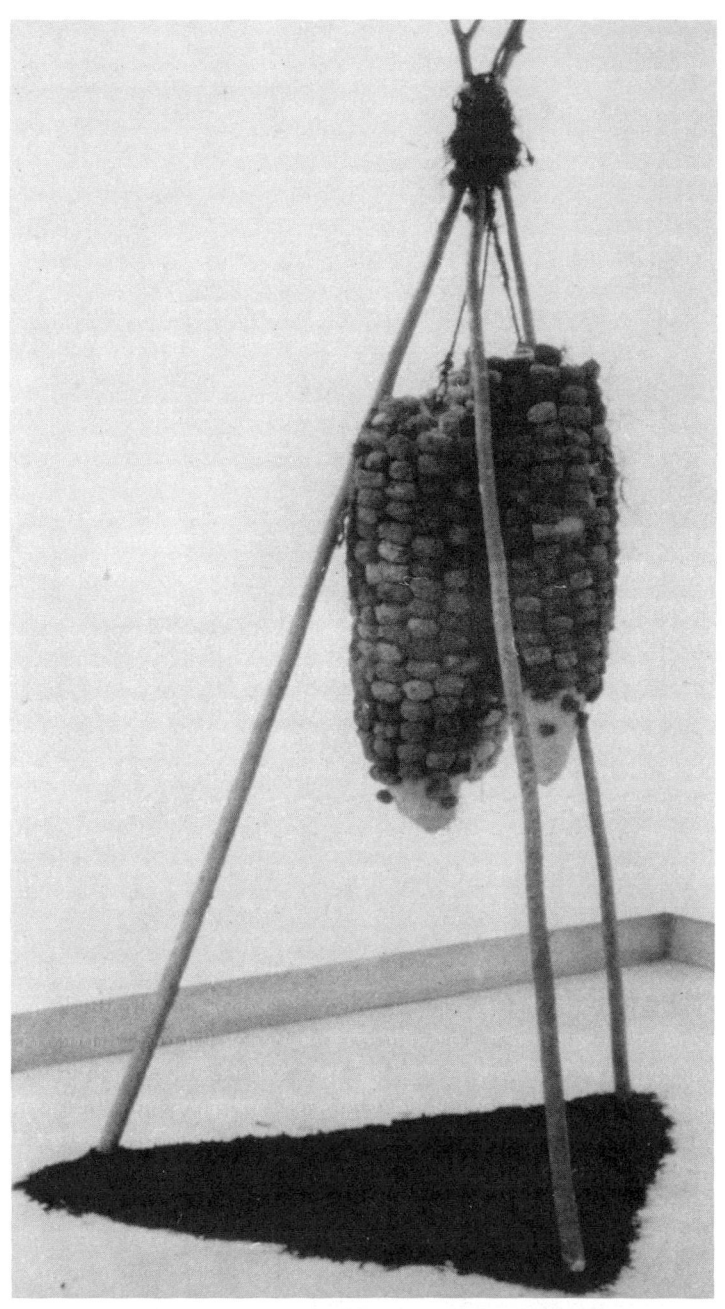

Juan Francisco Elso Padilla, Tierra, maíz, vida (Soil, Maize, Life), *part of an installation, 1982, 290 × 150 × 150 cm. Collection of Magali Lara, Mexico. Photo by the artist.*

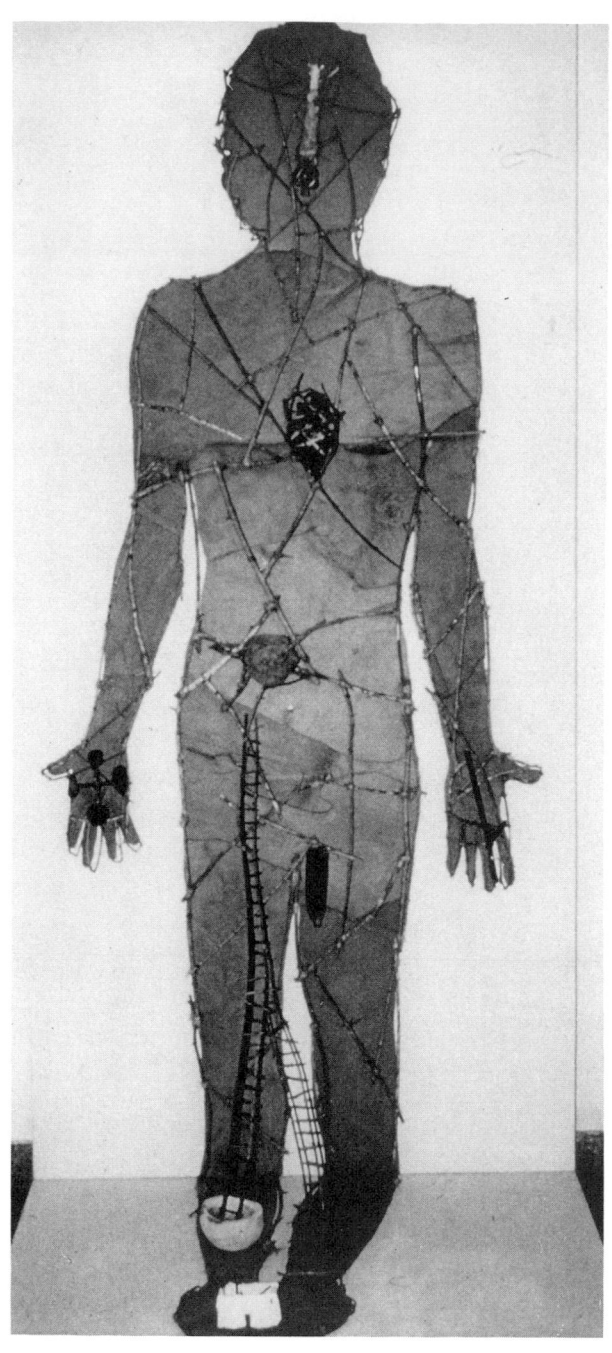

Juan Francisco Elso Padilla, El monte (The Forest), *1984, mixed media, 170 × 60 cm. Collection of Magali Lara, Mexico. Photo by the artist.*

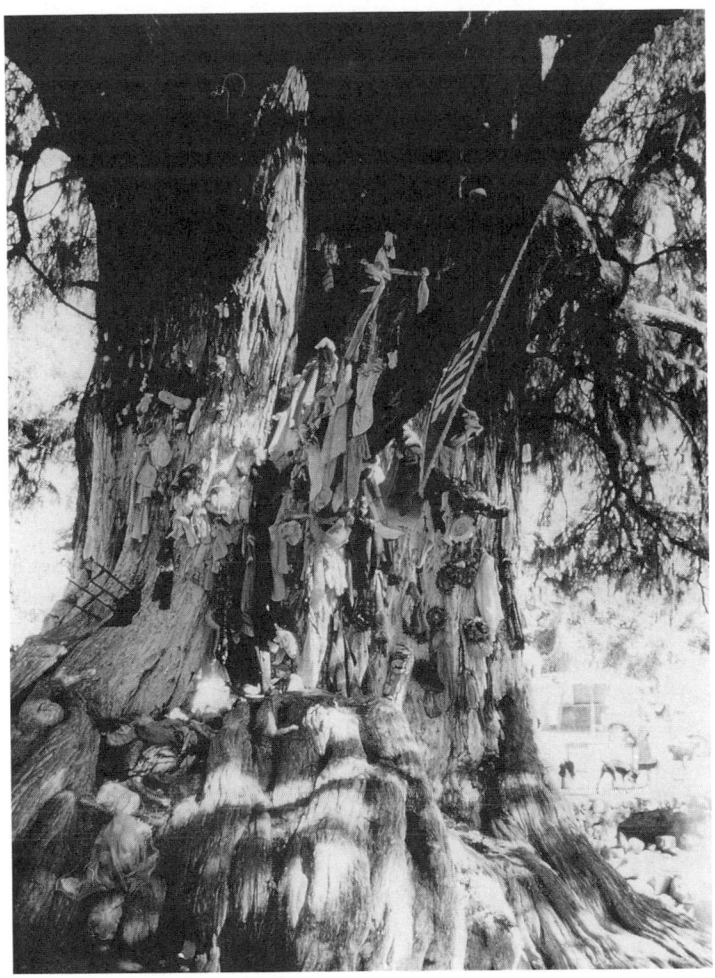

Sacred Ahuehuete tree, Chalmas, Mexico. Photo by Luis Camnitzer.

ones to explore the role of maize in some of the Amerindian cultures. Already symbolically loaded, connecting the maize to pyramids and calendars, the references addressed more customs than myths.

The maize work culminated in an exhibit called "Tierra, maíz, vida" ("Soil, Maize, Life") (1982), the show in which Elso felt he had finally got rid of his schooling and had become free to pursue his own unhampered language.[51] Utilizing texts and a sound track with songs by the Bari Indians, Elso tried to establish not only how the Indians depended on maize but also how maize depended on the Indians, illuminating their symbiotic relationship.

In 1984, at the First Biennial of Havana, Elso exhibited a piece that broke new ground. Called *El monte* (*The Forest*), it consisted of a human silhouette made out of burlap, with symbolic details provided by twigs. The piece formalized, for the first time, his interest in *Santería*, opening a second direction for his work, which later would merge with his interest in Amerindian traditions. Elso was his own most rigorous critic. While he acknowledged *El monte* to be an important personal breakthrough for himself, he felt it was too descriptive and that "the narrative parts of the piece did not add to a total and did not achieve the magic state I wanted."[52]

Both the *Santería* and the Amerindian traditions were subjects of Elso's intellectual curiosity. While the Afro-Cuban tradition was a live one for him, a part of the everyday social web, the Amerindian one was acquired from books and, at first, incorporated in his work in a superficial and idealized manner. It took him time to understand the meaning of good and evil in those cultures (as opposed to the stereotype of evil being Spanish and good being Indian) and to put this new awareness into place. The process of demystifying Amerindian cultures allowed him to approach them with increased respect, and thus they became part of his work. A subsequent trip to Mexico, where he had direct contact with artifacts from these cultures, was crucial to his development. The sacred Ahuehuete tree had a particular fascination for him. Located in Chalmas, the tree has been used by pilgrims since pre-Hispanic times to hang fragments of umbilical cords of their newborns, along with other mementos connected with birth, in order to ensure strength and good luck for their offspring.

Unlike many other Cuban artists, Elso had no initial direct contact with *Santería* rituals. His close friendship with Ricardo Rodríguez Brey allowed him more intense access to its inner workings. The experience made him draw ethical analogies between the new *Santería* experience and his socialist upbringing in the sense that both *Santería* and socialism aim at the betterment of people. (*Santería* rituals cannot be used for evil purposes, but are only to fend off evil.)

The combination of his experiences produced what is Elso's most memorable masterpiece: *Por América* (*For America*). A three-quarter-size effigy of Martí, the piece was built in the manner of colonial church saints, the sculpture partially covered with mud, with the body wounded by red and green darts—the first signifying the blood drawn by aggression, the second being sprouts of fertile rebirth. The work, which was awarded a Mention in the Second Biennial of Havana, was probably the most powerful entry among more than two thousand works exhibited, in that it sustained multiple political and religious

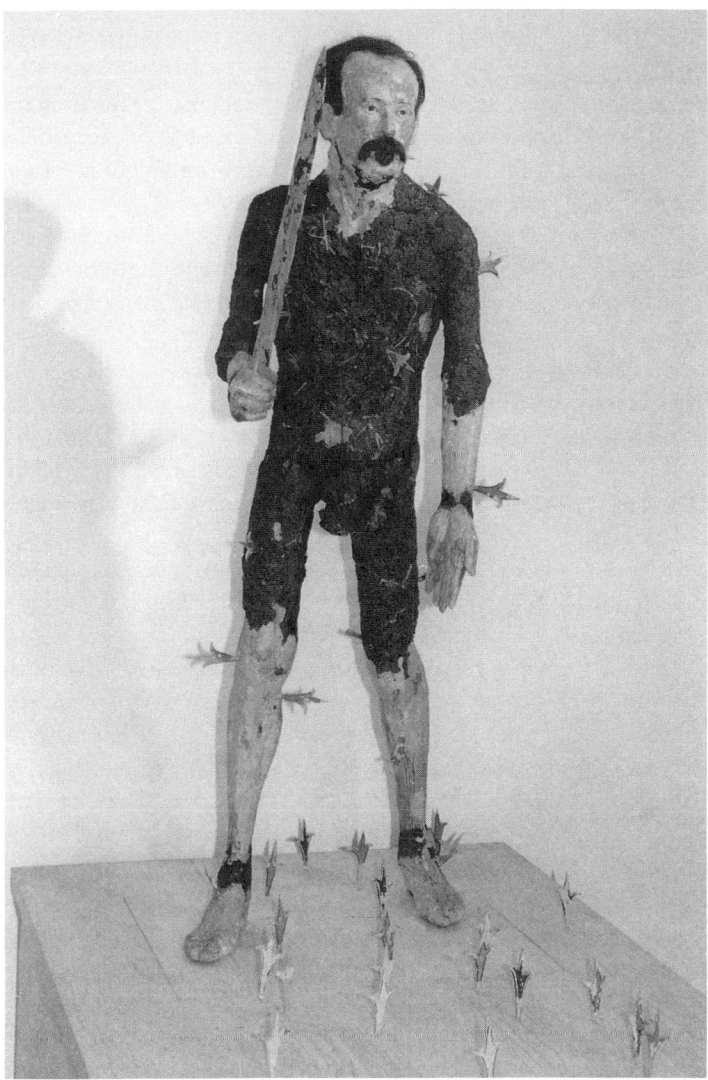

Juan Francisco Elso Padilla, Por América (For America), *1986, mixed media, 150 × 100 × 100 cm. Collection of Magali Lara, Mexico. Photo by Luis Camnitzer.*

readings within the deceiving simplicity of an icon. *Por América* was also a piece of Elso himself. Using *Santería* rites, he had "prepared" the sculpture for life by blending his own blood into the materials and by encasing potions and memorabilia related to himself and Mexican artist Magali Lara,[53] who soon after became his second wife.

The Biennial piece had been preceded by the work Elso exhibited in the 1986 Biennial of Venice. The Venice entry fit neatly between *El monte* and *Por América*. More literal in its narrative and more attached to basic myths, the work lacked some of the power of Elso's later pieces. Though nurtured by local traditions, it seemed to merge into what is by now an "international primitivism" trend. One of the pieces, *La fuerza del guerrero* (*The Warrior's Strength*), was an amazing recreation of the seventy-third illustration of the Latin Vatican Codicil 3738, though the document was unknown to Elso at the time.[54] The relative lack of repercussion of his Venice show could very well have been due to the modest size of the pieces and the way they were presented in contrast to the flashy presentations from other countries.[55]

During the last year of his life, Elso worked on a new project in Mexico City. Called *La transparencia de Dios* (*The Transparency of God*), it was based on Nahuatl educational principles. By the time he died, the installation comprised only three pieces: a seven-foot-high skull made out of twigs and canvas (*The Face of God*), a six-foot-high heart fabricated with intertwining branches (*The Heart of America*), and an equally large hand (*The Hand of God*). The face signaled the search for one's own way, the heart gave the energy to the way, and the hand symbolized the tools with which the world was created. It was Elso's intention that *Por América* be included in the total project to symbolize its attitude. Titled *Rostro-corazón* (*Face-Heart*), these three pieces were assembled together for the first time in Elso's posthumous retrospective. There, they seemed nurtured by the presence of *Por América*, even though they were displayed separately.

When I first saw the pieces, individually and cramped in a small studio, I had mistaken them for a sign of transition, a way for Elso to first absorb Mexico and then to launch himself into Latin America. Installed, this fragment of *La transparencia de Dios* shows Elso sharing his spiritual perception in a much more accessible manner than he did in *Por América*. In the sculpture of Martí, Elso's presence is secret. The *Santería* preparation is available to the viewer only if the anecdote is shared, but it is hermetic otherwise. *La transparencia de Dios* is transparent and, in a prophetic sense, terrifying. *The Face of God* is the face of death, a mask to be looked through in order that one may then see life in a forced perspective defined by the other two parts. Assuming this face of death and its point of view, we are in a position to understand the meaning of the cuts of the lifeline on the palm of the hand, and only then can we perceive life itself in perspective, once it is too late. In this work, Elso shares his experience on two levels. It presents a personal revelation that becomes accessible because it appeals to a relatively known and understandable

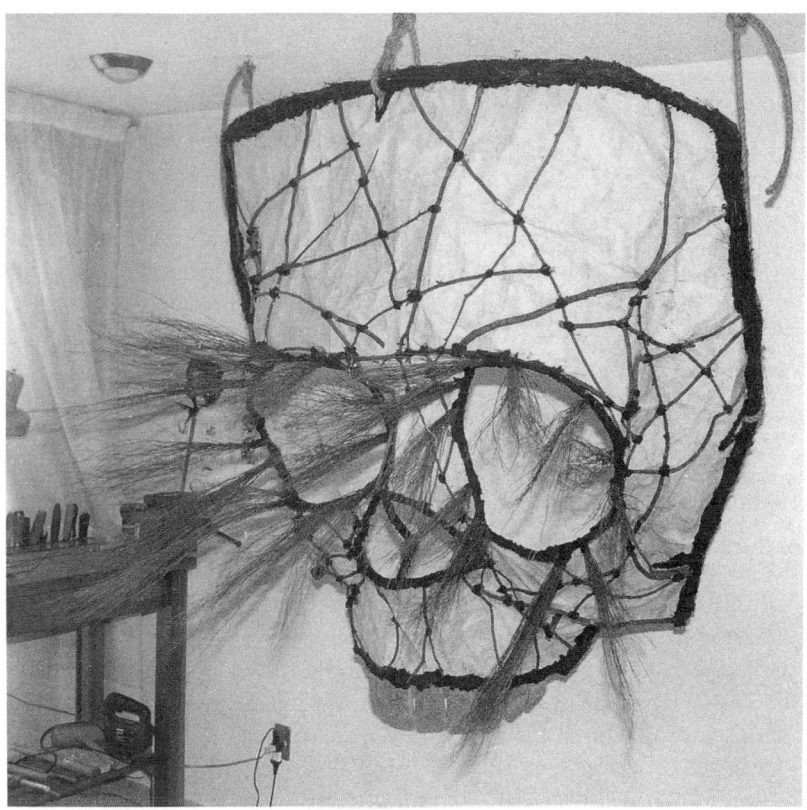

Juan Francisco Elso Padilla, El rostro de Dios *(The Face of God), (from* La transparencia de Dios) *(The Transparency of God), 1987–1988, paper and twigs, 128 × 128 × 50 cm. Collection of Magali Lara, Mexico. Photo by Luis Camnitzer.*

cultural repertoire. But, in a less intellectual and more immediate way, he invites us to peek through the actual eyes of death, to wear a mask usually forbidden. And one of the effects is that God is, in fact, transparent. Either due to omnipresence or because of absence, the reason for the transparency will be ours, not one imposed by dogma.

This installation would have provided a solid platform from which Elso would have evolved to his next highpoint. His incomplete piece on Simón Bolívar, *Caballo contra colibrí* (*Horse against Hummingbird*), was included in the retrospective and continued the premises of *Por América*. The horse represents European materialism, the hummingbird the defensive shield of indigenous spirituality. The evocations of the piece are more complex since both animals are connected by the beak of the bird and by an umbilical cord. But this piece was barely started. On November 27, 1988, they all became his unfinished last pieces. In another dialectical twist, Elso, in his gentleness, always considered himself a warrior—a spiritual one—and wanted to die fighting. But he had not expected his own body to become the battleground. The fact that he died of leukemia seems consistent with the use of his own blood in his art.

The Hand of God was modeled after Elso's own hand. Cuts he had made with emerging bundles of dried weed stems, symbolizing gushes of blood, interrupted the lifeline. When his wife returned to Mexico after Elso died in Havana, she found that the darts of *Por América* had fallen off Martí's body.[56]

THE INDIVIDUALISTS

It is unlikely that any Cuban artist would squarely place himself or herself in this category. Categorizing always implies some editorial violence, particularly transparent when it does not achieve neatness. The artists in this section may show some of this problem of organization, but in using the word *individualist* I merely want to point out that the problems of concern in their work are not yet being shared by other artists to the point of needing a separate heading.

These artists are not eccentrics in the Cuban context (otherwise I would have used that word as a heading), nor do they aspire to the romantic individualism often associated with the Western artist. They sometimes only seem individualists in the Cuban context because they use international references not shared by others.

Castro once differentiated between "private property" and "personal property."[57] The Cuban revolution is against the first, since it implies private possession of the means of production, but not against the second. Private property dynamics lead to the control of other individuals through possible monopoly. Personal property is geared to the needs of the individual, in this case defined by the well-being of the collective environment. The artist's individuality is defined by these same subtle constraints. Socialism, in this sense, aims at fostering individuality. Eccentricity, while conceivable, does not seem to serve any purpose.

Rogelio López Marín (Gory)

Gory (1953) was an orthodox realist from 1974 until 1980. Invited to participate in "Volumen I," he saw five days before the opening that he would be unable to finish his painting. It was out of despair that he decided to present it unfinished, with the photograph he was copying, placed on an easel.[58]

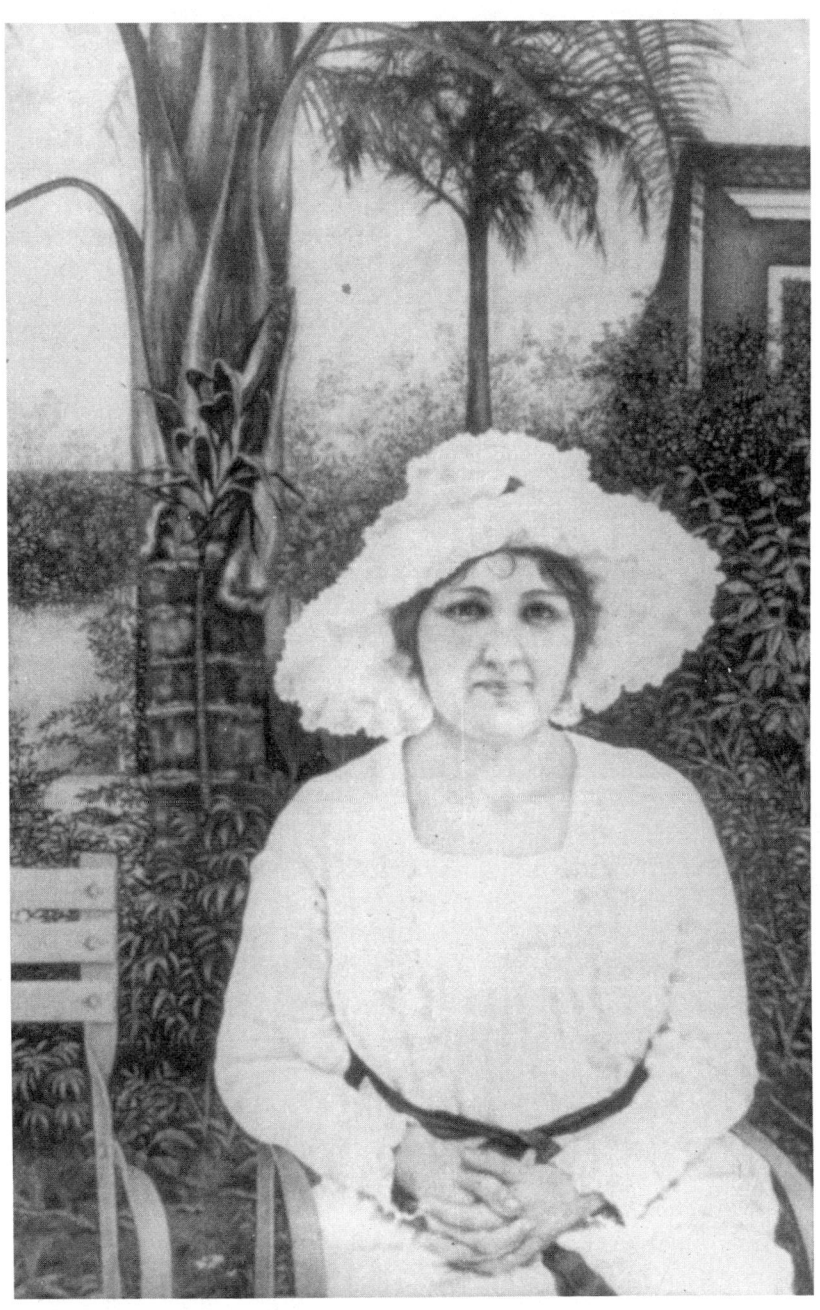

Rogelio López Marín (Gory), Ayer *(Yesterday), 1974, oil on canvas, 120 ×
80 cm. Collection of the artist. Photo by Gory.*

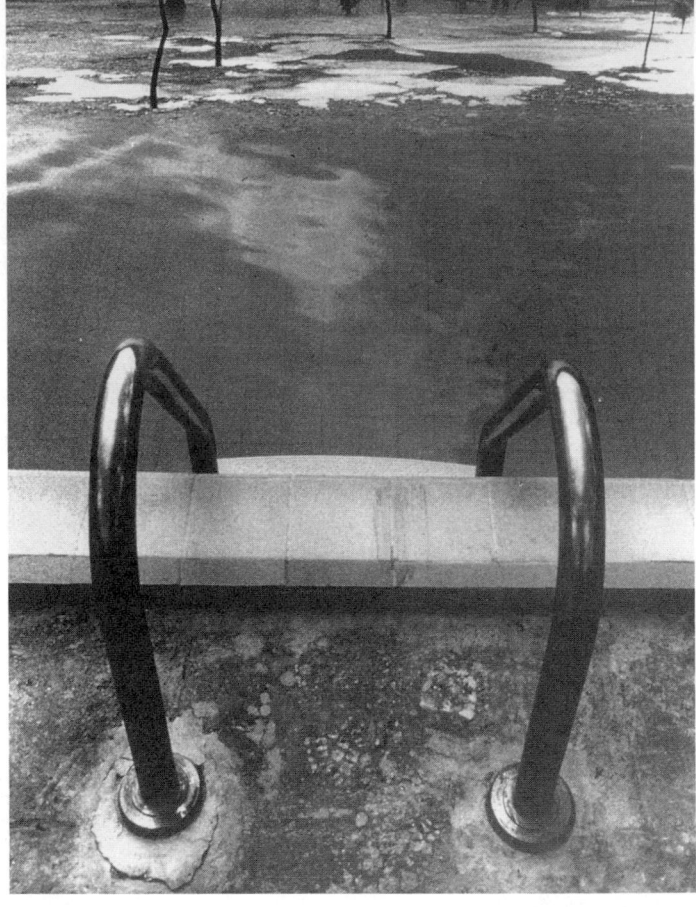

Rogelio López Marín (Gory), Es sólo agua en la lágrima de un extraño (It Is Only Water in a Stranger's Tear), *1986, gelatin silver photograph, 40 × 27 cm. Collection of the artist. Photo by Gory.*

It was the experience of the work of the others in the exhibit that then led him to the break with his hyperrealist painting. Always interested in photography, he had created photomontages since 1978 as models for his paintings and he decided to concentrate on these possibilities. For *Sano y Sabroso* he created a dining room that had a table with photographs of a wedding and a framed photograph of a meal hung on the wall. From this point on he went to the traditional photographic format with heavy literary involvement.

As a consequence, Gory allows himself to be inspired by readings or by his own meditations. Either one provides a text that acts as a support for his visualizations. Instead of photomontage he uses multiple exposures with several negatives in the darkroom to precisely depict his sometimes surreal imagery. He admires Jerry Uelsmann for his tech-

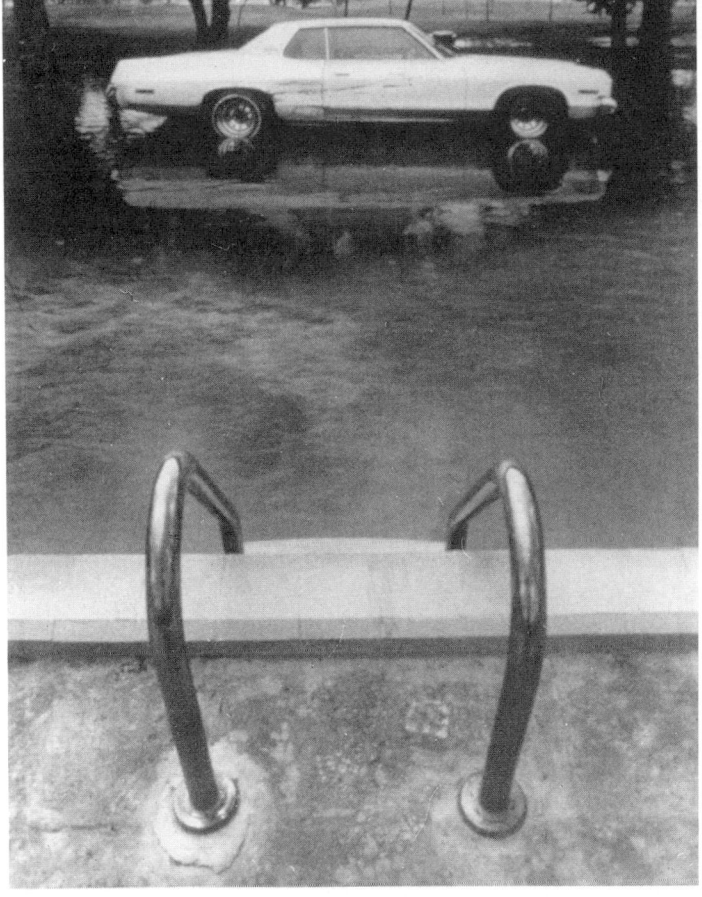

Rogelio López Marín (Gory), Es sólo agua en la lágrima de un extraño (It Is Only Water in a Stranger's Tear), *1986, gelatin silver photograph, 40 × 27 cm. Collection of the artist. Photo by Gory.*

nique and Duane Michaels for his connection with the text. His photographs are tinted blue and then airbrushed in detail with sodium sulphate, which gives the sprayed areas a yellow tint. The combination is mysterious and stunning and heightens the magic feeling of the imagery.

Paradoxically, Gory suffers from the prejudice that if things are not painted, they are not art. His hyperrealist period was a consequence of this attitude, and he only managed to make the break thanks to his colleagues. A student of the Escuela Nacional de Arte (ENA), he switched to the study of art history in the university while continuing with his painting and with photography as a separate trade (the source of his income). His attachment to painting went as far as rendering posterized photographs in painful detail, achieving an effect similar to Warhol's silkscreens but painted in oil (1979).

Gory is now firmly established as a narrative and poetic photographer. His sense of poetry is more connected with the Argentinean writers Jorge Luis Borges and Bioy Casares than with Cuban reality, and his work lives in its own world, abstracted from any nationalism. Manipulation seems less important in his newest work, and Gory concentrates further on the poetic component of his imagery.

Gustavo Pérez Monzón

Pérez Monzón (1956) combines personal art with the activity of teaching children. Interesting as an artist and part of the initial "Six New Painters," he has had an irregular production, particularly during the latter parts of the decade. Sometimes seen as a romantic version of Sol Lewitt's earlier work, Pérez Monzón's work of the early eighties had more to do with tarot cards and astrology than with a scientific approach to numbering.

His is a mystical and hedonist view of numerations. In an interview published in the form of one of the few advertisements used in Cuba (promoting the "Salón Permanente de Jóvenes," the "Permanent Exhibit of Young Artists," in the National Museum) he explained that what interests him is "the possibility of expressing a sensitivity beyond numbers, which in themselves are something cold."[59] Strings starting as geometric lines quickly become spiderweb-like structures trapping, but also signaling, mazes and spiral shapes.

In recent years, Pérez Monzón has worked little and has become more decorative. Using the same aluminum paper he often used earlier, linear designs made with silver paint laid down directly from the tube create patterns similar to the lead divisions of stained glass. The system of his earlier work, however esoteric, is missing—and much of the interest with it.

In his work with children, Pérez Monzón has created a pathbreaking activity in Cuba. Shying away from traditional media, he organizes activities that stress an interaction with nature. Twigs become children's antlers, trees are transformed into fantasy creatures through the application of found materials, monsters are built with rocks, and floating elements make designs in streams mingling with swimming young artists. Creativity becomes a tool for knowledge and respect for nature. Only then does he introduce art materials, to be merged into nature and to be used as an extension. Creativity becomes play and art an extension of it. With that, he radically departs from traditional children's art education, which treats the child as a dwarf artist.

The present lull in Pérez Monzón's work can only be seen as the temporary product of a personal crisis that hopefully will be resolved in the

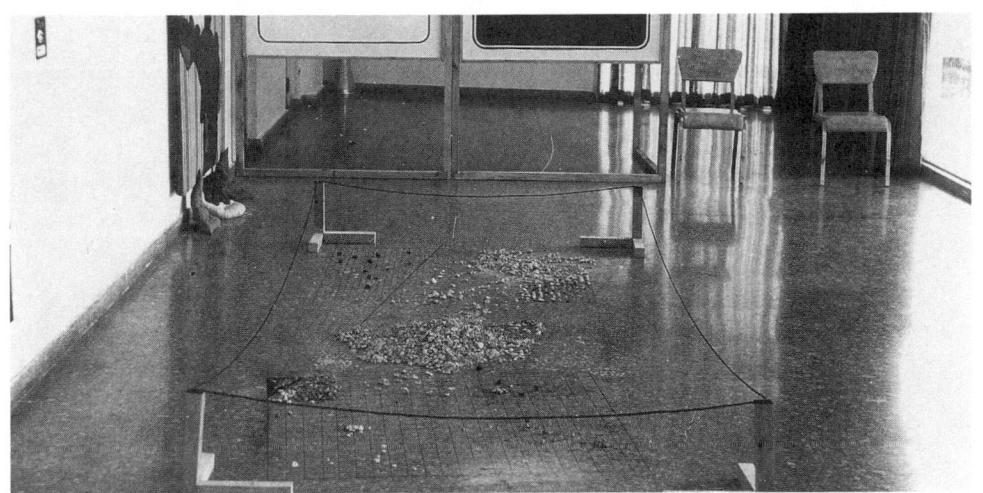

Gustavo Pérez Monzón, untitled, 1981. Installation in "Retrospectiva de artistas jóvenes" ("Retrospective of Young Artists"), Habana Libre, December 1981, Havana. Photo by José M. Fors.

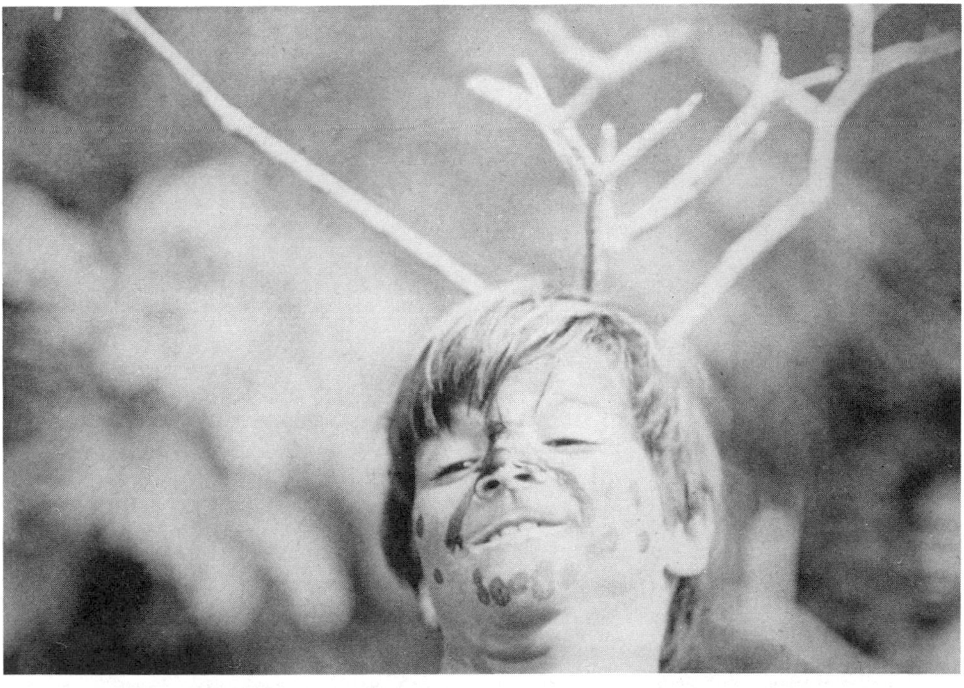

Gustavo Pérez Monzón, work with children, ca. 1982. Photo by Gustavo Pérez Monzón.

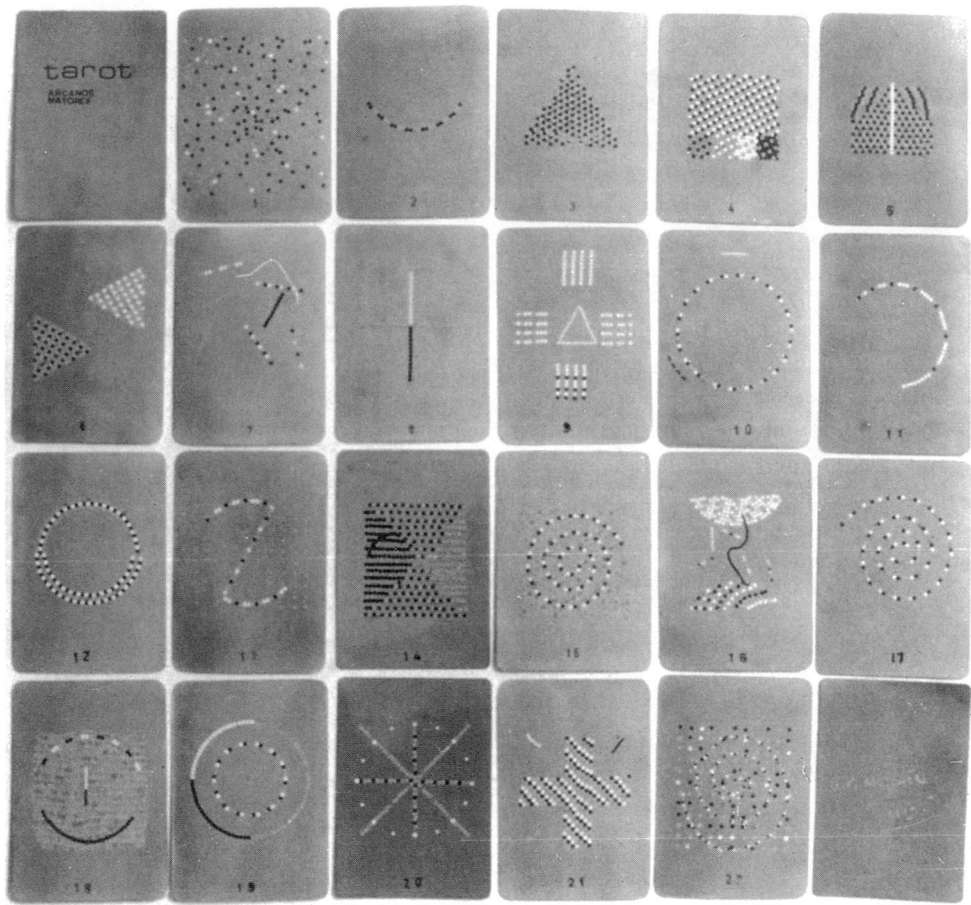

Gustavo Pérez Monzón, Tarot Cards, *1983, acrylic on cardboard, each card 10 × 7 cm. Collection of the artist. Photo by Gustavo Pérez Monzón.*

near future. His trip to Paris in 1982, when he represented Cuba in the Biennial of Paris, had a great negative influence. He discovered the competitive nature of art, an aspect of the trade that became overwhelming. He also was confronted with documentation about art similar to his, which made him feel futile. As a result, he reduced his art to the production of environments made as an homage for friends who come to visit him, which he disassembles after the meeting is over. These environments, among them the porch of his house in the outskirts of Havana, seem much better resolved and more profound than much of his previous work, but he refuses to acknowledge it. At the time of this writing he is in Mexico, integrated in a native community, occasionally involved in filmmaking and stage design.

Nevertheless, in 1989 Pérez Monzón did have an exhibition. Tanya Angulo and José Toirac, who had received use of the Galería Luz y Oficios (Centro Provincial de Artes Plásticas y Diseño) to have an exhibition, convinced him to use their space under their "curatorship." A project called "Eighteen Days" ensued, during which Pérez Monzón continually changed the environment and stayed in the gallery to talk to friends. The catalogue, entitled *Gustavo Pérez Monzón: DieSiocho días*—with a mysterious and intentional misspelling in Spanish—was done after the event and documented something that can be called a very tender artistic family affair. In the publication Angulo and Toirac say that they wanted to cite Gustavo in their work, using his works "like the references to African art by Cubism: as an acknowledgment of alternative aesthetic codes beyond tradition." With an indiscriminate and seamless mixture of parties and art-related situations, the artists-become-curators also tried to debunk what they saw as "the myth surrounding Gustavo's artistic inactivity," since they considered that he had only shifted the focus of his activities and not given up on being a creator.

2

CUBAN INFLUENCES
on the 1980s GENERATION

This chapter could be endless, covering most of the Cuban history of art. A selection of a few artists could be considered arbitrary, and for every one discussed, there may be several others ignored. The artists I selected, Raúl Martínez, Umberto Peña, and Ana Mendieta, are here for two reasons.

The first and simpler reason is that they were the most often mentioned when I asked members of the "Volumen I" generation who they considered crucial in their development. The second reason is that each one of them provides a metaphor for issues more complex than those limited to individual work or personality and thus stands as a symbol for theoretical issues, in both Cuban and Latin American art. They also typify three different Cuban art generations with the different roles they played in the Revolution, even, as in the case of Mendieta, while residing outside of Cuba. However, others were also mentioned; they will be discussed briefly here.

Antonia Eiriz (1929), who taught in the ENA during its peak period (1965–1969), deeply touched some of the younger artists, not only with her pedagogical gifts and moral fiber but also with her stunningly powerful neofigurative paintings of the early 1960s. Eiriz stopped painting in 1969, disappointed with the pressures of criticism. She turned her efforts to the CDR (the Comité de Defensa de la Revolución, or Committee for the Defense of the Revolution) in her neighborhood. She started with the children making decorative objects in papier-mâché. Eventually the activity integrated the parents of the children as well, and after making puppets, it grew into theatre performances with masks and props made by the participants, following texts written collectively by the group. She

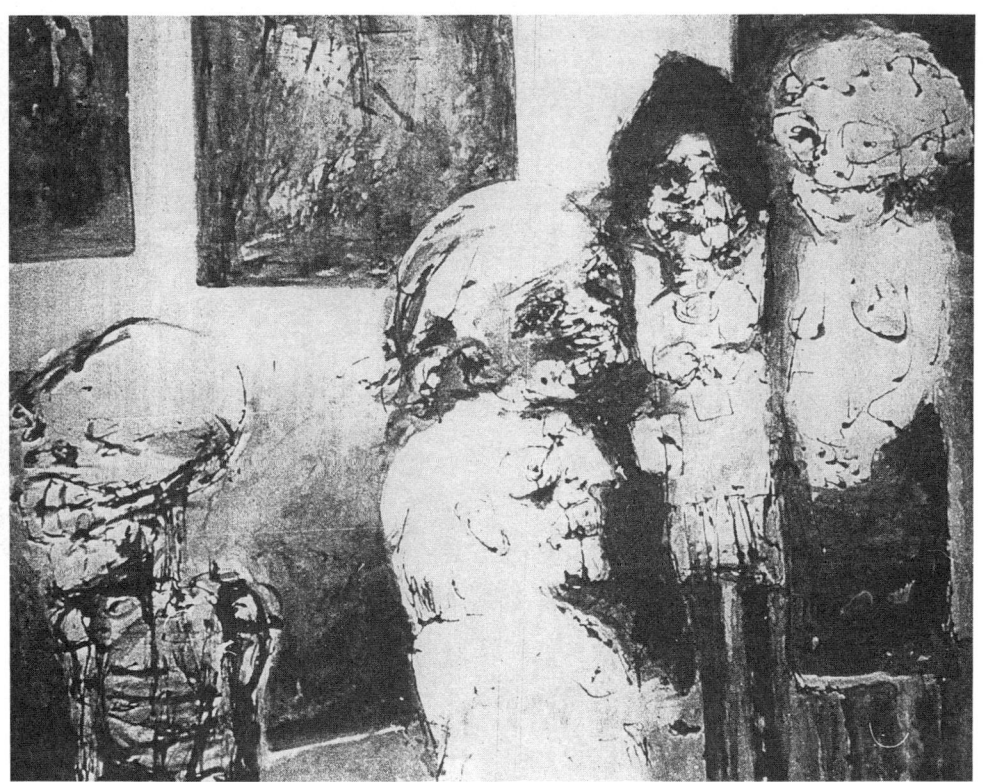

Antonia Eiriz, Mi compañera (My Comrade), *1962, ink on paper, 123 × 150 cm. Museo Nacional de Bellas Artes, Havana. Photo by Luis Camnitzer.*

bases her work on the idea that the lack of creativity is a social and not an individual problem.

Santiago Armada ("Chago") (1937) was primarily a cartoonist—in fact, he was the first revolutionary cartoonist of Cuba, since he was already working in the Sierra Maestra during the guerrilla period and was what could be called the guerrillas' art director. Chago did not teach and did not produce much "high" art, but humor drawing has a long and influential tradition in Cuba, and many important artists, including Eduardo Abela (1891–1965) and Rafael Blanco (1895–1955), were as important in that field as they were in the "higher" fine arts. They helped humor to permeate so called "serious" art, particularly in the newer art. Chago's drawings are quite overt about scatology and sex (one of his series is titled *La Chanson du Condom*), a point that reduced the frequency of exposure of his work during the early 1970s.

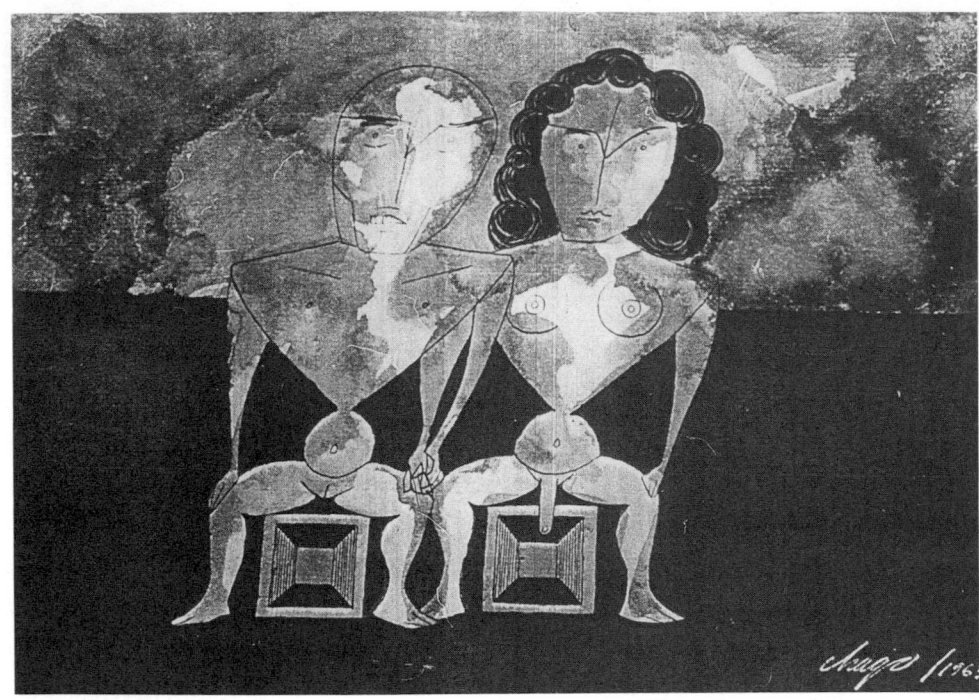

Santiago Armada (Chago), untitled, 1963, ink on paper. Collection of the artist. Photo by Antonio Eligio Fernández.

Jesús de Armas (1934) is another cartoonist, animation artist, and painter with some influence. In 1975 he decided to study whatever Native American tradition there was left in Cuba and to integrate signs and pictographs he gathered into his art. His work, mostly drawn with powerful and unhesitant charcoal strokes, is equidistant from Lam, Matta, Chago, and those Native American signs.

Flavio Garciandía, though considered a member of the 1980s generation, was also mentioned by some artists. Garciandía was already well established as a hyperrealist artist in the 1970s and always was a strong and influential theorist.

Raúl Martínez

BACKGROUND

Raúl Martínez, born in 1927 (son of a sugar-mill worker and a teacher), is an example of the "transitional" artist in Cuba. He exhibited for the first time in 1947, in the XXIX Salón de Pintura y Escultura of the

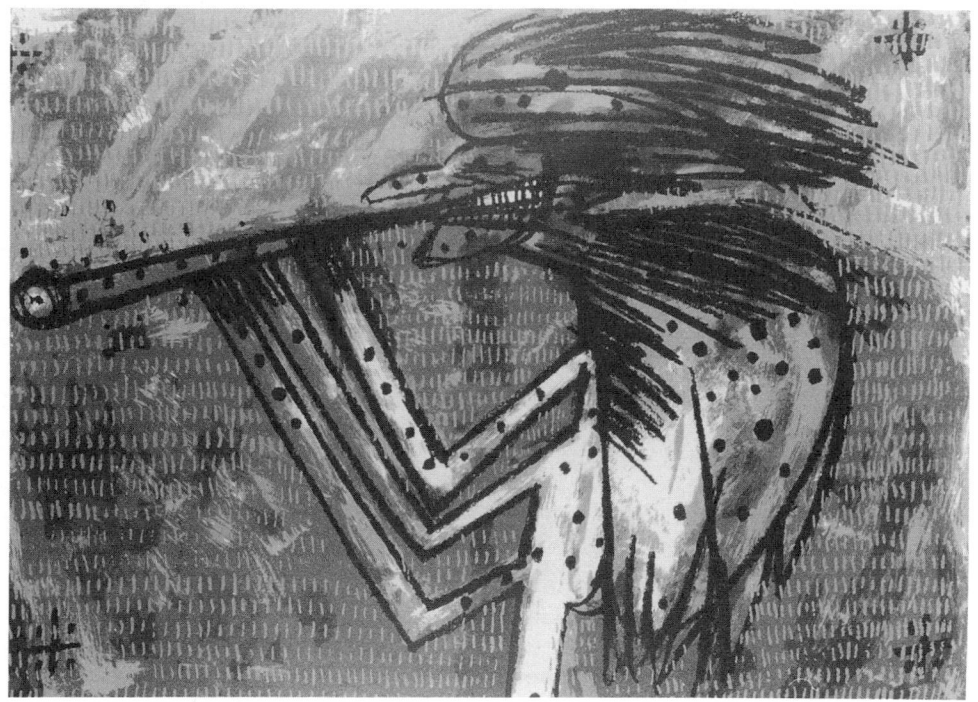

*Jesús de Armas, untitled, 1989, silkscreen, 50 × 70 cm. Private collection.
Photo by Luis Camnitzer.*

Círculo de Bellas Artes, with representational painting of figures in the
Cuban landscape. His first works were the outcome of a play with expressionist and postcubist devices, typifying the visual language of the
Cuban mainstream of the time. The paintings were competent, stereo-
typical, and forgettable.

Martínez dates his serious entrance into painting to 1956, when he
started his abstract-expressionist work. Previously a member of Los
Once (The Eleven), the group of artists active in Havana from 1953 to
1955, he subscribed to painterly painting: "Los Once aspired to 'painterly-
painting,' without any subject or literature. [They wanted] the expression of aesthetic emotion through plastic means—form and color—so
that the spectator faced with the work would be moved by its basic element: painting."[1] He spent a year in Chicago (1952, studying design at
the Art Institute), where he absorbed more information about contemporary trends. On his return to Cuba he continued painting in the same
style. In order to survive, he worked for a U.S.-owned advertising
company.

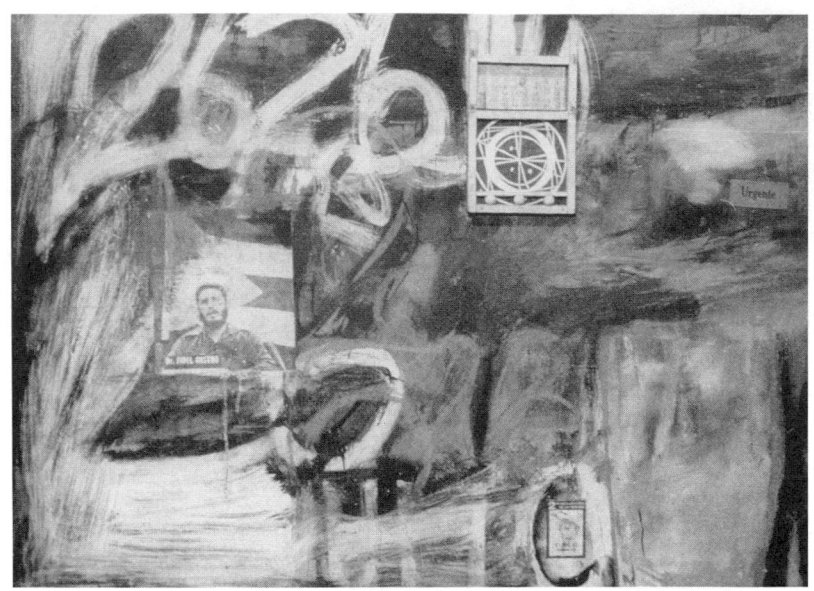

Raúl Martínez, 26 de julio (July 26), *1964, collage and oil on wood, 150* ×
180 cm. Museo Nacional de Bellas Artes, Havana. Photo by Luis Camnitzer.

THE REVOLUTION

Initially, the Revolution did not change his work much. Until the beginning of the U.S. blockade of Cuba in February 1962, Martínez continued doing advertising for Cuban tourism, and his painting remained the
same except for some titles (for example, *Sierra Maestra* in 1960). In 1963
he participated in the show "Expresionismo abstracto." By then his abstract paintings already had incorporated not only some topical titles but
also some symbols introduced by means of Rauschenberg-like devices.
In *26 de julio* (1964), he used the number *26* as a graphic scribble loosely
repeated over the canvas and blending into the gestural brush strokes of
the background, on which he also made a collage with some printed
matter that included a picture of Fidel Castro. He acknowledges Rauschenberg's great influence on his transitional work and, later, Warhol's.
The repetition of images on his canvas, however, did not derive from
Warhol's work but from an accidental experimentation with the image.

In 1965, Martínez started losing interest in abstraction, longing instead for closer communication with the public, although in a catalogue
of an exhibit he still used "old" language appropriate for his previous
art: "Magic always has been important for me, the magic of the surface
and the magic of an expressive life transmuted on it. By magic I define

the process of looking for the unknown, which is what I always have done." And later: "My method of work is to act directly on the canvas, without previous ideas, without a preconceived concept. The challenge rests on the animation of the unknown after it starts becoming outlined."[2] Figuration returned to his work. In an interview in 1964, referring to the previous five years he says, "The isolation in which we found ourselves has disappeared. Before, it seemed enough to maintain an honest individual behavior, without concessions to the regime. The work remained outside. Now we have a different sense of responsibility."[3] Asked why at this juncture he did not go with socialist realism, Martínez answered that Cuban artists were building something that had not been built yet. They were able to pick things they considered useful for this new situation; they could experiment, but they could not take anything for granted.

Martínez' previous work as a graphic designer made him realize that his graphic skills could be of more use to the revolutionary process than his painting. He became interested in the experiment of "selling" a vision rather than commercial merchandise.

THE DEVELOPMENT OF ICONS

The outcome was *Martí y la estrella* (*Martí and the Star*, [1966]), in which he repeated his subject sixteen times. The image of Martí, a rough, heavy, and schematic drawing, became a graphic symbol. In this painting Martínez achieved the rare mixture of painterly naivete with sophisticated graphic design, which became his brand for several years. It also determined his language in posters, such as the one for the movie *Lucía* (1968), considered a classic in Cuban poster making. Graphic skills, the popular art of the Committees for the Defense of the Revolution, and some awareness of pop art led him to define his new imagery. "Since I like landscape so much, I asked myself, what is Cuban landscape? The answer was, the heroes of the Revolution, the people."[4]

Martí's portrait is probably the most frequently seen in Cuba. Martí seems to satisfy a great variety of longings and functions. He certainly was the founding father of Cuba, a lucid politician, a poet who cofounded Latin American modernism in literature.[5] He also spent vast amounts of time and pages warning about the U.S. danger to Cuba, represented Latin American interests in the United States, and died while fighting for Cuban independence. In such a secular country as Cuba he has become the closest thing possible to a deity. He is a spiritual father to the people and particularly to the intellectuals. There are few gardens without his bust; indeed, his image plays the same role as kitschy garden dwarfs in capitalist yards.

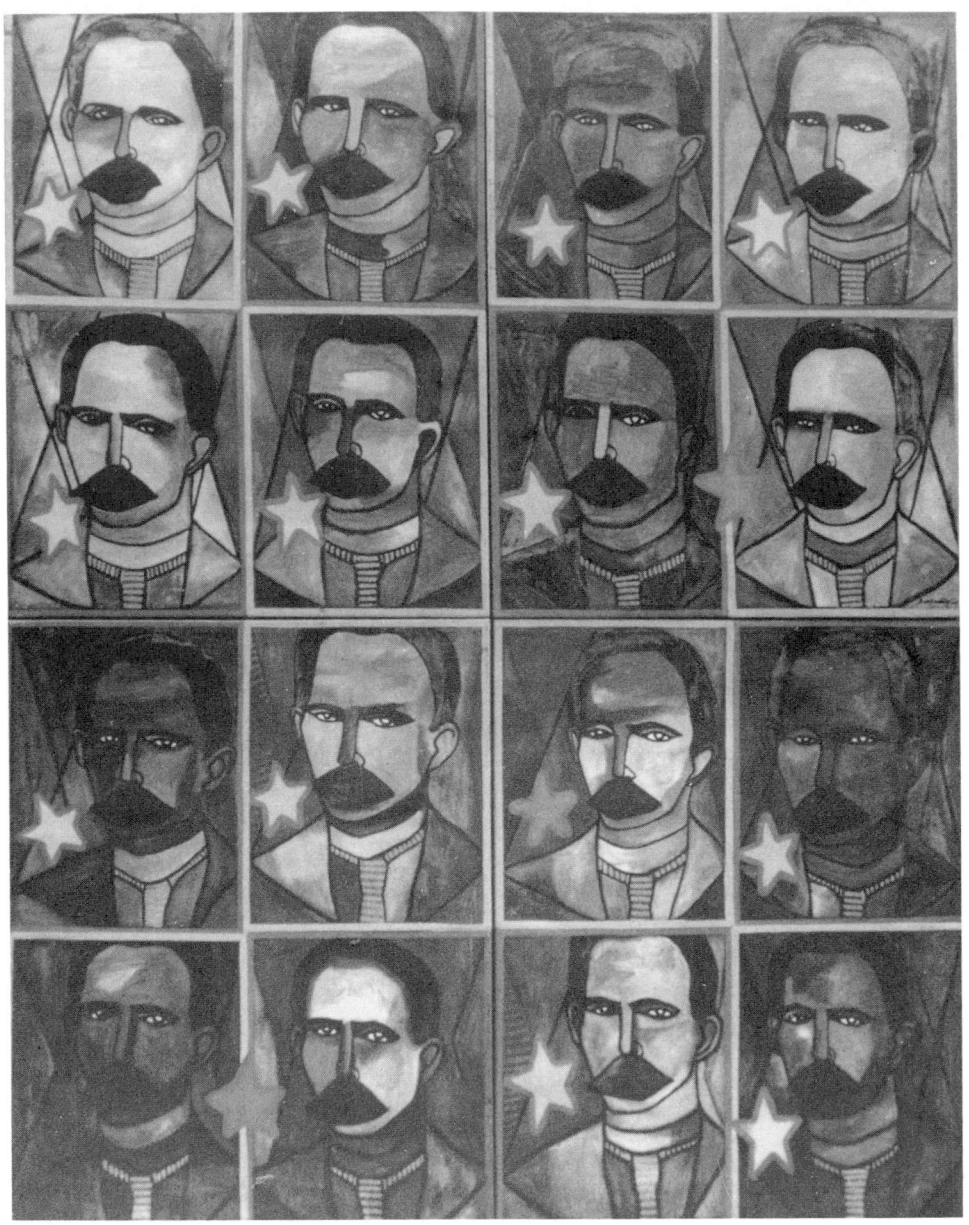

Raúl Martínez, Martí y la estrella (Marti and the Star), *1966, oil on canvas, 184 × 143 cm., Museo Nacional de Bellas Artes, Havana. Photo by Luis Camnitzer.*

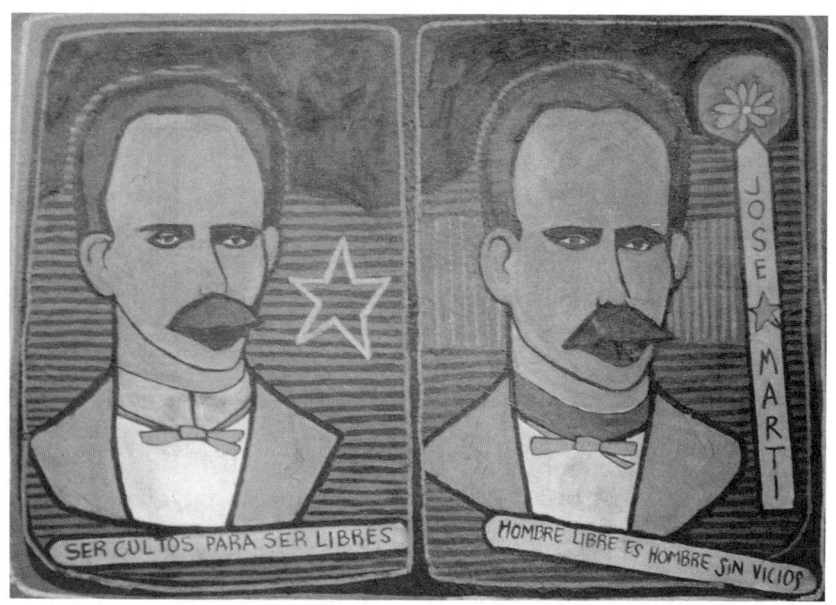

Raúl Martínez, untitled, ca. 1966, oil on canvas, 72 × 97 cm. Private collection. Photo by Luis Camnitzer.

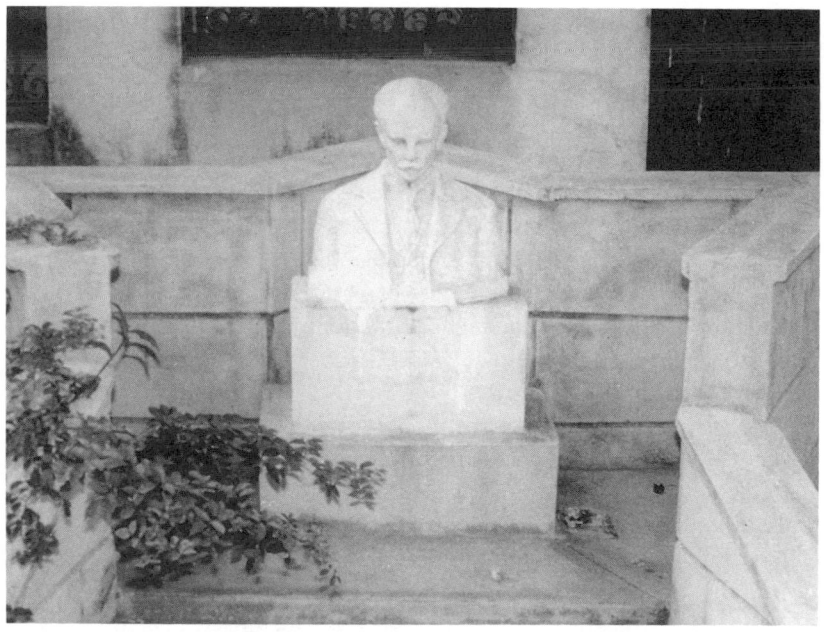

Anonymous, bust of Martí in a garden of Havana. Photo by Luis Camnitzer.

For Martínez to tackle this image and tamper with it was no small feat, a feat he later was able to repeat with the representations of Che and Fidel.[6] The work of this period places Martínez, while being influenced by some U.S. pop-art devices, as a creator of a very Cuban pop aesthetic. His strength was in taking popular icons and transforming and recirculating them with added power among the same people who had generated these icons. While not totally conscious and systematic in this regard, Martínez here is an heir of the Mexican José Guadalupe Posada. (An example of recycling the work into a new, enriched anonymity occurred when the scenic design of a New York Public Theatre production in 1986 used the repeated image of Fidel as a backdrop, without granting any credit to Martínez, assuming it was a popular image.) Martínez is an example for many of the younger artists interested in isolating popular elements in their own work with the hope of feeding them back to the people as the true and original owners of the symbolic goods.

THE RELATION WITH U.S. POP ART

The often mentioned relation of Martínez's work with U.S. pop art is relatively minor and heavily syncretic. Borrowing the serial structure, like the U.S. pop artists he uses a preexisting popular image. However, in his work of that period, he did not really delve into mass-media aesthetics nor into the visual "cooling" devices utilized by the North American artists. He sought inspiration in anonymous images taken from display cases in Workers' Centers and Defense Committees, images produced without artistic and technical skills. He did not share the "campy" attitude of North American pop artists. His "pop" work never did away with atmospheric qualities, even when the grid created by the drawing was rigid. His hard edges were graphic references but not industrial ones. His compositions did share the "lay-out" quality of contemporary Western art but did not erase his emotional individuality. In fact, they were often on the border of sentimentality, possibly as a consequence of his wish to appeal to a broader public. Unlike his U.S. counterparts, Martínez never used pop art's formal devices to banalize his subject matter.

Once he felt that there were enough good poster and graphic designers in Cuba (or, as others believe, once he became bored), Martínez decided to return full time to his paintings. Using many elements of his graphic repertoire, he projected photographs of his subjects onto the canvas to then find the right line and the right synthesis for his subject. The camera allowed him "to break away from my private little studio and my egotism" and to "see and document reality to ensure objectivity."[7]

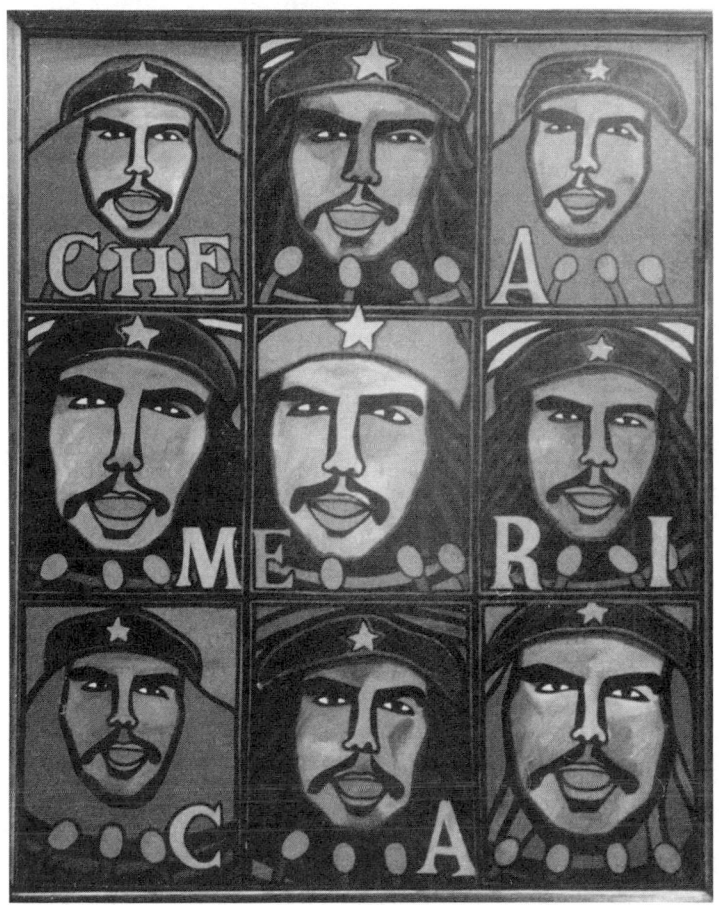

Raúl Martínez, Fenix, *1968, oil on canvas, 200 × 160 cm. Museo Nacional de Bellas Artes, Havana. Photo by Luis Camnitzer.*

INTERDISCIPLINARY AND TEAM WORK

His work has since become more overtly sophisticated, losing some of the charm of the initial crudeness and often giving the feeling of big illustrations. It also has become more ambitious. The Cuban entry for the Biennial of Venice in 1984 was a huge installation (ten-by-fifteen meters) done as a team effort with photographer Mario García Joya (Mayito), who had a predominant role in planning the project, and some papier-mâché objects made by members of CDRs (Comités de Defensa de la Revolución) under the direction of Antonia Eiriz. With this piece, Martínez reconnected with interdisciplinary work produced earlier by himself and other Cuban artists (including Mayito) and architects

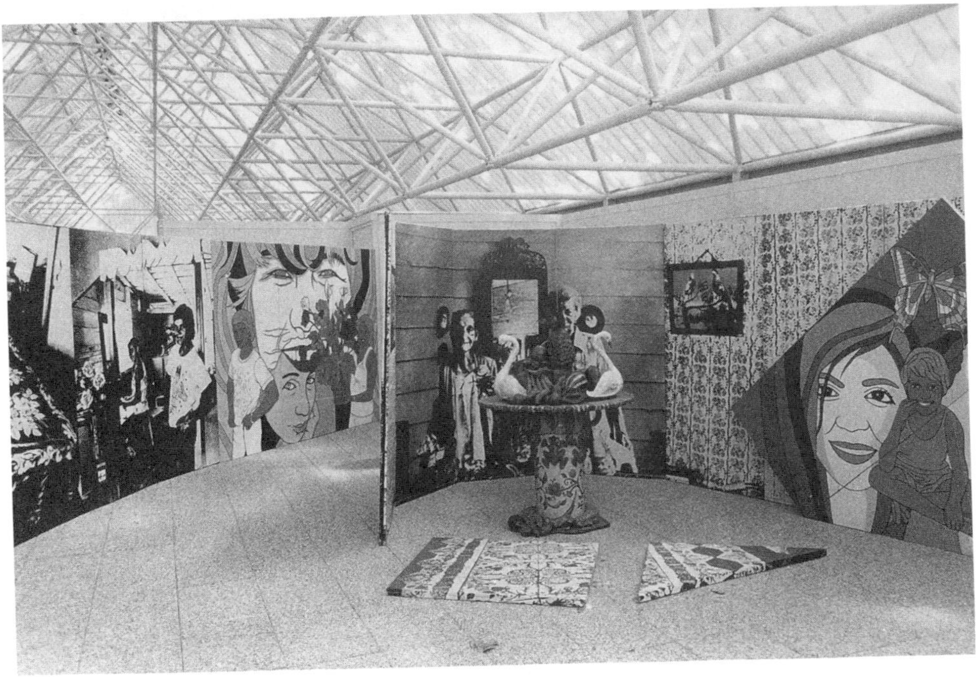

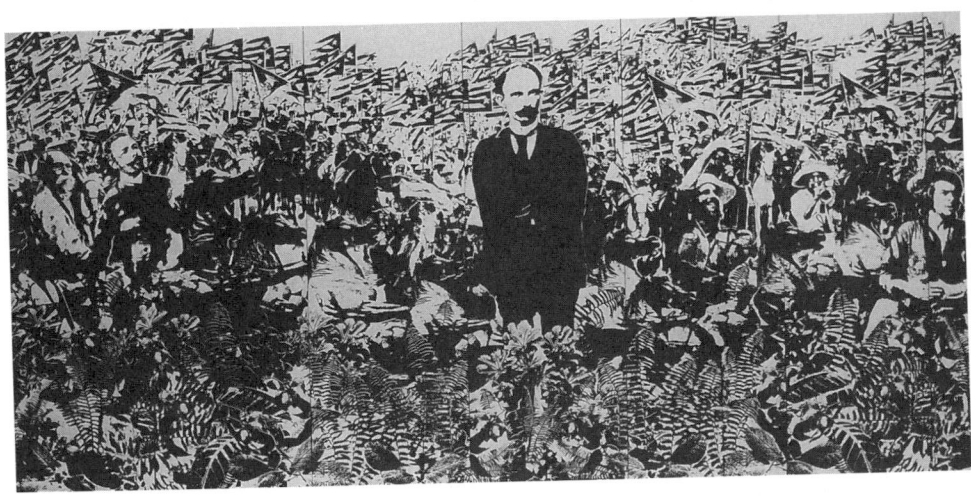

Raúl Martínez, Mario García Joya (Mayito), and Antonia Eiriz, untitled, 1984. Installation at the Venice Bienniale, 1984, 1,000 × 1,500 cm. Photo by Luis Camnitzer.

Mario García Joya (Mayito), De nacionalidad a nación (From Nationality to Nation), 1981, photomontage, 300 × 1500 cm. Collection of the artist. Photo by Vidal Hernández.

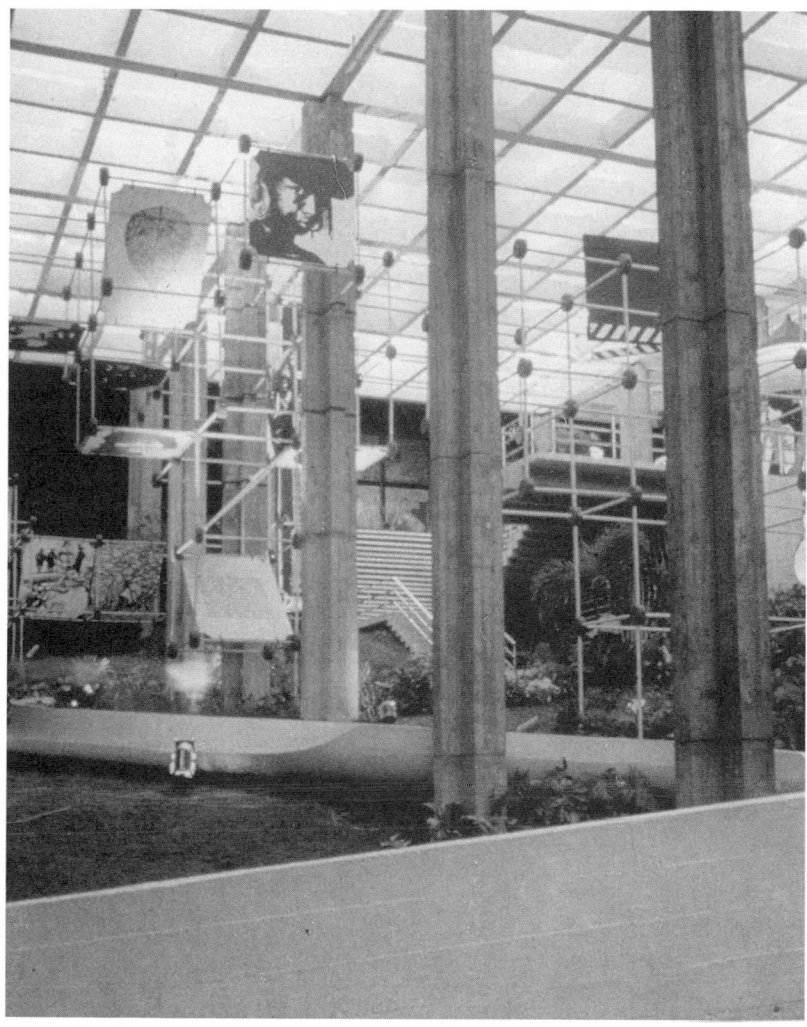

Pabellón Cuba (detail), 1968. Photo from the Segre archives.

during the 1960s. Among the works was *Tren blindado* (*Armored Train*, [1968]) in the square of the town of Santa Clara, which celebrated a military action by Che Guevara.[8] The installation included pieces of the derailed train, photographs projected on billboards, and music.[9] Other projects were the Third World Exhibition in the Pabellón Cuba and a system of billboards on buildings around La Rampa in Havana, in honor of the fight for Latin American liberation. The Cuban Pavilion in the World's Fair in Montreal (1967) was an example of this aesthetic as well, although Martínez did not collaborate on its execution.

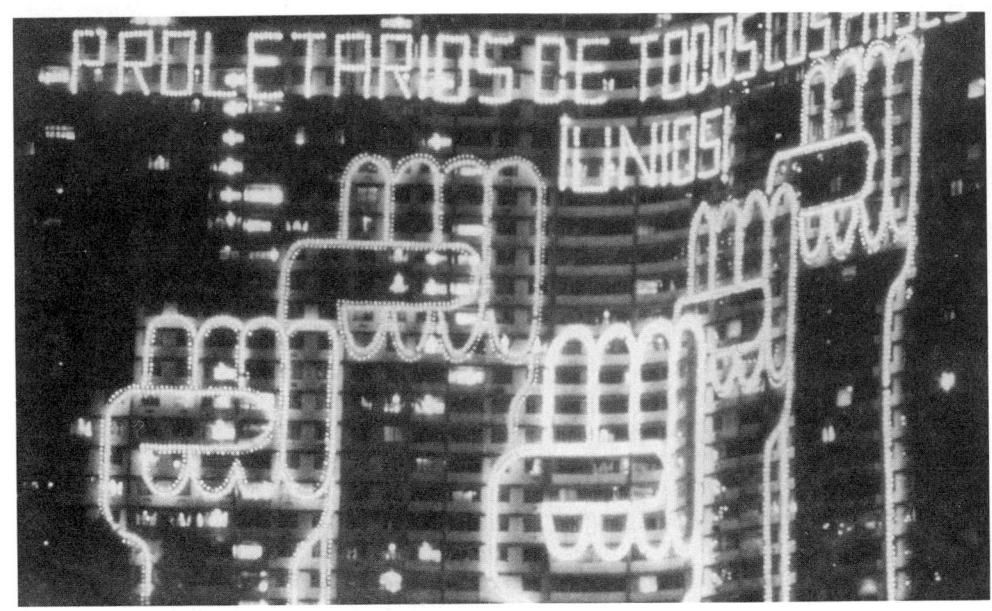

Light announcement in Havana, n.d. Photo from the Segre archives.

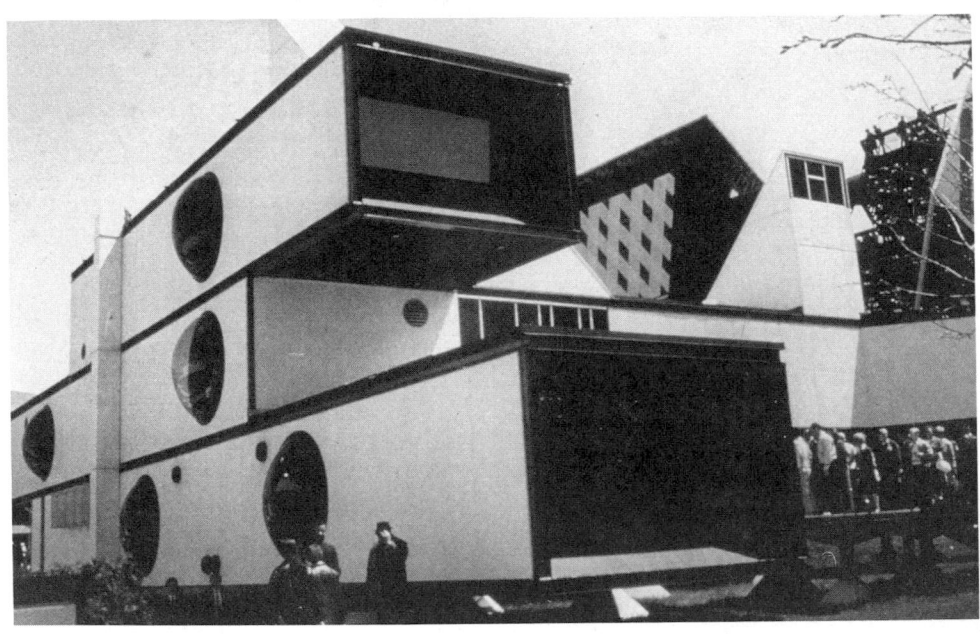

Cuban pavilion in the World's Fair of Montreal, 1967. Photo from the Segre archives.

The piece for the Biennial of Venice, while not totally successful, was imposing. It combined panels designed by Martínez with panels bearing photographs by Mayito, placed along two open and curved corridors that eventually defined two spaces hinting at home interiors. Titled *The Great Family*, it alluded to both the family nucleus and the people as family. The failures of the installation resulted from an excessive respect for the individuality of both artists, which prevented an adequate integration, and from a feeling that the final product was in fact an enlarged model. The interest of the piece was in the effort by two established artists with different languages and media to use popular culture as a meeting ground. Mayito is interested in kitsch and how it manifests itself in Caibarién, a small town known for its carnival floats. The attitude of both artists in this regard (and of most Cuban artists) is a loving and partly respectful one, as they try to identify valid points in kitsch. Kitsch, as we will see, is the central concern of Garciandía (a native of Caibarién) and has also played a great part in the work of Cuenca, Torres Llorca, and many other artists. But as critic Mosquera points out (without a value judgment), while their aim is to turn good forms into bad forms, Martínez takes bad forms and turns them into good ones.[10]

ART FOR THE PEOPLE

With Cuban art, it is easy to idealize how art may be made into a popular and classless tool. Cuba is "returning" symbolic goods to the people mainly through dissemination. There is an effort to distribute art as much as possible. To a certain extent this dissemination is also brought about by the effort to identify and develop talent everywhere. But there is an underlying assumption that "high art" is "the" art. As Vice President Carlos Rafael Rodríguez put it rather controversially in the 1988 UNEAC meeting, "Mass culture is not culture; culture has to be brought to the masses."* As such, the forms of production of artistic knowledge are not yet totally placed in the people's hands, are not totally "returned" to them, although the results are shared with them. It is an issue that presently is more of personal concern to some artists than a subject for government policy, and the work of Martínez is illuminating and influential in both its strengths and weaknesses in relation to this topic.

The influence of Martínez as a teacher is important in this context. Martínez taught stage design briefly at the ENA and influenced many of

---

*Quotes from speeches not otherwise cited are translations from tape recordings made by the author. For reference, transcripts of most of these speeches can be found in subsequent issues of *Granma Weekly Review*.

the first-generation artists. Some of them describe him as an intuitive rather than a rational teacher. While the curriculum was being designed and became more academic in the 1970s, he provided a mental opening that was more in tune with the younger artists. After he left his position due to the pressures that started during the late 1960s, he continued to meet privately with younger artists and encouraged them by contributing criticism, becoming a highly regarded extracurricular teacher. Martínez is a gatherer of information, and his house served as an informal library and clearinghouse.[11] The appeal of this environment and his personality helped to minimize the obvious danger of an intergenerational conflict with the emerging young artists.

Umberto Peña

Umberto Peña, born in 1937, is another name often mentioned by the younger generations as influential. Paradoxically, Peña has not exhibited much, has not taught, and is mostly known for his work as a designer for Casa de las Américas, particularly its magazine. He shaped the aesthetics of the publications of Casa de las Américas from 1963 until 1984. With a humility carried to the brink of paranoia, Peña refutes any possibility that his work may have been important or influential for other people. However, younger artists point to the example of his discipline and to his way of approaching visual research as important for their development. Peña dismisses as "hallway greetings" his highly appreciated critical comments about the work of others. He qualifies his retrospective exhibit in the Museum of Fine Arts in Havana in 1988 as anthological, since he never painted continually and claims to have stopped in 1984. The museum usually displays one painting, from 1960, and one print, from 1970, as part of the display of the Cuban Collection.

Peña studied for four years in San Alejandro, until 1959. He received a government grant in 1960 to study new materials in the Instituto Superior Politécnico in Mexico with Gutiérrez Leal, a former student and assistant of Alfaro Siqueiros. There he worked with new paint media. Simultaneously, he took courses in Byzantine mosaic techniques at the school La Ciudadela. Eight months in Mexico were followed by four months in Paris. When he returned, he started working as a designer at the Consejo Nacional de Cultura, a trade he learned on the job. In 1963 he began working for Casa de las Américas, where he defined that institution's visual public image.

An interest in Chaim Soutine, awakened in Paris, led Peña to focus on slaughterhouses, where he took photographs that served as the basis of his paintings. Because Cuban butchers display only meat pieces in

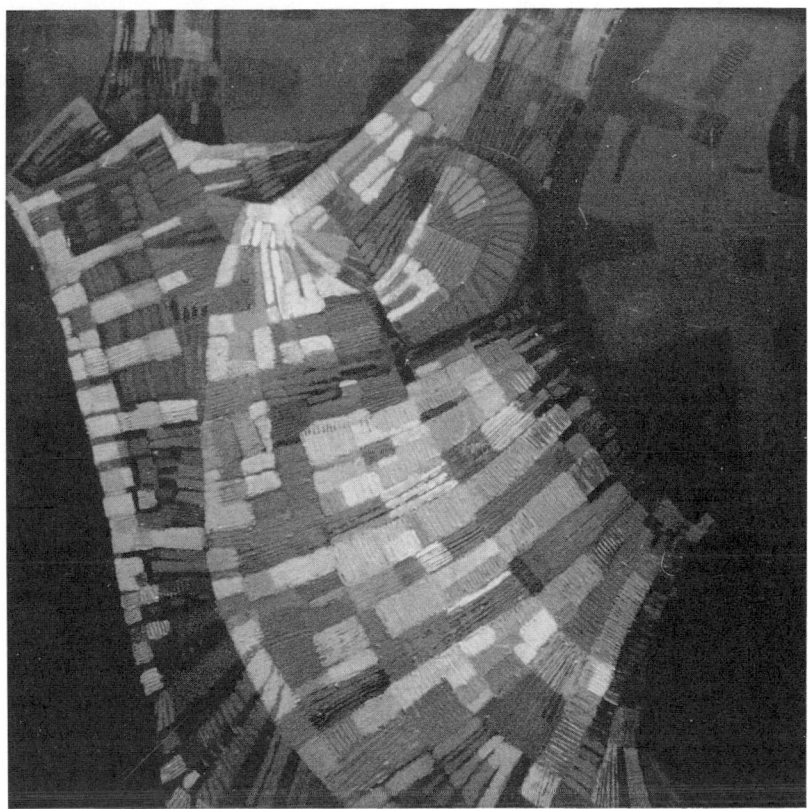

Umberto Peña, Buey desollado (Skinned Ox), *n.d., enamel on cardboard, 121.5 × 121.5 cm. Museo Nacional de Bellas Artes, Havana. Photo by Luis Camnitzer.*

their shops, Peña was shocked to see full carcasses in Parisian butcher shops. Initially interested in form and color, he put all his experiences together, using car enamel paint (a technique pioneered by Siqueiros and which he picked up during his stay in Mexico), organizing the brush strokes like a mosaic, and depicting hanging beef.

The paintings from this period, slightly decorative on a first approach because of the mosaic effect, acquire an extremely violent effect after longer observation. Violence and morbidity are frozen on the canvas and start thawing once they reach the spectator. His slaughterhouse research changed his ideas about the color of carcasses, which he presumed to be red from being covered with blood. Instead he realized that, covered with a layer of fat, they are white. This insight, and a developing interest in expression and action, led the paintings to evolve first into a

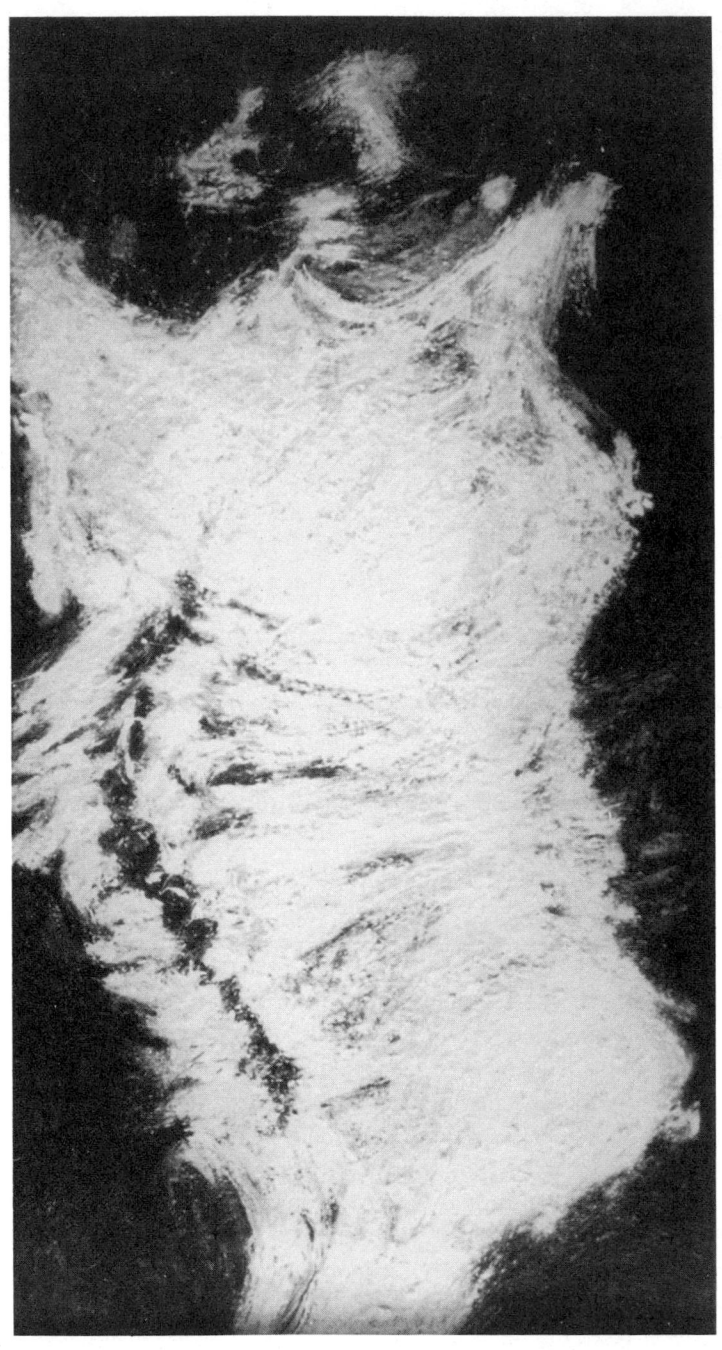

Umberto Peña, Buey #8 (Ox #8), 1964, enamel on masonite, 200 × 100 cm. Museo Nacional de Bellas Artes, Havana. Photo by Luis Camnitzer.

white stage and then into a surface with red gestural strokes evoking entrails. It is interesting that in a conversation about these works, Peña went into painfully precise descriptions of the models, although the paintings are not at all realistic and only vaguely suggestive of what for him was a traumatic experience. It is also noteworthy that the discovery of these models took place in Paris and not in Mexico, where he undoubtedly must have been confronted with similar manipulations of meat. Peña's body of work during these years neatly places him in the context of Latin American neofiguration of the 1960s,[12] an aesthetic that may have struck him in Paris and thus helped open his eyes to French butchers.

Animals evolved into physically vulnerable human beings toward 1965. The stress on vulnerability made him concentrate on physiological aspects of the body. He saw work by Tom Wesselman and Peter Saul, and particularly the latter led him to rethink his own work, which became more cartoonish in form and scatological in content. This change also allowed him to bring into line his graphic design, his prints, and his paintings. The works of this period have a pop-cartoon appearance with violent colors and strong, cold outlines. Bathrooms merged with bodies. Toilets became dentures, piping and intestines were integrated into long circuits where circulation was directed by arrows and expressions were underlined with onomatopoeic writings. In 1967 he represented Cuba in the Biennial of Paris with this work and received one of the six prizes, a grant that he used in Paris for six months in 1968. There he met the artists Antonio Saura (Spain), Erro (Iceland), Pierre Alechinsky (Belgium), Rómulo Macció (Argentina), and others. He picked up on a certain eroticism fashionable in Europe at the time, which he introduced as a further physiological function in his work after his return to Cuba at the end of 1968. He resumed his work in Casa de las Américas and worked less in painting. Difficulty in access to materials, visual fatigue, and a feeling that his "erotic" paintings had communication problems in the moralistic atmosphere of Cuba at the time led him to slowly stop painting and become a full-time designer. Peña himself states that what he considers a very personal process was later mistakenly interpreted as "not being able to exhibit because of the [shocking] erotic content of his paintings," creating a false myth of martyrdom. Still, his phallic paintings had been attacked, and even during his retrospective in the Museum of Fine Arts in Havana during 1988, the paintings elicited criticism from *Bastión*, a periodical of the armed forces, and a defense in *Granma* by Roberto Fernández Retamar, director of Casa de las Américas. In the introduction to the catalogue of his retrospective, Nelson Herrera Ysla comments, "The sexual symbols become independent to such a point that they seem ani-

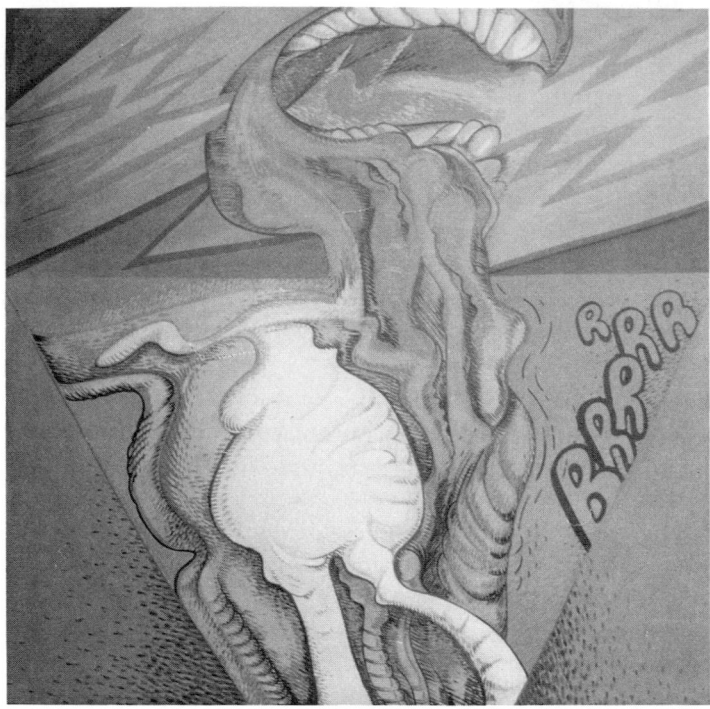

Umberto Peña, Tú haces brr con mi electricidad (You Make Brr with My Electricity), *1967, acrylic on canvas, 180 × 180 cm. Museo Nacional de Bellas Artes, Havana. Photo by Luis Camnitzer.*

mated with their own souls, possessed by a devil who pushes them to challenge the space they inhabit. With these pieces, Peña reached the doors of a limit that at the time could not be trespassed. It is 1971, and Peña stops making prints in the Taller Experimental [de Gráfica] (Experimental Print Workshop). Sketches for lithographs and canvases, which never would see the light, remain frozen on his table."[13] Regardless of the polemics at different times, as critic Antonio Eligio Fernández (Tonel) points out, Peña seems to enrich scatology with his good taste.[14] Reflecting on violence, he does not pick up on wars but rather on the rampage of a toothbrush. His mixture of scatology and humor will later bear fruit in the artists of the third generation.

THE "TRAPICES"

One day in 1976, while visiting a tailor shop, Peña discovered fabric leftovers that he took with him. He started a series of fabric mosaics,

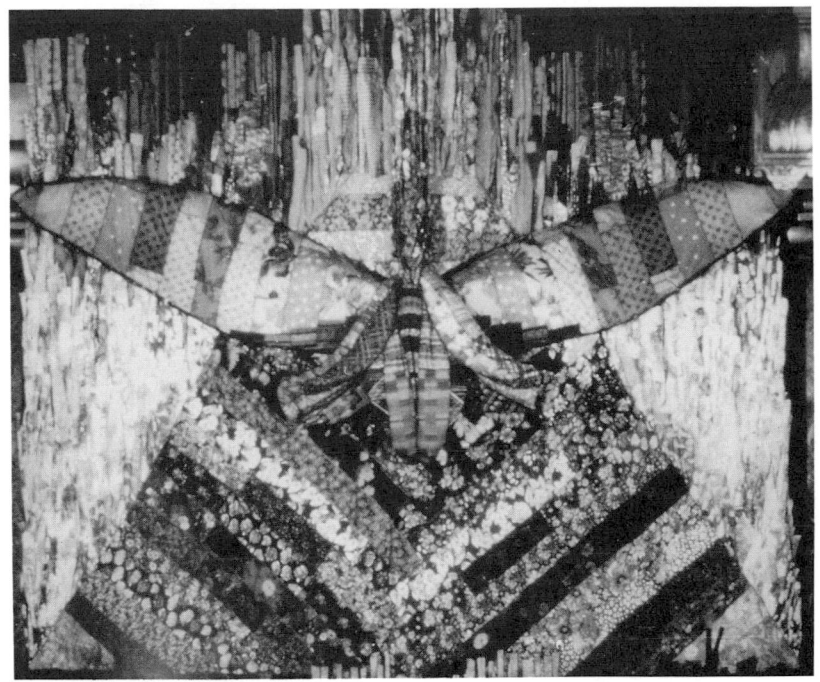

Umberto Peña, Trapiz, *1976–1980, 350 × 400 cm. Collection of the artist. Photo by Umberto Peña.*

"sewing like Penelope," which he worked on until 1980. The result of this four-year process was a group of twenty pieces, each about ten-by-five feet with sculptural effects. Called *trapices* (a contraction of *trapo*, rag, and *tapiz*, tapestry), they were based on erotic orchids and vaginas and were exhibited all together in a big space in the old National Capitol.

The exhibit took place in 1980 and can be credited with being one of the events that set the tone for experimentation in the arts to follow during that new decade. While art in Cuba always had escaped traditional technical confines with great ease, the examples usually occurred in non-artistic contexts, as in the public displays organized by the COR (the Comisión de Orientación Revolucionaria), such as the *Tren blindado* event.[15] Peña's "Trapices" exhibit took place not in the traditional context of art exhibitions but as part of a Festival of Ballet and in a space not normally used for exhibitions of this nature. Nevertheless, the work was recognized in its full importance and had a great impact on the younger artists. In particular it influenced one of the "Volumen I" artists, Rubén

Torres Llorca, who, at the time, was sewing for his own work. Except for one of the *trapices,* which hangs in the National Theatre, he gave away all the pieces because his apartment was too small for them.

PEÑA'S ESTRANGEMENT FROM ART

Peña now works as a free-lance designer for events such as the Biennial of Havana. He is also designing book covers and record jackets and has not produced "high" art since his Capitol exhibit. He claims that it is alien to him by now, a maze he is no longer interested in unraveling. He feels a fraternal relation with the younger artists but never had any interest in dealing with them as groups, preferring contact on an individual level.

As Peña himself says, most people did not know his work until the museum exhibit in 1988. They have a mythical relation with him enhanced by the feeling that he has an aura of tabu. His relation to his own art career is as if it consisted of a distant series of events parallel to his own life. While all this may be true to a certain extent, it is undeniable that Peña exerted an extremely strong perceptual influence. An active contributor to the Cuban poster tradition, a participant in many interdisciplinary projects (particularly the Third World Exhibition in Pabellón Cuba), designer of 120 magazine issues of Casa de las Américas, countless catalogues, and about 2,000 books, his work created a standard for Cuban design.

THE PERCEPTUAL LEGACY

Peña redirected pop-art devices to Cuban reality. He used Cuban comics as a reference, focused on Cuban everyday life, fashion, and texts and, as he says, "combined them in antagonistic and surreal forms." In the magazine issued by Casa de las Américas he tended to use a circle on its cover design as a constant formal reference, developing a kind of tropical "homage to the circle," an example of his use of idiosyncratic eclecticism. More profoundly, unlike any other Cuban designers, he deconstructed the industrial printing process to fit Cuban material conditions, making an aesthetic out of the color-separation process using magenta, cyan, yellow, and black as leading values; using halftone effects as themselves, and using "clip" art as a strong component to be transformed by the combination of the whole. With these elements, he created a visual system that reflects the poverty of means available and exploits eclecticism to his advantage, succeeding in making what normally is considered "poor" printing quality into an aesthetic in its own right. It is here that Peña lays down ideological roots for the succeeding generations.

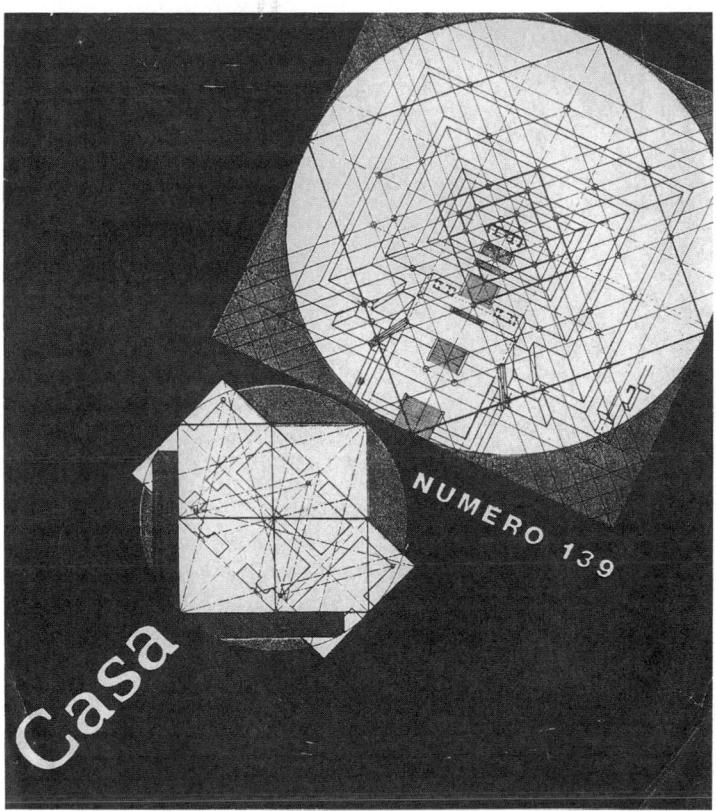

Umberto Peña, cover for Revista de Casa de las Américas, *No. 139, 1983.*

Peña claims that he works mainly using his taste and general intellectual information and that he has no methodological approach. His answer to a reputation for system and rigor is that it can be explained only by his passion for work and that there is nothing else behind it. However, once the work is seen as a body, it becomes clear why the younger generations perceive a deeper order in it than one dictated by Peña's individual taste.

Ana Mendieta[16]

The role of Ana Mendieta in the art of Cuba is different from that of Martínez and Peña. Because of her background, her self-evaluation in regard to the U.S. mainstream, and her need to reconnect with Cuba, Ana became the ideal mediator between the 1980s generation and the "outside." She did not influence artists aesthetically but provided a sounding board for ideas and gave moral support. She also became a two-way carrier of information about art between Cuba and the United States. Only slightly older than the members of the first generation of the 1980s, she is an influence, but she is not an antecedent of the Cuban artists. She represents the "extended nation" created by the diaspora in most of the countries of Latin America.

BACKGROUND

Ana's great-granduncle was Carlos Mendieta, a president of Cuba in 1934, strongly overshadowed by his army chief Fulgencio Batista.[17] Confronted with a sugarcane workers' strike, Batista defined the personality of the government with such bon mots as "If there is no sugar harvest, there will be blood harvest." Born in 1948 and sent with her sister to the United States by her family—two months before her thirteenth birthday—Ana experienced only a few years of the Cuban Revolution to compensate for Batista's tradition. She was then at the age when most adolescents start developing political opinions. Her father had political problems with Castro and landed in jail. (She suspected that he had worked for or collaborated with the CIA.) After spending some years in an orphanage, she was joined in the United States by her mother and brother in 1966, while her father remained jailed in Cuba. Eventually released, her father also came to the United States, where he died shortly after arriving due to a postoperation infection.

Reminiscing about her orphanage years, she often said that her choice in life was to become a criminal or an artist. Choosing the latter, her education continued in the United States. She received an M.A. degree in painting in 1972 and an M.F.A. degree in multimedia and video in 1977, both at the University of Iowa. Particularly the multimedia program, under the direction of Hans Breder (with whom she was to live for several years), had great impact on her, partially thanks to visits by multimedia artists Robert Wilson, Vito Acconci, Nam June Paik, and Mac Adams, art critic Lucy Lippard, and others.

ASSIMILATION AND ROOTS

Until the late 1970s, and except for an interest in feminism, she defined herself as apolitical (in terms of party politics). It took her a long time to fill the cultural gap caused by the circumstances of her emigration. Pondering about place and displacement marked her work, and she tried "to become one with the earth."[18] In 1980 she returned to Cuba for the first time, reconnecting with her past in a way that was easier than she had feared or expected.

Ana's work, a direct product of her U.S. education, has a different relationship with Western mainstream art than that of Cuban artists living in Cuba, although there are elements in common. Her decision to become an artist occurred in the United States within the mainstream's frame of reference, and her initial drive was to assimilate into that mainstream. Given her personal history, this drive was to be expected. But, given this same history, that assimilation was bound to be incomplete. Her maturation process as an artist was based on the development of a refined awareness of this incompleteness.

SPANGLISH ART

The term *Hispanic art* has been used to unify diverse ways of making art under one easy ethnic label,[19] and Ana's work is usually classed as Hispanic. But given the variety of origins and problems grouped by it, the label lacks subtlety. The concept of "Spanglish" is one that can be used to better focus on some of the "Hispanic" products.

Used in relation to speech, the term *Spanglish* has negative connotations, implying the absence of a functional tool and its substitution by a corrupt hybrid of two languages. The negative interpretation obscures the origin and the need that it fulfills. Used in relation to art, Spanglish represents the merging of a deteriorating memory with the acquisition of a new reality distanced by foreignness. It is in this sense that Spanglish becomes a good metaphor for Ana's art. Spanglish art is probably the most authentic alternative for the uprooted Latin artist. It accurately represents the fact that one came from one place and went to another, and it functionally bridges the abyss left by that travel.

Spanglish art is an individualistic and immediate solution that allows a release of the tension caused by the clash of two cultures and permits the integration of both experiences and the richness of both imageries into one iconography. It is not art that reflects a programmatic attitude or that evinces political awareness. Its cultural significance inheres in the witnessing of a shared destiny rather than in the activity of a shared aesthetic research, and its quality is dependent on individual effort rather than on group support or a community of interests.[20] The term *Hispanic art,* as well as, for example, *Feminist art,* presumes the existence of such a group support or community of interests.

THE CAREER

Ana had joined AIR (Artists in Residence), the feminist cooperative art gallery in New York, so her art has been seen in the context of both a feminist and Hispanic community of interests. But, in fact, she was working in a Spanglish manner and creating individually. The dual perception of her work as ethnic and feminist separated her two steps from

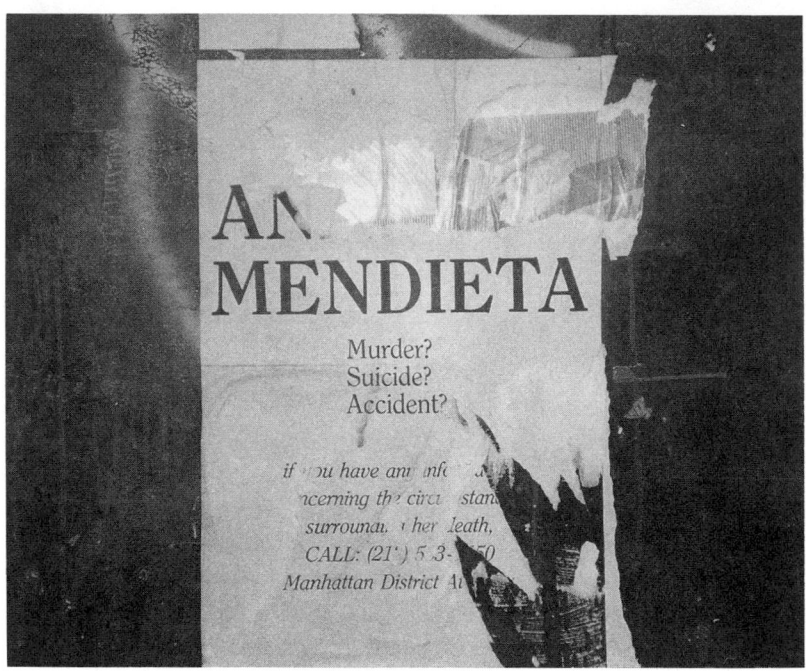

Anonymous, poster on the death of Ana Mendieta and trial of Carl Andre, 1987, New York City. Photo by Gaspar Noé.

the art of the U.S. mainstream. This same perception, on the other hand, also led her work to be seen as fulfilling two minority quotas, and the U.S. mainstream's quota system accounts for the velocity of her short career. Deserved honors accumulated at a higher speed than usual: between 1978 and 1983 she received a CAPS (Creative Arts Program Services) grant, three National Endowment for the Arts grants, a Guggenheim fellowship, a New York Council for the Arts grant, and the American Academy Fellowship in Rome.

The fact of her double separateness, along with the artificiality of the quota system, created a static that tended to interfere with a direct relation to her work by the audience. To this effect, the comments by two New York critics are revealing. Both quotes are taken from a cover story in *New York* magazine after her death. One is by Kay Larson, art critic for the magazine: "The remarkable thing to me was that Ana had been given a fellowship at the American Academy, considering the quality of her work, which was not that extraordinary." Barbara Rose, *Vogue*'s critic, comments, "[I] later went to a show of hers just because she was Carl's wife, and it was very bad. I asked a friend why anybody would show her and they [*sic*] said, 'Because she's Carl Andre's wife.' There was an opinion she had married Carl to gain entree into the art world."[21] The cover of the magazine bore the intriguing question, "Did Carl Andre, the Renowned Minimalist Sculptor, Hurl His Wife, a Fellow Artist, to Her Death?," reifying Ana in the anonymity of wifehood.

Ana died on September 8, 1985, as the consequence of a fall from the thirty-fourth floor of the apartment building where she lived with her husband, under circumstances that are still unclear. He was acquitted on February 11, 1988. After her death, she became a symbol for artists who shared her sense of separateness from the mainstream. In fact, because of the artistic status of her husband, the New York art scene polarized into pro-Ana and pro-Carl people.[22] It is not a polarization around individuals or about feminism versus machismo. It is a polarization along mainstream versus nonmainstream lines of thought.

THE LEVELS OF POLITICIZATION

By 1980, Ana's politics had become quite radical with a belated passion partially helped by her reconnection with Cuba.[23] Her sense of incomplete assimilation was symbolized in her use of "Tropic-ana" to sign letters to her friends, punning not only on a tropical country as her place of origin, but also on the squeezing of its economy. Nevertheless, her political views never entered overtly into her work.

For Ana, politics remained reduced to a vague atmosphere that generated opinionated discussions with her friends and helped her introspection while working.[24] Her work was often seen as a programmatic expression of feminism enhanced by a U.S. perception of mysterious exoticism. It was therefore also seen in the context of the superficial anthropologism prevalent in art. Some of her success within these perspectives can be attributed to a misunderstanding. Her work is not programmatic. It is, much more simply and modestly, a self-portrait.

THE WORK

In that work about herself, Ana sequentially portrayed the process of being wounded, then dying, the subsequent destruction of the image, the integration of the remnants into nature, and the reincarnation into objects. Without a preplanned scenario, that is the order of the different periods of her work, and it provides a chilling metaphor for her life. At the same time the work reflects, in a systematic and consistent fashion, an ideology. This ideology, when she had occasion to express it verbally, seemed rather confused and obscurantist. Among other things, she would talk about her attraction to earth as the outgrowth of the fact that she lacked a homeland, that she had been "taken from the womb." She would also express a mystical belief in an energy that flows through everything and in the healing power of spiritually charged objects.

Her first pieces started in 1972. Hans Breder, then her teacher, describes how she began: "Spontaneously, Anna announces that she has an idea for a piece. She undresses, lies on the lawn, and asks one of the students to cover her body with grass. Somebody takes photographs. In the photographs her body blends into the ground. From that point, she blended her body with the elements in innumerable ways."[25] In 1973 she performed a piece related to the rape of a fellow student in Iowa where "an unsuspecting audience of artist friends entered her apartment to discover her bloody, half-naked body."[26] This performance was followed by others in which she wrote on walls or left traces with mixtures of gouache and blood using her hands and arms, or covered her body with the blood of a beheaded white chicken to then roll over a bed of feathers that adhered to her body. While there are antecedents (e.g., the more frivolous Yves Klein body paintings and Ralph Ortiz' destructionism), these pieces establish the beginning of Ana's search for herself, both as a woman and as a cultural entity identified through its wounding. Shifra Goldman compares Ana with Frida Kahlo: "Both make reference to blood in the lives of women, Frida to birth and miscarriage, Ana to rape and menstruation."[27]

During 1974–1975, there were some performances related to death. A film clip shows her quasi-immobile face, strongly evoking a death mask, being marked by blood drops slowly seeping down from her hair. In another performance, her body floated inertly, subject to the force of the tide until it ran aground. She would also have herself filmed buried under stones, while some of the stones slowly rolled off her body due to minimal movements. In these works her own body symbolized, or was, the corpse. In works to follow, her body was absent. Only the silhouette remained, not unlike police drawings of corpse positions, which in turn disintegrated. Her body outline drawn with flowers slowly drifted apart floating in a lake; made with sand, it was washed away by the waves of the sea; drawn with a support for firecrackers, it burned away in sinister and unfestive fireworks; drawn with gunpowder, it became a *Palera* signature, a deity and personal identification sign that preludes the execution of good and bad deeds in Afro-Cuban rites.[28]

In a later stage, the image became so integrated with nature that it was practically imperceptible. She found silhouettes as readymades in the landscape and introduced subtle changes to stress cavities and shadows, which can be found only if one knows what to look for. She built an ever-so-slightly anthropomorphic island that can be seen as a totally natural event. She tried to become nature. Several trips to Mexico

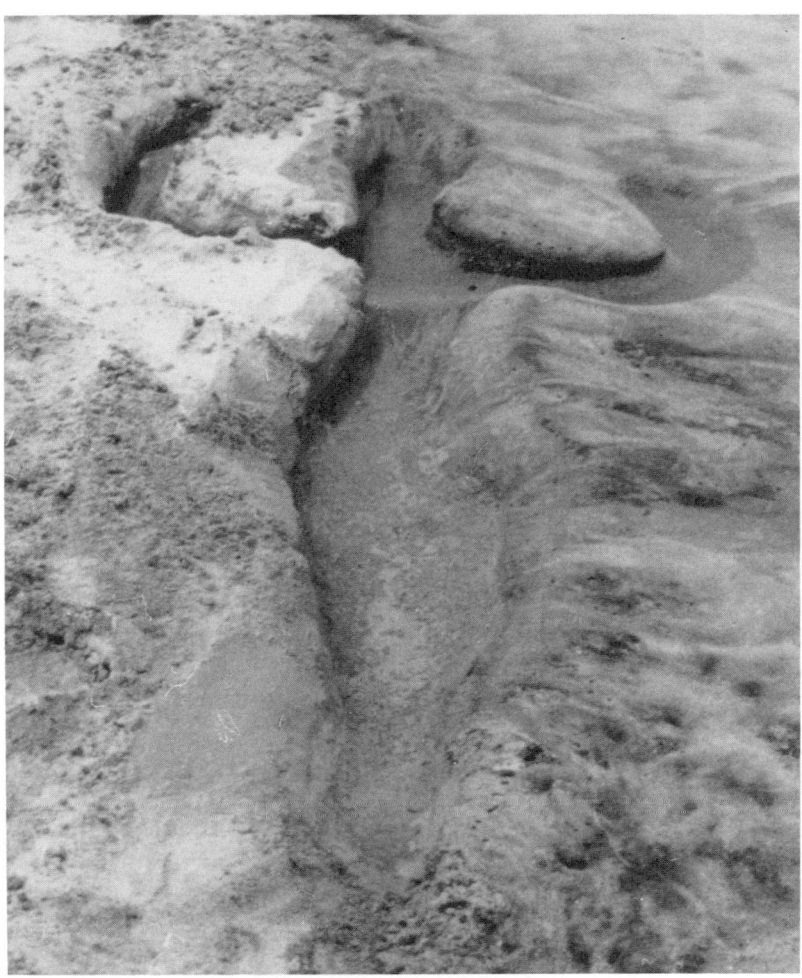

Ana Mendieta, Silueta Work in Mexico, 1973–1978, photograph, 50 × 33 cm. Estate of Ana Mendieta; Courtesy of Galerie Lelong, New York City.

strengthened her feelings of alienation in the United States; she wanted to integrate with Latin American nature and particularly with Cuban nature.

THE CUBAN WORK

In 1980 she made her first visit to Cuba and prepared her subsequent trip to Jaruco, where she carved her Rupestrian pieces. Jaruco is a hill with a forest, about twenty miles from Havana. It is where the Almendares River starts, and there are gorges and caves. The caves were first

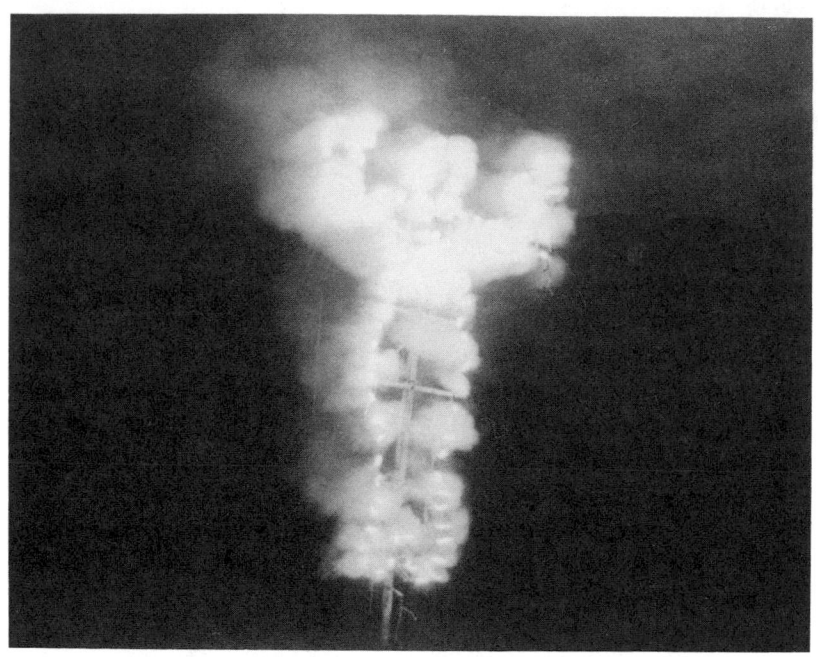

Ana Mendieta, Anima, *1976, bamboo armature and fireworks, photograph from the estate of Ana Mendieta; Courtesy of Galerie Lelong, New York City.*

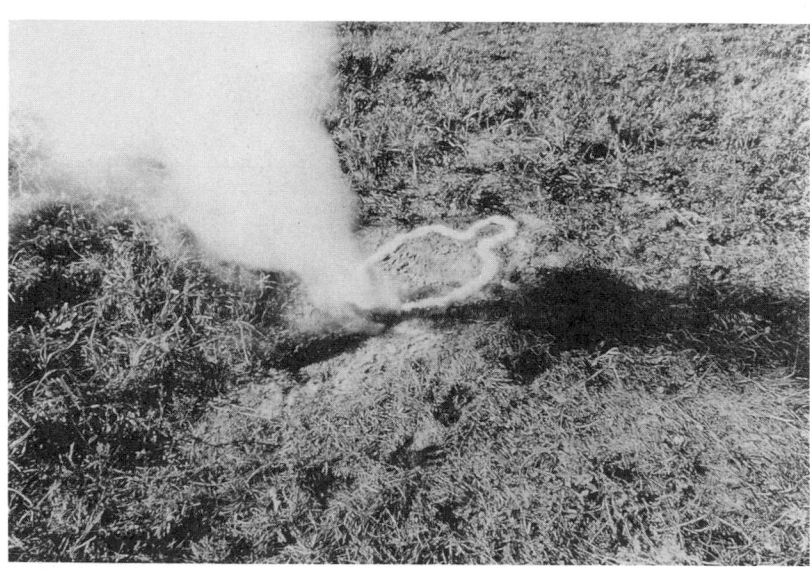

Ana Mendieta, Gunpowder Sculpture, *1978, gelatin silver photograph, 33 × 48 cm. Private collection. Photo by Luis Camnitzer.*

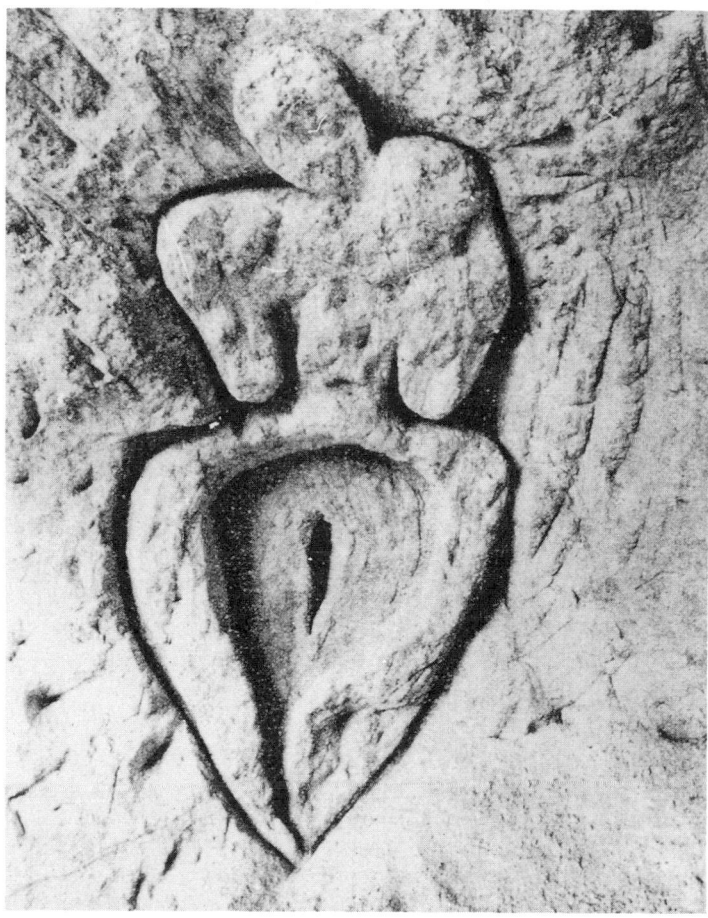

Ana Mendieta. Escultura rupestre (Rupestrian Sculpture) *at Jaruco, 1981, Photoetching, 13 × 9 cm. Private collection. Photo by Luis Camnitzer.*

inhabited by Indians and later by nineteenth-century fighters for the independence of Cuba. She was introduced to the place by Cuban artists, among them Ricardo Rodríguez Brey, who taught at the Casa de Cultura in the adjoining village.

At Jaruco, in 1981, she used limestone walls in the caves to find and retouch the forms that interested her. Her silhouette became reminiscent of the Venus of Willendorf, and the caves were an ideal setting, rarely disturbed by human presence. Possibly her sense of belonging allowed her to return to more defined images. She dispensed with her own outline, by now already dissolved in her work, and established her own link with tradition. But in actual art terms, the work did not exist in itself but only as documented memory. Thus, big photographs (sixty inches by forty-six inches) once more underline her sense of distance. The tension created by this sense resolves itself in her choice of materials. She framed some photographs and continued the photographed texture of sand or gravel in the background with real sand or gravel on the frame, creating a trompe l'oeil effect, which attempted to bring back reality. She used *amate* paper (made out of bark), leaves, roots, mud, and trees to draw or shape her figures, this time as objects independent of the natural environment, *being* nature instead.

It is this last period of her work in which one finds imagery hinting at thoughts of reincarnation. Since Jaruco her work had become more sexually detailed; the outlines started to contain sex and not just the void. Sexual symbols, or ornaments in their place, gave definition to the image and the outline. The veins of a leaf became the lines defining separation of legs and crotch in a kind of ambiguous conceptual trompe l'oeil as opposed to the explicit visual descriptive device previously used in the frames.

There seems to be a consensus among critics that this last period is her weakest in terms of art. But when viewed in the larger context over twelve years, this period can be seen as a logical extension, even a completion. The evocation of fertility goddesses often used in conjunction with her work only happened truly in this stage. The empty silhouettes made before Jaruco, if goddesses at all, were sterile, maimed, and emptied. Her last works attempted to make nature, at large and in any of its parts, the ultimate deity of fertility.

THE RELATION TO "VOLUMEN I"

It would be to idealize Ana in mainstream terms to claim that she created a new language. She did not. She was sensitive to contemporary aesthetics and appropriated them well, using them specifically for functions defined by her. In that, her attitude was very similar to that of her Cuban artist friends; rather than fight an overbearing flow of information, she and they picked those elements deemed useful for a defined purpose.

Ana was able to perceive her friends' work from within at the same time that she could lend a distance and a perspective to the discussion of their work. She initially arrived in Cuba with the same preconceptions about socialist art that other foreigners bring with them. One of her first encounters with the new Cuban art was provided by the "Volumen I" exhibit. The "Volumen I" exhibit radically changed her perception and also led to immediate friendship with most of the exhibitors. It became a two-way relation. Her work with tree roots can be traced to some of

Elso Padilla's work, her interest in *Santería* and Afro-American rituals to José Bedia and Ricardo Rodríguez Brey. In turn she provided fresh criticism and strong moral support in a period when the group was breaking new ground and disconcerting the public. She shared with them the belief that political positions can condition art without the need for pamphleteering content. Like her friends, Ana escaped the derivativeness endemic in making art in colonial situations. She, like they, broke with aesthetic servility and began to appropriate at will whatever she saw as pertinent to the creation of a syncretic culture. While there never was an opportunity for them to exhibit together, it would have seemed natural if they had. She was close in age and interests and otherwise lined up with them. The new history of the latest developments in Cuban art is fortunately recognizing the connection, and Ana is being listed with her friends based on this commonality.[29] At the time of her death, Ana was thinking more and more of Italy and Cuba as her places of residence.

Ana's work inhabits the gap between periphery and mainstream and is, in some deep sense, inaccessible to present value judgment, as there are not yet values set up to accurately and justly evaluate her work in terms of art. Her art is too early for nonmainstream values, and it is too much outside of traditional mainstream values because of the problems she addresses. What can be said is that she provided a vivid and powerful link that had been missing. She successfully started the formalization of a cultural rupture, which can be fully understood only once her work is placed in its true cultural context. In her case it is the rupture addressed by Spanglish that sets her apart from the 1980s generation. This cultural context has yet to be developed by other Spanglish artists.

3

ART within the
REVOLUTION[1]

Modernism, Internationalism, and Nationalism

"Volumen I" brought to the fore in visual form and through the surrounding controversies the essences of the many conundrums in which
cultures on the periphery find themselves when searching for their identity. In the Cuban case the issues were even more loaded with theoretical
stands because they occurred within a socialist context. On one side this
gave more credibility to the factions who advocate anticapitalist purism.
It also pointed out the many contradictions raised by the traditional art
object with its commercial potential placed in that kind of society. However, Cuba is the product of the influx of an incredible variety of cultural
currents and ideologies. The Russian Revolution's choice was to inherit
the bourgeois aesthetic of the nineteenth century or to invent something
new. It played with both possibilities and then settled with the first one.
The Cuban Revolution, instead, had a wider heritage available—the European and the North American avant-garde—and the knowledge that
Soviet art did not serve Cuban needs. By allowing art to evolve at its own
pace within the new society, Cuban leadership hoped to have the contradictions slowly go away on their own. The contradictions did not go
away, but the restraint of the government on aesthetic issues allowed for
a healthy and nonintimidating presence of these issues for all the artists.
"Volumen I" was a consequence of this policy, and the discussions took
place primarily with "the people," not with the government.

What strikes most foreign viewers as surprising—that the politically
explicit content of Cuban art today is minimal and that its products look
much closer to the Western mainstream than what one would usually
attribute to a "socialist country"—is therefore a logical consequence of
Cuban policy. Still, even sympathizers of Cuba, upon first contact with
Cuban contemporary art, have difficulty in believing that it is an art en-

couraged by the state. This makes Cuban art less easy to deal with than if it were clearly nationalistic or "typical" in its expression and separate from transnational trends.

The expectation of some exoticism, political or otherwise, is heightened by an odd use of geography. As Cuban critic Adelaida de Juan has noted, Cuba, according to the United States and following the beliefs of Columbus, is perceived as part of the "East" because of its politics, while Japan is treated as part of the "West" for economic reasons. The reality is that Cuba has been rather close to the United States, not only in geographic location but also in influence, and it shares most of the cultural conditions of the rest of Latin America. In that sense, as in the other countries of the continent, contemporary Cuban art is the product of a modernist tradition.

Among the conditions held in common with the continent is the permanent conflict between the assertion of national identity and the insertion into an international context. As in the rest of Latin America, this conflict was (and still is) accompanied by political positions that tried to elucidate the issues of contemporaneity, cultural penetration, imperialism, and colonization. The import of European modernist tendencies in the arts during the first decades of the century further fueled the discussion of these topics, with many attempts to blend international modernism with vernacular solutions.

The Introduction of Modernism

It is difficult to credit single individuals for the introduction of modernism into the visual arts in Cuba. Some authors attribute the initiation to Víctor Manuel García (1897–1969). Victor Manuel (his last name is usually dropped) traveled to France in 1925 and returned deeply marked by the work of Gauguin. Although his paintings, somewhat sentimental, deal with the Cuban countryside and its peasants, Victor Manuel expressed with clear words his position in his time: "One has to be a child of one's time, but not a bastard."[2] Painter Rafael Blanco (1885–1955), who doubled as a caricaturist (he was perceived as having changed the path of humor drawing in Cuba as early as 1910), is mentioned by others. His biting humor crosses over into his paintings both in content and by loosening his formal approach as compared to his contemporaries. His most interesting work is in a Goya/Daumier tradition. Ruptures introduced by both artists, though not radical from an international perspective, provided an alternative to the stuffy academicism of the School of San Alejandro (the Cuban School of Art, see Chap. 4) and influenced other artists. Both artists were connected with the maga-

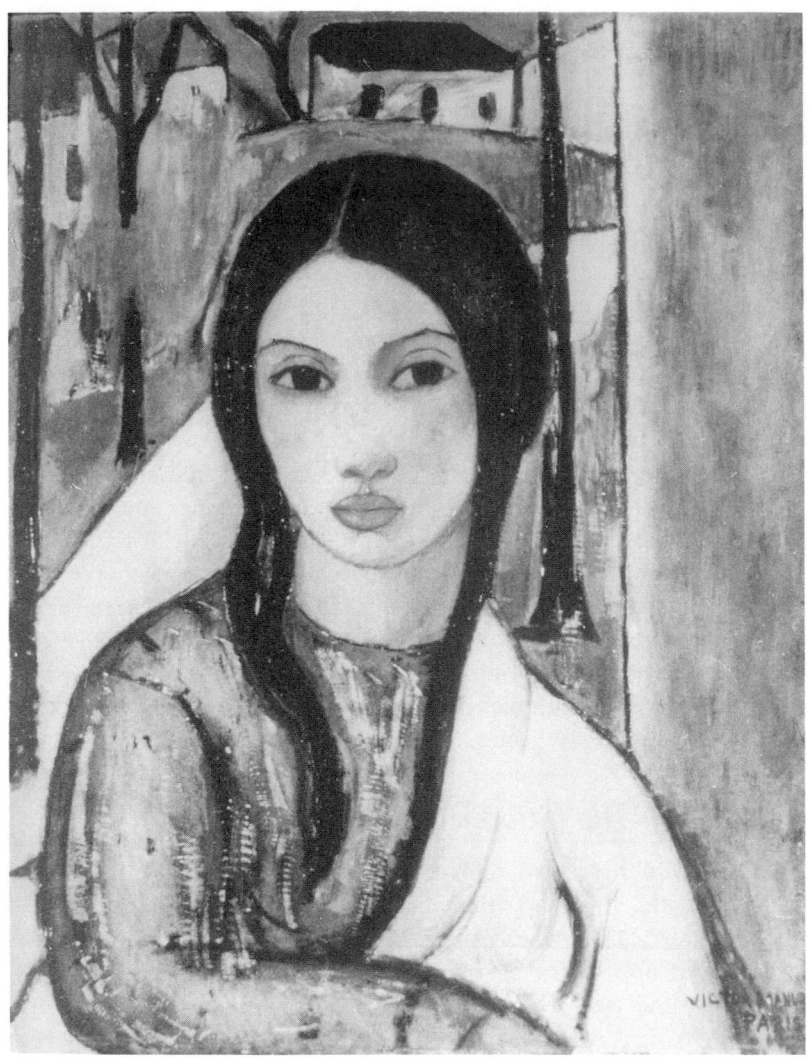

Víctor Manuel García, Gitana tropical (Tropical Gypsy), *1929, oil on wood, 46 × 38 cm. Museo Nacional de Bellas Artes, Havana. Photo by Luis Camnitzer.*

zine *Social* (published between 1916 and 1933), which may deserve a bigger credit for the introduction of modernism than any individual artists. The magazine became the voice of the Grupo Minorista, a nucleus of politicized artists and writers that in 1927, years after their organization, would proclaim the need for a "vernacular art and the new art in its manifold manifestations."[3]

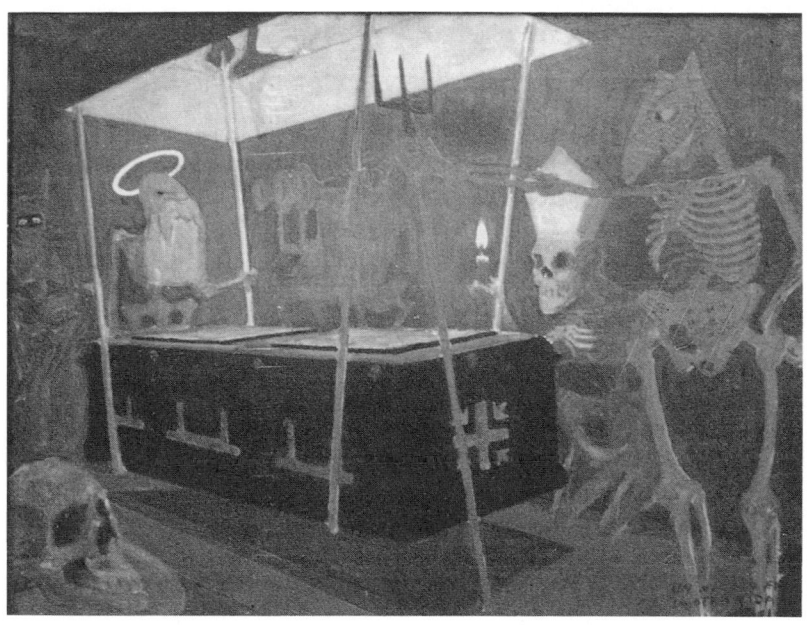

Rafael Blanco, Un novato en la otra vida *(A Novice in the Other Life), ca. 1920, oil on canvas, 48 × 61.5 cm. Museo Nacional de Bellas Artes, Havana. Photo by Luis Camnitzer.*

However, the big event that marked the official beginning of modernism was a group exhibit. When in 1927 the *Revista de Avance* sponsored the "Exposición de Arte Nuevo," the aim, again, was to place Cuban art in the context of the new European modernist trends without giving up identity. The accompanying "manifesto" affirmed, "[We are] artists of the new generation who, with a concentrated effort, fight to incorporate the great undertakings of our time without neglecting, however, [our] essential Cubanism."[4]

In addition to Cuban artists,[5] the list included foreign artists, particularly Alice Neel and Adja Yunkers from the United States, to show an intention "to transcend any local '*-ism.*'" The fear of excessive localism seemed justified since most of the Cuban artists were dealing with local subject matter. Eduardo Abela (1889–1965), the founder of the Estudio Libre (an antiacademic art studio), was painting in a vein that produced his *El triunfo de la rumba* (*The Triumph of the Rumba*) in 1928, and generally, most of the Cuban artists in the exhibit were representational and doing regionalist painting.[6] The use of European trends was more a move against the rigidity of academic education than against the more

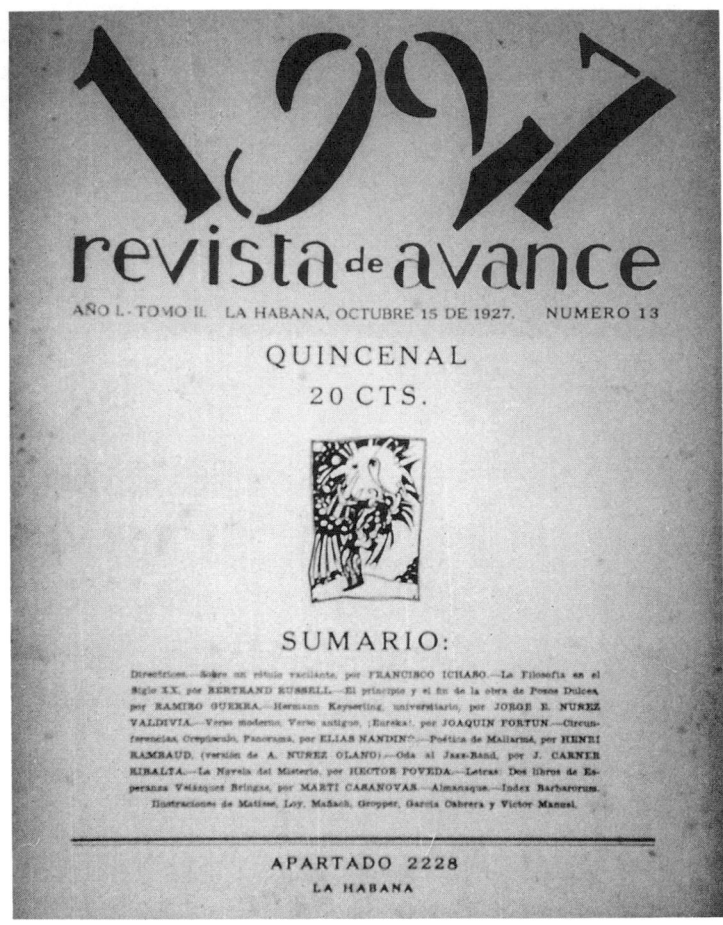

Cover of Revista de Avance, *1927. Photo by Luis Camnitzer.*

fundamental tenets that were informing Cuban art at the time. As Cuban writer Alejo Carpentier wrote, it was a matter of being nationalist and avant-gardist at the same time, "something difficult since all nationalism rests on the cult of a tradition while 'vangardism' signified a rupture with tradition."[7]

A superficial approach tended to use modernism as a novelty, as an exchange of an old and worn-out tradition for the creation of a new one. Cuban artists, however, perceived that the art tradition prevalent in the country was a false one since it ruled out the cultural validation of the multitude of ethnic and popular traditions coexisting at the time. Modernism thus served as a tool not only for rupture with a tradition but

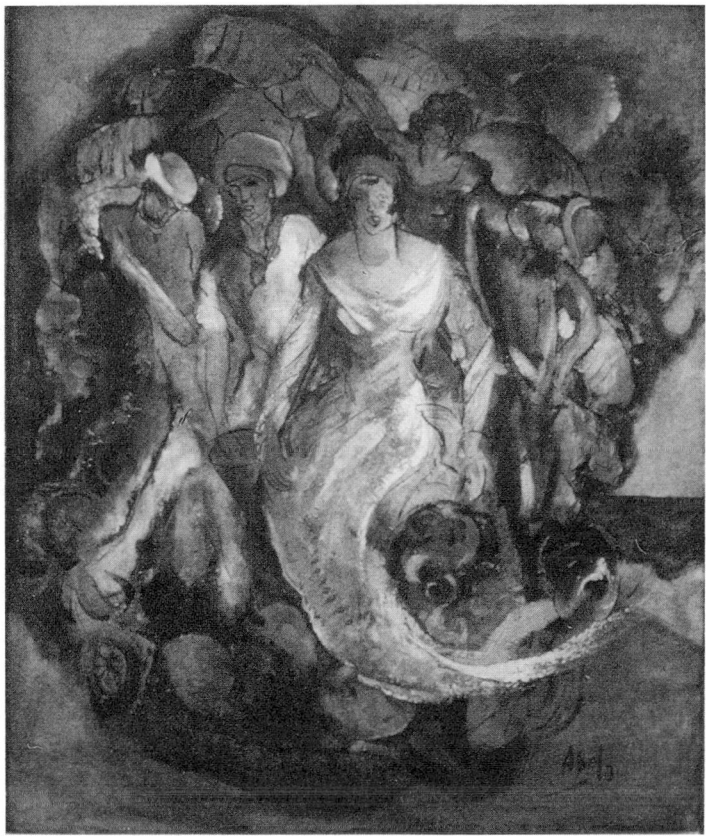

Eduardo Abela, El triunfo de la rumba (The Triumph of Rumba), *ca. 1928, oil on canvas, 65 × 54 cm. Museo Nacional de Bellas Artes, Havana. Photo by Luis Camnitzer.*

also as an opening for other traditions.[8] This fact accounts for this artistic generation's less radical approach in regard to formalist matters. Paradoxically, while the exhibit gave Cuban arts a new direction, it also coincided with the beginning of a temporary exodus due in great measure to the bloody dictatorship of Gerardo Machado, who ruled Cuba between 1925 and 1933. Many of the Cuban artists present in the 1927 exhibition traveled to Europe, some absorbing much of what was being offered (e.g., Carlos Enríquez, who in time made some collages adapting John Heartfield's aesthetics, and Marcelo Pogolotti, who became a member of the Futurist movement).

The ambivalence between nationalism and internationalism evident in the 1927 Manifesto has continued in Cuba until today, in both art and

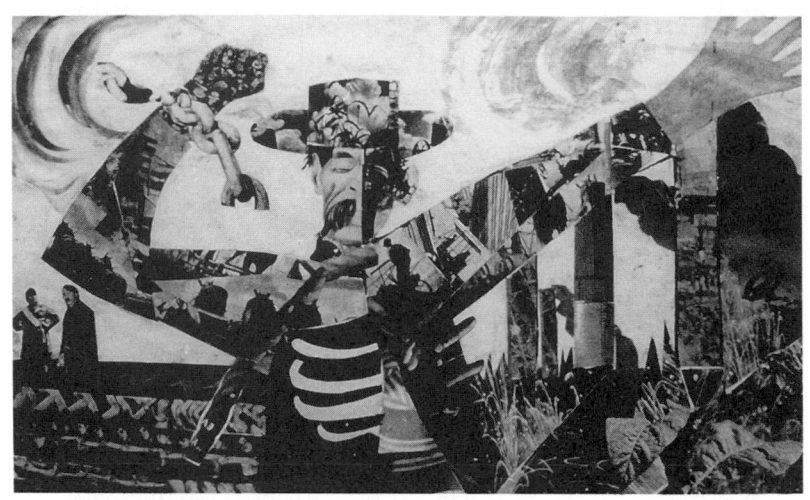

Carlos Enríquez, Nuevo ripalda (New Ripalda), *1934, collage on cardboard, 24.2 × 44.5 cm. Museo Nacional de Bellas Artes, Havana. Photo by Luis Camnitzer.*

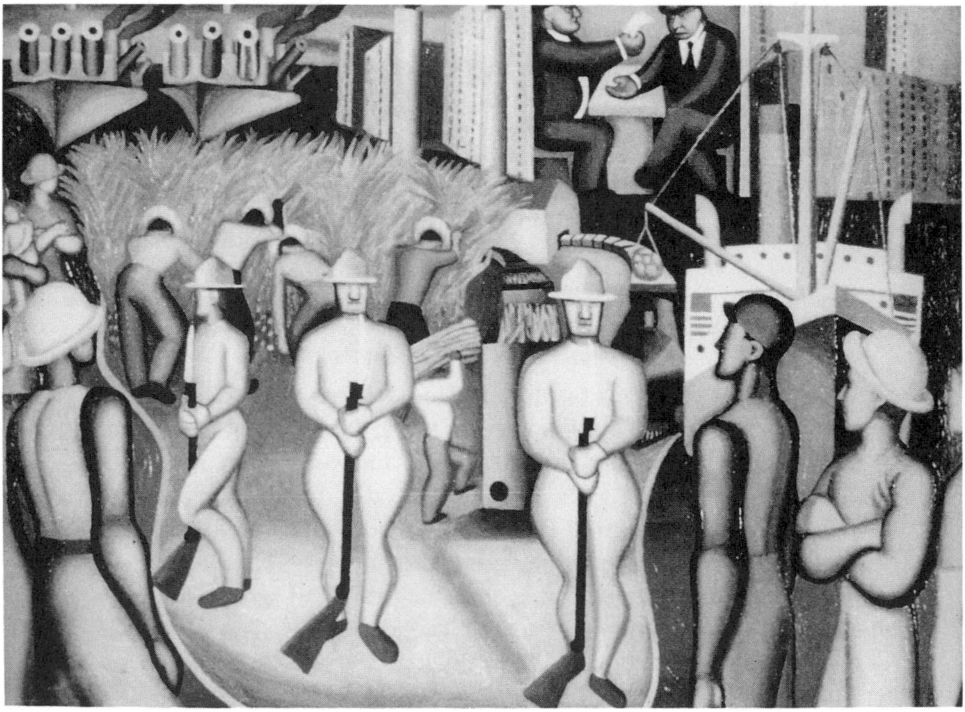

Marcelo Pogolotti, Paisaje cubano (Cuban Landscape), *1933, oil on canvas, 99 × 73.5 cm. Museo Nacional de Bellas Artes, Havana.*

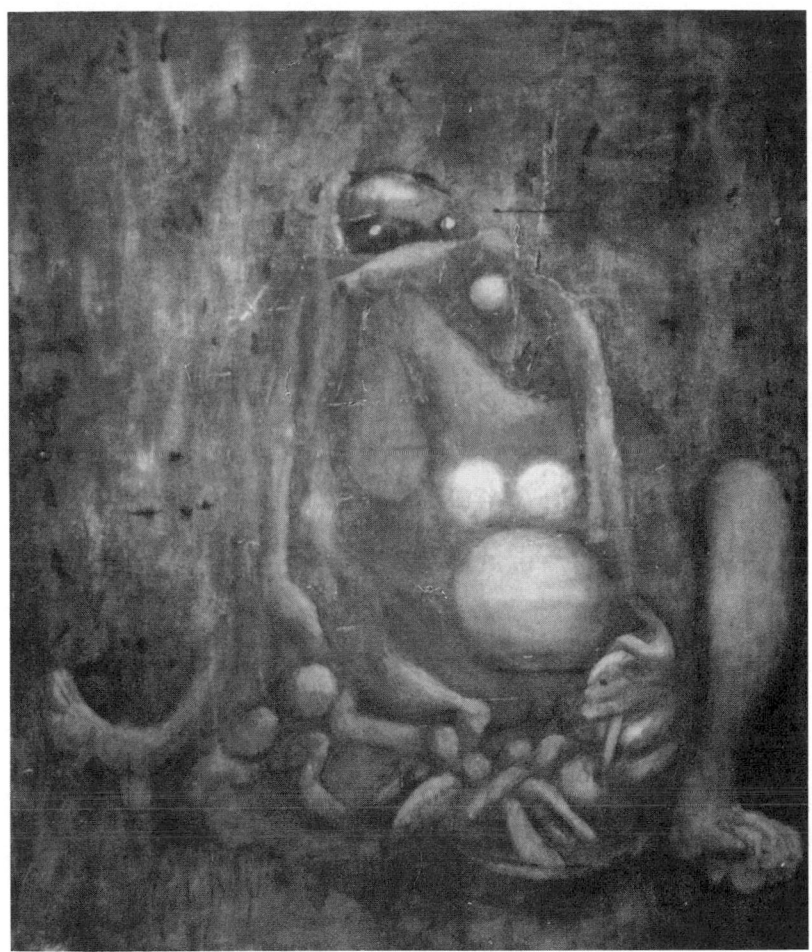

Roberto Diago, Maternidad (Maternity)*, 1945–1946, oil on canvas, 106 ×
97.5 cm. Museo Nacional de Bellas Artes, Havana. Photo by Luis Camnitzer.*

politics.[9] So has the close connection of artist movements with literary
magazines. *Revista de Avance* was followed by *Orígenes*[10] and then by
Lunes de Revolución. Orígenes, with writers Lezama Lima, Cintio Vitier,
and Eliseo Diego, and painters Mariano Rodríguez and Roberto Diago,
constituted a more ethical and less political avant-garde. At the same
time, the art stemming from this nucleus became more regionalist and,
with Amelia Peláez and René Portocarrero, became known as the
"School of Havana." It was a regionalism to serve as an alternative to
what was called the Cuban "School of Mexico," which reflected heavy
muralist influence.

Somewhat overlapping with *Orígenes,* several artists organized into the group known as Los Once. Reliving the feeling for a need of rupture of the 1927 generation, the artists this time referred to U.S. abstract-expressionism and beat literature. They reasoned that abstract-expressionism was a visual language uncontaminated by a political reality they opposed and hoped that it would give them a freedom denied in other areas of life. Raúl Martínez, a member of the group coincidentally born in 1927, painted in black and white as a reaction against the sweet colors of his predecessors. In the same process of reaction they accused writer Lezama Lima of being "French."[11] Los Once, however, had a bigger impact as an example of integrity than because of their aesthetics. Their organization of the Anti-Bienal in 1954 was an influential statement against dictatorship. Batista and Franco had promoted a Bienal Hispano-Americana to take place in Havana that year. The group encouraged the boycott of the exhibit and organized the alternative show. The artists further boycotted an exhibition to be held in Venezuela under the auspices of Venezuelan dictator Pérez Jiménez and the Panamerican Union as another metaphorical protest against Batista. As described by Raúl Martínez, "We believed that art is for art's sake, but what one does *with* art is a problem of individual conscience, and that is already political."[12] International art language was integrated with local political resistance and, out of fear of Batista's reprisals, the group then dissolved by its own accord in 1955, although in 1957 they once more participated in a protest exhibit. This time it was a sidewalk show against the "Salón Nacional," again a Batista-sponsored event. The same year, a museum in Camagüey—an inland city—organized an exhibition of some of the group's work for which they wrote a "declaration of principles" in which they proclaimed thematic and technical independence "free of all pseudo-Cuban elements."[13]

From 1959 on, *Lunes de Revolución,* with writers Guillermo Cabrera Infante, Carlos Franqui, Edmundo Desnoes, and Ambrosio Fornet, reacted to the "regional sweetness" of the School of Havana, which remained powerful in spite of Los Once. While committed to politics, the group advocated for an art more oriented toward artistic issues. The publication was stopped in 1961, as an aftermath of the polemic ensuing from the prohibition of *P.M.,* a short documentary film by a brother of writer Cabrera Infante, which showed Cuban nightlife in a way considered offensive by orthodox members of the Communist Party. The polemic generated Castro's often quoted dictum, "Within the Revolution, everything; outside the Revolution, nothing," and a commitment to aesthetic freedom in the arts.

Today's Cuban position on the relation of the vernacular with the issues of nationalism versus internationalism is represented by Minister of Culture Armando Hart's statement, "We are also part of the West, geographically and culturally, [and] we should not shut ourselves off from the rest of the world behind a border. We wage our cultural battle based on the principles that inspired Western culture and on its universal aspiration or perspective. . . . We don't forget that, and we're willing to wage our own battle within that culture's tradition of struggle."[14]

The Revolutionary Poster

Following the stereotypes about socialism and Latin America but ignoring the country's cultural history, foreign observers expected that Cuba would enter a period of Mexican-style muralism to communicate with the masses. Instead, the silkscreened poster took its place.

In this context, the important period of the Cuban poster (roughly 1965 to 1970) should be seen as a spontaneous and organic development, not as evidence of any public policy or self-imposed artistic canon. It reflects the clear definition of aims typical of advertising combined with a wise use of international models (e.g., Polish poster art and U.S. pop art).

Again, Cuban artists looked for international trends to help define national identity, and the blend of conditions created an art form peculiarly appropriate to the times in Cuba, with the stylistic consistency, elegance, and directness that characterized the Cuban poster of the period. Alfredo Rostgaard, one of the preeminent poster designers of the period, comments, "The Polish artists showed us that we could make completely political posters for the First of May or the anniversary of the October Revolution, with poetry, with beauty, with an indirect language."[15]

Painted murals would have demanded much more specialized labor[16] and created a permanence of messages that was not appropriate to the fluid Cuban situation. At the same time, the way the poster was used did not exclude the gigantic mural size that, when needed, was solved through piecing together, just as commercial billboards are produced. It is estimated that in 1972 alone about five million posters were printed.[17]

While the first cultural posters, which are the ones that eventually set the aesthetic tone of the Cuban poster, were produced by Casa de las Américas as early as 1960,[18] the posters created by ICAIC (the Cuban Institute for Cinematographic Art and Industry) were the ones that gave the strongest stylistic guidelines.[19] The ICAIC made it a policy to do its own posters rather than to use the posters accompanying the movies, which were designed in the capitalist world. The poster was to have a didactic function related to the film being announced, complementing rather than selling it.

The next organization to use posters on a wide scale was OSPAAAL (Organization of Solidarity with the Peoples of Asia, Africa, and Latin America), which blended more overt political messages into the developed graphic image. OSPAAAL was founded in January 1966 to fill a void created by the political rift between China and the Soviet Union. The posters took turns in propagandizing the various liberation struggles occurring in the Third World. After this, the "new" poster increasingly developed into a vehicle for internal politics, using all the power implicit in the medium.[20]

The atmosphere of poster creation was closer to the one in a good university design class than to a commercial advertising corporation. Artists spurred each other's creativity in search of elegant visual solutions, rather than concerning themselves with the translation of an image into future sales. Instead of following the descriptive rules of pamphletary information or using abstraction for idealization, the artists used symbolic integration and visual punning to create a new reality dedicated to the space provided by the poster. The lack of capitalist pressure was particularly beneficial for the film poster. There was no profit to be derived by drawing large crowds since people would go to see the film anyway. The posters therefore functioned as announcements and not as publicity, eliminating "any need for the lurid, garish poster art of our own film industry."[21] In a synthetic manner, the poster satisfied some of the same needs a good catalogue does for an exhibit.

Paradoxically, the poster design "market" was rather competitive, as different institutes had access to a general pool of talent and would commission particular designers to execute their projects. While many of the original designers are still working, the later relative decline of the Cuban poster is attributed by some to the fact that the artists eventually were permanently hired and monopolized by the different organizations or simply applied themselves to their own paintings. But it is also true that the settling of the revolutionary process eventually made the form somewhat obsolete, and consequently the poster as a creative entity lost some of its appeal.

The poster movement became the highest visual literacy accomplishment of the Revolution. Its aesthetic, considered intellectual and sophisticated to the point of being the prey of Western highbrow commercialization,[22] was readily accepted by the "masses" who, according to Right and Left dogma, were supposed to understand only pamphlets. Posters

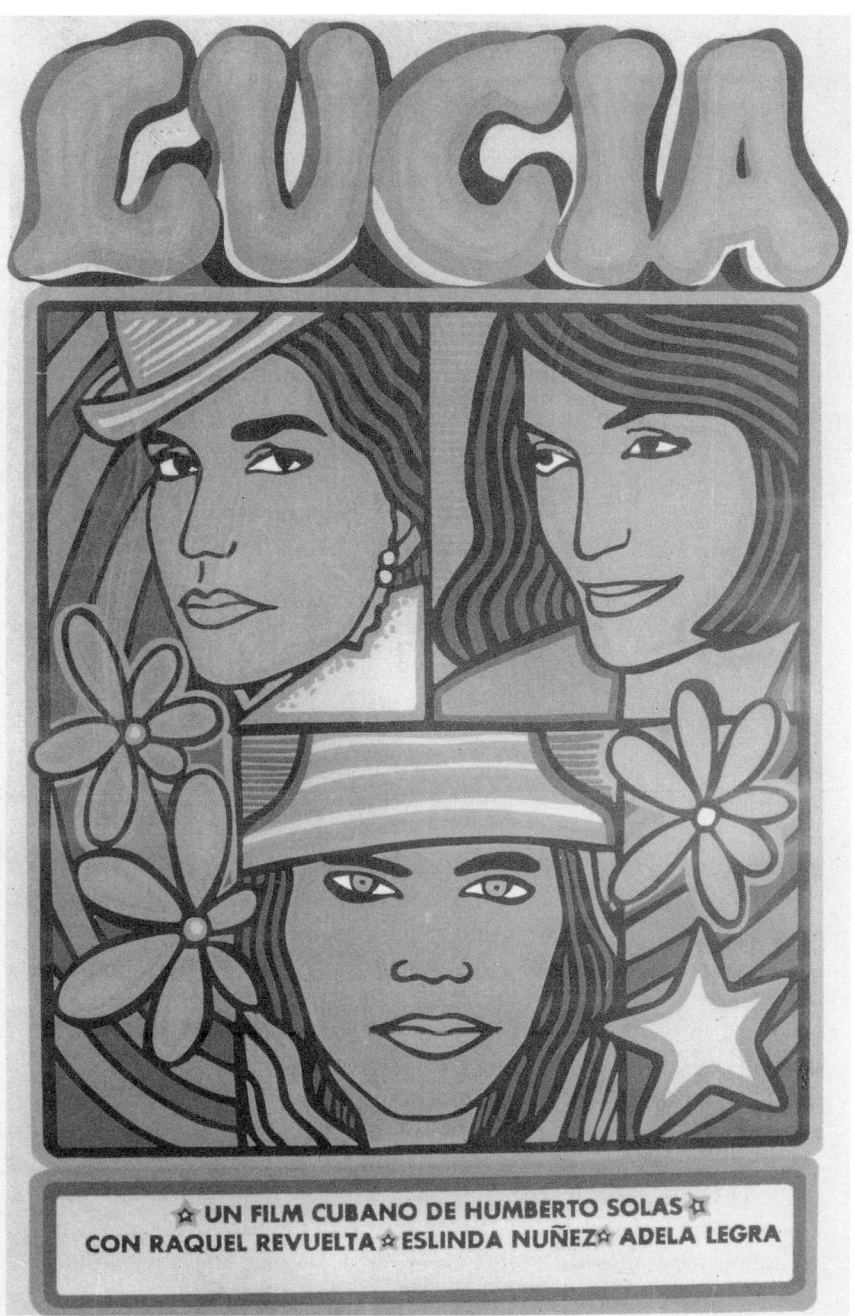

Raúl Martínez, Lucía, 1968, silkscreen on paper, 70 × 50 cm. Private collection. Photo by Luis Camnitzer.

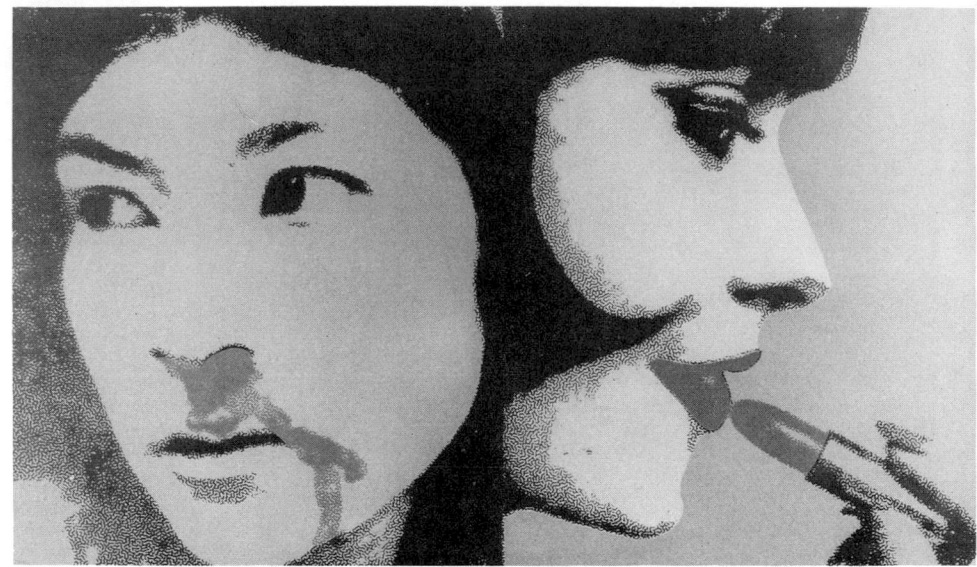

José Gómez Fresquet (Frémez), from the series "Burgueses" (Bourgeois), ca. 1969, silkscreen on paper, 34.5 × 58 cm. Private collection. Photo by Luis Camnitzer.

created a mutual feedback dynamic with much of popular art, which in turn was again utilized by "high culture," as exemplified in much of the work of Raúl Martínez, artists of the Grupo Escambray (who, in the 1970s, would organize mobile exhibits and incorporate discussions with the public into their art) and, more recently, Leandro Soto, among others.

The Campaigns for Literacy

The issue of literacy, both visual and straightforward, has been a permanent feature of the Revolution since its beginning. Neither Cuba of the last thirty years nor its art can be understood without an understanding of this point. Literacy has been, more than a narrow activity, a broad cultural concept that informed education at large. It was seen, next to economic independence, as a primary tool to achieve not only cultural autonomy but also the ability to create a new culture within the new social order.

Implicitly, this meant a heightened awareness of what amounts to a cultural tradition resulting from a long colonization process, which had to be changed. However, there is no implication that this tradition, greatly conditioned and influenced by the United States, was abruptly terminated by the Revolution and a new one artificially and automatically instituted. In 1965, Che Guevara wrote, "We revolutionaries often lack the knowledge and the intellectual audacity needed to face the development of the new man with methods different from those which are conventional and which suffer the influence of the society that created them."[23]

Since 1959, Cubans have undergone a process of introspection, trying to identify their own traditions and to bring them to the foreground. Nevertheless, they did not erase history. The cultural heritage was not cleanly subdivided into convenient and inconvenient components, although some efforts to this effect have occasionally been promoted. Cuban forms of artistic expression today continue to represent the tensions of contradiction with the awareness that the arrival of a purified revolutionary culture can, if at all, only emerge slowly. Guevara's analysis remains valid today, although with time it has acquired a pragmatic quality.

The kind of culture dreamt of at the beginning of the Revolution could not be simply and single-handedly achieved by one or a group of visual artists, no matter how enlightened. To achieve this, a rigid design for a course of action would be needed, a step that Cubans consistently have avoided in the arts and that probably could not be successful anyway.[24]

Such a grand design, however, seemed appropriate and feasible in some areas. High rates of illiteracy, for example, could be and were addressed by massive efforts to reverse the statistics in a short period of time. Illiteracy, which stood at 23.6 percent in 1953, was reduced to 3.9 percent in 1961.[25] The literacy drive was not strictly limited to problems of reading and writing. Questionnaires to be filled out by teachers included the search for information about the health of the learners. Thus, the campaign doubled as a census with the intention of subse quently also improving living conditions. A special flag was designed to indicate that illiteracy had been defeated in a particular village.[26] (This flag was flown by Cuba over the building housing their delegation to the OAS meeting in Punta del Este, at which Cuba was expelled from the organization. The flag's absence in the houses of the other delegations implicitly commented on their literacy status.)[27]

A parallel effort to the literacy campaign was undertaken in regard to cultural consumption with the Movimiento de Aficionados (Amateur Movement) and later the Casas de Cultura (Houses of Culture), which in 1988 numbered about two hundred all over the country. However, no comparable effort was directed at redesigning creativity in art. Aesthet-

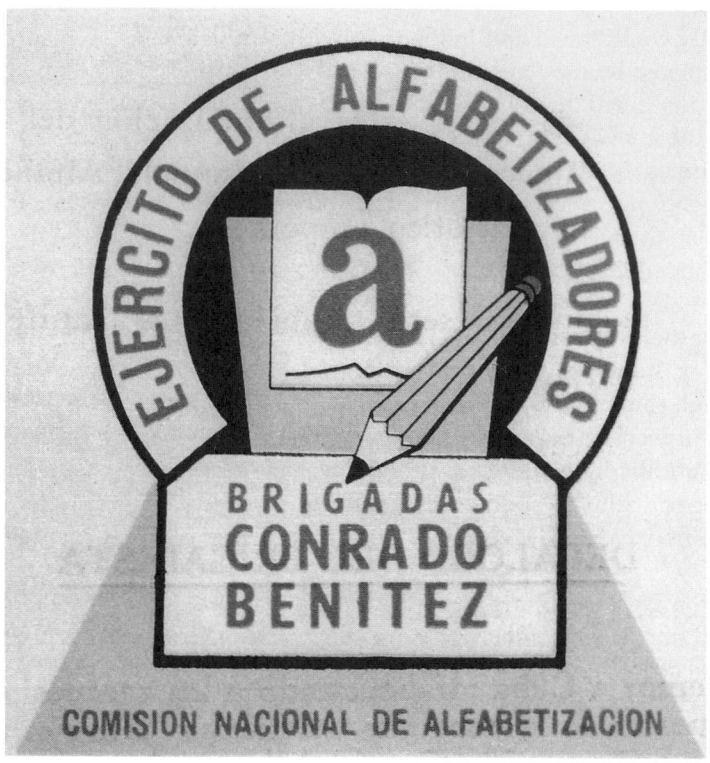

Guillermo Menéndez Madan, logotype for the literacy campaign. Photo by Luis Camnitzer.

ics were not made the object of dictated guidelines, and no directive on how to produce art has ever been provided by the government. For that matter, no such grand design has emerged from the artists themselves either, although the notion of a need for a new literacy campaign, this time in relation to art, is often invoked by Cuban artists. The closest attempt has been the Proyecto Pilón (see Chap. 5), initiated in 1989 but short-lived because of local party bureaucracy and resistance. Meanwhile, a second literacy campaign in literature, which began in December 1984, the National Campaign for Reading, had the aim of establishing a nationwide minimum of ninth-grade level.

Another Cuban experiment in mass distribution is offered by Telarte, a textile art activity of the Ministry of Culture which began in 1983. Cuban artists, and recently also international artists (among them Robert Rauschenberg), contribute designs for textile printing. With initial runs of ten thousand meters in 1983, more recently the designs are printed on

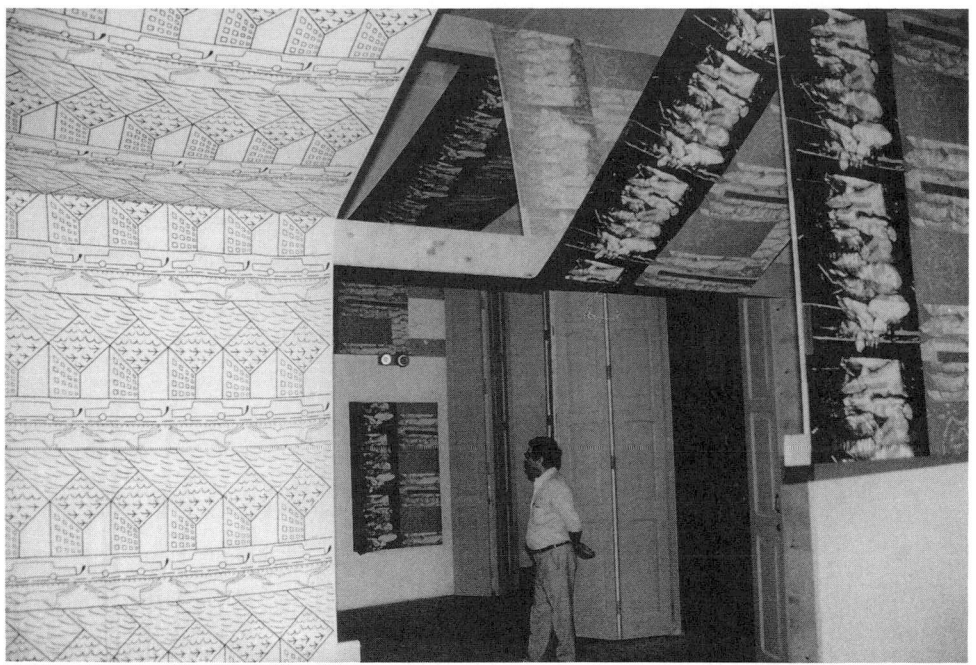

Exhibition of "Telarte VI," Centro de Desarrollo de Artes Visuales, 1989, Havana, with examples by José Bedia and Robert Rauschenberg. Photo by Luis Camnitzer.

twenty and thirty thousand meters of fabric and then used to tailor dresses, shirts, and sometimes banners, or sold by the yard.[28] During the Second Biennial of Havana the whole city was filled with Telarte banners bearing the Biennial's logo (based on a symbol by Wifredo Lam and designed by Umberto Peña). The same design filled billboards and posters, and many people wore dresses and shirts patterned with the logo to announce the event.

A precedent for Telarte was set in 1974 when Casa de las Américas produced artists' handkerchiefs on the occasion of the Meeting of Latin American Art. (The designs were later reprinted in 1979.) In 1980 some new designs by the same artists were added and used to produce sweaters. While the intentions were clearly part of a general dream of having art connected with industry and of having artists as part of the country's production process, the scope, at the time, was modest. Today Telarte is laying the groundwork for an activity that in time may have an impact on visual education parallel to what the poster movement had achieved in the late 1960s. A double demystification takes place. Museum artists

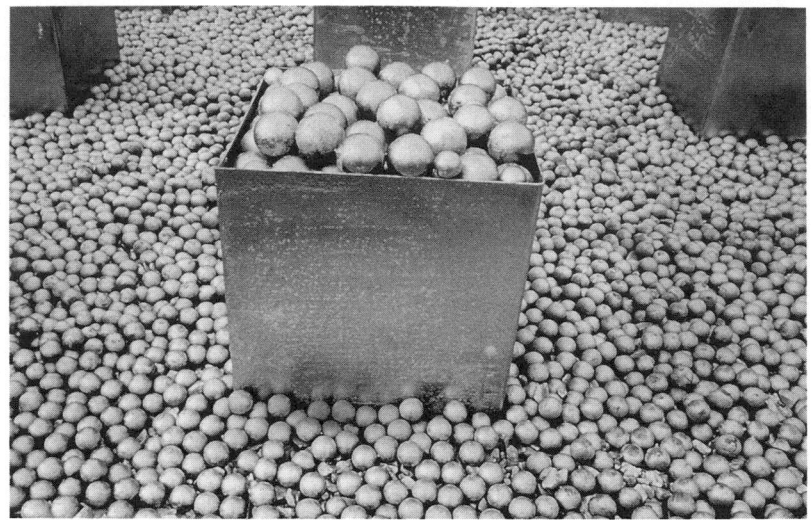

Grupo Hexágono, Arte en la fábrica (Art in the Factory) project, 1983, mixed media. Photo by the artists.

and images become approachable elements for the public, and the artist starts thinking of wrapping the spectator in desacralized art.

A parallel project, also started in 1983, was Arte en la Fábrica (Art in the Factory). Based on an idea of Flavio Garciandía, artists go to factories and plan work using available materials normally used for production. The execution of the art work involves the factory workers, and the results are mostly environmental pieces. The project followed a suggestion by Minister of Culture Armando Hart that art connect with industrial production. This activity lately has lost some of its initial energy, possibly because the artists tend now to focus more on their personal work and do not feel the industrial parameters as totally appropriate for their individual expression.

The Bourgeois Legacy

Along with artistic utopias of the twentieth century, one might expect that the borderline between high and low culture, or between fine and applied arts, is being erased in Cuba for the benefit of a more total and seamless culture. But the differences between the areas seem to be carefully kept, if not by planning then by lack of interest in the problem or lack of clarity about what the solution can be. Many artists, such as Raúl Martínez and Umberto Peña, are equally respected in the fields of poster making and book design and in the areas of fine arts, but there is a difference in the respect each field may elicit in the consumer.

The Revolution inherited a bourgeois art structure and so far has chosen not to radically change it, in order to maintain the freedom of the individual artist. Thus, to a certain extent, a market for cultural objects, with works chosen and valued by aesthetic criteria derived from a bourgeois public,[29] is still operating in Cuba. Cuban poet Cintio Vitier interprets the situation as a transition that inherits many of the conceptual problems and stereotypes of the past, sometimes masked by presumed "socialist" versions. He states that perhaps the last bastion of petit bourgeois hegemony might be located in the area of aesthetic taste. His solution hints at qualitative improvement through quantitative change. He feels that when a national culture, represented or directed by a hegemonic social class, is acted out by the immense majority of the people, there is a revolutionary culture. People as generators of their own history become the center of national culture; they have an accelerated access to the means of information and to creative expressive levels and become conscious recipients and producers of cultural values.[30]

Another author, the Argentinean writer Ezequiel Martínez Estrada, notes about revolutionary Cuba—maybe with too much idealization—that the entire apparatus of civilization is transformed, without touching any part of it, when it stops being private property and becomes collective and national property. Without any alteration of the structure of cultural artifacts, the system can shift from a restricted service to public service.[31]

Except for the possible audience for "testimonial art," the Cuban public for the arts may be defined as an enlargement of the traditional bourgeois audience. Referring to the effects of the literacy campaign, critic Gerardo Mosquera comments, "In that sense it is not a socialization of art since this demands not just the increase of the numbers of artists and spectators in the ranks of the people, but also the separation itself between those who make art and those who receive it be revolutionized."[32] The playing board remained the same, only the pieces changed. While the poster period had temporarily diminished the distance between art and public, gallery rituals had not disappeared, and they later regained strength.

Money paid for art work goes to the Fondo Cubano de Bienes Culturales (Cuban Cultural Goods Fund), which then pays the artists. The art work goes mostly to public buildings, rather than to private owners, but the overall market structure is unchanged. In fact, the Cuban need for hard currency after the barter agreements stopped being honored by Eastern European countries has led the government to see art as a form of income. As a consequence, a trend seems to be developing in the 1990s of having galleries focus on potential purchases by tourists. The recent success of the new Cuban art outside of Cuba seems to encourage this policy and thus, with an enormously regressive action, seriously threatens to alter the conditions that produced such successful art.[33]

The numerical enlargement of the public is achieved by the increased access to education, by the proliferation of exhibitions and exhibition spaces, and by the promotion of art events through publicity. This structure keeps certain artistic haughtiness in place; artists use their competence in the formal aspects of the execution of the work as quality control and run into the danger of neglecting rigor in issues of communication.

Normal exhibits open with a public of from 100 to 400 people, with a continual stream of visitors. The First Biennial of Havana, in 1984, had 44,000 visitors during the first six days and a total of 200,000 visitors in a city of 2 million inhabitants. The opening night of the Second Biennial had 5,000 people and by its end it had been seen by more than 300,000. The awareness that a large public comes to big spectacular events makes these group exhibits more desirable to artists than one-person shows. A foreign observer is likely to be confounded when reading the biographical information of a prominent Cuban artist. There usually is a proud predominance of group shows over one-person shows, an attitude that is a consequence of what Cubans call "eventism." "Eventism" gives priority to the size and public appeal of the event as opposed to the individual payoff of the exhibit.

Some of the traditional differentiations among the public still exist, a factor that became important in the controversies around the younger generation in 1988. In an interview, artist José Bedia comments,

> I think the three of us [Bedia, Garciandía, and Rodríguez Brey] are trying to open the audience. But artists always think they can take on the burden single-handedly. In reality, we are part of a mechanism that is the cultural life of the country, where we are only the workers who give the finishing touches to a product that will be offered to the people. Many people are needed to promote that work in this direction and help the art language to be understood on a broader level, something that never happened save in a few cultures. I believe it is a battle that some day will be won. All of that is still in diapers, and the advantage we have in Cuba is that the field is open. We spent twenty-five years trying this new approach. It is not just the task of the artists to think about it. We always speak about 'the people' as a totality, but there are many ways of understanding these

people, many subgroups with different needs and levels, which have different codes.

Later, Rodríguez Brey adds, "In my case, I have made work with the intention of reproduction, of making editions. But because I worked in a gallery context, those editions ended up in galleries again, therefore not reaching a broad audience, and once more the same elite had contact with my drawings, paintings, or installations. In relation to mass-media, I believe a minute of television is worth a hundred exhibits."[34]

Added to the problem of different levels of understanding by the audience, artists are faced with a subtle market pressure since they have to buy the materials for their personal work. An exception is made when they are commissioned for specific works or selected to represent the country in an international exhibit. Under these circumstances it is likely that the artist will give preference to the purchase of materials for new work that may finance future purchases rather than get lost in experimentations that may prove to be economic failures. The drive for hard currency is likely to make this problem even more acute.

Some of the remnants of the bourgeois tradition also affect art schooling. Art education has a basically conservatory orientation to the point of sometimes ideologically contradicting socialist aims, even when put in terms of reaching the masses with quality. In 1983 the graduation work in the printmaking department of the ISA (Instituto Superior de Arte, or Graduate Institute of Art), for instance, consisted of the production of a limited edition, luxury-bound portfolio of prints, thus using a bourgeois ritual without an effort to examine its meaning or to challenge it. (Requirements for graduation work have since changed.) In a society without a true and complete capitalist market for the arts, this is a good way of developing one, since it confirms the fetishism of individual property through limited availability.

The Opportunities for Exhibition

The Cuban gallery system offers the same ambiguities. Galleries are socialized like any other commercial enterprise, and access to exhibition space is open for any artist to apply. The artist is proposed for an exhibit by the Fondo Cubano de Bienes Culturales or goes to the gallery and asks for an exhibit on the basis of his or her work and is then accepted or rejected. Adding up Houses of Culture, municipal centers, lobbies of movie theatres, museums, and galleries, the network is quite large and offers a parallel structure to the one in capitalist countries, though without the high-powered pressure, since gallery survival is not based on profit and artists are not affiliated with the galleries. Tongue in cheek, Gerardo Mosquera wrote in the prologue of a catalogue: "As the work is exhibited in a commercial gallery, I don't want to leave without giving advice to the public. The right moment to buy an important work of art is when it has not yet been recognized as such in a generalized fashion. The market is always behind in relation to the artistic event. What I am telling you is not a prediction, but a reality worth money: buy these four [artists] *now* and not *later*."[35]

The pressure toward personal highlighting is there. Artists are concerned about the quality of posters and catalogues and about leaving a personal mark in what slowly is bound to become a market with price differentiation among the artwork. Galleries are ranked by the amount of space, by location (influential for the quantity of public to be expected), and by being national or municipal (the latter being less professional and subject to small-group politics).

The gallery network in a particular district is ruled by a major gallery, the "methodological gallery," which under a new plan (1989) aspires to museum-quality exhibitions. It is refreshing to see that this potentially negative dynamic of the Cuban "art market" has not resulted in serious individual rivalry among the artists. If any, there may be an aesthetic rivalry among groups, related more to what is sponsored in international events and to the interpretation of the meaning of that sponsorship in theoretical terms. But this rivalry can be better understood in generational and global aesthetic terms than in terms of envy among stars.

Since 1984 Cuba has organized the Biennial of Havana, which has become both a national and an international focus for the art of countries marginal to the cultural centers. The First Biennial included only Latin American art, while the Second Biennial became an artistic replica of OSPAAAL and tried to cover the art of the Third World, a model kept in the Third Biennial and planned for the Fourth. While picking up on what essentially is the structure of a capitalist trade fair, Cuba has tried to transcend the implicit limitations. Particularly in the Second Biennial, the "competition" exhibit started to be somewhat downplayed by putting it into a context of workshops directed by several international artists, along with one-person exhibits of prestigious Cuban and foreign artists scattered all over the province. Though, incongruously, prizes were awarded, the general drift of the Biennial came to be a laboratory of visual experiences where, because of the wide range and quantity of the work, artists could understand better how the conditions of underdevelopment affected their production and allowed them to extract a balance of positive and negative aspects in their work. But again, there were ambiguities. While the intent for a Third World identity separate from the mainstream market was clear, the general definitions of art operating in the Biennial were perilously close to that mainstream. Thus, countries presently undergoing Western colonization or countries that had just recently started to pursue their independence were encouraged to compete in a game defined by the rules of art as a set of collectible items, and they let their work be judged under values of quality that were not clearly defined.

The Third Biennial, which took place in November 1989, did away with prizes and picked up on those traditional or contemporary works in each country that best represent it culturally, regardless of art market considerations. To this end, the Biennial had the title of "Tradition and Contemporaneity." Budget cuts (50 percent on convertible currency) forced the Biennial to be more modest than the preceding ones. But modesty was compensated by rigor and a further stress on decentralization. In its third version the Biennial managed to establish itself as a feasible and stable alternative to the Biennials of the hegemonic centers eliciting international respect and interest. This success could be the bearer of mixed blessings, since it may attract commercial interests that in turn might transform the Biennial into a Third World marketplace for the international gallery system.

The Biennial has become a powerful showcase for Cuban art. Foreign visitors are drawn to evaluate it in the context of other Third World presentations, and Cuban artists are eager to present their work in it. Here "eventism" does come coupled with some form of individual reward. Artist Rodríguez Brey was invited to the 1992 Documenta in Kassel on the strength of his work in the 1989 Biennial.

Art and Dogma

The present ambiguities in the Cuban scene reflect, more than anything else, great caution and a fear of losing something valuable in the production of art for the sake of ideological precision. In 1987, the Centro Wifredo Lam, the institution in charge of organizing the Biennial of Havana, launched an in-depth study of the arts in Cuba. The study encompassed all aspects of art, crafts, and architecture and their production, circulation, and consumption. The preparatory document was designed to gather information but did not provide directives on what guidelines to be used for drawing conclusions from the data gathered and what uses might be given to those conclusions. The document stressed the importance of a correct definition of what constitutes the objective in art. Marxist-Leninist parameters were used to do this but in ways that do not seem particularly dogmatic or stifling. There were warnings against the danger of identifying the objective in art (the artistic appropriation of reality) with the objective of scientific research, since that would imply "to give the same importance to the subject in all spheres of reality, distorting art's function in regard to the gaining of knowledge." In doing so, the document explicitly leans on the aesthetic criteria of Marxist-Leninist thinkers such as Moisei Kagan, Dimitri Markov, S. J. Rappoport, and L. I. Stolovich "who recognize that the object for artistic appropriation is not all of reality, but is reduced to those aspects in a particular historical situation which have a personal meaning for the subject." According to the document, "To analyze art as a social phenomenon does not imply that art's characteristics have to correspond directly with those of social life." Also, it states that "the concept of ideological character and content as used in verbal means of expression cannot be mechanically transferred to other arts."[36] All through the document there is a pervasive awareness of the complexities permeating the issue given the existing individualities and the different media of the artists and the individual conditions of the consumers confronting the work of art.

The various documents that resulted from the study, "diagnoses" of the different areas, are, as intended, very critical. Criticism covered the disorganization of the support institutions for the arts and the concession to market conditions (in the case of painting, drawing, and installations), conservatism of the artists (sculpture), indiscriminate taste on the part of the public (crafts), lack of social recognition and therefore scarcity of talent (comics), and ignorance of aesthetic and ethnographic values (Cuban religious representations, particularly in the Afro-Cuban tradition). The documents provided a good starting point for future work. It is interesting to note that the overtly Marxist-Leninist directives present in the initial document led to conclusions not that different from those that might have been reached by any critical observer, regardless of ideology.

Marxist Aesthetics

Soviet Marxist-Leninist thought in aesthetics is widespread in Cuba, but not in the simplistic way in which we encounter it in the West, a presentation that tries to confine the thought to the Stalinist period and to exemplify it in a few rigid examples about realism. Several volumes of Soviet primary sources are available in Cuban bookstores. The magazine *Criterios*, dedicated to literary and aesthetic theory and "culturology," translates the latest theoretical contributions from all over the world (including authors such as Frederic Jameson, Umberto Eco, Moisei Kagan, etc.). Published by polyglot Desiderio Navarro, the scope of the magazine is limited only by his knowledge of languages, and he is fluent in fourteen. Initially, the strongest mediator of these theories, besides his own sizeable theoretical contributions, was the already mentioned (Chap. 1) Adolfo Sánchez Vázquez.

Sánchez Vázquez, a newspaper editor and a fighter in the Spanish Civil War, went into exile to Mexico in his twenties, studying there and graduating in philosophy. Intrigued by the initial art of the Cuban Revolution, he turned to Marxist aesthetics. His writings, in turn, shaped the aesthetic thought in Cuba during the 1960s. He stressed the "young Marx" writings and wrote from a perspective that includes Antonio Gramsci, Louis Althusser, and Galvano Della Volpe. His singularity at the time was based on an attempt to justify abstract art from a Marxist point of view. Attacking tendencies prone to illustration, the homologizing of art with science, and realism as an only possibility, Sánchez Vázquez states that art is really "artistic praxis" and cannot be confined to any "*-ism.*" He separates the artist's praxis from the observer's praxis, thus stressing the ambiguity and polysemic values of the work of art. He further makes a strong point differentiating the artist's ideology from the ideology of the work. He stresses the contradictions that can exist between the ideas an artist expresses in public life in regard to politics, morals, or art and the ideas for which the work may stand as the result of a "practical-spiritual process of creative transformation." The latter is beyond the artists' control.[37]

Sánchez Vázquez' influence waned during the 1970s, a Sovietphile period, but regained its former status during the 1980s. The internalization of his ideas forced the Cuban "dogmatics" who surfaced in the 1970s to connect with the more enlightened, post-1956 Soviet aestheticians such as Moisei Kagan. To the Cubans, Kagan seemed more open in writing than in person; early in 1988 he visited Cuba and gave several lectures that disappointed and totally bored the younger artists. In particular, Kagan's examples in art tend to be conservative to the point of being perceived as aesthetically reactionary.

From the very beginning of the Revolution, a majority of the Cuban artists distrusted socialist realism, a distrust shared by many political leaders. Che Guevara had warned against extreme dogmatism in the course of revolutionary change, as had happened in other countries:

"A summit interpretation of cultural aspiration was proclaimed, a formally exact representation of nature which then became a mechanical representation of the wished-for social reality: the ideal society, nearly void of conflicts or contradictions."[38] Guevara was not an art critic, and his personal taste probably was closer to the nineteenth century than to the avant-garde of the twentieth. Nonetheless, he recognized the dangers of government dogmatism in the arts and saw that socialist realism was not viable for Cuba.[39] With the possible exception of the photo-realist period in the seventies, which cannot be attributed to dogmatism, Guevara's observation held true through the whole of the Cuban process. If any planning emerges as a result of the research initiated by the Centro Wifredo Lam, it will in all probability not affect art making but will affect the social conditions that generate and determine art making, such as the level of education of the artist and the public, distribution systems, and the role of art in everyday life. This view seems to have been consistently maintained since the beginning of the Revolution; the variation of these factors rather than an ideological program has determined the aesthetic fluctuations during the life of the Revolution.

The analysis of the dangers and presence of dogma should also address the artists. The approach of Cuban artists to their art has not been particularly dogmatic either, at least not in a missionary sense. They seem to share the view that it is more likely that a new society will generate the art it needs rather than that art will generate the society that will support it. Discussing Russian constructivism, Mosquera remarks about the vision of the more radical artists of the period that "although they were based on perceptual laws with a universal character, people were not used to eating raw universal laws."[40]

Cuban artists relate strongly, but critically, to the mainstream of Western art. Art history and aesthetics are taught in the ISA from a Marxist-Leninist point of view, seeing Western artistic expressions in the context of a bourgeois-capitalist socioeconomic structure. Thus, while Western methods of creation are respected, they are always seen with the distance of social criticism. The internalization of Western values—such as individual success and competitiveness and the generation of mimetic attitudes—is therefore minimized. It should also be noted that the use of these Marxist-Leninist approaches by instructors is far from homogenous or guided by unifying directives. Instructors study in different places and use different sources as references, mostly gathered through individual research. Their work, not unlike the artists making art, reflects a theoretical eclecticism that introduces an unexpected richness and complexity in their teaching.

The Influence of the Government on the Arts

Despite the varied style and the individual tendencies prevailing in the arts in Cuba, the Cuban government continues to view art production as one dimension of social productivity and accords the artist an integral place in the social system. Thus, art is promoted and criticized like any other means of production.[41] In the speech in which Fidel Castro initiated the "rectification" process, a national drive against corruption sometimes misnamed "Cuban perestroika" (and in vernacular, "Castroika"), he attacked several professions. His main target was the construction industry, but he also addressed the arts, citing an example where an artist received undue monies for fraudulent commissions.[42] It was reported in January 1988 at the Fourth Congress of the National Union of Cuban Writers and Artists (UNEAC) that thirty-seven artists (of lesser importance) earned 100,000 pesos in two years and that four intermediaries were facing charges. The artists were spared prosecution since they had operated within the law. A consequence of this publicity was that artists walking into a store would be greeted with a "here comes the millionaire." But what is relevant here is that artists are treated in the same way as any other professional in the socioeconomic context.

Aesthetic direction remains a matter of individual choice, a point successfully stressed during the early years of the Revolution against those who demanded a party line in aesthetics. In his much-quoted speech of June 30, 1961, "Words to the Intellectuals," Fidel Castro addressed the issue of artistic freedom: "Freedom of form has been spoken of here. Everybody agrees that freedom of form has to be respected. I believe there is no doubt in regard to this point." He continued, "No one ever thought that every man, or every writer, or every artist has to be a revolutionary, as no one believes that every man, or every revolutionary, has to be an artist." That speech, though designed primarily to respond to the uproar caused by the proscription of the film *P.M.*, in effect solved the problems Cuban abstract and surrealist artists were facing at the time, mainly stemming from dogmatic artists rather than from the government.[43] Remembering the beginnings of the Revolution, Raúl Martínez comments, "Abstract artists were strong [as a movement] when the Revolution took place, and they were supporting the Revolution; therefore, there was no negative identification with abstractionism."[44]

Fidel Castro's speech (together with Guevara's "Socialism and Man in Cuba") remained a cultural spine for Cuba during the life of the Revolution, even during the most ideologically narrow moments,[45] and connects with his closing speech at the Fourth Congress of the UNEAC. His final words there were "Socialism's reason for being is to elevate man's capabilities and possibilities to a maximum, to also elevate the freedom of creation to its highest degree, not only in form, but also in content." Fidel Castro had not addressed artists' problems specifically between 1961 and 1988, and the remark on "content" was seen by the younger artists as a confirmation of their own searches.

Nevertheless, there were occasions in which dogma took over this liberalism, such as during the First National Congress of Education and Culture in 1971.[46] These deviations were not so much based on aesthetics as on politics and issues of nationalism (much of them catalyzed by the jailing of poet Heberto Padilla[47] and, in the case of the congress itself, on the moralism of the 1965–1967 period).[48] Castro concentrated on politics between his "Words to the Intellectuals" and 1976, neglecting the cultural sphere in which he apparently never felt totally comfortable. (It is rumored that Guevara influenced his 1961 speech.) The 1971 congress had more influence than it merited because it coincided with the period in which Cuba was isolated by the U.S. embargo, the release of poet Heberto Padilla after thirty-eight days in jail, the aftermath of the death of Guevara, and the ten-million-ton sugarcane harvest failure. Sensitive to world opinion, both the congress and Castro had a shriller tone than usual. In the closing speech (May 1, 1971) of the congress, addressing the Padilla affair, Castro affirmed, "Our way of valuing is political. There cannot be aesthetic value without human content. There cannot be aesthetic value against man. There cannot be aesthetic value against justice, against man's happiness. It cannot be!"

The Declaration of the congress, even in this loaded atmosphere, did not give direct aesthetic directives but laid out a socialist artistic aim of a different kind, which could be subscribed to by everybody in Cuba. "The Revolution frees art and literature from the inflexible mechanisms of supply and demand that rule over bourgeois society. Art and literature will cease to be merchandise, and all possibilities will be offered for aesthetic expression and experimentation in its most diverse manifestations, based on ideological rigor and high technical qualification."[49]

While the Soviet Union had been helpful to Cuba during the 1960s, there were serious discrepancies between the two countries about economic plans. The "ten million" harvest was geared to prove Cuba's points in how the economy was handled. The failure of the harvest thus placed the past on the utopian level of something creative and fertile but essentially chaotic and inefficient. At that point Soviet assistance was sought for corrections. The assistance was given, but with demands for a process of institutionalization. These demands included a centralization of the economy, the exchange of money (as opposed to bartering) between institutions, the acceptance by Cuba of the idea that Communism can only be achieved by passing through a socialist stage (a position originally rejected by Che Guevara), and the adoption of the military ranks used by the Warsaw Pact. However, while this form of hardening was taking place, the Revolution also started a process of democratization. "Popular Power" was introduced, an electoral system for national and regional assemblies where representatives are elected through secret balloting. With this move the Communist Party started to separate from the government.[50]

No explicit directives were given on how to deal with art issues, but people lost their jobs because of ideological discrepancies, and many artists exerted "self-control." Magazines typical of the 1960s, such as *Pensamiento Crítico*, stopped publication, and some artists, including Antonia Eiriz, stopped painting altogether (as mentioned in Chap. 2).

The First National Congress of Education, planned before these events, was then utilized as a "cleaning" instrument. Expanded to encompass "culture" as well, it became a vehicle to underline some points over others, and the interpretation of "ideological rigor" became slightly tricky. While Castro's statements about the role of the intellectuals were kept, the slogan of "art as a weapon" received particular emphasis. Many new bureaucrats came from military ranks, representing a hope for efficiency. However, instead of an overt change of mandate to the artists, in a subtle way a new breed of politically oriented artists was favored for promotion, and some more dogmatic publications became more easily available in bookstores. Previously, books by Western Marxist aestheticians such as the Austrian Ernst Fischer and the French Roger Garaudy, both friendly to Western modernism and avant-garde movements, were widely displayed along with the writings of Sánchez Vázquez, but these were now replaced by the books of a rather conservative Soviet aesthetician, Avner Zis.[51]

Zis attacked Fischer and Garaudy for being revisionists, deviationists, and "cultural agnostics," and, finally, for merging into bourgeois idealism.[52] Zis was not taken too seriously by the younger artists, and Kagan, who in his theories was closer to Sánchez Vázquez, remained the main influence. Kagan at least accepted Dalí's and Kandinsky's work as fitting Lenin's theory of art as a reflection of society.

The latitude permitted artists has remained fairly constant, even during this period, ensuring an enormous diversity not dissimilar to any other Western country, with fashion dictated through different channels. The activities of many institutions, particularly the ICAIC and Casa de las Américas, never changed their openness, and many tendencies coexisted during the whole of the revolutionary process. Both Alfredo Guevara, head of the ICAIC, and Haydée Santamaría, who directed Casa de las Américas, had a revolutionary stature that made them untouchable. Though often targets of criticism by the army publication *Verde Olivo*, their institutions became havens for those artists whose normal market had been affected negatively. What changed, from time to time, was the relative primacy of tendencies, without any profound change in the beliefs of the higher ranks of the government and the party.

Some years later, in a speech before the UNEAC in 1977, Minister of Culture Armando Hart said, "When government officials with responsibilities in the cultural area misunderstand their mission and feel justified in interfering with the artists' creative work, they lose prestige and influence and become unable to fulfill their duties."[53] While reflecting a general policy, his words also marked the beginning of the complete opening that climaxed in the 1980s.

The Ministry of Culture

In 1976 the Ministry of Culture was created, taking the place of the Consejo Nacional de Cultura (National Council of Culture). Hart's appointment to the Ministry of Culture followed Luis Pavón, director of the council. Pavón, who had come from the army, where he was a lieutenant, was responsible for the harshness in the treatment of Padilla in 1971 and was behind many of the anti-intellectual campaigns of *Verde Olivo* as its director and poetry critic. But before him, the first person to direct the council had been Edith García Buchaca.[54] She is remembered as probably the most rigid functionary to hold the position in the history of the Revolution and, even with that background, she was unable to radically affect Cuban culture at the time. García Buchaca's position was that criticism should demolish any work by an author at the service of imperialism, while the work of the friends of the Revolution should be criticized in a friendly and "constructive" fashion.[55]

During the thirty years after the beginning of the Revolution, dogmatism in Cuba meant that for a while some forms of art were more prominent than others, not that deviations from that prominence were abolished. The peak of dogmatism that occurred during the 1970s, relative shift of positions and particularly hard on many individuals, is severely criticized in Cuba today as a grave cultural mistake and considered as something akin to a "dark age." There have been and still are "hawks and doves" in Cuba. They have been present in the revolutionary process since its beginning. Their rivalry causes, to this day, some tension and these relative shifts. During the decade of the 1980s, the

Ministry of Culture became a haven for what I am here calling doves. It did so without losing any ideological consistency as it maintained an unimpeachable political stance and, as a consequence, fertilized the ground for the present art.

Contemporary Cuban art is the accumulated production of discrete artists. Many meet regularly to discuss their work and problems of communication and identity, but the final process of making art is a private one (with the exception of groups organized later in the decade such as Arte Calle and Grupo Provisional, discussed in Chap. 5). Political and ethical stands derive from personal insights within a loose framework of ideas provided by the Revolution. In the visual arts, what is required by this intellectual framework is not the mouthing of orthodoxies or the pandering to specified conventions; it is rather an attitude toward work, internalized by experience in the revolutionary society, which emphasizes the connection between individual activity and the "common good." This attitude may be less apparent in the work produced than in the work that becomes uninteresting for the artist to make. The common good is not defined; what is defined, implicitly, is the notion that the artist has an organic responsibility to think for himself or herself about what connections with the common good are possible, interesting, and individually satisfying. There is, in other words, a palpable moral dimension to the intellectual life of Cuban artists, a dimension that arrests the attention of an outsider stumbling upon their discourses. It is of course also a dimension often disturbed by the frustrations caused by the incongruence between the ambition of a project and the unavailability of resources. But, "whereas 'political art' in the U.S. almost always means art in opposition to the 'system,' to erosions of democracy currently encouraged by the Reagan administration, in Cuba it means an art integrated into the system."[56] The challenges expressed by the younger artists today are pointed against inconsistencies in the system but come from a profound commitment to the system. They consider themselves as the spearhead of the "rectification" process, much more dedicated and more advanced than any other segment of their society.

Censorship and Self-censorship

Fidel Castro's famous statement in 1961, "Within the Revolution everything; outside the Revolution, nothing," can be seen as more ambiguous and less ominous than it has generally been portrayed outside of Cuba by those unsympathetic to the revolutionary process. To Cuba's critics, the statement has represented a succinct recipe for totalitarianism and tyranny. The speech "Words to the Intellectuals," in which the phrase appeared for the first time, was not given under the most auspicious circumstances. *P.M.*, the already-mentioned documentary film on Cuban nightlife, had been produced and then proscribed in 1961 because it was considered frivolous and "counterrevolutionary." The proscription seriously divided Cuban intellectuals along former political divisions (Communist Party, represented by Anibal Escalante and García Buchaca, versus the Movimiento 26 de Julio, represented by *Lunes de Revolución*). It was this problem that Fidel Castro had to solve, and while the proscription of the film was not lifted, he did in fact try to reassure creative freedom—but without giving up governmental powers.[57]

Particularly for the visual arts, policy and practice in Cuba have since then mostly conformed to the more liberal interpretation of the statement. It is more a vague synthesis of patriotism and an attempt to make the common good sacred than a restrictive dictum. In the speech Castro discussed freedom of form, trying to elucidate the role of the artist in the new Cuban society. The context of the quote was one to ensure respect toward those artists who were not militant revolutionaries, explaining that nonrevolutionaries were not counterrevolutionaries, a stance repeated through many speeches by members of the leadership over time. These positions culminated in 1988 at the Fourth Congress of the UNEAC at which Minister Hart stated emphatically that reality is too rich to be limited by dogmas and theories. Vice-President Carlos Rafael Rodríguez said, "Those who are not against us, are with us" and "although liberalism is dangerous and complacency unacceptable, more dangerous still are intolerance and dogmatism." On the same occasion Secretary Carlos Aldana, referring to the role of the Cuban Communist Party in regard to art, stated that "our Party is not a Party of aestheticians, but one of politicians" and stressed "the unrestricted respect toward diversity in artistic activities," after acknowledging the mistake of allowing a limitation in the aesthetic platform during the 1970s when "a mirage was introduced that paralyzed art" in contradiction to Castro's ideas. And Castro himself underlined once more, "Nobody should fear that the Revolution or Socialism may asphyxiate artistic freedom" after referring to the "unlucky period with mistaken theories."

In 1961 *P.M.* was plainly forbidden. The controversy that ensued was as much the result of the content as of the use of authoritarianism to solve the problem. The Fourth Congress of the UNEAC marked the highest point in the process of erasure of the use of authority for problems in art and in opinion. Besides Castro's remarks on the need for freedom of form *and* content, there were several calls for the development of a more critical press. This point was specifically stressed by Carlos Aldana, whom many classify as a "hawk."

In spite of the congress, 1988 was a year marked by a feeling of increasing restriction on the side of the artists. At least according to the perception of many artists, the atmosphere started changing after an exhibit of work by Tomás Esson and was confirmed by some events that followed. (See Chaps. 5 and 6 for a description of the artist, the circumstances of the exhibit, and the events following.) None of the controversies pertained to problems of aesthetic form, and the discussion of content was relatively minor. The main issues discussed were in relation to what kind of public would see the work. Similar works of the same artist were shown in the Museum of Fine Arts at the same time that they were challenged as suitable for exhibition in a neighborhood gallery. There is an interesting parallel here to communication channels in the capitalist sphere. Public television in the United States (the PBS or Public Broadcasting Service) is much more critical and blunt about government policies and the interpretation of U.S. history than any commercial broadcasting station. While the faithful PBS audience does also see or listen to commercial stations, the reverse is very rare.[58] There is a social class difference between the two audiences stemming from levels of income and education, and the design and content of the respective messages are effective in keeping the classes apart. There is no need for subsidiary constructs. Audiences in Cuba have not yet reached a homogeneous level of sophistication; thus, what is acceptable for the normal public in the museum may not be acceptable in the gallery. In that sense, Cuba still has an intellectual class division that needs at least time to be erased. The separation of channels has been effective in practice to minimize tensions. The technique is debatable and often suffers from an acute and misguided paternalistic attitude that usually reflects more the lack of sophistication of the functionary than that of the "protected" public.

The issue of communication, or lack of it, was a subject of much discussion during 1988. The UNEAC organized an important meeting on this issue, and the press surrounded the event with interviews and articles (particularly *Granma*, the Party organ, and *El Caimán Barbudo*). Problems addressed were the lack of good art criticism, the use of national symbols in art, the performance of functionaries, and the uses of art. Art critics were accused of being excessively concerned with formalism. It was pointed out that national symbols are collectively, not individually, held and therefore should not be subject to tampering by artists (an allusion to Tomás Esson's exhibit and reminiscent of the flag exhibition in Judson Church in New York in the early 1960s, which led to the jailing of the organizer).[59]

Jorge de la Fuente, vice president of UNEAC, remarked that "generally the so-called taste of the people is really the sublimated taste of the functionary." Artist Arturo Cuenca made a distinction between research in art leading to the establishment of new codes and art for communication (the latter an issue that raised the dangers of condescending populism) and demanded encouragement for both. Artist Aldito Menéndez summed up the problems saying, "A counterrevolutionary artist criticizes all the problems of the Revolution but does not offer any solutions because he believes that the only possible solution is to change the political system. A revolutionary artist criticizes the problems of the Revolution and tries to offer solutions because he believes in the Revolution."[60]

During the height of the 1988–1989 crisis, rather than outright prohibitions of art exhibitions, there were amicable discussions in some cases and complex negotiations in others, but always aimed at reaching a consensus between functionaries and artists. In this regard the Revolution has created one serious double-edged sword. Functionaries and artists come from a common pool of intellectuals and are, more often than not, bound by friendship. Communication with the higher ranks in the power structure is easy and uncluttered by ceremony. This openness facilitates the circulation of ideas and minimizes corruption. On the other hand, it also creates an ambiguous situation in which genuine friendly advice can be misread as an order and vice versa. It is this ambiguity that causes artists, sometimes unwillingly (and sometimes more willingly), to react with *autocensura* (self-censorship).

It is difficult to measure whether any process of self-censorship is proportionate to the objective causes that generate it. Cuban poet and art critic Osvaldo Sánchez notes, discussing the problem and the role of bureaucracy in it, that "political paternalism engenders political infantilism" and that a way of dignifying and underlining the exceptional political experience of past years is to foster polemics with those implied moral and political requisites that force an ideologically mature intellectual atmosphere.[61]

Self-censorship in Cuba operates on two levels. One is in regard to the tenor of the actual creative work being produced; the other is what is said in meetings. Both modes do not necessarily happen simultaneously. Until recently, discussions were very open, and nobody seemed overly worried about making theoretical criticism and analyzing the situation. There is generally more insecurity about how far the artist can go with the creative work,[62] but as mentioned before, it is more an issue related to where the pieces will be presented than to what the pieces are communicating. In a discussion with Minister Armando Hart, artist Lázaro Saavedra illustrated the point by stating that art in Cuba mostly lands peacefully in galleries, but when the same work is spontaneously performed on a wall (referring to work made by the group Arte Calle), it causes irritation. By the end of February 1989, the potentially explosive situation seemed defused, and previously planned controversial exhibits took place with much debate and success, but, in due time, problems surfaced again.

As a form of reassurance for the younger and more controversial artists, the Ministry of Culture projected a cycle of exhibits in the Castillo de la Real Fuerza. The exhibits were to be accompanied by debates about the work and concerns of the artists. One of the exhibits showed work that was considered disrespectful of national symbols, including a drawing of Fidel in drag, bearing huge breasts and leading the masses (see Ponjuán and Rodríguez, Chap. 6). The ensuing controversy led to the shift of Marcia Leiseca, then vice-minister of culture in charge of visual arts and an opponent to the removal of pieces from the exhibit, to the vice-presidency of Casa de las Américas. She was responsible for the implementation of the enlightened policies used during the decade and bears responsibility for much of the flourishing of the arts of the period.[63]

The present lack of clarity (or the potential excess of clarity) of the limits of expression does not seem to affect the general notion of the artist as a fully participating member of the Cuban socioeconomic structure. If this comparatively privileged status of art is to suffer, it probably will be the consequence of a general economic deterioration. There has been no tradition in Cuba of attaching strings to stipends (salaries or grants) as one finds in Stalin's Soviet Union and, lately, in the initiatives of Senator Helms in the United States.

The Role of the Vernacular

It is clear that the general context for defining art in Cuba, even during the most conservative periods, is taken from the Western tradition. Most of the still very respected Cuban modernists studied in Paris. One of them, Eduardo Abela, even wrote from Paris in 1927 warning about what he considered to be excessive influence from the Mexican movement on young Cuban painters (an influence he would be subject to himself for a short while as exemplified in *Guajiros,* a painting from 1938 that followed Diego Rivera). But contemporary Cuban artists only work within Western art parameters as they perceive them from their own country. The ruptures achieved by some of them are primarily with this Cuban perception and tailored to the Cuban public. They are formal ruptures within the Cuban art historical context, focusing not only on

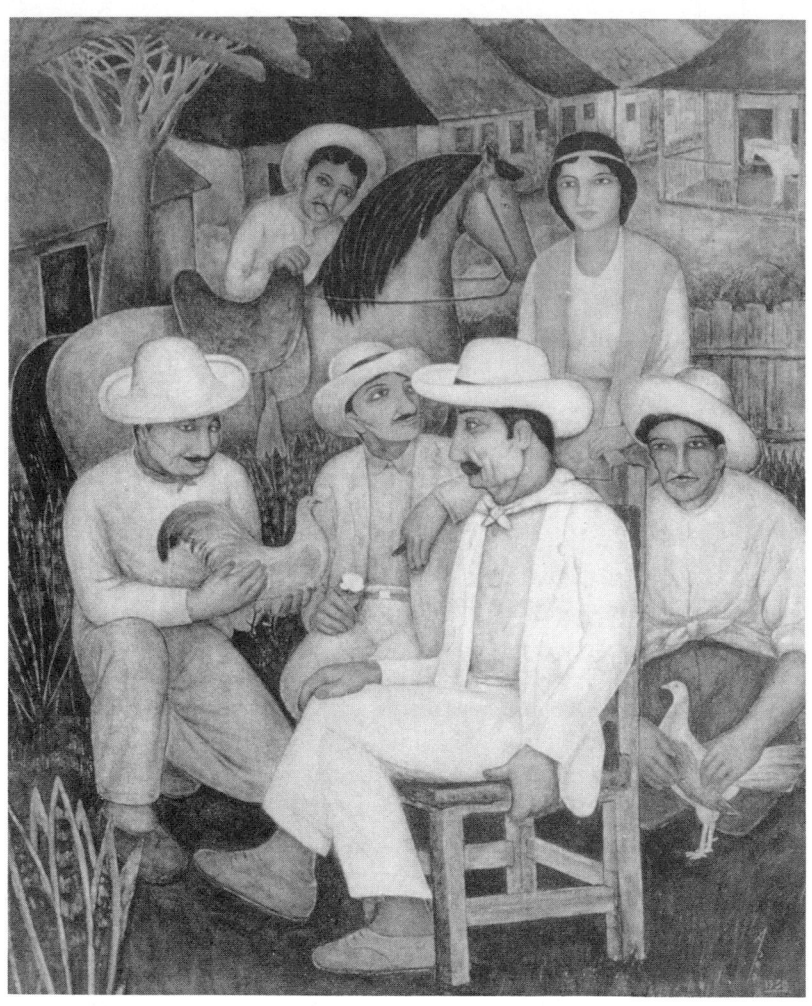

Eduardo Abela, Guajiros (Peasants), *1938, oil on canvas, 84 × 71 cm. Museo Nacional de Bellas Artes, Havana. Photo by Luis Camnitzer.*

the problems of forms but also on the new socioeconomic situation. Although they share processes developed in the Western mainstream, Cuban artists do not intentionally compete with the artists who actually belong to this mainstream. Even if shown internationally, the work is produced for the national reality. Thus, there are elements that separate Cuban contemporary art from parallel manifestations in other countries, even if the roots of the Western tradition have not been fundamentally challenged, and Cintio Vitier's analysis, quoted earlier, may prove to be right.

The absence of this challenge of the Western tradition by individual artists, regardless of the lack of specific official policy, is a matter worth pondering by any outside viewer interested in the tension between international culture and local culture, between the culture of the world capitalist system and the culture of the revolutionary societies. The outside viewer is apt to expect an underlining of local values, a promotion of vernacular culture, in defiance of canonic culture.

In Cuba, vernacular elements are integrated into the canonic frame of reference but do not take its place. It is possible that the exception to this prerevolutionary rule is starting to emerge in the third generation of the 1980s. Because in the last decade the ruling canon was postmodernism, a formal integration is made even easier and sometimes misleading. In an interview with José Bedia conducted by Benjamin Buchloh, the latter complains, "I feel I am not learning about *Cuba* through your art. I am only learning about *art* in Cuba and its connection with the mainstream international art of the late sixties and seventies." And later: "There must have existed some kind of authentic visual culture that was not entirely part of colonialism and the Batista regime. There must have been an art practice, either local or regional, in Cuban history." Bedia answers, "I use that: it is the Afro-Cuban component that is very real. . . . I don't have a distance. But there is a very heterogeneous appropriation of elements in that culture. . . . The 'lack of scruples' in the use of formal elements operates in real life when those rituals are executed."[64] For other artists the appropriation is applied, among other things, to kitsch or to popular scatological humor.

Painter Arturo Cuenca, who belongs to Bedia's artistic generation, defined his generation in the Fourth Congress of the UNEAC: "We don't ask ourselves anymore if this is or is not revolutionary. We are revolutionaries and that is internalized. We live in a period where ideology is integrated into culture." It was particularly interesting to have Cuenca say this and have the audience accept it, since the intellectual community sees him as an eccentric personality and as a very individualistic artist with idiosyncratic ideas.

What is consistently challenged in meetings of Cuban intellectuals is the use of art historical values for cultural penetration, but not the values themselves. Cuban artists have never expressed a wish to break radically with the Western history of art. There is a move to expand rather than to contradict or separate from this history. Therefore, and to a certain extent, Cubans feel that they operate within a common aesthetic world with the Western countries.

Aesthetics in Cuba became an independent discipline only in 1987. The faculty that teaches aesthetics recognized the impossibility of giving an exhaustive view of the Marxist history of aesthetics. They decided to limit themselves to providing access to a system and to defining the instruments that enable the understanding of the work of art, rather than enter a scholastic process. In order to achieve this, they use not only the already mentioned Soviet Moisei Kagan and Spanish-Mexican Adolfo Sánchez Vázquez, but also Frederic Jameson of the United States, Argentinean Néstor García Canclini, and Italian Umberto Eco.

In pragmatic terms, art provides Cuba with an internationally perceivable image. The Cuban government support of the arts addresses this factor with an interest in ensuring that Cuban artists excel in their trade on the international scene, very much as with Cuban athletes.[65] While criticizing the international market, the Cubans accept the rules of the game and promote their players.

It is admirable that the Cuban process did not fall into the pits of false populism, raising an indiscriminate mixture of spurious and authentic values to act as a canon. The state did not submit to the temptation of sponsoring what García Canclini catalogues as the confused cohesion of internal social sectors, an overindulgence of folkloric roots, and the exclusive attribution of culpabilities to foreign or mythical adversaries.[66] This is not to say that there is no populist art in Cuba. A longitudinal section of the history of the last thirty years will show populist artists present in every generation, and because of it, each generation has aesthetic (or aesthetic-politic) tensions.

In all three Havana Biennials that have taken place as of this writing (1984, 1986, 1989), the Cuban entry was by far the most powerful. This was in part due to the poor and unrepresentative selections made in many of the other countries, even though more than fifty countries participated in these Biennials. But Cuban art showed a shared clarity of formulation, a freshness of approach, and a lack of timidity in the formalization of the pieces that one did not see in any other national entry. In part this was due to a Western lesson that Cubans seemed to have learned better than artists from most other Latin American countries. The lesson pertains to how the work of art is "packaged," the finish of the work, the heroic scale, the spectacularity of the presentation, its media-perfection. In part it is due to the free use of artistic and nonartistic media; many of the Cuban artists disregard the limits of traditional techniques and jump into complex environmental installations. These installations, though not new in the Western tradition, constitute a start at a degree zero and a rupture with the Cuban history of art. Added to this, there was an amazing evolution in the work of those artists who were represented in more than one event, an evolution of maturation rather than the trendy dispersion typical of artists eyeing the international scene.

To understand this dynamism, one must try to separate the complex play of variables: the individual abilities of the artists themselves, the extensive government support given to the artists, and the relative absence of capitalist market pressures, to mention a few. Whatever the cause, it is fair to say that the new generations educated in the Revolution have brought about a Cuban Renaissance.

A more elusive quality is given by the society to which their art is addressed, different from societies to which art in the Western market is directed. Art functions as a dialogue, and its forms change their meaning, however slightly, according to the partner in the dialogue. A purely formalist critique of Cuban contemporary art is bound to fail since Cuban artists engage in a dialogue with their own society. Still, the products are close enough to the Western mainstream to invite extracultural judgment. What we have, in the end, is art in and for a new society, where the rules of the traditional art game have been refreshed by the absence of what Guevara called the "invisible cage."[67]

4

ART EDUCATION
in CUBA [1]

The Role of Art Education in
Contemporary Cuba

The absence of the "invisible cage" mentioned by Che Guevara is analyzed and underlined during a long educational process by most Cuban artists. Self-taught artists are rare in contemporary Cuba and are mostly reduced to the so-called primitive or naive artists. In Cuba they are referred to as "spontaneous" artists, avoiding the condescension of the other terms. Most of the artists exhibiting today have gone through between eight and twelve years of formal art education. After graduating, many students repay the state for their studies by becoming temporary instructors, and some continue teaching as a source of regular income. This makes education an intrinsic element of the Cuban art situation today.

On balance it may be said that the strongest point of Cuban art education is the extended immersion provided the student and the removal of extracurricular worries, such as economic survival. Many of the artists of the first generation of the 1980s (in particular the "Volumen I" artists) do not look back kindly on their years of study. They disliked curricula and often teachers as well, as occurs in any other country. Nevertheless, they achieved an outstanding level of professionalism at an early age, which can be explained less by the old curriculum and the vocational detection system than by the length of the course of studies. New curricular adjustments were introduced during the decade of the 1980s, and these can only improve this situation and provide even more startling results.

The Cuban government seems to be eager to improve art education. During the Fourth Congress of the UNEAC, Cuban Vice-President Carlos Rafael Rodríguez remarked that "we have a well-educated people, but not yet a cultured one," while Minister of Culture Armando Hart

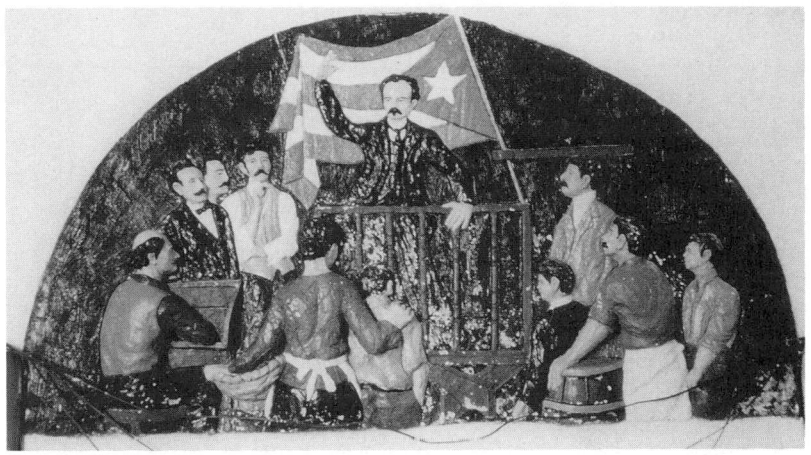

Anonymous, Martí Addressing the Tobacco Workers, *n.d., ceramic mural in a fire station in Havana. Photo by Luis Camnitzer.*

emphasized the importance of education versus patronage to foster the arts.

Cuba has not yet found all the answers to the questions related to art education. The country passed through a history similar to the rest of Latin America, full of the tensions produced by the dynamics of colonizing pressures. Modernization, one of the panaceas used by many of the ruling classes in the continent as a tool against colonialism, did no more than open the doors to other aspects of the same evil. Free of many of the problems that still act as obstacles to the process in Latin America, Cuba has achieved—sometimes in mysterious ways that defy logic—the preparation of a high-quality level of artists.

Cultural Dependency in Cuba and Latin America

Education has been an important part of the development of all of Latin America, both in connection with its colonization and with the presence of the "invisible cage," and also with the development of its idiosyncracies. But as much in prerevolutionary Cuba as in the rest of the continent, the educational process helped equally to distort the ideas of the student body as it raised its political awareness, providing, for many, the foundations for an anticolonial sentiment.

Over the centuries, art in Latin America has echoed art in the cultural centers, and therefore the Western mainstream has become a part of the tradition of contemporary Cuban art. At the same time, most of the artists in Latin America and nearly all of the artists in Cuba were (and still

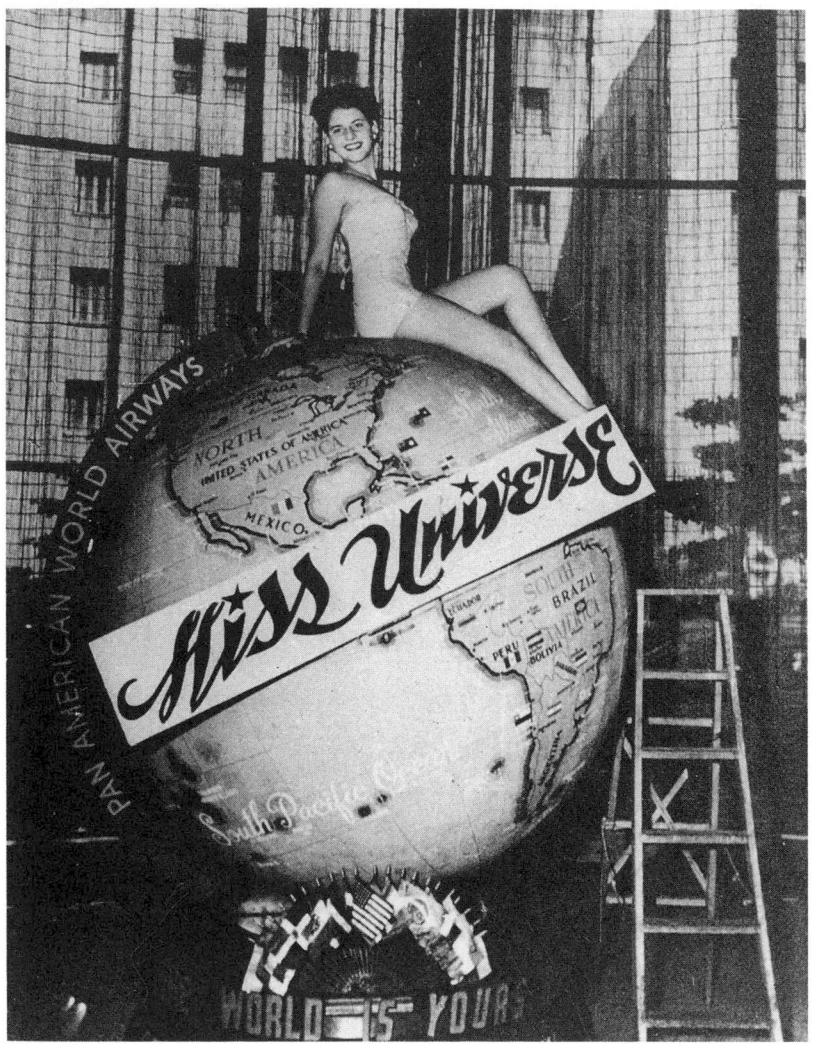

Constantino Arias, Miss Universe, *1950, silver gelatin photograph. From a negative in the Fototeca Collection, Havana. Courtesy of the Center for Cuban Studies Archives.*

are) concerned with collective identity problems and resent their artistic status inasmuch as it shows dependency.

The political and economic implications of colonialism in Latin America are obvious; the cultural implications, however, are more difficult to see. An overbearing flow of information has obscured cultural frontiers,[2] and the colonizers' interests have eroded or aborted indigenous identities. Metropolitan perspectives are internalized as authentic while affectation and mimicry become accepted as cultural patrimony and therefore part of national culture. In the movie *La hora de los hornos*, the Argentinean writer Manuel Mujica Lainez once said, referring to his classical education, "The point is not so much to know English, but to know English and have an Elizabethan sense." African drums were forbidden in public and private meetings after 1900 in Cuba—they were considered a sign of barbarism and a challenge to hegemony.[3] For many years some Cuban middle-class homes felt incomplete without a "fireplace" with plastic logs and an electric fire, and Cuba was the first Latin-American country to have television. The "national" anthem of Chile was commissioned to Spanish composer Ramón Carnicer, who was never in Chile and, indeed, all national anthems in Latin America were composed after European models fashionable at the time.[4] Diego Rivera cites a governor of the Federal District of Mexico, William de Landa y Escandón, who each morning would receive a telegram about the day's weather in London so that he could dress accordingly.[5] In 1932 Havana, a city full of low cottagelike buildings, banker López Serrano commissioned a fifteen-story dwelling and promoted it as a "modern residence building the same as North American buildings."[6]

More recently, U.S. companies in Brazil spend in advertising the equivalent of one-third of the government budget used for education.[7] On November 25, 1975, Dutch Guiana achieved its independence, becoming Surinam. An analysis of thirteen Latin American papers between November 24 and 27 shows that the news item merited 3 percent of the space allocated to foreign events. The telegrams came exclusively from news agencies belonging to industrialized countries. During the same period, 70 percent of the news referred to events that took place in the industrialized countries, and four-fifths of these items came from the same news services.[8] The monument to the Charrúas, the original native population in Uruguay, was made in Montevideo after a French etching. It illustrated the three last survivors of the tribe, sent to the World's Fair in Paris as a curiosity. In snowless Latin American countries, cotton decorates Christmas trees to make them seem closer to a totally unknown reality.

Commenting on Cuba's search for identity, Uruguayan theatre director Atahualpa del Cioppo said in an interview, "Our continent has become geography because it has stopped being history. To regain our geography, our economy, our culture, we have to become history once again."[9] Or, as Albert Memmi observes in his *Portrait of the Colonized*, a loss of history takes place with the effect that "the colonized is kept out of the objective conditions of contemporary nationality."[10] As we will see, it may be difficult to identify a coherent Cuban aesthetic at this point, but it is fair to say that Cuba, unlike the rest of Latin America, is working hard at answering these statements and trying to become history.

Once having secured his version of a people's history, the colonizer must next take steps to inculcate it. Education has always been a useful tool in shaping colonies, proceeding from the initial formation of local bureaucracies to the setting of the "brain drain" process and projects such as the notorious "Camelot" plan of the 1960s. Camelot was an attempt to involve both U.S. and Latin American universities in secret research on the potential causes of insurrection and how to eliminate them. The study, to be financed by the U.S. Defense Department, was discarded because of the outcry from Latin American universities when the plan was discovered.

What the architects of Camelot did not take into account is the historically close relation between education and politics in Latin America: because of its historical role there, education is regarded as integral to the realization of true independence. Students in Latin America, unlike those in the United States, have a class consciousness based on an awareness of full intellectual capability not yet compromised by everyday pressures from society. This awareness leads to the assumption of responsibilities toward social justice, and the history of Latin America's educational reform is a consequence of these attitudes. Already in the first half of the nineteenth century, Simón Rodríguez (Simón Bolívar's tutor) preached in Venezuela that education should not be about reading, writing, and counting, but about thinking. It was a time when segments of the "intelligentsia" considered taking the popular and distorted Spanish then in use as a standard language and dismissing the rules given by the Royal Academy of Spain about spelling and grammar. The implications of these thoughts were as much pedagogical as they were political. Rodríguez was succinct: "Nothing is as important as having a *people:* to shape it should be the only occupation of those concerned with social causes."[11]

The Legacy of the Reform of Córdoba

In 1918 a major university upheaval took place in Córdoba, Argentina. Called the Reform of Córdoba, it predated by half a century many of the things that were attempted unsuccessfully in Paris, Berkeley, and Columbia University. The Reform of Córdoba advocated free, nonclerical, egalitarian education. The university should become an autonomous state within the state, with participation by all students, alumni, and faculty in its government. These principles spread throughout Latin America over the following decades, hampered only by invasions and dictatorships.[12]

Universities rapidly underwent changes, including those in Lima (1919), Santiago de Chile (1920), Medellín (1922), and so forth. In both Argentina and Uruguay, the initial changes were partially a push by the middle class to enter the upper levels, although soon the movement was influenced by the Russian Revolution. In Peru, the student movement led to the creation of APRA (American Popular Revolutionary Alliance), the political party headed by Víctor Haya de la Torre, one of the continental leaders of the reform. Initially this party tried to stop the increasing impoverishment of the Indian and mestizo population. As these ideas received wide support in Latin America during the following decade, educational reform came to be regarded as a political act that challenged the distribution of power.

After the Reform of Córdoba, changes in Latin American education did not occur without strikes and bloodshed. (The massacre of Tlatelolco, with four hundred students killed by police in Mexico City in 1968, is one example.) The fights were both about university problems and in support of worker demands, and to this day there has not been a generation of students that has not participated in them.

Militancy has been as much an educational factor as courses. Each generation took pains in forming the next, as if knowing that upon graduation, people would be absorbed by the prevailing corruption and be unable to continue the fight for ideals on their own.[13] The First National Congress of Students in Cuba, in 1923, was quite explicit in the description of the "duties of the student." Its statement spoke of the need for brotherhood between the intellectual and the menial proletariats "to rid society of tyrants and parasites." "The student has the duty of being a perennial researcher of truth, without permitting the criteria of teachers or books to become superior to his own reason." "The student has the duty of always remaining pure because of the dignity of his social mission, sacrificing everything for the benefit of moral and intellectual truth."[14]

The Reform of Córdoba focused primarily on the distribution of power and only secondarily on teaching methods. The problem of education "for whom" was tackled mostly from a socioeconomic point of view. Even so, in 1960 only twenty-nine students per ten thousand inhabitants in Latin America went to the university, a figure comparable to the numbers in the United States in 1900.[15] But the introduction of governance changes and the liberalization of admissions in Latin America were seldom accompanied by far-reaching curricular changes.

The Reform of Córdoba had a second wind from 1959 into the 1960s, guided by a second wish for "modernization." Faculty traditionally working part-time and pursuing their professional interests at the same time they were teaching, became, in a great percentage, full-time. Simultaneously the administrative force was sizeably increased. The shift was caused by a massive student enrollment. In the span from 1950 to 1959 there was a world increase of 57 percent in primary school enrollment, 81 percent at the secondary level, and 71 percent in higher education. In the same period, Latin America had respectively an increase of 82 percent, 150 percent, and 109 percent. Cuba was the only country with a reverse trend, dropping 10 percent in the same period.[16] Faculty grew in Latin America from 66,000 to 388,000 between 1960 and 1976. The process of modernization was guided by principles of dependency (international funds were allocated to achieve a kind of *Gleichschaltung*, or uniformity) and democratization.

Cuba experienced processes similar to those that resulted in the rest of Latin America from the Reform of Córdoba.[17] Universities achieved autonomy and implemented many of the Córdoba ideas, though these were violated, more often than not, by the different dictatorships. The Cuban Revolution also did not fully respect the reform, since the autonomy of the university was formally abolished. Instead, the other, more social aspects of the reform were given a major emphasis. In 1960, the placement of art education into a politico-socioeconomic context became an immediate concern. For many of us who had worked on curricular reform in other Latin American countries, Cuba's chance to begin with a clean slate became an opportunity to be lived vicariously and to be observed with envy and with the frustration provided often by periodic disagreements and, always, by geographical distance. A long tradition inherited and cherished by many people like myself suddenly climaxed, not in the place where we were working but very far away.

The Development of Education in Cuba

Until the Revolution, Cuba had shared the Latin American educational conditions and background. But Cuba's history deviated somewhat from the rest of Latin America because of its prolonged colonial status, a condition that colored every step in the process of achieving a functional educational system.

Education had not been a priority for Spain in the colonies. In fact, in 1502 a royal decree limited the introduction of books into America. In the beginning, education was performed by Catholic seminaries, mostly

in connection with the preparation of priests. The University of San Jerónimo in Havana (1728) was administered by the Dominicans, and
though intended for the preparation of professionals, six of the fifteen
courses offered were oriented toward religion. Beginning in the late
eighteenth century, there were sporadic and modest student revolts
against excessive difficulty in exams. Those who failed exams were
forced into the army (at the time, the Spanish army). Repeated revolts
were accompanied by anti-Spain and anticolonial actions, usually in the
form of defacement of monarchs' portraits. Education was extremely
conservative, even by the standards of metropolitan Spain, since the reforms that took place there were not exported to Cuba. The main subject
taught was law, and the result was an overproduction of lawyers while
other fields of study remained untouched. The Cuban educational system evolved from another seminary, the Real Colegio Seminario de San
Carlos y San Ambrosio, founded in 1774, and access was not allowed to
those "who did not have 'old Christian ancestors' or who were Black,
Mulattos, or Mestizos."[18] In 1784 those who lived in or were born in
Cuba were forbidden by royal decree to complete their degree. Fears
raised by the slave insurrection in Haiti in 1791[19] led to increased racist
measures and projects to prohibit education for the black population on
the elementary level as well. In 1816, black teachers were forbidden to
teach white students, and by 1836, out of 8,900 children going to school,
only 456 were black, although the black population exceeded the white.[20]
As of 1892 a royal decree prevented Cuban institutions from granting
Ph.D. degrees.[21] The measure was to force members of the Cuban elite to
travel to Spain and refresh their commitment to the mother country, as
well as to exclude the impoverished segments of the population. The
move generated Cuba's first student strike.

Félix Varela is credited with opening up the teaching process. He was
a priest and a protégé of the relatively liberal bishop in Havana, Juan
José Díaz de Espada y Landa. The bishop, in his post starting in 1804 and
interested in Johann Pestalozzi's methods,[22] was a sponsor of the Colegio
Real de San Carlos y San Ambrosio, which became the "progressive"
institution of that moment. During his first class in his course on consti-
tutional matters in 1821, Varela explained its importance, declaring it "a
course on the freedom of human rights, . . . one that for the first time
reconciles law with philosophy" and "that stops the fanatic and the des-
pot."[23] Varela was an early abolitionist and later became an advocate of
independence. After he signed a document demanding the suspension
of the king for bringing foreign troops into Spain, he was forced into
exile. He died in the United States in 1853. He exerted a strong influence

on his students and shaped the beginnings of Cuban nationalism.[24] His teachings were further promoted by his writings in the exile paper *El Habanero,* which was smuggled into Cuba. One of the first leaders of Cuban nationalism, the poet José María Heredia, was one of Varela's most distinguished students. The highest cultural award in Cuba today bears Varela's name.

While the student revolts were anticlerical and pushed for curricular changes in the sciences and philosophy, the main drive was toward national independence. Unlike most other Latin American countries, the Cuban clerics were mainly born and trained in Spain and faithful to the Crown. Anticlericalism thus became a part of the drive toward independence and had strong Masonic support.[25]

Independence, here, was not a straightforward concept. For some Cubans it implied total autonomy, for others it only meant separation from Spain. Many favored independence from Spain in order to achieve annexation to the United States. The arguments used by annexationists were those of a "geographic fatalism" for Cuba and "complementary economies" for the United States and Cuba. While coinciding with the interest of many U.S. politicians, the latter argument especially served different Cuban interests at different times. Before the abolition of slavery, annexation to the United States implied the protection of the slavery system in Cuba, a system threatened by England's pressure on Spain but still espoused by the United States.[26]

After the U.S. abolition of slavery, annexation became a possible source of help for abolitionists in Cuba. The interest of the United States in annexing Cuba dates back to 1803, when Thomas Jefferson gave instructions to U.S. agents to investigate feelings in Cuba about this possibility. William Shaler, the consul of the United States in Cuba appointed by James Madison, negotiated the possibilities of annexation with rich Cuban landowners represented by José de Arango y Gómez del Castillo. Negotiations stopped eventually because the Cubans feared a British invasion would be the result. A British invasion was equally feared by the U.S. government, since one of the consequences of this invasion would have been the abolition of slavery in Cuba, with the danger of fanning slave rebellions in the United States.

Student leaders became independence leaders, in a long tradition that included José Martí and eventually Fidel Castro.[27] The rest of Latin America already had achieved national independence, and an active student body was free to address university issues. But Cuban students were sidetracked by issues pertaining to nationality. The ideas of the Reform of Córdoba reached Cuba in 1922 and were discussed in the First

National Congress of Students in 1923. The congress was presided over by Felio Marinello and Julio Antonio Mella.[28] It is interesting to note that, as a symptom of the continental character of the movement, Haya de la Torre was appointed honorary president of the congress. The following year the Student Confederation of Cuba was created. It was declared illegal by dictator Gerardo Machado in 1925, who followed with the closing of the university itself in 1928. That year, shortly before his death, Mella had written, "Every student, like every teacher, is the owner of a certain amount of intellectual riches. If he only uses them to his own advantage he is selfish, an individual guided by the criteria of the exploitative bourgeois. . . . [T]he University is a social organ for collective benefit, not a factory where we search for private wealth with a diploma."[29]

By the 1940s reformism was as entrenched in Cuba as in the rest of Latin America. In the 1950s, the university politics were fragmented by major groups such as the Directorio Universitario, the Movimiento 26 de Julio, and groups representing political parties, with different claims on the university's ideology and later on the prerevolutionary process. After the victory of the Revolution and partially because of a continuing fragmentation, the emphasis of the Córdoba ideas in Cuba shifted in 1960 from autonomy to social commitment, setting the process apart from the rest of Latin America. While autonomy was a sacred issue in the other countries, the Latin American Left accepted (not without reluctance) Cuba's approach, acknowledging the radical change in historical conditions. Cuba has since systematically reinterpreted the tenets of Córdoba to make them function with the general ideological direction of the country. It should be noted that in 1959, Cuba was way below the Latin American average, with 17,000 university students (about seventeen per ten thousand inhabitants versus an average of twenty-nine in the rest of Latin America).[30] Presently there are 200,000 university students, or about two hundred per ten thousand.[31]

With the exception of Cuba, the process of democratization initiated by the Reform of Córdoba affected mostly the Latin American lower middle class, which became the prime beneficiary of the process.[32]

Unlike the development in Europe and the United States, the course of studies chosen by the new students did not follow market patterns or correspond to changes in material production. The enrollment in the social sciences increased to a third of the choices, followed by education and the humanities, while the numbers of applicants for medicine and law decreased. The "prestigious" professions were therefore not affected by the democratization. The sudden proliferation of universities created a stratification of hierarchies similar to the one in the United States. Democratization was further blocked by the assignment of different values to diplomas given by different institutions.

The increase in full-time faculty also affected the number of researchers (from thirty thousand in 1960 to eighty thousand in 1980). In spite of the increase, the new ratio (230 per million inhabitants) remained twenty times less than the ratio in the United States in the mid-1970s. The lack of a solid "peer society" led these researchers to seek recognition in the cultural centers, therefore increasing dependency. Meanwhile, student militancy remained strong. The political activity provided institutional cultural identity, like football and basketball teams in the United States.[33] At the University of Uruguay, for example, the School of Law was known in the 1960s as leaning toward communism, the School of Fine Arts was considered anarchist, and the School of Architecture, while mixed, provided forty of the seventy-two votes for the Trotskyite Party in national elections.

The effect of these patterns explains two events in Cuba. One is the extraordinary role of the student movement in the riddance of Batista. The other is the relative fragility of many of the professionals who decided that they would not be able to perform (or earn up to their standards) during periods of national economic duress.

The Development of Art Education in Latin America

Art schools were mostly untouched by the changes introduced by the Reform of Córdoba. Modeled after the idea of conservatories, where access started at the level of secondary education, they were an oddity in the university structure. Many art schools were (and still are) accountable to ministries of culture in hiring and decisions on minor expenditures, and the main achievement of the reform was to bring some of these schools under university tutelage, thus providing them with administrative autonomy. But even then, prereform curricular structures remained unchanged.

Although the spirit and philosophy of the Reform of Córdoba persisted as an important part of Latin America's cultural heritage, the primary structural and methodological influences on present-day Latin American universities came from the Napoleonic era in France. Inspired by Napoleon's emphasis on centralization, Latin American governments and upper- and middle-class interest groups promoted the notion of stringing together a loose conglomerate of career-oriented schools under one umbrella. Because powerful classes resisted state prerogatives, these efforts to create national university systems were more tentative, and the resulting university structure became much less centralized than in France.

In art schooling, the reference point was the nineteenth-century French Academy, which held that art was informational and transmittable by way of skills, which were teachable. Quality control was therefore easy—results were close to the model and good, or removed from it and bad. The models were recognizable and easy to define. They fit into a reality accepted as truly perceivable and ruled by causality. In an ambience already receptive to French democracy, French positivism, and even French masonry, the simplicity of the French Academy made a lot of sense and satisfied most of colonial Latin America's needs of the time. The accent on skills gave art a certain democratic aura since in theory anybody could learn them. But by defining which skills were valid for making art and which were not, crafts could effectively be debased and an elitist market tightly defined, counteracting the democratic aura. By following a model validated by Western European history, the products were guaranteed a relative acceptance. The model was ambiguous enough to foster a sense of independence while ensuring a continued colonial dependency.

Latin America's art school rebellions against the French Academy were partial, cautious, and secondhand, and for the most part motivated by a vague sense of having missed the European modernity boat. Latin American artists who traveled brought back some ideas about impressionism and, eventually, even some postcubism, although not always from the most distinguished models. (Andre Lothe, for example, exerted far more influence than his stature warranted.) Most of them were sent and financed by their governments to study institutional art teaching, and it was expected that, upon returning, those artists would funnel their newly acquired knowledge into local institutions. Thus, the majority, as critic Cardoza y Aragón puts it, "copied from marbles what they already had copied from copies in plaster."[34]

The few new influences were carefully inserted into art teaching with minimal disruption of the traditional canon. In Argentina, art schools introduced theoretical courses for the first time in 1958. As late as the mid-1970s, the National University of Colombia still offered drawing courses with the nineteenth-century approach, but now combined with fashionable theoretical courses on "Means of Communication" and "Psychology of Teaching."[35] By leaving the overall academicist structure untouched, the main objective remained the acquisition of skills—*how* to do art, not what *is* art.

Primarily spurred by the Bauhaus (and also by Maria Montessori and other reformers), the spate of challenges in the early part of the twentieth century had less impact than might have been expected. The reasons are unclear. Possibly it was because reforms were equated with the production of avant-garde works, which the power structure regarded as subversive, the aesthetically conservative faculty regarded as too challenging, the Left-leaning student body regarded as too elitist, and the already overextended local art market deemed not worth supporting.

Reform primarily arrived through architecture, and though architecture schools did change as a consequence, the overall effect on the arts in general was limited. Architects and architecture students always considered their field the most cultured among university studies. It was said that architects were the only professionals who, because of their wide culture, did not have to use professional jargon in an intellectual discussion and thus could not be traced to their studies. Consequently, there were many who pursued the studies for an intellectual challenge in the arts and not necessarily with the intention of practicing architecture, a profession with a limited perspective in an impoverished market. Much was thought about curricular problems and the function of the arts in these circles, but the ideas were infused with an architectural bias. Consistent with Walter Gropius' concept that the architect is the thinking and creative head who supervises and directs all the input into a building, artists and craftsmen were thought of as potential members of the architect's team and under the architect's control. Moreover, most of the changes in architecture were intended to bring local expression into line with the international building style. In spite of these limitations, architecture schools tended to have a more enlightened approach to curricular matters than art schools.

Renewed attempts at structural overhauls in Latin American art schools began in the late 1950s (Uruguay and Argentina) and continued into the eighties (Colombia and Cuba) and nineties (Venezuela). Most of the other Latin American countries have kept the nineteenth-century structure, into which faculty who espouse contemporary views fit awkwardly. The Bauhaus influence became stronger after it was validated in the United States, particularly through the Chicago Institute of Design and the publication of the books by Lazlo Moholy-Nagy and Giorgy Kepes. Some design exercises based on their publications (particularly *Vision in Motion* by the former and *Language of Vision* by the latter)—as well as on Wassily Kandinsky's books, Paul Klee's *Pedagogical Sketches*, and rumors about Johannes Itten's *Vorkurs* (the foundation course in the Bauhaus)—thus entered some Latin American classrooms. Skills were extended to include ceramics, textiles, and photography. But crucial ideological problems, such as the rift between Itten's mysticism and Gropius' conversion to industrial servicing, were never reflected in curricular planning. Thus, Latin America imported a fragment of secondhand, predigested superficial formalities that originated in the Bauhaus but lost the spirit of the teachings on the way.

The lack of rigor in analyzing the implications of reform alternatives to what was offered by the French Academy created other problems, for while the structure of the French Academy was designed around the implicit idea that art *can* be taught, the Bauhaus was organized around the idea that art *cannot* be taught. The foundation course was intended to be a filter, to identify those who, in some mysterious way, could become artists or creative artisans on their own. The institution as such was a place conducive to the development of those chosen people. While advanced placement in the academy was achieved by skill development emphasizing virtuosity, advanced placement in the Bauhaus was through the school's consensual perception of creativity. Once identified, creativity was consistently nurtured through problem solving and the development of appropriate skills.

By the 1950s, the many contradictory ideologies within the Bauhaus had been blunted by time. On the one hand, the Bauhaus could be read as a socially progressive institution, since many of its concerns were with social problems; on the other hand, it also could be interpreted as a kind of enlightened fascist institution, given how functionalism connected with German interests of the time. This ambiguity, coupled with excellent public relations, was undoubtedly responsible for the spread of the Bauhaus influence in Latin America, as well as for the perception that the only options in art education were either the French Academy or the Bauhaus. Most Latin American art schools declined to choose one or the other and developed into strange hybrids, retaining the emphasis on skills but also identifying a "chosen few" to develop on their own. Thus, the average student learns some "how-to-do things," the skills that in all probability will not be of any use once he or she decides on "what things to do." Meanwhile another issue, the "for whom," the definition of an audience, remains in the hands of a central hegemonic marketplace far away from where the student is working. Many of these ills permeated Cuban art education as well, with the relative exception of the power of the marketplace.

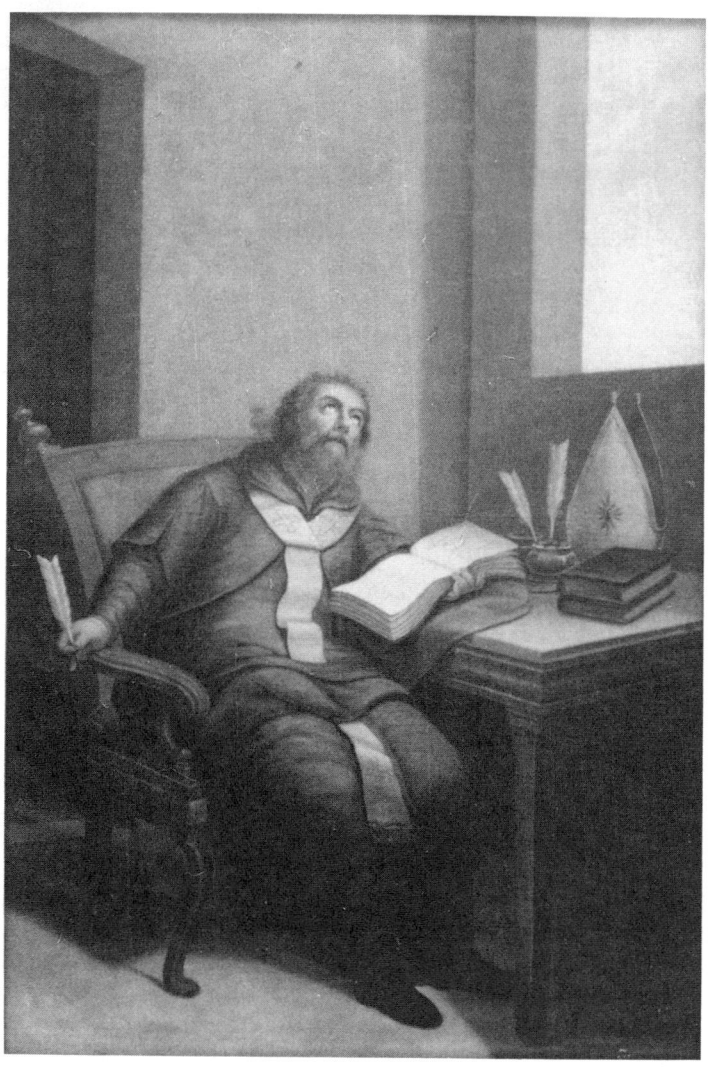

Juan Bautista Vermay, San Atanasio (Saint Atanasius), n.d., oil on canvas, 184 × 123.5 cm. Museo Nacional de Bellas Artes, Havana. Photo by Luis Camnitzer.

Origins of Art Education in Cuba

Initially art in Cuba was considered a menial activity and left primarily to black people. There was much "anonymous" art, and many of the streets of Havana were named after the subjects portrayed in murals.[36] A change in the concept of the social status of art led to organized schooling. A Frenchman, Juan Bautista Vermay, created the Academia de San Alejandro in Havana in 1817;[37] one year later the school received official recognition. It rigidly followed the French model for about a century. Vermay was a student of the French painter David, and there are unsubstantiated reports that he may have been a friend of Goya. It is said that this friendship put Vermay in contact with the bishop in Havana, Juan José Diaz de Espada y Landa,[38] who encouraged him to go to Cuba. Vermay, aged thirty-one, arrived in Havana, a city with eighty thousand inhabitants, in 1816. He had received a medal in the Paris Salon of 1808 but was a rather undistinguished painter, a fact that did not preclude obituaries from referring to him as "the Raphael of the Antilles" upon his death from cholera in 1833.[39]

The Academia de San Alejandro offered geometrical drawing, life drawing, and "antique figure" drawing. It emphasized drawing mainly because it lacked the materials for any other technique. Vermay tried to promote his school through public statements: "Modern governments must understand the importance of teaching sketching and the fine arts related to architecture in temples, palaces, and houses, and to the development of medicine, anatomy, botany, and all industries."

When Vermay died, Francisco Camilo Cuyas, age twenty-nine, became the interim director. Cuyas brought "new ideas" into the institution. He criticized the mechanistic approach to drawing and painting and the search for perfection in the copying of busts.[40] In his criticism, Cuyas may have reflected some of the pressures of romanticism on the French Academy at the time, as well as some of its internal rifts,[41] but he did not challenge historical paintings, which were the main objective of the curriculum. Cuyas was followed by another student of David, a French painter named Colson, after whom he became interim director once more. The first native Cuban director, Alejandro Melero,[42] took the post in 1878, but the Academy's approach remained the same. His contributions were the introduction of gas light, nude models, and access for female students.

San Alejandro was the place where most Cuban artists studied, including Wifredo Lam, Amelia Peláez, and René Portocarrero.[43] Like most academies in Latin America, San Alejandro provided education for many valuable artists through a negative process. Opposition was elicited against the prevailing ways of teaching, and alternatives were sought.

One of these alternatives was the Asociación de Pintores y Escultores, created in 1915, which had nonacademic exhibition space. Among others, Lam exhibited there while he was studying in San Alejandro (1920–1923), and later it displayed the "New Art Show" sponsored by

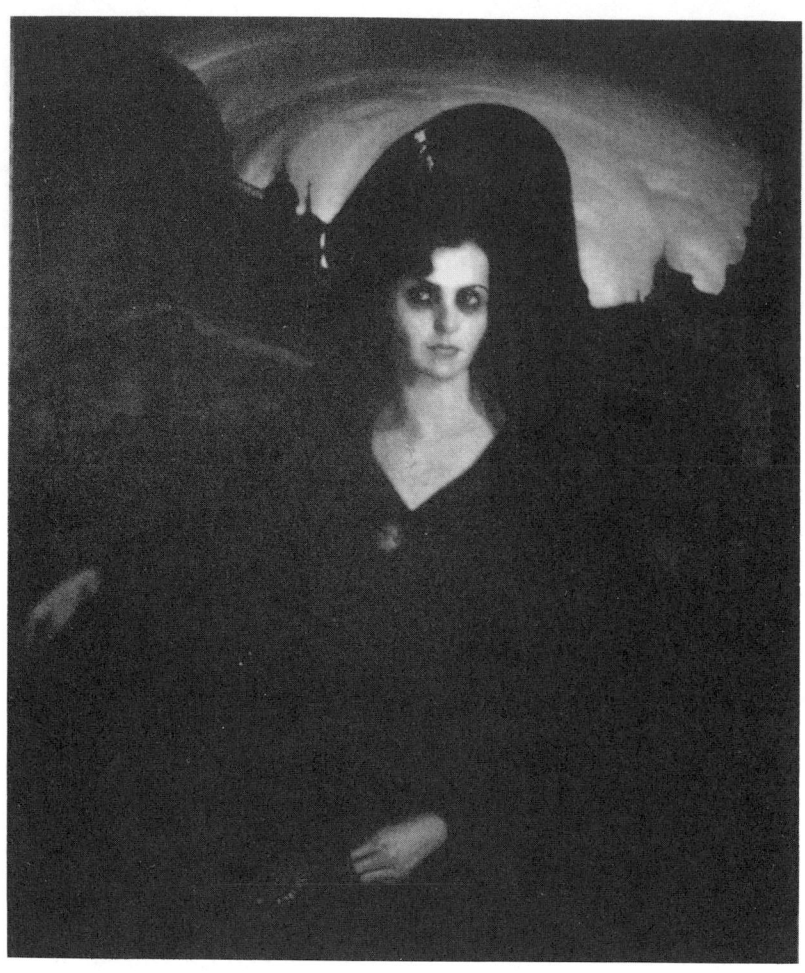

Wifredo Lam, Eulalia Soliño, *n.d., ca. 1925–1927, oil on canvas, 119 × 100 cm. Museo Nacional de Bellas Artes, Havana. Photo by Luis Camnitzer.*

Revista de Avance. A second antiacademic attempt consisted of the creation of open-air schools. A Spanish painter, Gabriel García Maroto, inspired by an educational experience that followed the Mexican Revolution of 1910, introduced these schools in Cuban rural areas. Then, in 1933, a group of artists tried (and failed) to persuade the government to create a new institution to help "spread the interest in painting among the poor classes" and "to raise the Cuban artistic level."[44]

The antiacademic drive culminated with the creation of the Estudio Libre (Free Studio) by Eduardo Abela (1891–1965). In 1936 the government established the General Administration for Culture, and Abela, until then consul in Milan, returned to work in the new institution. He organized what first was called the Escuela Libre de Artes Plásticas (Free School of Plastic Arts) and later became known as Estudio Libre. The school, which, unlike San Alejandro, was not to charge any tuition, received two hundred applications in ten days. Because of space limitations, only eighty students were accepted.

The new school was open to some of the European avant-garde ideas of the time, but its main aim was to promote "a national art in the context of the utmost creative freedom."[45] In addition to free tuition, students received free materials and technical assistance. The school functioned more as an open studio than as a structured program but was threatening enough to the academic teaching prevalent in Cuba that the Academia de San Alejandro prohibited its faculty from participating in any activity of the new institution. Abela therefore resorted to young artists working outside of the Academia de San Alejandro (Portocarrero, Mariano Rodríguez, and others) to serve as "orienting faculty." Aesthetic decisions were left up to the students. Many of the students were studying at San Alejandro and went to the Estudio after their regular classes to enjoy a freer atmosphere.

Seen from today's point of view, the Estudio was not particularly radical in its approach, and the opposition raised gives a measure of how academic the Academia was at the time. Students were given skill instruction and then led to interpret their models freely. To learn how to feel became more important than to learn how to paint.[46] One of the teachers, Romero Arciaga, would describe a flower vase to his students as "a well-known character"[47] about whom they had to discuss its manner of dressing, its psychology, and several other anthropomorphic attributes. The feelings derived from this analysis then were to be poured into their paintings.

Initial financing for the Estudio was provided by money left over from the budget of the Ministry of Education. After that, Abela continued to finance it personally as long as he could. The Estudio lasted less than a year but had a great impact and is still used as a reference for some curricular matters.

Art Education in the Revolution

Art education in Cuba fit the traditional mold until roughly 1962, when the Escuela Nacional de Arte (ENA) was created. Until then, the more prominent Cuban artists had been conspicuously absent from teaching and had no direct influence on newer generations. Through their travels, those artists had contact with new teaching trends but had relatively little interest in and opportunity for affecting curricular reform. With the Revolution, attitudes changed and curricular matters became more important. Initial changes were content-oriented and primarily concerned with creating a Marxist-Leninist frame of reference. Courses about muralism and the making of monuments were introduced, but fortunately without much effect on the students, since even in these courses there was no concerted effort to direct issues of taste or aesthetic solutions. The Escuela Nacional de Arte tried to change art education into what had been practiced at both Abela's Estudio Libre and the Bauhaus. Prominent Cuban artists such as Raúl Martínez, Servando Cabrera, Martínez Pedro, and Antonia Eiriz, as well as many foreign artists, were hired to teach.

The ENA maintained both drawing from nature as a basic introductory course and the traditional technical division of the arts, but a basic design course was introduced. In it, students worked in all techniques before they chose the one to their liking, and they were free to work on independent projects after the second year. Muralism soon became an optional course and was centered on one particular faculty member, Orlando Suárez, who had worked with members of the Mexican School.

At the time, the ENA became a focus for the arts, and many artists and critics visiting Cuba in the 1960s contributed with lectures, exhibits, and courses. The Chilean painter Sebastián Matta, the Spanish painter Antonio Saura, and Wifredo Lam participated in many discussions with the students. In 1967, Lam brought the May Salon from Paris to Havana, and the exhibit was accompanied by many of the participating artists. The Salon included works by Picasso, Miró, Magritte, Adami, and Arroyo, and examples of pop art and op art. Students of the ENA served as guides for the exhibit, thus having intimate contact with work hitherto known only through reproductions. Art critic Herbert Read, after a visit to Cuba, was impressed enough to praise the school as the most inspiring art school of the moment.

The ENA produced graduates working in all aesthetic directions. A particularly interesting experience was the one of *cuadrodebates* (painting-debates) started in 1973 by Alberto Jorge Carol and Juan García Miló. Both painters joined the Grupo de Teatro Escambray and organized mobile exhibits of "modern figuration with expressive distortion,"[48] which addressed specific regional problems. The exhibits were presented with an organized structure that encouraged debates with the audience.

Grupo Teatro Escambray had been formed in 1968 by several people who felt that Cuba's reality needed a direct-action form of theatre rather

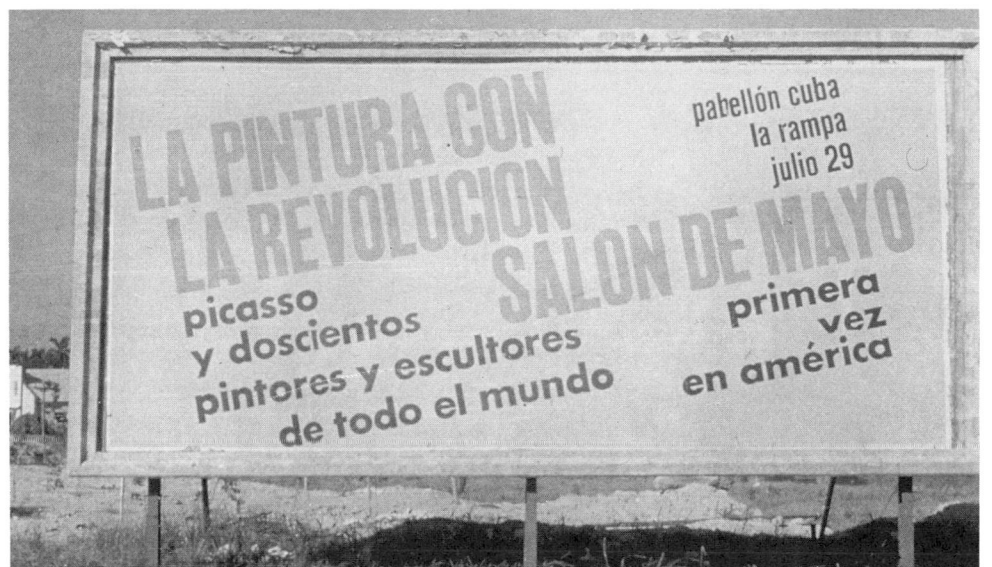

Billboard for the "Salón de Mayo," 1967. Photo from the Segre archives.

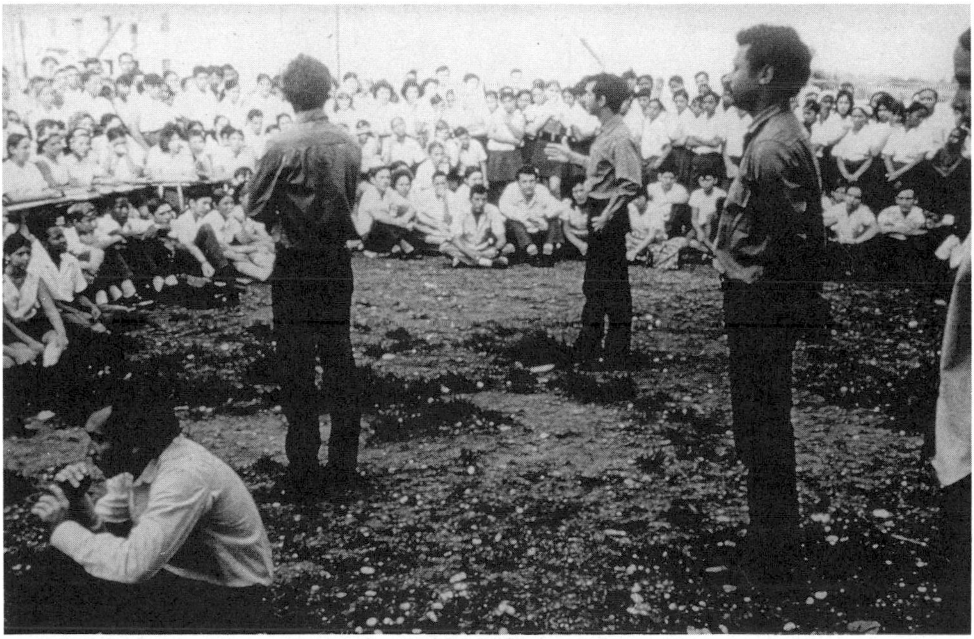

Performance by the Grupo de Teatro Escambray, ca. 1972. Photo from the Segre archives.

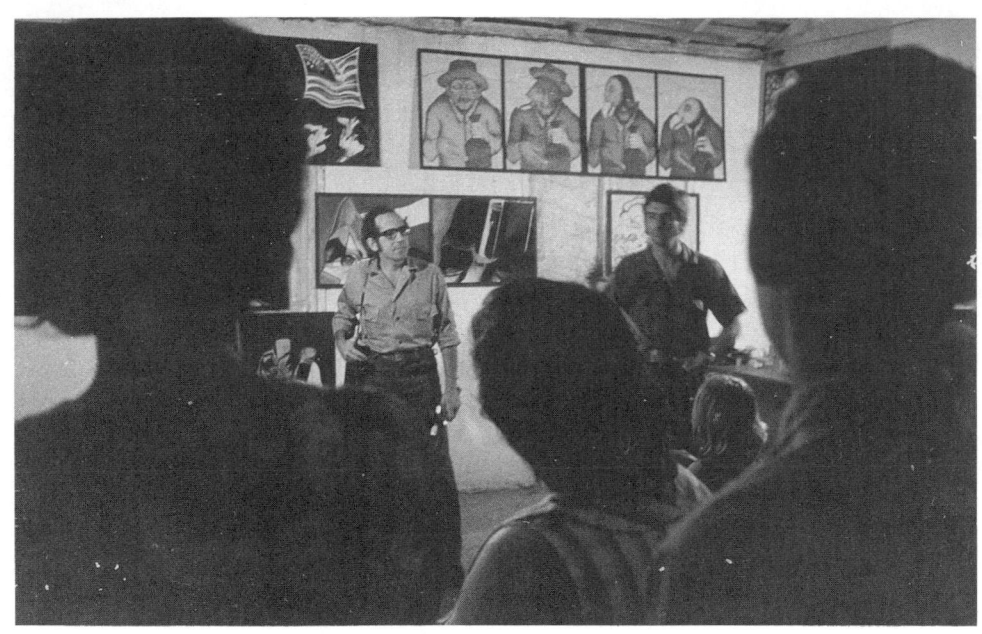

Cuadrodebate meeting, with works by Alberto Jorge Carol and Juan García Miló, 1974. Photo by Pirole for Revolución y Cultura.

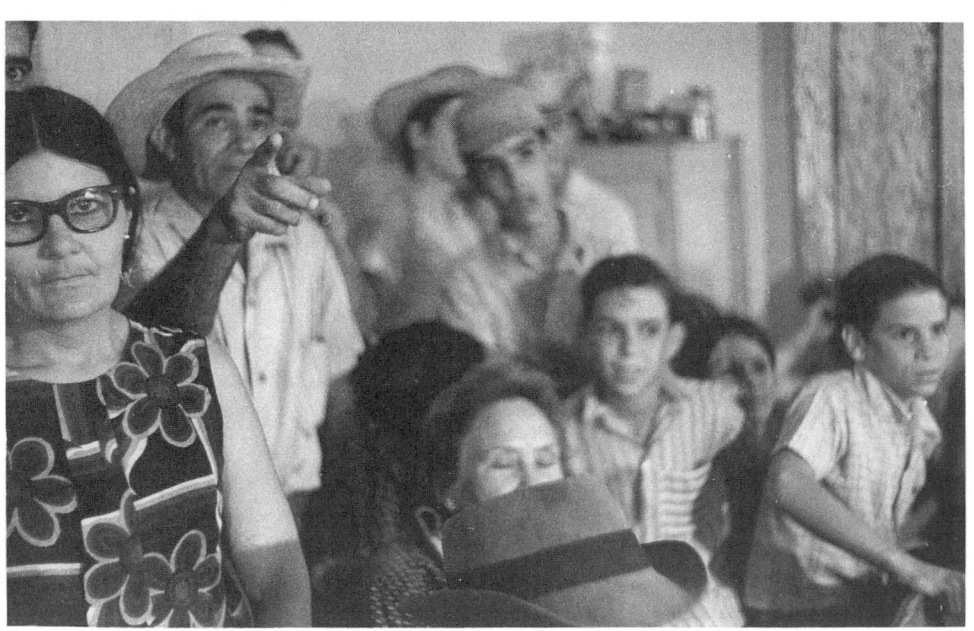

Cuadrodebate meeting, 1974. Photo by Pirole for Revolución y Cultura.

than packaged spectacles. They picked the Escambray region to start their experiment and, with help of the inhabitants in each village, performed plays that related to local history and events. Some performances drew up to four thousand people. One of the concerns of the ensemble was to raise political awareness in the rural areas and counteract the proselytizing of Jehovah's Witnesses, who were preaching nonparticipation in the military service.[49] Carol joined the group in 1971, followed by Juan García Miló in 1972. Both painters decided to expand the activities of the group into the visual arts. In order to achieve their goals of political discussion, their paintings were high in literary content.[50]

The dynamic of the school continued until approximately 1973. Around 1970, as a reaction to the U.S. blockade and as a consequence of the failure of the ten-million-ton sugar drive, tendencies toward isolationism and dogmatism became more pervasive. Cuban pro-Soviet sectors became more influential in cultural policy, and the combination of these factors finally reached the ENA. The curriculum was changed in 1974 to reflect the combination of these ideas and in an effort to unify curricula all over the country. The ENA is still functioning today with this conservative approach.

The Creation of the
Instituto Superior de Arte (ISA)

In 1976 a higher level for art education was created in Havana. Named the "Instituto Superior de Arte" (Graduate Institute of Art) and known by its acronym ISA, it groups visual arts, theatre, and music, has a faculty/student ratio of one to seven, and provides the final degree in the arts after five years of study. Since 1981 it has been undergoing increasingly progressive curricular reforms. A complete art education from entrance to the basic art curriculum until graduation from the ISA presently takes twelve years. Cuban students who are perceived as talented are offered the chance to double their curriculum with art studies during the two educational levels that precede the ISA. Since 1980, students interested in starting in the art curriculum take an aptitude and an imagination test, based on a work with subject matter and a free-choice work. Technique is evaluated in relation to the objective of the work and not as a free-standing skill. Still, evaluation is at the discretion of individual teachers, and therefore there are serious variations among the different schools, not to speak of the universal problem provided by the lack of a definition for "talent." One of the elementary art schools, which is part of secondary education in Havana and is called Elemental de 23

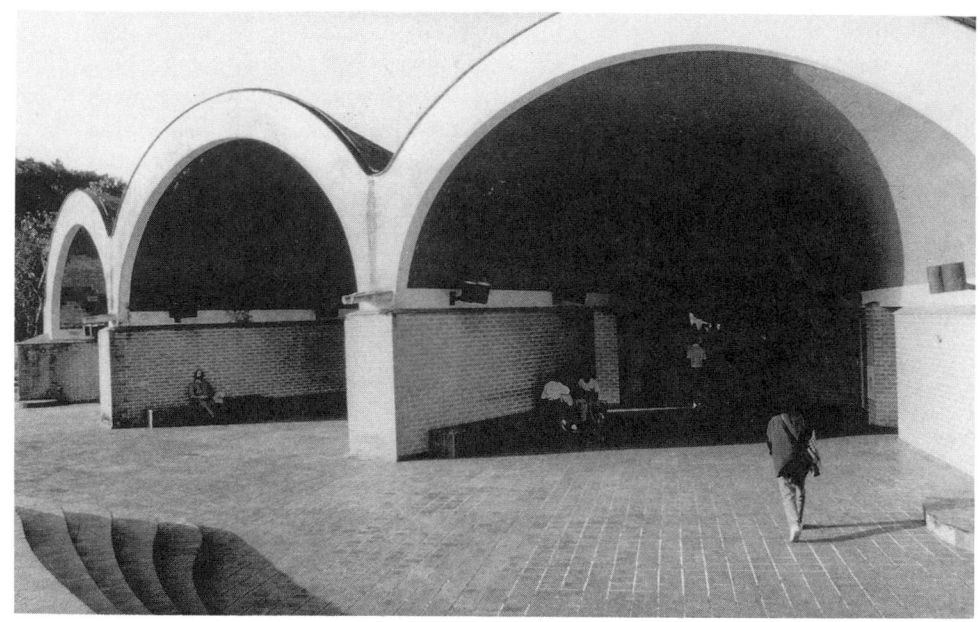

View of the Graduate Institute of Art (ISA), Havana. Photo by Luis Camnitzer.

y C, is particularly concerned with these issues. Under the direction of Heber Rojas, it developed a National Methodology Center in 1983. Exercises are designed to be applied in other schools, though, as yet, the program has had limited success. Sponsored by the ISA, a group of psychologists is studying the meaning of "vocation" and "talent" as conditions for admission to an art school and how to channel talent.[51]

While most of the students go through the whole sequence of elementary and middle art schools before applying to the ISA, acceptance only requires passing the university entrance exam and a professional quality test. Different from other university schools, the ISA considers its students to be professionals already, who are there to perfect their education. Thus, ISA students play an active role in the Cuban art scene and have access to exhibition spaces before graduation, especially during their fifth year of studies, the "thesis year."

However, changes are being contemplated in spite of the success, or rather because of the success of this structure. The present system has generated too many artists for the Cuban "market," and a plan was considered to cut off the elementary level toward 1992. The Elemental de 23 y C would be one of the casualties. The middle-level schools were to be reoriented toward applied arts (ceramics, printing, and casting, with industrial application) to help students find better placement in employment. Thus, "real artists" would only be those who graduated from the ISA. It is hoped that the "fifth" year dedicated to the arts in the formation of teachers (announced by Castro at the Fourth Congress of the UNEAC, see below) may, at least culturally, compensate partially for the losses produced by the cut.

The latest economic developments, however, are threatening the structure. Although the number of applications to the ISA remains constant and undeterred by an uncertain future, the school was to accept only half of them in 1991 for budgetary reasons.

The Access of Women to the Art Scene

As in the rest of Latin America and much of the world and for the same reasons of discrimination, women historically were not a quantitative factor in the production of Cuban art. In 1884, the Academia de San Alejandro had 28 percent women students, but few of them pursued the activity into the professional area. Juana Borrero (1878–1896) died too young to leave a serious mark, although the two paintings that hang in the National Museum of Fine Arts in Havana are very interesting. Amelia Peláez, born the year Borrero died, is by far the most important woman artist Cuba has produced. She lived until 1968 and shaped Cuban art as much as Wifredo Lam, whose stature she shares. Other notable women artists are Antonia Eiriz (1929) and the younger Nélida López (1950), Flora Fong (1950), and Zaida del Río (1954).

The effects of the Revolution were slow in shaping the role of women in the production of art. Only two women out of twenty students graduated from the first generation in the ISA in 1981. From 1982 onward the percentage rose and has oscillated at around 25 percent. While the "Volumen I" artists did not include women, the jump starts making itself felt from the second generation of the 1980s onward.[52]

Alternative Art Education

Alternative instruction exists in Cuba, but, with the exception of the Movimiento de Aficionados (which will be discussed below), it occurs in a different context than that offered by other Latin American countries. The instruction complements, rather than challenges, the official system. Casa de las Américas, founded in 1959, is an institution primarily concerned with Latin American culture. Its Visual Arts Division regularly invites artists for exhibits, and they generally give lectures about their art and other issues. The Centro Wifredo Lam, in charge of the Biennial of Havana, is oriented to the Third World. It conceives of

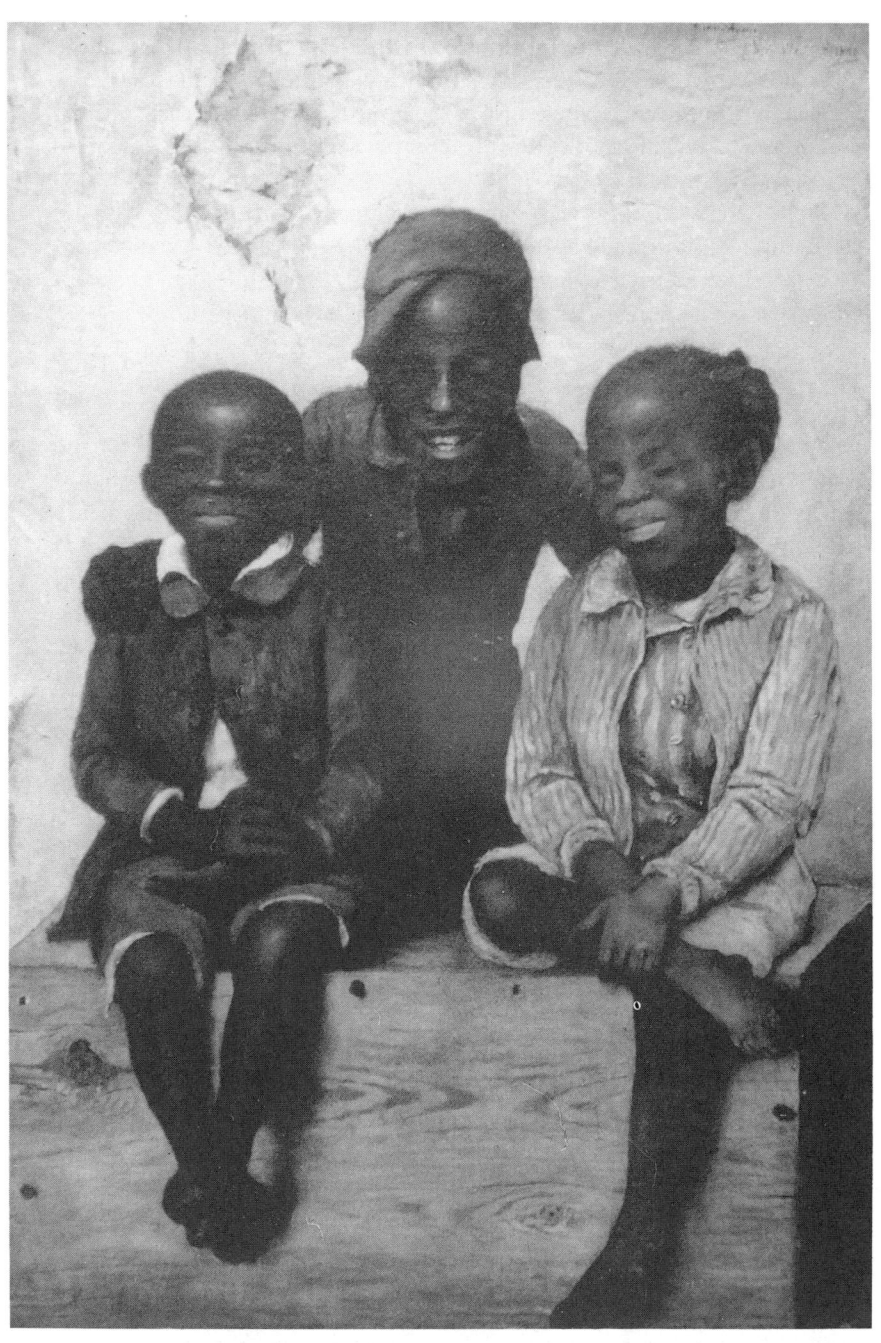

Juana Borrero, Pilluelos (Little Rascals), *1896, oil on canvas, 76 × 52.5 cm. Museo Nacional de Bellas Artes, Havana. Photo by Luis Camnitzer.*

the Biennial as not just an international exhibit, but as a complex of activities, with lectures, panel discussions, and workshops. The Visual Arts Department of the Ministry of Culture organizes other international art events, equally enriched by lectures, panel discussions, and workshops. During the Second Biennial (1986), Mexican artist Marta Palau offered a textile workshop, organizing her class into teams that produced environmental pieces woven out of ropes and elements taken from Cuban vegetation. At the same time, Argentinean artist Julio Le-Parc led a group to work on a "fun park" where the public could play with the sculptures. During the Third Biennial, workshops were offered as well—by Mexican photographer Gerardo Suter and Uruguayan Carlos Capelán, among others. Taller Portocarrero, the silkscreen atelier that produces highly sophisticated prints by Cuban and foreign artists, was created with the assistance of Colombian artist Pedro Alcántara in 1983. All these activities are a way of bringing international talent to the Cuban population, and they attract large numbers of high-school and university students. While these activities are not organized from a pedagogical vantage point nor do they fit into any particular pedagogical structure, they are broad enough to allow the entrance of challenging ideas.

Survival after Graduation

In socialist Cuba, where unemployment was for many years considered inconceivable (today there are "changes" in employment when a field cannot fully occupy its workers),[53] artists are still guaranteed employment upon graduation. Graduating art students become instructors, art consultants, graphic designers, and gallery directors. Art thus becomes a career as serious as any other course of studies, and market pressures are removed to a great extent. While this security is being increasingly challenged, by the end of 1990 the arts appeared to be more protected from unemployment than other fields. The political shift in Eastern Europe is bringing about the sudden return to Cuba of many artists who were studying and working there. This factor will further affect the situation of the arts in Cuba.

Income is ensured by employment, and secondary earnings, though desirable, become less important. The issue of copyright and author dues, one of the possible sources of side income, is still unresolved on a theoretical level. Proposed laws to accept and regulate what constitutes individual profits have been passed in regard to the use of reproductions of works and designs.[54] A law on copyright passed in 1977 is presently being revised with the idea of introducing a flexible taxation system to avoid excessive profits and extending it to include all intellectual activities. While maintaining the intention of fostering the arts, the revisions are geared to equalize income to a certain extent. Another current project is a preliminary study of ways to equalize artists with other workers in their pension rights. A step in this direction has been the recent institution (1989) of an *oficina del cuño* (office of the stamp) in the Fondo Cubano de Bienes Culturales, which attests to the professionality of the artist by stamping his or her document of identity. It is, in fact, a certification given out without any restriction.

Art in Cuba is considered national patrimony. This notion that somehow the work of art belongs to the country gives the Fondo the right to establish prices for the work and to distribute it. The Fondo is aided in its work by Artex, a corporation that previously had primarily handled records, and the Consejo Nacional de Desarrollo de la Escultura (National Council for the Development of Sculpture), in charge of deciding the destiny and emplacement of environmental and monumental art pieces.

The increased opening of an international market for Cuban art is having an impact. The Fondo is not yet equipped to handle international market conditions and, at the same time, is placed in a situation full of conflicts. While the capitalist artist is relatively free to individually judge and decide the payoff of prestige versus price, the Fondo officially negotiates in Cuba. As a consequence, there are cases in which artists feel that they were sold below a fair price for the sake of a prestige they do not feel is sufficiently rewarding.

The perception of Cuban art as being sold below value is also spreading internationally, attracting unscrupulous dealers. As a consequence, many Cuban artists are taking a dim view of the commercialization of art. In many cases they resent that museums in Cuba may lack the funds or the perspective to ensure that what they themselves see as important work remains in the country.

The artist in Cuba is facing the decade of the 1990s with a particularly disconcerting panorama on the horizon. On one hand, commerce will start having some effect on the work. The Cuban decision to encourage tourism as a source of income will, unavoidably, have some repercussions on the art market as well. On the other hand, there is the whole drive against corruption led by Castro under the name of *rectification.* Rectification, as we will see, encourages voluntarism. The use of art as a source for hard currency, if well handled, probably will not transform artists into capitalists. But it will introduce the notion of feasibility of aesthetics into the desired market and will therefore pose a serious danger, if not of artistic corruption, then of artistic alienation.

The Rectification Process

Cuba is now undergoing a process of "rectification" to stamp out corruption, and with it there is a revival of Che Guevara's moral incentive theory.[55] Until the Fourth Congress of the UNEAC there was a fear that this revival might do away with the prospect of individual rewards through royalties. The fear was dispelled by several speeches at the congress. The rectification process, which started in April 1986, tries to eliminate errors and "stupidities" and to find "new solutions for old problems." Observers see it as an original enterprise, different from the *perestroika* process in the Soviet Union in the sense that it is a movement promoted by those responsible for the errors.[56] As Carlos Aldana (Party secretary in charge of ideological matters) said when addressing the UNEAC, "It is not a fight against persons but against mistakes," and "There is not a change of policy, but of methods."[57] In this context, the Soviet process was initially seen by Cuban officials as one that could lead to instability, a process to be observed rather than to be prematurely applauded. It is an experiment with uncertain results, and it should be completed before value judgments can be made. Over the last years, Cuban caution seems to have proven well founded. Besides the unresolved situations in Eastern Europe, the effects of Soviet *perestroika* did damage Cuba economically. The break of contracts by many of the Soviet Bloc countries and the shift to hard-currency contracts with the Soviet Union did force Cuba to allocate funds designated for education and public health into the development of basic production.[58]

The "errors" to be corrected in Cuba are seen as a consequence of a careless economic liberalization started in the early 1980s, a factor that Castro stressed in the congress by remembering Guevara's warnings about tampering with the socialist economy.[59] The 1970s had seen a reaction against the romanticism of the 1960s, when planning was more guided by the notions of budgeting than by considerations of profit, and thus Cuba adopted positions closer to Brezhnev in the Soviet Union. Several mistakes led the rectification process to view many of the results of this shift as dangerously close to an inefficient capitalism. Nevertheless, rectification seems more concerned with productivity and careful adjustments of the existing economy than with radical changes. A stable course of action is seen as crucial in the face of U.S. pressure, which, paradoxically, "impedes the evolution that the leaders and the people would like to undergo,"[60] since any serious mistake could greatly weaken Cuba. The rectification process also stressed voluntarism once more. Workers volunteer to leave their normal jobs to work on projects that require extra labor, while they receive the pay they get in their regular jobs. "Microbrigades" solve particular problems such as the construction of more child-care centers. The absence of workers from their regular workplace is approved and covered by their co-workers. They, in turn, make up for the missing work by extra productivity within their normal work time. In addition to this basic structure, voluntary work has been encouraged beyond normal working hours, increasing productivity even further. A project to create artists' microbrigades has been discussed, where artists would be able to integrate art into new buildings while taking a leave from their paid jobs. The economic problems have put those plans on hold, and, instead, artists participate in generalized microbrigades following the model of the 1970s.

Overall, the total meaning of "rectification" as a systematic approach and as a concept is not yet completely clear, even for Cubans.[61] But it cannot be ignored here since it has become part of the rhetoric of many of the younger artists in an effort to have ethics precede politics and determine economics. This is not to say that these artists see themselves as identified with the present process. On the contrary, they tend to believe that the true rectification is taking place in their art and that what is happening in the country at large is only a timid and insufficient attempt. In that sense many see the young artists as the true and unexpected political avant-garde in Cuba today.

The effects of the rectification process on education are as unpredictable as on other fields, although Castro did address some issues in his speech at the UNEAC. He pointed out that art schools are the "Cinderellas" of the educational system and that galleries and museums must be considered part of the improvement of national living standards and not just as social expenditures. While primary school teachers had been required to have a minimum of a ninth-grade education plus four years of studies before teaching, future teachers should have a fifth year added to address the aesthetic education of children. This "aesthetic year" will not be appended but will be distributed along the teacher's curriculum. While this is not a part of the rectification process, it is a byproduct of a continual rethinking process applied to education and of a conception of art as a part of social production.

The Power of the Urban Centers

In spite of continental rhetoric, the awareness of colonialism tends to be colored by nationalism in Latin America. Problems directly affecting the region at large are not read in patterns but only in their local incidence, and sometimes they are not read at all. In Latin American countries, the rural areas are subcolonies. Cultural values are measured by urban standards, and the flow of talent is from rural areas to urban centers, the same as it is from colony to metropolis.

The Cuban answer to these problems has been multipronged. A general planning program through decentralization has managed to stop the growth of Havana due to rural migration. Coupled with the creation of centers of interest in the interior, the process of subcolonization of the countryside was reduced. There is an effort to bring culture into the inland and, also, to generate it there. However, the process is slow and difficult. During the decade of 1977–1986, out of 124 titles of first editions by Cuban authors, 99 belonged to authors residing in Havana.[62]

The distribution of art schools is also intended to help cope with the problem. One elementary art school takes students from age eleven to age fifteen in each of the provinces (with two in Havana). There are middle art schools for students ages fifteen to nineteen, one each in Holguín and Santiago de Cuba and two (ENA and San Alejandro) in Havana. The Instituto Superior de Arte (ages nineteen to twenty-four), also located in Havana, along with the ENA and San Alejandro, make Havana the place with the highest percentage of Cuban artists. There is now a drive to create a second ISA in the province of Oriente to correct the situation. While on the surface this seems like a good solution, other problems arise from the project. The ISA in Havana is just now updating its faculty and curriculum, and there is a fear that a second ISA might become an extremely conservative and provincial institution, thus promoting a pedagogical setback that may make present problems even worse. Both the demand for decentralized higher education and the problems involved in its implementation are common to most Latin American countries.[63]

The capital-inland rift is a serious one and was one of the major subjects for complaint at the Fourth Congress of the UNEAC. One delegate asked rhetorically if the frequent mentions of the "interior" implied that Havana was located somewhere externally. Another pointed out that while books and films do go from Havana to the provinces in an organized way, art work is distributed haphazardly. Still another said that the urban view of folklore made it appear to be a dead expressive form rather than a live and self-renewing activity.

The Movimiento de Aficionados provides a parallel structure of art education through a network of Casas de Cultura started in 1978. The aim of the network is to open communication between artists and the public, to facilitate access to art, art education, and art production on the broadest base. Talent may be discovered here and directed into professional life. The program aims particularly at workers, and both the middle schools and the ISA have evening courses designed to accommodate students coming from the Casas de Cultura who continue working during the daytime.

The Soviet Influence

From 1976 to 1980, Cuban art education included some Soviet teachers.[64] Their teaching was primarily technical in a very academic tradition and did not have a major influence on the development of artists. During the decade of the 1970s, a period that can be characterized as particularly Sovietphile, a Soviet adviser by the name of Anatole Tishenko had some input in curricular planning in the ENA, but most of the Soviet contributions came through Cuban artists who had studied in the Soviet Union. These changes were promoted by Carlos Suárez, a former art director of the periodical *El Caimán Barbudo*. At the time, he was in charge of art education and, ironically, later left Cuba as a *Marielito* (an exile who left via the harbor of Mariel) during the Carter administration. Some of the Cuban hyperrealism present in old work by José Bedia and exemplified in work by Flavio Garciandía of the 1970s or in the current work of Tomás Sánchez, can be better understood through the influence of U.S. trends rather than in the context of Soviet socialist realism. Students of Soviet teachers accepted instruction with humor, drawing information from them and ignoring dogma. They saw Soviet painting as muddy in color and in finish. Jokingly, they taught the teachers the slang word for muddiness but without telling them its meaning. Thus, Soviet teachers, nonproficient in Spanish, would ask students to paint more *patiñero*, more muddy, believing that they were using a term belonging to good Cuban art jargon. Humor and aesthetic discrepancies did not, however, affect human relations, and the teachers are remembered fondly as individuals.

The many tendencies operating in Cuba during the 1960s and 1970s were not just idiosyncratic—they also reflected splits in the Latin American Left. Latin American art critics in the Left, during the 1960s, had criticized Raúl Martínez' paintings of Martí as vulgar and Antonia Eiriz' neofigurative paintings as counterrevolutionary. However, there was a whole tendency in the same decade, possibly with excessive romanticism, to socialize art through collective actions and to break down the divisions between public and artists through "truly socialist" concepts as opposed to "bourgeois" concepts. As Gerardo Mosquera writes, these tendencies corresponded to a utopian perspective of ultraradical and ultra-Left positions related to the original Soviet Proletkult ideas.[65] Artists belonging to the Proletkult movement (Proletarian Culture movement) proposed art as a direct weapon to build socialism. Their theories were based on ideas of Bogdanov, but also on Lunacharsky and Gorky.[66] There were unforgivable casualties such as Antonia Eiriz, who stopped both teaching and painting. There were affirmations of art previously ignored, such as that produced by "spontaneous," naive artists. But, more than anything else, the time became one of settling down. It prepared, through a sometimes awkward and painful process of institutionalization, the foundation for present Cuban art education and the art resulting from it.

The Cuban Search for Answers

Technique, or the "how to do it," is still a primary factor in Cuban art education. Students are led to commit themselves to either painting, sculpture, or printmaking at age fifteen. The structure encourages them to remain faithful to whatever technique they may choose initially. The faculty at the ISA perceived the dangers of this construction and during recent years was working on a new curriculum for the first year of studies. The year is intended to be interdisciplinary and common to all students before they group into the technical streams. It is clear that the present rigid technical division is out of step with the art made by the new artists. In their work, these artists seem to be fighting against their own education and tend to mix different media without any consideration for traditions.

Nevertheless, the work made under this system always has been fairly varied. In 1981, Raúl Navarro Padrón, then dean of the School of Plastic Arts of the ISA, described the history of Cuban arts as having leaned strongly toward abstraction since 1953, with influences of pop art and neofiguration in 1963, entering hyperrealism in 1967, and simultaneously reevaluating the avant-garde movements with particular emphasis on neofiguration and neoexpressionism, but keeping figuration, abstraction, kineticism, and performance art as part of the options.[67]

The audience, or "for whom," is, in theory, the most clearly defined issue in the system. The curriculum in the ISA has among its objectives an application of Marxist-Leninist economic theory to the interpretation of practical problems derived from the construction of socialism. The bourgeois economic concepts about the development of capitalism and socialism are to be criticized from the vantage point of the working class. The dialectical relation is to be established between culture and the social class that conditions it, and a scientific understanding of the Cuban historical process is to be developed to achieve a correct interpretation of the traditions in artistic research, creation, and criticism. The effects of these points in the application of the arts is not yet as strong as one might expect, because the distribution system for the works has not been sufficiently redesigned. The alternative channels to the traditional gallery structure have not yet been adequately developed.

The form and subject, or "what to do," is the least directed issue in the preparation of professionals but has some importance in the amateur programs. Programs for the Casas de Cultura (they include dance, music, and theatre as well) focus on many patriotic and historical events to be used for its activities. But at the higher professional levels, such as the ISA, content is absent from the curriculum. Instead, there is a stress on logical thinking, articulation of ideas, objective evaluation, the development of a system of aesthetic concepts and criteria to guide the search for and adoption of a personal language, and on stimulating imagination and creative talent using a maximum diversity of expressive means. These objectives are part of the 1987 plan, the result of a gradual curricular evolution started in 1981 which probably reflects the presence on the faculty of artists belonging to the newer generations.[68] The new five-year plan, to start in 1992, is introducing some changes in the curricula of sculpture and printmaking.

Previous plans also had included monumental sculpture and muralism, which, while giving no guidance in regard to content, were liable to produce particular results due to the models available in the field. Muralism faded once it became an optional course in the early 1980s, and monumental sculpture has received an emphasis in environmental design and spatial signalization processes, thus removing previous "heroic" implications. The more conservative monuments occasionally produced in Cuba are mostly by artists who studied in the USSR and not by ISA graduates.

No doubt, the new developments in Cuba, both political and economic, will have some influence on art education. It is unlikely that the methodological principles developed in the ISA will be overturned. But the shrinking economy will probably affect the possible utilization of artists in society and make a career in the arts less desirable. And, if the wave of censorship and self-censorship endures for an extended period of time, it is likely that some elements of the more conservative aesthetics of the 1970s may receive more attention than they merit, slowing down the exceptional development of the 1980s. However, many Cubans do not feel there is a real threat to the accomplishments. They see a transitional period due to economic circumstances with tempers running hot politically and with fears of yet unproven corruption of artists through their deals with other countries. But they are confident in the future. The optimism is supported by the fact that all of the artists who had problems with censorship are still sponsored by the government, many of them hired for teaching in the ISA itself.

5

THE GENERATIONS FOLLOWING "VOLUMEN I"

The Categorization in Generations

It might seem artificial to speak of three generations within the short time span discussed. However, there are enough disparate elements to make it awkward to speak of all the artists in the 1980s as a homogeneous group. The development of artists in Cuba is an accelerated process; "old work" sometimes refers to pieces produced three months earlier, and the long educational process continually pumps in new individuals, sometimes not yet "mature" by traditional art standards. In some ways, Cuba seems to have gotten rid of a sense of "exquisiteness," of the traditional aura of preciousness that typically surrounds art activities. Promotion is applied to beginning artists as it is to mature ones, and this may very well be one of the techniques to redistribute "symbolic goods" and make the right to production widely democratic. All this makes the generational break more blurry than usual, a fact particularly noticeable between "Volumen I" and those artists immediately following.

Definition of the Second Generation

There is a fairly clear division between the first generation and the third one; interests, self-awareness, and sense of mission are all different. Defining the second generation is more problematic. The age of its members often overlaps with the first generation (in fact, Bedia, a participant in "Volumen I," is younger than many of the artists of the following group), and the group dynamic is not really of the same character as in the first and third generations. In that sense, it is a generation by default and more of a transitional group. Their work appeared fully blown only some time after "Volumen I," and though close to the artists of the first generation, they did not merge with them. At the same time, the third generation sees itself as definitely apart from them. While the artists of the first generation graduated from the ISA in 1980–1981 (Bedia, Garciandía, and Torres Llorca), the others graduated in successive years. In an intangible way it has become a group of artists "condemned" to be a second generation.

The second generation contributed a number of excellent artists but lacked a group vision or action. The first generation, primarily through "Volumen I" and the activities that preceded and followed that show, had a collective impact that acquired its own importance, regardless of the actual quality of the individual work. The third generation, with its generational political stand, achieved a similar status. It is possible that the second generation had to pay the price for a period of stable and peaceful flourishing. The possibilities for an aesthetic rupture were laid out by the first generation, while the time for the political analysis brought about by the rectification process only arrived in time for the third generation. Thus, the second generation served to refine the potential of the first generation through individual artistic achievements and to help focus what was to come for the third generation (such as Grupo Hexágono and the sex happening at the UNEAC—see section on "Happenings and performances"—both discussed below). This relatively low generational profile leads some Cuban critics (Osvaldo Sánchez, Antonio Eligio Fernández) to merge them into the first generation.

Artists within the second generation are Consuelo Castañeda (1956), Gustavo Acosta (1958), Humberto Castro (1957), Moisés de los Santos Finalé (1957), Magdalena Campos (1959), José Franco Codinach (1958), Carlos Alberto García (1959), Antonio Eligio Fernández (known as "Tonel") (1958), and Marta María Pérez (1959). The work of most of them will be discussed in the next chapter.

The group activity of the second generation has been minor. The ground opened by "Volumen I" allowed for more individual statements within the parameters given by the first generation. This led to the erosion and eventual disappearance of group activity among the first generation and became less needed among the artists immediately following.

THE GRUPO HEXÁGONO

The only group event worth mentioning in the second generation is the Grupo Hexágono, which was formed in May 1982, somewhat by accident. Humberto Castro, a painter; "Tonel," a cartoonist; and Sebastián Elizondo, a photographer, had all received a prize consisting of a trip into the inland. They went with their wives, Consuelo Castañeda, a

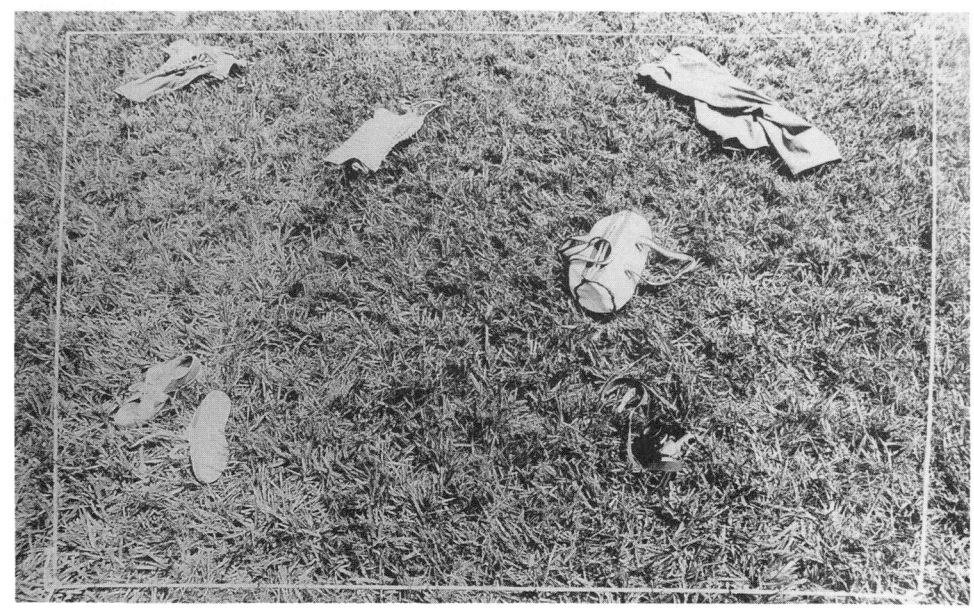

Grupo Hexágono, Seis amigos visitan un paisaje (Six Friends Visit a Landscape), *installation, 1982. Photo by the artists.*

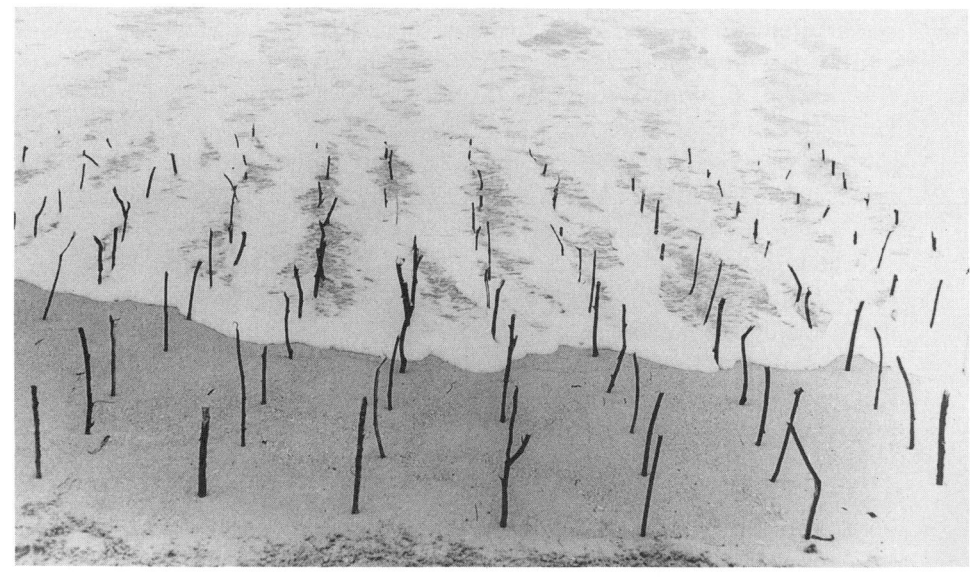

Grupo Hexágono, Arena y madera (Sand and Wood), *installation, 1983. Photo by the artists.*

painter; María Elena Morera, a museologist; and Abigail García, a photographer. On that trip they decided to become an interdisciplinary group. Inspired by the landscape, the work was to be connected with nature.[1] The pieces they made consisted of white canvas squares placed among the trees and other interventions into the landscape. With that approach they participated in the Arte en la Fábrica project and produced a huge environment in a metallurgic factory with the help of the workers. The first public showing of their work took place as part of the "Salón Paisaje '82" exhibition. Their first exhibition followed in May 1983, in which they introduced relations between materials and their photographic documentation. In 1984, a second exhibition with installations and photographic documentation also related to nature and with an ecological bent had the title "Hexágono." The group worked as a collective, trying to maintain individualities but merging together in the final work. After this exhibit, individual art concerns (which had been maintained during the group work) took over for each of them, and the group ceased operations.

Aside from this experiment, the activity of the members of this generation is individualistic, in both theoretical and practical approaches. They cement the openings of "Volumen I" and enrich them, but they do not expand on them in a collective dynamic. What separates the second generation slightly from the first generation is the introduction of humorous, erotic, and scatological elements in some of their work, a trait that has been picked up more blatantly by the generation following. Many of them unintentionally became more internationalized in their work while neither seeking nor trying to avoid it.

The Third Generation

The third generation, with a median age of twenty-five years old today, is radically different. Although also exhibiting individually, they were organized in even more intense groups than was the first generation. They are highly conscious of belonging to one generation and of a need to find their own generational expression. In that sense, even if most of the distinct groups we will discuss were extinct by the end of the decade, the generation itself still carries a kind of "group identity" as a generation. As José Franco put it, this is the first generation in Cuba that is able to do in school the same kind of work they do at home, at least in regard to those who presently are studying in the ISA. They are also aware of the process of "rectification" and feel that they are visually advancing this process.[2]

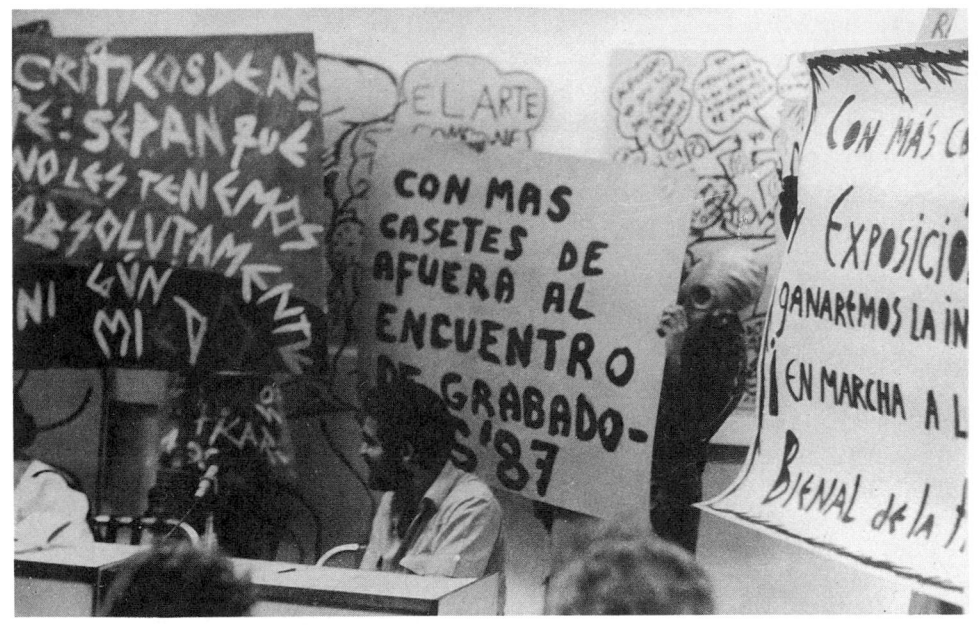

Arte Calle, performance, 1987, with text: "Art critics, know that we absolutely have no fear of you!" Photo by González Vidal.

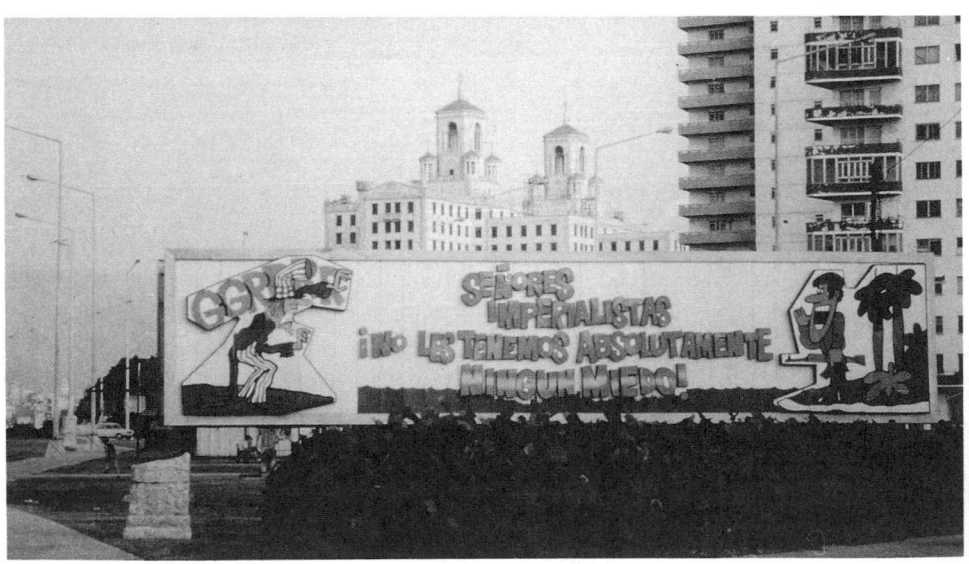

Billboard facing the U.S. Interests Office in Havana, with text: "Messrs. Imperialists, we absolutely have no fear of you!" Private collection. Photo by Luis Camnitzer.

THE NEW GOALS

One of the main concerns of the third generation is to "desloganize" Communist Party language, which they feel has gradually been frozen to death. They look for ambiguities and irreverent puns. A sign in Old Havana that reads, "Nothing can be done anywhere without the presence of the Party," is deconstructed into its oppressive possibilities by shifting the emphasis in the reading of the slogan. Another example is a sign used at an unannounced happening staged by Arte Calle during the awards ceremony of the UNEAC in 1987: "Art critics: know that we have absolutely no fear of you," punning on a billboard facing the Office of U.S. Interests in Havana, which stated, "Messrs. Imperialists, we absolutely have no fear of you." While previous generations of the 1980s are, to a great extent, concerned with aesthetics, this generation is concerned with ethics, including those governing the art market. It is here where they distance themselves from the older artists.

HAPPENINGS AND PERFORMANCES

Happenings became one of the trademarks of this generation, although the events functioned differently than what was expected from them in the Western mainstream. The performance as an aesthetic construct had and has a lesser appeal among visual artists, and only Leandro Soto can be seen as one who showed a serious interest in the field. When used by the members of the third generation, happenings became more of a humorous guerrilla theatre than an exercise in carefully staged aesthetics. Critic Osvaldo Sánchez cites an event in 1986, by Consuelo Castañeda and Humberto Castro, as the guiding example for similar interventions by the younger artists. Both artists "burst into a conference on sex held at the headquarters of the UNEAC (National Union of Cuban Writers and Artists) masquerading as giant penises and spraying milk on the participants and distinguished panelists."[3]

From then on these events became, for a while, accepted enrichments of intellectual gatherings. In time they were put to political use by groups trying to impress political dissatisfaction on the international press through staged spontaneity. The most prominent example of this was the stepping on a portrait of Che Guevara during an opening, an event that will be discussed below under "Arte Calle."

THE GROUPS

The third generation is (or was) loosely formed by six groups: Grupo Provisional, Arte Calle, Grupo Puré, a less-organized group named "1.2.3 . . . 12," Grupo Imán (formerly called Grupo Reunión), four artists who work collectively without a group name (Tanya Angulo, Juan Pablo

Ballester, José Angel Toirac, and Ileana Villazón), a team of two artists (Eduardo Ponjuán and René Francisco Rodríguez), plus some individual artists. Except for Arte Calle and the Angulo, Ballester, Toirac, and Villazón team, they are fairly open, and there are collaborations and crossovers. The parenthetical "was" in the first sentence is there because when I interviewed members of Arte Calle they told me that on that day they had decided to stop their activities as a group. From then on, and for different reasons, the other groups ceased their collective activities during the writing of this book. Arte Calle is less open in the sense that members are screened and excluded if not up to expectations. In the case of Angulo and team, the four artists worked on rigidly organized appropriation schemes in which they operated as a single artist.

Grupo Provisional

Grupo Provisional (Provisional Group) has a core of only two members, Carlos Rodríguez Cárdenas (1962) and Glexis Novoa (1964). Initially they worked with a third member, Segundo Planes (1965), but his personality proved too strong for team work. Nevertheless, the three are very close and continually discuss their work together. They decided to call themselves "provisional" out of fear of becoming institutional and also because, according to the project, they may invite other artists to participate. They often complemented, disturbed, or overlapped the activities of other groups, particularly the ones organized by Arte Calle. For example, they helped paint a graffiti mural, cosigned by them with Arte Calle, and performed happenings within some of the happenings organized by them.

Grupo Provisional members consider the whole generation as a pool of human resources, an attitude that has eventually prevailed over all the groups. The "group" exists only while they perform an activity and ceases immediately afterward. It is reconstituted each time for a specific purpose, without the burden of a permanent existence.

The main concern of Grupo Provisional is the routine into which the Revolution has fallen. They see the dangers of mechanical repetition of the original ideals over the course of thirty years. While they feel very positive about those ideals, they feel that it is time to create new, "alive" strategies to guide the revolutionary process. "Those educated by the Revolution are more daring, and audacity is revolutionary," they say.[4] Members of the Grupo Provisional are critical of the "Volumen I" generation to the degree that they feel its only contribution was aesthetic renewal. While they admire "Volumen I"'s will to break with the past and feel that they are continuing that process, Grupo Provisional members apply themselves to bigger and more substantial issues than aesthetic research. Both Planes and Rodríguez Cárdenas studied in the ISA and were admiring students of Consuelo Castañeda and Garciandía while they were active in Havana. It is interesting to note, however, that as an influence on their art, Planes and Novoa (who studied in the ENA) mention only the work of Arturo Cuenca and his conceptual stance.

All three see some of the "Volumen I" generation's work, and that of Castañeda, as excessively dependent on international influences. They are primarily interested in looking inward into Cuba, although they do not refuse information about art produced in other countries. The speed of the influx of international information is perceived as high enough to exclude dependence; it is a reservoir to be used before it can exert influence through frozen and obsolete products. Nevertheless, they fear the absorption of foreign prepackaged work that might lead them to an unwanted "propriety" in what they do.

Novoa and Rodríguez Cárdenas work more closely together between themselves than with Planes. They perceive Planes as more secure in his work and as able to run personal risks as an artist, maybe unwittingly accusing him of being an artist in a more traditional sense. While Planes believes that artwork is an individual expression, Novoa and Rodríguez Cárdenas do not differentiate between their individual production and their team work; one activity is not seen as taking away time from the other. They share ideas for their individual work and discuss it with the same intensity that they invest in the team projects.

Their biggest identification is as a generation. Interviewed early in 1988, they accepted the possibility that their work was still immature, but they felt that the intentions they espoused were more ambitious and varied than the ones of the preceding generations. They felt that the first generation of the 1980s now has its work guidelines and follows them; in that sense they are "establishment." "They produce ruptures, but in the same way the generation of *Revista de Avance* did in 1927—they take into account what is happening in art a little after the facts. They appropriate things from outside Cuba to produce ruptures in Cuba." About themselves, Novoa, Rodríguez Cárdenas, and Planes state, "We don't have a distance; we are afraid of assimilating things foreign, and thus the work we do as a reaction may only be understood nationally, but we don't care."

Happenings organized by Grupo Provisional are friendly and humorous. When the UNEAC had a conference about the concept of art in 1987, members of Arte Calle barged in, their faces covered with gas masks as they wielded signs bearing transformed slogans, critical of art. The gas masks were to prevent their contamination during this artistic event. Grupo Provisional then took over and changed the situation into

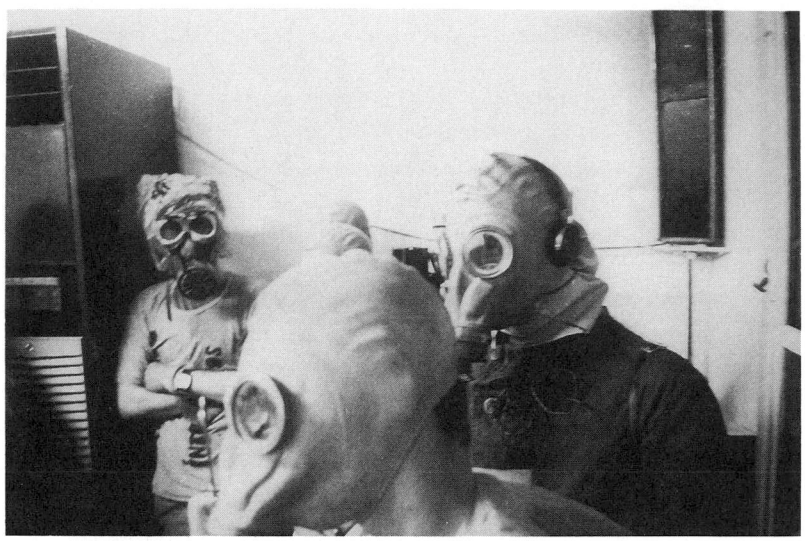

Arte Calle, performance, 1987. Photo by González Vidal.

an award-offering ceremony. After a willfully pompous introduction through the microphone, they called Garciandía for an award for his teaching; Gerardo Mosquera, for his art criticism; and Aldo Menéndez, for his support of the younger artists. Menéndez, an artist who was prominent during the photo-realist period, is the director of the Taller Portocarrero, where he employs many of the artists of the third generation and helps them to obtain materials for their work. The awards were Halloween-like skeletons with the word *artist* on the forehead of the skull, silkscreened in Menéndez's workshop and then personalized for each award recipient.

Another action of the group was also connected with an event organized by Arte Calle in early 1988, a fake opening. Arte Calle had taken a gallery space and announced the opening of a nonexisting exhibit. The public received drinks and a Cuban version of punk rock and could watch each other, but there was no artwork. The exhibit was supposed to be the opening ritual itself. Grupo Provisional came in with a banal video providing a false focus for the audience, shifting the original intent of the other group, and "making fun of a fun-making activity." The group was expanded with the presence of another artist, Francisco Lastra, and a nine-year-old hyperactive neighbor of Novoa, who is expected to "become a natural member of the arts when he grows up, although he doesn't know it yet." Grupo Provisional is now often invited by other artists to give life to their gallery openings. At a lecture given

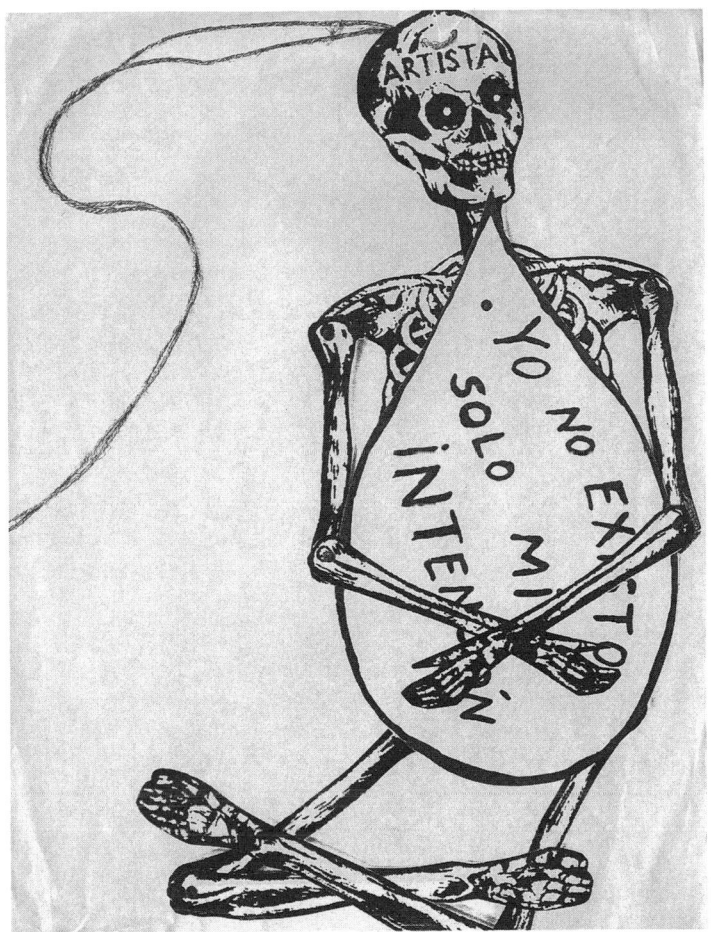

Grupo Provisional, artist award, 1987, with text: "I don't exist, only my intention does."

by Rauschenberg in the National Museum of Fine Arts in 1988, Novoa, Rodríguez Cárdenas, and Lastra appeared with a big banner bearing the profile of an Indian saying, "Very good, Rauschenberg," pointing out how the setup around the admiration for Rauschenberg put the young artists in the role of being colonized.

Arte Calle

Arte Calle (Street Art) is a more organized, rigid, and ideological group. It has a clear leader, Aldito Menéndez (1970) (son of Aldo Menéndez), who acts as the undisputed spokesman and who has achieved some sort of mythical stature in the Cuban art scene. Garciandía relates that when Aldito was four years old he approached him with a heavy book on Cranach in his arms. "Do you like him?" the boy asked. "Yes," answered Garciandía. "He is OK," said Aldito, and then he added, "So is Dürer. But all the others are shit-eaters."

Arte Calle, with a core of eight members, started a little before the Second Biennial of Havana in 1986, while most of them were in elementary art school. Some wanted to protest, others to make big paintings, and still others were interested in graffiti. As a group they tried to unify purposes and language, excluding anybody suspected of being interested in using the group to enter the arts. One of their first slogans on a wall at the time was, "We don't need biennials, we have [exhibition] space." The short history of the group is a mixture of recognition (including TV interviews) and warnings against vandalism (including a short detention). These mixed signals led to the development of an even more acute sense of skepticism and distrust toward the art establishment. When officially invited to paint a wall, they were given washable paints so that the work could be hosed down.

The group has been much more interested in art issues than in art making. The "murals" produced, heavy on scribbles and words, are reminiscent of any other graffiti piece around the world, with the differentiating appeal that they are not made with spray paint, but by brush. As Aldito stresses, it is not the final painting that matters, but the act of making it and, possibly, the text.[5] They worked with music, sponsored discussions with the public during their work, and invited bystanders to participate. What mattered was the idea and the challenging of the rituals that accompany traditional art making.

The group's original aim was to involve the uninterested, general public as much as possible. Realizing that they were not really reaching the large audience in any meaningful way, they decided to work on a more realistic scale. The acknowledgment of the failure of their first strategy led the group to shift its attention to the art system itself, using its particularized audience and some of its tools. That is how the "artless opening" came about. Later, some members prepared events to take place in theatres and, eventually, shifted into music. Aldito himself became concerned with pedagogy and prepared a "lecture on art for the elite" and an "experimental art workshop." One of his individual works consisted of a painting bearing the text "Reviva la Revo" (Revive the Revo). With a plate on the floor, the piece asked the public to contribute to finish the work, in this case the Revolution itself. On the occasion of Robert Rauschenberg's lecture during 1988, Aldito sat in the first row staring at the speaker, clad only in a loincloth, with feathers on his

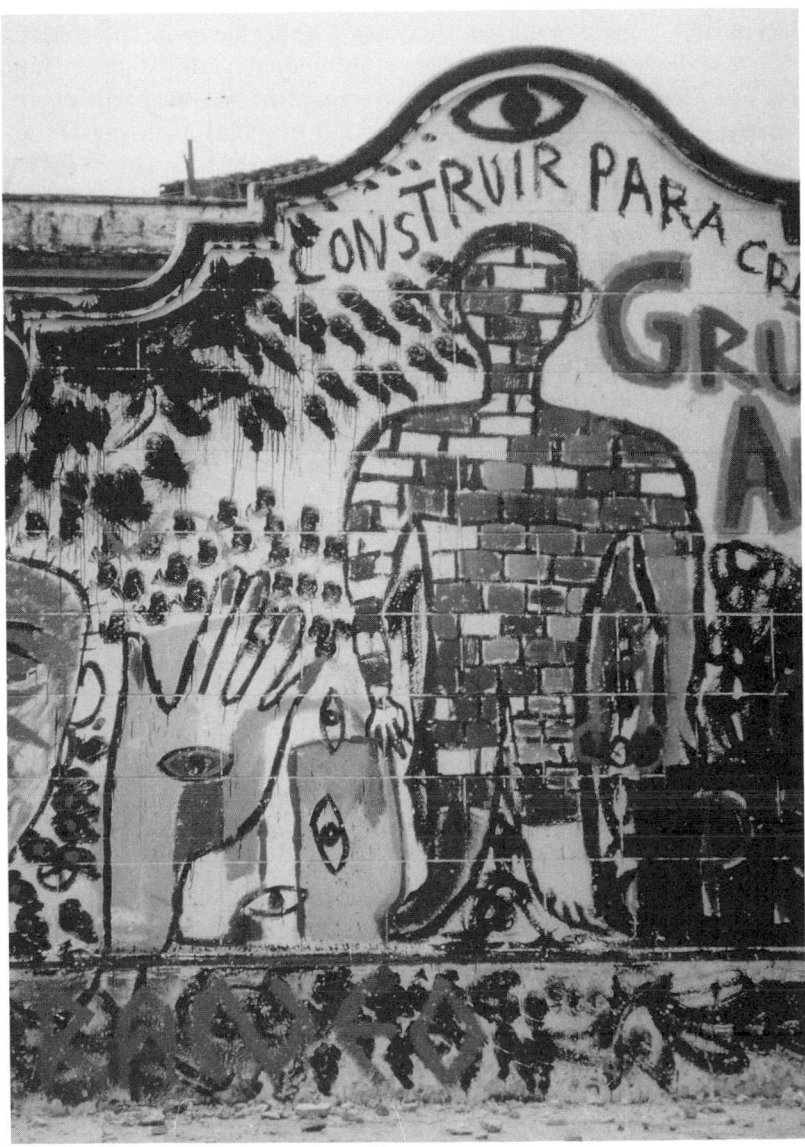

Arte Calle, mural painting (detail), 1987. Photo by Luis Camnitzer.

head—an ironic commentary on colonial respect toward the international star, thus echoing the Grupo Provisional banner on the same occasion.

Members of Arte Calle became more and more aware that they could not have an effect on the public if they acted individually. Shortly before the Fourth Congress of the UNEAC, they felt that the name and concept of Arte Calle had already become an "individual name," a personality that was identifiable and placed on the same shelf that other artists were occupying. As a consequence, they decided to abolish the name and to merge into their generation. The use of the generation at large as a resource was to become the only way possible to leave a mark in the broader public. Thus, they joined the philosophy espoused by the Grupo Provisional. However, after their dissolution they participated in one more, very controversial, event in September 1988. Since Arte Calle did not officially exist anymore, they used the name but crossed it out ("Arte Calle Tachado," "Arte Calle Crossed Out").

The event was an exhibit in the Galería L with work by many artists, including members of the Grupo Imán and others. It was scheduled to last one day, followed by a debate. One of the pieces was a huge drawing portraying Che. The drawing was too big for any of the walls and was displayed on the floor in the center of the gallery. For unexplained reasons, the director of the gallery decided to extend the exhibit and have the debate on the following day. What normally would have generated a public from between fifty to one hundred people led to a packed gallery, including the presence of the foreign press. What can be reconstructed from the different versions about subsequent events makes the following story. A man dressed in police uniform[6] and wearing an earring started walking over the portrait of Che. Three scantily clad dancers then improvised a choreography on the drawing. Outraged, members of the public proceeded to beat up the policeman and the dancers, and the event deteriorated into total chaos.

Arte Calle is now completely dissolved, the result of disillusionment provoked by this incident. As Aldito Menéndez writes, "The mistaken attitudes held against the new and young art born after and within the Revolution have resulted, as a consequence, in the enemies of the Revolution taking advantage so as to confuse and antagonize a sizeable part of the youth against the Cuban government."[7]

Grupo Puré

The Grupo Puré, though linked to the other two groups, always focused on the art scene. An older organization (it started in January 1986, while the other two began in November of the same year), its members addressed the issues they felt were going wrong in Cuban art at the time, but without negating art. They wanted to destroy the "special aura" of art and artists, stardom and individualism. As a group they aimed at the production of collective work while still respecting the possibility of individual production, so that most of the members were developing as

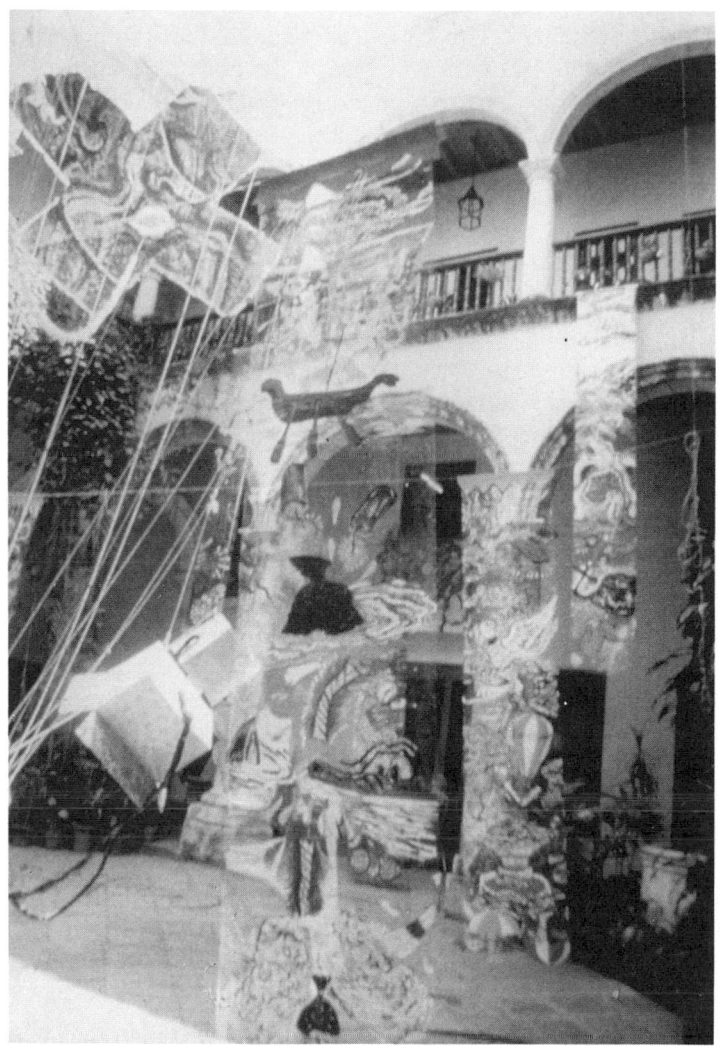

Grupo Puré, first exhibit, 1986.

individual artists as well. With a basic core of five members (Adriano Buergo, Ana Albertina Delgado, Ermy Taño Carrillo, Ciro Quintana, and Lázaro Saavedra), most of them were still studying in the ISA while they were active as a group. There were also overlaps, since the Grupo Provisional and Segundo Planes also worked with Grupo Puré. *Puré*, which means *mashed* (and usually refers to potatoes) was arbitrarily chosen as a name, partly because they liked the sound, partly because they wanted to mash art to restart it.

While Arte Calle was philosophically opposed to art imports, Grupo Puré stood for the total assimilation of international languages, going as far as direct appropriation of images by others, hoping that from the mixture something personal and identifiable would emerge. Information about contemporary U.S. multimedia artist Jonathan Borofsky's work became very influential and changed their awareness of how to work with the space of the gallery and how to integrate it into their work. Courses in urban studies taken by most Puré members in the ISA led them to focus on the city and on everyday life. One of their last projects, synthesizing their concerns about space and daily experience, was Art in Garbage (a reference to Art in the Factory). The idea was to create an aesthetic situation in the street with garbage found on location. They were unable to gather the needed support, and the project was shelved.

In its beginning stages Puré hoped to be able to break down artistic codes, but they realized later that they were condemned to address a specialized public. The group, after a process of self-analysis, came to the conclusion that it had become a shell in which the individual artists were working in isolation. An experience with television provided a shock. The group received a commission to design the sets for a musical TV program, a project that forced them into a series of intolerable concessions. After its first presentation, the sets were reused and changed without consultation, totally distorting the original intent.

By 1989 most of Grupo Puré's members were working on their graduation theses and thus unable to continue group activities. They coincided with Arte Calle in deciding to stop their activities and to merge into their generation. Particularly in the case of Quintana and Saavedra, their new, individually produced work seems to suggest that the group had functioned as a repressive force. Their individual work flourished above any of the group projects.

Grupo "1 . 2 . 3 . . . 12"

The "1.2.3 . . . 12" group was more amorphous than the preceding three groups, and already a year after its beginning, it became debatable if they should be classified as a group at all. Their work, with the exception of that of Lázaro Saavedra and later Pedro Vizcaíno, is less mature than that of the other groups. However, their guiding ideas are very illustrative of the generation's thinking. Maintaining their mention as a group here is partly a device to illustrate the interests of another sector of artists, otherwise in danger of being omitted.

The group originated in December 1987 when one of its members had the chance to exhibit in a gallery (Casa del Joven Creador, or House of the Young Creator) and decided to share the space with eleven friends. The title of the exhibit was "1.2.3.4.5.6.7.8.9.10.11.12," which then became the collective name.[8] The only overlap in this group with other groups was Lázaro Saavedra, who also belonged to Grupo Puré. Most of these artists were, at the time, studying in San Alejandro or had failed entrance into the ISA.[9]

Unlike the preceding groups, the "1.2.3 . . . 12" people only work on individual pieces, on occasion loosely knitted together by a common subject or aim. Visually, the work of these artists refers to Magritte (images with disconnected text), to graffiti, and to the use of slogans. Most of the production goes back to traditional formats, such as painting and drawing, in order to "challenge art from within," and there is a strong reliance on titles ("men and books resemble each other in that both need titles").

Saavedra's pieces, which bring this reliance on titles to an extreme, are full of written comments about the work itself ("This is important, it was published"; "These things are unrelated, but look good together"). Members of the group talk about focusing on the everyday human "landscape" to elicit thoughts about reality and to force the analysis of codes (what does a knife, a ladder, or plain humor mean as a form of communication?).

Their frequent use of humor is not connected with the Cuban humoristic tradition but is one more element of everyday imagery and a factor in normal life. They resist the expected "presentation" of art (oil on canvas, museum, reproductions) and work primarily on paper. Like Grupo Puré, they invoke Borofsky as someone who helped them to challenge things, to dispense with expected elements. Aggression becomes important if done competently, and a good instrument is the use of unusual, "tabu" themes. They feel constrained by the fact that art distribution is still confined to galleries and a particular specialized audience. Their main resentment is against the San Alejandro school, which, instead of teaching them ideas, teaches them to copy objects and how to decorate walls.

Grupo Imán

The Grupo Imán (Magnet Group) became prominent more because of a political scandal than because of the quality of the art of its members. Started in March 1988 as Grupo Reunión (with Juan-si [Juan Enrique González], Eliseo Valdez, and Jorge Crespo), the group switched names for the Galería L exhibit (the exhibit with the dance over Guevara's drawing), where Ernesto Ocaña and Amauri Suárez were added. After the "L" incident, the group asked for and was granted permission from the city to use the park at the streets G and Twenty-third in Havana for some happenings, activities sponsored by the Asociación Brigadas Hermanos Saiz (a junior version of the UNEAC). Participation in the events at G and Twenty-third streets was spontaneous,[10] open to anybody, and not necessarily artistic, although paintings were also exhibited. Again, the public perceived a level of desecration and offense that could invite violence, while most of the art people witnessing the events found artistic merit noticeably absent.[11]

The authorities decided to create a committee of peers (three artists—of whom two belong to the youngest generation—one "Volumen I" artist, one aesthetician open to avant-gardism, and one contemporary art historian) to help the group devise means for the securing of quality control for future events. Grupo Imán accepted the committee and expressed pleasure in the choice of individuals whom they knew and recognized as aesthetically friendly, but then they failed to pursue any meetings. The project of G and Twenty-third ended with this failure, adding some fuel to the controversies caused by the Galería L incident.[12]

ABTV Team

Tanya Angulo, Juan Pablo Ballester, José Angel Toirac, and Ileana Villazón constitute possibly the most rigorous group in Cuba today. Their lack of a group name makes referral cumbersome, and here they will be called ABTV for expediency.[13] Though they occasionally produce individual work (particularly Toirac), the group as such applies itself to appropriating other artists' work to make theoretical criticism about culture and society. The team started with Ballester and Villazón, with Toirac joining a little later, and then Angulo. By 1989 they decided to split up again, although temporarily. They regrouped in 1991.

Ballester and Villazón set the direction of the group with a team project realized while they were studying in the ISA. Using the visual structure of the appropriations of Consuelo Castañeda (their main teacher at the time, 1987) they constructed a piece with penises painted in the various styles employed by the artists of the new Cuban generations.

The integration of Toirac and Angulo into the team was apparently seamless; the group agreed on an idea, and research and labor were farmed out among its members. In the process of their research, they sometimes unearthed uncomfortable information—for example, the history of one of the most famous photographs taken of Che Guevara. A photograph taken by the Cuban photographer Alberto Díaz Gutiérrez (Korda), it was neglected until it was chosen by publisher Giangiacomo Feltrinelli to accompany the Italian edition of Che's diary after his death. The point they pursue in the corresponding piece (which they wanted to exhibit in the cycle at the Castillo de la Real Fuerza) is how the (revolu-

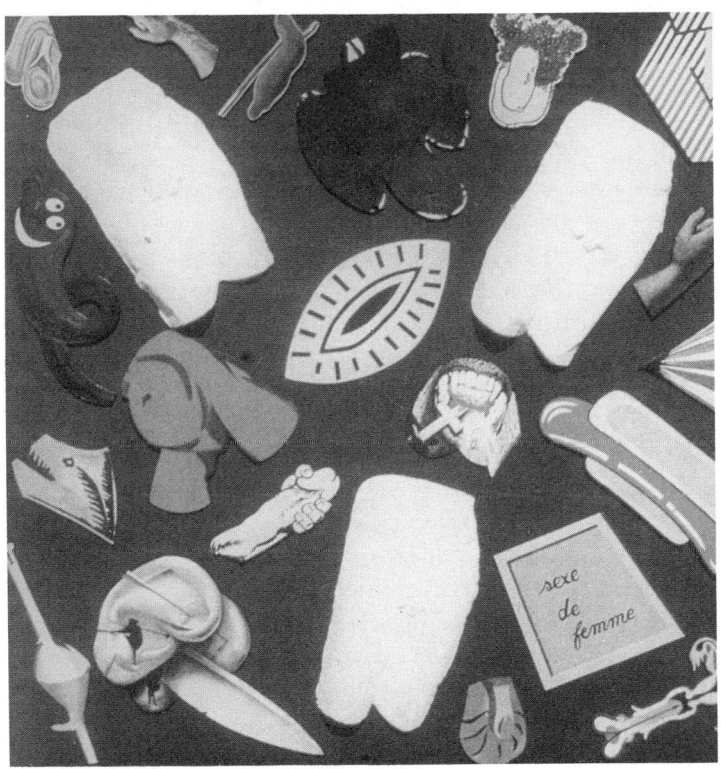

(Juan Pablo) Ballester and (Ileana) Villazón, untitled, 1987, acrylic on canvas, 150 × 150 cm. Collection of the artists.

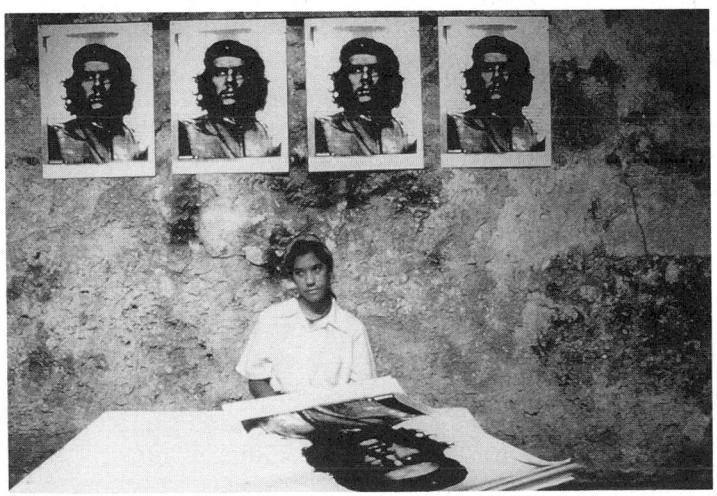

ABTV Team, "Che" project, 1989, Castillo de la Fuerza, Havana.

tionary) iconic character of that particular photograph was created by a capitalist enterprise. More work by ABTV will be discussed in the next chapter.

Ponjuán and Rodríguez

Finally, a team of two artists (which broke up in 1990), Eduardo Ponjuán and René Francisco Rodríguez, should be mentioned here. They worked as an individual artist, reminiscent of the methods of Soviet artists Komar and Melamid. Working together since January 1986, they made mostly paintings and drawings characterized by a unified handwriting.

In the process of achieving this unity, they describe three periods of their own development. First was a period in which either one repressed himself in order to allow for the primacy of the other. In a second period they each tried to work freely, while merging elements. Finally, in the third and last phase, they worked with more personal initiative, having one partner wait until the idea was clear enough to be worked on by both. The works make ironic commentaries about historical and cultural Cuban issues—for example, one pictures a samurai cutting sugar cane. This particular painting alludes to a team of samurais that purportedly traveled to Cuba in 1970 to help in the famous ten-million harvest (a fact I could not confirm with anybody else).

Occasionally, Ponjuán and Rodríguez allowed the participation of other individuals. Friends including Segundo Planes and Tomás Esson have worked on some of their projects. The pieces, though, seem less successful than when either is on his own. The invitation of friends happens mostly when they see somebody close to them in distress, and the working in common becomes as much an act of therapy as it is of creation. All these artists are bound by strong friendships that include intense critical dialogues among themselves, and this kind of teamwork can be seen as an extension of the dialogues. The work of Ponjuán and Rodríguez will be discussed in more detail in the next chapter.

THE SELF-PERCEPTION OF THE THIRD GENERATION

The whole of this third generation feels quite separate from the first and second generations. On the surface, this is a puzzling situation. The age difference is ten years or less, and while there may be some anarchic ingredients in the third generation's actions, all the artists of this decade agree that they are not challenging the ideological platform of the Revolution but, instead, that they are profoundly committed to improving and refining it.

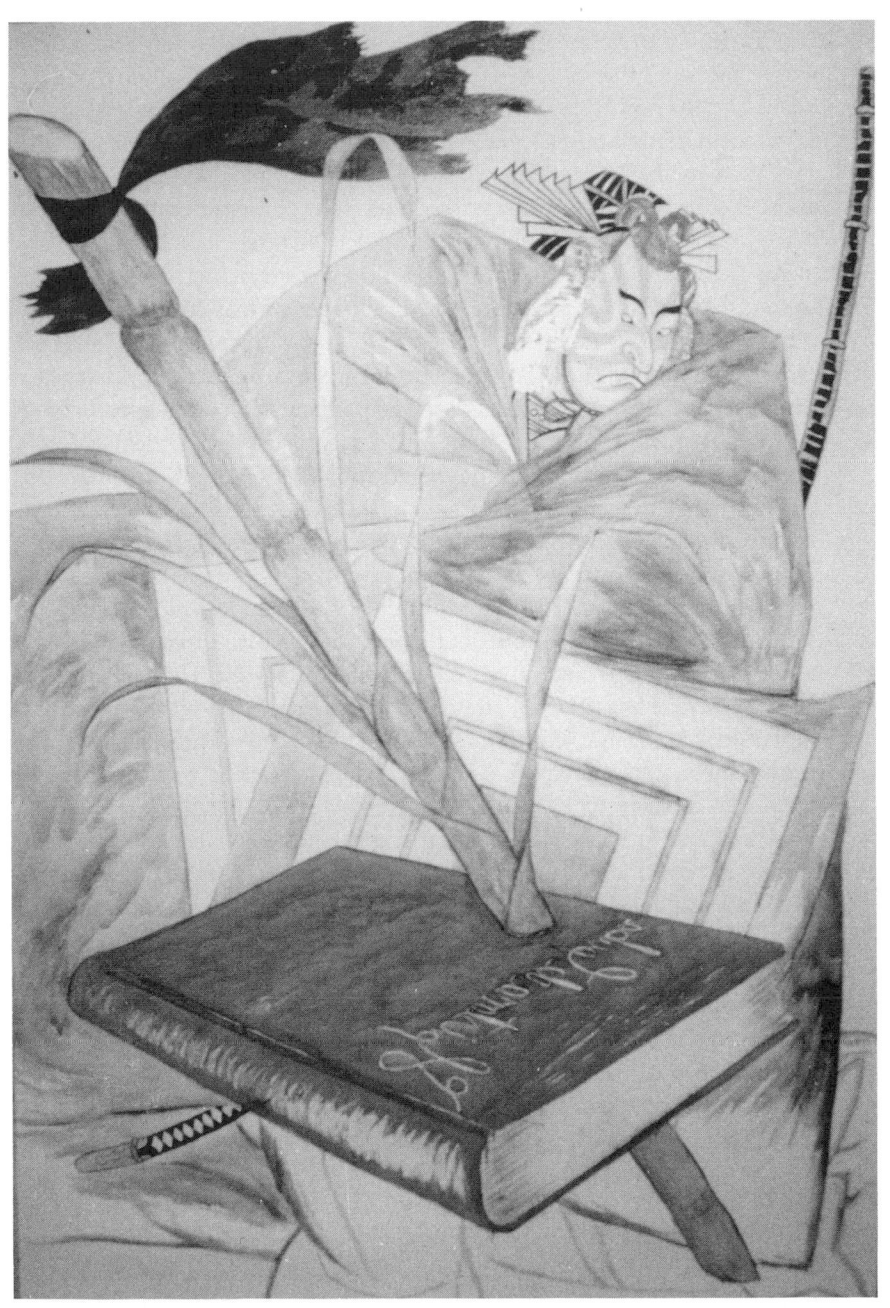

(Eduardo) Ponjuán and (René Francisco) Rodríguez, Samurai, 1988, acrylic on canvas, 150 × 200 cm. Collection of the artists. Photo by Luis Camnitzer.

One might presume that within a socialist frame of reference, artists would perceive themselves as members of an extended team working toward a common goal. Rabid individualism or, on a different level, generational confrontations are not only obstacles to achieving a common goal but can also be considered as negative bourgeois imports. In spite of these considerations, the break between the third generation and the preceding two is serious enough to have precluded teamwork among them. Teamwork had existed in the first generation and in parts of the second generation, and is a strong component in the third generation. While generational identification is an understandable process in these groups, it is the present self-enclosure of the third generation that may curtail some of its effectiveness in the implementation of its aims.

Many artists of the first generation are members of the UNEAC. None of the third generation belonged to it at the height of the group activities, and this absence was seen as a serious qualitative difference. The third generation perceives the UNEAC as "the establishment" and as being old and stuffy.[14]

As Alexis Somoza (1966), a sculptor of this generation, describes it, "Volumen I" artists are seen as creating an aperture in art but also as subsequently neglecting the search for new objectives.[15] Their new codes stopped having any efficacy, and while their work matured as individual expression, it became less functional in social terms. The implicit criticism in these statements is that the preceding generations essentially regressed to the making of bourgeois art.

According to Somoza, the historic mission of the new generation is to create a new opening. The entire generation is dissatisfied with weakness and inefficiency; the national "rectification" process is a consequence of this dissatisfaction. What these artists feel they are doing is an "artistic rectification," although they question not just art, but everything. Aggression in this case represents a functional approach where an emotional attitude should serve to elicit and foster a critical spirit in the audience through the shock produced by its violence.

While the rectification process is applauded, it does not escape criticism. There is a fear of further development of fetishes, particularly around the image of Che Guevara, whose presence is becoming something of a renewed slogan. The issue of nationalism versus internationalism is on everybody's mind. "Volumen I" artists are perceived as being internationalists, using codes that have become nonfunctional for Cuban reality.

The third generation wants to use national issues in a direct and local way, and some of the artists are unconcerned about how the end result of their works looks. For example, much of the written text in the artwork is full of intentional (and unintentional) misspellings; the artists, rather than wanting to correct them, use the mistakes to criticize what they feel is an imperfection in the educational system, thus using their work to publicly push for improvements.

In their process of questioning, the younger artists end up challenging political rectification as well by introducing a playful irony, something that professional politicians could not afford to do. The interests of the third generation seem different enough to impede a fusion into the other two. Nevertheless, there are connections. Garciandía and Castañeda are admired teachers who are influential through the teacher-student relationship. Cuenca is respected because of his conceptual approach, seen as a force of liberation from formalism. Bedia, another teacher in the ISA (since 1987), is also appreciated for his approaches to indigenous cultures. Torres Llorca, on the other hand, is the only artist who consciously organizes group meetings with them and organizes exhibits where he merges his work with theirs. While Gerardo Mosquera promotes the generation in his writings, they do not consider him as "their" critic, possibly because of the difference in age. The generation is developing their own critic in Abdel Hernández (1964), who doubles as an artist but who has not yet been published.[16] Save for Torres Llorca, the other artists of the first generation reciprocate the feeling of distance. They admire and encourage some of the younger artists, are happy about their existence, and accept some of the criticism as valid, but they do not see any way to break down the generational division.

THE RELATION WITH THE UNEAC

The main possible instrument for an intergenerational connection is the UNEAC, and the speeches by Aldana, Hart, and Rodríguez were seen as hopeful signs. Membership in the UNEAC is not easy (presentation of potential members by two current members, and eight months waiting for acceptance after a careful evaluation of the candidate's work), nor is exiting, which explains the predominance of older members. In 1988, the artists of the third generation were preparing a banner to be hung in the UNEAC exhibition organized in coordination with the Fourth Congress, but they did not finish it in time. The banner was to bear a kind of "testament" bringing together all their thoughts pertaining to the group activities that subsequently were to cease. Preparatory work consisted of having all members of the generation who were willing to do so explain what their work was about and then to proceed to construct a common platform. It is interesting to see some of the individual quotes collected for the preparatory work, which not only illustrate the points discussed but also show a lot of near-messianic motivation.

INDIVIDUAL STATEMENTS (1987)

Aldito Menéndez: "I am not interested in any art expression. I want to question institutions, art for the elite, the copy of foreign artists. I want the repercussions of my work to go beyond the realms of art."

Luis Gómez: "I want to tell the world that I am a believer, even if I am not. I want to redeem the mysticism that exists in every man. The important thing is to be valiant and consistent, and through these qualities, my work acquires a pedagogical quality."

Abdel Hernández: "My future work can be synthesized in the fact that a body of basic hypotheses can be a secure instrument for the practitioner [of art] without implying that the theoretical analysis should portray, in itself, the ultimate image of reality."

Nilo Castillo: "I want to deal with everyday life and to criticize commercialized art and everything else that is in the way of the fundamental sense of art."

Adriano Buergo: "I want to stop criticizing problems, something I have done until today, and find solutions."

Erik Gómez: "I want to research why art does not reach the masses."

Lázaro Saavedra: "I want to become an unconscious and automatic bearer, telling the good and the bad with total crudeness and frankness."

Tania Bruguera: "To transform work into a personal therapy and cure, useful for others."

The incidents of 1988 and the new perception that there are "hawks and doves" (not yet reflected in the statements) helped the third generation, at least for a while, in developing strategies to affect Cuban society. The demise of the group structure brought with it a weakening of the generational barriers with the third generation (though not of its generational identity). The major exhibits of Umberto Peña and Raúl Martínez have created more contact between the third generation and these artists (the ABTV team appropriated Martínez' work for an exhibit with his help; Peña, who until recently was a myth, now is a presence). Consuelo Castañeda's approach to art started off the first projects of the ABTV artists. Torres Llorca worked on a team exhibit with Saavedra on equal footing (the show is partially dedicated to "Saint" Joseph Beuys, guided by an archeological point of view: it is found and displayed in the twenty-second century). Garciandía, with his new plays on hammer, sickle, penis, and flamingo, suddenly appears much closer to the interests of the young generation.

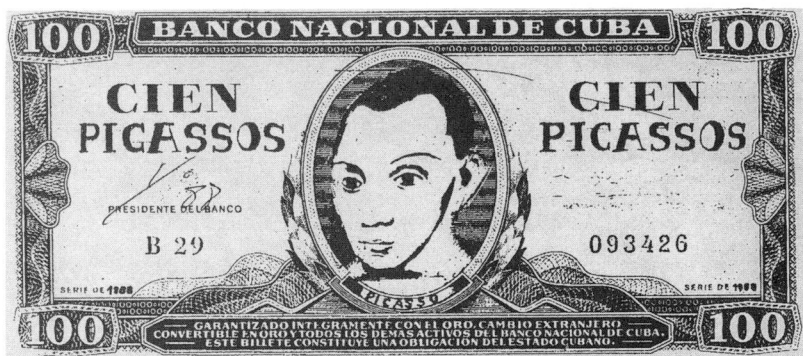

Nilo Castillo, Picasso, *1988, silkscreen, 7 × 15 cm. Private collection. Photo by Luis Camnitzer.*

The experience of censorship, the pondering about self-censorship, the (often reluctant) perception of the Ministry of Culture as a protective and encouraging institution, and the facing society as individual artists, are all factors that seem to lead to some unification.

A first reaction to the perceived limitation of their freedom of expression led the artists to organize a set of three exhibitions. The first was to be an "abstract" show, the second about still lifes, and the third about Cuban landscapes. The proposal caused dissent among the artists themselves, since many felt that the shows might be taken at face value and not as signs of distress. The proposal was eventually dropped, and, instead, artists organized a baseball team, with the idea that in this activity they might be seen as socially more useful and less subject to pressure than when making art.

Even if these exhibits never took place, they had some consequences. The one on abstract art had a review in *La Gaceta de Cuba*, with the pompous title, "La retroabstracción geométrica: un arte sin problemas: Es sólo lo que ves" ("Geometric Abstraction: An art without problems: It is only what you see"). Desiderio Navarro, author of the piece, laid out empty spaces in place of the essay, sprinkled with numbers referring to footnotes. The footnotes were fully printed and dealt with hypothetical comments of the public, references to other (critical) exhibits that included the same artists, and pseudoerudite and sarcastic remarks. The same issue also brought an article by Gerardo Mosquera, "Trece criterios sobre el nuevo arte cubano" ("Thirteen Criteria on the New Cuban Art"), in which he reaffirmed the connectedness of the young Cuban art with the Revolution.[17] The exhibit on Cuban landscape appears listed in many artists' vitae.

More productively, three projects originated by artists of the third generation (sponsored by the Ministry of Culture) were designed to give the generation a stronger voice and to help them find more rigor in their expression. The projects were the Castillo de la Fuerza cycle of exhibits, Proyecto Pilón, and the Proyecto de las Guaguas.

THE CASTILLO DE LA REAL FUERZA CYCLE

The Castillo de la Real Fuerza (Castle of the Royal Force), an old Spanish fortress, was designated as an exhibition space for contemporary art in 1989. Part of this space is used for experimental projects, and three artists (Alexis Somoza, Alejandro Aguilera, and Félix Suazo) approached the ministry with the idea of curating a series of exhibits. Originally intended to focus on sculpture, the curatorial idea has been shifted as a result of the climate created by the Esson exhibit in January 1988 to exhibits dealing with what the artists perceive as a crisis. In conjunction with the visual arts teams of the Ministry of Culture, they decided to organize a set of five exhibitions exploring iconoclasticism and how far it can be taken without losing an educational function by becoming offensive. Each exhibition was to be followed up by a public debate on these issues. Mosquera refers to these exhibitions as "a full artillery schedule."

As we will see (Chap. 6), some of these exhibitions encountered problems. As a consequence, the yearly schedule to follow, originally planned with twelve exhibits, was reduced to six. The situation worsened when half of the original exhibition space was given to a ceramics museum. These moves express a certain caution but not a shift of commitment. One-person exhibits planned include Alexis Somoza, Glexis Novoa, and Carlos Rodríguez Cárdenas, along with a major review of the art of the 1980s to be curated by Jorge Rodríguez.

PROYECTO PILÓN

The Proyecto Pilón was community-oriented with no intention of an exhibition as a final product. Pilón is a city in the extreme eastern end of Cuba. The area has cattle and produces some coffee and sugarcane. There is no television, and other comforts of modernity have barely reached the town. A group of artists (visual artists Lázaro Saavedra, Abdel Hernández, Hubert Moreno, Nilo Castillo, Alejandro López, and musician Alejandro Frómeta) decided to study the place and work with the people living there to generate art with them. With the help of sociologists and psychologists, the team determined the conditions for their work. A month's stay in 1988 allowed them to establish contact with political and religious leaders (the area is highly involved in *Santería*, with influence from Haiti), to get acquainted with the local history, and to verify that the project was welcome. Some of the topics they identified concern the contradictions between religions and revolutionary ideology, a distrust toward public institutions, and a lack of understanding of the problems of housing and food distribution.

The second step included work on theoretical proposals and setting up budgets for materials. Then, each artist would think of individual projects (some were considering the creation of billboards, others were thinking of performances, as well as using the spaces provided by schools and factories for art). Early on, the group developed a consensus that no matter what project, the official institutions (Casas de Cultura, museums, etc.) would not be employed in the implementation of their ideas.

Pilón is the town in Cuba that offers a picture closest to poverty. There are no galleries to speak of, so that the equivalent for the people is their own home and whatever decoration they have there. With the exception of some pictures of heroes, some still lifes, and some decoration on refrigerator doors, a tradition of direct painting on the walls is the primary visual form in the area. Paintings of different subjects are executed in a rather banal manner but invariably with an ornate frame painted around them. According to Saavedra, the "artists" are identified by their frames, into which they pour their personalities.

The artists entered the project aware that it was meant to be long-term, not to be abandoned halfway, and that it would seriously hinder their personal work. Meanwhile, the Ministry of Culture showed its commitment to the idea by paying them normal salaries for this work.[18] The dynamics of this project promised to create a new formalized group, the "Pilón Group." (The members liked to speak of themselves as an aesthetic platoon.) However, the political leaders in Pilón started to offer resistance to the project, and it finally had to be abandoned by 1990.

PROYECTO DE LAS GUAGUAS

Finally, 1988 also saw the development of another example of the interest in broadening the public for art. This project, which transcended the third generation, was the Proyecto de las Guaguas (the Buses Project). Artists made drawings to be produced as silkscreens that would then be affixed in the space reserved for advertising above the bus windows. The idea was to have the artwork regularly changed and to have a continuous link of communication with many people who might not otherwise be interested in art. The preliminary designs were mostly critical of the state of public transportation in Havana, and the project, though backed by the Ministry of Culture, was stopped by the administrative offices in charge of the buses.[19]

A parallel project fared no better. While the Proyecto de las Guaguas envisioned a mobile gallery of sorts, younger students of San Alejandro were concerned with the environment of the driver. Lirca Catasú (1968), a former member of Arte Calle, is preoccupied with how the decoration in the home can affect people's lives, and she decided to use the driver's taste to create an improved setting around him and in view of the passengers. The challenge was to take the elements usually used by the driver for his decoration and change them enough so that she could genuinely enjoy them without offending the driver. The project was to be designed by several students and friends and then silkscreened and installed. Lirca herself was able to decorate one bus for her graduation thesis, but she never saw it again after photographing it once. She likes to believe that the driver took the pieces home.

COMMUNICATION WITH THE PUBLIC

This united concern for communication with a public not traditionally prepared to deal with the "fine arts" with concern for the political content of this communication, is what sets the third generation most apart from the preceding ones. Aldito Menéndez is probably the artist who wrote most lucidly about the issues and problems his generation is facing. "If we are intensely preoccupied with communication, if we want to convey urgent and constructive criticism—a revolutionary SOS—we can't afford to be ambiguous, because the seriousness of the problem does not allow it. . . . We have to find new poetics, not based on ambiguity." Menéndez wrote this in a not-yet-published piece to explain why he had decided not to go through with a planned exhibition of his work (he suddenly felt that his pieces were not a valid answer for everybody in relation to the questions he was raising). He continues, saying that the young Cuban art is hampered by the contradiction of using classic modernist poetics of aperture in order to express specific problems. The artist should not be forced to have to choose between "art" and "communication." If people are not prepared to receive a message, the solution is not to resort to ambiguity but to use subtlety instead, and to go slowly.

> The degree of urgency and of ambiguity of a message are in inverse proportion. It has been agreed in the capitalist system that the poetics of ambiguity should be used because it eliminates the possibility of art becoming an efficient weapon against

the system. . . . Isn't it strange that when the art of the [capitalist] world had reached its highest revolutionary level [during the 1960s and 1970s], at its highest degree of freedom . . . it stopped, to regress several decades? . . . Artists don't exist. Art doesn't exist. There are only people who work according to the dictations of the capitalist or the communist systems. Among them, there are people who pollute the environment the same way the industrialists do.

He concludes that socialism does not yet exist since "we are not able to put into practice all the beauty and the just things we can think of." And "Che Guevara was an artist. . . . Art is a nameless trade, a secret organization, with an infinity of shapes, to which some people belong, from street sweepers to poets. That is why true artists always deny both being artists and their existence."[20]

This lengthy quote sums up the direction that the new generation is trying to pursue. Individual success is becoming less and less relevant, and communication without compromise is taking over. The traditional artist's haughtiness is disappearing for the benefit of culture-building. The subtlety of communication is not always there, and unpleasant tensions can arise from its absence, compounded with ambiguity and the traditional expectations of sectors of both public and bureaucracy. Art, for many people—as in the rest of the world—is still defined by traditional techniques, and any deviation added to misunderstood messages becomes heresy. As one functionary said, people accept the image of a penis on TV but hit the ceiling when they see it in a frame. Another functionary (who asked not to be named) synthesized the responsibility of the artists with the statement, "Talent is not enough. Many tend to trust their artistic ability without evaluating correctly the message, without analyzing its effect and consequence. If the piece is totally accomplished and its politics are debatable, one can debate the politics. If it is not an accomplished piece and the politics remain ambiguous, one is forced to discuss the piece as a failure."

In a set of interviews organized by *El Caimán Barbudo* (July 1988) exploring the question of what united the third generation, some of the answers were as follows: "To create a new culture based on aesthetic values" (Ponjuán and Rodríguez); "Art as a weapon and not as an indifferent decorative object" (Lázaro Saavedra). In the same interview, Lázaro Saavedra remarked that "today we paint the same things that formerly were not painted but spoken." He also noted that free education gave access to people coming from popular levels, thus bringing everyday life into art. Added to some ideological puzzles for these artists (the Cuban flag was hanging half-mast for three days because of the death of Emperor Hirohito, as part of Cuba's attempt to be considered a "respectable" nation among equals), this generation may be faced with no more than a heightened version of the art conundrum. The public will tend to reduce a piece of art to parameters already known, to the comfortable commonplace, while in the same piece the artist tries to open things toward the unknown.

THE INDIVIDUALS

Introduction

The artists discussed here are only some of those directly related to the "Volumen I" generation or belonging to the streams generated by that group in the generations that followed them. Much more art is being produced in Cuba today than I can discuss here, but it has a weaker linkage to the issues raised by the generations discussed in this book.

It should be noted that traditional sculpture has never been an important medium in Cuba. This is not a subjective evaluation; it becomes clear in the National Museum of Fine Arts in Havana, where paintings are hung in room after room, while sculpture is reduced to one hallway between two of the painting sections. It is also symptomatic that one painter expressed himself by saying, "Oh yes, he is one of the 'intelligent sculptors,'" referring to a member of an upcoming generation and consciously condemning the work of all preceding sculptors.[1] All this accounts for the fact that only two artists in this book, Somoza and Aguilera, are connected with this medium in relatively traditional terms.

Somehow, from the "Volumen I" group onward, painting remained painting or jumped into installations decreeing the freedom of media. Sculpture students in the ISA are mostly bypassing the traditional sculptural media and dealing with environmental problems. The installation format seems to have liberated Cuban art from much of the past by taking it out from traditional technical divisions. While shaped by a familiarity with foreign installations, the format served as a new starting point. Although much of the art does refer to art problems, it usually does so in the context of other, broader issues.

As in Chapter 1, the "Kitsch," "Afro-Cubanism," "Nationalism," and "Individualism" categories will be kept to organize the artists. I refer to the corresponding introductions for three of those terms in that chapter. The one for "Nationalism" will appear here. Again it should be kept in mind that most Cuban artists may fit into more than one group or may have shifted during their evolution. Cuenca, for example, who for many years was concerned with perceptual problems and abstract aesthetics, is putting his previous experience to work on fashion and kitsch and, lately, also on national issues.

KITSCH

Arturo Cuenca

Cuenca (1955) was not part of the "Volumen I" exhibit; however, he is generally considered not only part of that generation but also as one of the artists who was most instrumental in shaping this Cuban decade. For some years the most rigid Cuban conceptualist, his interest moved toward research about taste and fashion, including kitsch itself, in relation to perception and cognition. His interdisciplinary interest produced much excessively hermetic writing, but more importantly, very interesting artwork.

While Garciandía's approach to kitsch is strategic and analytic, Cuenca's approach is anthropological. Cuenca's interest in kitsch is the result of a more recent development in his work and linked to his long-standing interest in perception. After a short period of photo-realist painting that quickly led him into photography, he focused on how reality is perceived and how the spectator "sees" the art object. A realist painting from 1979, *El futuro como espacio* (*The Future as Space*), a visual collage of different vanishing points blended into one spectator's view, already showed his theoretical concerns. His use of photo-realism in the 1970s was for conceptual purposes.

Each Cuenca exhibit is accompanied by catalogues with long explanations of his theories, which become an important part of his work. In fact, he considers those texts an intrinsic part of his art. In the catalogue of a 1983 exhibit in Havana's Museum of Fine Arts, called *El espectador*, he explained some of his ideas, separating three-dimensional from two-dimensional vision as they relate to art. According to Cuenca, the three-dimensional art object is an intrinsic part of the space surrounding it.

Perception is neither absolute nor limited but is a constant sense of infinity given by a mixture of sensorial and conceptual elements where a two-dimensional art image conforms to the retina's way of registering information. Thus, the "window" quality normally attributed to a painting is really part of the spectator's visual makeup, and the Renaissance use of perspective is no more than the identification and overlapping of the viewer's convention with that of the artwork.

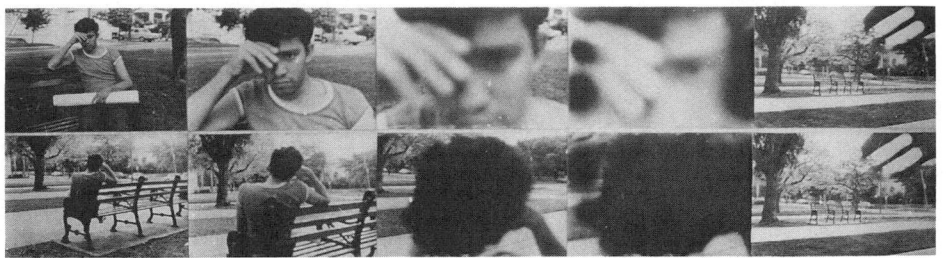

Arturo Cuenca, Conocimiento (Knowledge), *1983, silver gelatin photographs, 60 × 200 cm. Collection of the artist. Photo by Sebastian Elizondo.*

Cuenca cites the Larousse dictionary for a definition of landscape: "Fragment of space offered to vision." He extends this to be "the structure of a space possible from the viewpoint of the subject." Accordingly, Cuenca uses this concept of "landscape" as a bridge for the different implications of two-dimensional and three-dimensional perception. "Landscape" becomes a "total-possible-sculpture" shaped by the "image-landscape" of the viewer.[2]

For Cuenca this theoretical platform is more important than the actual visual work. Minimal prodding of Cuenca elicits lengthy, dense, and passionate lectures. Meanwhile, the visual work often, and mostly unfairly, runs the risk of being interpreted as a collection of didactic illustrations. His theories give him a seed to conceive the work. When he superimposes text about his theory onto window panes in front of fragments of reality framed by the window (1983), he illustrates the idea in a tautological fashion but also creates a haunting situation where perception is made rational and thought processes are made visible. Like much other good mainstream conceptual and postconceptual work, Cuenca's pieces engage the viewer in a participatory experience.

Since 1983 and for several years, Cuenca has increasingly used photographic media, synthesizing all the desired space qualifications onto one surface. In a series of large photographs titled *Conocimiento* (*Knowledge*) and exhibited in the First Biennial of Havana, a house slowly broke through the soil until it stood fully on the ground in the last image. With a sense of undoing an earthquake and the evocation of giving birth, the piece also hinted at the destruction of the horizon as a visual limit. Photography, for Cuenca, is "the external conscience of man, the materialization of his conscience."[3]

Interested in his own personal brand of metaphysics, Cuenca may very well have been until recently the artist most oblivious of problems

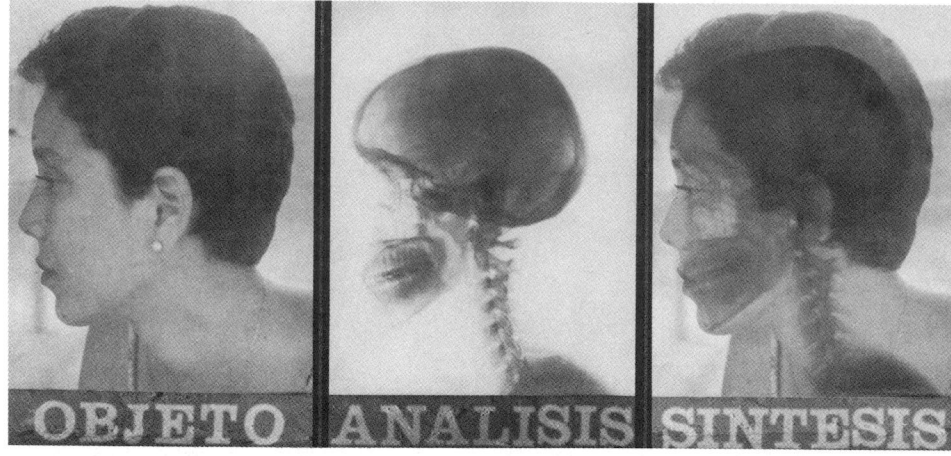

Arturo Cuenca, Conocimiento: objeto, análisis, síntesis (Knowledge: Object, Analysis, Synthesis), *1983, handcolored silver gelatin photographs and X-ray, 40 × 60 cm. Collection of Ninart Centro de Cultura, Mexico. Photo by Arturo Cuenca.*

about nationality and cultural identity in Cuba.[4] His honest belief that his generation has internalized the revolutionary process, and thus that anything he does is part of that process, allowed him to neglect thinking specifically about those issues for some time. In 1986 when he started addressing problems related to fashion and kitsch, his attention shifted to subjects more pointedly related to Cuba, but without losing sight of his previous work. "When I work I try to take your image of reality and change it into mine. But I also need to transform space into ideas. I think that the human being does not have pure sensations, and if that is true I make use of cultural prejudices and already-established categories so that you, the spectator, look through the hole in my work and see the world. Sometimes it is I who look through the spectator."[5]

On the occasion of an exhibit in 1987 (in the Centro Provincial de Artes Plásticas y Diseño), Cuenca asked in his catalogue, "Why is it that science-fiction artists never anticipate the art of the future? Why isn't there an 'aesthetic-fiction'?" In the same piece, he proposed to understand modernism as all that has had a relationship with capitalism since the middle of the nineteenth century, and to use the term *contemporary* for the transitional culture that "contemporizes" two antagonistic cultural systems in "peaceful coexistence." He wrote, "Many qualitative aspects of contemporaneity are still waiting for a harmonic realization. The only context that has the conditions to transform them into a cul-

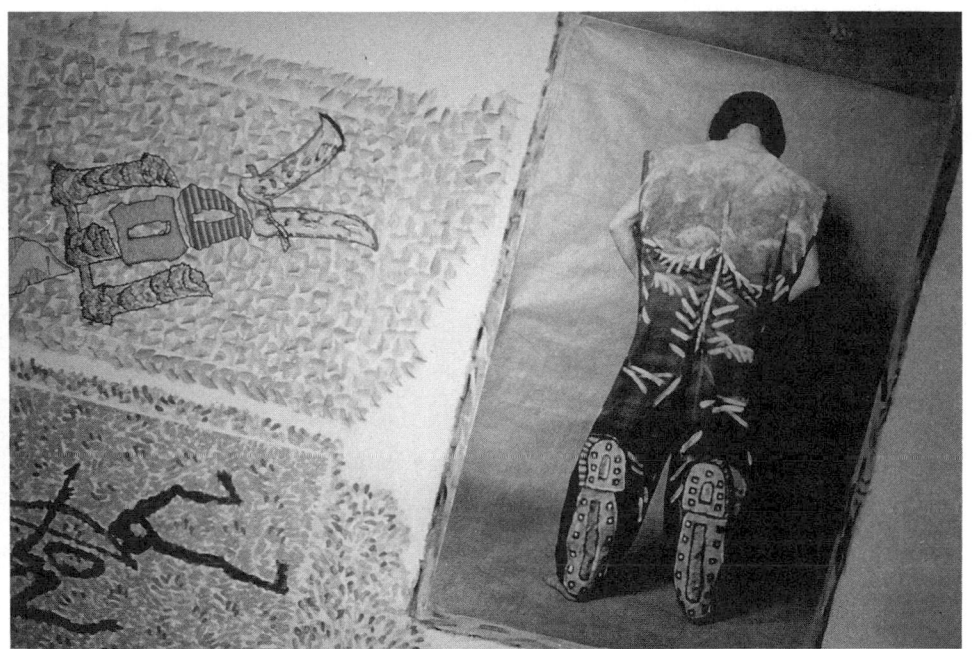

Arturo Cuenca, Estética de la moda (Aesthetics of Fashion) *(detail), 1986. Installation at the Second Biennial of Havana, 400 × 400 cm. Photo by Luis Camnitzer.*

tural system is socialism, whose revolution is essentially an anthropological one."

Distinguishing *Fashion* (as the cycling of taste) from *fashion* (in its restricted garment meaning), he considers the first the phenomenon that best describes the "economist anthropological essence" of the social system in the capitalist market. In *fashion,* on the other hand, form as function minimizes the importance of past and future and defines an empirical formalistic attitude, devoid of any content, which climaxes in present postmodernism.

As a consequence, Cuenca wants to achieve the "universal theoretical generalization of aesthetics in the praxis of an individual work of art . . . achieving not an aesthetic that describes art, but one that proposes itself as a new code for anthropological communication. . . . I would like to revolutionize fashion by means of a theoretical platform whose essence is fashion as a system of content, emitting a complex discourse of symbolic, anecdotal, and conceptual meanings that becomes a new artistic meaning."

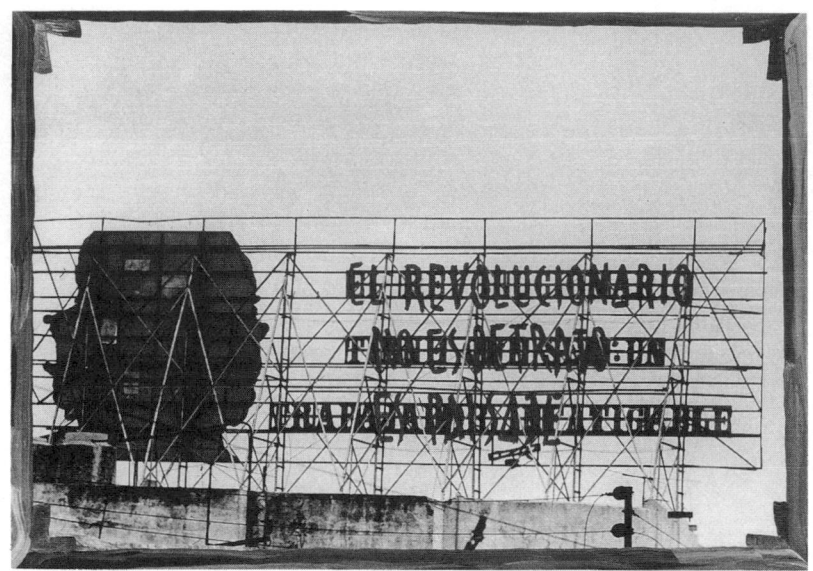

Arturo Cuenca, untitled, with text: "The revolutionary is not a portrait, he is a landscape," 1987–1988, handpainted silver gelatin photograph, 50 × 60 cm. Private collection. Photo by Luis Camnitzer.

It is questionable if Cuenca's art has ever accomplished the complexity that he strives for in his writing, although his work does not preclude the possibility of success in the future. His work is not always totally satisfying but, over the decade, it has systematically come closer to his writing. His ambitious piece for the Second Biennial of Havana tried to juggle all these ingredients into one major work.

A large wall installation, it comprised photographs of models with garments designed by Cuenca (bearing images of foreshortened parts of the body to indicate, for example, a kneeling position, although in fact the model is standing) and small paintings of humanoids formed by the letters of the word *moda* (fashion), which had painterly effects evoking U.S. "pattern" painting of the 1970s. But, despite wonderful fragments, the piece did not manage to hold together.

In a series of hand-colored photographs, Cuenca integrated the word *kitsch* into animal furs. The word becomes part of the pattern, but it also becomes the essence decoded and revealed once the fur is transmuted into a translucent veil. While most of the other Cuban artists working on issues related to taste allow their work to become "contaminated" with the tradition of the subject matter (work about kitsch becomes somewhat kitschy), Cuenca tries to keep an aesthetic distance. If some of the work

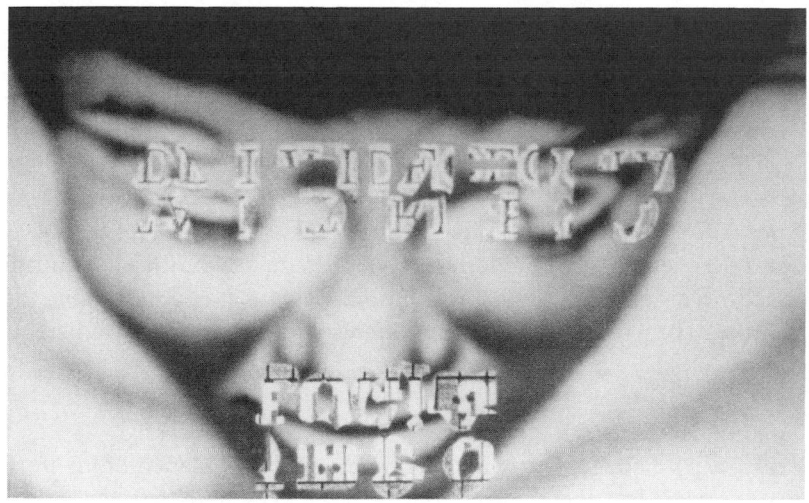

Arturo Cuenca, Ciencia e ideología (Science and Ideology), *1989, acrylic on canvas, 70 × 110 cm. Collection of the artist. Photo by Arturo Cuenca.*

is reminiscent of kitsch, it is so because he took what he perceived as being irreducible units and arranged them to then create a new entity— a product of dissection. The work represents an unemotional postmortem kitsch that, rather than equipping the viewer for perception, helps plan a strategy for perception. Considering that art should become "an objective and natural process, unquestioned by cultural subjectivisms of any aesthetic tendencies, it seems that Cuenca intuits changes in the basic function of art and not in the superstructure."[6]

In 1988, Cuenca started working on a new series based on a billboard about Che Guevara. The original billboard, portraying Che's face in a huge dimension, bears the words, "The revolutionary has to be a tireless worker" as a slogan made with cut-out letters. Cuenca photographed the billboard from the back (the outline of the portrait is a strong enough icon to be recognizable without the information of the face) and wrote over the structure of the letters his own slogan: "The revolutionary is not a portrait: he is a landscape." An elaborate ornamental and kitschy frame is painted around the photograph, synthesizing his concerns about landscape and kitsch with an interest in politics.

In April 1989, Cuenca had an exhibit in the Castillo de la Real Fuerza cycle: "Ciencia e ideología" ("Science and Ideology"). The fortress itself became the symbol of ideology, in its representation of transient interests: defense building, museum, cafeteria. The outside reality symbolized science in its technological presence. It was perceived on photographs that, hung on the walls, portrayed what would be seen if the walls were not there. Cuenca painted shadows of himself using tools on several places and then performed dances reminiscent of Kabuki in front of them to have the shadows of his movement interact with the painted one. Since that exhibit, Cuenca has been residing in Mexico, painting a series of canvases with the title *Naturaleza moderbunda*. *Moderbunda*, a contraction of modern and moribund, expresses his vision of the death of modernism and postmodernism as a platform to launch a "socialism based on an anthropological revolution."[7] Somewhat apocalyptic, the paintings seem to be a transition in Cuenca's work into an unpredictable future.

José Franco Codinach

Franco's main subject matter is fur patterns. The relation of his work with kitsch is less obvious and may be more debatable than that of the other artists discussed, since the patterns he works with can also be interpreted as painterly formalistic speculations.

It is not yet fully understood how fur patterns occur, and present theories are still based on the 1952 speculations of Alan Turing (of Turing machine and computer fame) about morphogenes in a reaction-diffusion model where small spatial disturbances are created that allow a pattern to grow.[8] The growth pattern is not alien to what can happen on the surface of a canvas guided by the abstract inquisition of a painter, and Franco comes from an abstract tradition. But in his work, Franco has always had a humorous streak, incorporating foreign elements into an otherwise consistent pattern.

What had started as a way of possessing the space defined by the limits of the canvas evolved into the creation of fake surfaces. The references became not live animals rendered through realistic devices but twice-removed abstractions from the original model through the use of imitation furs as a primary source.

Franco's work reconstructs reality through the arrangement of formal stereotypes derived from a preexisting imitation. The units forming the totality have an abstract quality and do not imitate the model. The surface, often broken by a three-dimensional addition functioning as a tail, becomes the animal's rear end, thus setting itself apart from what at first might appear merely decorative. One of his pieces in the Second Biennial, an installation, portrayed the back legs of a cow where the pink udder merged into the black and white pattern. Unusual in his work, the piece included a pail, alluding to an action beyond the animal itself. While not totally resolved, the construction stressed the more latent whimsical aspects in his other works. Franco creates what amounts to a

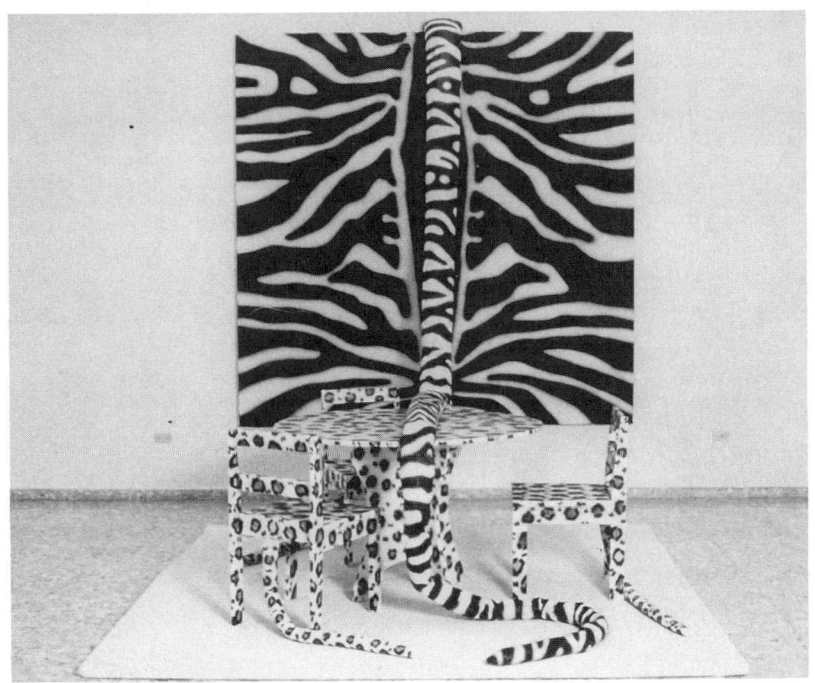

José Franco, Cobra y leopardos somos todos (We All Are Cobras and Leopards), *1989, installation, 250 × 300 × 350 cm. Collection of the artist. Photo by José Franco.*

metareality parallel to the one of cartoons and life made out of plastics, and informed by both.

However, Franco's work does not have a theoretical platform. This creates some dangers for his way of painting. Seduced by the painterly effect, he sometimes wanders away from his more solid criticism of taste to enter into playful exercises. Pleasant to the eye and with improved craftsmanship, his latest work flirts with recreating the pleasure of a hide on the floor, instead of making a statement about the implications of that pleasure and its substitutes. Franco's work is increasingly closer to plain hedonistic painting, losing its edge and keeping only its power of attraction.

Nevertheless, when he delves in installations, he seems to be on firmer ground. His *Cobra y leopardos somos todos* (*We Are All Cobras and Leopards*), presented at the Third Biennial of Havana, regained some lost ground. A set of four life-size chairs with leopard skin and tails, surrounding a leopard table bearing a tail coming from a zebra-covered wall, produced a piece both hilariously funny and elegant.

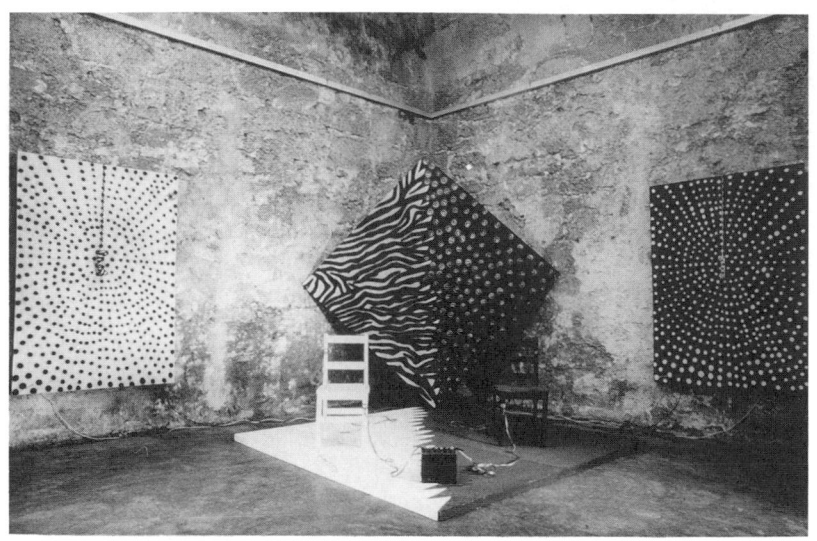

José Franco, En el día natural (On a Natural Day), *1990, installation. Collection of the artist. Photo by José Franco.*

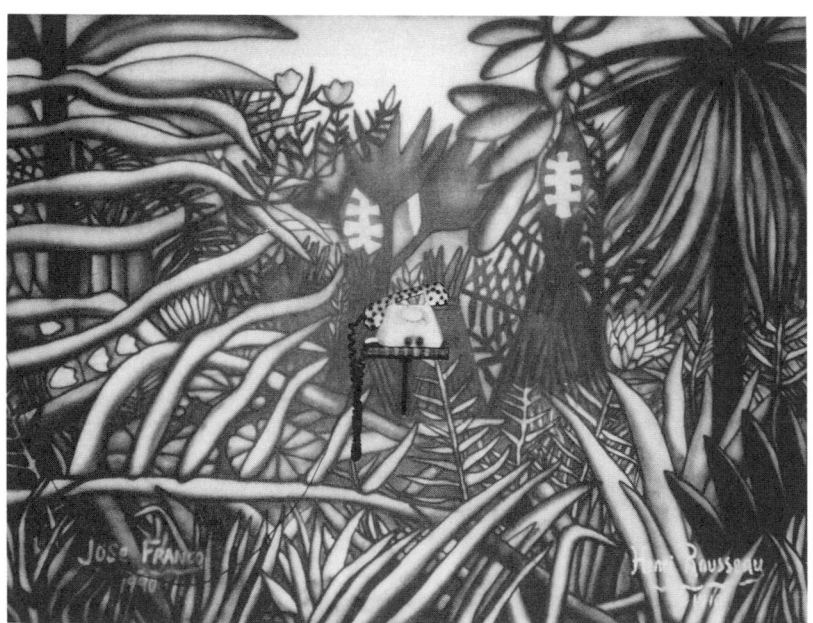

José Franco, Conversación 1910–1990 (Conversation 1910–1990), *1990, acrylic on canvas, 150 × 200 cm. Collection of the artist. Photo by Luis Camnitzer.*

AFRO-CUBANISM

Magdalena Campos

Campos belongs to the second generation of artists and is among the youngest in that group. Born in 1959, she graduated from the ISA in 1985. Campos believes that myths show more erotic freedom than what is offered by actual practice. It is this freedom she continually looks for in her work. Originally a music student, she was guided into art by one of her teachers in the town of Matanzas. Her beginnings were under the influence of Picasso's Blue Period, and it took her until her third year at the ISA to work with abstract shapes. These shapes, in turn, began to take on heavy connotations, oriented toward both sexuality and *Santería*.

Campos' grandmother had been strongly involved in *Santería*, but the tradition was interrupted with her parents, and today she is unable to trace back to her African roots. Unlike the case of many other Cuban artists, her interest in *Santería* evolved purely from artistic pursuits. However, the process acquired such an intensity that she now has come to wonder about the power of her grandmother's spirit. Nevertheless, she continues to define herself as a materialist in the Marxist sense.

Campos does not see any conflict between *Santería* and Marxism. *Santería* may expand the frontiers of Marxism and enrich it, and Marxism, in order to function in Cuba, has to take account of all the traditions that define Cuban reality.[9] As a result, her work becomes an ongoing process of synthesis. By using herself as a center, these objective tensions are made meaningful and are softened with a personal erotic veil.

Because Campos happens to be black, the immediate and simplistic assumption, especially outside Cuba, has always been that she works in an Afro-Cuban mode. However, this is only a recent and coincidental development in her work. Interested in myths like many of the other Cuban artists, she saw parallels between some stories of the Bible and of the Mayan Popol Vuh. Her first exhibit, called "Acoplamientos" ("Couplings"), in 1985, had works in this direction. In a text (in fact, a poem) written for the catalogue, she stated: "I select the images with which I reorganize the myth, the symbols with which I construct these 'couplings'; a drop of saliva extracted from the Popol Vuh loses its innocently fecundating character and transforms into a spermatic drop, which lives as an object in its entirety . . . [The] forms allude to and simultaneously somehow deny the myth."[10]

Campos' selection of myths is always guided by a sense of eroticism. It was this sense that eventually led her to investigate African and Afro-Cuban traditions. Spears and shields become bearers of sexual significance, as in *Cinturón de castidad* (*Chastity Belt*, [1985]), a piece she de-

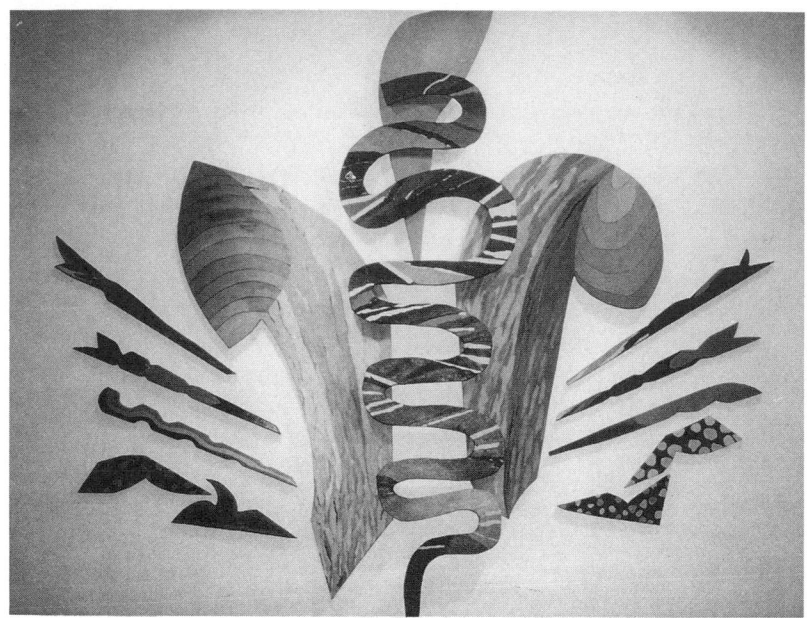

Magdalena Campos, Anticonceptivo (Contraceptive), *1987, acrylic on canvas, 350 × 350 cm. Collection of the artist. Photo by Luis Camnitzer.*

scribes as "based on the idea of oppression of feminine sexuality."[11] Stories about *Santería* deities are used as inspiration for parables about fertility. For example, Yemaya, the goddess of the flowing waters, one of her favorites, dies when her abdomen explodes and releases fifteen new deities.

Primarily abstract, her installations formed by shaped canvases have sexual connotations, often clarified by the titles. Her use of abstraction is more oriented toward the possibilities of ambiguity than toward formalist composition. The lack of definition of squiggly elements thus allows a shape to survive as a form—a snake, a sperm—or helps by providing contextual forms, (for example, a penis). Expanding her statement, some of the forms she employed during the late 1980s were based on intrauterine devices. The ambiguity of the abstraction with the literary aura given by the possible meanings makes the knowledge of the context a crucial element for the full perception of the work, which, otherwise, could be unjustly misunderstood as decoration. In her own mind many pieces are detailed descriptions of sperm, Fallopian tubes, vaginal space, and pubic hair. As a consequence, she dismisses any parallel to abstract work by other artists as a misunderstanding of her own art.[12]

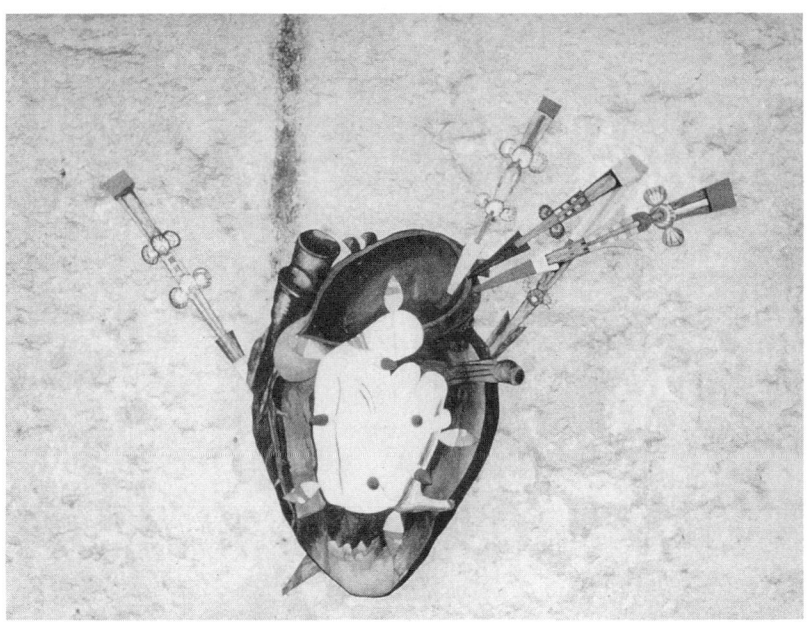

Magdalena Campos, La ofrenda de la propia sangre (The Offer of One's Own Blood), *1989, mixed media, 300 × 250 cm. Collection of the artist. Photo by Magdalena Campos.*

Over the years, Campos' work has acquired a pantheistic quality in which parts of her body appear blended with parts of the world. Together they signify myths and deities. In this mixture, symbols lose their hierarchy. The water "separating everything" (as in her 1990 piece, where body and house are cut, forming a triptych with the separator) is no more than one object among many, rather than the violent actor the narrative of the work implies. The viewer's attention is attracted by the use of symmetry and centering, but not by size or accentuation.

The abstract discipline of Campos has led her to create a layout system that contains and expresses her narrative ideology. She manages to do so either without resorting to overt literal descriptiveness or, when doing so, without losing the abstract rigor. Her narrative ideology is a product of the stories provided by the many cultural streams that converged in Cuba over the centuries. Her form of abstraction is a product of the Western legacy in Cuba, a synthesis she had been working on in a relatively intellectualized fashion.

According to her own view, Campos' latest work has lost some of this intellectualism and stressed more her emotions. Aided by readings about Frida Kahlo, "in this latest work I felt less of a pleasure in intellec-

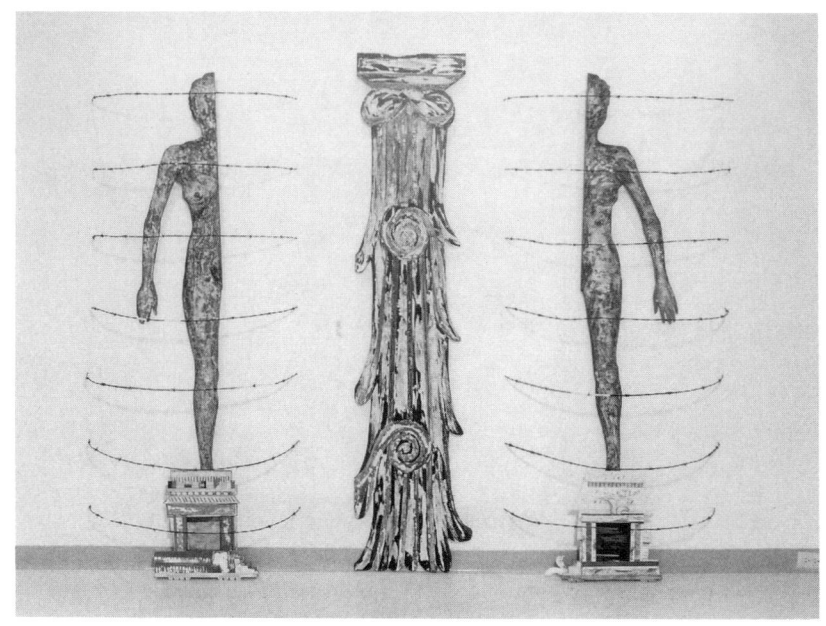

Magdalena Campos, Todo es separado por el agua. Incluso mi cerebro, mi corazón, mi sexo, mi hogar. (Everything Is Separated by Water. Including My Brain, My Heart, My Sex, My House.), *1990, mixed media, 180 × 240 cm. Collection of the artist. Photo by Magdalena Campos.*

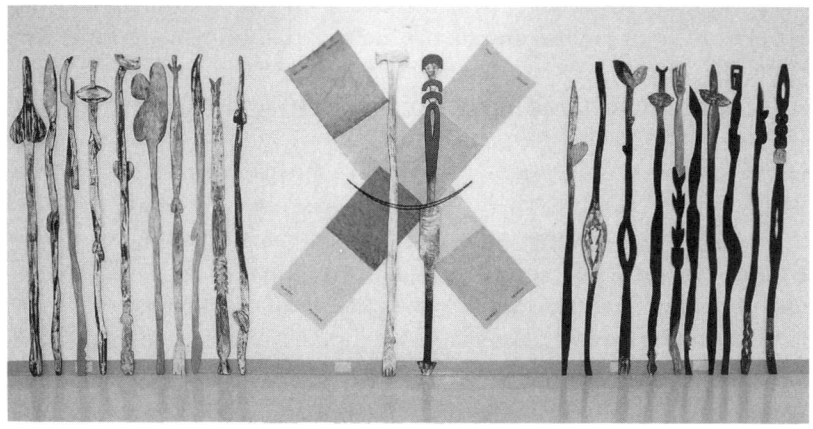

Magdalena Campos, Hablando de árboles, pino negro, pino blanco, especie endémica (Speaking of Trees, Black Pine, White Pine, Endemic Species), *1990, installation. Collection of the artist. Photo by Magdalena Campos.*

tual discourses and more of a desire to let my feelings run."[13] This shift in her work is accompanied by an increasingly feminist focus in her thought process. She is now revising her views of her past production in this light and honing her strategies for the future.

No matter which of the possible multiple readings one may choose, Campos' works act as unified containers for Cuban everyday eclecticism. Contradicting forces, beliefs, and cultures are placed into a continuum, their potential explosion tamed into communication.

Marta María Pérez Bravo

Also born in 1959, Pérez Bravo graduated from the ISA a year earlier than Campos. Her work is resolved in photographs that act as documents for carefully constructed situations. She employs a process of "photographic thinking," in which work is conceived to be formalized into the confines of a photograph, rather than using the camera to record found reality.

Pérez Bravo's connection with the Afro-Cuban tradition is more indirect and anthropological. The Afro-Cuban tradition is all around her, and she not only cannot ignore it, but she feels she must respect and record it. Her interest initially was oriented toward peasant traditions and superstitions, many of which in turn have Afro-Cuban influence. In the mid-1980s the superstitions addressed by her work were connected primarily with water and with the protection of the harvest from the weather.

Water is an important element in Cuban folklore, not only through Yemaya, the *Santería* goddess, but also through the "Mother of the Waters." According to different versions, the "Mother" ranges from a snakelike creature to a fairylike motherly old woman, to a mushroom-shaped thing that inhibits water from drying, to an entity able to summon tornadoes ("cloud tails"). A myth of both African and Amerindian origin, the "Mother" can be a killer or a benefactor.[14] Pérez Bravo took the benign interpretation and used forms of snakelike streams, which she built out of shredded paper and integrated into the landscape, to then document photographically. The snakes are no more than two yards long, but they appear monumental in the photographs. Text added to the photographs consists of quotes from women talking about the "Mother" ("There it is where it appears. I have never dared to look when the water whirls"). She also used shredded paper to recreate peasant rites in the form of crosses in the fields, which, according to tradition, are made (with ashes placed by the left hand and deposited without looking back) to fend off disasters that might affect the crop. Phrases

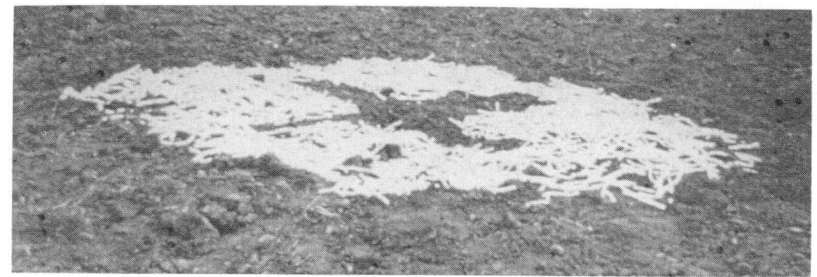

Marta María Pérez Bravo, installation with shredded paper, 1983, silver gelatin photograph. Collection of the artist. Photo by Marta Pérez.

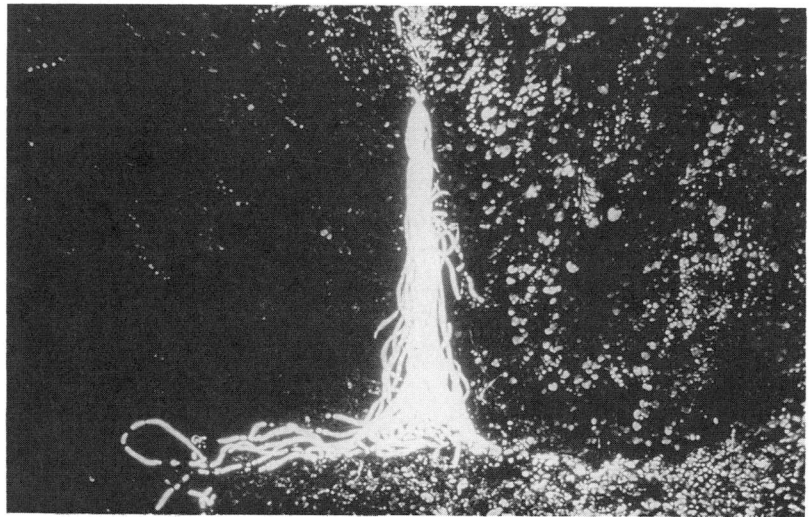

Marta María Pérez Bravo, Cascada (Waterfall), *installation with shredded paper, 1984. Photo by Marta Pérez.*

from the text include "I cut you, cloud," "without a knife or dagger," "with the nine words," and "sacrament of the altar."

Cuban photographer María Eugenia Haya (Marucha) considers both the peasant pieces and Pérez Bravo's recreations to be installations complemented by nature.[15] Some pieces were purely visual. Again using shredded paper, she built a series of cascades in the forest to be seen later only in her photographs.

In 1986 Pérez Bravo, who is married to Garciandía, had twins. The process of pregnancy was a difficult one with long periods of bed rest. Added to birthing and nursing, the experience led to a series of photo-

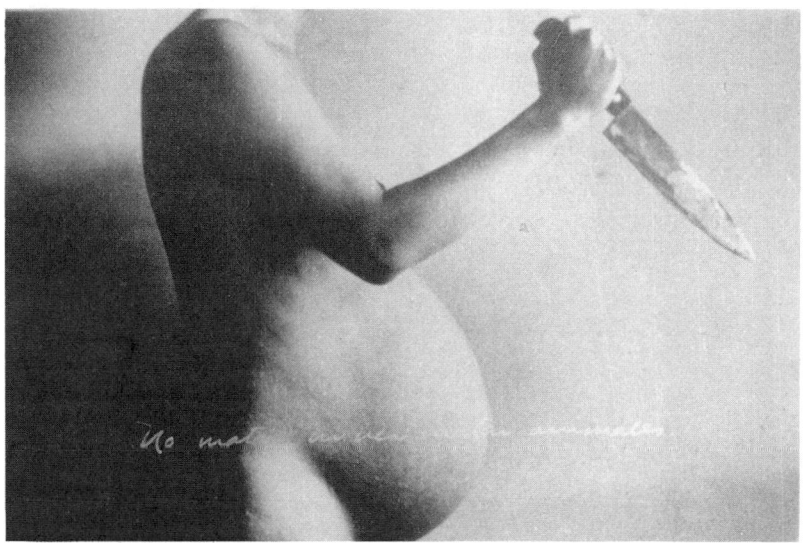

Marta María Pérez Bravo, No matar ni ver matar animales (Neither to Kill nor to Watch Animals Being Killed), *1986, silver gelatin photograph, 24 × 30 cm. Collection of the artist.*

graphic works in which her body becomes the new landscape. It is depicted as ravaged by sucking dolls, scars, and knives, demystifying motherhood and bringing it into the context of the actual physical violence undergone in real life.

This work, reminiscent of the Italian artist Gina Pane and Brazilian Iole Freitas (both unknown to her) constitutes what may be interpreted by a foreigner as Cuba's strongest feminist art today. For Pérez Bravo, however, the work is no more than an autobiographical piece that also records many of Cuba's old wives' tales and *Santería* beliefs about conception. By letting herself be photographed during the pregnancy process she hoped to give expression to feelings that superstitions, fears, and shame would keep locked in other women. She does not perceive the work or herself as feminist.[16] Feminism for her would be a limiting label with a danger of forcing her into pamphlet art. Instead, she likes to believe that a man "under the same conditions" would produce the same kind of work.

A subsequent series, using her face and the little baby dolls, depicts different feelings. Her head lying on a pillow, with a brick on her ear and the two little dolls on the brick, represents *Prejuicios* (*Prejudices*). Her face covered with half dried mud and the dolls covering her eyes is *Miedo a la muerte* (*Fear of Death*).

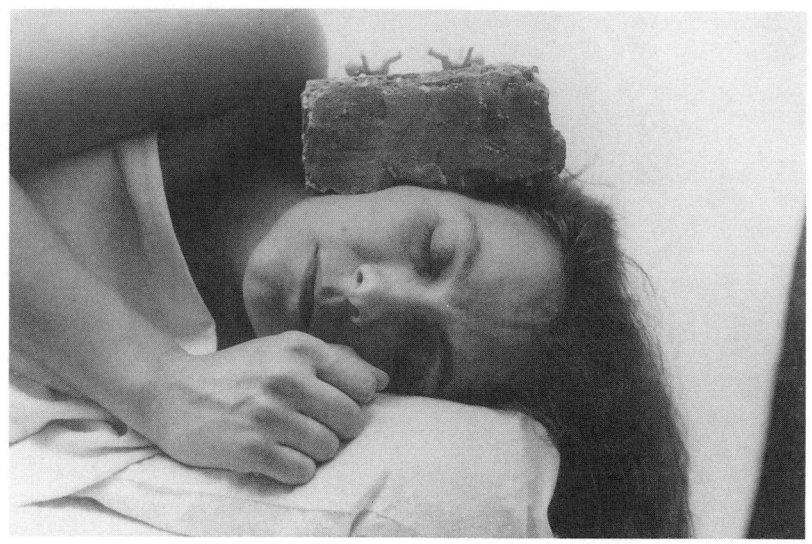

Marta María Pérez Bravo, Prejuicios (Prejudices), *1987, silver gelatin photograph, 24 × 30 cm. Collection of the artist.*

About both series, "Concebir" ("To Conceive") (1985–1986) and "Memorias de nuestro bebé" ("Memories of Our Baby") (1987), she wrote,

> I attempt to develop through the use of both suggestive and precise images a parody of an album, not to recall moments, but rather constants charged with contradictory elements— strength and weakness, sleep and waking, etc.—along with other elements that might be suggested by the images themselves, such as the sensuality of the strong sex, to the physical violence childbirth itself implies and the sensation of sacrifice before the image of a scar, to name some examples. In other words, it will become an album of images of carnal categories independent of feelings; that is, the material recording of maternity, and in some way the questioning of the spectator with regard to what lies beyond that "mission."[17]

A third, more recent series, "Cultos paralelos" ("Parallel Cults") (1990), transforms her body into a place of miracles and rituals. (Mosquera refers to her as working on her body as an altar.)[18] She lifts her blouse to discover her body covered with ceiba tree spines, or she leans over two *Santería* cauldrons, fitting her breasts into them as offerings while protecting the two dolls that represent her twins.

Over the years her work has slowly accumulated to form a violently powerful popular illustrated dictionary in which the imagery gives a new life to eroded words—words that should not just stand for, but should *be* emotional and psychological forces and processes and that are able to absorb even the most uninitiated viewer.

NATIONALISM

While most of the artists in contemporary Cuba are concerned with *Cubanía* or Cubanism, it is approached primarily by the artists of the third generation, who are trying to discard international art values or are using them as a background, providing a counterpoint for what they consider to be their real task. The "real task" is not always explicitly put in terms of nationalism, but it often shows as an ingredient in the problems and subject matter chosen for their art. In this sense, there is a radical departure from the attempted nationalism in the late 1920s,[19] the later work of Amelia Peláez,[20] and Cuban art of the 1970s, which treated art with great respect, maintaining its "sacred" character.

In the 1980s Cuban art opens to vernacular humor, language, and irreverence coupled with the political concerns of the rectification process. Thus, issues become of primary importance and relegate formalist speculation to a second plane. Cuban art has become unafraid of topicality and rejects the wish for survival in posterity. The image may survive no longer than the same short instant of a flippant remark. The cultural impact, devoid of pomposity, may be smaller than that of an "ambitious" piece of art and may move culture a shorter distance than traditional art. But the artists are aware that this short distance belongs to what they consider the correct direction, and they see it as more useful. Misspelling, as discussed before, prevalent in much of the writing, becomes a symbol for this tendency toward the ephemeral. The visual components are also often "misspelled," and the lack of permanent perfection becomes one more element in the constellation of aggression.

It is, of course, debatable whether or not, in a long historical perspective, nationalist art still makes sense today. A long-range view may tempt us to think that, once the whole world is immersed in the same technological communication system where time lags in information are totally erased, the values stemming from this progress-oriented dynamic will totally dislodge local identities. The passage of time seems to have made events acceptable that at a particular moment were seen as ethical cataclysms connected with nationalism. Armenians seeking revenge today for the Turkish genocide are seen as extreme and obsolete fanatics. Any Colombian wanting to fight for the reannexation of Panama, or any Mexican demanding the return of Texas, would be seen as a

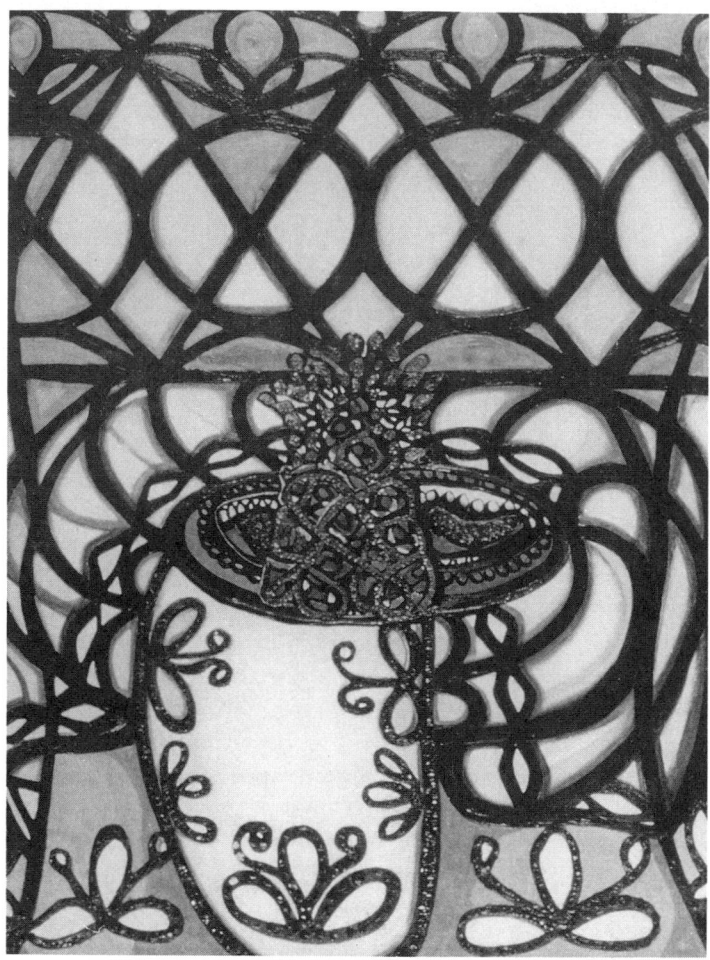

Amelia Peláez, Naturaleza muerta con piña (Still Life with Pineapple), *1967, oil on canvas, 119 × 92 cm. Museo Nacional de Bellas Artes, Havana.*

kook. Since "progress" and historical pragmatism in this sense are Western values, it is no accident that good mainstream art is supposed to be depoliticized and as timeless as possible. These values fly in the face of the drive for identity, which is characteristic of self-asserting cultures. For some groups and in given historical moments, nationalism is still the link with identity—i.e., Palestinians and Native Americans—and has to be respected as such.

Regardless of what the actual future will bring in terms of a world society, at present internationalist values have not completely permeated peripheral cultures. Local ethics, and many political beliefs that still derive from those ethical beliefs, provide a platform for an aesthetic language that, because of colonial influences, never was allowed to develop freely. And regardless of what the international future holds, to develop this language is absolutely necessary if a peripheral culture is to integrate into any global culture as an equal partner.

Cuba is carefully balancing its ideological internationalism with that nationalist sense, which it perceives as a crucial tool for survival. The Fourth Biennial of Havana is titled "The Challenge to Colonization"; thus, even when not espousing a narrow-minded nationalism, it raises the questions and warnings about a passive acceptance of indiscriminate internationalism. It recognizes that underdevelopment cannot afford the luxury of the internationalism of developed countries, based on the sense of security offered by having nonthreatened cultures.

In this regard, Cuba may be functioning on a slightly different level than the rest of the Latin America countries. The term *cultural deterritorialization* is becoming common, and the notion that popular nationalism is an unrealistic romantic concept is taking hold among sociologists. External debt is seen as a new web to define identities.[21] Meanwhile, in Cuba some believe that the competition of cultures leads to deculturalization on the periphery. The culture with the highest power of distribution of information will prevail. The antidote to this is seen in popular expression as a form of nationalism.[22]

It is premature to affirm that Cuba will achieve the level of "equal partnership," although the chances clearly seem better than for the rest of Latin America. It is also premature to affirm that the resulting art, if it ever happens, will come from this "nationalist" stream in Cuban art. It is more likely that it will be the product of the cross-pollination of all the streams discussed in this chapter.

Meanwhile, the outlook of all of Cuban art is changing, particularly due to the input of the youngest artists. Exhibits are organized around subjects related to how information enters Cuba and is processed by Cuban artists. "No por mucho madrugar amanece más temprano" ("Dawn Does Not Come Sooner by Waking Up Earlier") was the title of a group show addressing many of these issues, including plagiarism and influences caused by the influx of foreign information. The title satirized the tendency to believe that with less time passed between the execution of an original and its copy, the latter acquires more credibility. One of the pieces (by artist José Luis Alonso), symbolizing the point of the exhibit, was a mock-up of Eco's book *The Name of the Rose*, with the author's name changed to "The Echo of Umberto." Another typical event was an officially sponsored mural painted as part of a ceremony during a mass rally honoring the birthday of Che Guevara in June 1988. Members of the third generation were invited to conceive and execute a project. Their solution was to paint, in huge letters, the word *MEDITAR* (*MEDITATE*).

Tonel

Tonel is the pseudonym for Antonio Eligio Fernández (1958). Cartoonist and art critic, graduated in art history in 1982, he merges all those activities into his artwork. Tonel is one of the few prominent Cuban artists from 1980 onward who was not trained in an art school. His high school studies were at the Escuela Media Vocacional Lenin, a school created in 1973 for students with an average above 86 and oriented toward science. With 4,500 students, there were art facilities to satisfy secondary interests, and it was there that Tonel defined his future. Eventually interested in entering the ISA, he was dissuaded by one faculty member and chose art history instead. As a consequence he became a respected art critic who contributes regularly to the magazine *Revolución y Cultura*.

Tonel started doing newspaper cartoons during 1980. His initial style was reminiscent of sloppy versions of Saul Steinberg drawings that were well liked by the "Volumen I" artists. His contact with the artists and the trip that led to the creation of the Grupo Hexágono shifted his creation into a more ambitious artistic context, placing him squarely into the second generation.

Tonel credits Consuelo Castañeda with helping him develop a certain mental rigor, but his aesthetics come from the long tradition of Cuban populist humor, and the work of Chago (a subject for his theoretical research and with whom he exhibited in 1981) became his primary influence. Chago exemplified a continuation of Martí's example of combining politics with creative activities, but he was also intriguing for his ability to work on the fringes of art, in areas not validated by the fine-art tradition. Tonel stopped focusing on the newspaper and magazine conditions for publication in his work and explored those same fringes.

While Tonel's work often includes kitsch, he is not interested in its typological implications but only in kitsch as a component of vernacular expression. He records popular ingenuity and humor as expressed in language, particularly in the use of multiple meanings of words leading to double entendres. *Dos Mojones* (*Two Milestones* [1985]), plays on the two meanings of the word in Spanish, *milestone* and *turd*, bringing to the foreground the lost funny metaphorical value of its second meaning. *Cumbres del Arte* (*Summits of Art* [1984–1985]) bears a painter's palette on the top of a mountain, illustrating the sentence in its most banal interpretation possible. In *Pingüino ordinario*, an "ordinary penguin" flaunting a human penis plays on the intricacies of the word *ordinary*.

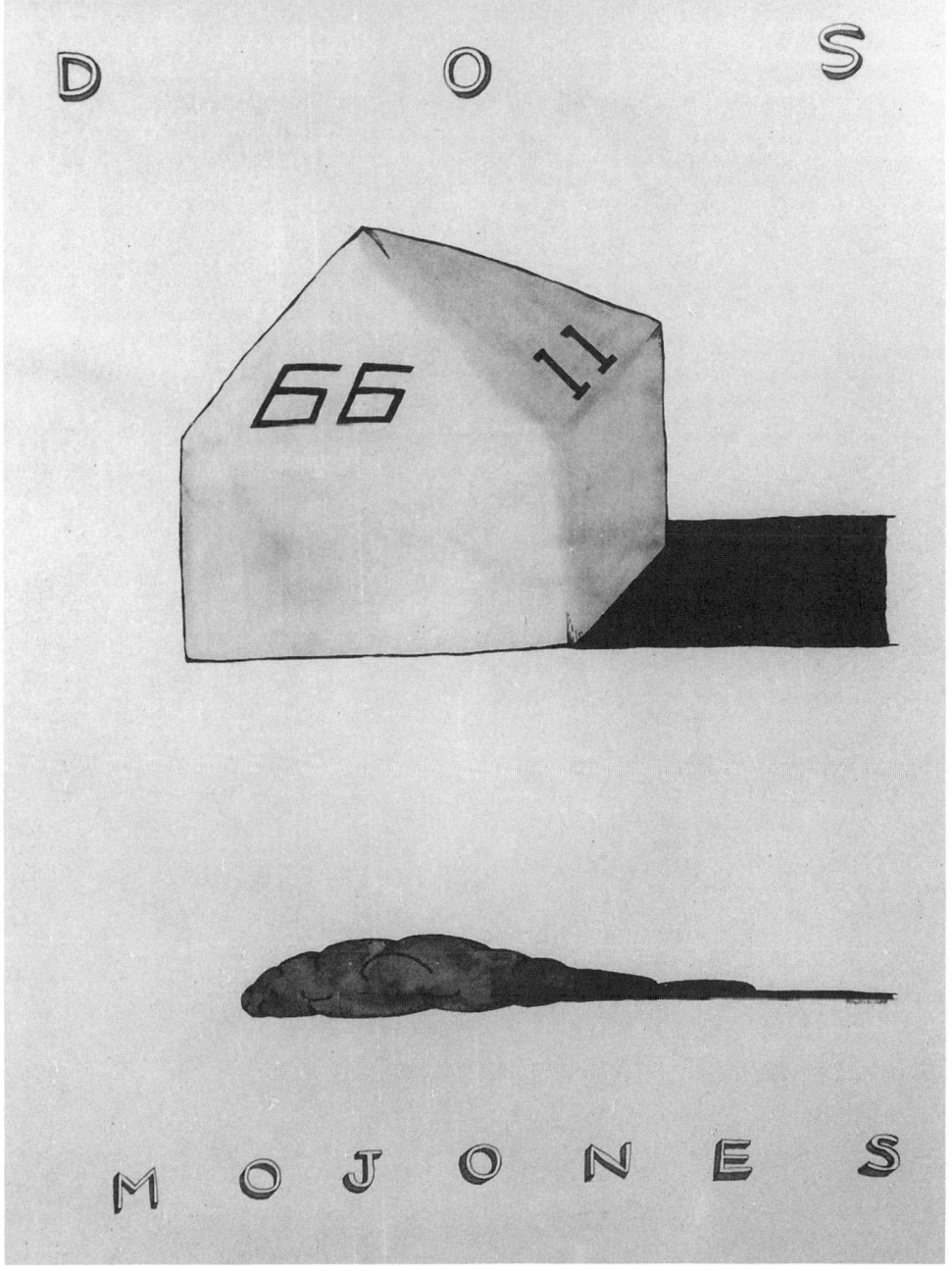

Antonio Eligio Fernández (Tonel), Dos mojones (Two Milestones/Turds), *1985, watercolor on paper, 65 × 45 cm. Private collection. Photo by Luis Camnitzer.*

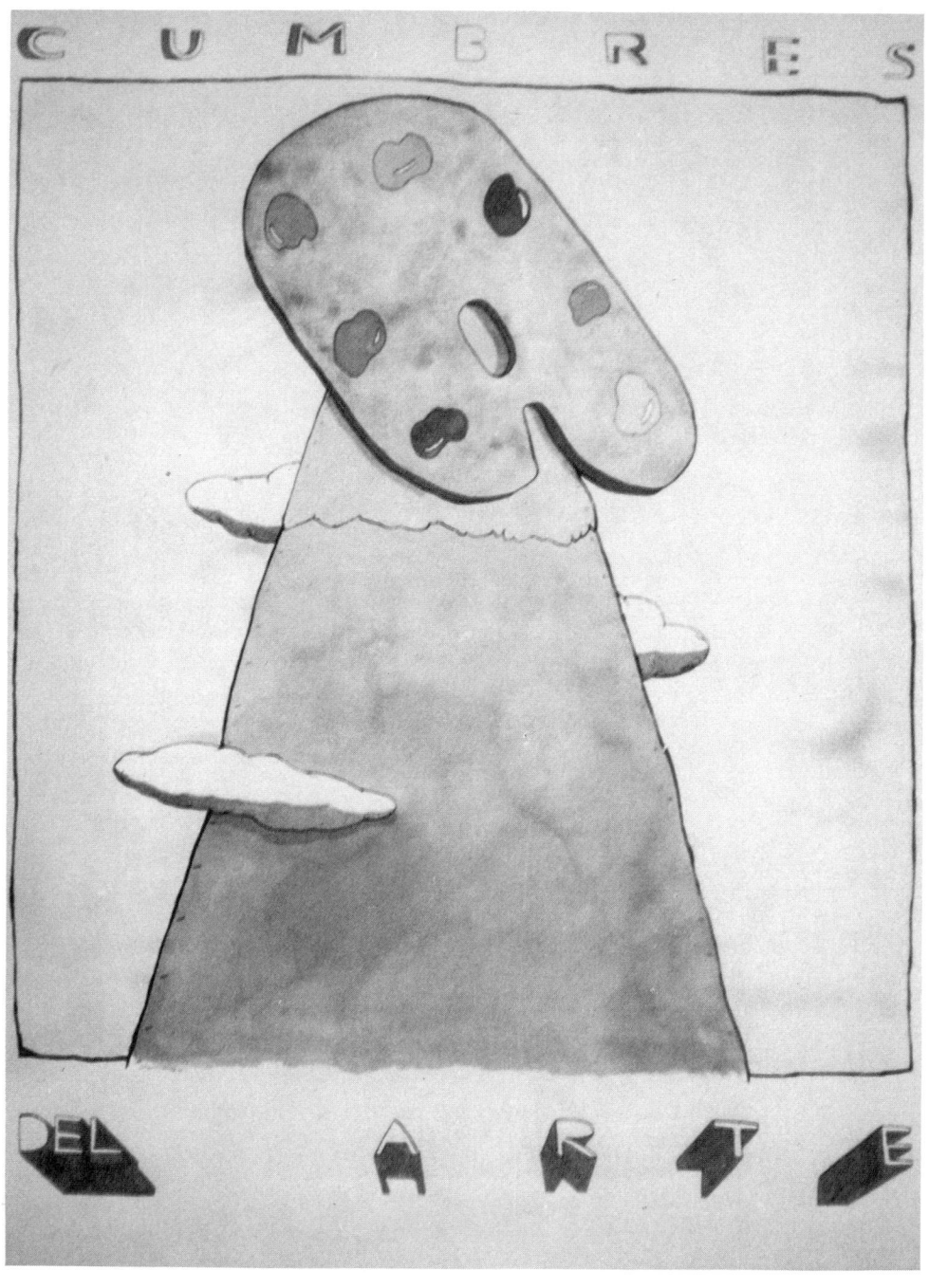

Antonio Eligio Fernández (Tonel), Cumbres del arte (Cusps of Art), *1985, watercolor on paper, 65 × 45 cm. Collection of the artist. Photo by Tonel.*

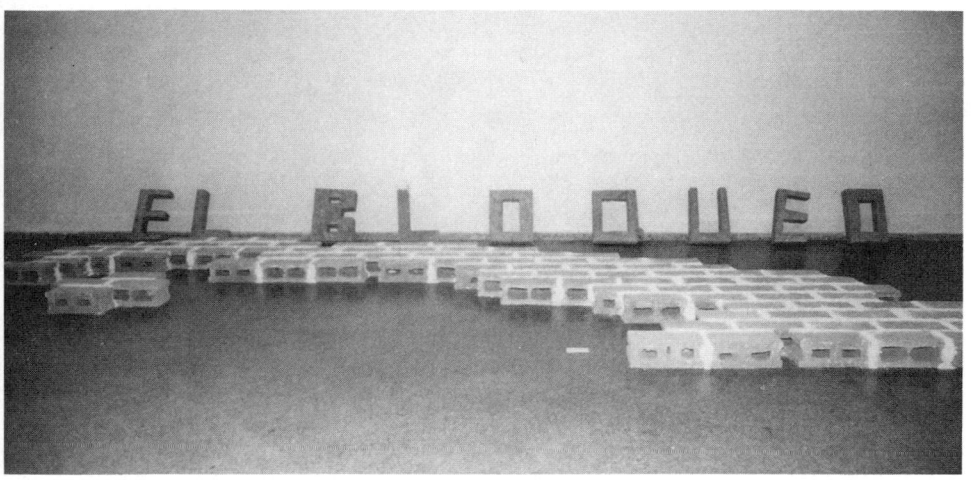

Antonio Eligio Fernández (Tonel), El bloqueo (The Blockade), *1989, installation at the Third Biennial of Havana, 50 × 800 × 200 cm. Photo by Luis Camnitzer.*

Tonel is interested in the reification of women in a male-controlled society and records flirtatious street comments attached to objects with female organs (something that Aldo Menéndez calls "erotic malice"). The images are composed to create an iconic synthetic symbol, sometimes with echoes of Magritte, set into a poster format and painted with gently toned watercolors. They achieve the credibility of the commercial object offered for sale in an advertisement. But in this case the ad is not a slick agency ad—it is a vernacular view of the act of advertising, a reelaboration of the aesthetic after it has undergone popular digestion.

With punch lines minimized by banality and twists reduced to the effect of puns (mostly only understood locally), Tonel's work sometimes evokes the covers of the *New Yorker* magazine, with all the trappings of a visual joke but without the joke. Tonel's dulling of the punch line brings the visual elements to the foreground to a point that the work becomes a link between popular expression and art, but a link that clearly has been designed on the art side of the frontier that separates them. Without giving up drawing, Tonel is now starting to explore all of this three-dimensionally.

Tomás Esson

Esson (1963) is the most painterly artist of his generation. The work exudes his pleasure in painting; however, his subject matter denies the pleasurable, hedonistic surface. Esson's most aggressive images deal with distorted copulating buffalo-like creatures, a topic that sometimes

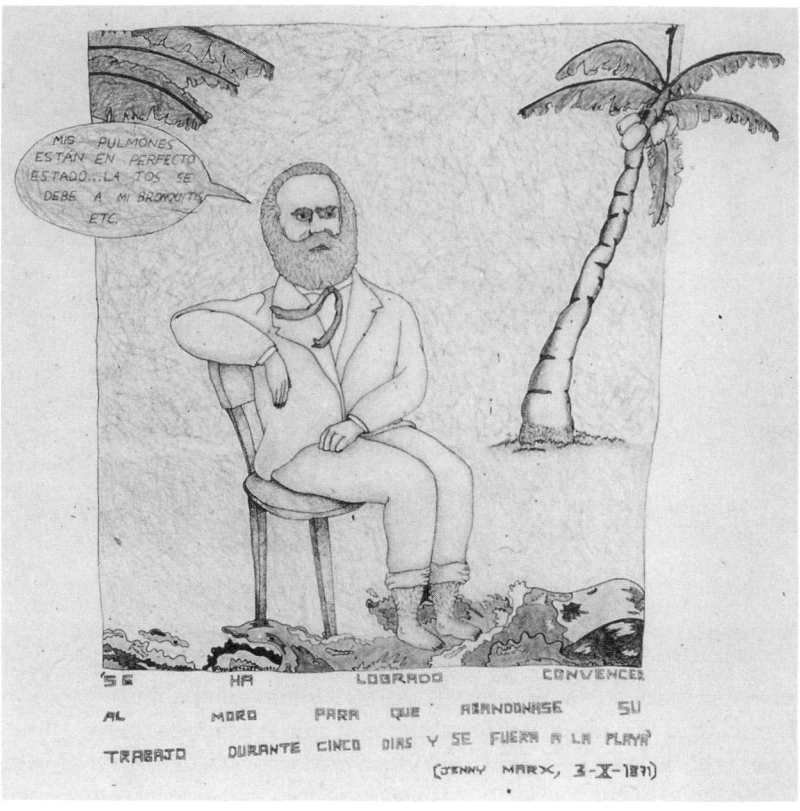

Antonio Eligio Fernández (Tonel), Marx (en sus cartas a Kugelmann)
(Marx, in His Letters to Kugelmann), *1990, watercolor on paper, 70.5 ×
50.5 cm. Collection of the artist. (Text in bubble: "My lungs are in perfect
shape . . . the cough is due to my bronchitis, etc."; text under drawing: "It has
been achieved to convince the 'moor' to leave his work for five days and to go
to the beach.")*

causes great controversy and even scandal. During the week before the
Fourth Congress of the UNEAC he became a "cause célèbre."

Esson had opened a one-man exhibit in a municipal gallery situated
at the corner with the most traffic in Havana.[23] One painting depicted
two of his copulating creatures at work in front of a portrait of Che Guevara. Another work had the bars of the Cuban flag shaped into ambiguous fleshy tubes. These then penetrated the star-bearing triangle in the
same flag, which became a vagina, while the star was composed of five
little horns.

The director of the gallery, which is controlled by a neighborhood

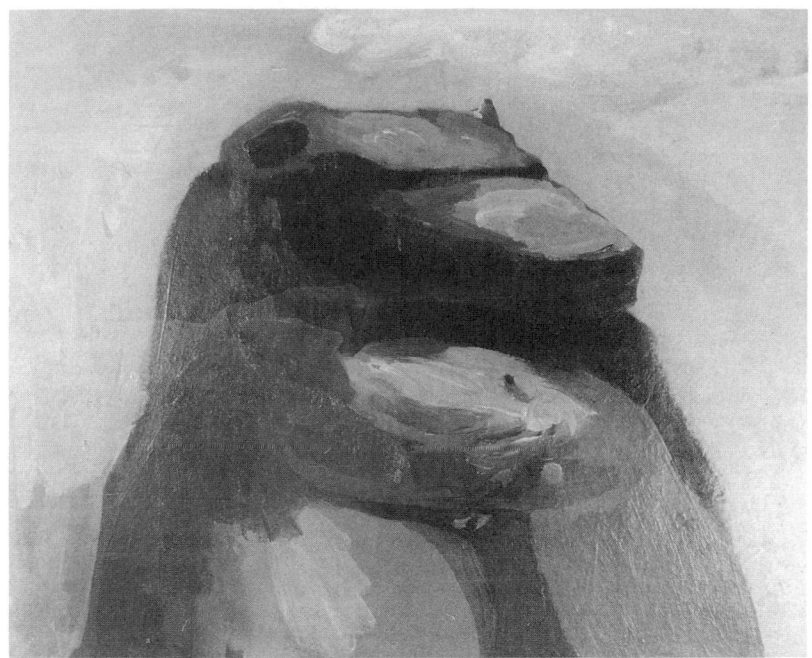

Tomás Esson, untitled (from the Portrait Series), 1981–1982, tempera on cardboard, 48 × 59 cm. Private collection. Photo by Luis Camnitzer.

committee, had irresponsibly neglected to look at the work before the opening, panicked, and contacted the committee. Doctrinaires in the committee then called Minister of Culture Armando Hart, demanding the removal of the offending two pieces. An awkward censor or not-to-censor situation was created. The assault on the taste of the sectarian committee members was unimportant. Because of the populated placement of the gallery, there were fears of not only offending the public but also of creating, either way, an issue bound to distract the proceedings of the upcoming UNEAC congress and endanger many of the liberal propositions to be discussed there. Esson was therefore requested to remove the offending pieces. He felt that the integrity of the exhibit would be jeopardized and chose to take down the whole exhibit.

The affair created ripples throughout the art community. Esson was by no means suspect of counterrevolutionary leanings since he was a leading member of the Communist Youth at the ISA. A remarkable discussion process ensued. Esson and Hart had a long public exchange trying to make their points, followed by further discussions involving vice-ministers and ISA personnel to see what could be done.

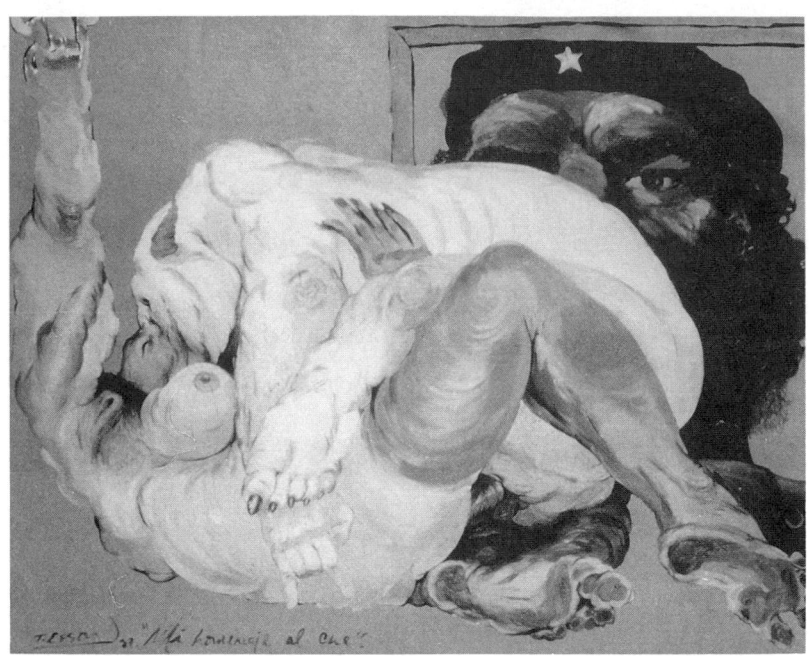

Tomás Esson, Mi homenaje al Che (My Homage to Che), *1987, oil on canvas, 170 × 200 cm. Collection of the artist. Photo by Luis Camnitzer.*

One of the possibilities considered later was to move the exhibit to the ISA itself (some of the work had already been shown there as part of his graduation thesis) and have it accompanied by a public panel discussion about the work and the incident it caused. According to his concept, one of the pieces had to cover a full wall. The walls at ISA were bigger, and some of the paintings (on cardboard) had suffered when removed so that it would have required an enormous amount of new paintings for the new location. He therefore discarded the suggestion. Instead, he had an exhibit in the ISA the following April, with work he had done in childhood between his fifth and twelfth years. The exhibit of his childhood drawings was named "ESSONSISEHACE," punning on "eso sí se hace" ("that can be done indeed"). To the surprise of his censors, they discovered that all the subjects of his mature work were already present in those drawings.[24]

The controversial exhibit had been preceded by a similar one in 1987 in the Museum of Santa Clara without any censorship problem (though with plenty of discussion), and a video was shown on the provincial TV channel.

Esson's paintings are grotesque without falling into caricature. His

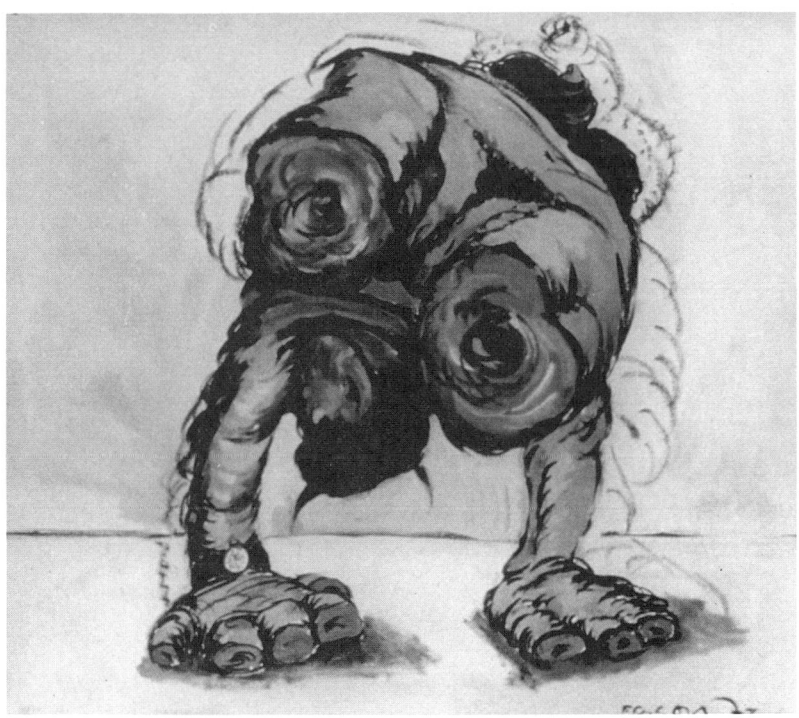

Tomás Esson, Vuelta de carnero (Somersault), *1988, tempera on paper, 93 × 101 cm. Collection of Fernando Alvarez Pérez, Miami. Photo by Charles Merewether.*

painterly handwriting is strong enough to give his creatures a presence in their own right, devoid of illustrative references and weaknesses. As Mosquera writes, "His beings seem to live in mythical primogenital time; at the same time they become undesirable contemporaries."[25] It is this jumping over time, the elimination of the distance that protects us from mythological figures, that makes his creatures particularly vile and threatening.

Esson had a very academic education. Into his initial realism, he slowly incorporated distortions and vegetable forms. Combining this formal repertoire with social concerns and a sense for expressionism (Munch, Van Gogh, Ensor, Bacon, Chia, Servando Cabrera, and Lam are his references, later completed with Mendive, Chago, and Tonel), he evolved into his present manner of painting. His literary sources are García Márquez and the Marquis de Sade. Guided by Garciandía, he became interested in symbolism, and from then on he planned the content of his paintings to the smallest detail. The vegetable forms became

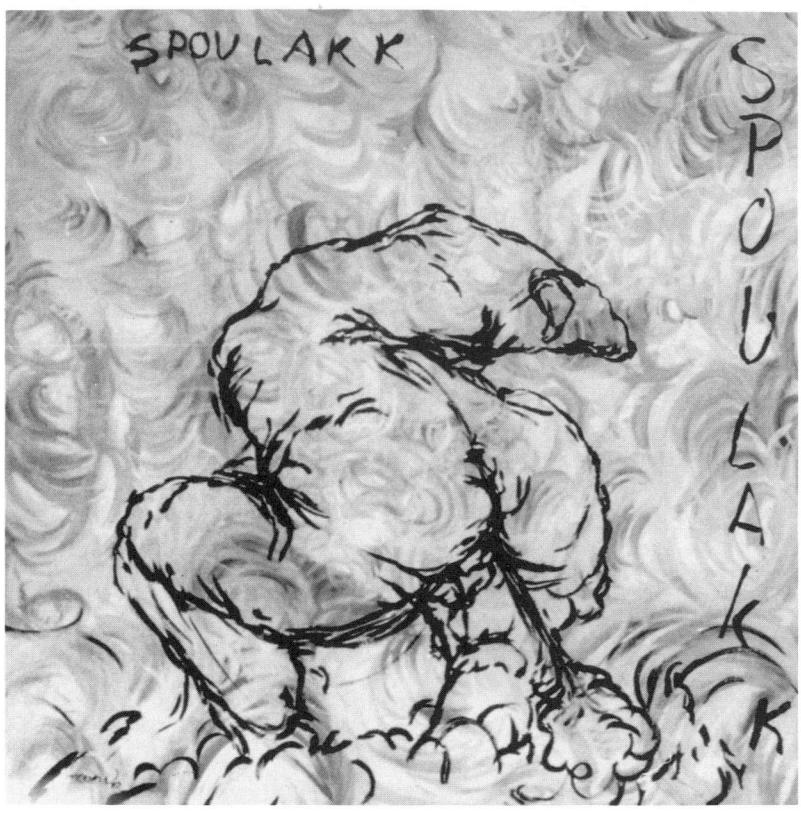

Tomás Esson, SPOULAKK, *1987, oil on canvas, 150 × 150 cm. Collection of the Fredric Snitzer Gallery, Coral Gables, Florida. Photo by Luis Camnitzer.*

increasingly sexual, thanks to the associations made by the public, which led him to become more explicit (both in imagery and titles, always conceptually fused in his work) and interested in hypocrisy.

SPOULAKK is the image of a farting and defecating humanoid. Esson explains that "the subject matter, which could be described as scatological, refers to a human biological process presented in an exaggerated form, underlining the grotesque nature of an action that is an intrinsic part of man."[26] The pronunciation of the letters of the title becomes "Ese peo uele a kaka," a version in sound meaning "that fart smells like shit."

Esson admits that his manner of painting with all its violence and morbidness is just his painterly handwriting, something beyond his control. For him, though, the interpretation of the paintings was quite clear. The painting with the portrait of Che (*Mi homenaje al Che,* or *My Homage to Che* [1987]) was about the hypocrisy of those people who applaud political speeches and then leave, like the *Marielitos,* or of those bureaucrats who speak in one way and act in another. And he purposefully painted Che as a mulatto, to identify him with himself. In regard to the other painting (*Bandera cubana,* or *Cuban Flag* [1988]), it was connected with his sense of strength and virility.[27]

The incident around Esson's work marked the rest of the Cuban art year. Any criticism or controversy around the work of young artists was suspected of being part of a pattern, a fact that was exploited by some of the foreign press. A vicious circle of sorts was created, which led to a relative hardening of positions on both sides of the issue. The debates around this show and subsequent events demonstrated that there is a strong religious feeling around many Cuban issues, often encouraged by middle and lower ranks of the bureaucratic structure but not denied by the upper levels either.[28] Particularly these middle and lower levels have a paternalistic attitude toward the public and often protect it from nonexisting threats.

The situation also made it clear that there is no room, except with a misguided ethnocentric attitude, to project values about relative "freedoms of expression" defined in other political and cultural contexts onto Cuba. The problem seems to be set not by the need for freedom of expression but by a common agreement on where the limits for tolerable and productive offense may be. It is not a simple determination and will require all the subtlety Aldito Menéndez had asked for in his earlier quoted "Revolutionary SOS" essay, more discipline and study of the use of communication elements by the artists, and more opening by those enclosed by dogmatism or ignorance.

Meanwhile, Esson's neighbors did not seem to mind his paintings on the street while we were taking slides, and the guest book in the exhibit had friendly opinions outnumbering negative ones at a three-to-two ratio. Esson continues to paint in his irreverent manner and to rub bureaucrats the wrong way. Together with Rodríguez Cárdenas and Glexis Novoa, he had an exhibit in the Castillo de la Real Fuerza (March–April 1989). The title of the exhibit was "Patria o Muerte," a sacred national slogan. One of his pages in the catalogue depicts Fidel in a manner suspiciously close to *SPOULAKK.*[29]

Glexis Novoa

My first reaction to Novoa's (1964) work was artistically negative. The works seemed rushed, careless, and halfbaked, and I was more interested in his ideas than in his products. Over time, however, I was placed in a defensive situation. It was very conceivable that I was em-

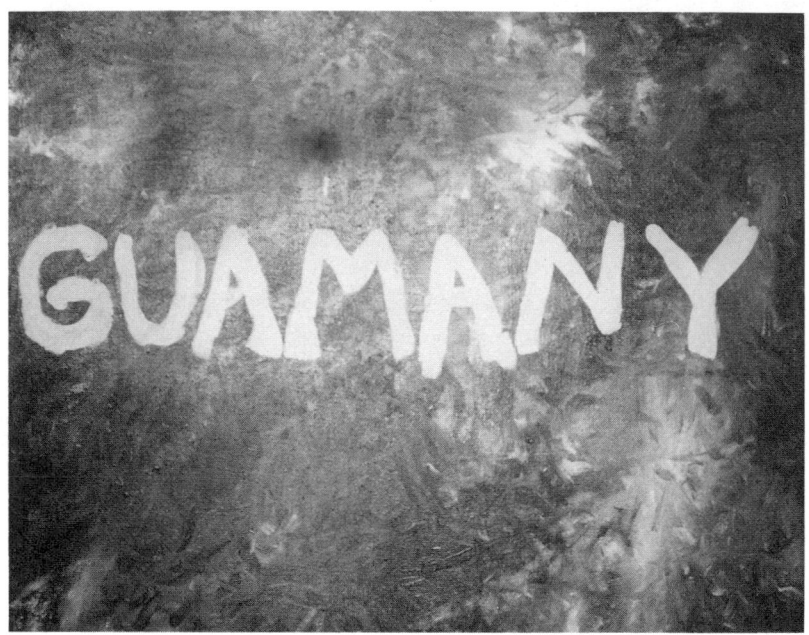

Glexis Novoa, Guamany, *1988, oil on paper, 50 × 70 cm. Collection of the artist. Photo by Luis Camnitzer.*

ploying my cultural distortions to evaluate work that was willfully evading them. I had to concede to myself that I might be too old and very foreign to Novoa's taste. I felt on shaky ground, forced to review my own values, and I had to respect his work for forcing me into this position.

Over time, seeing his evolution (not exactly toward good taste), I have even had moments in which some of the work gives me pleasure. It is clear that Novoa does not care about taste in most of his work. In fact, he once expressed his ambition of becoming the "worst painter in history." When he uses abstract-expressionist effects, which he does frequently, it is not because he likes them or because the aesthetic provides grounds for artistic exploration. The whole abstract-expressionist movement is reduced to existence as a functional symbol, which in Novoa's repertoire only signifies "the foreign" and "the imported."

The paintings are slapped on with fake gestures, rendering a superficial impression of "something abstract-expressionist," without the artist caring about really being abstract-expressionist. This symbolic surface then becomes the support for the second message, usually a text. He proceeds to paint words on that background, which in turn guide the perception of the totality. Often nonsensically made-up words, which

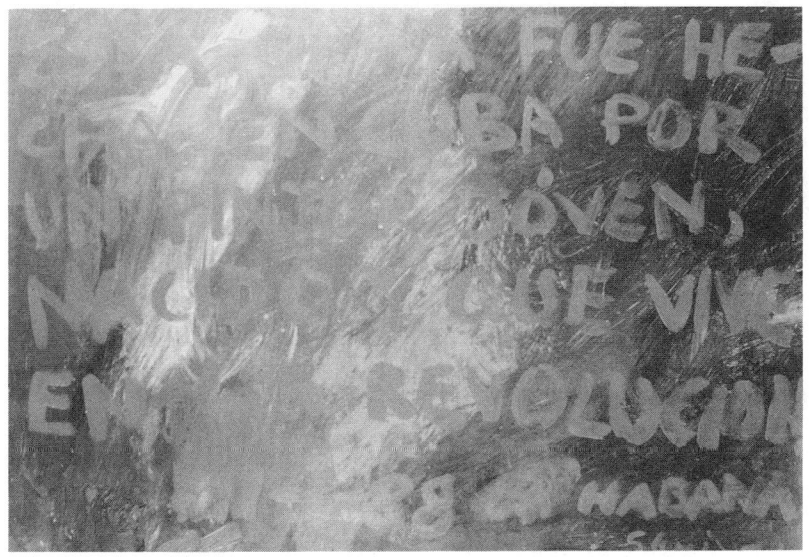

Glexis Novoa, Esta obra fue hecha en Cuba por un pintor joven, nacido y que vive en la revolución (This Work Has Been Made in Cuba by a Young Painter Who Was Born and Lives in the Revolution), *1988, oil on paper, 50 × 70 cm. Private collection. Photo by Luis Camnitzer.*

Novoa calls "abstract texts," they sound foreign or Latin American depending on his intentions. The word *Guamany* written in sloppy violent pink letters over one of these backgrounds sounds like "it could be" some Indo-American language. Other times the text is philosophical with apocryphal quotes, such as "'And man created a piece of art to convince himself,' St. Augustine."

Novoa deconstructs art to identify cultural values and prejudices, disregarding formal canons. A work from an earlier period, *Horóscopo chino, calendario azteca, panteón yoruba"* (*Chinese Horoscope, Aztec Calendar, Yoruba Pantheon* [1987]), is no more than a roulette-type contraption activated by an electric button, where the numbers, placed on a dial filled with hermetic symbols, correspond to a series of arbitrary everyday objects. The process becomes more poignant in subsequent work. A series of scribbled surfaces, also from 1987, bear the title *Painting is . . .* followed by a dotted line ready to bear a definition, which in one case is "a hobby."

Other works, from 1988, over an abstract-expressionist background, have the inscription "This work has been made in Cuba by a young painter born and living in the Revolution," or "Suddenly it turns out that I am a postmodernist like you." Work often is signed with the word *sig-*

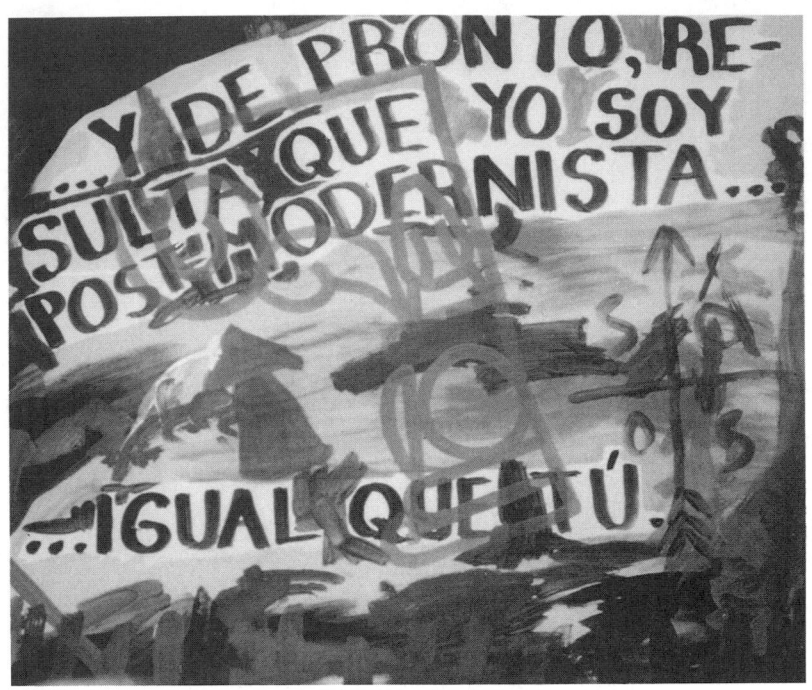

Glexis Novoa, Y de pronto resulta que yo soy postmodernista . . . igual que tú (And Suddenly It Turns Out that I Am a Postmodernist . . . the Same as You), *1988, tempera on paper, 50 × 70 cm. Collection of the artist. Photo by Luis Camnitzer.*

nature, and the writing has the same careless and awkward quality of slogans brushed on a street wall.

Novoa's work is aggressive, though in a teasing way. A *Gran pintura* (*Grand Painting*), made in 1988, covered an entire large wall in a gallery. He painted the work in the gallery and kept nagging officials from the Fondo Cubano de Bienes Culturales to buy it, also haggling over how much they would pay. With humor and irreverence he points out what he considers untrue; in that sense, it is primarily pedagogical work. Novoa speaks strongly for his generation and is appreciated by his peers as doing so. The interest of this work relies on the fact that it already challenges all the notions that are supposed to lead to a definition of what a mature artist is.

Novoa, like many of his contemporaries, suffered a process of deaesthetization. Up to 1986 his work was aesthetically pleasing and artistically acceptable. A deceptively naive-looking piece, somewhat akin to sophisticated Mexican folk painting, has the image of Martí and some

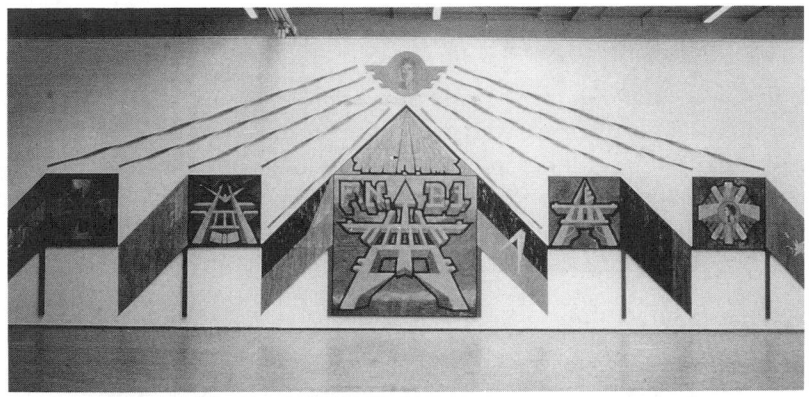

Glexis Novoa, Practical Stage, *1989, 10 × 4 m. Installation at the Kunsthalle Dusseldorf.*

benign-looking animals. The text around it says, "I painted a poem for Martí, and he once posed for me for a painting of himself. Now I am giving a leopard to the good friend." From this tender harmlessness, he evolved into visual and intellectual assault. For his exhibit "To Be or Not to Be" (in English in the original) (Galería Habana, November 1988), he introduced his own prologue to the catalogue with a quote of Li Thu Schen: "The lotus will not allow us to see the fish / even more beautiful than its leaves." Both author and text are made up. Followed by a rambling text that you must read three times before you discover that it does not make any sense, he closes with, "I have nothing more to say; I want to express my gratitude for coming to my exhibition. I believe that the most important thing is human contact, warmth, sympathy, solidarity, brotherhood, the correlation of strength, friendship, fornication."

All this madness was eventually shelved into what he calls his "theoretical stage" or "romantic period." Novoa is presently in his "practical stage." IIis painterly skills returned, this time to execute huge multipanel installations in the fashion of Soviet socialist-realist pomposity. Many of the panels bear unintelligible inscriptions written in a Cyrillic-looking alphabet created by himself, which with a little effort can be decoded into PCC (Partido Comunista Cubano) and into "Patria o Muerte," the national Cuban slogan. The work is totally cynical, made to measure to satisfy the expectations of a *perestroika*-contaminated international market while making a devastating criticism of it.

The ruse worked, and his *Practical Stage* installation in the Third Biennial of Havana became the star of the exhibition, to then travel to Pori in Finland, to Düsseldorf, and to Boston. Novoa once had a nightmare. He dreamt that he suddenly had become an avant-garde artist.[30]

Carlos Rodríguez Cárdenas

Rodríguez Cárdenas (1962), Novoa's partner in the Grupo Provisional, works in different veins. Using very small formats, his work is always carefully finished, with great, nearly obsessive respect for craftsmanship (little wrappings he makes for the transport of the work are as elaborate as the work itself). Interested, like many others of his generation, in destabilizing stereotypes and stressing the ambiguities of what are intended to be clear statements, his work initially took two forms. One, visually less interesting, consisted of the isolation of printed titles from catalogues and magazines, which he combined with images cut out of nineteenth-century wood engravings, collaged together in Max Ernst fashion. The work was treated in a quasi-ascetic manner, avoiding any temptation and trace of baroqueness and exploiting the emptiness of the page. The other path illustrated popular sayings on postcard-size boards. With a faked naive look, he incorporated cartoon elements and truck-decoration aesthetics into surreal, cataclysmic, sometimes erotic and scatological situations suggested by the text.

The text in this series became a point of departure for the image, which confirmed, denied, or carried its conclusions to the point of absurdity. *Que el ahorro entre por casa* (*Apply Savings to the Home* [1987]), refers to energy saving. A black sky with light bulbs instead of stars surrounds a home lit by the lights of a car pointing through the door. *Que nadie se mueva de su puesto de trabajo* (*Nobody Is to Move from His Workplace* [1987]), shows a cartoon character frozen in his place because of two lions. *Donde nace un comunista mueren las dificultades* (*Difficulties Perish Where a Communist Is Born* [1987]), depicts a torso bearing the emblem of the Union of Communist Youths as its face breaks out of a pregnant woman's belly. In front of the birth scene are several tombstones attesting to the death of different quantities of difficulties (ten and thirty).

This series grew to fifty-two cards commenting on most of the "revolutionary watchwords" applied to Cuban life. No symbol was left intact, and the potential exhibit caused controversy before it even had a chance to happen. The amount of discussion led Rodríguez Cárdenas to decide, with some frustration, not to exhibit the works although the catalogue was already printed. The incident was taken as an example of censorship by some, who interpreted the advice he received as a veiled prohibition, and as a worrisome case of self-censorship by others. In either case, justified or unjustified, Rodríguez Cárdenas' situation was symptomatic of the post-Esson atmosphere.

In fact, the series was irregular. To be read as a whole, the spectator had to shift without warning from appreciating puns about slogans, to enjoying the illustration, to picking up on serious criticism of concepts.

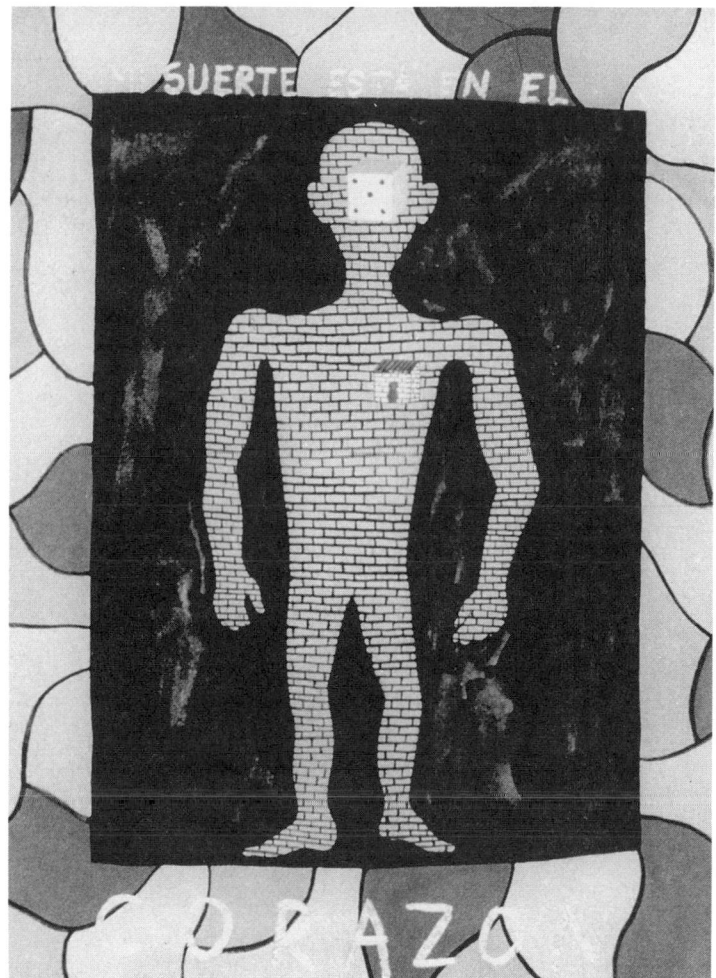

Carlos Rodríguez Cárdenas, Mi suerte está en el corazón (My Luck Was in the Heart), *1987, tempera on cardboard, 19 × 14 cm. Collection of the artist. Photo by Luis Camnitzer.*

Any mistake by the reader led to a misreading of the critique offered by Rodríguez Cárdenas, which he did not intend or share. A blatant example was a piece literally illustrating a slogan about the institution of family doctors, from which the only possible and rather absurd conclusion to be drawn was that family doctors are the product of the exploitation of the people.

For a while, and more than others in his generation, Rodríguez Cárdenas seemed project-oriented and lacking in unity, except for an overall

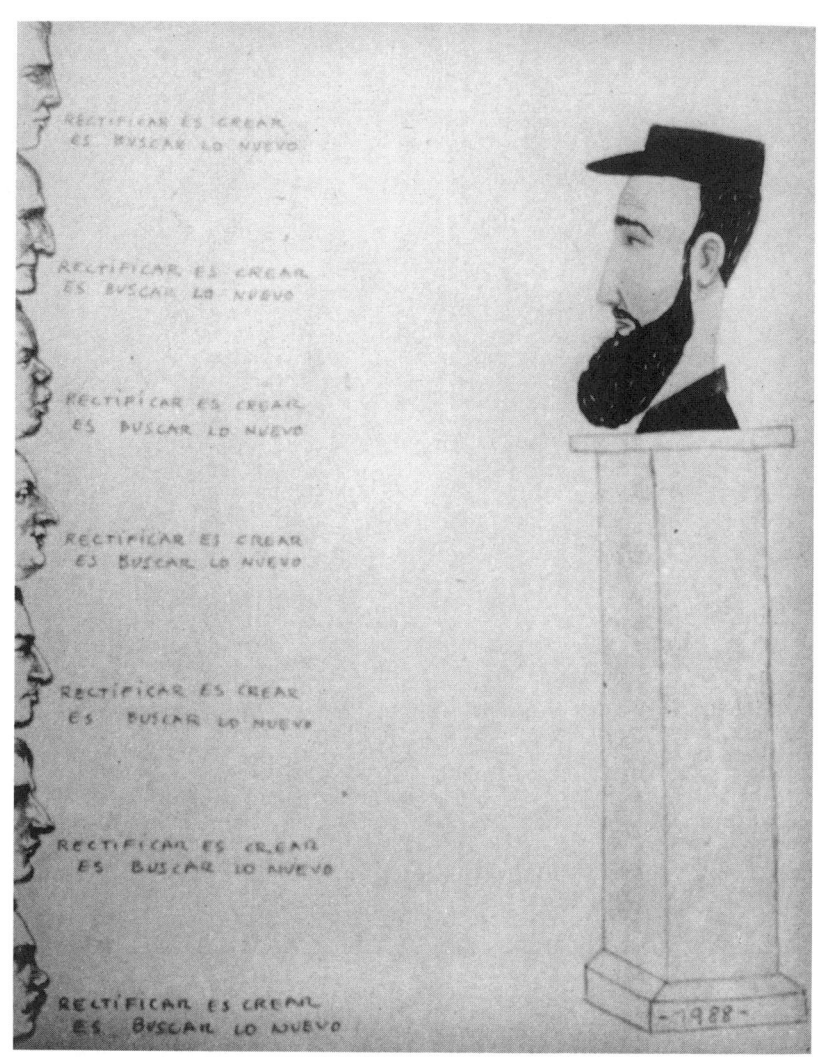

Carlos Rodríguez Cárdenas, Rectificar . . . , *1988, tempera on cardboard, 19 × 14 cm. Collection of the artist. Photo by Luis Camnitzer.*

sense of humor, care, and charm. As a student in San Alejandro in 1985, he had produced a series of incredibly slick and appealing watercolors that would have ensured him a formidable market. It is a sign of his integrity that he rejected the easy attractiveness of that work and pursued deeper problems. In that he paralleled up to a certain point Novoa's deaesthetization process.

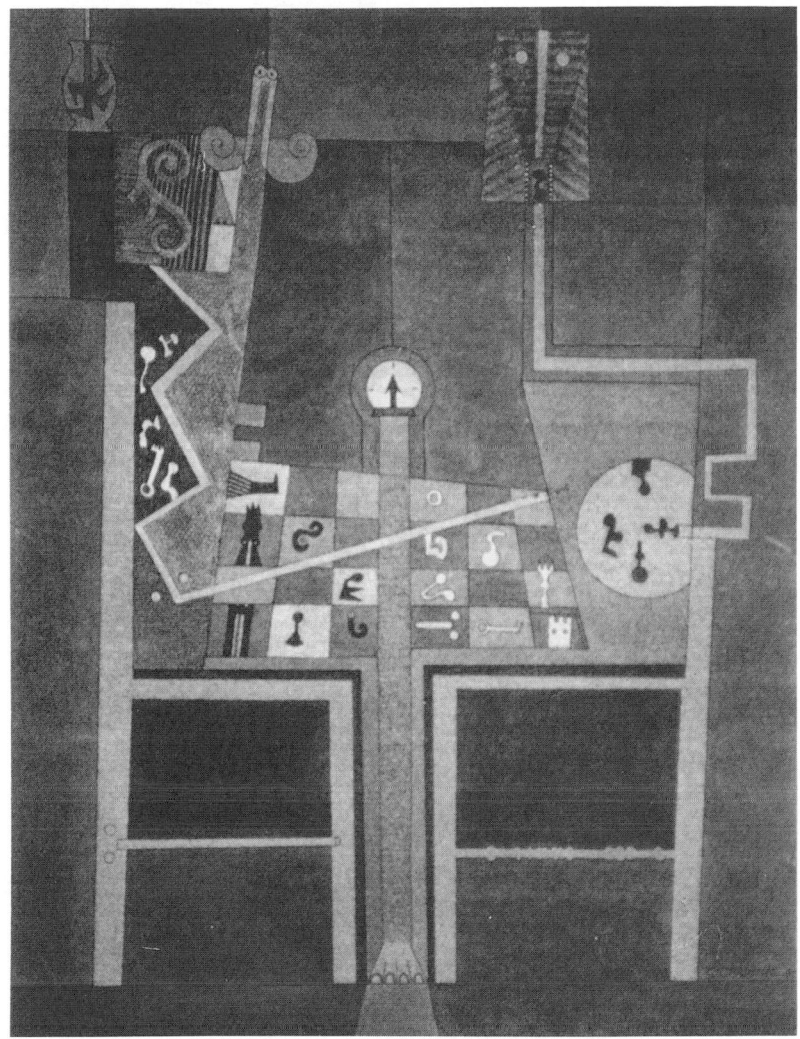

Carlos Rodríguez Cárdenas, untitled, 1985, watercolor on paper, 20 × 30 cm. Collection of the artist. Photo by Luis Camnitzer.

Rodríguez Cárdenas used the Third Biennial of Havana to pull things together. He built his own exhibition room and titled it "Popular Philosophy." Visitors entered through curtains painted on wood and were then invited to contemplate a series of small scatological paintings that, following the style developed in his postcards, depicted variations of possible relationships between human beings and feces. The series of

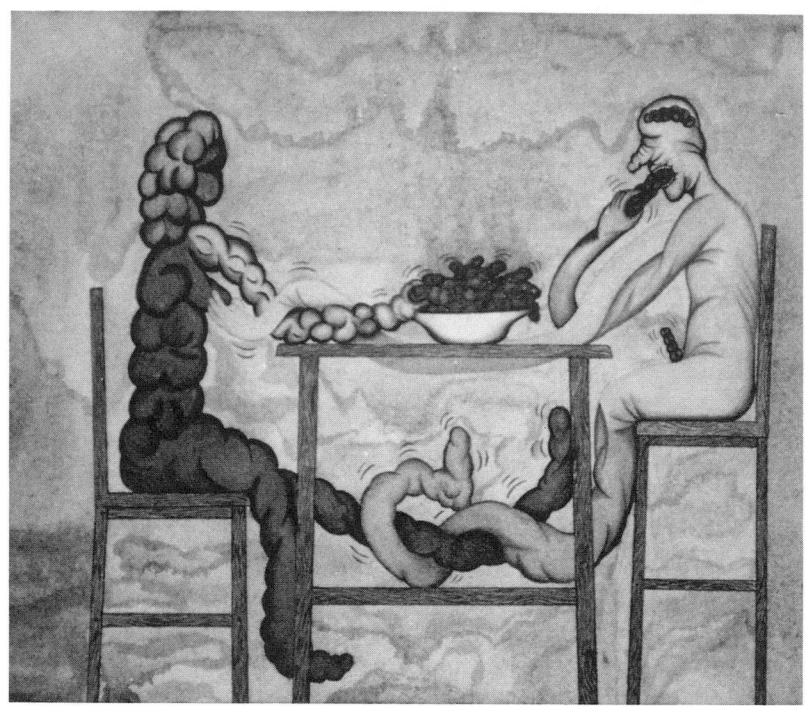

Carlos Rodríguez Cárdenas, Filosofía popular (Popular Philosophy) *(detail), 1989, acrylic painting, 20 × 30 cm. Collection of the artist. Photo by Luis Camnitzer.*

images was interspersed with such positive and optimistic texts as "The word that contains the truth doesn't have to be beautiful." However, the sentence appeared to be written with fecal matter. In another canvas the artist asserted that "the world is not shit" in a sentence surrounding an image of the globe depicted as a mosaic of little brown pellets. The same pellets, although larger, were used to ornament the exit of the room, which acquired a rocky texture.

Rodríguez Cárdenas' use of humor parallels and is indebted to much of Tonel's often tautological punning and feigned literalness, which in turn is typical of much of Cuban humor. But, like Tonel, he does not shy away from poetic images. *Construir el cielo (To Build the Sky,* [1989]) depicts a wall being constructed with blue bricks on a black background bearing the title in digital letters.

His true humor and attitude is summed up by one of the phrases that led into the text of the catalogue for the canceled show: "And each morning the sun discovers the marvels of every day."[31]

Lázaro Saavedra

Saavedra (1964) is the most overtly humoristic artist of the third generation. Unlike Tonel, who decidedly has an "art" point of view, he shows a refreshing disregard for the borderline between joke and art or, for that matter, for any borderline. Often drawing with ballpoint on scraps of paper, he develops endless series of hominoids working around variations on a theme.

Possession of quantity and qualities of eyes, for example, becomes the excuse for power struggles, racist divisions, and ethical crossroads. Pinned on a wall, they become his contribution to an exhibit. But while this example shares some of the international humor, Saavedra's hominoids are mostly bearers of written messages and, with their vernacular comments, invade any seemingly more ambitious artwork and sometimes become the artwork itself.

Painted in a neoexpressionist manner on a TV-screen shape, a dozen of them look disconcertedly at a bigger character who boasts (in English), "I know speak English." But mostly, the hominoids become an effective link of communication between the viewer and the artist. They point at details of the work, bearing comments in their speech or thought bubbles that represent possible reactions of the public observing the work or skeptical ideas about the art process coming from Saavedra's mind while he works. He is the first and instant viewer of his own creative process and seems to take the viewer's side in teasing himself as an artist.

Saavedra describes his artistic form as the product of context and the destruction of style, elements that made him confident about the results of his participation in the Proyecto Pilón mentioned in the preceding chapter. It is a trait that he sometimes may carry too far. After the demise of the Pilón idea he stopped making art to become part of a construction microbrigade.

Many of Saavedra's pieces are outright cartoons. A painter is about to start a still life with a flower. A friend shows him a cover of *Art News* with the same image he is about to paint. The painter, in despair, screams, "Why didn't I do it earlier? Why?" But his humor takes other forms as well. The meaning of a textured cave painting (painstakingly recreated with oil paint) is explained with the comment that cave people did not particularly care about mass communication. Another cave painting is attributed to a prehistoric child prodigy. In a group show he hung a text explaining that he did not have a piece important enough to express his gratitude for the honor of being invited to exhibit in such a prestigious exhibition.

For the team exhibit with Torres Llorca, he prepared the didactic part

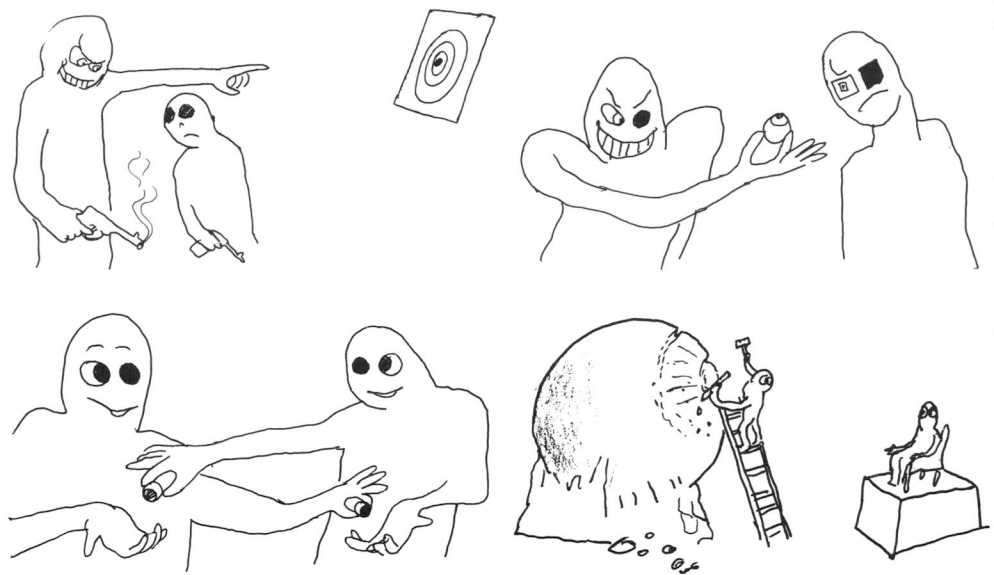

Lázaro Saavedra, drawings from Te estoy mirando (I Am Watching You), *1987, ink on paper, each drawing 19 × 14 cm. Private collection. Photo by Luis Camnitzer.*

of the display with sociological graphs and added a "work gage" (later renamed *Ideology Detector* [1989]) with a needle that moved over a dial going from "without problem" all the way to "diversionist," passing through "problems" and "counterrevolutionary" (with an "unconscious" and a "conscious" part). *Mesa sueca* (*Smorgasbord* [1989–1990]), an endless accumulation of ideas presented on tables in the form of scraps and sometimes finished work, includes a portrait of Karl Marx. One of Saavedra's hominoids rips off an eye to reveal an anatomical drawing beneath. "Gentleman, don't you see? He was made of flesh and bones."

Ciro Quintana

Quintana (1964) perceives his own work as mostly autobiographical. A relative definition, in his case it signifies the drawing on his own experience of how culture affects him, rather than the traditional anecdotal interpretation. Trained to be "a Picasso and to have contact with people lacking any relation with life,"[32] he decided to study these failed dynamics and to consciously comment on them in his work with a good addition of irony.

He shares with other artists of the third generation the use of titles

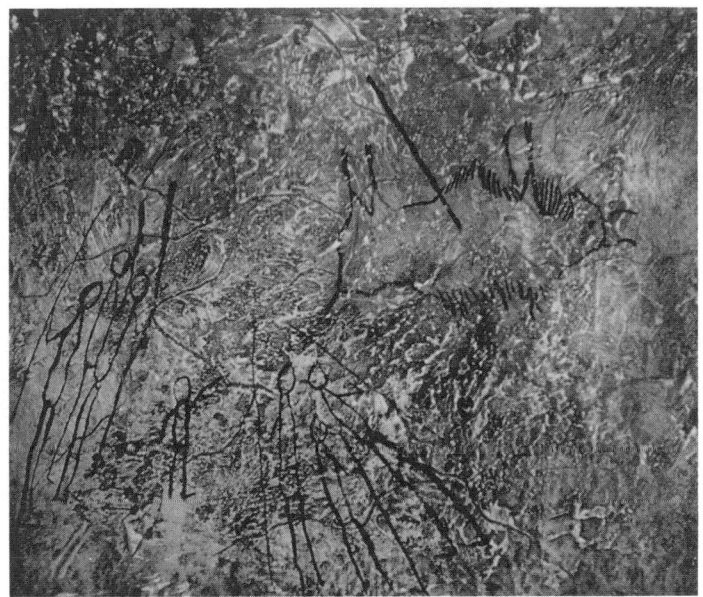

Lázaro Saavedra, Pintura rupestre que representa a un niño prodigio (Cave Painting Depicting a Child Prodigy), *1988, acrylic on paper, 50 × 70 cm. Collection of the artist. Photo by Luis Camnitzer.*

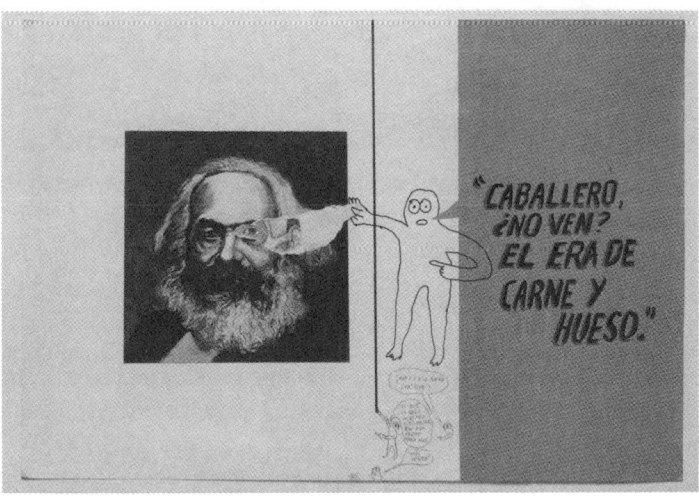

Lázaro Saavedra, Caballero, no ven? El era de carne y hueso. (Gentleman, Don't You See? He Was Made out of Flesh and Bones.), *1989, acrylic and collage on paper, 40 × 60 cm. Collection of the artist. Photo by Luis Camnitzer.*

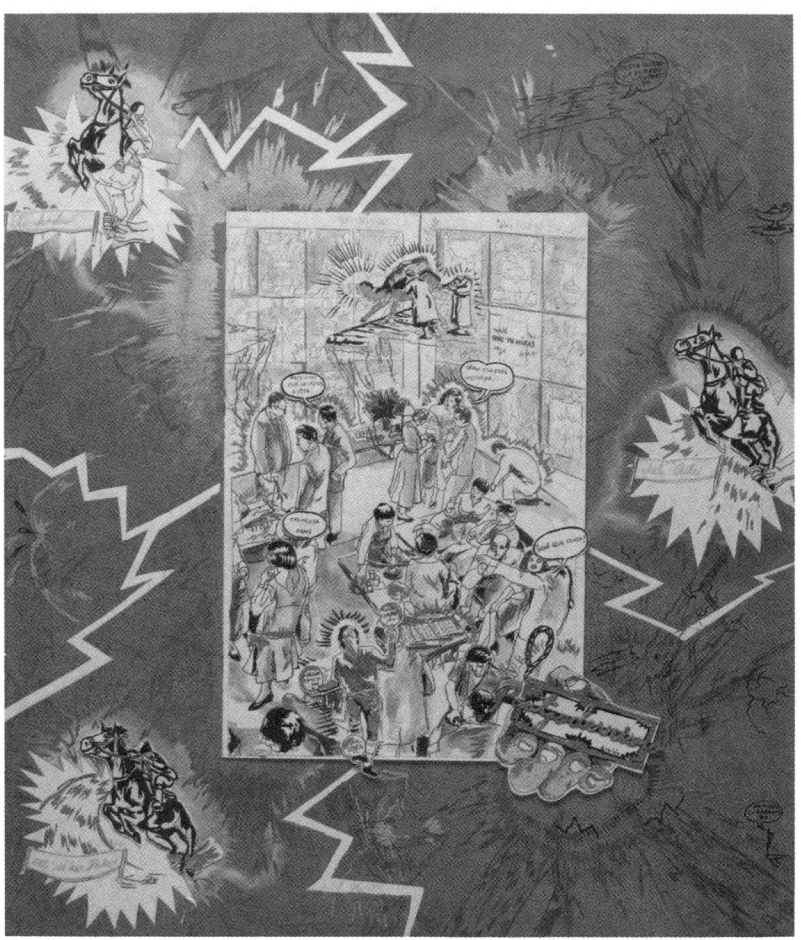

Ciro Quintana, Las maravillas del arte cubano (The Wonders of Cuban Art) *(fragment), n.d., collage and drawing on paper, 70 × 50 cm. Collection of the artist.*

as a fundamental element in his work. The title sometimes becomes a determining container that puts order and meaning into an otherwise chaotic configuration. When Quintana titles a piece *It Is Not a Borofsky, It Is a Ciro,* it no longer matters *what* is named because the title becomes a statement that appropriates any work to which he may give it.

From the very beginning, Quintana's work was "a search for a system into which I could fit everything, with a language apt to express what I want to say, while including the viewer in the whole process." This may sound like a statement by any artist, but in the case of Quintana it becomes a quite specific statement. A very active member of the Grupo Puré, when one sees his pre- and post-Puré work it becomes clear that the group work was an interruption. There may have been an enrichment of his repertoire thanks to the collective experience, but his own development picked up at the precise point he had stopped. From a formal point of view, his work seems to illustrate his statement.

Many of his works of art start with big simple outlines that subdivide into smaller orders as one approaches them, to finally get resolved into a multitude of little characters talking to each other or to the viewer and commenting about a variety of issues ranging from politics to art. "I am crazy about information." "Shit, Ciro, change! You always do the same thing." "Nobody can be better than anybody else, nobody can bug anybody else." "Elementary, Ciro, you are a postmodernist." The characters comment incessantly, and the closest analogy for his work is the sound of chatter. The characters, which are what amounts to aesthetic units, are mostly traced with carbon paper from newspaper drawings, cartoons, or photographs and mixed with collaged-on photos from magazines. Their combination, while spitting out cataracts of comments that spin in Quintana's head, create a rococo pattern. With the addition of some gold and silver paint, this ornateness negates the cheapness of the newsprint and construction paper he uses in much of his work.

Quintana's work could be classed under kitsch as much as under nationalism. This is because his definition of nationality includes kitsch, in the same way that for others it includes Afro-Cuban rituals. Though keenly aware of the borderline between kitsch and nonkitsch, his approach is much less intellectual than that of many of his colleagues. Perceiving this, Aldo Menéndez wrote, "Perhaps he is one of the 14 million [sic] Cuban kitsch agents who operate in the art circuit. Who is this Ciro?"[33]

Saavedra often can be placed in cartoon making, Novoa can be defined as opposed to art languages, and Rodríguez Cárdenas can be accused of exquisite perfectionism even in his explicitly vernacular imagery. Quintana, who participates in all the same uses and misuses as his friends, however, can be placed only within himself and seems immune to references. Swedish contemporary artist Ovynd Fahlstrom's work sometimes may come to mind, but it is a reference both remote and coincidental.[34] In this sense it is possible that Quintana may have internalized the art game much better than his friends and found a much less elitist way of expressing himself. Seeing his work and the name of Borofsky appearing in it leaves one pondering whether Borofsky may not have more popular acclaim in Cuba than in the United States.

Lately, Quintana identifies himself with the Grupo Provisional and

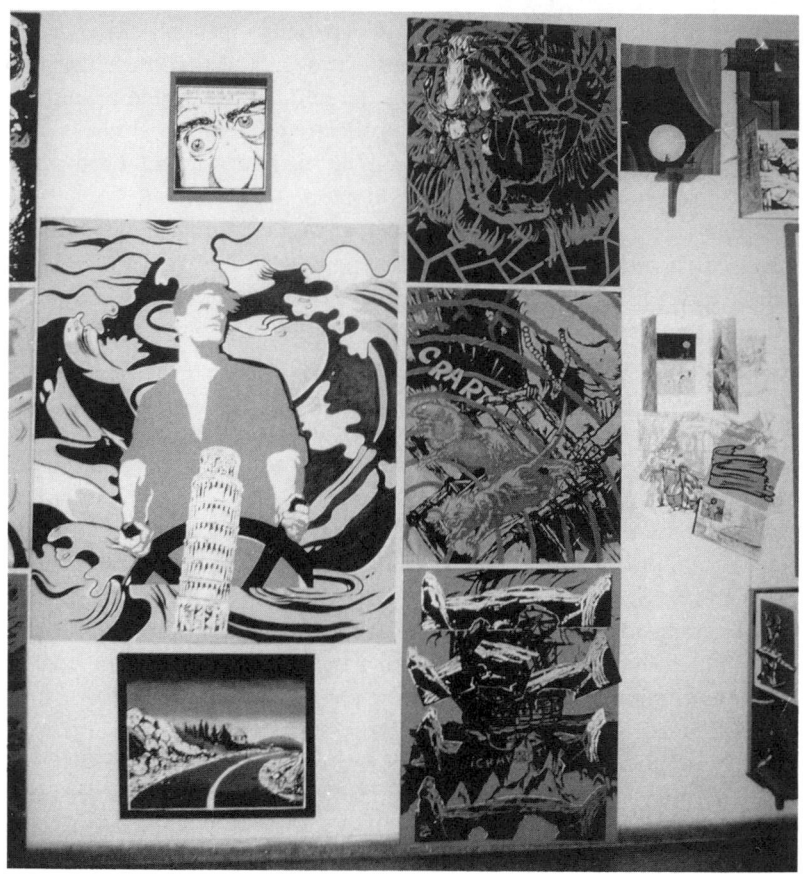

Ciro Quintana, Made in Cuba *(detail), 1989, installation. Collection of the artist. Photo by Ciro Quintana.*

works with it on events. His contribution to the previously mentioned exhibit about influences and plagiarism consisted of a performance during which he explained the work of artist Joseph Beuys to the audience. He read the explanation in English while in the background a tape with English lessons was being played to assist the audience in the understanding of his lecture. Following the concerns of this exhibit, he worked on *Made in Cuba,* a four-by-eight-yard composite painting, and a series titled *Snowing in Cuba.*

Made in Cuba was presented at the Third Biennial of Havana and addressed the flow of information directly. The clue to the idea that information flows in one direction, from the United States and the developed centers to Cuba, was given by a small brush stroke executed in the

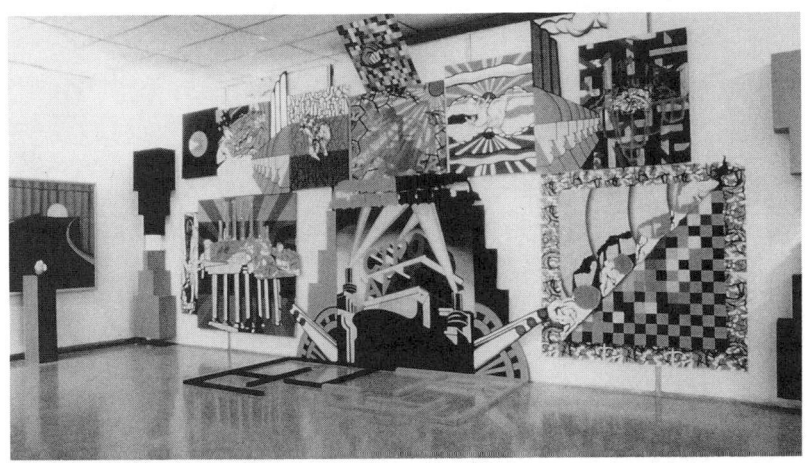

Ciro Quintana, Adiós a las armas (Farewell to Arms), *1990–1991, installation. Photo by Luis Camnitzer.*

fashion of U.S. artist Roy Lichtenstein, with the comment "Magazine texture and Western brush stroke."

Quintana worries about the possible commercialization of his generation. As another artist put it, they may stop being "rectification" artists to become collection artists. The only possible antidote is a humor that transcends painting. With Novoa and Torres Llorca he is considering an exhibit of a fictitious naive painter from the province of Oriente, "who is making the biggest painting in the world." They would display some fragments of the work and, primarily, documentation.

A remark by a bureaucrat, indicating that the state should acquire more work by the young "in case something happens," led Quintana to speculate about his own death. He would die officially, have a formal funeral, and have things arranged so that proceeds of the sale of his work could go to the members of the Grupo Puré.

Robaldo Rodríguez

Rodríguez (1964), perhaps more than other artists who grew up in Cuba's inland, suffers from the split with the capital. Close in feeling and ideas to the Grupo Puré, he did not join the group "because Puré is from Havana and I am from Holguín."[35] Much travel to his hometown and difficulty in finding living quarters and studio space in Havana made him feel unsettled and apart from the Havana environment.[36] He thus symbolizes the unresolved city-centricity still operating in Cuba.

Primarily a student of Garciandía—he graduated from the ISA in 1988—his early work was heavily influenced by his teacher in the way

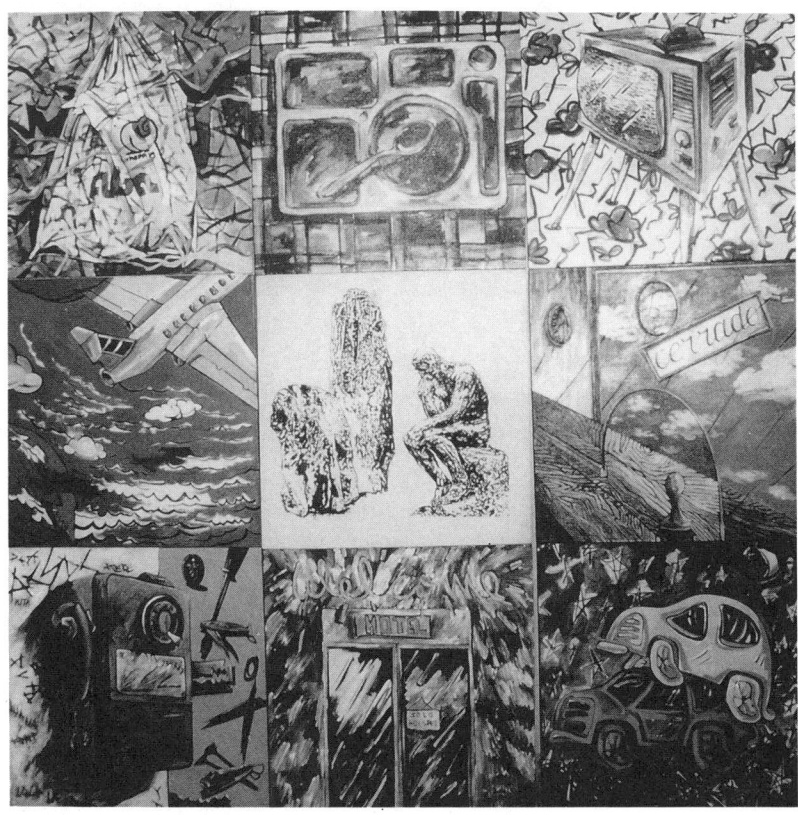

Robaldo Rodríguez, untitled, 1988, acrylic on canvas, 150 × 150 cm. Collection of the artist. Photo by Luis Camnitzer.

he painted, even if his subject matter was different. He is interested in what he calls "metaphorical permutations," in which images, shapes, and meanings connect emerging patterns. He explains, "The basic intention was determined by the need of having a broader public approach my work. The image had to respond to common sense with established codes, while also allowing a richness of mediation that could go beyond a plain visual translation." He wants "coincidence and redundancy to play an important role in the message, helping a banalized approach that aids intelligibility and restricts the ambiguity of representation."[37] In plain English, this would lead to populism with sophistication, which is Rodríguez' point of contact with Grupo Puré, except that Rodríguez believes in the finish of the product far more than do his friends. In this point, Garciandía's painterly mastery became a magnet for him.

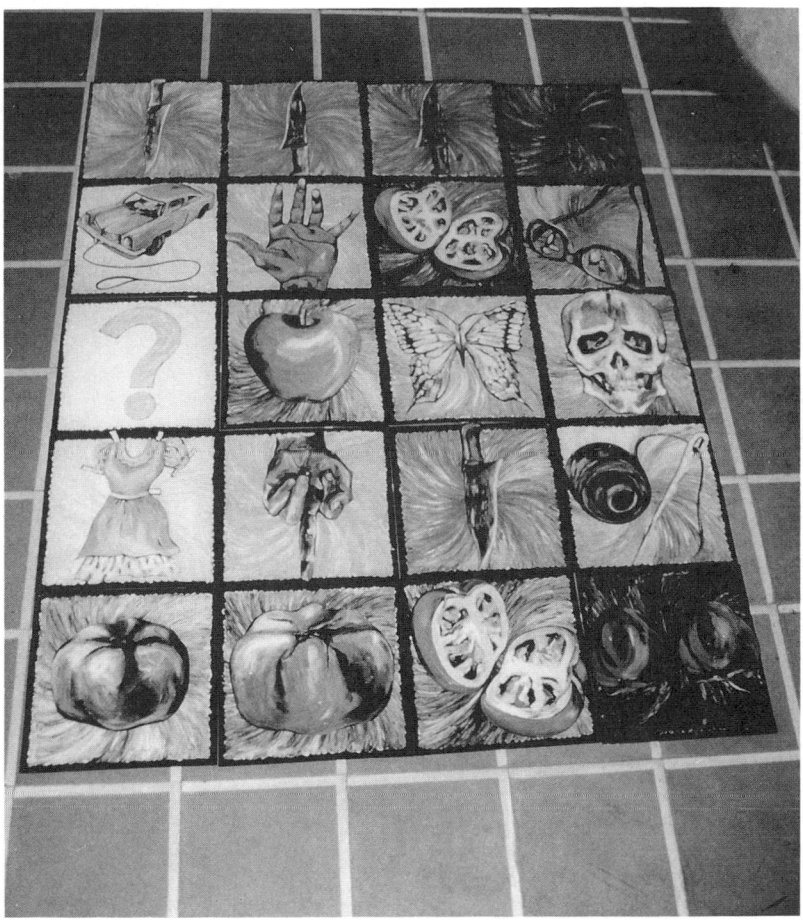

Robaldo Rodríguez, untitled, 1988, acrylic on paper, 170 × 140 cm. Photo by Luis Camnitzer.

Rodríguez takes his painterly language from Garciandía's "proverbs" and applies it to the tile system used in the same artist's *El lago de los cisnes* (*Swan Lake*). What saves him from being derivative is the manner in which he uses the connectors that define a tiling system and their kind. His connectors are multiple, not reduced (as in normal floor tiles) to the ornamental contact of formal devices that ensure the regularity of a pattern. There are literary and descriptive connectors as well. Thus, three different systems of interconnection may operate at the same time, in mutual support, but each visible only within its own mode of reading the work of art.

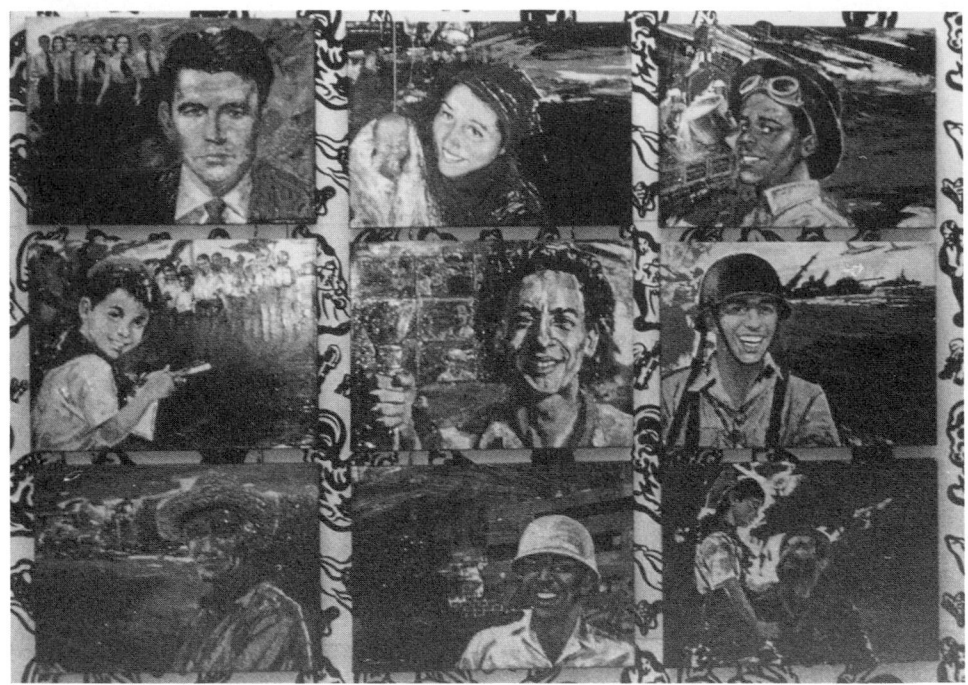

Robaldo Rodríguez, portfolio of posters, 1988, displayed on a wallpaper by Adriano Buergo in the exhibition "Kitsch," 1989. Collection of the artist. Photo by Luis Camnitzer.

The mixture of populism with sophistication is potentially a metaphor for Rodríguez' split between background and education, but it is a point he has not clearly assumed and exploited, at least not yet.

His most interesting work actually broke away from all this. On the occasion of the thirtieth anniversary of Castro's entry into Havana, a portfolio of posters by René Mederos was published. Mederos is an artist who was popular in the 1970s with an aesthetic as close to Soviet socialist realism as is conceivable in Cuba. The posters are portraits of contributors to the Revolution. Mostly generic portraits, there is "the" worker, "the" nurse, "the" student, and so on. Rodríguez noticed that "the" artist was missing. He mounted each poster on canvas, painted over the text, carefully blending it into the background, and varnished the surface of each one heavily with brush strokes to make them look like original paintings. In the manner of the portfolio, he then added his self-portrait, completing the series. The piece related Rodríguez to some of the appropriationists in Cuba but also allied him with the political direction of many of his peers in the third generation.

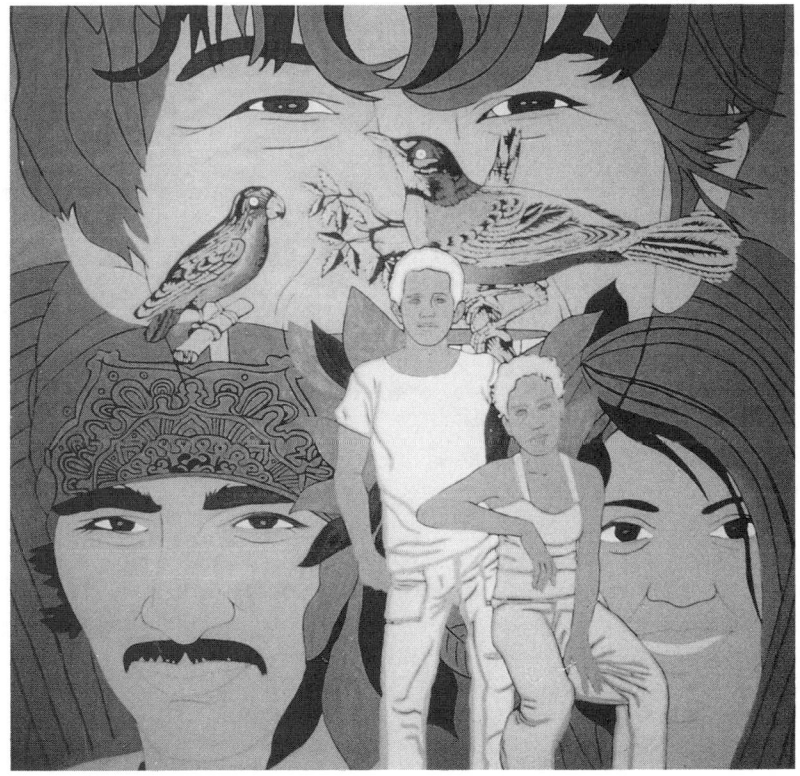

ABTV Team, Nosotros *(after Raúl Martínez), 1988, acrylic on canvas. Collection of the artists. Photo by Luis Camnitzer.*

The ABTV Team

Tanya Angulo (1968), Juan Pablo Ballester (1966), José Angel Toirac (1966), and Ileana Villazón (1969) formed a group of artists who, as mentioned above, worked without a name. The team dissolved in 1989. They worked together in such a seamless manner that they cannot be ignored in this chapter. Clearly influenced by U.S. appropriationists, they started a process of second-generation production with Cuban work and third- (and sometimes fourth-) generation work with U.S. artists. As mentioned in the previous chapter, they initiated their path with a Consuelo Castañeda (see below) version of possible renditions of penises painted in the styles of various Cuban artists of the new generations. The piece started a body of work that was put together in an exhibit titled "He Who Imitates Fails," which was written in Garciandía's handwriting as used in his Cuban proverbs. The pieces in the exhibit[38] were all credible creations in the manner of Cuban artists successful in Cuba since "Volumen I." The introduction to the catalogue was a collage of writings by Gerardo Mosquera taken from different publications and on different subjects, all woven together into one consistent piece that seemed to extol this particular exhibition.

A subsequent, less interesting piece, a remake of Sherrie Levine's photographs, was taken in the manner of U.S. photography masters. The twist in this piece is that the artists followed with extreme precision not only the rephotographing of Levine's pieces but also the layout of the reproduction in the magazine from which they worked. Thus, they emphasized also how the information had gotten to them. What is interesting in the work of this group is that they do not use the appropriation process as a recipe. Instead, each project has its own distinct structure and point, all carefully researched. The ABTV team can be better understood, in their present work, as a counterpart to the U.S. Group Material than as followers of Sherrie Levine.

"Nosotros" was the title for an exhibit of the work of Raúl Martínez in the National Museum of Fine Arts in 1988. "Nosotros" is also the title of an ABTV exhibit in 1989 of Martínez made with the help of the artist. The conscious choice of Martínez in itself has some political implications since he had some difficulties during the UMAP period (see Chap. 3, note 47), and the new generation identifies with the artists who were in that position. The second reason is Martínez' success as a selling artist. This second "Nosotros" exhibit included work not exhibited in the museum, filling in gaps in the history of Martínez because they wished to present a more militant, antiestablishment vision than the museum show. Of all the images he painted of Che, they chose the one used in the homage to him that took place at Cárdenas Square in 1968 to stress Martínez as an accessible painter, not as a valuable one.

The vita they prepared, while factual, makes a point of including such data as 1982, the year Martínez managed to live off the sales of his work and became a "self-sufficient artist."[39] The exhibit also included a fake of a work by Martínez, executed by the team. The original plan went as far as having Martínez sign the fake and then offering the painting for sale to the Fondo Cubano de Bienes Culturales. After all, they explained, Martínez has assistants who prepare his paintings up to the finishing point, and the difference with their own painting is only a matter of degree. Martínez balked at this point and did not want to get involved in that particular piece.

For the cycle at the Castillo de la Real Fuerza, ABTV worked on several projects, to be presented in an exhibit titled "Homage to Hans Haacke." The phrase "Every artist has to find his own formula to express the Revolution" was the starting point for one of the projects. The phrase

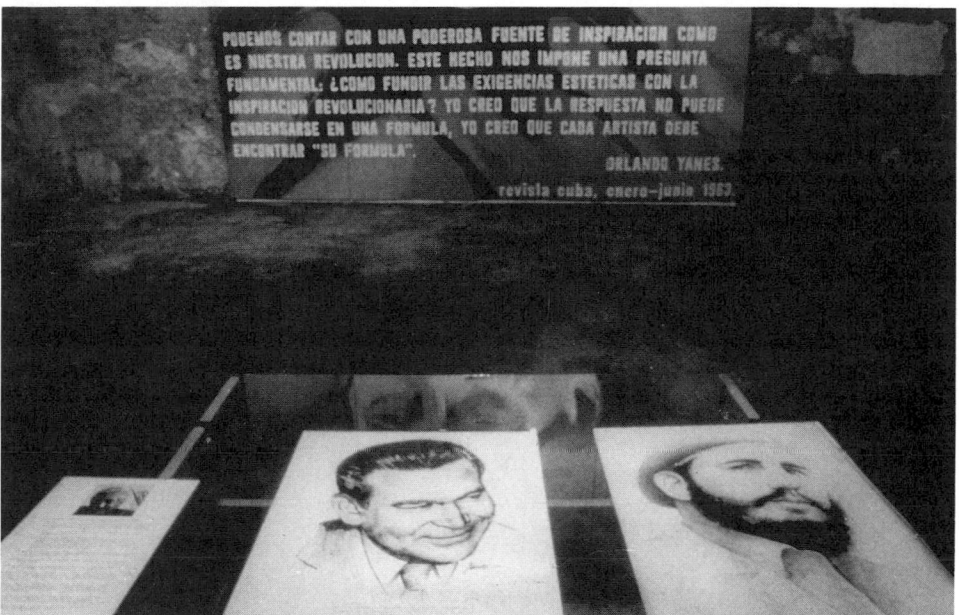

ABTV Team, Homenaje a Hans Haacke (Homage to Hans Haacke), *the Yanes project, 1989, mixed media. Collection of the artists. Photo by ABTV Team.*

was created by an artist who now specializes in portraits of political figures and who, as it turns out, had also made portraits of Batista and his wife before the Revolution. What irked the team was that the artist, Orlando Yanes, used the same visual formula to depict both Batista and Fidel Castro, in spite of claiming that every artist had to find "an individual blend of aesthetic needs and revolutionary inspiration." According to the team, Yanes received a prize in the Batista exhibit boycotted by Los Once and also is the creator of the logo of the Cuban Communist Party. The installation comprised documentation about works from both periods and was accompanied by a banner with a portrait of the artist done in his own style.

A second piece consisted of the burning of a work of Cuban painter Mendive. Mendive's *El pavo real* (*The Peacock*) was burned publicly by José Juara, a Cuban exile and former parachutist during the Bay of Pigs invasion, in Miami in 1988. Juara had bought the work in an auction and then burned it to express his dislike for the Cuban Revolution. His justification was then published in *Opiniones*, a Miami newspaper. In it, Juara warns that any work produced by a Marxist constitutes ideological penetration because it leads youth to associate culture and beauty with Marxism: "Therefore, when *The Peacock* was burned publicly, what was burned was the Marxism associated with the Cuban Marxist painters." ABTV intends to reproduce the burning as a performance but in the Cuban context, associating the piece with its monetary value, symbolizing a capitalist commodity, since Mendive is one of the best-selling Cuban artists alive, particularly in the international market. As a text ABTV slightly rewrote Juara's article and printed it like a newspaper article.

The catalogue text explains, "The FCBC [Fondo Cubano de Bienes Culturales] focuses its commercial work in a type of market whose dynamics are alien to the economic structure of our country. . . . As an institution and not just as an enterprise, the FCBC should function in a 'cultured' manner, not to idealize the value of use, but at least to defend its symbolic function. . . . By burning Mendive's silkscreen we are burning the hyperbole of its exchange value and we are pronouncing ourselves against the fetishism with which the FCBC exercises its commercial policy."[40]

The third project was based on the already-mentioned photograph of Che Guevara taken by Korda. The photograph had been taken by Korda on March 5, 1960, during a rally against the sabotage of the ship *Le Coubre*. Publisher Feltrinelli, visiting Havana after Che's death, met Korda and received two copies of the photograph to make a poster. Subsequently the poster was printed in editions of tens of thousands. Feltrinelli took the royalties and did not credit Korda.[41]

Finally, the team invited Glexis Novoa to exhibit, although (and because) he already had exhibited in the cycle of Castillo de la Real Fuerza. In that way they appropriated the selection process of exhibitions.

Given the density of criticism the exhibition carried, both in the catalogue and in the material shown, the artists felt that some censorial move could be on the way. They hung the exhibit, photographed it, and closed it before the opening, thus also appropriating the act of censorship. The choice of German artist Hans Haacke as the recipient of the homage was due to the empathy the team felt with his plight to make art that criticizes society's mechanisms without being coopted. The last line of their text states, "Paradoxically, our criticism of the institutional framework can also be registered as institutional self-criticism."[42]

ABTV works with appropriation, or with the appropriation of appropriation, but there is always an ethical component in the work, an element of social criticism. The reference to art becomes a metaphor, not an end in itself, at least not in formalistic terms. A particular tension is created by the use of a procedure traditionally considered unethical, as plagiarism would be, to transmit messages based on moral indignation.

After the Castillo de la Real Fuerza nonexhibit, the team broke up temporarily into Angulo and Toirac on one side and Ballester and Villazón on the other (but by 1991, they were working together again). Both couples were present in the "Kuba o.k." exhibition in Düsseldorf in 1990, and both returned to issues of the appropriation of art, making exhibits within the exhibit. Angulo and Toirac titled theirs "Kangaroo?" which is claimed to mean "What are you saying?" in the language of the native Australian who was asked by a sailor of Captain Cook's expedition what that animal was. Angulo and Toirac faked work of the artists included in the exhibition, with this question in mind. One of them was Rodríguez Cárdenas' poster for the exhibit, which therefore appeared twice in the catalogue, once on the cover and then as the fake, with miniscule variations, under their name. Ballester and Villazón complemented the exhibit with art by artists not originally included by the curators, thus extending the scope of the exhibit.[43] They also reproduced works by U.S. artist Louise Lawler and organized the whole exhibition following her "Arrangement of Pictures."

Eduardo Ponjuán and René Francisco Rodríguez

Ponjuán (1956) and Rodríguez (1960) work in the tradition of the Spanish Equipo Crónica (a team of three artists who worked as one) and the Soviets Komar and Melamid. The resulting product is totally unified and seems made by one author in spite of the use of personal styles. They blend their styles into each other until the unity is achieved.

In their work, too, as in other examples discussed, the borderline between kitsch and *Cubanía* is often imperceptible. Although older than the artists of the third generation, the date they became public (they started working together in 1986) and their use of political issues make them a part of the movement of the third generation. Both studied in the ENA and the ISA; Ponjuán graduated in painting and Rodríguez in printmaking.

Their work has political elements fairly consistently. But when these elements appear, it is in such an ambiguous or even hermetic way that a straightforward reading becomes impossible. They explain this as being a product of their working system, which tries to capture a dreamlike state that is never completely formalized; these are "controlled dreams which, without becoming hermetic, do not become open messages."[44] For example, in many paintings they use areas painted like camouflage fabric, with clear allusions to the military but where any value judgment is left to the viewer (they claim it to be equally a symbol of defense and of attack). The earlier mentioned Samurai painting uses a piece of camouflage cloth attached to a piece of sugarcane as a symbol for the wars

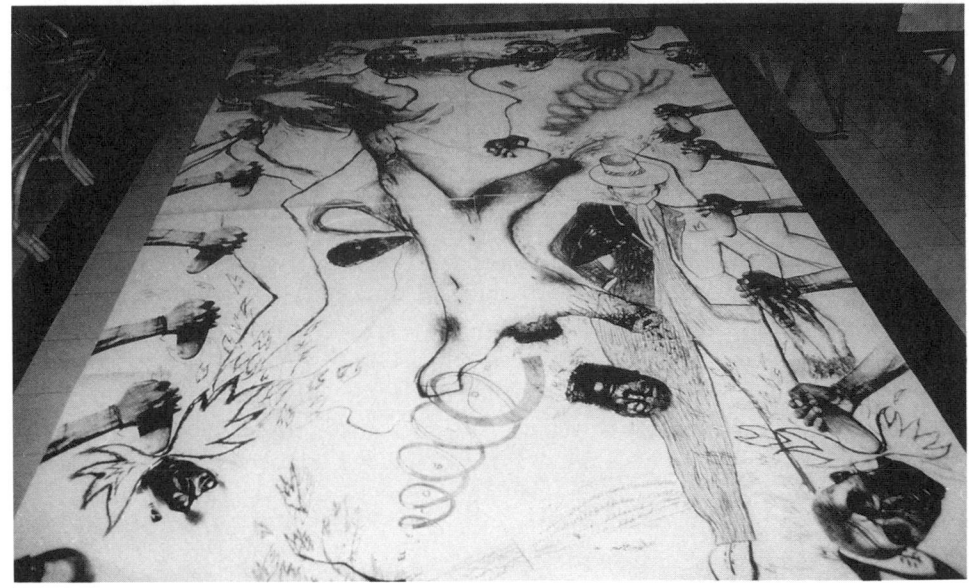

Ponjuán and Rodríguez, untitled, 1987, drawing on paper. Collection of the artists. Photo by Luis Camnitzer.

conducted around sugar. The unrealized dream quality thus absorbs the viewer and leads to a continuation (though not a completion) of the dream.

In *Lectura 2* (Reading 2 [1987]), a diptych, the paintings are separated by a pulley system that moves three flags—USA, USSR, and Movimiento 26 de julio—in a way that, regardless of position, the 26 of July flag remains equidistant from the others. The painting depicts Martí with a second-grade reading book, which justifies the title. *Cuadro de un pintor apátrida* (*Painting by a Stateless Painter* [1988]) is filled with Cuban kitsch and a landscape with snow. The title is written on the frame but with many letters missing, expressing a slow process of decay. *No Smoking* (1988) copies a Malevich stage figure and adds the title in Russian (without translation). *Utopía* (1988) realistically depicts a donkey-eared Soviet official kissing the 26 of July flag while a woman hangs a portrait of Cuban proindependence and abolitionist hero Antonio Maceo (1845–1896) out to dry on a clothesline.

In spite of the use of politically loaded subjects, the work of Ponjuán and Rodríguez has an art meditation quality underlined by an aestheticization that is reminiscent of the work of contemporary American-British painter R. B. Kitaj. Aggression or any overt manifestation of a wish to communicate seems covered by a layer of introspection, a baf-

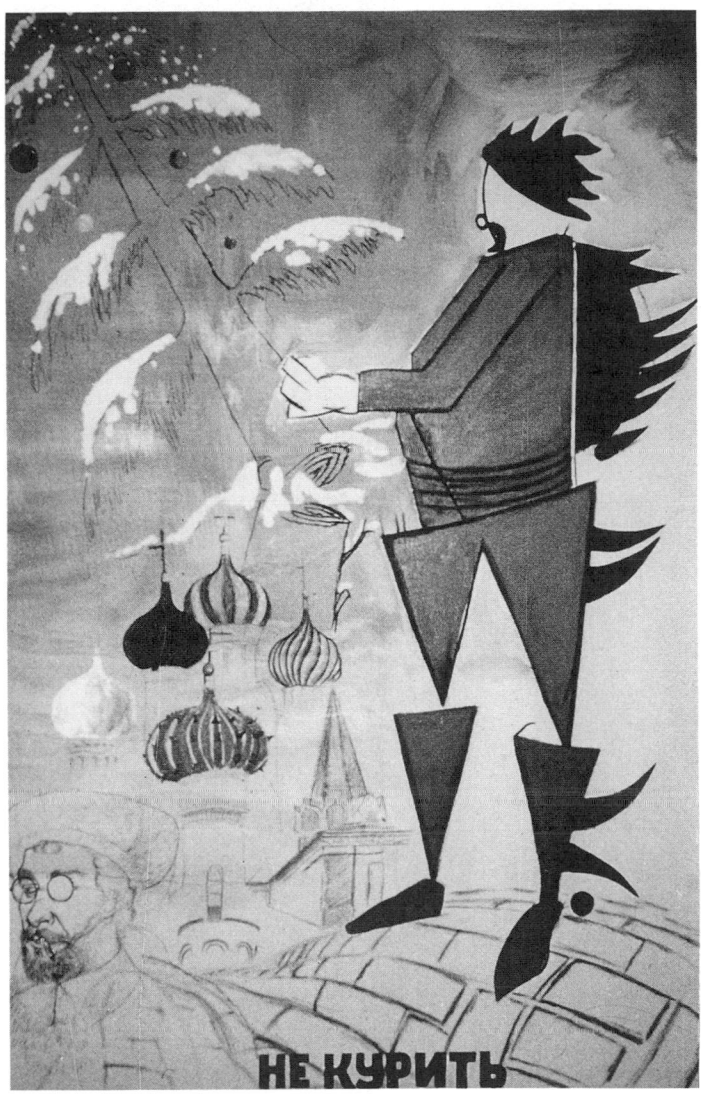

Ponjuán and Rodríguez, No Smoking, *1988, acrylic on canvas, 150 × 100 cm. Collection of the artists. Photo by Luis Camnitzer.*

fling quality in a work produced by a team. There seems to be an absence of a master plan into which the works can be fit. They "happen" individually and unconnectedly. Nevertheless, they seem to belong to a consistent discourse, explainable only by an extraordinary nonlogical communication between both painters, which they explain as the product

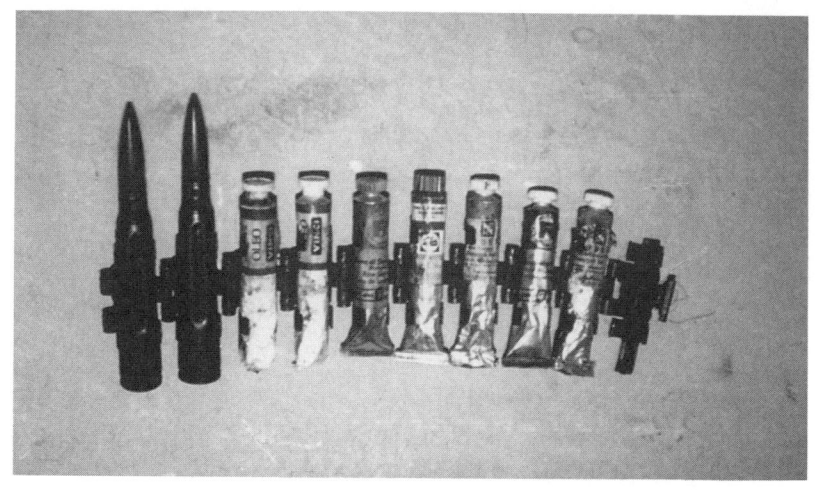

Ponjuán and Rodríguez, Línea de fuego (Firing Line), *1989, mixed media, approximately 15 × 80 cm. Collection of the artists. Photo by Luis Camnitzer.*

of the confluence or intersection of zigzagging states of chaos and peacefulness.

Their exhibit in the Castillo de la Real Fuerza during 1989 created another minor scandal. While most of the pieces in the exhibit were totally harmless, some were problematic in the view of censorial bureaucracy. One drawing, depicting Fidel Castro dressed as a woman with enormous breasts and leading a big rally, was seen as particularly offensive. As a result, the rest of the exhibition was read differently than it otherwise would have been. The effect was so obvious that one was left wondering if the artists were not actually inviting censorship.

Details of the affair vary according to the teller, but shortly afterward Marcia Leiseca, vice-minister for Visual Arts in the Ministry of Culture, was shifted to Casa de las Américas. The issue of censorship became the subject of important polemic both in newspapers and in the UNEAC. Both Ponjuán and Rodríguez participated in the latter, where their arguments were ultimately accepted.

Some time after the incident, during 1990, they decided to work as individuals. Rodríguez went to Spain for a while (October–December 1990) and installed himself in Avila, where he painted by request. Villagers would come to him and ask for a painting of a relative, a landscape, or a dream, and he would comply with their requests. At the end of his stay he borrowed the pieces for an exhibit in the same village and made a catalogue describing the project. Ponjuán, after a standstill, worked on a series based on van Gogh's relations with light and paint. They started

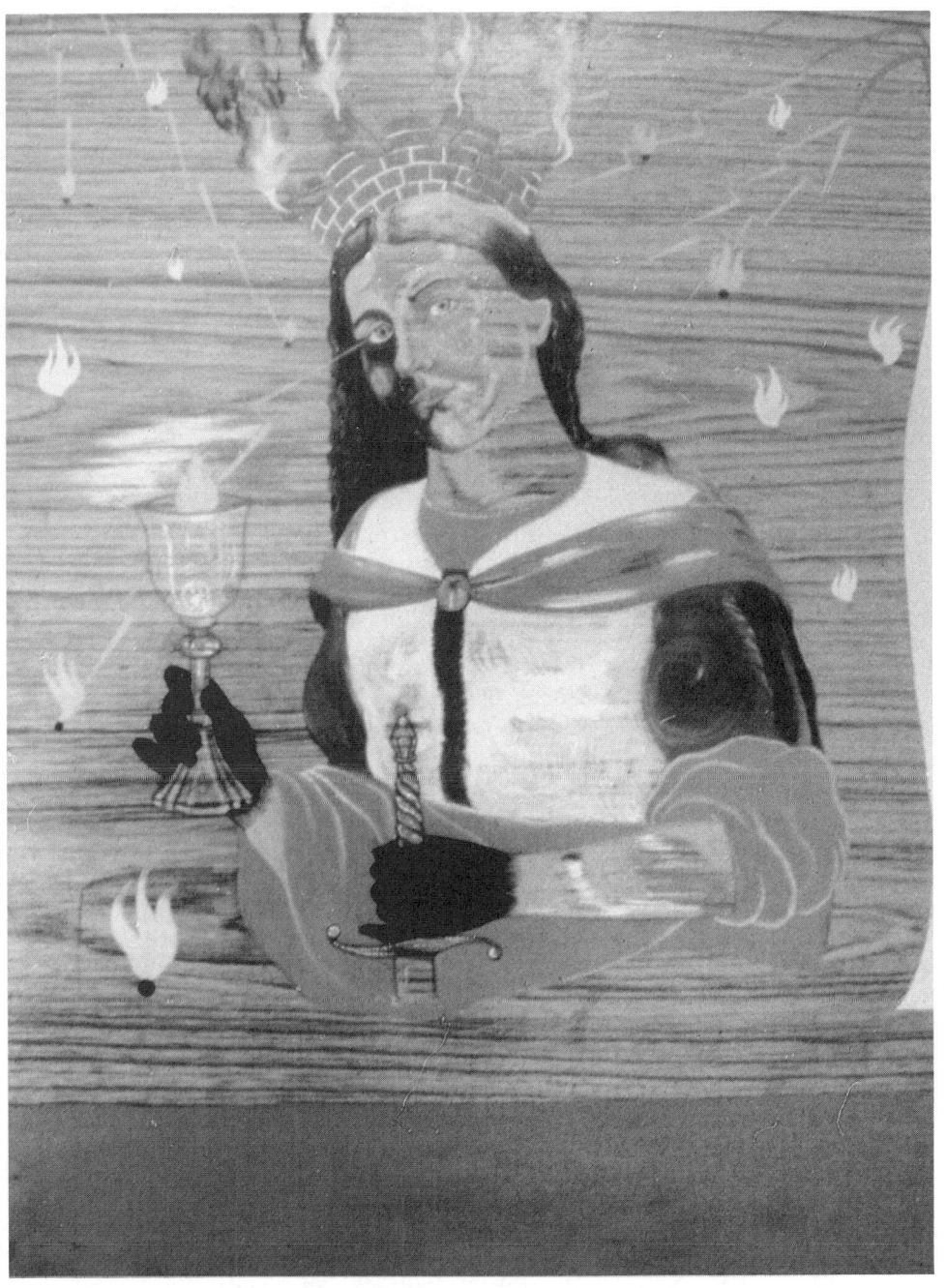

René Francisco Rodríguez, Souvenir, *1990, acrylic on wood, 50 × 40 cm. Collection of the artist. Photo by Luis Camnitzer.*

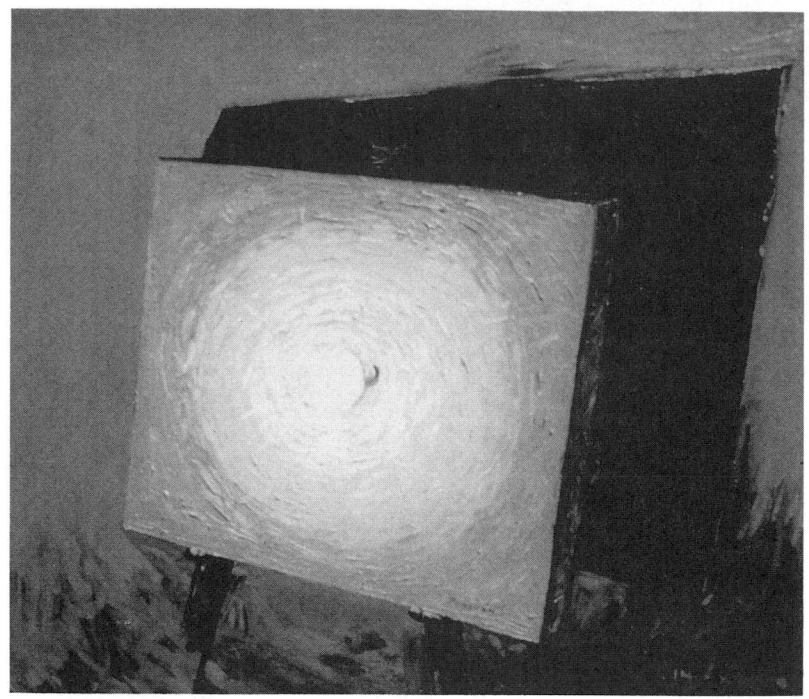

Eduardo Ponjuán, Iluminación (Illumination), *1990, acrylic on canvas, 70 × 80 cm. Collection of the artist. Photo by Eduardo Ponjuán.*

to work again on team projects, and they teach in the ISA, a sign that their official standing was not harmed by the 1989 incident.

Alejandro Aguilera

Aguilera (1964) is one of the few straightforward sculptors among contemporary Cuban artists. Coming from a strict Catholic family—he himself was a believer until the age of twelve—his first pieces were connected with religion, though according to him, mostly connected with medieval aesthetics and more as a way of understanding myth and the history of art. Aguilera's evolution has been quite linear, unshaken by trends or speculations about art-historical traumas.

His first, more conservative pieces have traditional concern about form and materials (carving and casting) and vaguely resemble the works of Yugoslav sculptor Yvan Mestrovic. Primarily based on pietàs and crucifixions, they have some ingenuity in their construction (a window opening in Mary's belly with Christ installed behind it), but they are nevertheless hopelessly dated in style. Aguilera's excellent skills were not enough to validate the work.

A transitional piece, a cosmonaut version of Christ covered in plastic wrap (as such, transformed into a scientist, he would come to redeem us all) failed again. Enormous in size and with some interesting details, the piece had an unintended precariousness that was out of sync with the somewhat pompous statement. However, this particular work was important because it opened the doors for the use of materials looked down upon by traditional sculptors.

Aguilera's next works became clearly focused. His interest in Christian mythology was transfered to Cuban and Latin American history. His sculpture, now produced with wood scraps, forced him to study joints and connections that became interesting on their own and at the same time were functional in relation to the images. His aesthetic clearly went, for a while, on a parallel course with the older and more interesting work of Venezuelan artist Marisol (whose work is familiar to him). They shared the same mixture of folk-art roots with art-historical sophistication.

The pieces, like characters on a stage, hint at three-dimensionality while demanding frontal view. The heroes—Che, Don Quixote, Bartolomé de las Casas, Simón Bolívar, and others—do resemble wooden church saints, but they keep their humanity in an endearing way. Unlike Marisol, Aguilera tries to keep his work free of any secondary speculation about art itself. "Mythological characters with subversive attitudes become freedom fighters, shifting their reason for existence toward terrestrial problems," he says. Aguilera's own description of one of his pieces probably best explains why his work, in his apparent simplicity, did not fall into banality.[45]

Subsequently, Aguilera experimented with a variety of materials as a support for political messages and symbols. The first in this vein was *El tiempo histórico del símbolo es el tiempo histórico de su portador material* (*The Historical Time of the Symbol is the Historical Time of its Material Support* [1989]), an installation five yards long that included seven parts. The parts were variations on the bullet-ridden facade of the Cuartel Moncada (place of the first guerrilla action of Fidel Castro on July 26, 1953, considered the initiation of the Revolution), the last one just an empty, luminous rectangle made of fluorescent tubing. The title underlines or "walks" the seven stations.

A more recent installation (1990) bears the title *They Still Will Know How to Defend It* over a dozen arms with fists, cast in concrete, which slowly evolve into pure abstraction. With these pieces, Aguilera seems

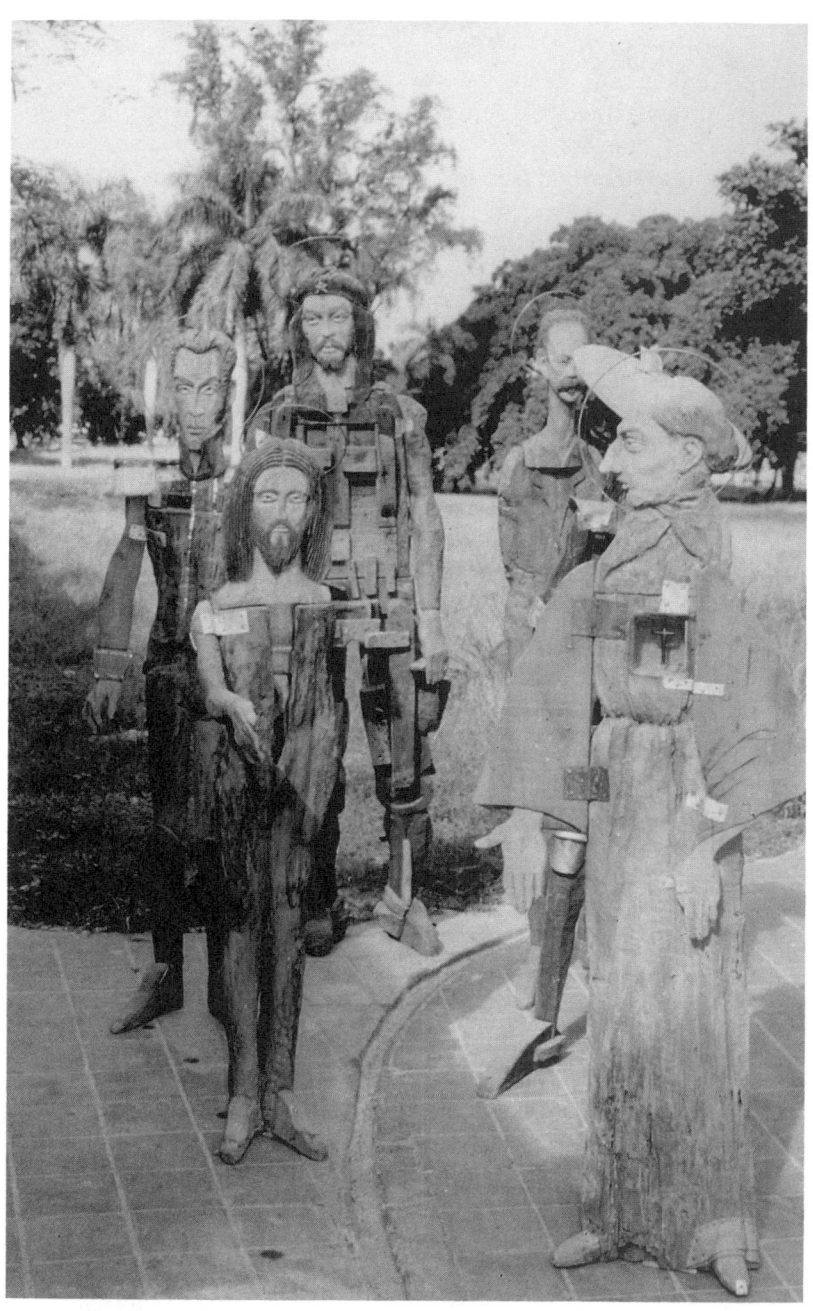

Alejandro Aguilera, En el mar de América (In the Sea of America), *1988, wood carving. Collection of the Centro de Desarrollo de Artes Visuales, Havana. Photo by Luis Camnitzer.*

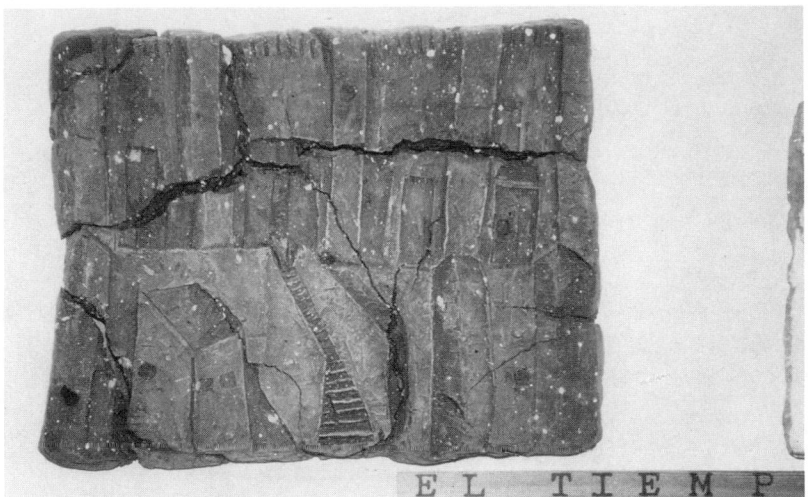

Alejandro Aguilera, El tiempo histórico del símbolo es el tiempo histórico de su portador material (The Historical Time of the Symbol Is the Historical Time of Its Material Support) *(detail), 1989, mixed media, 60 ×
400 cm.*

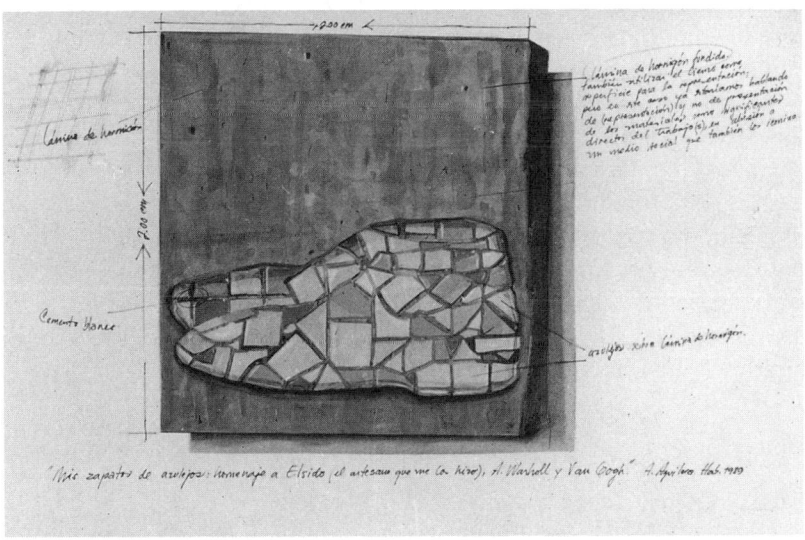

Alejandro Aguilera, Mis zapatos de azulejos: homenaje a Elsido (el artesano que los hizo), Andy Warhol y Van Gogh (My Tile Shoes: Homage
to Elsido [the craftsman who made them], Andy Warhol, and Van
Gogh), *1989, watercolor on paper, 50 × 70 cm. Private collection. Photo by
Luis Camnitzer.*

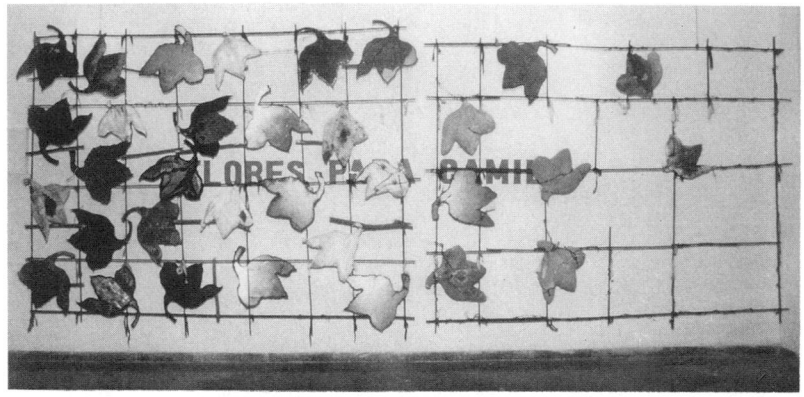

Alejandro Aguilera, Treinta y tres flores para Camilo (Thirty-three Flowers for Camilo), *1991, mixed media, 200 × 400 cm. Collection of the artist.
Photo by Luis Camnitzer.*

to be searching for a new, fresh sacralization of the national symbols,
which is possible only because of the deconstruction of his colleagues in
his generation.

Together with Alexis Somoza and Félix Suazo, Aguilera was one of
the initiators of the Castillo de la Real Fuerza exhibition cycle. The original idea came from their perception that sculpture never had an important role in Cuban arts and that, compared to the other arts in the 1980s,
it had not evolved accordingly. The three artists felt the need to bring
this problem to the foreground, surrounded by debates that might help
diagnose the reasons and cures for the problem. The very attempt to
discuss sculpture in those terms, narrowly focusing on it as a technical
problem, may be in itself a clue to the answers they were seeking. But
the idea that had preceded Esson's exhibit was subsequently changed
and adjusted to what they perceived to be a new climate deserving its
own discussion. The technical approach was dropped and the communication issue was addressed instead.

THE INDIVIDUALISTS

Gustavo Acosta Pérez

Acosta (1958), an exceptional draftsman, has transversed a variety of
unconnected periods. His first interesting series was based on old photographs of scenes of Havana in the 1920s. They were rendered in strong
and vibrant lines, yet realistically faithful, and set on black pages, thus
recalling old photo album pages and increasing their nostalgic value.

In the Second Biennial of Havana, Acosta's work shifted in size and

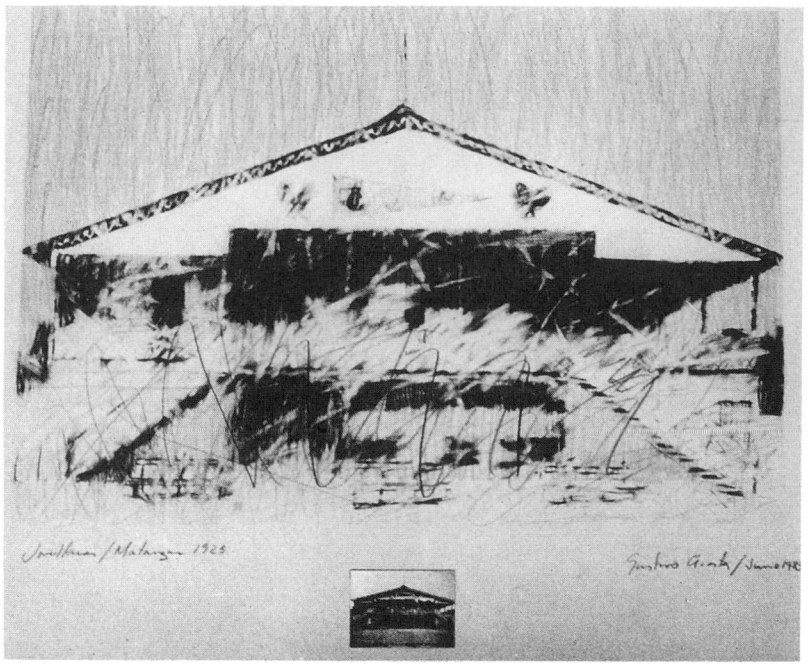

Gustavo Acosta, Jovellanos *(from the series "Album Cuba, 1925"), 1983, graphite on cardboard, 50 × 60 cm. Collection of the artist. Photo by Gustavo Acosta.*

subject matter. A canvas roughly seven-by-fourteen feet, *Día de sol con molino* (*Sunny Day with Windmill* [1986]) depicted a house with a windmill, done in his realist style. The air was covered with stylistically dissonant brush strokes, seemingly the rays of the sun whirled by the wings of the mill. Thus, nostalgia seemed applied to the present.

In a subsequent period, he used acrylic on squares of paper that accumulate to form a large square. The image, ignoring the structural grid, was now symbolic, ambiguous, maintaining figuration but lacking realism. In *La capacidad de aguantar lo que caiga* (*The Ability to Bear What May Fall*), a pillar or armlike shape created a powerful dark division on a nearly pointillist background, with the title integrated on the top and bottom of the painting. Both the use of the title in the image and the treatment of the painting are reminiscent of some of Bedia's work.

The pillars slowly coalesced into Roman nostalgia, which merged with feelings about Havana. Works in an exhibit with the title "The Roads to Rome" (January 1990) portrayed Roman-like buildings with Latin sentences and a sense of decay typical of some constructions in

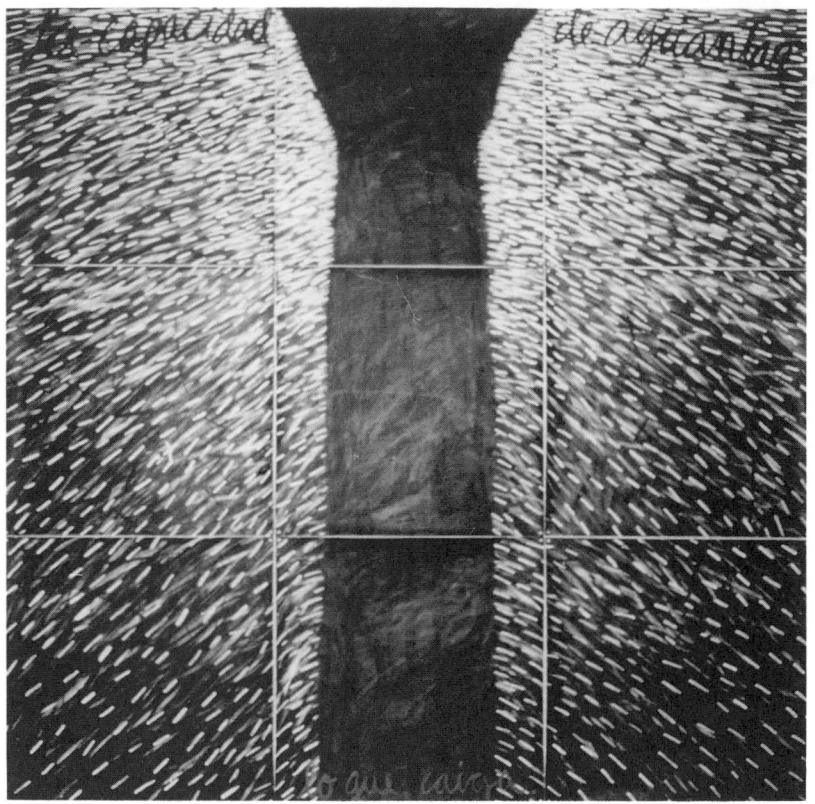

Gustavo Acosta, La capacidad de aguantar lo que caiga (The Capability of Bearing What Falls), *1988, acrylic on paper, 207 × 207 cm. Collection of the artist. Photo by Luis Camnitzer.*

Old Havana. The work reconstituted into big-size canvases, maintaining some echoes from the gridding developed by the small-size papers. The latest work of Acosta synthesizes his career as a painter in sizeable dramatic depictions of large, unpopulated architectural spaces with a Mussolinian atmosphere. They are his most successful pieces to date.

Humberto Castro

Castro (1957) is the Cuban artist most easily classed as an expressionist, a style consistent with his interest in violence. Both elements have a Latin American root. The expressionism is linked with the work of Argentinean painters Luis Felipe Noé, Ernesto Deira, and Rómulo Macció, and with Venezuelan painter Jacobo Borges, all of whom developed a style that in the early 1960s in Latin America was called neofiguration or

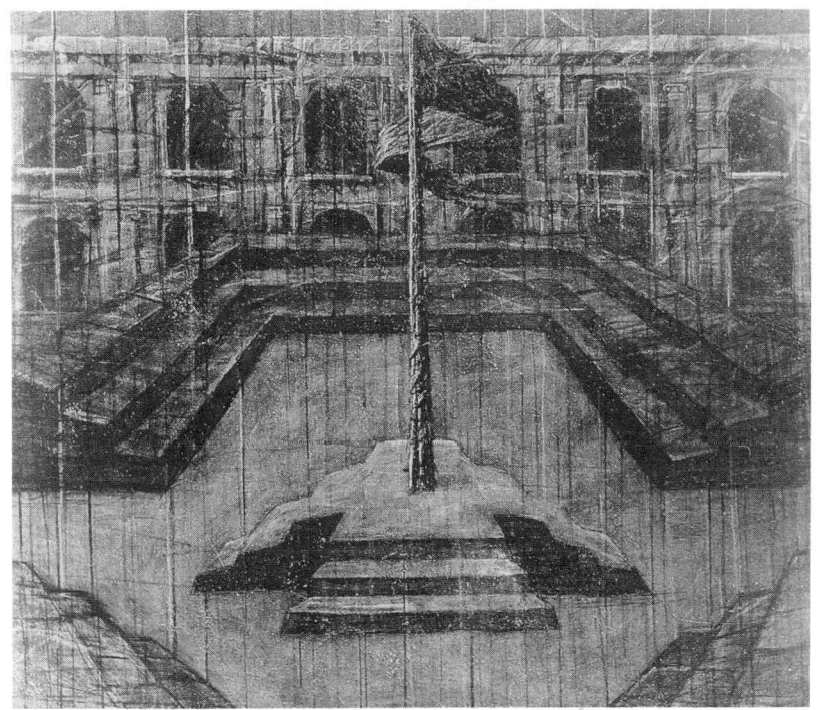

Gustavo Acosta, untitled, 1991, acrylic on canvas, 180 × 200 cm. Collection of the artist. Photo by Romulo Fialdini.

neoexpressionism. Castro's violence was inspired by the extermination of the native population in Cuba and other genocidal activities in Latin America. "I am a mirror, and what I want to do with my work is reflect violence in a filtered form. I use it to demonstrate an expressionism of our period that is much more charged with man's inner feelings than the previous one,"[46] he says.

Castro developed a style early on in his work which, while competent and undeniably powerful, suffers from a certain repetition and reliance on formula. His work becomes more interesting when he deviates from his excessively formalized style. Two clear examples of this are provided by his entry in the Second Biennial of Havana and the work he made for the "Salón de la UNEAC," the exhibition accompanying the Fourth Congress in 1988.

The Biennial piece, though not completely successful, was, to say the least, a powerful installation. Three hideously green life-size sculpted bodies appeared crushed into a bed of broken mirrors and surrounded by panels painted in a manner looser than usual. The resulting total had

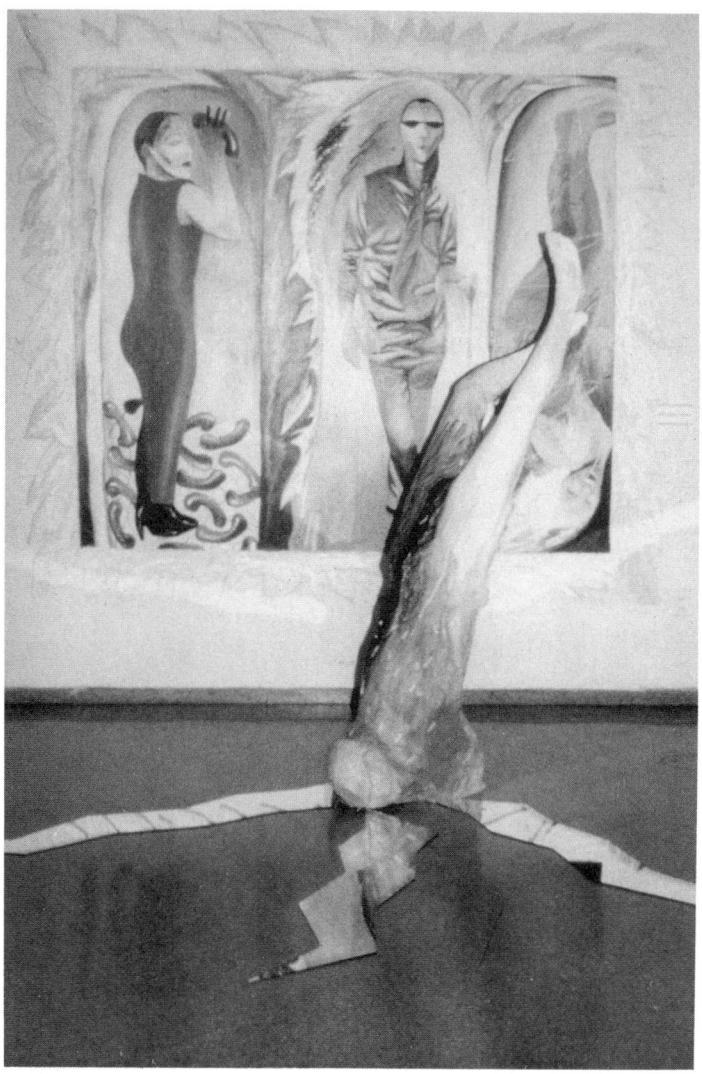

Humberto Castro, La caída de Icaro (Icarus' Fall), *1984, acrylic on canvas. Museo Nacional de Bellas Artes, Havana. Photo by Humberto Castro.*

a Rosenquist-like quality of disconnected imagery, but without the billboard slickness. The weakness of the piece was mainly provided by the mannequinish look of the sculptures.

The UNEAC installation, *Los lobos y el hombre* (*The Wolves and the Man*), was totally successful. Involving panels at the outside hall of the Pabellón Cuba and the three-story-high wall of a neighboring building,

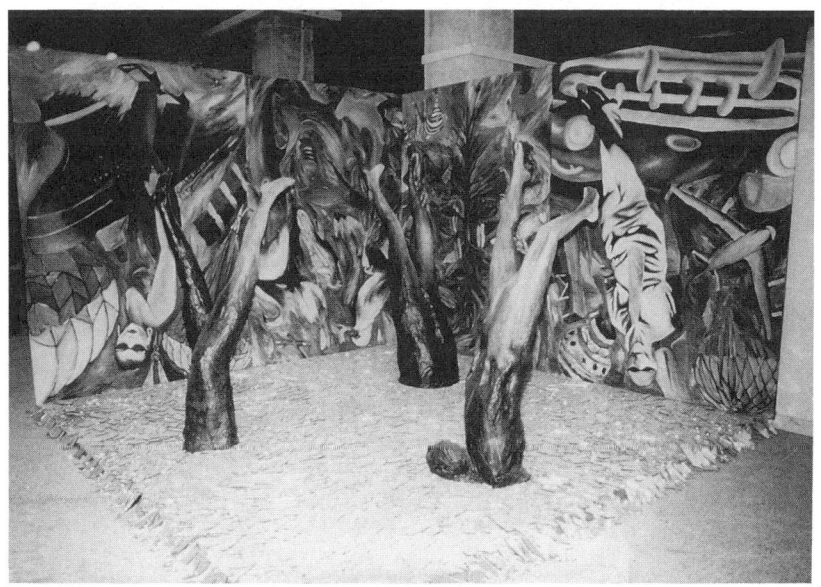

Humberto Castro, La caída de Icaro #2 (Icarus' Fall #2), *1986, mixed media installation at the Second Biennial of Havana, 400 × 400 × 400 cm. Photo by Luis Camnitzer.*

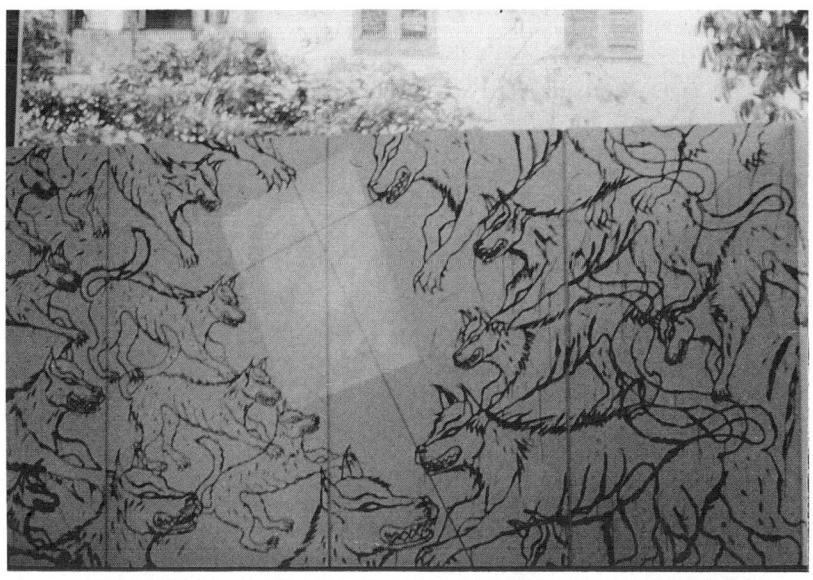

Humberto Castro, Los lobos y el hombre (The Wolves and the Man), *1988, installation at UNEAC, Havana. Photo by Humberto Castro.*

the surfaces were covered with savage-looking wolves slowly encircling an area on a panel where a slide projector screened photographs of Che Guevara's dead body. The impact of the piece in Cuba was much greater than that suggested by the description, since those photographs are rarely seen, maintaining the tradition that Che's presence in spirit is stronger than his bodily death.

Castro's current work continues to have violence as a thread. In a catalogue prepared for an exhibit traveling in Canada (1988), he wrote a sequence of views on violence: "violence as the most elegant weapon that dwells in the heart of the feeble. The violence of the brilliance of glass that breaks the spectator's eyes. Your violence."

Consuelo Castañeda

Until recently, Castañeda (1958) appropriated different styles without any transformation. Three-dimensional sharks navigate through a mosaic of Hokusai waves where shells taken from Botticelli's *Birth of Venus* complete the marine landscape painted in 1986. In *Lichtenstein y los Griegos* (*Lichtenstein and the Greeks* [1987]), she employs Roy Lichtenstein's *Temple II* of 1965 as a backdrop for images and casts of Greek sculptures. In *La creación de la creación: Da Vinci y Jenny Holzer* (*The Creation of Creation: Da Vinci and Jenny Holzer* [1987]), Leonardo's presence is indicated by mirrors that reverse Holzer's text while in the back of the accordion-like structure, characters of Michelangelo frescoes stare into their own faces.

Critic Osvaldo Sánchez refers to her work as being *mestizaje artístico*, the product of intermixing, giving it roots in the mestizo character of Cuban culture, but Castañeda's work seems more rationalist than that. Castañeda's work is risky. It can be interpreted as following the post-conceptual appropriationist trend, artificially introducing it into Cuba. But it also can be seen as a didactic effort designed to save future artists from directly submitting to the influence of Western mainstream art by predigesting it and putting it into a Cuban context. In that sense, what she does is a follow-up on book and magazine culture. There, she picks what she considers basic components to assemble a new, clarified (and humorous) grand total. As she explains, "In Cuba everyone learns from reproductions. We see very few original works of art. Consequently, many works have the finished quality of a print. We like our work to look slick, like reproductions in a magazine. It all takes place unconsciously. That's why we had to found a movement that concentrated on style, on the mode of presentation."[47]

André Breton once observed that Mexico was a surrealist country and consequently was interested in what belated surrealists produced

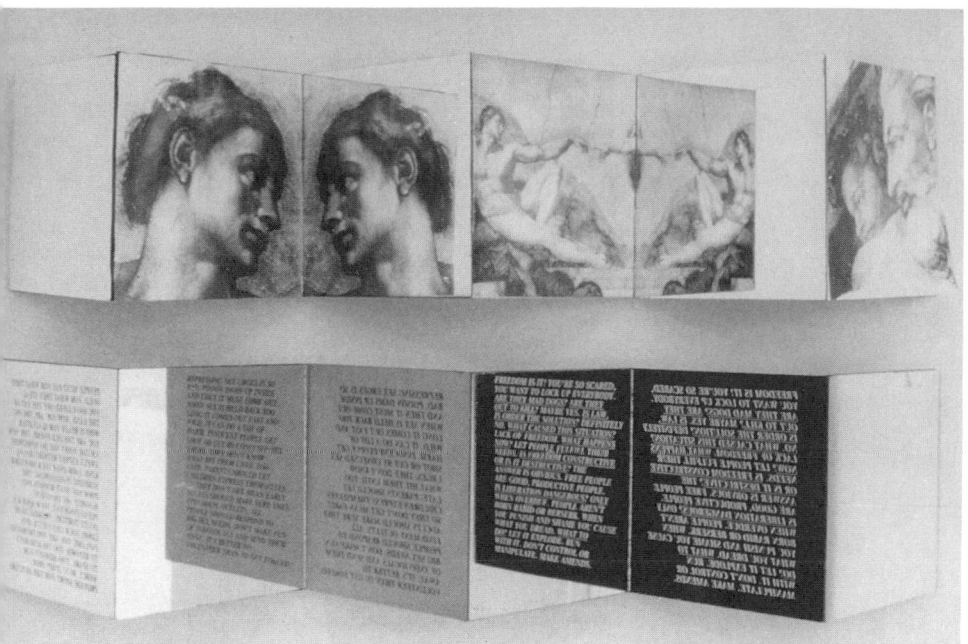

Consuelo Castañeda, La creación de la creación: Leonardo da Vinci y Jenny Holzer (The Creation of Creation: Leonardo da Vinci and Jenny Holzer), *1987, mixed media, 30 × 124 × 25 cm. Collection of the artist. Photo by Charles Merewether.*

there. Several aesthetic movements in this century have been representative of peripheral cultural needs, either revealing local identity or helping to cope with hegemonic influences. Pop art, conceptualism in its Italian *Arte Povera* form, and appropriationism were all movements that followed surrealism and that could have been generated locally.[48] Pop art was a tool to handle the artificial cultural overlay created by the massive influx of prepackaged consumer goods. Arte Povera gave the chance to work with "unapproved," easily available, nonartistic materials and to incorporate meaningful ideas. Appropriation presented a way of structuring the colonizing information stream and opened the possibility of digesting information without submitting to it. It is a symbol of the intensity of cultural dependence that these movements had to be imported through the same channels as the aesthetics they opposed, rather than being generated without the need of an example. They thus lost some of their potentially liberating power and contaminated the results by always forcing a comparison with the work of the artists who started the movements in the hegemonic centers.

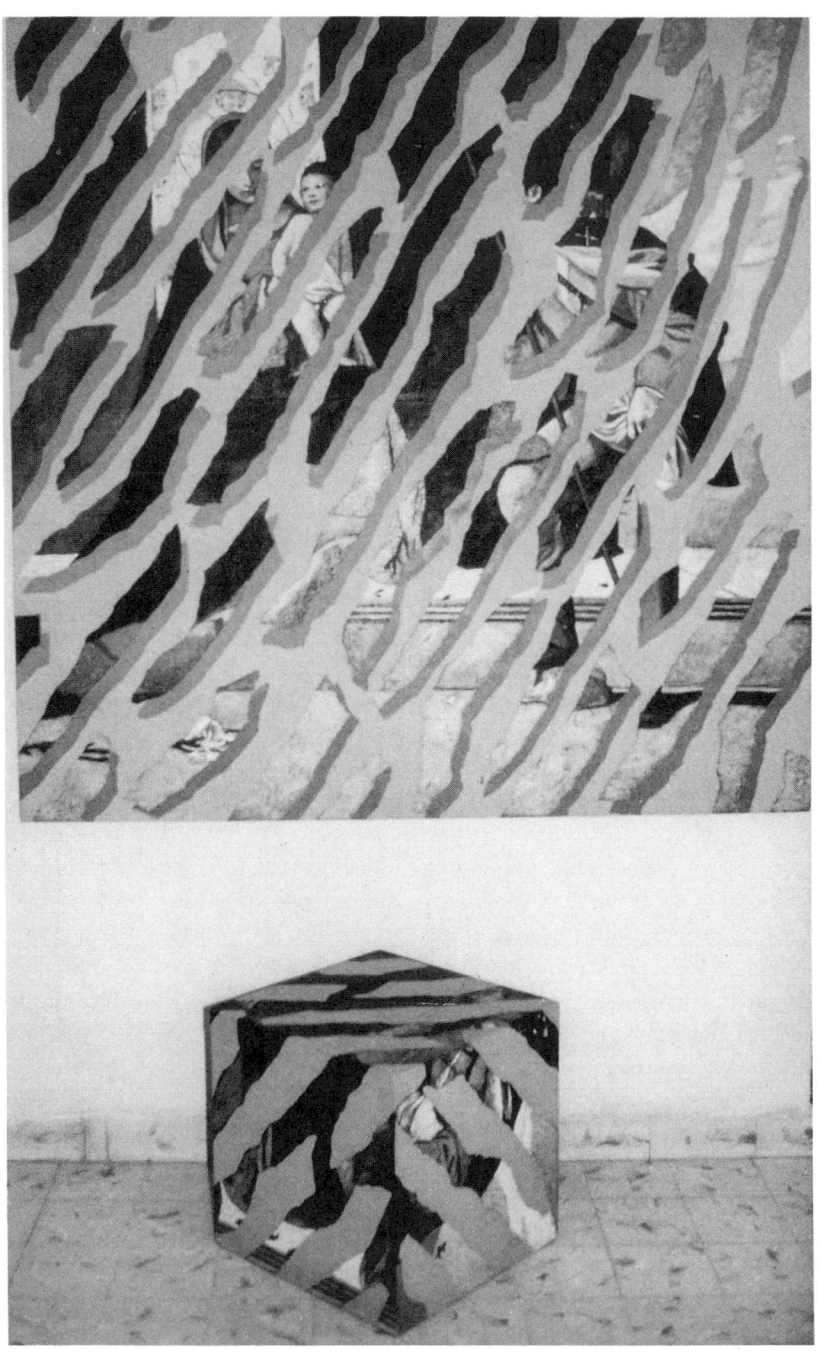

Consuelo Castañeda, untitled, 1984, acrylic on canvas, 180 × 180 cm. Collection of Antonio Eligio Fernández. Photo by Luis Camnitzer.

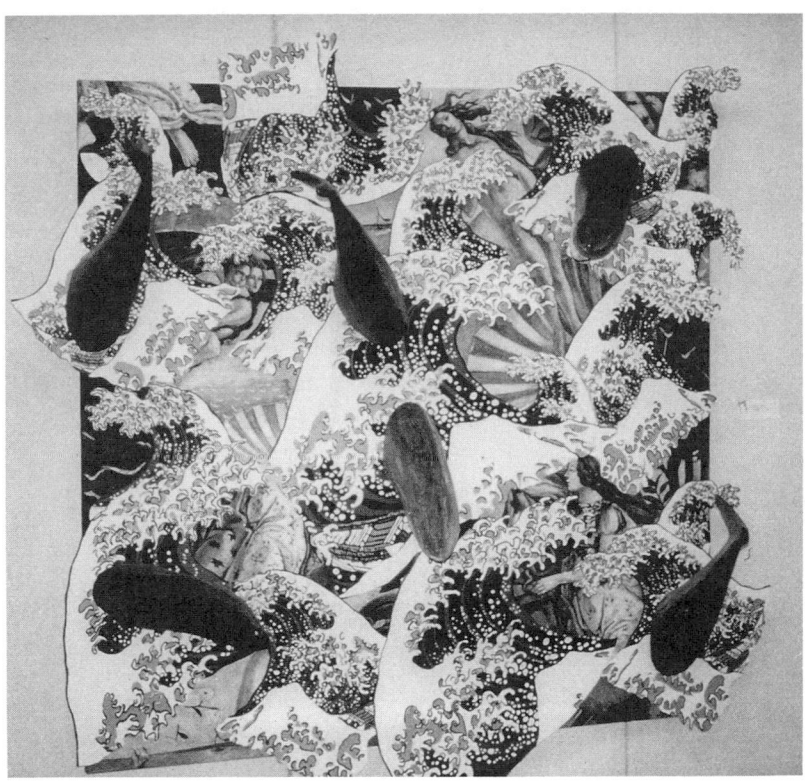

Consuelo Castañeda, untitled, 1986, acrylic on canvas. Collection of the artist. Photo by Luis Camnitzer.

Castañeda's work, up to this point, can be seen as self-sacrificing for the benefit of a collective need. She reduced herself to conducting an orchestra formed by members of the art-historical repertoire who all play their own instruments, loosely fitting into her grand design. In this process of reassembly, much becomes demystified and accessible, and in that sense her work fills a void. Cuban art would not be the same without her work. She created catalysts for other people's creations, confirming her reputation as a teacher, an activity in which she seems to perform the same function.

In 1988 her interest started to shift from the artistically referential to the self-referential. Roughly painted and sculpted concentric circles, nearly alluding to fingerprints, were stacked in apparent crowdlike rows. The act of painting became a public observing the viewer. Creating, maybe unwittingly, a metaphor of her path, she made a spiral sculpture in ceramics (1989) with the text "The signs change according to the

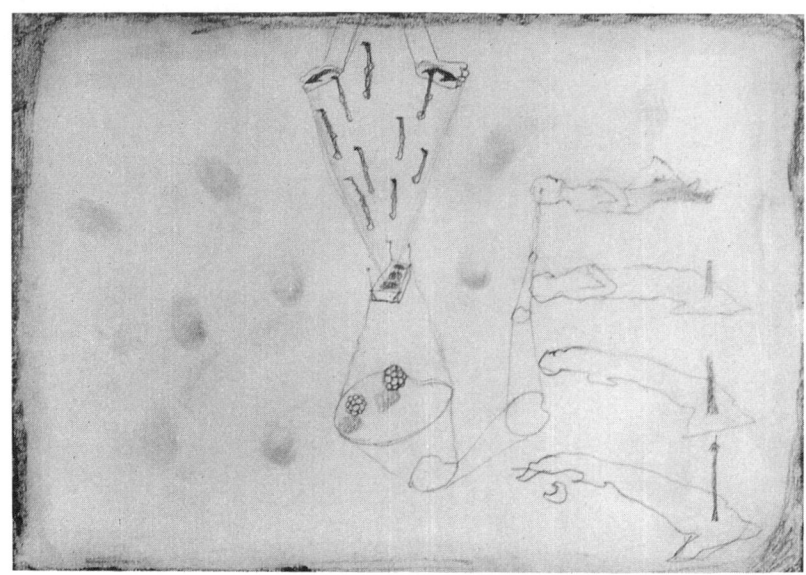

Segundo Planes, untitled, 1986, drawing on paper, 45 × 65 cm. Private collection. Photo by Luis Camnitzer.

materials used in their representation." The piece recalls tautological conceptual art of the sixties and Aguilera's piece about historical time. But it also leads very pointedly to another work, *Retrato de mi madre y yo: Una historia en setenta páginas* (*Portrait of My Mother and I: A Story in Seventy Pages* [1989]), in which Castañeda for the first time confronts a private emotional issue—a detailed analysis of her aged mother, though in as detached a manner as possible.

Segundo Planes

Planes (1965) is at the opposite extreme from Castañeda and, with Arturo Cuenca, the closest thing to an individualist artist in Cuba. Working in a stream-of-consciousness fashion, he combines extensive self-portraiture with philosophy, politics, sex, scatology, and poetry in an endless flow of baroqueness. Art critic Mosquera links his work with Hieronymus Bosch and the Latin American carnival tradition, calling it "supersurrealist, superexpressionist, and superbaroque."[49]

At first view, the work seems somewhat self-indulgent and therapeutic. A facile draftsman, he often relies on Dalí-like recipes and fashion-drawing effects, which weaken his pieces. But the apparent chaos is supported by a method and a search for a system. As he told me in an interview, "My concern is not so much to be a good painter. If I am one,

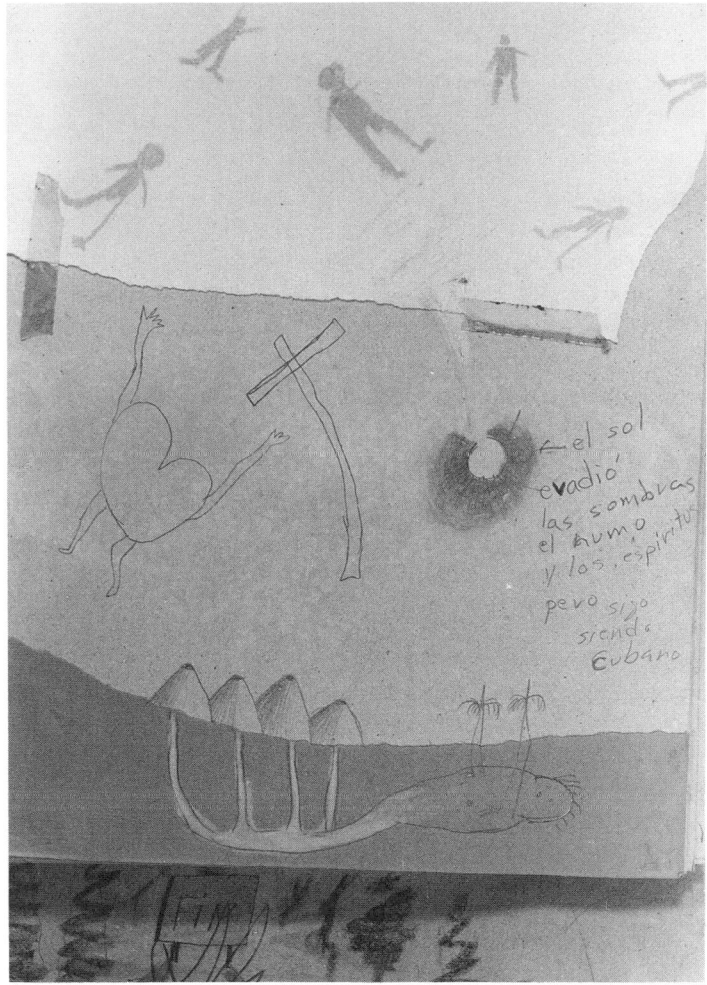

Segundo Planes, untitled page from the book Jugando a ser loco (Acting Like a Fool), *1987, drawing and collage, 60 × 40 cm. Private collection. Photo by Luis Camnitzer.*

it is only because that is what I know, but what I want is to find a consistent system for my body of ideas. I am interested in the process of doubting, in things such as whether or not humankind will survive, in the relation of the rational with irrationality."

Contradictory to the apparent egotism of his work, he signs it "nobody," since "the concept of the personal is only based on a name or a word. . . . Marx was totally unimportant as a person. What matters is the work he left. . . . One should make art to express that art doesn't exist."[50]

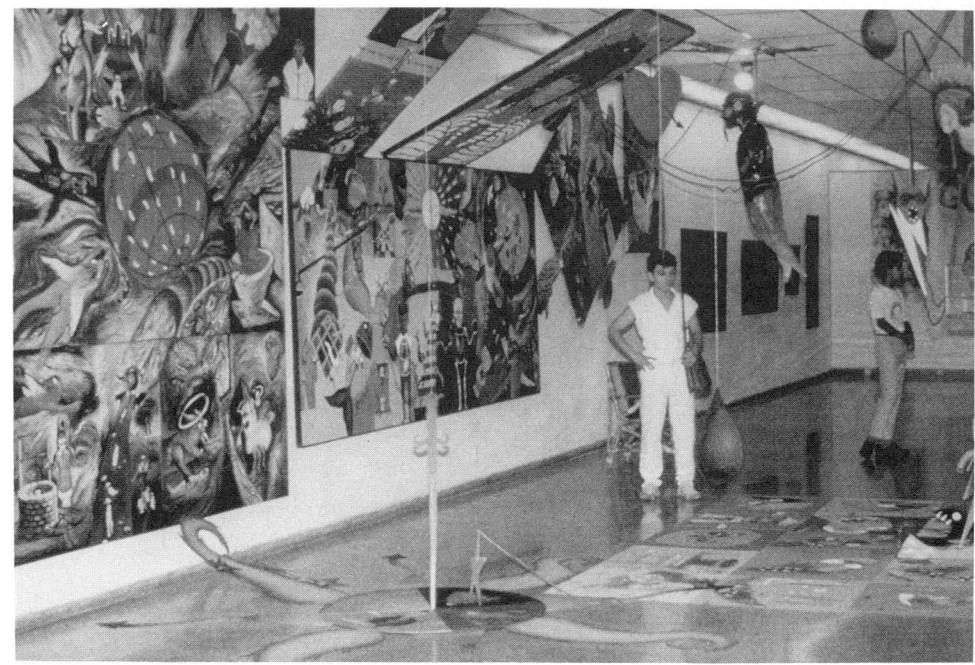

Segundo Planes, untitled installation, 1988. Collection of the artist.

Planes' baroqueness takes several shapes. It can appear as a complex canvas, as an overwhelming installation (he is aware of Borofsky's work), or as endless pages with drawings, collages, and written comments and humor seamlessly integrated. A 1986 drawing follows the evolution of the map of Cuba into a man taking his siesta. A 1987 drawing and collage with the title *Con los brazos abiertos* (*With Open Arms*) pointedly separates a hammer from a sickle.

In the case of Planes, it really seems futile to analyze individual pieces. His output is continuous and diluvial. To catalogue his work would be equivalent to choosing some words over others in an encyclopedia. In time, patterns will emerge that will help both him and the viewer to organize the work.

Planes, maybe more than others, had already been fully accepted into the Cuban art world at the time when he was still a student at the ISA. That fact, coupled with his diarrheic form of working, unavoidably leads to a degree of self-indulgence. It can be expected that, forced to measure up, he will become more rigorous and distrusting of his own facility. Meanwhile, he continues working under the motto "Life is shit and the world is crazy, or viceversa."[51] His work is liable to reveal his precise mood and state of mind at the instant it was produced. If that instant has any relevance—and it very frequently does—so does the corresponding piece.

Alexis Somoza

Somoza (1966) derives his work primarily from an analysis of and resentment toward the Cuban sculpture tradition. Believing that Cuban sculpture's stagnation is due to an excessive respect for traditional materials and that these condition the imagery, he set out to challenge it. He cites Sol Lewitt's statement, "If words are used which derive from ideas about art, they are art and not literature."

In 1987 he had an exhibit "Formas bajo la luz" ("Forms Under the Light"). The pieces exhibited were flat and used banal materials (concrete, paint, tar, tin, masonite, wax, etc.). The titles invariably referred to unrelated traditional Cuban sculptures, including the materials. Therefore *Nude, Marble* was made out of concrete, tar, and tempera; *Roosevelt, Artificial Stone* was done in masonite, wax, and tar.

In January 1988, Somoza had a one-hour exhibit called "Pollock." An homage to the artist, it consisted of a pile of wax-sealed envelopes to be taken by the public. The envelopes contained relevant information—among other things, Jackson Pollock's curriculum vitae, a poem by Mimo Rotella, a text by Carl Jung, and reproductions of works of British artists Tony Cragg and Gilbert and George. One of the projects he is working on involves only sound, an aural sculpture in which sounds transmitted through a quadrophonic system organize the space without any visible elements.

Somoza is extremely articulate about the third generation's identity and sees himself as a representative of the aims of the "rectification" process: "Antibureaucratism is not only the outspoken criticism of the errors and weaknesses of the apparatus but also the support of the forms of combat against its monolithic character in the areas of its interests; that is, incapacity, laziness, fragmentation, and backwardness, which are all related to those serving the state structure." He cites Ernst Fisher's writing: "We need heretics." "One has to defend heresy against any orthodoxy."[52]

While Somoza attacks the "Volumen I" generation for having, to a certain extent, joined the establishment and limited themselves to concentrating on formal changes in art, the same criticism can be applied to his work.[53] Focusing on a particular medium as the area for change, he has not yet integrated his general view of the world into his art. The work still lacks the passion that many of his colleagues have achieved. In its place he has developed the "finish" of his pieces, which stress his

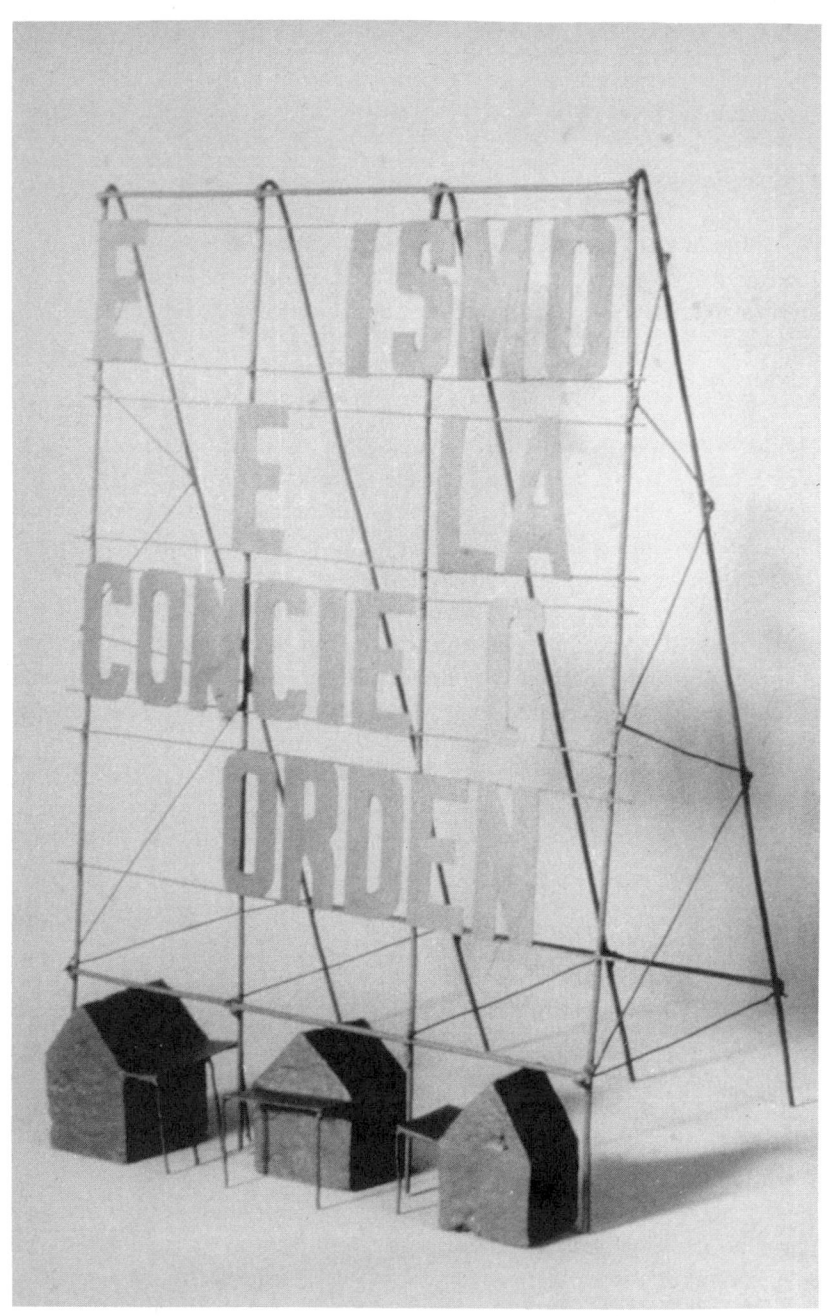

Alexis Somoza, El ilusionismo de la conciencia y su desorden (The Illusionism of Consciousness and Its Disorder), *1989, mixed media. Collection of the artist. Photo by Conchita Pedrosa Morgado.*

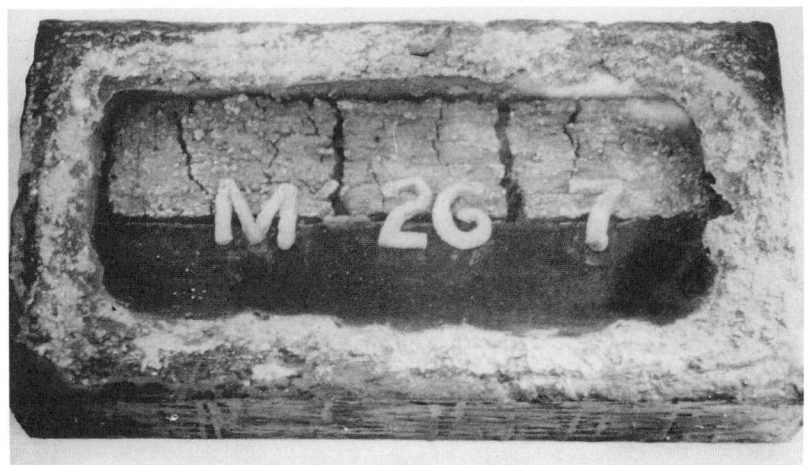

Alexis Somoza, Movimiento 26 de julio (Movement 26th of July), *1990, mixed media. Collection of the artist. Photo by Conchita Pedrosa Morgado.*

artistic rigor and intellectualism but are left functioning in a vacuum inconsistent with his writings.

As seen previously, Somoza had an important role in the development of the Castillo de la Real Fuerza cycle. Subsequently, during 1990, he helped organize an exhibit under the title "El objeto esculturado" ("The Sculptured Object"),[54] trying to bring back the focus on sculpture that had been lost in the previous attempt. The exhibit, harmless in itself from a political point of view, engendered its own scandal. During the night of the opening one of the visitors decided to add his own sculpture to the show. He carefully laid out newspaper in the middle of the room, lowered his pants, squatted, and deposited an odorous offering.[55]

Somoza's present work tackles patriotic symbols with a sense of irony, which he expresses through the use of cheap and crude materials. The work is not intended to be disrespectful; he is patriotic in his own way, representing the "rectification" process in opposition to the official patriotic stuffiness. His work is now more in line with that of Aguilera and might also fit him into the nationalism stream in this same chapter, an indication of how powerfully the national reality interacts with the production of art in Cuba.

José Angel Toirac

Toirac (1966) did to printmaking what Somoza was doing to sculpture, except that his approach was more conceptual—so conceptual, in fact, that he mostly used prints discarded by others, which he found in

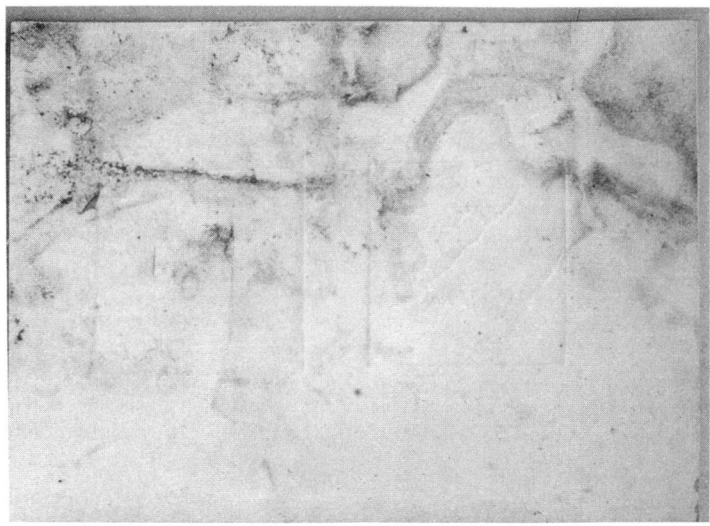

José Angel Toirac, untitled, 1987, etching on paper, 50 × 70 cm. Collection of the artist. Photo by José A. Toirac.

the ISA's garbage cans when he was a student. These "prints-trouvés," soiled and ripped, are torn into pieces, cut into squares, folded, collaged, or arranged in multiple copies. Whatever is done to them is random, without any particular taste or compositional determination.

Toirac believes that the imprint of the viewer's mind on the print is the ultimate and most powerful act. It is also the purest. He detechnified the technique while remaining outside of the generating process, and he recontextualized the object within its own frame of reference. Unlike Marcel Duchamp and followers, who appeal to transmutation through a shift of the levels of perception and association, Toirac tried to expand and enrich the level initiated by the found print. The approach is intellectual, but the overlay of age, usage, and, even more, misusage, leads the viewer to imprint an emotional response on the work, which the original normally would not have elicited.

In a statement attached to one of his pieces, Toirac says, "What matters is the mind's process, which conceives of the prints. These prints represent this process, as well as the intellectual process they spur in the observer. In the traditional sense, I did not create them. They came to me as ruinous objects, devoid of the meaning that had created them. I imprinted another content on them. They are, simultaneously, a ruin of prints and a print of ruins."

Though originally interested in printmaking, Toirac did not remain bound by specific media. He works within a self-constructed system that

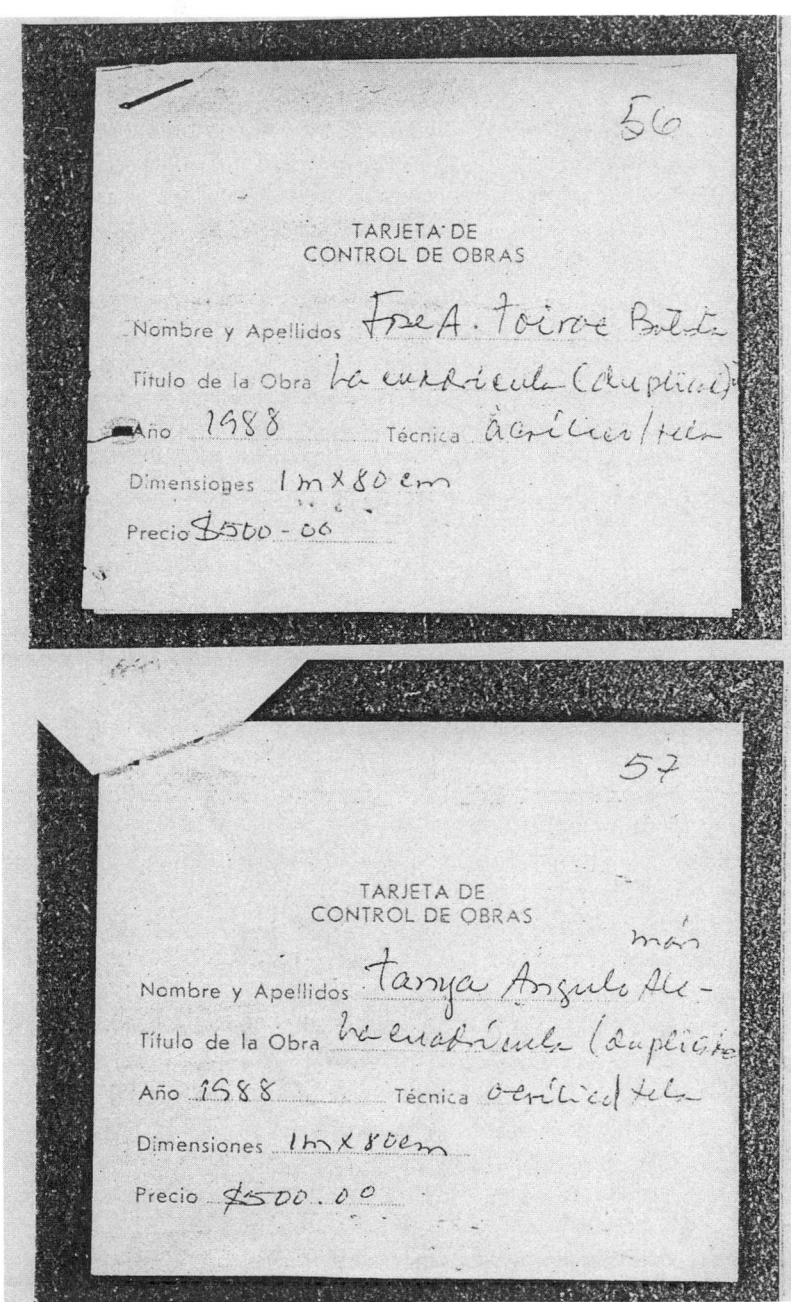

José Angel Toirac and Tanya Angulo, labels for Una cuadrícula, duplicado (A Quadricle, Duplicate), *1988. Private collection. Photo by Luis Camnitzer.*

connects with the work of John Cage and some early conceptualists. Illiterate in music, he constructed a composition, *Scènes pittoresques* (1988), picking fragments of scores that he selected and combined using purely visual criteria. The piece was then performed by a professional concert pianist and had a better aural consistency than anybody might have expected. With Tanya Angulo he prepared two identical abstract paintings and submitted them, under different assumed names, to a competition (unfortunately without their being accepted).

Operación Yagruma is his most ambitious project to date (except for his collaboration in ABTV and later with Angulo). It is an object and video work still in progress. Yagruma, a popular tree in Cuba, becomes an art-historical object of profound importance. Monet painted it in the early morning, at noon, and at sunset. It takes the place of a palm tree in a poem of Cuban poet Nicolás Guillén and also appears as an underpainting, only visible with infrared photography, on a Rembrandt painting. Seen from the front and the back, it becomes a metaphor for Octavio Paz' description of Duchamp's *The Bride Stripped Bare by the Bachelors Even*. Nineteenth-century woodcut artist Hokusai included it in a woodcut in front of a Japanese landscape in a close-up rendition that made the tree appear out of focus. Goya mixed its sap with pigment, integrating the intimate perfume of the Duchess of Alba in the *Naked Maja*. And Barbara Kruger, in *Untitled*, uses it for an effective comparison with male rationality.

Of the four members of ABTV, Toirac is the artist who maintains the strongest commitment to individual art. The fact that he works with distinct ideas and within technical and stylistic freedom helps him avoid conflict in this dual track.

Dania del Sol

Del Sol (1966) works, in a rare occurrence for contemporary Cuban art in her generation, in a conceptual-constructivist tradition. She is deeply involved in mathematical philosophy and logic. Images taken from her studies are counterpointed with trompe l'oeil effects and discourses about magic. While Pérez Monzón challenges logic with numerology, she takes the opposite stance and underlines the poetry of rigor. Illusionistic effects initially seem to challenge the rational structure, only to reappear intact in a virtual image. Or reality appears as virtual, while the accessories take bodily presence, something she also exploits when creating photograms, where lights and shadows directly projected on photographic paper create a form initially absent. A pyramid, projected on the wall by means of a slide, casts a perfect painted shadow on the floor. Using fixed points of view, she forces the viewer to reconstruct

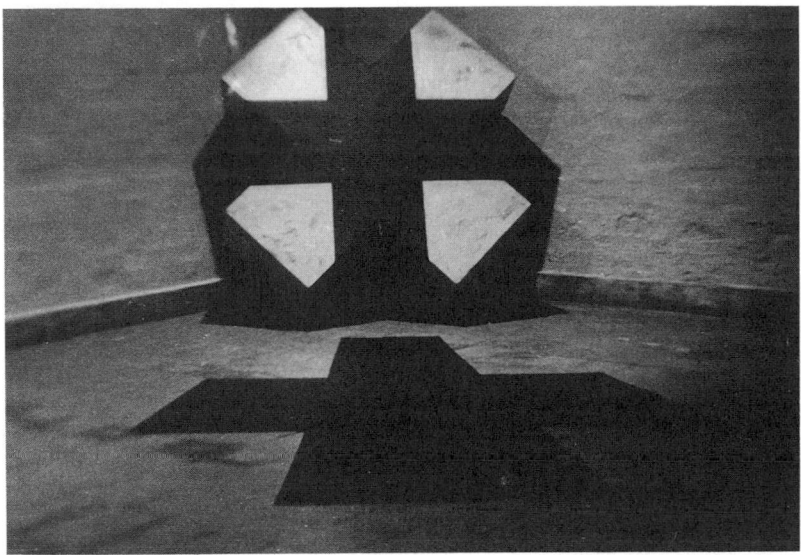

Dania del Sol, untitled, 1988, installation. Collection of the artist. Photo by Dania del Sol.

three shapes into a cube that bears the coordinates of the real cube placed in front of it.

Del Sol's use of logic tends to be used against reality as normally perceived. But, even when she uses gestural strokes, they are part of a logical discourse in which the physical appearance is destroyed on the surface level to allow the other definitions of that reality to come through with greater power. Thus, geometric solids, especially in her earlier work, are covered with expressionist brush strokes and have an equally patterned flat echo on the wall. The resulting shape, with the help of an outline, reconstructs the three-dimensional reality.

Her path in Cuba has been a lonely and somewhat frustrating one. She has little peer input and great technical problems. Her aesthetic requires in many cases a quasi-industrial finish that is not easily achievable for Cuban artists. As a consequence, she increasingly resorted to photography to "represent" her projects and bypass production. She also turned to the identification of numbers with nature. For a time the results included illustrations, texts, and diagrams, which often gave a dangerously didactic feeling. Her commitment to her research, under the circumstances, has been admirable in that it has not wavered even minimally over the years. What may constitute her own brand of ivory tower has also saved her from the dizzying speeds of transformation that affected many of her peers.[56]

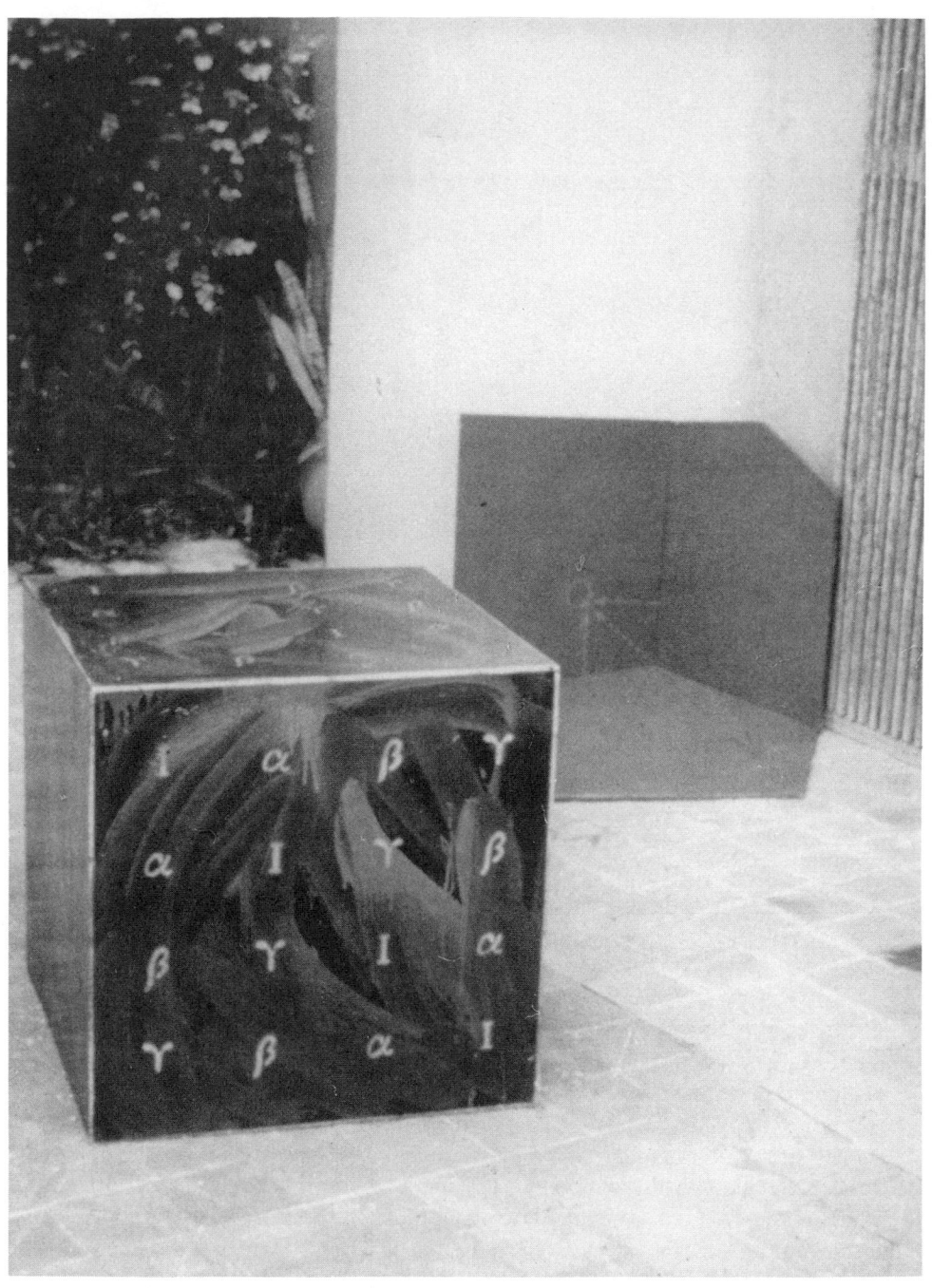

Dania del Sol, Isomorfismo (Isomorphism), *1989, oil on wood, each 80 × 80 × 80 cm. Collection of the artist. Photo by Dania del Sol.*

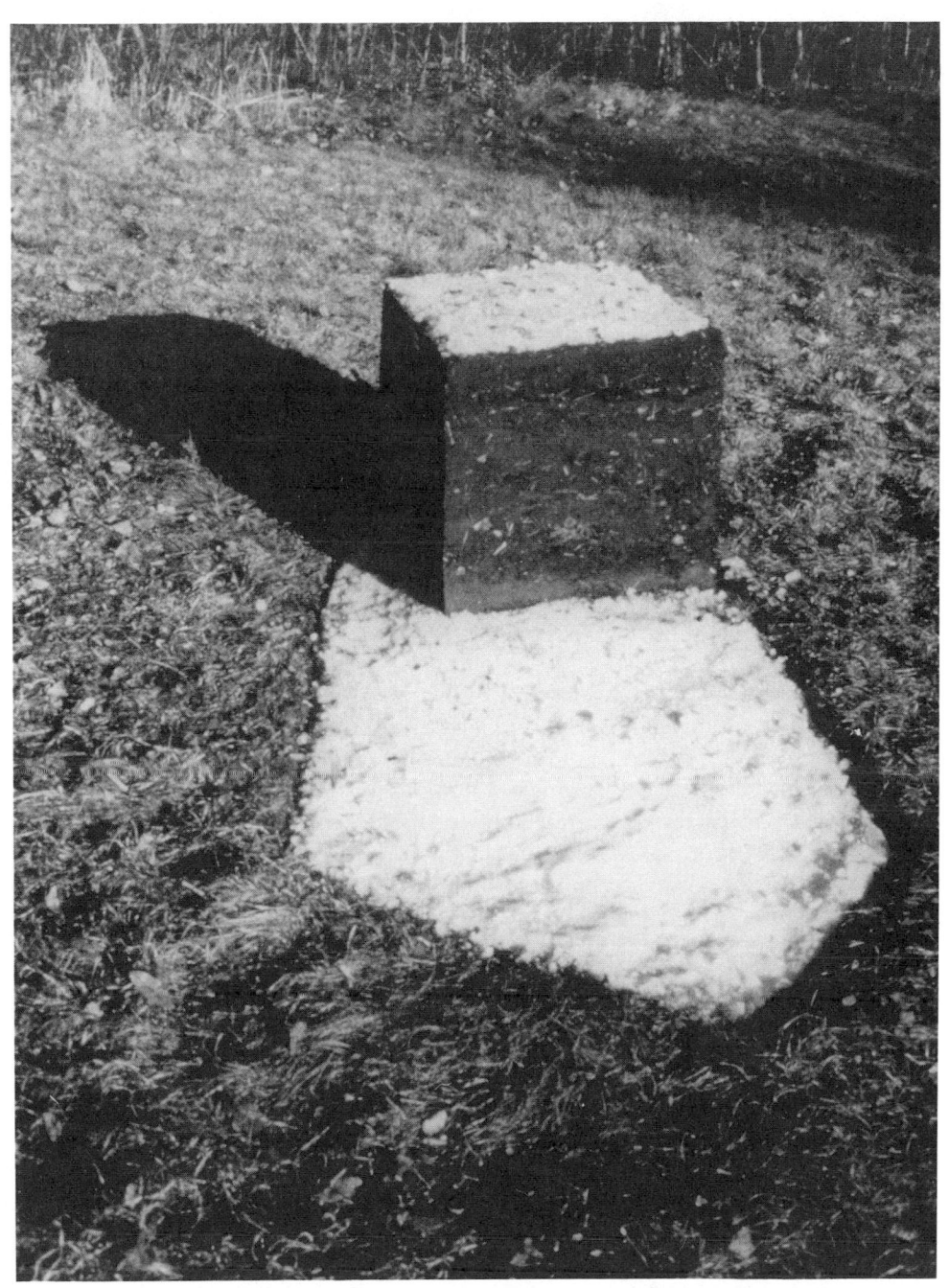

Dania del Sol, Oposición naturaleza (Opposition Nature), *1991, soil and paint, 50 × 60 × 100 cm. Collection of the artist. Photo by Dania del Sol.*

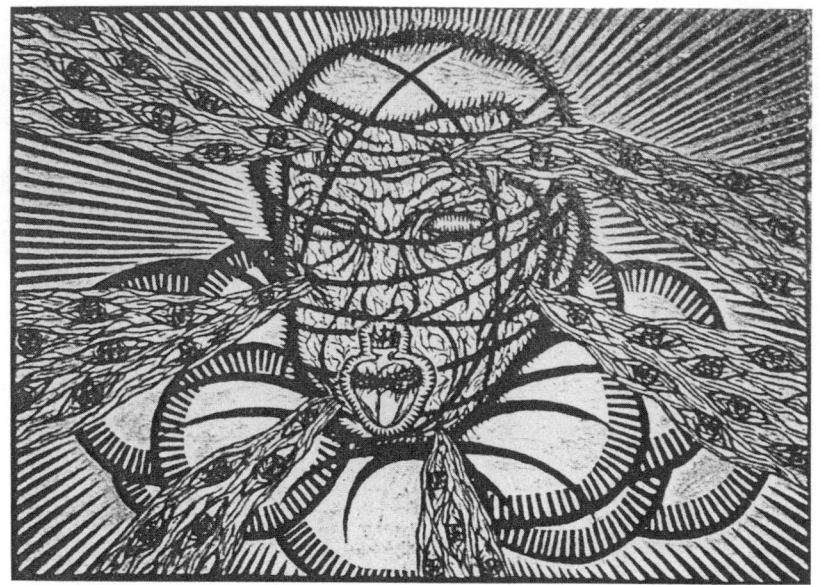

Ibrahim Miranda, untitled, 1990, woodblock for printing, 30 × 40 cm. Collection of the artist. Photo by Luis Camnitzer.

Her shifting the search to the counterpoint of intuition versus reason further enriched her work. Her view is that intuition is a process as rigorous as rationality: "Intuition definitively does not belong to the zone of error or underdevelopment. Intuition is not a theoretical action; it challenges all the categories of rational thought. Its logic is not commensurate with our conception of scientific truth." Her interest is to create work that exists between both universes, "between demonstration and showing."[57]

Other Artists

Meanwhile, new names are emerging in the Cuban art scene at a breathtaking pace. The exhibit "Kuba o.k.," for example, already included two artists who appeared during early 1990 and may become prominent during the coming decade: Ibrahim Miranda (1969) and Lázaro García (1968), both still students at the ISA.

Miranda makes woodcuts in which he combines sex, religion, and mythology. They seem influenced both by fifteenth-century cuts and by the drawings of Uruguayan artist Carlos Capelán (who exhibited in the first three Biennials of Havana).

García describes himself as "assimilating styles," preferably Gothic, Romanesque, and neoclassic, to make religious portraits. He feels he is

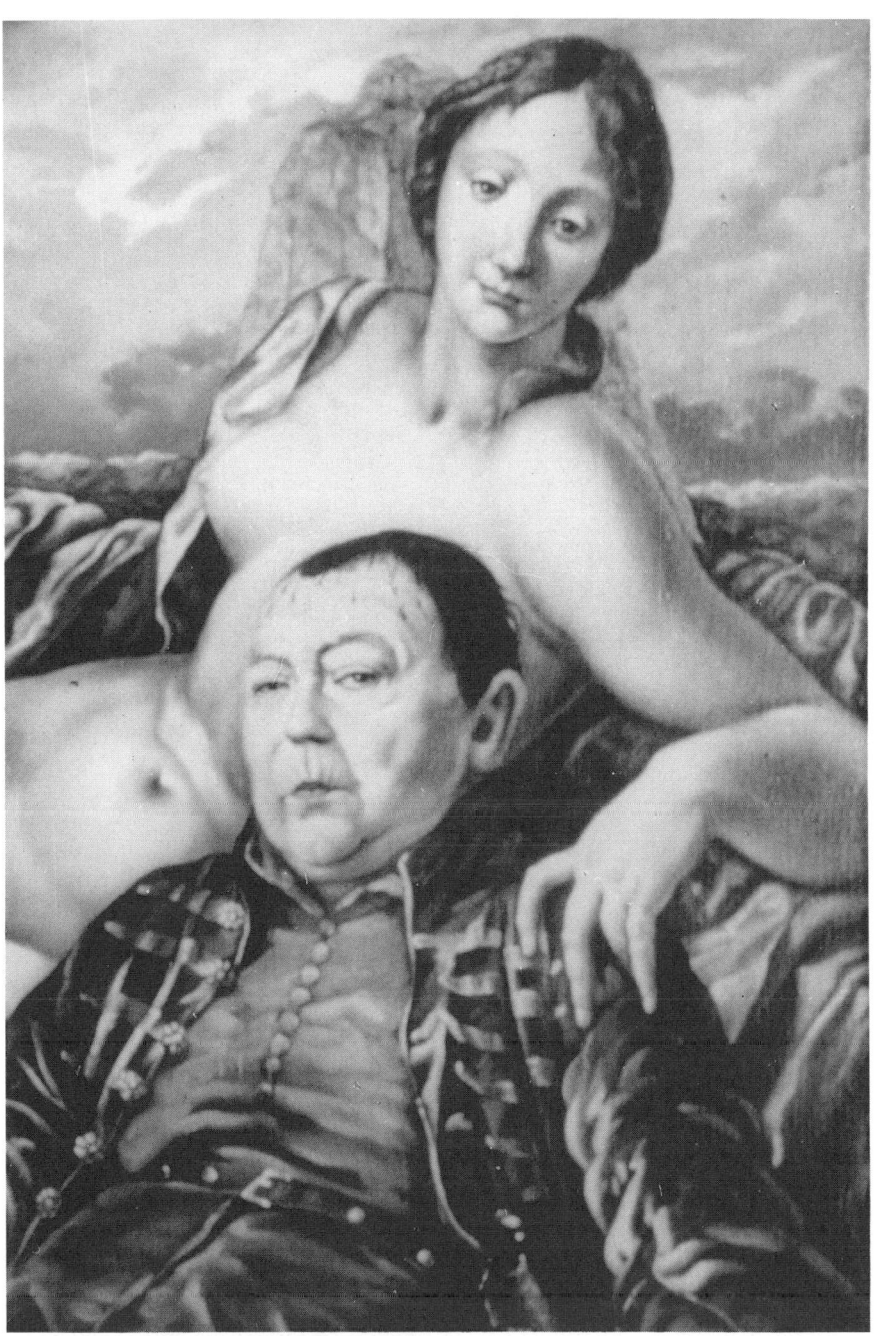

Lázaro García, Jesús y Magdalena, *1990, oil on canvas, 67 × 45 cm. Collection of the artist. Photo by Lázaro García.*

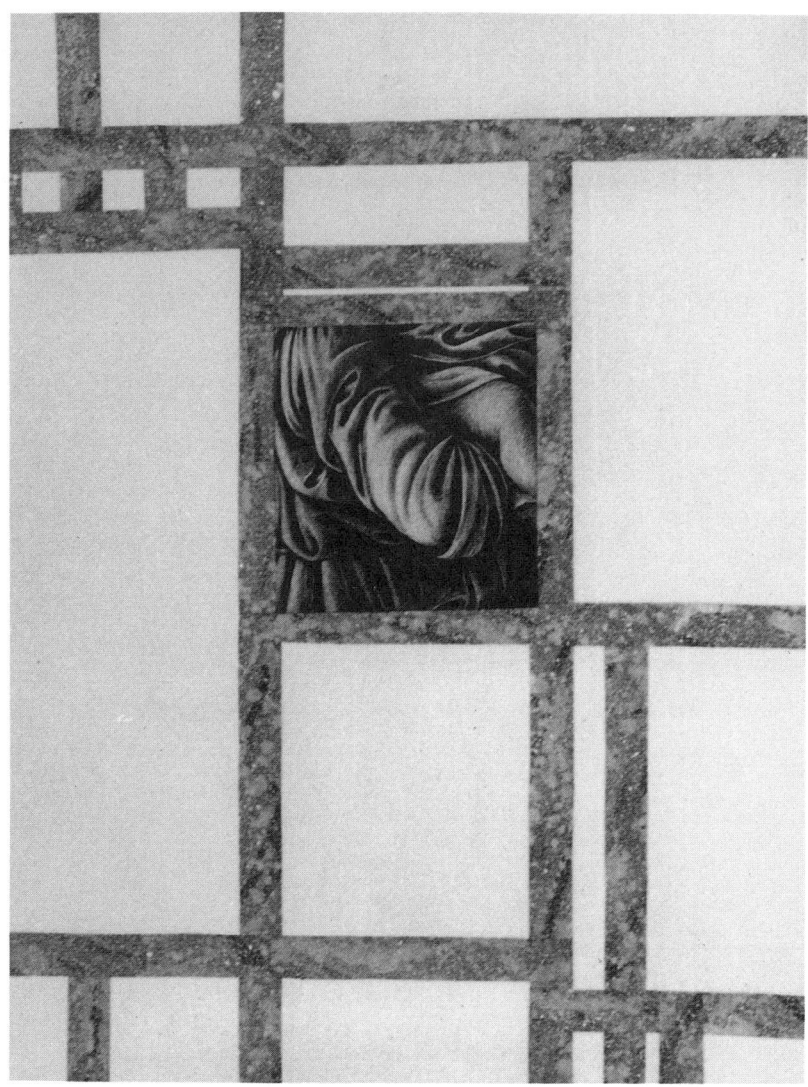

Lázaro García, Simbolismo abstracto (Abstract Symbolism), *1991, tempera and ink on paper, 51.5 × 37 cm. Private collection. Photo by Luis Camnitzer.*

repeating the process of early Latin American colonial art—much of the work shares that look—an art "that was supposed to be the same as that of the metropolis, but which always turned out different, new—I believe because it was the product of an environment very different from the European."[58] What initially seemed to be an extremely well-made recipe

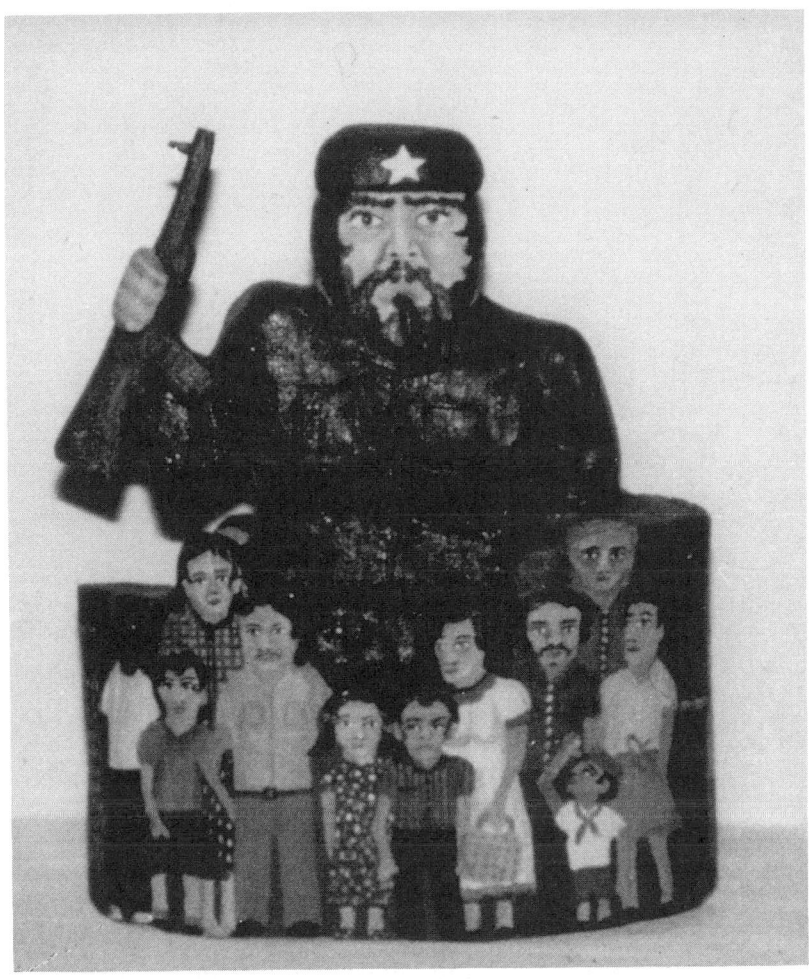

*Fernando Rodríguez/Fransisco de la Cal, Che, painted wood carving, 28 ×
30 × 9 cm. Collection of the artist. Photo by Luis Camnitzer.*

for where Dalí met Raphael became a much more rigorous analysis of
the possibilities of combination of styles. In a more recent series, García
followed Dutch painter Mondrian's grids with lines painted in a Jackson
Pollock mode and the rectangles framing Dürer drawings.

Fernando Rodríguez, a student of the ISA (like Miranda and García),
created Fransisco de la Cal, a fictional blind friend who dictates to him
what to do in art. The results of the teamwork are extremely credible
and seductive "naif" pieces, both in sculpture and in painting, about
Che, Castro, and other national heroes. The pieces are exhibited with a

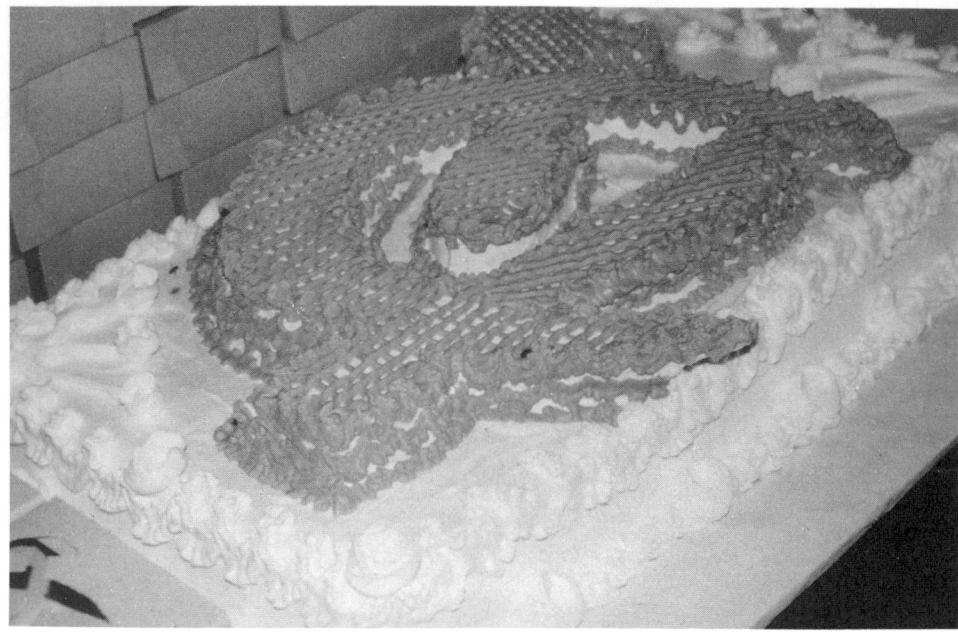

Nestor Arenas, Cake (after Flavio Garciandía), *1990, 15 × 80 × 60 cm. Photo by the artist. (The cake was eaten during the exhibition.)*

small handwritten biography of de la Cal in which he also thanks Rodríguez for his empathy ("I sometimes feel we are the same person") and shows a little self-portrait that makes him look like Ray Charles. Rodríguez drew from his social work with the blind, a community service component connected with his studies.

Nestor Arenas (1967), another eclecticist, is integrating Cuban symbols into canvases faithfully painted in the style of Magritte. He had previously worked on the formal elements of Garciandía's work, constructing tables and chairs with the shapes cut out. The outstanding piece of that series was a big cake (the frosting reproduced one of the paintings), which was eaten during the opening of Arenas' exhibition.

Luis Gómez (1968) explicitly follows the work of Elso Padilla. In *El herrero, el artesano, el creador* (*The Blacksmith, the Craftsman, the Creator* [1991]) he intends to create the counterpart for Elso's *El Guerrero.* In his work, Gómez also tries to define a form of spirituality, but he is more focused on Cuba than his model. He sees Elso's *Por América* as the pivotal piece that unleashed the elucidation of the meaning of national symbols in the generations following.

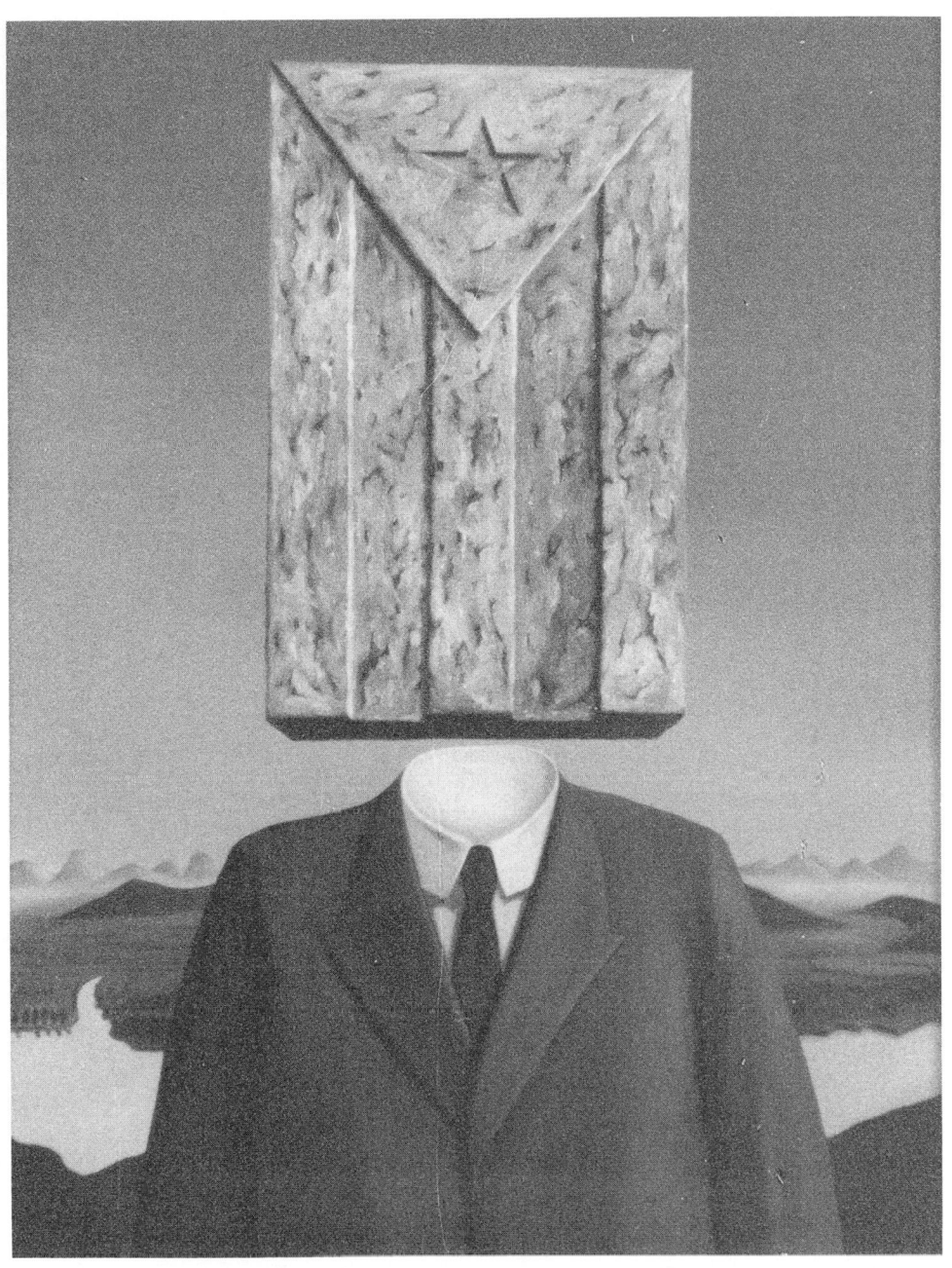

Nestor Arenas, La idea fija (The Fixed Idea), *1991, oil on canvas, 100 ×
80 cm. Collection of the artist. Photo by Luis Camnitzer.*

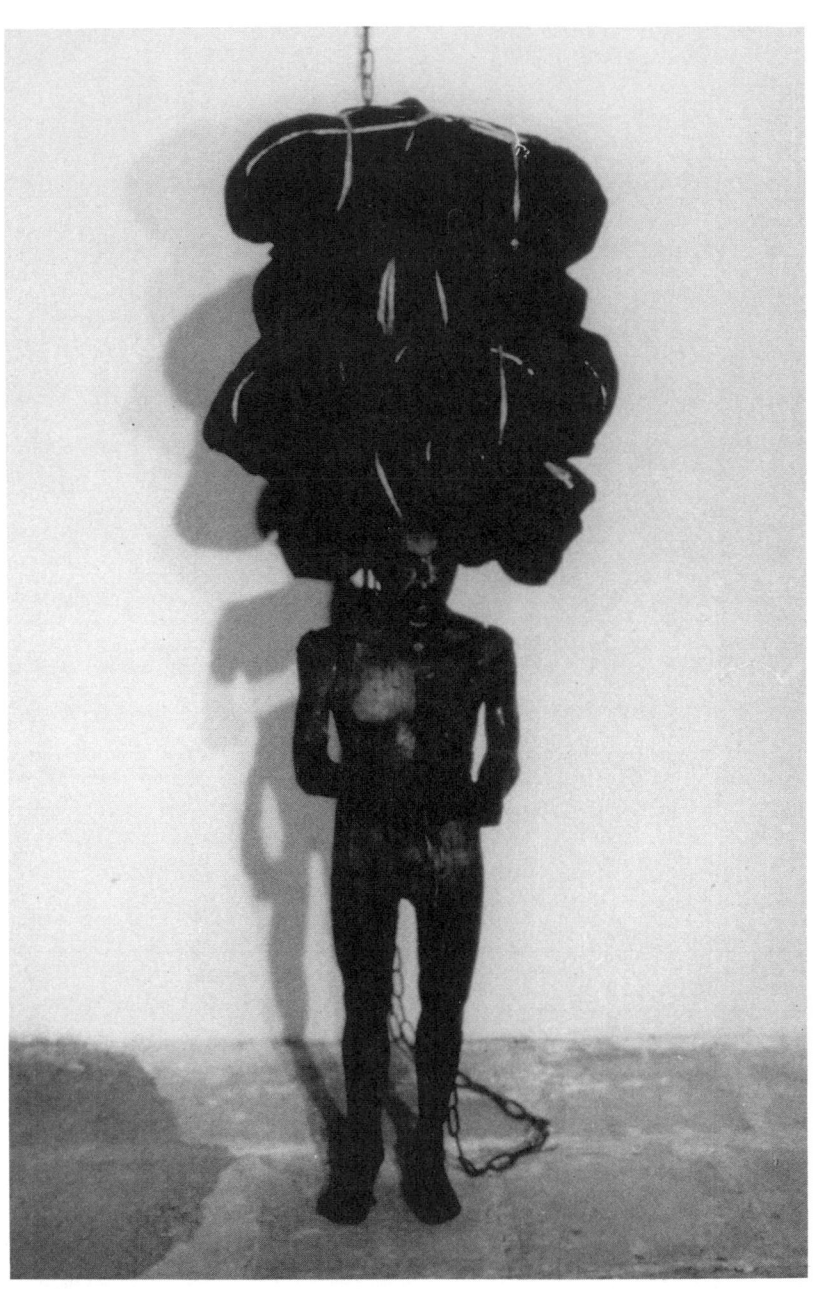

Luis Gómez, El herrero, el artesano, el creador (The Blacksmith, the Artisan, the Creator) *(detail, 60 cm. high), 1990–1991, mixed media. Collection of the artist. Photo by Luis Gómez.*

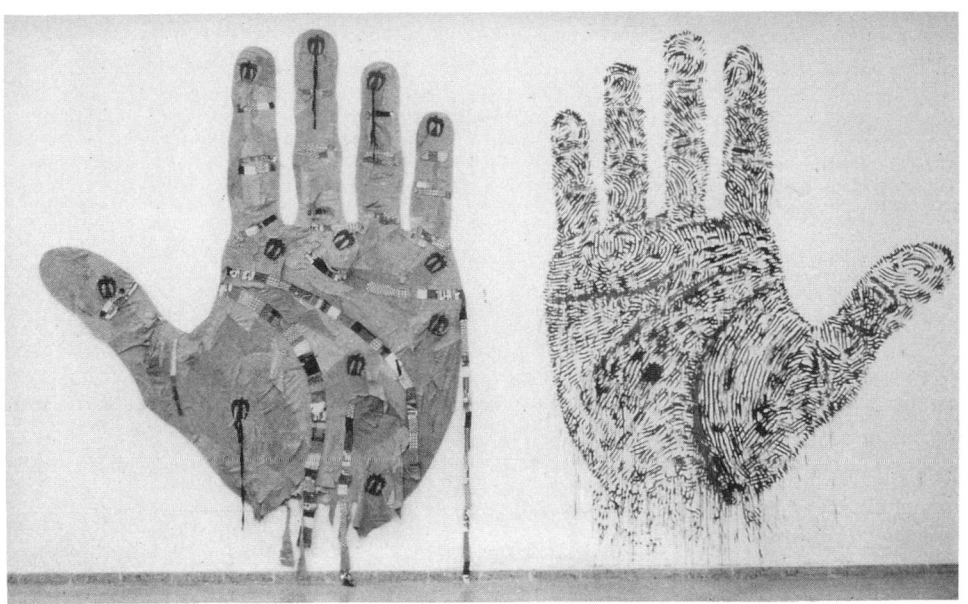

Luis Gómez, Y nada nos pertenece (Nothing Belongs to Us Anymore), *1991, mixed media installation at the Fourth Biennial of Havana, 200 × 500 cm. Photo by Luis Camnitzer.*

An example of this influence is provided by the work of Alexis Leiva (Kcho) (1970), an artist who, using basic materials such as twigs and paper, makes large irreverent sculptures about the map of Cuba. In *La peor de las trampas* (*The Worst of Traps* [1991]), he presents a ladder with the steps made out of machetes with the cutting edges pointing up.

Another artist in this new generation is Eryk González Litvinov, who is experimenting with electric brain stimulation to generate phosphenes (light sensations on the retina) in the spectator. He wants "to cater to the spectator's wish for intimacy" and instead of "the work stimulating the viewer, stimuli should work within the viewer."[59] He envisions that through the use of computerized stimuli he may some day create figurative "phosphenedramas."

Two artists, Ana Albertina Delgado (1963) and Adriano Buergo (1965), who were active since the latter part of the decade and were part of Grupo Puré, are, in my judgment, only now starting to mature as individual creators. Delgado, after an overly shy and hermetic period, is now being more explicit in her description of a Cuban repertoire of femininity. It is a subject matter that no other artist has yet approached.

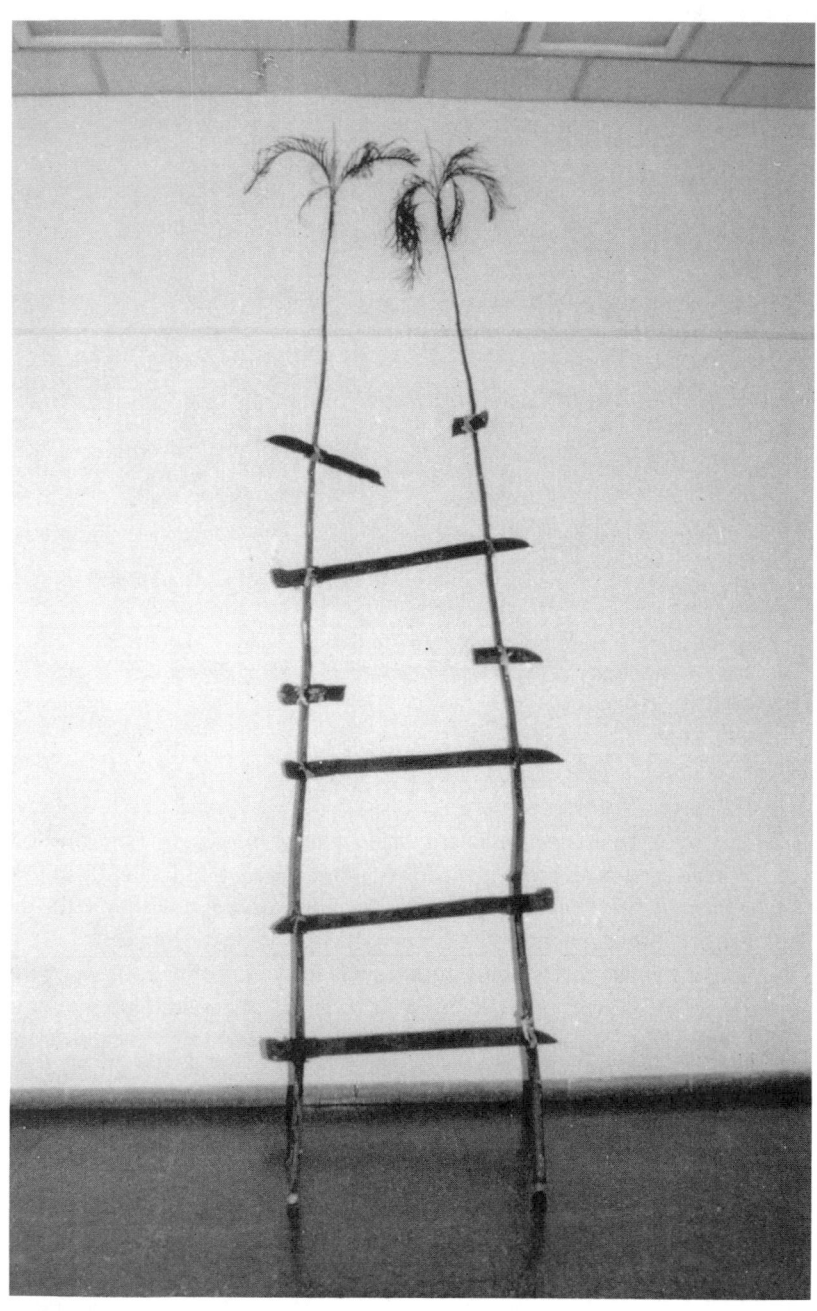

Alexis Leiva Machado (Kcho), La peor de las trampas (The Worst of Traps), *1991, mixed media, 390 × 100 cm. Collection of the artist. Photo by Luis Camnitzer.*

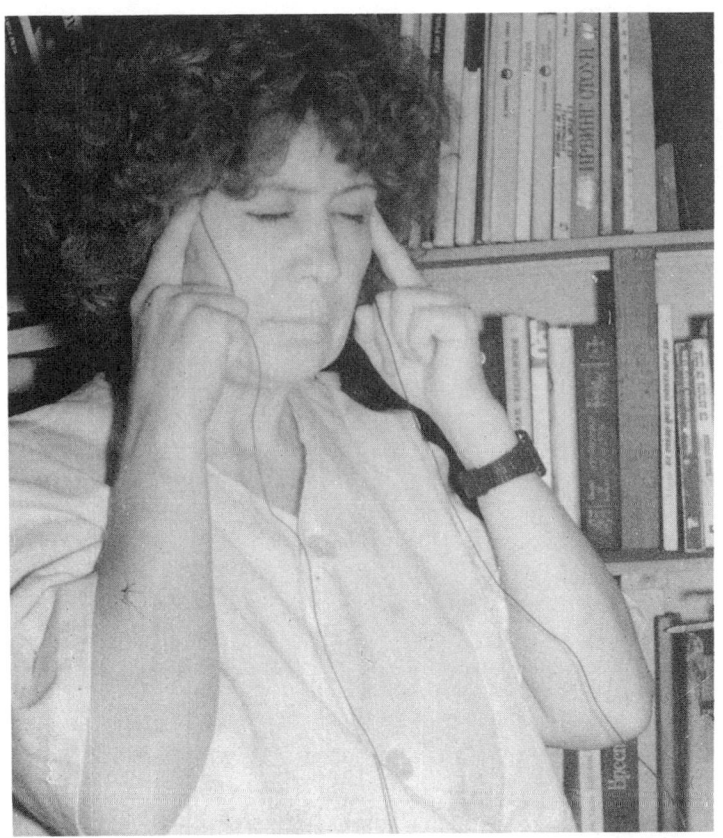

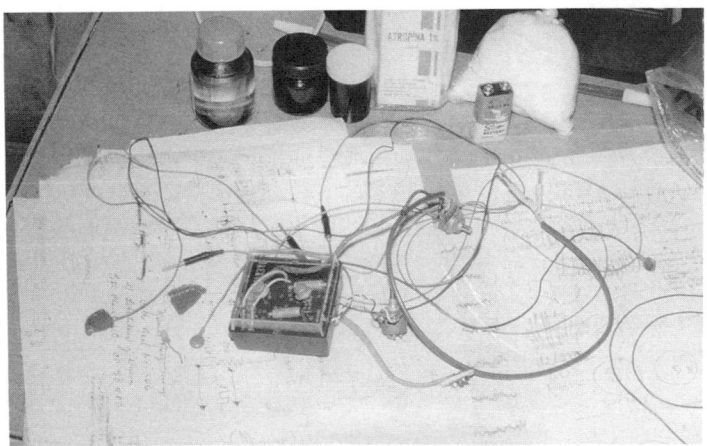

Eryk González Litvinov, setup for "Fosfenáutica," 1989–1990. Collection of the artist. Photo by Eryk González Litvinov.

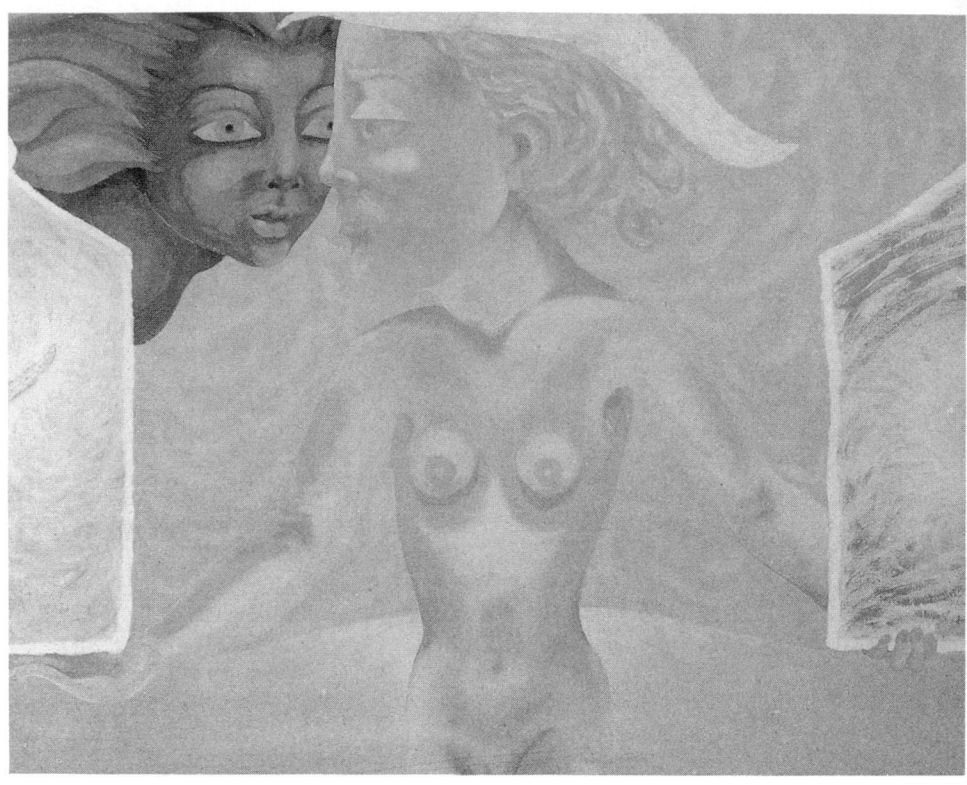

Ana Albertina Delgado, Nuevos oficios para Isabel, Lázara y Bertica (New Skills for Isabel, Lázara, and Bertica), *1990, oil on canvas, 69 × 88 cm. Collection of the artist.*

Buergo had pursued many venues about Cuban kitsch and pop culture through comics and other devices, all interesting, but incoherent (at least for me) as a total discourse. In one piece of his entry in the Third Biennial of Havana—a floor installation connected with demolition and decay that looked as if the ceiling had caved in—he satirized Garciandía's *Swan Lake* by sharing the title. Demolition and decay now seem to unify his newer work and "Roto" ("Broken") is the name of the protagonist of his latest series about a "bricolaged" fan, who appears both in paintings and installations.

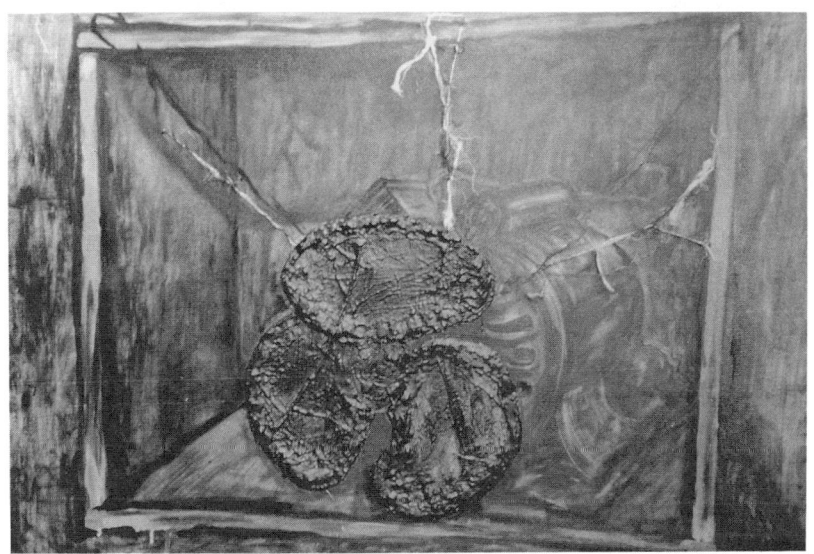

Adriano Buergo, Roto, *1988, oil on canvas, 120 × 150 cm. Collection of the artist. Photograph by Luis Camnitzer.*

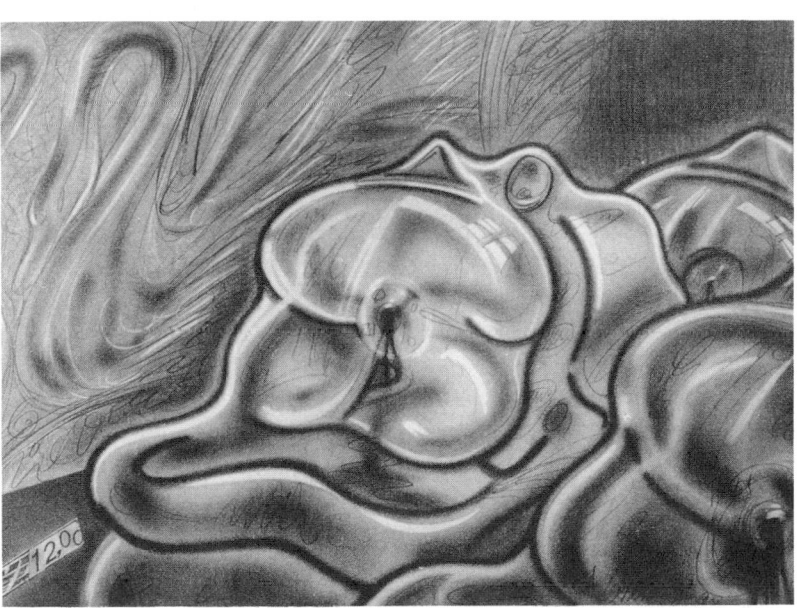

Adriano Buergo, Roto se vende (Roto for Sale), *1990, graphite on paper, 51 × 70 cm. Courtesy of Nina Menochal. Collection of the artist.*

7

CUBAN ART
and POSTMODERNISM[1]

Cuba's culture encountered more U.S. influence than many other Latin American countries, but it also found better and less traumatic ways to absorb that influence and put it to its own use.

Some of Cuba's idiosyncracies are the product of having undergone a socialist Revolution and therefore pose a radical qualitative difference from the rest of the Latin American countries. However, many achievements are merely the consequence of a more rigorous application of ingenuity and inventiveness after a recognition of the constraints imposed by a forced economic underdevelopment. This underdevelopment, first in common with the rest of Latin America as a consequence of colonization, undiversified production, and exploitative trade agreements, was in the case of Cuba later worsened by the U.S.-organized blockade. Without the blockade, the situation of Cuba roughly paralleled that of Chile under the government of Frei, when the United States subsidized that country by about the same amount that the USSR gave to Cuba. It is interesting that both economic models, socialist and capitalist free market, no matter how heavily subsidized by the superpowers, have suffered a nearly simultaneous collapse during recent years.[2]

While the effects of these changes are being felt in Cuba, it is too soon to predict what the final impact will be in general and on the role of the Cuban artists in particular. At present, Cuba is still the only country in Latin America that seems to accept art as a form of social production. With no internal collectors' market of any importance and no possibility for corporations to function, public funding takes care of nearly all art activities, both as a sponsor and as a customer. Cuba, in the present situation, may still be accused of not having radically redefined the traditional role of the artist as used in the Western mainstream. But, as we have seen, the social usage of the artist goes well beyond what is standard in other countries: that of a dedicated hobbyist or a manufacturer of profitable collectibles.

Although artists are not directed aesthetically in any way, the hope for Cuban art production is eventually to develop a visual language that corresponds to cultural identity. Because of the unusual length of the art education process, this goal requires an even higher investment by the Cuban economy than is necessary in other countries where education is also free. Compensatory moves, such as shortening the course of studies and commercializing the gallery system even more, designed to alleviate the economic problems, seem to evade the responsibility of finding more interesting alternatives for the application of art. At least, however, they are respectful of the artistic persona. This respect, coupled with the full support of the artist at a time when there is a constant threat of having to regress to the stage of considering art a luxury, make a mixture that signals the fragility of this hybrid construction.

The Artist on the Periphery

That the Cuban artist is not yet a "new artist" but a hybrid is a symptom of much of the history of Cuba. This hybridization shows both what Cuba has in common with the rest of Latin America in terms of attitudes toward incoming information, and Cuba's gradual efforts to develop independence, getting rid of the malaise intrinsic to its placement on the periphery.

Traditionally, the flow of information from the center to the periphery has been overbearing and has far exceeded the digestive capacities of its recipients. On the part of the center, this informational overkill is as much a product of commercial motivations as it is part of a strategy of cultural control. On the part of the periphery, the acceptance of the flow of information, inasmuch as it is voluntary, is a consequence of the assumption that this information carries with it progress, modernity, and cosmopolitanism.

In most countries, including the United States, people often suffer from collective provincial inferiority complexes that lead them to attribute an aura of special quality to things imported. The U.S. consumer seems to consider Parmesan cheese labeled "imported" so far superior to the local version that sellers do not even bother to specify the country of origin. Imported versus local in this case becomes an issue of dogma or passive belief and not a subject for analysis. Labeling takes the place of evaluation of quality.

In a more sophisticated stage of submission, quality considerations do occur. The imported product is ranked against its peers (as in the case of whiskey) or copied with the aim of making a dignified comparison (as in the case of Californian wines). While the standards remain imported, the expertise becomes local and slowly merges into a cultural structure. After an initial period of affected mimicry, the values may be genuinely absorbed and put to constructive use, in the sense that they may develop a cultural identity beyond the creation of an avid consumership of specific products.

But it also may happen that the values are not put to a constructive use, which is dependent on the context into which the values are absorbed and the primary aims of that absorption. The context is defined by whose cultural identity is being developed: one's own, or that of the hegemonic center. The aims are defined by the purported function of the values to be absorbed: to enrich one's life, or to open the market for a better sale of imports.

Modernization and Dependency

The whole process of "modernization" in Latin America, for example, was pushed by the region's leaders, with the intention of making their countries better contenders in a competitive world market. Initial colonialism had seeded metropolitan values and simultaneously ensured that these values would not bloom into threatening competition. Thus, a concept of independence evolved that, based on the metropolitan values, limited itself to breaking away from only the mechanical constraints inhibiting fiscal viability. Coupled with these commercial dreams, there was a longing to be considered culturally an "equal partner" with the former colonizers. As early as the nineteenth century these economic and cultural developments were inescapable. However, they constituted a reactive and adaptive process that condemned the countries to a continuing superficial selection from among various hegemonic standards at the expense of the vernacular. In that sense, this process helped develop the center's cultural identity and was expected to lead to a more efficient production and thus to expand the metropolitan market. The influx of information from the center was received on the periphery as a welcome aid, needed for the successful accomplishment of the chosen mission to achieve the ill-defined independence.

Artists were drawn into this dynamic along with everybody else. Local primary information was inevitably masked by the imports, and artistic products started to become echoes, postponing culture instead of generating it. Art on the periphery under these conditions became more a postcultural than a cultural phenomenon. It is primarily the product of an adopted or an imposed culture rather than a contributor to a culture in action. Primary artistic information is presumed to exist mostly in museums and galleries located in the "cultural capitals" of the world. Artists on the periphery are conditioned to accept travel grants to study those primary sources as an honor and a reward for their achievements. The grants reward a body of work that shows its readiness to enter the cultural mainstream. At the same time, the work reveals an incomplete knowledge of all the conditions informing that mainstream—thus, the need for travel. Culture is to be acquired as a packaged product, and the real work of art will be produced only after that acquisition and will be a postcultural artifact.

The Eclecticism of
Survival Versus Postmodernism

However well-designed the process, total resignation on the part of societies on the periphery seems unattainable. Instead, these societies have developed what could be called an *eclecticism of despair* in which elements are merged through appropriation. Subservient and fragmentary mimesis blends with a defensive syncretic use of resources and with recontextualization. The result is an aesthetic that long predates postmodernism[3] but that often matches it in visual terms.

Postmodernism, however, is considered by the mainstream to be a postindustrial aesthetic, one that responds to the instantly available and omnipresent information distributed by supertechnology and able to cancel out the appearance of distinct styles. Hegemonic postmodernism absorbs all identities into an amorphous conglomerate. On the other hand, when eclecticism is used on the periphery, it is, at least partially, a way of attempting to define an identity. The misperception by the mainstream of the postcultural eclecticism on the periphery as a rehashed product of postmodernism is a poor and self-serving simplification of a much more complex and tortured process. A struggle for cultural survival is dismissed under the cover of a dishonest construction of history. Unfortunately, with their eyes set on the hegemonic market, many artists on the periphery try to benefit from the misunderstanding instead of helping to clear it.

The surprise experienced by Western observers upon viewing Cuban art during the decade of the eighties—its lack of Soviet socialist realism and its apparent formal closeness to the products of the capitalist mainstream—was glossed over by labeling the art as postmodern. This label, often used by Cuban artists themselves, seems to facilitate an easy connection between two cultures. It provides an easy cataloguing from the outside and a sense of a validating context from the inside. As with much of the art on the periphery, superficial viewing of the work seems to confirm the classification, since in many cases there is a conscious appropriation and use of borrowed art solutions.

In the Cuban case, just as in the rest of Latin America, this appropriation is not focused on an abstracted research around the topics of historicism and recycling as it is in the West. It is a process of appropriation connected with a long tradition of attempts to syncretize unstoppable imported influences with the surrounding reality. In that sense, the application of the term to Cuban art from the outside is ethnocentric; used from the inside, it is a sign of a (usually unacknowledged) dependency.

The Afro-Cuban Tradition and Appropriation

Cuba has undergone the process of appropriation in a particularly powerful way over the centuries, and the omnipresent Afro-Cuban component of its culture is one of the many examples of this. Both the *Regla de Ocha*, or *Santería* (of Yoruba origin), and the *Regla de Conga*, or *Palo Monte*, the main African rituals still alive in Cuba today, are examples of cross-cultural appropriation.

In *Santería*, deities are identified with Catholic saints, the Christian cross is one of the ceremonial symbols, and the Yoruba vocabulary used has often been translated from publications in English. In the *Palero* ritual, the original African animals used for the ritual were replaced with Cuban animals. Good and bad deeds can be executed in the ritual, and bad deeds—in a remnant of the Spanish Inquisition—are called "Jewish work."[4]

Both rituals use Western mass-produced objects in their ceremonial setups, including items such as plaster casts representing Sioux Indians, and both rites require Catholic baptism for the initiation of their members. Elements of Spiritism, a custom of European–North American origin, were absorbed as well, particularly by the *Palero* ritual. In turn, *Santería* was then absorbed by much of the Cuban white population. Another African import, the secret male fraternity *Abakuá*, became a society of mutual aid, instrumental in the matter of job protection among Cuban dock workers.[5] The ceremonies of this group also borrowed heavily from Catholicism.

The resulting mélange constitutes, with all of its referential and readapted material, a very original and authentic culture. Though the original intent was to conserve a tradition and keep deviations to a mini-

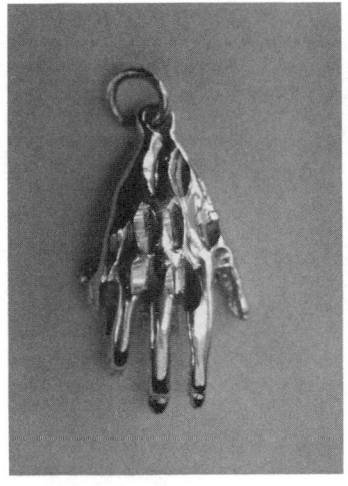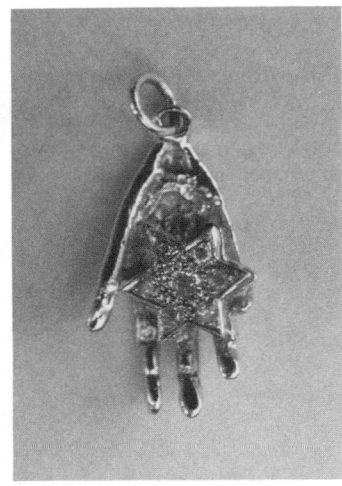

Jewish/Santería *jewelry, 14 karat gold. Collection of Ellen Wolfe, Cambridge, Mass. Photo by Ellen Wolfe.*

mum, these deviations and reinterpretation serve as a potential for a development of identity.

While less frequent in art, this is a process ubiquitous in other fields in Latin America, ranging from theoretical studies to everyday objects. For example, the Liberation Theology movement can be seen as an example of theoretical adaptation, in which traditional religion is made to function in a concrete social situation. The same process is present in more banal examples of everyday use. Coca-Cola bottles, in another instance, are subject to something that can be called a "design by substitution" technique. The drink has a widespread use as a contraceptive device among "ignorant" segments of Latin American populations. The contents of the bottle alter the acidity level of the vaginal fluids, and the bottle itself, well-designed for this purpose and helped by the carbonation of the liquid, becomes a practical douche after it is shaken.[6]

Victor Papanek, a design expert concerned with the economic use of resources for a betterment of living standards on the periphery, in his classic book *Design for the Real World,* used only one Latin American example to illustrate creation through recycling, a Mexican brazier made out of old license plates. Cuba could have provided many more cogent examples through the production of the ANIR (National Association of Innovators and Rationalizers) and its antecessors, and this organization itself is a model of its kind.

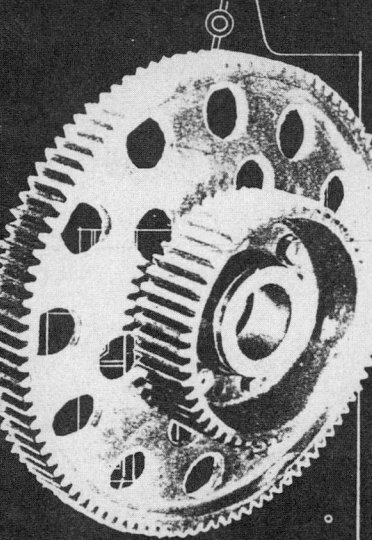

Ministry of Industry silkscreened poster, 1961, 70 × 50 cm. Photo courtesy of the Ministry of Industry, Havana.

ANIR

Cuba shares with Third World countries the simultaneous conditions of dependence on imported technology and lack of currency to acquire the needed replacement parts. Cuba's plight is sensibly worsened by the blockade instituted by the United States. The ANIR is a group of scientists and technicians organized to find alternative solutions to the problems created by scarcity or unavailability.

Although the ANIR in its present form was established in 1976, its precedents predate the victory of the Revolution. Still in the Sierra Maestra, Che Guevara had organized both a weapon factory and a shoe factory in the hills, operating on the basis of recycling and cannibalizing old units. In 1959 Parts Committees were established to find solutions for missing parts in factories. The movement came from an initiative by workers and not through government planning. A year later, Consulting Committees were created to assess the feasibility of the production of parts. By 1961 the project became more ambitious, and posters were made stating, "Worker, Build Your Own Machinery," a slogan promoted by Guevara himself. By 1965 a Convention of Innovators and Inventors was created. In 1975 the slogan became "To Beat Imperialism in the Battle of Replacement Parts."

The ANIR was created on October 8, 1976, in honor of Guevara, who became the closest thing to a patron saint for the institution. Contributions over the years ranged from a plywood substitute made out of bagasse to a flexible foot support for medical use and eighteen counterweights for a freight elevator cast single-handedly by one Antonio Nicholás in 1975 in honor of the First Congress of the Cuban Communist Party.[7]

The process is not limited to the ANIR but has achieved a quasi-folkloric dimension. Any old motor with rotation power together with any reasonably flat and attachable object will product an effective ventilation fan in a Cuban household. What is remarkable, beyond the fact that the contraption works, is the pride of the inventors about the triumph of ingenuity. The objects, aesthetically fascinating and deserving a study of their own, so far have attracted the interest of only one artist, Adriano Buergo (1965), who is working on a series of still-life paintings of such objects.

Cuban Eclecticism

Words such as *pluralist* and *pastiche*, taken from the postmodernist jargon, have been suggested for appropriate recent Cuban art. While one

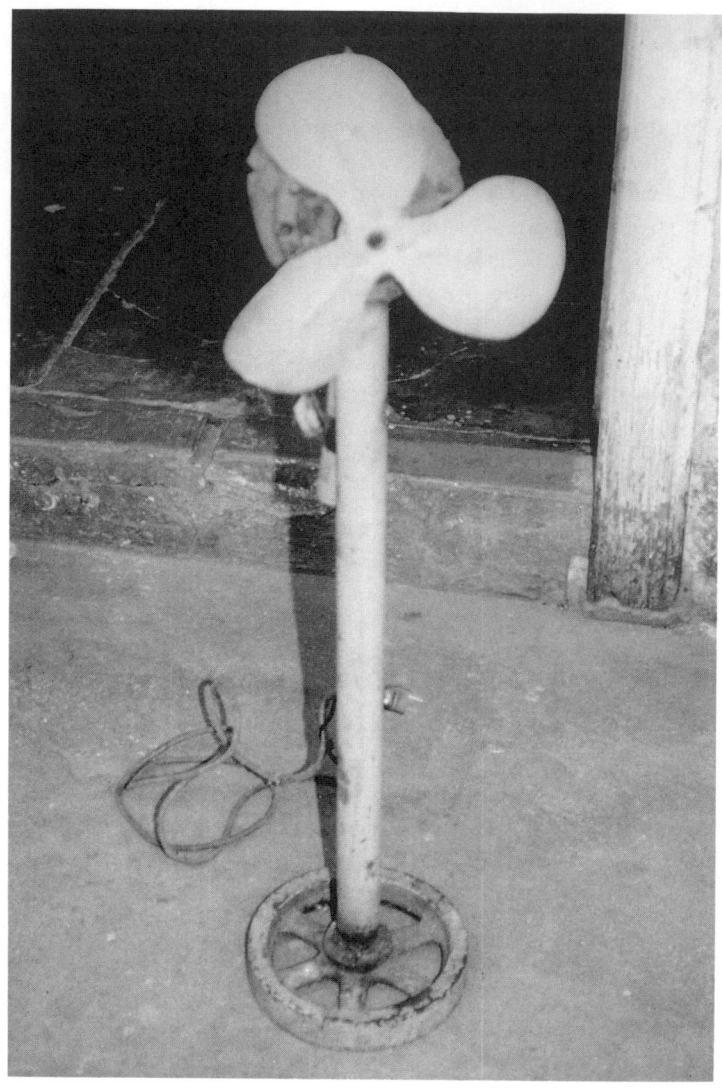

Anonymous, fan in Havana home. Photo by Luis Camnitzer, 1989.

could expect that a socialist government such as the one in Cuba would sponsor some kind of collective style, this has not been the case. Thus, art in Cuba is pluralistic, in the sense that there is no predominance of any particular aesthetic dogma. There is a focus on individual art production and a great receptivity to imported information, which is recycled in much Cuban work. The motivation and the work of the ANIR constitute a very accurate metaphor for Cuban aesthetics. But, while present, pluralism is not a concept that captures the essence of recent Cuban art.

The second term, *pastiche*, as explained by Fredric Jameson, is a symptom of the disappearance of creative individuality and of the impossibility of finding new styles ("the failure of the new and the imprisonment in the past").[8] Therefore, it is not an accurate term either.

Contemporary art in Cuba, like the Afro-Cuban rituals, has stressed the elements of deviation from models and reinterpretation of information acquired. It is not the salad quality that defines it, but the use to which that salad is put. *Eclecticism*, a term that seems to have less passive connotations, therefore seems a more accurate description of the new Cuban art. In some instances this eclecticism can achieve total integration, in which case the traces of origin become irrelevant and something is achieved that the Cubans call *mestizaje*. Coming from *mestizo*, the offspring of white and Amerindian couples, it refers to a perfect integrative blend.

Eclecticism, in Cuba, is an instrument for survival in a context in which a plethora of cultural crosscurrents defies the creation of a unified language. Past, present, and envisioned future are all too complex to permit the luxury of exclusion. As Cuban critic Osvaldo Sánchez puts it, "Recontextualization appears like a 'leitmotif' in Cuban social life. It is normal to see a 1940s Chevy with a driver wearing shoes modeled after the 1950s who is necking with a 'mulata' with bleached blond hair and painted lips reminiscent of the innocent sexual aggression of the 1960s, while they hum a song of the 1970s in duet with the feigned glamour of the 1930s."[9]

Both semantically and visually, the notion of eclecticism still leads to a simplistic temptation to connect the new Cuban art with the Western mainstream. Eclecticism is presently flourishing in the Western market as a tool to refresh production, somehow replaying the end of the nineteenth century. As a consequence of willful historical "referentiality," the market is introducing a string of neo-isms purportedly signaling freedom and lack of prejudice, but in fact rehashing and confirming an array of well-digested aesthetics.[10]

The production of cultural objects, within the context of the market with an emphasis on individual initiative, takes primacy over cultural actions as a response to social demands. Those expressions representing marginal social dynamics thus only gain acceptance inasmuch as they are able to merge into the market and camouflage themselves in it. Because Cuba is not as market-oriented as capitalist countries, eclecticism there provides an experimental arena that ensures the freedom to search for the as yet undefined future language.

Pseudo-postmodernism

This element of search and the parameters within which it occurs make it dangerous to apply Western postmodern standards when talking about this art. If confined to the use of Western market terminology, we have to say that what is presently functioning in Cuba is a *pseudo-postmodernism*. This, however, is an inappropriate term because, both referential to and reverential of mainstream terminology and concepts, it casts a pejorative light on the Cuban mode of expression. Essentially, Cuban artists are embarked on an effort to maintain ideological consistency while reserving the right to use any instrument available, even if it is formally inconsistent and even if it belongs to somebody else's fashion. As artist Glexis Novoa called it when, in his "romantic period," he wrote on top of his paintings, it is *postjodernismo* (*postbuggerism*).

While Cuban artists are keenly aware of Western trends, and while they are consciously influenced by these trends, the issue is more complex than a simple observation of formal symptoms would suggest. Twentieth-century modernism always had a utopian component, a belief that art would eventually lead to the betterment of society. Modernism, in an idealist way, expanded on the philanthropism of the nineteenth century, when museums were promoted to somehow raise the culture of the average man and help him become a citizen.

Modernism tried to provide a language for that ideal construct while conservative, nonmodernist tendencies were lurking in the background. The antimodernist work of Balthus, of the late Giorgio De Chirico, of the more decadent period in Francis Picabia's work, all are used today to build an illustrious and validating genealogy for the conservative stream of present postmodernism. In fact, these antimodernist works constitute a line parallel to modernism in this century. Much of what is called postmodernism in art is not an aesthetic developed as an answer to modernism but one picked by the market to occupy modernism's place upon its exhaustion.

The indiscriminate use of *postmodern* in reference to art tries to ignore the existence of two distinct streams of production following the demise of modernism in the Western market. One of these is the essentially reactionary movement that coexisted with modernism, envious of its predominance and opposed to its premises. The other developed as a contestation not so much of the principles that generated modernism but of the misuse by the establishment of the art produced under those principles. It is this process of instant art history by nomenclature that places the work of Julian Schnabel in the same bag with graffiti art.

Much of twentieth-century modernism was based on a search for a universally understandable language, on the use of art to create a classless society, on art as a tool to improve life. Free of market conditions, these modernist premises are much closer to the Cuban political and social ethics than the formal chaos and libertarianism espoused by the reactionary stream of Western postmodernism. This stream, as manifest in a successful market and as it was sponsored by the Reagan administration, was a born-again nineteenth-century laissez-faire ideology, and as such, a close visual representation of it.[11] The production of cultural objects, within the context of the market and with an emphasis on individual initiative, takes primacy over cultural actions formed as a response to social demands. Those expressions representing marginal social dynamics thus gain acceptance only inasmuch as they are able to merge into the market and camouflage themselves in it.

Cuban artists formed under the Revolution are far removed from this latter ideology. They are imbued, to a great extent, with the romantic mystique of the Revolution and, while critical of some of its modes of implementation, they agree with and endorse the revolutionary platform and ideals. Their art is individually oriented but also concerned with the greater problems of an ideal society and with the need to provide a visual articulation of it.

Nevertheless, postmodernism is a highly discussed issue in Cuba, and there is disagreement even among artists with otherwise similar concerns. Osvaldo Sánchez remarks, "One often confuses identity with tradition and tradition with underdevelopment. Therefore to proclaim that we are authentic, to underline that we are *us* taking as an exclusive point of departure a *nonothers*, should be a temptation long overcome. It is a form of dependency through opposition, usually masked by a spirit of confrontation." He warns about this attitude leading to the same provincialism that in the 1960s hid the true contributions of such artists as Antonia Eiriz, Umberto Peña, Chago, and Cabrera Moreno.[12]

The Role of the Notion of "Progress"

Postmodernism also surfaced in the rest of Latin America, but much more as a product of colonial influx than in Cuba. There is a difference in degree between Cuba and the rest of Latin America in regard to the role this colonial influx and the use of appropriation play in the development of art today.

Artists in most Latin American countries operate under the assumption that art-historical processes are linear and develop progressively in the search for quality. Progress and quality are defined by the hegemonic center, and whatever fills the media about these issues achieves pervasiveness and becomes immediately the canon. The desirability of the canon is internalized, and to follow it finally seems spontaneous, instinctive, indigenous, and authentic when in fact that submission to the canon is the product of an artificially created need that distances the artist from his or her reality.

Postrevolutionary Cuba was saved from some of the "progress" devices used in other Latin American countries in relation to the arts. In many countries, particularly Argentina, industrial corporations made new materials available to artists in order to promote their products. The Chamber of Plastic Industries, for example, invited fifty-five artists in 1966 to produce works in plastic. The Argentinean Industrial Union organized an exhibit in the Museum of Fine Arts under the title "Materiales, nuevas técnicas, nuevas expresiones" ("Materials, New Techniques, New Expressions") in 1968. The introduction to the catalogue commented that "the present concept of art is generated in a parallel fashion to the one of industry" and "when that occurs, it also occurs that the traditional concept of industry is transformed."[13]

Broadly, Cuba has progressed—in the sense that it came closer to its goal—remarkably over the last three decades. Cuban artists therefore do not share the skepticism about "progress" that prevails in the developed "West" and that serves as a basis for recent postmodernist trends. Thus, their basic spirit is still more connected with modernism and its belief in a possible improvement. If there is any modernist attitude still alive in the rest of Latin America, it is a product of historical lagging, but in Cuba it is a product of the present.

Functionalism

An issue rarely discussed in cultural terms is the role of functionalism—an aesthetic of modernity and progress—in design in Latin American culture. Obviously present to some degree in any utilitarian artifact, post-Bauhaus design has pushed functionalism to become a deep-seated internalized ideological factor in Western culture. It is, more than an application of rationality and economy, an evaluative tool for aesthetics that helps define good taste in the direction of a new classicism.

To a certain extent, functionalism has become the counterpart to kitsch. In Latin America this has had several consequences. Functionalism provided a relatively stable compass signaling the "correct" direction of taste in everyday life. The cultured middle class was exempted from its self-created need to be informed about latest fashions. Functionalism also helped to join an internationally acceptable aesthetic with the saving of money. After all, a set of cyclic war economies promoted all this in the first place.

On the other hand, elegance, a class attribution, became part of the thinking process ("elegant solution" in design), and obsolescence became an intrinsic aesthetic factor (a scratched or dirty well-designed functional object became aesthetically unpalatable and had to be replaced as quickly as possible). The aesthetics provided by aging, usage, and repair became a symbol of poverty and lack of cosmopolitanism. Under the guise of "modernity," functionalism thus became one of the doors opened for consumerism and one more tool for the erasure of identity.

With a reduced consumer market, the pressure in Cuba in this regard during the last thirty years has been a more modest one. While functionalism is, unavoidably, a part of the ideological makeup, its emphasis has been more on a pragmatic than on an aesthetic aspect. (Those aesthetic elements that today might coincide with the Western mainstream's postmodernism stem from a criticism of a possible Cuban tendency toward consumerism rather than from a search for a market expansion and better sales for the work of art.) What is really occurring in Cuba is a new aesthetization of the pragmatic aspects of functionalism. This does not immediately and totally decolonize the products, but it starts a process toward decolonization.[14]

Art and Rebellion

In Hilde Hein's terminology, Cuban artists are producing "propaedeutic" art, art as "a paradigm source of understanding for most people as to what lawfulness and order really are."[15] Such an attitude would produce conservative art in a conservative society. It is interesting that the visual results in Cuba overlap with what a benevolently minded and uninitiated viewer in the West would consider "challenging," if not an art of rupture.

Members of the newest Cuban generation, now in their early and mid-twenties, are both somewhat more skeptical and more militant than their immediate predecessors. While still embracing socialism and the general revolutionary tendencies, they are much more sensitive to the stereotypes and myths that have slowly crept into the revolutionary path. As a consequence, they are interested in a process of demystification of the rote aspects of the Revolution. Demystification is a common trait among many artists of the equivalent generations in the rest of Latin

America. Significantly, though, the Cuban demystification is essentially constructive in reaction to the present political system, while the process elsewhere in Latin America seeks alternatives to that system. The art of these Cuban artists, again in Hein's terminology, is "propulsive." The artist is a "critic of the existing system and an architect of the future."

Cuban art continues to be both the product of the belief in and a tool for striving for the betterment of society, and it uses any means available to fulfill this purpose. This fact explains why it has this hybrid quality of modernism disguised by a postmodern repertoire of forms. It also stresses the importance of seeing this art within the social context for which it was produced, rather than as an exercise in aesthetics.

The Nationalization of Devices

Most of the information about international art comes to Latin America through secondary sources. Incompleteness, delay, and transformations are the consequences of information brought by reproductions of primary sources. They bring no more than a mirage to the peripheral culture. Juggling and contortions are required to fit solutions originated by a rich infrastructure into a poor one and to make them appear as true statements. It is this process that so often leads to the affected and derivative products that characterize colonial art. As Umberto Eco stated, "The basic form of provincialism does not consist of the maintenance of relations of dependence with other cultures, but is a continual elaboration of a neurotic sense of being dependent."[16]

In Cuba, particularly among the youngest artists, there is a growing awareness and recognition of the process through which information is spread and the distortions it suffers. José Angel Toirac (1966) discovered a reproduction of the Mona Lisa that was mistakenly printed in mirror image. He promptly drew a moustache and a small beard on it and labeled it "Marcel Duchamp, L.H.O.O.Q. [1919]." His writing, though, in a pun that reached Leonardo himself, was in mirror image as well.

To classify Cuban work as truly postmodern disregards the fact that "appropriation," one of the major devices utilized in postmodernism, is also a major device for answering the problems of poverty. As such it predates postmodernism and has a different function. Without much to be mentioned in favor of economic poverty, it can at least be said that it fosters ingenuity and some inquisitiveness. It elicits questions such as How does this work? and How can I use this? and, if this research is fruitful, What can it do for me? When this process occurs in technology or science it is considered perfectly valid unless it infringes on some patent law or implies industrial spying, and nobody would dream of call-

Cuando Leonardo pintó la **Mona Lisa** traspuso creativamente en el plano la imagen física de alguien de carne y hueso, llevó a dos dimensiones a ese ser vivo y tridimensional y le dejó para siempre en el lienzo con su sonrisa inquisitiva y eterna.

52

Marcel Duchamp
L.H.O.O.Q. [1919]

43. Leonardo de Vinci (1452-1519). **La Gioconda o Mona Lisa.**

La célebre obra de Leonardo muestra una armoniosa transición de luces y sombras.

Los artistas, junto a los elementos plásticos enumerados, hacen uso de determinados materiales y técnicas que caracterizan no solo su estilo personal sino incluso el de su época.

Si nos retrotraemos en el tiempo hasta el siglo XV nos encontramos con que es la técnica de la pintura al temple el método más usado. En esta se mezclan pigmentos con yemas de huevo diluida con agua, que se seca en pocos minutos y forma una película áspera de color luminoso y puro, extendida a pinceladas cortas, superpuestas. Con este método no se podía someter a rectificación lo pintado, ni se permitía extender el color en amplias pinceladas, ni la textura aparecía con las variaciones expresivas con que más tarde fue representada. Materiales y procedimientos influyen directamente en la naturaleza de una composición y de sus elementos plásticos. Por ejemplo, sin la presencia del óleo y su uso acendrado por siglos, difícilmente gozaríamos de obras donde el color fuese un relumbre de luces e iridiscencias.

José Angel Toirac, untitled, 1988, pencil on printed page, 20 × 30 cm. Private collection. Photo by Luis Camnitzer.

ing Brazilian-made tanks (apparently in higher demand than U.S.–made tanks in today's weaponry market) as colonial or derivative products. When this process occurs in art, judgment becomes harsher, primarily because of the difficulty in keeping apart the two dynamics operating: the internalized drive to be part of the hegemonic culture, and the utilization of imported devices for one's own good.

Latin American artists, no matter what their ideology, still perceive the art process through the veil of market constraints. At this point, this colors the work of many Latin American artists with a heavier dose of postmodern veneer in an often unconscious effort to assimilate into the mainstream. This veneer becomes a needed quality to qualify as a contemporary artist. But Cubans and other Latin Americans do have in common the way in which they accede to the information about mainstream art, which they do in a fragmentary and delayed way, mostly through reproductions.

Eclecticism in Cuba is a consciously assumed stance rather than a colonial, internalized consequence of outside pressure.[17] What separates Cuba from the rest of Latin America on these issues is the predominance of the second dynamic—the use of things for one's own good. Because of the U.S.–orchestrated blockade, information from the outside world is even more delayed and incomplete than in the rest of the region. It is often mistrusted for its origin and perceived as cultural penetration of imperialism. Marianela Boán, a delegate in the Fourth Congress of the UNEAC, warned about the damaging consequences of this attitude when used without discrimination and underlined that foreign (meaning Western) literature on art should also be considered technical information, not just a colonizing influence.

To understand an aesthetic through fragmentary information often requires actual experimentation to verify things. Resources are often lacking, and great ingenuity is required to compensate for this deprivation. The result is that art making in Cuba, where the intent is not so much succeeding in the market place as generating cultural identity, has much more in common with scientific and technological research than it has elsewhere. Experimentation becomes crucial, and the artist perceives borrowing as morally justified, as it is in technology, as long as the results are socially useful. Gerardo Mosquera comments, "His compass will consist in projecting the voice of his people, taking advantage of the most efficient artistic methodologies of today, *nationalizing* them the same as transnational enterprises are nationalized today."[18]

The distinction between appropriation and piracy that is demanded by this is well illustrated—as already mentioned—by Cuba's handling of international copyrights in a moment in which publishers of the world were forced to respect the U.S. blockade and when Castro announced Cuban policy on the matter in 1967.

The Cuban view of appropriation, an eclecticism not only of survival but also of despair, is a form of truly interdisciplinary thinking. It is based on integration and not on accumulation. The activity of the ANIR, as described earlier, exemplifies this interdisciplinary thinking at its

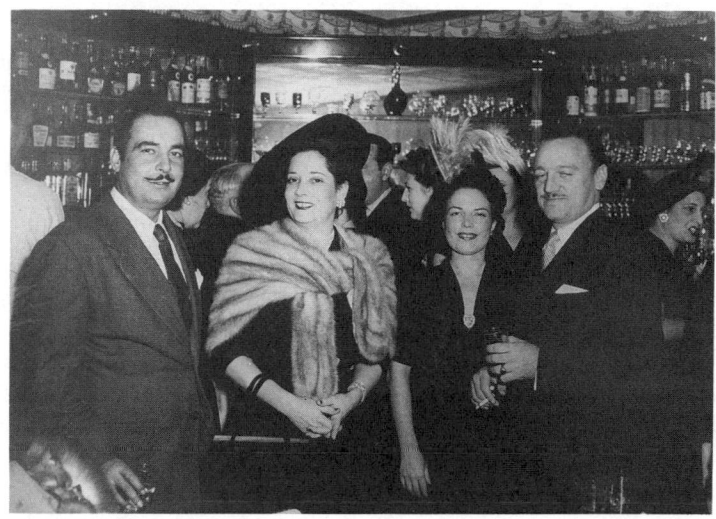

Constantino Arias, Joyas y pieles (Jewels and Furs), *1948, silver gelatin photograph. From a negative in the Fototeca Collection, Havana. Courtesy of the Center for Cuban Studies Archives.*

most refined level. Need and scarcity unify reality by exacting an ingenuity for survival. On a more theoretical level, the attitude exemplified by the ANIR is interesting in that it helps redefine what is called "derivativeness" in art as a device for negative judgment coming from the hegemonic centers.

It becomes clear that there are two kinds of appropriation in this regard. One is spurious, stemming from a drive toward affectation, a process of mimesis of the cultural center. This is graphically illustrated in a work by Cuban photographer Constantino Arias. He portrayed a Cuban prerevolutionary upperclass woman wearing a fur coat in tropical Havana. It also shows in much of the art production of peripheral countries. The other attitude stems from the urgency of solving immediate problems, where existing devices take the role of replacement parts in a broader aesthetic context.

While it is difficult to establish a formal borderline between the two attitudes, the conceptual difference is clear enough to help find the dissimilarities when analyzing a work of art, and, clearly, the second attitude primarily informs contemporary Cuban art. It is the use of imported elements without being used by them. And it is the creative nonuse of imported elements when they are not available. In an interview, Cuban painter Amelia Peláez reminisces about a visitor who, seeing a painting in progress, expressed surprise and admiration about the sudden elimination of black in her work. He interpreted it as an unexpected creative renewal of the artist, while the real reason was that her supply of black had run out and she was unable to replace it (a fact she did not reveal to the visitor).[19]

The Integral Work of Art, the Artist as Both Aesthetician and Constructive Critic

Formal solutions, particularly among the youngest Cuban artists, are the product of ethical speculations. Their work is comprised of an indissoluble web of humor, social criticism, political positions, ethical stands, and formal play. The web is so tight that the removal of any of the parts would lead to the collapse of the work. The work thus achieves in many cases a sense of integrality. It is a *Gesamtkunstwerk,* but not one based on Wagnerian megalomania or on Gropius' architectural overlay. It is an integrality based on the use of all levels of communication connecting the artist with the environment, where kitsch and vernacular joking become as important as refined design. Cuban art therefore is not postcultural like most art on the periphery, but cultural. It is proactive work, not reactive.

Regardless of the sometimes rocky trajectory of the Revolution, its ideological and social conditions have been internalized by the artists. In addition, the youngest generation of artists in Cuba now consists mostly of individuals coming from segments of the population that before the Revolution did not have access to education. The traditional monopoly of the middle class on art has been broken, and their art unites a sophisticated education with political awareness and grass-roots sensitivity. It is not surprising then that some traditional borderlines that characterize art are erased. The younger artists see themselves not only as artists but also as a part of a political spearhead, hence the attraction of rectification.

Rectification has not yet achieved a level of ideological cohesion or precision that would make it easily describable or permit conclusions about its effectiveness. Recent events in Eastern Europe and a concurrent straining of relations between Cuba and the socialist and formerly socialist bloc, added to internal problems leading to the execution of General Arnaldo Ochoa[20] and members of the Ministry of the Interior because of corruption and drug trafficking, all muddled the issues.

In fact, rectification may have had a greater impact on artistic discussion and production than on politics and administration. The younger artists identified with the premise and felt that their medium was ideally suited to challenge political commonplaces and revolutionary slogans that had died of overexposure, and to help move lazy bureaucrats.[21]

Thus, visual artists, traditionally considered the intuiting intellectuals, took over the role formerly assigned to writers and philosophers, those usually considered the reasoning intellectuals. This erasure of traditional borderlines between reason and intuition has also been one of the implicit aims of the Biennial, where most of the subject matters are discussed in the context of identity and cultural autonomy.

While a contextual awareness is usually present in a majority of Latin American artists, there is often a lack of articulation and clarity in regard to the complexity of the issues involved. The Latin American artists tend to be confined to their specialization instead of being nourished into the role of full citizens with the ability to make art.

Critic Gerardo Mosquera described the position of the new Cuban artists as "informed by a variety of languages," with ethics coming to the foreground and "a wider sense of a concern about human conduct, a faith in human betterment, the absence of nihilism, alienation, or an existential cynicism. It implies a libertarian spirit of openness, the widening of postmodernist poetics, which have been assimilated in order to confront local situations. All this coexists with a utopianism of human and social transformation closer to the aspirations of the sixties and the old vanguards, a deconstructionist impulse with regards to political rhetoric and stereotypes, the wide spread of humor, a waning interest in the aura of art."[22] In fact, the balanced blend these artists achieve in their work makes them safe from the pitfalls of self-righteousness, doctrinaire politics, and formalism in their art, all forms of terrorism when unduly stressed (according to Habermas).

The resulting mixture of political challenge and irreverence by the young Cuban artists' pointed use of art and ethical and political languages became, in some instances, too much for parts of the political establishment. As a consequence, some works of art that intentionally reattributed meanings to national symbols were censored when the artists exhibited them in public places with excessive circulation. On the occasion of the Third Biennial of Havana, during November 1989, the most aggressive work was confined to a section titled *The Tradition of Humor in Cuban Art*, which effectively dulled many of the barbs.

Despite unfortunate incidents of censorship, containment of information, and self-censorship, it is a remarkable success of the Revolution that this generation of artists exists in Cuba. Equivalent generations in other socialist countries have resorted either to the maintenance of a party-line aesthetic, to copying of Western art, or to adoption of nihilist positions, while the Cuban artists feel that they are refining their own political and social process. In Cuba, art has developed into an increasingly sophisticated tool of constructive criticism and improvement of the system. Even when aesthetic ruptures occur, this awareness gives Cuban art a sort of steady continuity. Even considering the recent incidents of censorship, Cuban art can largely be defined as a blend of individual freedom within a collective sense of responsibility.

The Cuban approach presents an alternative to the capitalist model followed in the rest of Latin America. It is clear from the Cuban experience that public funding dealing with the artist as a totality—not just financing some of the produced collectibles—can be successful not only in helping the artist individually but also in raising a general level of culture. It is also clear that this success is optimized if there is a belief in culture as an intrinsic, active part of society's productivity and not just as a decorative appendix. Without this belief as a formative part of the social philosophy, it would not be possible to have this type of support nor these results.

The process presently employed by Latin America, based on a competitive market that it cannot afford without the help of the hegemonic center, clearly is at a disadvantage. Those artists who are successful owe their fortune to a certain fit with international demands and values. Those artists preoccupied with affecting cultural conditions in their immediate environment have a lesser chance for economic survival.

It is interesting that the "free market" artist is seen as a free individualist at a time when in the economic centers some creative areas are suffering a dynamic of increasing collectivization and anonymity. Presidential speeches are created by teams, books are written by ghostwriters, works of art are made by assistants or ordered in factories, and, lately, a camera has appeared on the market with a bar-code reader. The user selects a photographic example from a catalogue with a particular depth of field, blurriness of background, and preferred exposed area and feeds the encoded information of the page into the camera.

The result is a collectivization according to preset artistic values, one whose social advantages are not totally clear. A style of correctness and acceptability is given that in turn will define an identity devoid of any individual decision. Until now, this capitalist Orwellian perspective has been avoided by Cuba in an exemplary manner. Because of the ethical grounding of many of the artists in Latin America and the Cuban success, there is hope that they too may be spared that future. Culture cannot help being a collective enterprise. The choice is not between making "individual" or "collective" art but in the kind of collectivism to be employed.

POSTSCRIPT

September 1991

There are many artists missing from this book whom somebody else might have included, and there may be many present whom other writers would have excluded. But beyond this normal situation, a product of the arbitrariness inherent to any author's taste, there is the Cuban situation. The fluidity and speed of art production in Cuba during recent years has made it very difficult to keep up. Every trip I undertook during the process of this book forced me to make serious rewrites and to add new information that cast light on old information. The individual work of Cuban artists evolves and matures (and may wither) in a matter of months. Some of the names appearing here were completely unknown two years before I wrote them down. Some were known but not yet interesting, and had I written a book then from a directory point of view, it would have been quite a different directory. By the time this book is read, the leap may be worse, given the acceleration of the Cuban process.

Regardless of possible mistakes in cataloguing and except for natural or political catastrophes, however, the issues touched by the artists in this book should remain valid for a while. They address concerns of all peripheral cultures, no matter whether they are in countries far away from the hegemonic centers or whether they coexist in the same geographical space. As long as there is a global imbalance of power, Cuba's history, because of the achievements and the mistakes, will remain a fertile ground for study and a good metaphor for the possibilities in the Third World.

An issue that may not have been stressed enough in the previous chapters is the importance of the Biennial of Havana. Cuban authorities are keenly aware of the problems posed by the unidirectionality of the flow of information, and the Biennial of Havana has been one of the measures taken to solve the problem. The Biennial has increasingly become a center of attention, both inside and outside Cuba. It has helped Cuban artists by providing them with an international stage as well as providing them with contact with work produced in other Third World countries. The Biennial itself is a subject for experimentation and has been through changes in each one of its presentations. These changes were an issue for discussion not just among the Cuban organizers but among participants coming from all over the Third World as well.

The present format downplays the importance of the traditional central exhibit concept and emphasizes the role of panel discussions, workshops by invited artists, and smaller exhibits that are presented all over the province of Havana. The Biennial is thus becoming more and more a clearinghouse of ideas and a laboratory of creation, where the structure of the Biennial itself remains one of the topics for analysis.

When it first started, the Biennial was limited to Latin America. In the two subsequent events (1986 and 1989) it became a Third World Biennial. In a time in which the hegemonic centers are changing the meaning of the term *Third World* to have racial and racist connotations, it seems important that Cuba reasserts the historic origin (the Conference of Bandung) and the political importance of the concept (the common front of dependent nations against the hegemony of the superpowers). The Biennial thus becomes a reminder of our own history and a warning against a cooptation of the name. This cooptation is already showing signs of success among some minority populations in the First World countries. Ignorant of the history, they are accepting the overlaid racist interpretation as valid and consequently abandoning *Third World* as a rallying title.

In Latin America the Biennial is now counted (together with Venice, São Paulo, Kassel, and Sydney) among the major international artistic events. The mutual feedback has weakened some of the grip held by the hegemonic centers in regard to aesthetic decisions. Chilean artists are developing their own brand of political art, many of the artists in Brazil are groping with nonurban culture, and in Argentina some artists are trying to combine Western abstractionism with pre-Columbian aesthetics. In other words, many artists are shifting away from the production for a market and concentrating on the generation of culture relevant for their own environment.

Cuban artists, in turn, have been quick in perfecting the presentation of their work, consistently providing the most stunning installations of the Biennial. Nevertheless, still focused on Cuba, they have not wavered from their initial task of working for their own audience.

The initial intention was to finish this book in 1987. My first version—a kind of sketch for this book—seems, in retrospect, excessively utopian and idealized. The first seven years of the decade had shown such a linear evolution within a path of enlightenment that they had a ring of panacea. The obstacles that lately appeared in that path and rounded the decade make perceptions of Cuba more realistic and make it a place where Revolution cannot rest. If the positions of the parties involved do not harden beyond the present stage, sifting through them in an undogmatic way should fertilize, not hamper, the creative process. In that case it may require a quick succession of volumes to keep up with the production.

Cuba was confronted in 1989 and 1990 with an array of internal and external crises, and their resolution could have serious negative consequences on the development of Cuban art. The process against Ochoa, a national hero executed for corruption and drug trafficking, is still too recent for a clear perspective. On one hand, the proceedings, shared with the public via extensive television coverage, were a symptom of the rectification process in action. On the other hand, the incident is a symbol of the pressure imposed by the United States through the blockade, which shows how an illegal action leads to other illegal actions and how these can corrupt individuals. Lastly, it was an embarrassing incident for the armed forces and became a missionary flag to help eliminate other corruptions. It is through this latter path that dogmatic hardenings can occur that might damage the arts.

Then there is the deterioration of relations with the Soviet Union. The process of revision of history that took place in the USSR was definitely perceived as threatening to the Cuban vision of history as proposed by the Revolution during these thirty years. The threat was seen by some sectors as big enough to achieve the prohibition of circulation of the Soviet magazines *Sputnik* and *Moscow News*. This, in turn, led to the paradoxical situation of having Radio Martí beam readings of chosen Soviet articles from Miami into Cuba. It was an action that, in fact, confirmed the position of those suggesting the prohibition. According to the Cuban Communist Party paper *Granma*, the Soviet publications were written for the capitalist public and do not fit Cuba, and "in their pages one discovers an apologia of bourgeois democracy . . . as well as a fascination with the U.S. way of life. Imperialism has disappeared."[1] Late in 1990, *Moscow News* retaliated, calling Fidel Castro a "Caribbean Saddam Hussein."[2] However, the Soviet publications are not representative of the full political spectrum of the USSR, and the relation of both countries is still considered friendly, even if strained.[3]

This strain leads some sectors in Cuba to draw superficial and incorrect parallels. The former Soviet Union, while undergoing ideological upheaval, is also undergoing a cultural opening similar to that initiated in Cuba a decade ago. The temptation is to connect what these sectors consider Soviet political "deviations" with the mature Cuban art solutions initiated a long time ago. In this context, the manipulation of patriotic symbols becomes particularly sensitive.

In an exchange between Carlos Aldana and secretaries of the UJC (Unión de la Juventud Comunista, or Young Communist League), Aldana addressed worries expressed by those from the municipalities where the ISA and the Castillo de la Real Fuerza are located. In his remarks he expressed confidence in both institutions (which are the ones seen as originating problems). *Juventud Rebelde* reports that

> Aldana said it would be extremely absurd and irrational to express regrets about the artistic potential we have, which has developed under the Revolution. He added that this potential needs to be 'decanted,' but so far this process has been hampered by a series of unsolved problems such as promotion, incompetence of some officials, and certain cliquish behavior, which explains the coexistence of exponents of an artistic vanguard in gestation with manifestations of grandstanding and opportunism. . . . There are genuine voices of those who are committed to the Revolution and touch on sensitive and contradictory aspects of our reality. They legitimately claim our attention, although they don't always manage to overcome the tendency toward hypercritical and iconoclastic attitudes. There are others who, when we try to understand them and when they must assume social responsibility for their work, hide behind the so-called 'diversity of interpretations.' The latter can't be taken seriously.[4]

The length of the quote is merited because it expresses both a sense of caution and respect toward the controversial artist, while it leaves open the possibility of deciding who is expressing well-intended hypercriticism and who is falsely hiding behind a diversity of interpretations. It should be stressed here that the artists who have shown signs of being iconoclasts continue to be well sponsored. Ponjuán and Rodríguez both received teaching appointments after their scandal. Esson, Rodríguez Cárdenas, and members of the ABTV team are all promoted outside of Cuba with work similar to that which caused problems in Cuba. Quintana, another "rectification" artist, has been appointed director of the silkscreen workshop Taller Portocarrero.[5]

All the problems and tensions mentioned become particularly noticeable in moments of economic tightness. In the past Cuba was able to acquire two tons of crude oil from the Soviet Union with one ton of sugar. Presently it costs Cuba two tons of sugar to buy one ton of oil. Thus, the income of hard currency coming from the sale of oil refined in Cuba has practically disappeared. In relation to the arts and artists this has created a new, transitional situation. Artists are not exempted from the call to the microbrigades organized to cope with the situation. But they are not dissuaded from working in other countries either. At the time of this writing Torres Llorca, Soto, Pérez Monzón, Castañeda, and Planes are in Mexico; Campos is in Canada; Garciandía and Pérez Bravo are in Germany; Rodríguez Brey is in Belgium; Esson, del Sol, Quintana, and Aguilera had a long stay in the United States; and Novoa and Rodríguez Cárdenas have been traveling between Mexico, Europe, and the United States.

This high circulation of Cuban artists, partly due to the recent success of their exhibits in the international market, is a mixed blessing. On one side it counteracts a traditional Cuban insularity problem, something that under duress tends to become more acute and that can lead nationalism to distort into chauvinism. If insularity prevailed, the Latinamericanist drive of many Cuban artists and the precisely measured use of nationalism as a springboard toward a Third World and truly internationalist expression would be lost. But, on the other side, it makes Cuban art overly vulnerable to the mainstream market and may slowly separate Cuban artists from their own audience. It could become something critic Mosquera already calls the "danger of papinization," a reference to Los Papines, a group of Cuban drummers who have been performing all over the world for many years, officially representing Cuba, but without touching base.

It would be dishonest on my part not to acknowledge that some of the changes in Cuba have affected my vision of the decade. When I started writing this book I did so in the belief that I was witnessing an open and endless road of artistic flourishing and development. By the time the book was being finished, because of all the later events, I was forced to revise my image and to acknowledge at least that there are some obstacles on the road. Hopefully these obstacles will disappear, or at least will be handled successfully so that they do not become a complete roadblock. Russian constructivism comes to mind as a possible precedent, a movement that wanted to be part of the Russian Revolution and eventually ended up encapsulated, both isolated and insulated, in an alien development of visual history. The art of the Cuban artists of this last decade is too representative of Cuba itself to be in that danger.

Leaving the future aside, the Cuban decade, such as it has been, has left at least two important lessons in relation to the insertion of the arts in society. One, which surprised my own prejudices, is that the ease of access to the course of studies in the arts and the length of immersion in that course seems to be more important than the actual methodology employed in the teaching. Although there are no studies offering quantitative data, Cuba gives the impression of having more good artists per capita than other countries.

The other lesson, assuming that the preceding impression is correct, is that nonrepressive socialism is more conducive to good art than nonrepressive capitalism. But what is most impressive is that Cuban artists have—unlike artists in other countries—an actual cultural and social influence in their country. A history of revolutionary Cuba would be seriously lacking without an understanding of this unusual full partnership. That Cuba was able to achieve this with relatively few overt programmatic constraints and mostly by means of sponsoring creativity has to be seen as one of the greatest achievements of the revolutionary process.

SECOND POSTSCRIPT

February 1992

My final work on this book took place shortly after the Fourth Biennial of Havana, and oil shipments to Cuba had been cut to a minimum by the new "Commonwealth of Independent States." Bicycles are becoming the main form of transportation, calories being burned accordingly but with little food available to provide the extra energy. More than fifty Cuban artists are working in Mexico, not as a sign of ideological dissension but for economic reasons. Most of the artists mentioned in this book are out of Cuba now. While this diaspora somewhat relieves the government in a moment of economic crisis, the cultural impact may be devastating—the feedback from the more mature artists on the emerging ones is interrupted.

The teachings of the "Volumen I" generation succeeded in creating a collective cultural dynamic focused on Cuban social and national identity. It was remarkable that this was done by a group of artists often accused of being aestheticists and that it was achieved without sacrificing the individual originality of the artists participating. This originality and diversity, presumably only possible in a capitalist and competitive environment, was implemented by artists educated within the Revolution and with socialist goals.

Critical to their success in this was the continuity of the process during the decade described here. This continuity now seems about to be broken, and not because of a lack of new talent; the new names already mentioned and what one could see in the many exhibits surrounding the last Biennial attest to the presence of an apparently inexhaustible flow of creativity. What seems threatened is the web that unites those artists and enables them to build a culture.

For the newer artists, particularly the youngest generations in the

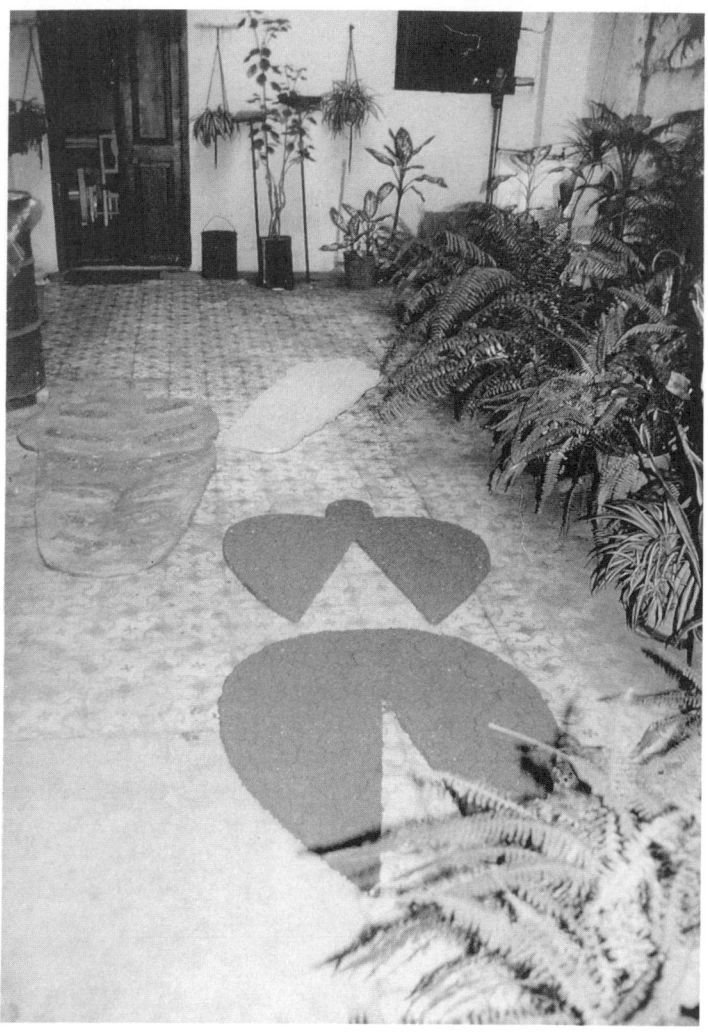

Tania Bruguera, recreation of the work of Ana Mendieta, 1987–1991. Collection of the artist. Photo by Luis Camnitzer.

ISA today, referentiality no longer functions as a form of eclecticism for survival, but as a new style. Individual work is successful and pleasant, and it is often difficult to level criticism on it when seen out of context. Some, such as Tania Bruguera, continue working in the spirit of the decade. Bruguera has been working on a recreation of Ana Mendieta's work for several years now, trying to reconstruct it from reproductions, but also creating "in the spirit" of her work, not unlike the Borges' story about Pierre Menard's efforts to recreate, word for word, *Don Quijote de la Mancha*. However, other artists, such as Marcos Castillo, do work connected more with the mainstream than with Cuba. Castillo uses photographs of Robert Smithson's earth works to create large canvases that look like Eric Fischel's work. The ingenuity and skills of his work are wonderful, but when seen in the context of a trend in which witty quotes and visual puns become the essence, the work is weakened.

The government, officially still in the rectification process added to what now is called a "special period of peace,"[1] is still trying desperately to keep the arts going. In 1991 there were fourteen hundred exhibits in Cuba, two thousand artists exhibiting in 136 galleries. The Fourth Biennial, although smaller in scope than the preceding ones, was generally considered the best to date, and the Centro Lam is already working on the Fifth Biennial.

While employment for artists seems to be more protected than that of other disciplines, the effects of the economic crisis are noticeable. The ISA is running out of materials for its students, and materials for the artists are scarce. The effect is that artists in Cuba are increasingly looking for sales outside of the country. The decade of the 1980s somehow had prepared artists to believe that living off the sale of one's art was feasible. The temporary opening to a mixed economy held on in the visual arts but never was fully thought out in strategy or in its consequences. With the international success of Cuban art and the opening of markets (including the United States after the legal ruling that confirmed that art is information and thus should not be covered by the embargo), this lack of planning left the commercial responsibility in the hands of the artist. With the economic problems inside Cuba, the hope of living off sales was displaced to outside of national borders, intensifying the ambition to travel. For the first time in more than ten years, an artist presented me with a calling card. Also for the first time I heard a painter comment that he was going to stick with his manner of painting for a while, in order to establish an image and not to confuse the market. Both incidents show a shift in attitudes and an emphasis on searching for crutches.

Bureaucratic paternalism has also shifted focus. What during the 1980s had been a facilitating paternalism, which subsidized artists and made them relatively free, is transforming into a paternalism that is only protective of the hypothetical viewer who could be offended or confused, with two effects. One is that the artist feels relatively unprotected and sometimes even paranoid. The other is that the issue of censorship and self-censorship continues to be unresolved. The first issue reinforces the artists' attention to market and survival issues rather than collective culture problems. The second one, in a continuing ambiguity that has not changed much since the Esson exhibit in 1988, signals the possibility of an underlying political danger in dealing with collective culture as the "rectification artists" of the third generation did. The temptation then becomes to make art for art's sake.

Lázaro Saavedra was to have an exhibit in conjunction with the Fourth Biennial. His project was to hang photocopies of his catalogues and documents of his achievements as an artist, accompanied with a letter in which he offered himself for grants and his work for sale. The exhibition, a direct satire of what he perceived as corruption in some of his colleagues, did not open on time in the gallery where it was planned. Rumors of censorship spread widely and, although some problem existed, it never became clear what exactly happened. It is believed that the censorship was confined to the opinion of a gallery administrator who, as a consequence, was punched in the face by Lázaro with what others called "the fist of his generation." However, Lázaro was promised to have his exhibit in another prestigious gallery, and he was not accused of physical assault. Simultaneously, the exhibit of Alexis Leiva (Kcho) was taking place, with work that was much more sacrilegious since it dealt with national symbols, without raising any complaint.

Thus, "hawks" and "doves" are still at work without a clear victory on either side. In a recent conversation, a ministry functionary expressed clearly a belief in the need to "guide" exhibits, taking into account what they may elicit from the people. An example given as improper work was the ABTV team's Orlando Yanes project, in which the artists had negated Yanes' right to change his own political views from pro-Batista to pro-Castro. The irony was that, accordingly, the freedom to change beliefs by one artist could only be ensured by curtailing the freedom of exhibition of other artists.

It is undeniable that the international pressure on Cuba is nurturing a form of political fundamentalism that is not helpful for a free development of culture. It is not clear, however, how far this fundamentalism will go. The 1980s decade in Cuba taught that artists committed to their society and nurtured to create freely can create culture and not just art objects. It can only be hoped that the generations of politicians following accept the lesson and try to keep that dynamic alive.

NOTES

INTRODUCTION

1. Martí resigned as Consul in 1892. Uruguay maintained friendly relations with Cuba at a time when Martí was publicly fighting the Cuban government. He resigned to avoid a potentially embarrassing situation for Uruguay. A street was named after him in Montevideo in 1916. The School of Fine Arts is located on that street, so I walked in the shadow of his name for many years.

2. "The general tendency of design is based on a strict and ascetic economy of forms and materials, in order to reduce costs to a minimum, and on a functionality denying any symbolic or stylistic reference, thus opposing, as an educational, functional, and moral alternative, the remaining prestige of the 'artistic' or 'generational' artifact" (Roberto Segre, "El significado de Cuba en la cultura arquitectónica contemporánea," *Cuadernos Summa-Nueva Visión: Arquitectura Cubana*, no. 46–47 [March 1970]: 11).

In a more recent analysis, Cuban architect Tamargo González, after relating functionalism in the West to profit motives, states,

> The mistake, of course, is not the use of the most efficient techniques, but to have them as the end and not as one of the means. In Cuba, where the above-mentioned problems don't apply, architectural activity also leans dangerously toward technocracy. Construction plans are big, . . . and the Cuban architect is not privy to a solid conceptual base to confront such structural transformations. . . . The way we have looked in Cuba toward developed socialist countries seeking new experiences and solutions for new approaches, we should have first looked into countries in our area. . . . [The area] that is closer culturally and economically is a richer and more certain source for specific solutions, even if this is not the case for development programs or guidelines. . . . The architect should not be a convinced imitator nor an impotent observer when faced with popular architecture. The first position means to become an accomplice to an architecture sprung from extreme economic limitations, from poor technical skills, from the lack

of knowledge in general; the second means alienation. . . . Vernacular architecture should give direct solutions to direct problems . . . the sincere answer to the form of life, to culture. (Jorge Tamargo González, "De la arquitectura en el Caribe hacia la arquitectura del Caribe" [Paper presented at the International Conference on Visual Arts of the Caribbean, Havana, 1986])

3. The process, however, does not supply enough material to satisfy Cuban publishing needs, and the economic crisis spurred by the events in Eastern Europe during 1989–1990 led to serious cuts in Cuban newspapers, magazines, and books.

4. In 1989 over half the population was under thirty years old.

5. Thanks to a grant from the Ford Foundation, Flavio Garciandía, José Bedia, and Ricardo Rodríguez Brey visited SUNY College at Old Westbury during the spring semester of 1985. During their stay they produced the exhibit "New Art from Cuba," which was shown at the College at Old Westbury, the Massachusetts College of Art, the Montserrat School of Visual Arts, the University of Massachusetts at Amherst, SUNY College at Purchase, and the Museum of the University of Puerto Rico at Río Piedras.

6. That retrograde art is still alive in Cuba as well is demonstrated by the recent monument built in honor of the thirtieth anniversary of Che Guevara's liberation of the town of Santa Clara. A work by sculptor José Delarra unveiled in December 1988, it consists of a plaza with a surface of 10,400 square meters, which, among other things, includes a seven-meter-high sculpture portraying Che, standing on a ten-meter-high column. The irony is that if Che were alive today he probably would have vetoed that kind of project.

7. The bulk of this book was written during the winter of 1987. The speed of events and development of artists in Cuba has forced many rewrites. It is probable, however, that the initial vantage point still permeates the book as a whole.

I "VOLUMEN I"

1. Even the short introduction to the exhibit, written by art critic Gerardo Mosquera, was amazingly cautious compared to his usual style, possibly attempting a studied form of understatement: "It is, simply, the presentation of some of the more significant work within the present creation of young artists."

2. The remaining four were Fernando Gómez, Israel León, Pedro Hernández Torres, and Manuel Daza. Julio Izaguirre Vichot (untitled Ph.D. diss., Universidad de la Habana, 1987) and Enrique Alvarez Martínez, "Volumen I: Primer volumen de una renovación esperanzadora," (Havana, 1986, Typescript). I am drawing on both essays for some of the historical information in this chapter.

3. Teresa Crego, who was responsible for the decision, interviewed in 1986 by Izaguirre Vichot, (untitled Ph.D. diss.).

4. Angel Tomás, interview with the author, January 1988.

5. Angel Tomás, "Desafío en San Rafael," *El Caimán Barbudo*, March 1981, p. 7. San Rafael is the street where the gallery is located.

6. Gerardo Mosquera writes in regard to this topic:

Identity as action, not as exhibit. In the "search for our identity" an "expression of our roots" has frequently been proclaimed which leads to a grave lack of cultural focus. It was believed that the problems of our own expression could be solved by showing folklorisms, local colors, traditions. . . . A dangerous error, because the solution is not in showing identity, but in *acting* from it, from inside toward the outside. . . . Wole Soyinka said, "A tiger doesn't announce its tigritude—it leaps." . . . Our dilemma is not resolved by throwing [capitalist instruments] into the garbage can, to then go back to precapitalist options. But neither is it a matter of arriving at the third millennium following [capitalist culture], adapting it, or even nationalizing it, which may be a transitional solution. We have to make it ourselves with our own criteria, or at least participate actively in its evolution. Slowly and more each time. And once this happens, it will have stopped being a Western culture. ("Identidad y cultura popular en el nuevo arte cubano," [Havana, 1987, Typescript])

7. During 1989–1990, three figures prominent in the administration of Cuban visual arts changed jobs. Marcia Leiseca, vice-minister of culture for visual arts, was removed from her position to become vice-president of Casa de las Américas. Gerardo Mosquera, head of the advisory committee to the Centro Wifredo Lam, resigned to become a free-lance writer. Beatriz Aulet, director of the Centro de Desarrollo de las Artes Visuales, was transferred to Artex, a government agency that promotes Cuban cultural products for commerce, as an advisor. Although known for their support for the new generations, none could be accused of being excessively partisan or of working to the detriment of traditional artists.

8. This does not preclude that the art produced was sometimes used by political sectors to their advantage in the perennial discussion about national and social identity.

9. See Victor Casaus, "El género testimonio y el cine cubano," in *Cine, Literatura y Sociedad*, ed. Ambrosio Fornet, p. 91.

10. "Protest Song," the title of a song festival in Varadero, Cuba, organized by Casa de las Américas in 1968, is a term mainly used outside Cuba. As a style in songwriting it covers much of Cuban music at the time, but the notion of "protest song" in the sense of its literal meaning, referring to the content of the lyrics, was never accepted as having application in Cuba.

11. I must credit Charles Merewether with the insight of placing Rodríguez Cárdenas in this context.

12. Soviet socialist realism had been, to a certain extent, a writers' contraption proclaimed by the First Congress of Soviet Writers (Moscow, August 1934). Adolfo Sánchez Vázquez, a Spanish-Mexican aesthetician and philosopher who was extremely influential in the thought process informing Cuban art during the 1960s (see Chap. 3), describes the events in a way that coincides with Cuban perception of the time. The idea of a party aesthetic went against a Communist Party

decision of 1925 that had established the free competition of artistic schools and tendencies, the refusal to proclaim one of them as an official and dominant tendency, and the confidence that the traits of a new art would come out of the struggle among different aesthetics and artistic tendencies. See Adolfo Sánchez Vázquez, *Estética y marxismo*, pp. 55–56, and *Art and Society: Essays in Marxist Aesthetics.*

Consequently, it was not so much party politics or the role of party officials as internal discussions in the avant-garde which debilitated the original Soviet movements. Malevich had insisted on the departure of Chagall and Kandinsky, while Rodschenko forced the conflict between the Productivist program and the Constructivism of Gabo and Pevsner due to their excessive aesthetism (Benjamin Buchloh, "Cold War Constructivism," [1987, Photostat], pp. 5–6).

Sánchez Vázquez sees the subsequent process as follows. In 1932, through the organization of the Soviet Union of Writers and Artists, all diverse groups of intellectuals were put under one umbrella and thus opened the way for future party interference or guidance. The definition of realism had been part of many discussions over the preceding years, and the hardening into dogma was the consequence of a process helped, but not caused, by Soviet bureaucracy. Stalin once spoke of language as indifferent to class, as serving all classes equally, as having a specific character that distinguishes it from economic infrastructure and ideological superstructure. Based on these remarks, some Soviet aesthetic thinkers in the early 1950s extended these ideas to art. Trofimov, for example, came to the conclusion that Greek art maintained its aesthetic significance after both the ideological content and the infrastructure based on slavery had disappeared (Sánchez Vázquez, *Estética y marxismo*, pp. 32–33). The conundrums generated by all of this, including, as a consequence, the possibility of absolute and eternal values in art, became the subject of revision in Marxist aesthetics from the mid-fifties onward.

13. Gerardo Mosquera, *Trece artistas jóvenes*, pp. 54–55.

14. Departamento de Orientación Revolucionaria del Comité Central del Partido Comunista de Cuba, *Sobre la cultura artística, literaria: tésis, resolución*, Proceedings of the First Congress of the Cuban Communist Party (Havana, 1975). Bowing to progressive intellectuals in capitalist countries, the statement continues, "This reality does not preclude that humanist, progressive works are produced under capitalist conditions, but such works can only be produced in spite of existing conditions, and not seldomly at risk—in every sense—for the artist who, in order to create them, has to elude or deny, if not challenge, the norms imposed by capitalist society (p. 14).

15. Cinematography was a priority of the Revolution from the beginning, not only in terms of production of national films (the ICAIC, the Cuban Institute for Cinematographic Art and Industry, was one of the first cultural institutions to be organized) but also in terms of screening. By 1975 there were 620 showing places for sixteen-millimeter films and 449 for thirty-five millimeter. Sixteen-millimeter films were shown also through mobile units, 112 specially equipped trucks, 22 in mule driven carts, and 2 "film boats." Fidel Castro, "Report of the Central Committee of the Communist Party to the First Congress," in his *La primera revolución*

socialista en América, p. 146. Particularly because of the market conditions, the blockade on one end and bartering on the other, Soviet films were easily available and shown frequently.

16. The flyer for the show, written by Mosquera, said, "Each artist (we can't speak here of painters or sculptors anymore) has presented a personal vision of the world of the home and of daily life. They go from irony to nostalgia, from love to mystery, from banality to poetry. But the principal aim of this show is to attempt a language of greater popular reach, which allows for a more direct and natural communication between artist and people. The artists aspire for the visual arts to become, some day, as normal, as fresh, as daily, and—why not—as healthy and tasty as a good recipe by Nitza Villapol." Nitza Villapol is a well-known Cuban cook who had a cooking and nutrition column in the newspaper *Granma*.

17. Angel Tomás, "Ni sano ni sabroso," *El Caimán Barbudo*, November 1981, p. 26.

18. Eduardo Torres-Cuevas and Eusebio Reyes, *Esclavitud y sociedad*, pp. 25–27.

19. Marion Muller, "Chinese Paper Gems," *Upper and Lower Case*, February 1988, p. 32.

20. The origin of the word is not clear. Some authors (anthropologist Fernando Ortiz, among others) believe that it is a distortion of the Spanish *picudo*, which means "beaked," but also "prattling." The image of childish babbling seems a good one to put a product into a perspective of elementary crudeness, while keeping an affectionate disposition toward it.

21. Photographer Mayito (Mario García Joya) in a conversation with Shifra Goldman, quoted to the author.

22. Benjamin Buchloh, "Interview with Flavio Garciandía," in *New Art from Cuba*, p. 27, catalogue for the exhibit, SUNY, College at Old Westbury, New York, 1985.

23. Erena Hernández, interview with Flavio Garciandía, in *Vereda Tropical*, catalogue for the exhibit, Fondo Cubano de Bienes Culturales, Havana, November 1982.

24. Gerardo Mosquera, "Bad Taste in Good Form," *Social Text* (Fall 1986): 62.

25. Buchloh, "Interview with Flavio Garciandía," p. 27.

26. Coco Fusco and Robert Knafo, "Interviews with Cuban Artists," *Social Text* (Fall 1986): 47.

27. Abdel Hernández, "Magie oder Post-Kunst?," in *Kuba o.k.*, p. 94, catalogue for the exhibit, Städtische Kunsthalle, Düsseldorf, 1990.

28. Leandro Soto, "La historia como material artístico," in *Retablo Familiar*, essay for the poster of his exhibit "Retablo Familiar," Casa de la Cultura de Plaza, Havana, April 1984.

29. Ibid.

30. Miscegenation between the native population and black slaves also started very early, especially when blacks escaped to join Amerindian rebellions, which started in 1520. These rebellions did not last very long. The rebels operated from the woods with limited supplies that were quickly depleted by freely roam-

ing Castilian pigs brought earlier by the Spaniards. Black rebellions are reported from 1533 onward. Jesús Guanche, *Procesos etnoculturales de Cuba,* pp. 147–148.

31. Slavery initially was a "color blind" system and included white criminalsas well. An important original condition (1501) was that anybody coming to the colonies had to be christened; thus, only black slaves from Spain could be imported to Cuba. The African trade started in 1580 on a bigger scale, with the participation of all major European powers, and in 1618 a British company was created with the wonderful title "Company of Adventurers of London Trading into Africa." Slaves were considered dehumanized commodities. In 1783 the captain of the British ship *Zong* was short of drinking water and threw 132 slaves over board. Subsequently the owners of the ship brought suit to receive insurance compensation under the clause "perils of the sea" and were granted thirty pounds for every slave lost. Eric Williams, *Capitalism and Slavery,* pp. 32, 46.

32. Between 1850 and 1860 the suicide rate in Spain was fifteen per million. During the same period in Cuba it was 340, the highest known in the world. Of these suicides, 92.5 percent were committed by Chinese people. Guanche, *Procesos etnoculturales,* pp. 319–320.

33. Williams, *Capitalism and Slavery,* p. 29.

34. Ex-votos are still being actively manufactured today in Cuba. Shaped out of sheet aluminum, they seem more primitive and less elaborate than their Mexican counterparts but have a synthesis in the image that sets them apart and gives them their own appeal.

35. Rafael López Valdés, *Componentes africanos en el etnos cubano,* p. 81. The word *bozal* referred to "imported" blacks.

36. The first black artist accepted by the Cuban establishment was Vicente Escobar, who eventually married a white woman. His birth certificate registered him as black, but according to his death certificate he died white (a "privilege" he apparently was able to buy). An admired painter in the early nineteenth century who made portraits for the establishment, he was a slaveholder himself. Jorge Rigol, "Apuntes sobre el grabado y la pintura en Cuba," in *Panorama de la cultura cubana,* ed. Marilú Moré de Castro, p. 124.

37. Cited by Alvaro Medina in "Lam y Changó" (Paper presented at the International Conference on Wifredo Lam, Havana, May 1984).

38. For an analysis of *The Jungle* in relation to *Santería* motifs, see Medina, *Lam y Changó.*

39. A *babalao,* a higher *Santería* priest, explained to me that *Santería* is a ritual that is defensive against evil, while the *Palo* is offensive against evil. I witnessed a discussion on this subject by two practitioners of the respective rites in which the *Palero* denied this division. He claimed to have witnessed a *Santero* putting a paper with the name of an enemy in the mouth of a lizard and then slowly impaling it until it died—something his ritual would never do. The *Santero* retorted that he watched a *Palero* cutting open the bulb of a cactus, turning the sharp spines inward and reclosing it over the written name of a victim. The last word of the *Palero* was that he had tried everything, including voodoo, against his father-in-law, but to no avail.

40. Gerardo Mosquera, "Art and Anthropology," *Granma Weekly Review*, April 15, 1984, p. 7.

41. José Bedia, interview with the author, New York, 1985.

42. Some weeks after arriving in the United States in 1985, Bedia happened to hear from critic Lucy Lippard that a "Cherokee artist" was going to have an exhibit in Soho under the title of "Bedia's Basement," in honor, it seemed, of some Cuban anthropologist. José was baffled, since he was the only Cuban he knew in whom was combined the name "Bedia" and an interest in anthropology. He mused about it through the evening while the rest of us present shared in the amusement, teasing José about his delusions of grandeur.

At precisely the same time an old friend of mine, unconnected with the arts, phoned my home leaving a message with my wife. He had called to report a bizarre coincidence—that a few days ago, while killing time in a dentist's waiting room, he picked up a magazine and read an article of mine that mentioned Bedia. Just now at a group show in New York, he had made the acquaintance of an artist named Jimmy Durham, who had invited him to attend the opening of his one-man show, which, he explained, had been conceived in homage to some Cuban guy named "Bedia." Upon returning the call to my friend, we planned to engineer a meeting of Bedia and Durham, without their prior notice. As planned, the evening of Durham's opening of "Bedia's Basement," a group of us, including Bedia, Garciandía, and Rodríguez Brey, went to several openings that evening until we "just happened" to find ourselves in Durham's gallery. There, in an appropriately unfinished and dimly lit basement, a man stood, quietly and alone, in front of a large wall hanging announcing his homage to "Bedia." My friend confirmed that this was indeed Jimmy Durham, whereupon I brought José to him and said, "I would like to introduce you to the real Bedia." Durham looked at him and without changing expression said simply, "I thought you would show up." Their friendship dated from that moment. Durham explained that, having been deeply impressed by some work of Bedia he had had occasion to view several years earlier in an exhibit of Cuban art at the Westbeth Gallery, he had subsequently constructed his own mythical anthropologist with Bedia's name. Otherwise, he had known nothing of the real Bedia, of his work or his whereabouts, let alone that he happened to be in the United States and in New York. Durham then engaged sculptor Claes Oldenburg's generosity to fund Bedia's trip to the Sioux Reservation.

43. Gerardo Mosquera, *Crónicas Americanas III*, catalogue for an exhibit of José Bedia, Centro Wifredo Lam, Havana, April 1987.

44. Renate Loeschner, "La presentación artística de Latinoamérica en el siglo XIX bajo la influencia de Alexander von Humboldt," in *Artistas alemanes en Latinoamérica*, ed. Renate Loeschner, pp. 21, 29.

45. Benjamin Buchloh, "Interview with Ricardo Rodríguez Brey," *New Art from Cuba*, p. 36.

46. Erena Hernández, "El único sitio posible," interview with Rodríguez Brey, *Revolución y Cultura*, no. 9 (September 1988): 73–74.

47. This segment was published in article form as "An Art of Secular Mysticism: The Legacy of Juan Francisco Elso Padilla," in *New Art Examiner*, November

1990, pp. 28–30. I had started writing about Elso for this book while he was alive and with presumed good health. His sudden death transformed this section into a eulogy that expresses my pain, but that also has a different voice than the rest of the writing here.

48. In spite of his condition, Elso had decided to apply for a Guggenheim Fellowship. The quote is taken from the proposal written for the grant.

49. February 7 to March 28, 1990. The exhibit then traveled to MIT List Visual Arts Center, February 23–April 14, 1991.

50. Guggenheim proposal.

51. Interview with the author, January 1988.

52. Ibid.

53. *Santería*-practicing friends of Elso were upset by what they considered an irresponsible misuse of the rites and the employment of his own blood. He had chosen the elements with poetic criteria instead of following established traditions.

54. The illustration was later found by Gustavo Pérez Monzón in a book (*Cuerpo humano e ideología*) and subsequently mailed to Elso, who was already in Mexico. It depicted a man with lines radiating from his chest and bearing twenty symbols that gave power over all men and that were used to dispense medicine.

55. One of the serious handicaps Cuban artists have when working in Cuba and exhibiting internationally is size. The Soviet-built airplanes of Cubana airlines have four-feet-high doors, a limitation that poses a serious obstacle for large assembled artwork. The lack of hard currency limits the possibilities of subsidy for work on location. Thus, Cuban art seen outside of Cuba tends to be more modest than that exhibited in Cuba and is often conceived as an accumulation of modules. Elso's Venice pieces showed this limitation.

56. Magali Lara, interview with author, Mexico, January 1989. Magali, who reported the fall of the darts to me, is a completely secular person who saw Elso's use of *Santería* as part of the mystical poetry and symbolical refinement in his work.

57. Fidel Castro in NBC television interview conducted by Maria Shriver on February 24, 1988; reprinted in *Granma Weekly Review,* March 13, 1988, pp. 1–12. Castro states, "We only accept personal property: the home, the automobile, everything people want for their personal use. But over the means of production, we do not accept private property over the means of production, those are collective property. . . . Individuality and individualism are not the same thing. Our conception does not worship individualism; it may worship the individual, his capability, the development of his intelligence."

58. Rogelio López Marín (Gory), interview with the author, Havana, January 1988.

59. Erena Hernández, "Un joven en el salón," interview with Gustavo Peréz Monzón, *Cartelera*, August 5–11, 1982, p. 3.

2   CUBAN INFLUENCE ON THE 1980S GENERATION

1. Alejandro G. Alonso, "Raúl Martínez: El tiempo que vive," *Revolución y Cultura* (October 1986): 45.

2. Quoted by Graziella Pogolotti, "Raúl Martínez: El arte como exploración sentimental," in *Oficio de leer*, ed. Victor López Lemus, pp. 56–57.

3. Interview by Graziella Pogolotti in *Bohemia*, cited by Alonso, "Raúl Martínez."

4. Shifra Goldman, "Painters into Poster Makers: Two Views Concerning the History, Aesthetics and Ideology of the Cuban Poster Movement," *Studies in Latin American Popular Culture* (1984): 167.

5. Latin American modernism was somewhat connected with French symbolism and had deep baroque roots. Both Martí and Rubén Darío are the movement's strongest examples.

6. With the Revolution, Cubans developed a sometimes intransigent respect for national symbols. Elso Padilla's version of Martí in *Por América* and Tomás Esson's rendition of a mulatto Che created controversies among many people because they thought that the tampering with the images had gone too far. This became, later, an issue for the controversy around censorship.

7. Raúl Martínez, interview by Sandra Levinson, Havana, 1984, videotape produced by the Center for Cuban Studies, New York, 1984.

8. Guevara's forces had taken over a train carrying a million dollars' worth of arms sent by Batista in the hope of defeating the revolutionary movement. That action, coupled with the taking of the town of Santa Clara, was fundamental for the victory of the Revolution.

9. The work was done by a team comprising Niko, an artist known for his posters, who designed the general environment; Fernando Pérez O'Reilly, an architect; painter Raúl Martínez; Mayito as photographer; Héctor Veitia for film; Angel Díaz for sound; and Rebeca Chávez for the script.

10. Gerardo Mosquera, essay on Raúl Martínez, in *Nosotros*, catalogue for an anthological exhibit of the work of Martínez, Museo Nacional de Bellas Artes, Havana, July–September 1988.

11. In the text for *Nosotros*, Mosquera writes, "I want to recognize a virtue [in Martínez] for which nobody has credited him: he has been one of the best and most opportune importers of North American culture." Mosquera considers Martínez instrumental in shifting Cuban artists' attention from Europe to the United States.

12. This point was strongly made to me by Shifra Goldman after I had overlooked it.

13. Nelson Herrera Ysla, "Palabras (sin título)," introductory essay for the catalogue *Umberto Peña*, for the retrospective in the Museo Nacional de Bellas Artes, Havana, 1988.

14. Antonio Eligio (Tonel), "Umberto Peña expone," *Revolución y Cultura*, no. 9 (September 1988): 28.

15. The COR, Commission for Revolutionary Orientation, was a part of the Central Committee of the Communist Party.

16. This part has appeared in article versions in *Arte en Colombia*, no. 38 (December 1988): 44–49; and in *Third Text*, no. 7 (Summer 1989): 47–52.

17. Hortensia Pichardo Viñals, *Documentos para la historia de Cuba* 4:59–62.

18. Quoted by Hans Breder in a letter to the author.

19. In "Homogenizing Hispanic Art in Houston," *New Art Examiner*, Septem-

ber 1987, pp. 30–33, Shifra Goldman cites Rodolfo Acuña, who (in *A Community under Siege*) attributes to the Nixon administration the initiation of the practice of "consolidating Latin Americans into a national minority called 'Hispanic' in order to manage them more easily."

20. See Luis Camnitzer, Introduction to *Convergences*, catalogue for the exhibit, Lehman College Art Gallery, New York City, 1988, where some of these ideas first appeared.

21. Both quotes are from Joyce Wadler, "A Death in Art," *New York*, December 16, 1985, p. 45.

22. During the Second Biennial, one of the exhibitions was of a collection of works donated by artists residing in the United States. One of the pieces on display was a portfolio of prints made by both Ana Mendieta and Carl Andre. During the opening night of the exhibit, someone from the public wrote "Carl Andre asesino" (Carl Andre murderer) in red ink on the first page.

23. In a letter to the author, written in Italy, October 29th, 1983, in reference to the invasion of Grenada, she comments, "All of Europe is under shock. Imagine how hard it is to be in *The* American Academy in Rome. This institution is leasing a villa across from ours to the *U.S. Envoy to the Vatican.* We are always surrounded by police, and in '68 they placed a bomb here in the Academy. . . . People here are *super* reactionary, and one cannot talk politics with them. They are really *BRUTTAS FIGURAS.*"

24. When I refer to politics in Ana's work, I do so thinking primarily of the traditional categories and polemics related to the Right and the Left and less so of their connections with gender, spiritual, and ethnic issues. Obviously, all those issues have important political implications, and many were touched upon by Ana in her work. It is the more narrow problem posed by the ideological differences between the regimes of Cuba and the United States, respectively on the Left and on the Right, that never entered her work overtly and that were only voiced by her later in her life.

25. Breder, letter to the author.

26. Petra Barrera, "Ana Mendieta: A Historical Overview," in *Ana Mendieta: A Retrospective*, catalogue for her retrospective exhibit in The New Museum, New York, 1987, p. 28.

27. See Shifra Goldman's review of Ana Mendieta, "A Return to Natal Earth," *Artweek* 20, no. 15 (April 15, 1989): 1.

28. Shifra Goldman comments, "It is also possible that Ana's body floating in water might have poetic references to Ophelia's dead body (suicide after rejection) in Hamlet; and the fire and gunpowder silhouettes (as well as burning an iron cast of her hand into objects) testify to the need for women to assert their (invisible) presences in society, for which the earth becomes metaphor" (letter to the author, April 23, 1991).

29. "(Elso, Bedia, Ana Mendieta, Brey, T. Llorca, Gustavo P. Monzón, L. Soto, Martha María . . .) The importance of the mythic, the cosmogonic, the ritual in Cuban art of the 1980s can be derived from an urgency to instate spiritual archetypes and to possess models of greater consistency between the *ethos* and the *ethnos* of social life" (Osvaldo Sánchez, "Synkretismus, Postmodernismus und

Kultur des Widerstandes," in *Kuba o.k.*, edited by Jürgen Harten and Antonio Eligio (Tonel), p. 24, catalogue for the exhibit, Städtische Kunsthalle, Düsseldorf, April 1990.

3 ART WITHIN THE REVOLUTION

1. Parts of this chapter are based on Luis Camnitzer, "Between Nationalism and Internationalism," an introductory essay in *Signs of Transition: 80's Art from Cuba*, catalogue for the exhibit with the same name organized by the Museum of Contemporary Hispanic Art and the Center for Cuban Studies, New York City, 1988, curated by Coco Fusco.

2. Víctor Manuel, quoted by Oscar Hurtado in *Pintores cubanos*, p. 14.

3. Artist Umberto Peña considers that the cumulative effect of the design of the magazine may have done more for Cuban modernism than individual painters. The Grupo Minorista financed Victor Manuel's trip to Paris. About the Grupo, see Pichardo Viñals, *Documentos* 3:391–395.

4. Pichardo Viñals, *Documentos* 3, p. 393.

5. The artists in the exhibit were Eduardo Abela, Rafael Blanco, María Capdevila, Gabriel Castaño, Carlos Enríquez, Víctor Manuel García, Antonio Gattorno, María Josefa Lamarque, José Hurtado de Mendoza, Luis López Méndez, Ramón Loy, Alice Neel (at the time married to Enríquez), Amelia Peláez, Rebeca Peink de Rosado Avila, Marcelo Pogolotti, Domingo Ravenet, Lorenzo Romero Aciaga, Alberto Sabas, José Segura, Jaime Valls, and Adja Yunkers. Rebeca Peink was from Mexico and Segura from Spain. The editors of the magazine were Alejo Carpentier, Martí Casanovas, Francisco Ichaso, Jorge Mañach, and Juan Marinello. Most of the work in the exhibit, although antiacademic and feeding on some formal liberalization provided by European movements, was relatively conservative and representational and dealt with Cuban national subjects. Adja Yunkers spent three years in Cuba at the time, working as a salesperson in a shop and as a friend of the artists of this group and, particularly, of writer Alejo Carpentier.

6. Abela had traveled first to Spain, where he intended to exhibit his paintings. Through friends he found out that nobody in Spain was interested in Cuban regionalism and that he should loosen his brushstroke and paint in the Spanish manner, which he did. Subsequently in Paris, after a similar experience, he produced ten impressionist paintings. José Seoane Gallo, *Eduardo Abela cerca del cerco*, p. 178. Abela had been strongly influenced by artist Jules Pascin, who made many trips to Cuba during the 1910s.

7. Alejo Carpentier, introduction to *Ecue-Yamba-O* (Havana, 1933), cited by José Antonio Navarrete and Ramón Vázquez Díaz, "En torno al surgimiento del arte moderno en Cuba," in *La vanguardia: Surgimiento del arte moderno en Cuba*, catalogue for the exhibit, Museo Nacional de Bellas Artes, Havana, December 1988–January 1989.

8. Navarrete and Vázquez Díaz, "En torno al surgimiento."

9. This ambivalence is a recurring problem in the ideologies of the Left, and many see the national-international polarity as unresolvable. Pablo González Ca-

sanova, in *Imperialismo y liberación*, p. 117, analyzes the shifts of Latin American Communist Parties on the subject. In 1919, there is total support for "national revolutionary" movements; between 1919 and 1921, the tendency is internationalist; from 1922 to 1927, there is renewed support for nationalist reform, implying alliances with progressive noncommunist parties; and this was again reversed from 1928 to 1935. Fascism, in turn, brought about the need for new alliances. Throughout this process, directives came mostly from the Soviet Union. After a period of uneasiness and debate caused by the emergence of Eurocommunism and, later, the changes in the Soviet Union, it is only in 1988, in a meeting of Latin American Communist Parties, that it was decided that each Party should be creative and adapt to local conditions rather than follow directives. The reasons for this move, however, may have been more related to the Soviet *glasnost* and *perestroika* process and the reluctance of some parties to join them, than to true national versus international issues.

10. *Orígenes* appeared between 1944 and 1956, with an edition of only three hundred, in an amazing disproportion with the intellectual influence it carried.

11. The first exhibit of Los Once, in 1953, included René Avila, Francisco Antigua, José I. Bermúdez, Agustín Cárdenas, Hugo Consuegra, Fayad Jamis, José Antonio, Guido Llinás, Antonio Vidal, Tomás Oliva, and Viredo Espinosa. Raúl Martínez joined the group after this exhibit.

12. Goldman, interview with Raúl Martínez in "Painters into Poster Makers," p. 165.

13. Edmundo Desnoes, "1952–62 en la pintura cubana," in *Pintores Cubanos*, p. 40.

14. Armando Hart Dávalos, *Changing the Rules of the Game*, interview by Luis Báez, pp. 32–33.

15. Goldman, "Painters into Poster Makers," p. 169.

16. Edmundo Desnoes, *Cuban Posters*, p. 2.

17. David Kunzle, "Public Graphics in Cuba: A Very Cuban Form of Internationalist Art," *Latin American Perspectives* 2, no. 4 (1975): 92.

18. Actually, the first posters were the first pages of the paper *Revolución*, designed as tear-off posters.

19. The ICAIC's influence on the arts beyond filmmaking was remarkable. Not only was it felt in the poster movement but in writing, stage design, and music as well. The "Nueva Trova," the most popular type of music in Cuba today, with Pablo Milanés and Silvio Rodríguez, is a product of the ICAIC, and Leo Brouwer, Cuba's foremost composer, has produced many film scores. The guiding slogan of the ICAIC was "that no viewer remain the same after seeing one of our movies." Alfredo Guevara, the first director of the ICAIC, has been a contradictory figure in the history of Cuban art. He was influential in the proscription of the film *P.M.* in 1961, a decision that at the time split Cuban intellectuals, but on the other hand he affirms that "the only social function of a work of art is to exist" (statement at the Film Festival of Rio de Janeiro, 1986).

20. An interesting description of U.S. posters during World War II, showing their power of persuasion as perceived in the West, is quoted by Margia Kramer in "Cracking the Concrete: Interventionist Posters," *Upfront*, no. 12–13 (1986): v.

Kramer reported, "The U.S. government hired the advertising firm of Young and Rubicam to write a pamphlet, *How to Make Posters That Will Help Win the War*, which said that posters '. . . can help speed up production, prevent waste . . . sell bonds, dramatize the things we are fighting, increase . . . enlistments, stop rumors and gossip, create a better understanding between this country and our allies, and help any other job necessary . . .'"

21. Dugald Stermer, "The Agit Pop Art of Cuba," *Ramparts* 7, no. 9 (December 14–27, 1968): 33.

22. Kunzle mentions the displeasure of many Cuban artists on the occasion of the publication of *The Art of Revolution: Castro's Cuba 1959–1970* by McGraw Hill in 1970 with an introduction by Susan Sontag, who saw it as contributing "to the 'aesthetization' of the poster and a diminution of its political value," referring to a review by Roberto Segre (1971) on the point ("Public Graphics," p. 92, n. 3).

23. Ernesto (Che) Guevara, "El socialismo y el hombre en Cuba," a letter to Carlos Quijano printed in *Marcha* (Montevideo), March 12, 1965.

24. Artist Flavio Garciandía says, "I do believe that eventually the result will have some consistency with these conditions. But it is not something that worries me too much. I try to take from here and from there, with the hopes of making art that functions in my environment and my time. . . . Even if we are concerned about these problems, the solution is not ours alone. The solution has to come from all the channels involved, including the power of the state" (Buchloh, "Interview with Flavio Garciandía," in *New Art from Cuba*, p. 7).

25. Mark Richmond, "Education and Revolution in Socialist Cuba: The Problem of Democratization," in *Education in Latin America*, edited by Colin Brook and Hugh Lawlor, pp. 15–16.

26. The flag and the logo for the literacy campaign were designed by Guillermo Menéndez Madan.

27. An interesting mass-culture project, connected with the literacy campaign and continuing today, dates back to a workers' victory of the nineteenth century. While tobacco workers roll cigars, an elected co-worker sits at a dais and reads to them from world literature.

28. In 1983 there were sixteen designs; in 1984, twenty; in 1985, twenty-one; in 1986, thirty-one; in 1987, thirty-two; in 1989, thirty-three. In 1989 the production of Cuban and international artists was combined, making actually two programs, which accounts for the gap shown in 1988. The fabric used is cotton, sometimes mixed with synthetic fibers, intended for wear in warm climates. The two main printing facilities are the textile factories Combinado Textil "Desembarco del *Granma*" with four thousand workers, and the Textilera Ariguanabo, with five thousand workers. An exhibit of the designs took place in the Amelie Wallace Gallery at SUNY College at Old Westbury during March 1990.

29. Néstor García Canclini, *La producción simbólica*, p. 74. He continues, saying, "With the appearance of an autonomous market for art, there also appear the needed places to exhibit the merchandise, where it can be seen and purchased: museums and galleries. While in other economic systems artistic practice was inserted in the total social life, in capitalism it separates and creates special

objects to be sold, because of its formal beauty, in differentiated places."

30. Cintio Vitier, "Apuntes para el encuentro de intelectuales por la sobe-ranía de los pueblos de nuestra América," in *Ponencias: I encuentro de intelectuales por la soberanía de los pueblos de nuestra América*, ed. Reynaldo González, pp. 286–289.

31. Ezequiel Martínez Estrada, "Por una cultura popular y socialista cu-bana," in *En Cuba y al servicio de la Revolución Cubana*, ed. Martínez Estrada (Ha-vana: Ediciones Unión, 1963), quoted by Pamela María Smorkaloff, *Literatura y edición de libros*, p. 196, n. 3.

32. Gerardo Mosquera, *El diseño se definió en octubre*, p. 202.

33. The "Kuba o.k." exhibition, a selection of Cuba's newest art, which took place in the Städtische Kunsthalle in Düsseldorf during April 1990, was practi-cally bought in its entirety by German art collector Peter Ludwig. The purchase gives individual prestige to the artists chosen and a validation from the hege-monic mainstream to Cuban art at large. At the same time, this success threatens to shift the Cuban artists away from the public they were addressing, distancing them from the Cuban environment from which they derive their strength. It also may solidify the traditional aspects of the Cuban gallery system.

34. Buchloh, *New Art from Cuba*, pp. 8–9. A Cuban filmmaker, Julio García Espinosa, once wrote an essay with the title "The Four Means of Communication are Three: Film and Television" (quoted by Mosquera, *El diseño se definió en octu-bre*, p. 212).

35. Gerardo Mosquera, *Cuatro*, catalogue for the exhibit of José Bedia, Gus-tavo Pérez Monzón, Ricardo Rodríguez Brey, and Rubén Torres Llorca, Fondo Cubano de Bienes Culturales, Havana, July 1982.

36. Centro Wifredo Lam, "Proyecto metodológico para la investigación ra-mal del arte en Cuba," a working paper for the members of the research team, Havana, 1987.

37. Jorge de la Fuente, "Praxis, ideología y arte en Adolfo Sánchez Vázquez," *La Revista del Sur*, no. 13 (1987): 18–19. De la Fuente is a professor of philosophy and aesthetics at the University of Havana.

38. Guevara, "Socialismo y el hombre."

39. The realist art of the nineteenth century is also class art, perhaps more capitalist than the decadent art of the twentieth, which expresses the anguish of the alienated man. Capitalism has given its everything, and there is nothing left but the announcement of a foul-smelling corpse. . . . But why try to seek the only valid recipe in the frozen forms of socialist realism? One cannot oppose "freedom" to socialist realism because it doesn't yet exist; it won't exist until the complete develop-ment of the new society; but one should not condemn all the art forms that followed the first half of the nineteenth century from the pontifical throne of unflinching realism, because one would fall into a Proudhon-ian mistake of return to the past, shackling the artistic expression of the man born and built today. (Guevara, "Socialismo y el hombre")

In a discussion with students during a visit to the ENA in 1967, Carlos

Rafael Rodríguez said, "I have defended socialist realism in the past. But I have to say, and always said, that generally speaking Soviet novels and paintings of that time [1940–1950] weren't very good. . . . I don't think I was mistaken with my criticism; I did not believe that Soviet painting was an expression of socialist realism. . . . I am not interested in the title now because I believe that socialist realism has come to represent so many bad things in art that it will be very difficult to change the people's mind about the idea of that bad socialist realism." From Desiderio Navarro, *Cultura y Marxismo: Problemas y polémicas*, p. 332.

40. Mosquera, *El diseño se definió en octubre*, p. 186.

41. In that sense it does not seem inconsistent with government policy to try to channel the arts into being hard currency earners.

42. "I would not like to cite, on a day like this, many of the shameful [examples] of those who in apparently licit ways have earned 100,000 pesos and even more in one year . . . because I know that some, painting or making decorative work primarily for State institutions, have earned even more than 200,000 pesos in one year. This is to speak of an example of exaggerated income, which doesn't seem to me the fruit of real work, because they are not, *compañeras* and *compañeros*, paintings by Picasso or Michelangelo" (Fidel Castro, "Speech on Occasion of the Twenty-fifth Anniversary of the Socialist Character of the Revolution and of the Victory of Playa Girón," *Granma Weekly Review*, April 21, 1986, supplement, 8 pp.).

43. Surrealism in particular elicited irate reactions in many circles that survived Castro's "Words to the Intellectuals." Mirta Aguirre writes in 1963, "Surrealism presupposes absurd associations of delirious ideas, conceptual proximities that are incompatible with logic. . . . When André Breton writes that the most accomplished and vigorous surrealist image is the one that presents 'the highest degree of arbitrariness,' he is telling us already that surrealism and dialectic materialism, surrealism and socialist realism are incompatible from the roots" ("Apuntes sobre literatura y arte," in *Revolución, letras, arte*, ed. López Lemus, p. 216). However, in 1976, the same author takes an interesting position in regard to realism: "Realism in art is to give shape to the reality of things, not to the things belonging to reality."

44. Raúl Martínez, interview by Sandra Levinson, Havana, 1984, videotape produced by the Center for Cuban Studies, New York, 1984.

45. The thought of the speech was incorporated in the Cuban Constitution in 1976. Point (d) of Article thirty-eight states, "Artistic creation is free as long as its content does not oppose the Revolution. Forms of expression are free."

46. In the Declaration of the First National Congress for Education and Culture in 1971, there were statements such as "Art is the weapon of the Revolution; a product of the moral combat of our people; an instrument against the penetration by the enemy," after which came this: "Socialism creates the objective and subjective conditions for true artistic freedom, so that those tendencies should be condemned and rejected whose criteria stem from libertinism and whose aims are geared to conceal the counterrevolutionary poison, who conspire against the revolutionary ideology on which the construction of socialism and communism is based, to which our people today feel irrevocably committed and under whose

spirit the new generation will be educated." The declaration further warned against snobbery, extravagance, and homosexuality, among other social ills. It should be explained that the congress was in fact only about education ("culture" was added later to the title), and its participants were secondary education teachers coming from one of the first promotions after the literacy campaign and therefore not overly sophisticated, thus having *machista,* or sexually repressive and moralist elements present in their thinking. Imports of fashionable apparel were seen as creating cultural dependency in a moment in which Cuba was moving inward. The congress asked intellectuals to focus on revolutionary topics, but it also demanded schools for handicapped children and the education of parents on subjects of hygiene.

47. The jailing of poet Heberto Padilla in April 1971 (purportedly unrelated to his poetic activities) had polarized foreign intellectuals originally sympathetic to Cuba. Padilla received a prize by an international jury in the 1968 competition organized by Casa de las Américas for his book *Fuera del Juego* (*Out of the Game*). The book of poetry, interpreted as expressing anti-Cuban sentiments, was published with an introduction criticizing the author. According to his enemies, Padilla exploited the situation to portray himself as a martyr in order to achieve international prominence. According to his friends, he was a plain victim of censorship. Matters were worsened by a "confession" delivered by Padilla that seemed to be a caricature of the confessions and recantations delivered by intellectuals under Stalin.

Authors including Jean-Paul Sartre and Julio Cortázar (who later changed his position) criticized the Cuban government for the jailing, and Cuba entered a "hard-line" period culminating with the Declaration of the First National Congress of Education and Culture in 1971, with effects that lasted several years. A substantial amount has been written about Padilla by himself and by others about the affair, and it is probably impossible to arrive at an objective evaluation of the events. But the official reactions in Cuba are a symptom of the direction of thought of the government at the time. Cuban essayist José Antonio Portuondo, considered a hard-liner, is a good example of the prevalent thinking at the time. He refers to this period (from the Cultural Congress in 1968 onward) as

> an opportunity [for foreign intellectuals visiting] to establish their revolutionary credentials and also to come and "teach" us what we have to do, how the Revolution has to be conducted in the aesthetic and cultural areas. We have always been good hosts and received everybody with open arms, giving them the opportunity to say what they want, and we even allow ourselves to be easily seduced by a name, a figure of international notoriety, etc. . . . Thus, some negative consequences resulted, such as some young writers and artists feeling seduced by those figures and trying to assume a sometimes hypercritical attitude toward our things, confronting the Revolution; and when that attitude had to be rectified, immediately those writers and artists protested, stood in front of us, signed documents against the Revolution, and, well, you all know the incidents that happened around the "Padilla"

case. ("Itinerario estético de la revolución cubana," in *Revolución, letras, arte,* ed. López Lemus, pp. 160–187)

Portuondo, who is particularly known and respected for his essays on aesthetics, was possibly a political dogmatist at the time. However, he cannot be described as a "dogmatist" in art, though his taste probably is conservative. He espouses that "social order should be changed; changing the social order, a new expression will appear." From this position he attacks Russian constructivism for having tried to change only the form in art. While he sees abstraction as a process of alienation, he emphasizes his abhorrence to any dictum telling an artist what to do or labeling an abstract artist as a "counterrevolutionary." One of his favorite quotes, which may put his thinking in a proper context, is Martí's: "When freedom cannot be enjoyed, the only excuse for art and its only right to exist is to service freedom," which also sums up the thought of Latin American student militants. See José Antonio Portuondo, *Ensayos de estética y de teoría literaria,* p. 133.

48. During 1965–1967 Cuba underwent a moralist period about which many Cubans are still reluctant to talk today and which is seen not only as a grave mistake but also as an unexplainable accident. It is the period of the UMAP (Unidades Militares de Apoyo a la Producción, or Military Units of Production Support). A confluence of several factors—the negative perception of elements from U.S. counterculture that were reaching Cuba at the time; the claimed manipulation of these elements by the CIA; the reluctance of the army to enroll some individuals who were not seen fit for military service; the machismo and homophobia still present in Cuban culture at the time; the need for assertion of authority in regard to law and order in an anarchic atmosphere mostly held together by revolutionary mystique; the need for increased productivity—all led to the creation of what ended up being a network of "rehabilitation" camps. Initially conceived as a way of satisfying the army service requirements through alternative civilian work, many of the camps degenerated into harassment centers against individuals seen as not conforming to the "revolutionary" image. Denounced by Jean-Paul Sartre and by Cuban writer Roberto Fernández Retamar in an issue of the magazine of Casa de las Américas, in 1967 they were ordered dismantled by Fidel Castro, who is presumed to have been unaware of the excesses. While it is known that Felipe Guerra Matos was in charge of closing down the camps, nobody takes responsibility for their creation. Although some individuals related to the arts suffered during this period, there was no connection between the UMAP and aesthetics of any kind. Homophobia and machismo were not confined to these years. Many homosexuals left with the *Marielitos* exodus, and still today there is a reluctance to be open about nonheterosexual preferences in Cuba.

49. First National Congress of Education and Culture, "Declaration of the First National Congress of Education and Culture," translated from a reprint in *Cuadernos de Marcha,* no. 49 (May 1971): 84. Castro's speech appeared in the same issue.

50. This does not mean that the Communist Party lost power. In 1976 a So-

cialist Constitution was approved by referendum, establishing the Communist Party as "the superior force in society."

51. Among other things, Avner Zis contends that "multiple attempts to soften the contradictions between realism and [Western] modernism, to bring them together or to 'enrich' the first with the artistic discoveries of the second, form a peculiar aesthetic variation of the 'theory of convergence' which in the aesthetic sphere is no less unacceptable than in any other part of ideological life. Modernism as a phenomenon is interlocked with the disintegration of art in imperialist society." Avner Zis, *Fundamentos de la estética Marxista.*

52. Ibid., pp. 48–55, 250–255.

53. Cited in Víctor López Lemus, ed., *Revolución, letras, arte.*

54. Edith García Buchaca had first been married to Carlos Rafael Rodríguez, who had already been high ranking in the prerevolutionary Communist Party and presently is the vice-president of Cuba, and then to Joaquín Ordoqui, at the time vice-minister of the armed forces. She was a member of the Aníbal Escalante faction, the old orthodox section of the pre-Castro Communist Party, which often clashed with Castro, and she was very committed to a faithful Soviet line. Both García Buchaca and Escalante disappeared from powerful positions in 1962. García Buchaca is considered responsible for stopping the publication of *Lunes de Revolución* in 1961.

55. García Buchaca's statements are in her publication *La teoría de la superestructura* (1961), quoted by Angel Rama in "Una nueva política cultural en Cuba," *Cuadernos de Marcha* (Montevideo): *Cuba: Nueva política cultural, el caso Padilla,* no. 49 (May 1971): 50.

56. Lucy Lippard, "Made in U.S.A.: Art from Cuba," *Art in America,* April 1986, p. 35.

57. Castro had not seen the film and was not so much addressing its content as, much more, the right of the state to make this kind of decision, something which, rightly or wrongly, he was not about to give up.

58. According to the Nielsen Media Research, the share of the public by PBS remained set on a constant 4 percent between 1982 and 1989.

59. The exhibit had pooled a series of artists who "tampered" with the flag to make an antiwar statement. After that, an incident took place in the School of the Art Institute of Chicago: "The flag was displayed beneath photographs of flag-draped coffins and flags burning. Viewers were asked to record their impressions on a ledger. But to get to the ledger most people found they had to step on the 34-inch by 57-inch flag, thereby directly confronting their own feelings about patriotism and symbols" ("Veterans Protest Flag Exhibit at Art Institute," *New York Times,* March 2, 1989, p. A19). The exhibit elicited the protest of veterans and the American Legion and was subsequently closed for nearly a week, to be reopened later with admittance restricted to faculty and students.

60. Aldito Menéndez, "La Revolución del arte y no el arte de la Revolución," (Havana, 1988, Typescript). He continues, saying that "we, the young artists, not finding an art criticism on the level of the needs of our time, not only have presented the problem but have also become our own art critics; hence, our high theoretical preparation."

61. Osvaldo Sánchez, "Elogio de Poncio Pilato," *El Caimán Barbudo*, June 1988, pp. 16–17.

62. Early in 1989, an artist made a painting where the triangle of the Cuban flag bearing the star was filled with the part of the Soviet flag with the hammer, sickle, and the small star. It was intended as a pro-*perestroika* statement. The artist felt that, given the official policy of dissociation with the Soviet *perestroika*, it would not be wise to exhibit this particular piece at present. It is not clear, however, if the fears are based on solid grounds. Castro's statements about *perestroika* address its inapplicability in present-day Cuba and do not offer ideological criticism. The possible controversy around the piece would probably come more from a feeling that the flag should not be tampered with and from a sense of wounded national pride. Two decades ago there was an unsuccessful motion to change Cuba's name to "Socialist Republic of Cuba"; a sense of national independence prevailed.

63. On the occasion of the Third Biennial, during November 1989, a group of foreign artists and critics met with Minister Hart to express their concern in regard to the future of Cuban policy toward art and their appreciation of Leiseca's work. Hart reassured them that there was to be no change of policy. A year later, new cultural appointments in administrative posts seemed to favor individuals with a more conservative personal taste, but the effect on overall art policy, if any, is not yet clear.

64. Buchloh, "Interview with José Bedia," in *New Art from Cuba*, p. 18.

65. In fact, Fidel Castro attacked the elitism in sports in his speech at the Fourth Congress of the UNEAC. He pointed out that there are twenty thousand teachers for one hundred thousand sports-persons, and there is an "emphasis on medals while there is a neglect toward the rest of the population."

66. Néstor García Canclini, *Políticas culturales en América Latina*, pp. 36–37.

67. "If the rules of the game are respected, all honors can be obtained: those which a monkey inventing pirouettes might get. The condition is not attempting to escape from the invisible cage." Guevara, "Socialismo y el hombre."

4 ART EDUCATION IN CUBA

1. Part of this text is based on an article published under the title "Art Education in Latin America Bypasses Cultural Identity Problem," in the *New Art Examiner*, September 1986, pp. 30–33.

2. "UNESCO estimates that between 50 percent and 70 percent of what is considered basic culture in the West comes from radio, film, and television controlled directly or indirectly by transnational corporations. They decide what is seen on over four hundred million television sets and listened to on more than nine hundred million radio sets. The United States controls . . . 75 percent of the TV programs, 65 percent of advertising, 55 percent of movie houses, 60 percent of records and cassettes, 65 percent of the news, and 35 percent of publishing in Latin America" (Miguel Barnet, "Identidad cultural y liberación nacional," in *Ponencias*, ed. González, p. 65).

"Between 1950 and 1972, the U.S. Department of Defense trained 61,032 Latin

American officers and soldiers" (González Casanova, *Imperialismo y liberación,* p. 42).

3. Smorkaloff, *Literatura,* pp. 74–75.

4. It is interesting that in the United States the first musical club was the "Handel and Haydn Society," founded in Boston in 1815.

5. Alfredo Cardona Peña, *Conversaciones con Diego Rivera,* p. 75.

6. Luz Merino, Pilar Fernández, and Roberto Segre, "El Art-Deco en la Habana" (Havana, 1987, Typescript).

7. L. S. Stavrianos, *Global Rift: The Third World Comes of Age,* p. 478.

8. Ibid., p. 481.

9. Atahualpa del Cioppo, interview in *Brecha* (Montevideo), November 29, 1985.

10. Albert Memmi, *Retrato del colonizado,* p. 106.

11. Cited in Angel Rama, *La ciudad letrada,* p. 62.

12. One of the biggest issues of the reform, the students' voice in matters of governance and the appointment of authorities of the universities, came from the tradition of the University of Salamanca in Spain. Since the Middle Ages students there have had a voice in the election of the rector.

13. In the late fifties, a highly regarded professor in the School of Architecture in Montevideo was asked by his students to resign his post because he had ignored a strike in another institution where he was holding a second job. He did so with grace and understanding after a moving meeting with the students, where his personal circumstances (the father of nine children) were pitched against the students' reality (the need for ethical role models). Teacher and students parted weeping and promising friendship.

A poll taken in Uruguay in 1964 showed that more than half of the students "strongly agreed" and a third "agreed" with the idea that big problems in the country can only be solved by means of profound changes in the political, social, and economic structure. The same poll taken in the United States in 1967 had only 28 percent of the students in both categories combined. Mark Van Aken, *Los militantes,* pp. 238–239.

14. Dardo Cúneo, ed., *La reforma universitaria,* pp. 55–56. See also Pichardo Viñals, *Documentos* 3:197–219.

15. Darcy Ribeiro, *La universidad latinoamericana,* p. 91.

16. In 1980, Cuba had the biggest increase in Latin America, with 27.6 percent. J. J. Brunner, *Universidad y sociedad en América Latina,* p. 73.

17. One difference with the structure achieved in other countries was that graduates were left out of participation in the university government.

18. Antonio Bachiller y Morales, "Apuntes para la historia de las letras y de la instrucción pública de la Isla de Cuba," Havana, 1859; cited by Hortensia Pichardo Viñals, *La actitud estudiantil en Cuba durante el siglo XIX,* p. 4.

19. As a consequence of the insurrection, Toussaint L'Ouverture, leader of the movement, declared the abolition of slavery in 1801.

20. By then there were 222 schools for white children and 12 for black children. By 1861 there were 620 black children in school, compared to 16,800 white

children. López Valdés, *Componentes africanos en el etnos cubano*, p. 46.

21. Pichardo Viñals, *La actitud estudiantil*, pp. 82–83, 111–114.

22. Olivia Miranda, *Felix Varela: Su pensamiento político y su época*, p. 132.

23. Pichardo Viñals, *La actitud estudiantil*, p. 29.

24. Until 1837, Cuban nationals were considered Spanish nationals and had representation at the Spanish "Cortes," where Varela was one of the Cuban deputies. In 1837 Cubans were stripped of these rights and declared colonists.

25. In 1822 Spain accused Philadelphia Freemason organizations of inciting revolution in Cuba through their connections with Cuban masonry. Philip Foner, *Historia de Cuba y sus relaciones con EEUU*, 1:118–119.

26. "United with this strong and respected nation, whose interests in the South identify with [Cuba], tranquility and future would be guaranteed; wealth would increase, doubling the value of plantations and slaves and tripling that of land; it would give freedom to individual action, and would eliminate that hated and pernicious system of restrictions which paralyzes commerce and agriculture." From "Unos Cubanos," a proclamation by Bentacourt Cisneros, Havana, April 20, 1848, quoted by Foner, *Historia de Cuba* 2:17.

27. Cubans today see the Cuban Revolution as the one that achieved independence, culminating an uninterrupted struggle started during the last century.

28. Mella (1904–1929) was a crucial figure in Cuban Leftist history. He was killed five years later at the age of twenty-five by order of dictator Gerardo Machado (who ruled 1925–1933) through what may have been the first Latin American "death squads" acting internationally. An active opponent of the dictator and the founder of the Student Federation and cofounder of the Cuban Communist Party, he had depicted Machado as a "tropical Mussolini." He was shot while walking on the streets of Mexico with his friend Tina Modotti, the Mexican-Italian photographer. See Christiane Barckhausen-Canale, *Verdad y leyenda de Tina Modotti*, p. 165.

29. Cúneo, *La reforma universitaria*, p. 271. See also Pichardo Viñals, *Documentos* 3:183–193.

30. This was so in spite of having the highest investment in education in Latin America. In the 1950s Cuba had over 3 percent of its budget invested in education. But while other countries (Chile, Uruguay, Argentina, etc.) investing close to that percentage had over 50 percent of the population between five and twenty-four years of age going to school, Cuba enrolled only 36 percent.

31. The push for education had paradoxical side effects. There is presently one doctor specializing in family medicine for every 150 families. The ideal proportion is considered Great Britain's ratio of 1 to 350, since this figure provides correct statistical experience feedback for the doctor. Cuba thus has a surplus of medical doctors in this area and resorts to export of personnel.

32. As a reference, in a 1988 study about the student body in Uruguay, 34.4 percent of the students belonged to the upper strata of society, 44.5 percent to the middle class, and 17.7 percent to the economically lower classes.

33. Brunner, *Universidad y sociedad*, p. 108.

34. Luis Cardoza y Aragón, *Orozco*, p. 23.

35. Edward Lucie-Smith, "A Background to Latin American Art," in *Art of the Fantastic: Latin America 1920–1987,* ed. Holiday T. Day and Hollister Sturges, p. 23.

36. Jorge Rigol, *Apuntes sobre la pintura y el grabado en Cuba.*

37. It was named "Alejandro" after the mayor of Havana at that time, Alejandro Ramírez. Jorge Rigol, "La Academia de San Alejandro," in *Revolución, letras, arte,* ed. López Lemus, p. 506.

38. Espada y Landa, though quite liberal in other areas, was totally committed to neoclassicism in the arts and had ordered much of the art produced previously to be destroyed. He invoked the need for visual order to represent what he saw as a general divine wish for order in the universe. Rigol, "Apuntes sobre el grabado," in *Panorama de la cultura,* ed. Moré de Castro, p. 122. According to Miranda, *Felix Varela,* p. 133, Espada y Landa was, in reality, fighting against the Jesuit influence, which in the arts manifested itself through the baroque.

39. Rigol, in *Revolución, letras, arte,* ed. López Lemus, p. 513.

40. Ibid., p. 523.

41. Albert Boime, *The Academy & French Painting in the Nineteenth Century,* pp. 14, 43, 79–80.

42. His appointment was blocked by Spanish opponents who successfully demanded a second competition for the position, but Melero won a second time.

43. Among students of San Alejandro who did not finish their art studies were José Martí (1867–1868) and Camilo Cienfuegos (1949–1950).

44. Yolanda Wood, *De la plástica cubana y caribeña,* pp. 43–44.

45. Ibid., p. 62.

46. Rafael Suárez Solis, "Un estudio libre de pintura y escultura," cited by Wood, *De la plástica cubana,* p. 64.

47. Wood, *De la plástica cubana,* p. 63.

48. José Veigas, "Nuestra pintura joven," *El Caimán Barbudo,* September 1979.

49. Collective document, "El teatro, un arma eficaz al servicio de la Revolución. Recuento del Grupo Teatro Escambray," *Revolución y Cultura* (August 1974): 11–23.

50. Alberto Jorge Carol, "Cuadrodebate," *Revolución y Cultura* (August 1974): 24–29; and José Veigas, "Estas láminas dicen mucho," *Revolución y Cultura* (August 1974): 30–35.

51. Nuria Nuiry, then director of the ISA, in an interview with Mireya Castañeda, "Artistic Freedom in Cuba," *Granma Weekly Review,* March 16, 1986, p. 7.

52. The role of women in Cuba was an early revolutionary concern. In an address to textile workers in Ariguanabo in 1963, Che Guevara complained bitterly about having had to relieve a female functionary from some of her duties because her husband did not want her to travel alone. "Liberation of women is not complete, and one of the tasks of our Party is to obtain their total freedom, their internal freedom," and later, "the proletariat doesn't have gender." For 1989 the following statistics were available: women were 40 percent of the labor force, 48 percent of labor leaders, 57 percent of technical and professional workers, and 37.6 percent of deputies (following Sweden with 38.1 percent and both Norway and Romania with 34.4 percent) *Granma Weekly Review,* October 22, 1989.

53. Official statistics placed unemployment at 6 percent in 1988, up from 3.4 percent in 1981. Many of the unemployed are voluntary. Available jobs are sometimes ignored because of lack of interest or sufficient family income. With the change of the economic relations between Cuba and the Eastern European countries, the figures are worsening, but there are no statistics available at the time of this writing. Relief for the new problem is found in shorter working days and shift into the microbrigades.

54. The issue of copyright has been clearer with regard to books, though policy has shifted over the years. With the blockade, publication of foreign books became increasingly difficult. "Western" publishers would not agree to sell rights of their books to Cuba, a policy that had a great negative impact, particularly for textbooks, and threatened to impair the educational process. The only solution was to disregard copyright laws. Explained by Cuban authorities as an act of fairness and reciprocity, the same principle was then applied to Cuban authors. During the 1970s the policy was reversed and copyright benefits were reinstituted. They are low and not designed to live on but serve as restitution for expenses incurred during the production of the book. (See Smorkaloff, *Literatura*, pp. 165–171.)

Castro had announced his cancellation of copyright laws in a speech of April 29, 1967: "We . . . consider as a right of our people—of all the underdeveloped peoples—the use of all technical knowledge that is available throughout the world, and we therefore consider ourselves entitled to print any book of a technical nature that we need for our development. . . . Cuba can and is willing to compensate all its intellectual creators; but, at the same time, it renounces [internationally] all the copyrights that it is entitled to. . . . If all countries did the same, humanity would be the beneficiary" (Fidel Castro, "Communism Will Be Abundance without Egoism: On Intellectual Property," in *Communications and Class Struggle,* ed. Armand Mattelart and Seth Siegelaub, pp. 288–295).

55. As Minister of Industry, Guevara had seen sugarcane as the symbol of a monocrop economy imposed by imperialism. His initial reaction was to radically shift the economy to an accelerated industrialization process. In order to achieve this goal, he developed a moral incentive model as opposed to the material incentive. Guevara's ideas created a polemic during the years 1962–1965 when his major opponent was Carlos Rafael Rodríguez, then Minister of Agriculture.

56. Francis Pisani, "La rectificación cubana," *Nexos* (Mexico), no. 119, (November 1987): 51–59.

57. In his closing speech of the Third Congress of the Cuban Communist Party, December 2, 1986, Fidel Castro indicated the direction of those methods: "[There was] the blind belief . . . that the building of socialism was fundamentally and essentially a problem of [economic] mechanisms." Instead, the issue should be "fundamentally the development of the consciousness and the education of man."

58. Complicated by war games conducted by the United States from April 20, 1990, on—Operation Global Shield, Ocean Venture (a surprise aerial attack), and Dexter (an evacuation of the Guantánamo base)—the situation led Castro to proclaim "a special period of peace, a special period of war." A week earlier,

commenting on the situation in Eastern Europe, he said, "The socialist camp, indeed, is gone. What socialist camp can we speak of today? . . . 'Revolution' seems to be a dirty word, unless it is confused with that grotesque thing called counterrevolution because they've even twisted concepts, ideas, words, and the meaning of words." Speech at the Fifth Congress of the Federation of Cuban Women on March 7, *Granma Weekly Review,* March 18, 1990.

59. During the early 1980s street vendors had become popular in Havana, establishing what was seen as a capitalist distortion of the system. Called *merolicos* (a term taken from Mexican soap operas seen on Cuban television), they offered their products in the free market, including well-organized street fairs. After stories about doctors who neglected hospital duties in favor of profits through crafts, the fairs were abolished in 1986. The same happened to produce markets, where intermediaries started to earn disproportionate monies. Critical observers attribute the failure of the liberalization, based on economic decentralization, to the lack of flexibility in reinvestment by the enterprises who earned the money and to an absence of a sound taxation system for excessive profits. Solutions stem more from morals than from pragmatic approaches. (See Marifeli Perez-Stable, "Castro Takes the Economy in Hand," *The Nation,* September 26, 1987, pp. 298–300.)

60. Pisani, "La rectificación."

61. Possibly there is an exception given by the drive against bureaucracy and the will to maintain independence. It is interesting to note the parallels between statements by Castro in 1965 and the present. In his address of January 2, 1965, on the occasion of the sixth anniversary of the Revolution, he attacked both bureaucracy and dependency. "Bureaucracy has many causes; it is an evil of both the past and the present. I genuinely believe that socialism has as much to fear from bureaucracy as from imperialism. Never forget that it is even more dangerous because it is a hidden enemy." And "it is also very important that no one, anywhere, tell any Party what to do in any specific circumstance; it is the Party and the people alone that must decide what is to be done by the revolutionary party in that circumstance" (Fidel Castro, *Apply Theory to the Particular Conditions of Each Country*). In his speech of July 26, 1988, he stated, "That is why every country on the basis of its own history, its concrete experiences, must draw up its own formulas, and we respect the formulas drawn up by each country, we have the fullest respect for them. We are glad of the efforts being made by the socialist countries to overcome their difficulties, the problems that have been created for them throughout history; yet there are many problems that arose in other countries that didn't arise in our country; our problems are different, of another type, precisely because we don't copy from others, because we were creative and didn't simply copy from others" (*Granma Weekly Review,* August 7, 1988).

62. Smorkaloff, *Literatura,* p. 231.

63. In a speech at the University of Oriente in December 1968, Fidel Castro had envisioned that "in the future practically every factory, every farming area, every hospital, every school, will be a university. And the graduates from the middle levels will pursue the higher levels. And what will happen with present universities? They will then become centers of higher studies for postgraduates."

64. Cuban artists and functionaries today underline very pointedly that Soviet advising, at the time, was requested by Cuba and not imposed by the Soviet Union.

65. Often this idea corresponded, and corresponds, with an ultraradical, ultraleftist and utopian perspective, which dreams of revolution as a total, immediate change instead of understanding it as a critical moment in an evolution, imagining it as catapulting into the future and not as a transformation from the present into the future. The revolutionary experience demonstrates that the metamorphosis of lifestyle and consciousness is much more gradual than the one of the material base. The will to transmute everything after an ideal should not make us lose the realism of praxis. Already in his time, Lenin had correctly warned against Proletkult's laboratory voluntarism. (Gerardo Mosquera, "Función social de nuestra plástica," El Caimán Barbudo, July 1985)

Lenin had written on this subject, "[The Soviet Union] needed not the invention of a new proletarian culture but the development of the best forms, traditions, and results of existing culture from the viewpoint of the philosophy of Marxism and the living conditions and struggle of the proletariat in the period of its dictatorship" (Leninsky Sbornik 35:148, as cited by Louis Fisher, The Life of Lenin, p. 492).

66. Christina Lodder, Russian Constructivism, p. 75.

67. Raúl Navarro Padrón, "La investigación y la producción artística y sus relaciones con las necesidades culturales del país" (Paper presented at the First Latin American Meeting on the Teaching of Plastic Arts, Universidad Autónoma de México, Mexico City, November 1981).

68. The direction the curriculum is taking can be exemplified by some assignments designed by Osvaldo Sánchez, who joined the faculty very recently. In a set of ten exercises for the second year in the ISA he includes the following: "The Scalpel. A manipulation of the artistic heritage: The Avant-Garde in Cuba. A plastic reflection of Modernity in Cuba through the deconstruction of a . . . work of the 1920s. The Yoke. The fetish of everyday life. The manipulation of an everyday object through ready-made. A reflection on morality and desire through daily objects as a repressive or liberating symbol of an anonymous subject, or as a yoke of a social bond."

5   THE GENERATIONS FOLLOWING "VOLUMEN I"

1. Julio Izaguirre Vichot, (untitled Ph.D. diss., Universidad de la Habana, Havana, 1987).

2. José Franco, interview with the author, Havana, January 1988.

3. Osvaldo Sánchez, "Children of Utopia," in Young Cuban Art, p. 58, catalogue for the exhibit, Museum of Pori, Pori, Finland, May 1990.

4. Glexis Novoa, Carlos Rodríguez Cárdenas, and Segundo Planes, interview

with the author, Havana, January 1988. Subsequent quotes are from the same interview.

5. Aldito Menéndez, interview with the author, Havana, January 1988.

6. Some versions claim that he was a real policeman and a former art student from San Alejandro.

7. Menéndez, "La revolución del arte." While there is no proof, many people suspect that much of what is seen as provocation is organized by elements close to Ricardo Bofill, the self-appointed leader of a "Pro–Human Rights Party," who are eager to create a climate designed to prove the existence of Soviet-like dissidents in Cuba. He refers to his group as "enemies of the Revolution." Menéndez continues in his paper, "If from the beginning we had analyzed the phenomenon of young art not only from a political point of view but from a social and artistic point of view as well, everything would have been different. We would have concluded that one of the most cultured, talented, and prepared sectors of a generation born much after 1959, nourished, raised, and educated by the Revolution, could not be counterrevolutionary. If it were, the sector would act like certain groups of supposed artists have, who openly stand against the Revolution and make their exhibits (very conventional and mediocre) in private houses." Instead, Menéndez says, artists like himself go public with their work and seek the deepest possible communication with the people to discuss what they perceive as communal problems.

8. The exhibit actually had fifteen artists: Alejandro Arrechea (1967), Manuel Arenas (1964), Miguel Dotres (1962), Víctor González (1963), Leonel Borrás (1966), Ernesto Arencibia (1963), Lázaro Saavedra (1964), Ezequiel Suárez (1966), Denis Núñez (1967), Angel Delgado (1965), Pedro Vizcaíno (1966), Agustín Valdés (1967), Roberto Alemán (1966), Eduardo Lozano (1967), and Alexis Linares (1966).

9. The ISA requires 90/100 as a total academic score to be accepted.

10. The group also invited some other artists to participate. Tomás Esson, one of the artists invited and whose work would have problems of its own, refused because he saw that there was no quality control in the project.

11. Nevertheless, the event had a short, favorable review in the newspaper *Juventud Rebelde*.

12. Concurrent with these events, Juan-si had a performance in the National Museum of Fine Arts without any problems. He stripped naked and shaved his chest in the pattern of the Cuban flag. He then entered a clear acrylic cylinder and painted it from the inside until he could not be seen.

13. In discussing their lack of name, they suggested that they would prefer to be considered an *equipo* (team) and not a group.

14. About 50 percent of the members of the UNEAC are over forty years old, a fact heavily criticized by, among others, Vice-President Carlos Rafael Rodríguez in his speech during the Fourth Congress, in which he pointed out that most of the members of the initial cadres of the Revolution were under thirty when Batista was deposed. By 1990 a correction in the UNEAC was under way, and new artists such as Ciro Quintana and others were made members.

15. Alexis Somoza, interview with the author, Havana, January 1988.

16. "It is imperative that contributions to art criticism come from the creators themselves." Abdel Hernández San Juan, "Sobre la crítica de arte y de como Elso Padilla, Rubén Torres, José Bedia y Arturo Cuenca parecen estar de acuerdo por telepatía" (Havana, 1987, Typescript). The essay is also interesting because it connects Cuenca's work, usually seen as internationalist, with three artists deeply concerned with national and Afro-Cuban issues.

17. Desiderio Navarro, "La retroabstracción geométrica: Un arte sin problemas: Es sólo lo que ves," La Gaceta de Cuba, June 1989, pp. 22–23; and Gerardo Mosquera, "Trece criterios sobre el nuevo arte cubano," La Gaceta de Cuba, June 1989, p. 24. Among the artists who "participated" in the exhibit were Adriano Buergo, Ana Albertina Delgado, Carlos Rodríguez Cárdenas, Tania Bruguera, Arturo Cuenca, Aldito Menéndez, Tonel, Tomás Esson, Abdel Hernández, Glexis Novoa, Segundo Planes, Ponjuán, Ciro Qintana, Lázaro Saavedra, Sandra Ceballos, Félix Suazo, Ermy Taño, Rubén Torres Llorca, Pedro Vizcaíno, and Carlos García.

18. An immediate precedent for this project, which also took place in 1988, was the "Cultural Invasion" sponsored by the Asociación Brigadas Hermanos Saiz. Group of artists went into different cities and villages in the inland and produced "instant" forms of art. Some activities were well received; others, such as defacing the façade of a church or running through the street in underpants, had a less favorable reception. (Minister Hart commented, "It may be art, but it still is a man running around in his underpants.") The Proyecto Pilón seemed to channel a good idea into a more serious context and to remove a certain element of colonization typical of city culture going to the inland, which tainted the "Cultural Invasion."

19. Lack of parts has decimated buses in Havana and created a serious problem and long waiting lines. Popular ingenuity created the two-line system, now institutionalized with signs at each stop. One line is for sitting and the other for standing only. The city of Milan gave three hundred buses to Havana in 1989, improving the situation somewhat.

20. Aldito Menéndez, "S.O.S. revolucionario" (Havana, January 1989, Typescript).

6   THE INDIVIDUALS

1. It would be unfair not to mention that interesting sculpture is being made by "spontaneous" artists. Angel Iñigo (1957) started a "Stone Zoo" in 1977. Today it counts 187 pieces carved out of existing rocks on a hill near the city of Guantánamo, and the hill has been converted into a national park. The sculptures depict animals from all over the world in full size. Partially sculpted out of the stone with a machete, Iñigo has an acute sculptural instinct and a sense for meticulous finish. Though naive in image, he easily links up with the grand tradition of sculpture. He has no art knowledge, and a guided tour led by him consists of remarks such as "This is a horse; there is an alligator." Ramón Moya (1950), also from Guantánamo, is an obsessive carver and painter. He started working in 1984, and like Iñigo, he "sees" the image in the material he is about to work

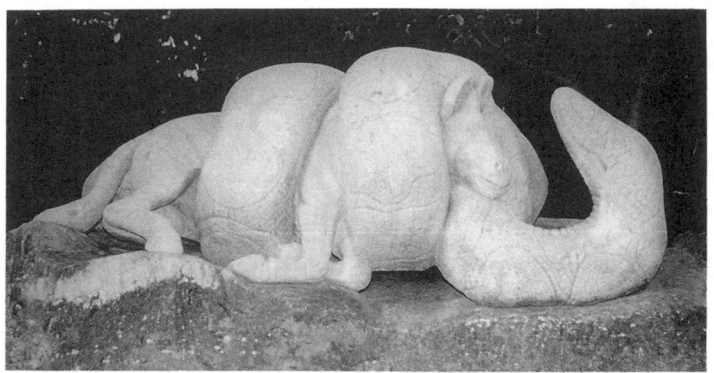

Angel Iñigo, sculpture at his "Zoológico de Piedra," Guantanamo. Photo by Luis Camnitzer.

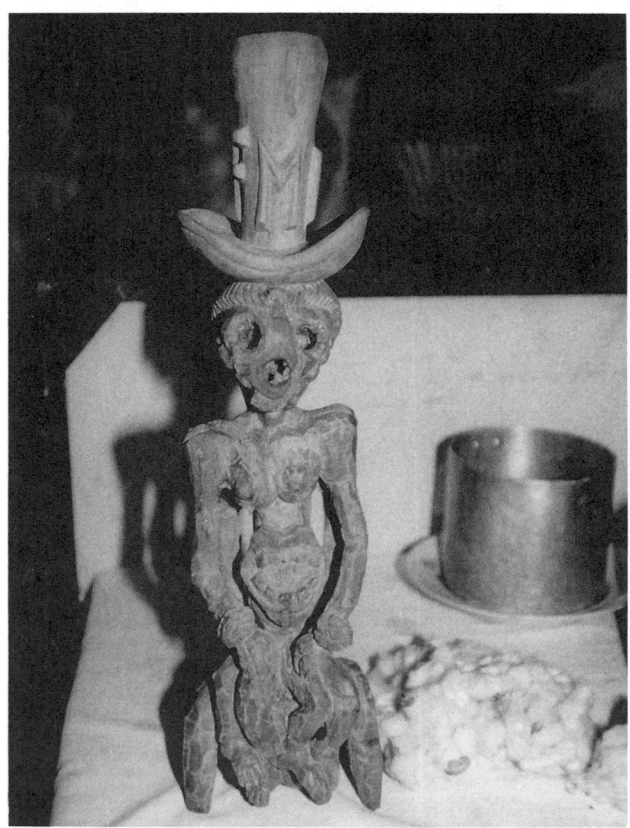

Ramón Moya, F.M.I., 1988, wood and sealing wax, $50 \times 15 \times 15$ cm. Private collection. Photo by Luis Camnitzer.

on—in his case a piece of old fabric, a tree, or a piece of wood. A frustratingly irregular artist, some of his pieces are totally crude and unresolved, while others are masterpieces. Though he will not acknowledge it, his pieces seem to be not just influenced by *Santería* rites, but part of them. In a stream of his own that could be called "magic pamphletry," he makes sculptures exorcising the International Monetary Fund and dealing with imperialist subjects.

2. In a text of 1973, "Utopia," Cuenca already had written, "This present presence of me, what order does it belong to? From which part of myself or of this landscape do I come? What do I do here, sitting, alone, as if my being was a perfect axis in the anguish of everything visible? What do I signify for my vision: this rain, this landscape, only mine from this angle? What is the use of this landscape if it is placed between what I feel and its realization: it is a terminal that never shall be my end." From *Ciencia e ideología,* catalogue for the exhibit, Castillo de la Real Fuerza, Havana, January 1989.

3. Rogerio Moya, "The Reality and Dreams of Arturo Cuenca," *Granma Weekly Review,* September 23, 1984, p. 9.

4. It is ironic that in 1988, and after the suspension of a section of the McCarran-Walter Act, Cuenca was denied entry to the United States to attend an opening of his one-man exhibit in New York under one of the only paragraphs to be still legally invoked, prohibiting visas to those individuals engaged in terrorist activities. He finally was allowed to visit the United States in 1990. In time Cuenca seems to have had a change of heart about Cuba. Early in 1991 he arrived in Miami and stated that he was seeking political asylum in the United States after a stay in Mexico of over a year. He claimed that since Mexico has diplomatic relations with Cuba, he did not feel safe there. He announced his decision in a press conference, which earned him some publicity.

5. Moya, "The Reality and Dreams."

6. Abdel Hernández, "Sobre la crítica de arte."

7. Gerardo Mosquera, "Arte y filosofía en Arturo Cuenca," *Catalogue for the Exhibition of Arturo Cuenca,* Galería de Arte Mexicano, Mexico City, August 1990.

8. James D. Murray, "How the Leopard Gets Its Spots," *Scientific American,* March 1988, p. 80.

9. Afro-Cuban rituals do place the government in an odd situation. From one point of view, it is a nonmaterialist obscurantist custom that may slow down the achievement of an ideal "enlightened" society. From another point of view, it is intrinsic to the makeup of Cuban culture and has to be fostered to achieve any possibility of a true identity. In Havana and the suburbs there are over three hundred *babalaos* who meet at least once a year, but not openly, and who feel they are not well seen by the government. On the other hand, there were talks with the government about making Havana an official continental center for *Santería,* a proposal seriously considered partly out of a feeling of rivalry with the Cuban community in Miami, which was competing for the post.

10. Magdalena Campos, *Acoplamientos,* Catalogue for the exhibit, Galería L, Havana, May–June, 1985.

11. Magdalena Campos, letter to the author, December 22, 1990.

12. Ibid. Cuban critic Gerardo Mosquera, for example, had pointed out a parallel with the work by U.S. painter Elizabeth Murray.

13. Ibid.

14. Samuel Feijoo, *Mitología cubana,* pp. 186–187.

15. María Eugenia Haya (Marucha), "Autorretratos?" introduction to *Marta Pérez Bravo,* catalogue for an exhibit, Havana, 1989.

16. Feminism in Cuba is a complex issue. The Revolution has established the equality of women as a goal, and an analysis of the Cuban structure confirms that great strides have been made in this direction. On the other hand, there are still deep-seated internalized *machista* traditions, particularly offensive to visiting U.S. feminists, who often project their own experiences onto Cuban reality and sometimes alienate potentially sympathetic Cuban women. When some years ago a group of U.S. feminists organized a consciousness-raising meeting in Havana, some Cuban women discussed the possibility of coming with deep décolletés, heavy make-up, and loads of jewelry. They dropped the idea out of politeness.

17. Marta Pérez Bravo, from Charles Merewether, *Made in Havana,* catalogue for the exhibit, Art Gallery of New South Wales, New South Wales, Australia, October 1988.

18. Gerardo Mosquera, "The 14 Sons of William Tell," in *No Man Is an Island: Young Cuban Art,* ed. Marketta Seppälä, p. 48.

19. Referring to the period, Aldo Menéndez writes, "And too much Chagall, who—as it is known—was not precisely a master from Guanabacoa. . . ." Aldo Menéndez, "Tonel Nacional," introduction to *Clásicos de Tonel,* catalogue for the exhibit, Galería L, Havana, March 1986.

20. In her later work, Amelia Peláez used ornamental devices taken from the decorative glass windows placed over traditional Cuban doors. While at first view the paintings seem decorative, they in fact only use the borrowed decorative style to reinterpret and reorganize reality, attempting a form of Cubanism. Nevertheless, painter Wifredo Lam criticized her work from a class point of view: "It reminds me of the colonial world and the creole bourgeoisie. . . . It is Cuban, but from the culture of those who held power" (Interview with Gerardo Mosquera, *Bohemia,* no. 25, June 20, 1980, reprinted in Gerardo Mosquera, *Exploraciones en la plástica cubana,* pp. 187–188).

21. See Nestor García Canclini, "Escenas sin territorio," and "6 preguntas a José Joaquín Brunner," both in *Revista de Crítica Cultural* (Chile), no. 1 (May 1990): 9–12; and 21.

22. Llilian Llanes, "Cultural Policies in the Area of Professional Formation in the Visual Arts" (Paper given at the UNESCO meeting, Caracas, November 1990). As a consequence, Llanes sees some advantages in the long blockade of the United States against Cuba.

It is interesting that the only "nonpartisan" promoter and distributor of culture on an international level, UNESCO, has a grand total of four million dollars available for this purpose for the whole world and for all the fields (1990). More than half of these funds were donated by Kuwait, Iran, and Saudi Arabia. India contributed $62,000 and Holland $15,000, while private foundations donated a total of $100,000 to the fund.

23. The corner also has symbolic importance and is revered by many in Cuba. It is the place where Fidel Castro announced Cuba's turn to socialism in 1961.

24. Tomás Esson, interview with the author, Havana, January 1989.

25. Gerardo Mosquera, "Mitología y vulgaridad," *Revolución y Cultura*, (September 1986): 78.

26. Esson, interview with the author. In a subsequent letter of 1990, he also stated that *SPOULAKK* was intended to sound like the name of an Eastern European country.

27. In some notes about the exhibition, Tonel comments about the Che painting: "That monstrous sexual relation is also dirt, an exaltation of instinct over reason, the absence of moral principles. . . . It is a Che omnipresent in daily reality—with all the bitterness and despicable qualities it may have—apprehensive and expectant (demanding) confronted with the negative aspects of this reality." About the flag he writes that it is a feminine flag, where the fabric covers the maternal body, which bleeds with the loss of its children. According to Esson, both descriptions reflect his intentions.

28. *Bohemia* of October 20, 1989, published an interview conducted by Juan Sánchez with Minister Hart under the title "Cultura cubana, escudo ideológico y moral," in which some of the problems here discussed are addressed.

> The art movement which broke with the Academy in Cuba arrived simultaneously with the social movement. . . . The broadest creative freedom does not mean liberalism. It [the freedom] moves on the foundation of the sense for social responsibility, for moral demand and for patriotic consciousness. . . . We have to articulate the new with what precedes it. Between both is the historical memory and the continuity of social, political, and cultural processes. Absolute, antidialectic, and abrupt denials with pretentions of ideological veracity, constitute a danger we have to stop. . . . No country with self-respect accepts an inadequate treatment of its patriotic symbols. In this regard it is not only a question concerning art; it is also a matter of a principle that addresses society's ethical and political values. We have respected and underlined the importance of the procedures and the styles of professional work in art. We have to demand respect for the deepest ethical, political, and cultural principles as well. Often, when there is carelessness in the treatment given to patriotic symbols, it is the result of the fact that the right artistic form hasn't been found, [but no matter what] for ethical reasons it is necessary to be careful to present the symbols of our society in a dignified manner exalting the highest values of Cubanism.

29. Tensions between Esson and Cuban authorities mounted, and finally Esson, who had gone to the United States in conjunction with "The Nearest Edge

of the World" exhibit of new Cuban art, decided in April 1991 not to return to Cuba.

30. Glexis Novoa, quoted by Carlos Rodríguez Cárdenas, "Pero se mueve," in *To Be or Not to Be,* catalogue for an exhibit of Glexis Novoa, Galería Habana, Havana, November 1988.

31. Carlos Rodríguez Cárdenas, *Artista de calidad,* catalogue for the exhibit, Galería Habana, Havana, 1988.

32. Ciro Quintana, interview with the author, January 1988.

33. Aldo Menéndez, introduction to *Hacer arte a lo cubano,* catalogue for the Ciro Quintana exhibit, Centro Provincial de Artes Plásticas y Diseño, Havana, 1989. The cover of the catalogue had a silhouette of a worker hammering on an anvil.

34. Quintana saw Fahlstrom's work for the first time on a trip to New York toward the end of 1990.

35. Robaldo Rodríguez, interview with the author, January 1988.

36. The lack of studio space is endemic in Havana. Even established artists work in fragments of rooms and often piece things together as a consequence. It is understandable that with the housing problems in Havana, artists cannot aspire to have comfortable home and studio space under one roof. But there is no rational explanation why some centralized collective studio spaces can not be made available to artists.

37. Robaldo Rodríguez, (untitled M.A. thesis, ISA, Havana, 1988).

38. Galería L, Havana, May 1988.

39. "1982—Raúl Martínez starts living off his work and becomes a professional." ABTV claims that the importance of Martínez is established by the fact that the Fondo Cubano de Bienes Culturales started selling his work at exchange value and not at use value, changing what was interesting work into a valuable signature.

40. Tanya Angulo and ABTV team, *Homenaje a Hans Haacke,* catalogue for the exhibit, Castillo de la Real Fuerza, Havana, 1989.

41. Ibid.

42. The team in fact criticized the Ministry of Culture for sponsoring the Proyecto Pilón. They felt that an alternative route was being coopted and closed. As the development and failure of the project proved, the criticism was unfair on a short-term strategic level. Without the ministry's financial help, it would have failed even earlier or would not have been able to start.

43. The artists added were Consuelo Castañeda, Arturo Cuenca, Adriano Buergo, René Francisco Rodríguez, Tomás Esson, Tonel, Hubert Moreno, and Pedro Alvarez.

44. René Francisco Rodríguez, interview with the author, Havana, January 1988.

45. Alejandro Aguilera, untitled M.A. thesis, ISA, Havana, 1988.

46. Humberto Castro, interview with Toni Piñera, "In Black and White," *Granma Weekly Review,* October 14, 1984 (p. 16 in Centro Wifredo Lam press dossier).

47. Fusco and Knafo, "Interviews," p. 52.

48. It is revealing that most of the pop artists working in New York in the 1960s came from rural states and that Arte Povera was created by Italian artists who were reacting to the commodification process imposed by the hegemonic centers.

49. "Visiones posmodernas de 2º Planes," *Huella* (Santa Clara), August 1987, p. 3.

50. Segundo Planes, interview with the author, Havana, January 1988.

51. Mosquera, "The 14 Sons," p. 34.

52. Alexis Somoza, "La individualidad artística en la sociedad socialista" (Havana, August 1987, Typescript).

53. In a letter to the author, May 2, 1989, Somoza focuses more on his interpretation and accepts that "'Volumen I' contributed content-oriented factors" and that "it would be a crass mistake to reduce 'Volumen I' to a contributor of solely formal elements. . . . Nevertheless, its contribution unites content and codes; but its historical usefulness resides in the opening of horizons, not in its role in regard to content."

54. The title is taken from an unpublished paper on Somoza's own sculptural work by Abelardo Mena, "El objeto escultorizado: reflexiones sobre la escultura de Alexis Somoza, Havana 1989, Typescript.

55. As a consequence of this incident, Beatriz Aulet, director of the Center for the Development of the Visual Arts and responsible for the exhibit, was transferred to another job. Aulet was, with Leiseca and others, in the forefront of those who helped Cuban arts flourish during this decade.

56. In 1990 Dania del Sol came to the United States as part of an exchange program with the Massachusetts College of Art and subsequently decided not to return to Cuba.

57. Dania del Sol, "Ad infinitum" (M.A. thesis, ISA, Havana, 1990), p. 7.

58. See Antonio Eligio Fernández' interview with Lázaro García, in *Kuba o.k.,* edited by Jürgen Harten and Antonio Eligio (Tonel), p. 90, catalogue for the exhibit, Städtische Kunsthalle, Düsseldorf, 1990.

59. Letter to the author.

7 CUBAN ART AND POSTMODERNISM

1. Part of this chapter appeared as an essay under the title, "The Eclecticism of Survival: Today's Cuban Art," in *The Nearest Edge of the World: Art in Cuba Now,* pp. 18–23. Catalogue for the exhibit, Massachusetts College of Art, Boston, November 1990.

2. James Petras, "Las transformaciones globales y el futuro del socialismo en América Latina," *Brecha* (Montevideo), April 20, 1990, pp. 15–18. It is interesting to note that of all countries, capitalist and socialist, Romania was the one that applied IMF conditions to the letter, without managing to cure any economic ailments.

3. Brazilian poet Oswald de Andrade, for example, published an "Anthropophagite Manifesto" in 1928, in which he wrote of the "absorption of the sacred enemy" and "I am only interested in that which is not mine. Law of man. Law of

cannibal." See de Andrade, "Manifesto antropófago," in *Claves del arte de nuestra América*, compiled by Lesbia Vent Dumois, Hugo Rivera, and Lourdes Benigni, vol. 1, document no. 8.

4. Rafael López Valdés, *Componentes africanos en el etnos cubano*, p. 112. López Valdés also shows the imprecisions of the term *Yoruba*, first used as a general name in 1832 by J. Raban (*The Eyo Vocabulary*, p. 66) as the product of a linguistic analysis made by Christian missionaries in the early nineteenth century.

5. *Abakuá* activities were often at odds with the plights of workers' unions, which tried to transcend small-group interests. Once port activities were systematically unionized after the 1940s, *Abakuá* influence waned. Guanche, *Procesos etnoculturales de Cuba*, pp. 443–450.

6. A design process stemming from affluence, as opposed to design by substitution, is one that stresses an aesthetic overflow from unneeded objects to functional ones, but is used to disguise the function. The best present example is the array of new telephone designs, ranging from Mickey Mouse to spike heel shoes and model Ferraris. Transformers, the polymorphous robot toys, provide another example while being a paradigm for capitalist postmodernism. Appropriated from Japanese designs and repackaged for the United States, their aesthetic power relies not on the particular look of each stage of their transformation but on the seamless transition from one appropriated image to another, always within a lethal militaristic context.

7. The information about the ANIR is taken from "25 años de innovaciones y racionalizaciones, 1959–1983," an unpublished study of the Department of Publication of the Ministry of Agriculture.

8. Frederic Jameson, "Postmodernism and Consumer Society," a lecture given in the Whitney Museum, New York, 1982, republished in Hal Foster, ed., *The Anti-aesthetic: Essays on Postmodern Culture*, pp. 111–125. The same title in Spanish, *Antiestética*, was used by the Argentinean painter Luis Felipe Noé for a book published in 1965 (Buenos Aires: Van Riel). Multiple morals may be drawn from this. One is that *pastiche* relieves people from the responsibility to give credit. The other, quite obvious, is that whatever happens in Buenos Aires has no relevance in New York. And finally, underdevelopment creates or can create conditions that generate results superficially related to those in the hegemonic center, but earlier and responding to completely different needs.

9. Osvaldo Sánchez, "La llama de la parodia," *El Caimán Barbudo*," April 1988, p. 3.

10. In a painting of 1984, *The Snake*, Swiss artist Ben Vautier inscribes, "If the new isn't new anymore, is not to make something new a new thing?"

11. There is even a certain parallel between the structure of Reagan's speeches and the paintings of Julian Schnabel. Both use repeated false endings in their discourses, one verbally and the other visually. They seem to announce a conclusion that is then followed by another and yet another, leading to a confusion of the audience and a feeling of emptiness. It is a device that Mahler used playfully in his First Symphony. The fourth movement, "Stürmisch bewegt," threatens to end about seventeen times before its actual conclusion.

12. Osvaldo Sánchez, "La llama."

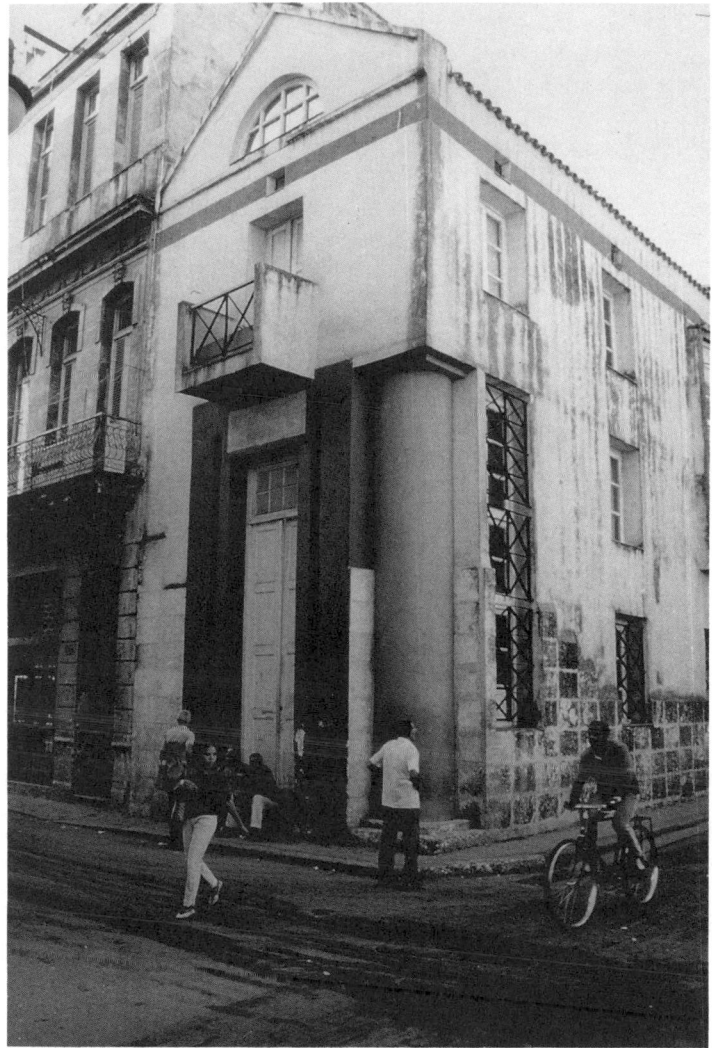

Eduardo Luis Rodríguez, house for a family doctor, corner of Sol and Compostela, Havana, 1988. Photo by Luis Camnitzer.

13. García Canclini, *La producción simbólica*, pp. 75–76. García Canclini continues to show how the technical changes failed to affect the ways work is distributed or the quality of the public addressed, compared to the art made previously.

14. Nevertheless, there is style leakage as well. A house for a family doctor was built in the center of Havana with the aesthetic proposition to reflect architectural elements from buildings in a four-block radius. However well intended, the result fits the new international tympanum and column look.

15. Cited by Georgia Collins, "Masculine Bias and the Relationship between

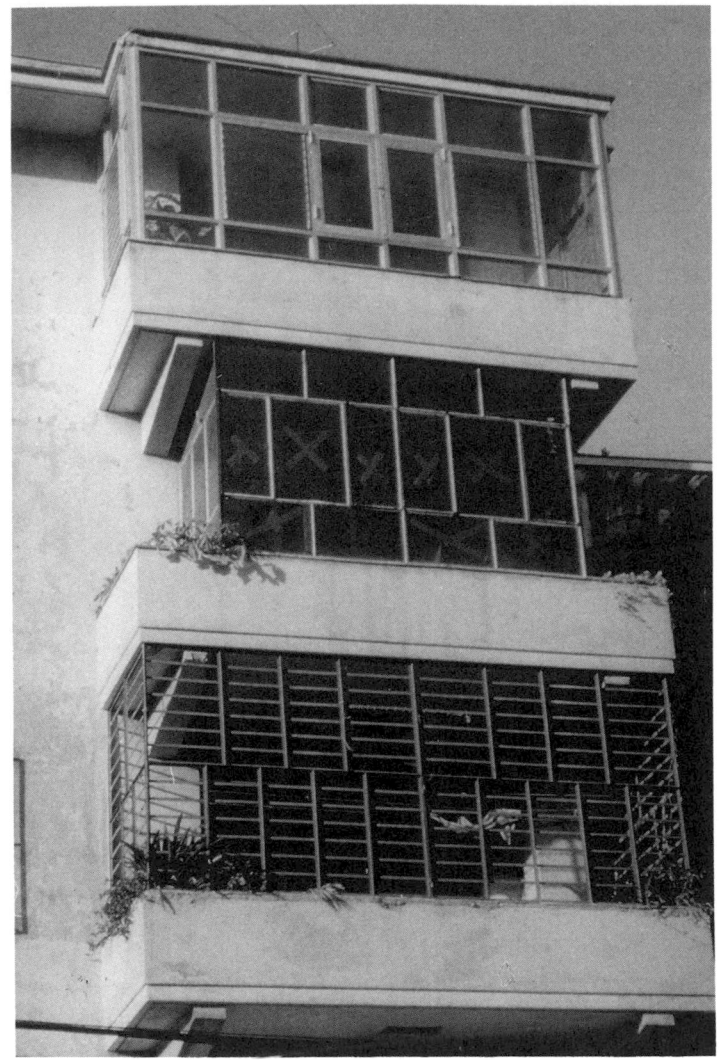

Three balconies in the same building, Havana. Photo by Luis Camnitzer, 1991.

Art and Democracy," in *Art and Democracy*, ed. Doug Blandy and Kristin Congdon, p. 30.

16. Umberto Eco, *L'Espresso*, September 21, 1970, quoted by Damián Bayón in *Aventura plástica de Latinoamérica*, p. 278.

17. Tamargo González elaborates on the same topic in relation to architecture: "What first jumps out in Caribbean architecture is its constant eclecticism. Eclecticism understood not as a Europeanizing or North Americanizing style, although there is much of it, but as an eclectic intention facing the fact of making

architecture. This eclecticism, which acquires unthought-of magnitudes and contributes very original solutions because of its vernacular essence, surpasses the limits of any norm and becomes a naive action with roots in cultural syncretism. . . . Yes to eclecticism if it implies freedom, no to eclecticism if it implies slavery" ("De la arquitectura en el Caribe").

18. Gerardo Mosquera, "Introduction," in *New Art from Cuba*, pp. 1–3, catalogue for an exhibit, Amelie Wallace Gallery, State University of New York, 1985.

19. José Seoane Gallo, *Palmas reales en el Sena*, pp. 192–193. In a parallel example, there was a time in which Cuban posters made a great aesthetic use of unprinted areas, really in order to use less ink. See Goldman, "Painters into Poster Makers," p. 170.

20. Ochoa had been a "Hero of the Republic of Cuba," prominent in Angola, and scheduled to be in charge of the military of the Western region of Cuba. He was convicted of trafficking in drugs and of operating a black market in Angola, and he was executed on July 13, 1989, together with José Martínez, Tony de la Guardia, and Amado Padrón. (For detailed information about the trial, see *Vindicación de Cuba*, or Center for Cuban Studies, *Cuba Update*, 10, no. 4–5 (Fall 1989).

21. The perception also was picked up by musicians. Carlos Varela, a young singer (1963), became famous because of his song "Guillermo Tell." The lyrics express Tell's displeasure when his son requests that the apple be on his father's head so that he can use the crossbow himself.

22. Mosquera, "The 14 Sons of William Tell," in *No Man Is an Island*, ed. Seppälä, p. 42, catalogue for the exhibit, Pori Art Museum, Pori, Finland, May 1990.

POSTSCRIPT

1. *Granma Weekly Review*, August 13, 1989, p. 13.

2. *Moscow News*, no. 44, 1990, quoted by James Petras in "Amigos Distanciados," *Brecha* (Montevideo), January 17, 1991.

3. Castro acts as a reminder of socialist consciousness toward the Third World whenever he addresses Soviet matters. In his letter of congratulation to Gorbachev on the occasion of his appointment to the presidency, he stated, "Working for peaceful understanding and for the reconciliation of the interest of the great powers with the aspirations of Third World people is another important task in your post" (*Granma*, April 1, 1990, p. 8).

4. Reprinted in *Granma*, November 26, 1989, p. 8.

5. Aldo Menéndez, the founder and original director, is in Spain starting a branch of the Taller.

SECOND POSTSCRIPT

1. The "special period of peace" is defined in opposition to the "special period of war." Both terms were created in relation to the grim economic perspectives caused by the collapse of the socialist bloc, when it was not clear if the future held peace or war with the United States.

BIBLIOGRAPHY

Achugar, Hugo. "Cuba: Las iniciales del cambio." *Brecha* (Montevideo), October 7, 1988, p. 26.

Acosta Julián, Vivian. *10 años del ISA.* Catalogue for the exhibit, Museo Nacional de Bellas Artes, Havana, May 1986.

Acuña, Rodolfo. *A Community under Siege.* Los Angeles: UCLA, Chicano Research Center, 1984.

Agriculture, Cuban Ministry of. "A.N.I.R.: 25 años de innovaciones y racionalizaciones, 1959–1983." Havana, n.d. Typescript.

Aguilera, Alejandro. Untitled Master's thesis, ISA, Havana, 1988.

Aguirre, Mirta. "Apuntes sobre literatura y arte." In *Revolución, letras, arte,* edited by Víctor López Lemus, p. 216. Havana: Editorial Letras Cubanas, 1980.

Aharonian, Coriun. "Silvio de vuelta." *Brecha* (Montevideo), December 11, 1987, p. 22.

Aldana, Carlos. "As Much as the Air We Breathe We Need Art, Its News and Prophecies." *Granma Weekly Review,* February 14, 1988, p. 8.

Alonso, Alejandro G. "Amelia Peláez." Catalogue for the exhibit, Museo Nacional de Bellas Artes, Centro Wifredo Lam, Havana, November 1986.

———. "Un éxito: El I Salón de pequeño formato." *Juventud Rebelde,* September 17, 1981, p. 2.

———. "Exponen nuestros más recientes creadores." *Juventud Rebelde,* October 20, 1981, p. 4.

———. "Una muestra y once caminos." *Juventud Rebelde,* January 25, 1981, p. 4.

———. "Raúl Martínez: El tiempo que vive." *Revolución y Cultura* (October 1986): 40–51.

———. "Sano y sabroso, ahora para una nueva muestra." *Juventud Rebelde,* August 11, 1981.

———. "A Tour around Cuban Rooms." *Granma Weekly Review,* April 17, 1988, p. 7.

———. "Visiones de Bedia." *Revolución y Cultura* (October 1987): 40–45.

Alvarez Martínez, Enrique. *"Volumen I: Primer volumen de una renovación esperanzadora."* Havana, 1986. Typescript.

Amnesty International. *Cuba: Arrest of Human Rights Activists*. New York: Amnesty International, 1987.

———. *On the Human Rights Situation in Cuba*. New York: Amnesty International, June 27, 1984.

———. *Political Imprisonment in Cuba*. London: Amnesty International, November 1986.

Angulo, Tanya, et al. *Homenaje a Hans Haacke*. Catalogue for the exhibit, Castillo de la Real Fuerza, Havana, 1989.

Angulo, Tanya, and José Toirac. *Gustavo Pérez Monzón: DieSiocho días*. Catalogue for the exhibit, Centro Provincial de Artes Plásticas y Diseño, Havana, March 1989.

———. *Pinturas Cubanas*. Catalogue for the exhibit, Galería Cultural Plaza, Havana, October 1988.

Areito (Miami). 1, no. 3 (July 1988): 4–25. Issue on Afro-Cuban religions.

Ashton, Dore. Introduction to *First Look: 10 Young Artists from Today's Cuba*, pp. 5–7. Catalogue for the exhibit, Westbeth Gallery, New York, November 1981.

Ballester, Juan, and José Toirac. *"Nosotros": Exposición antológica de la obra de Raúl Martínez*. Catalogue for the exhibit, Centro Provincial de Artes Plásticas y Diseño, Havana, January 1989.

Ballester, Juan, and Ileana Villazón. *El que imita fracasa*. Catalogue for the exhibit, Galería Extensión Universitaria, Havana, May 1988.

Baranik, Rudolf. "Bringing Metaphors and Dreams to the Cuban Revolution." *Old Westbury Review*, no. 2 (Fall 1986): 161–168.

———. "Forum: Art in Cuba." *Artforum* (December 1982): 2.

Barcia, María del Carmen. *Burguesía esclavista y abolición*. Havana: Editorial de Ciencias Sociales, 1987.

Barckhausen-Canale, Christiane. *Verdad y leyenda de Tina Modotti*. Havana: Casa de las Américas, 1989.

Barnet, Miguel. "Identidad cultural y liberación nacional." In *Ponencias: I encuentro de intelectuales por la soberanía de los pueblos de nuestra América*, edited by Reynaldo González, pp. 286–289. Havana: Casa de las Américas, 1985.

———. "Peacock or Phoenix? [Manuel Mendive]." *Granma Weekly Review*, June 12, 1988, p. 7.

Barrera, Petra. "Ana Mendieta: A Historical Overview." In *Ana Mendieta: A Retrospective*, pp. 28–41. Catalogue for the exhibit, The New Museum, New York, 1987.

Bayón, Damián. *Aventura plástica de Latinoamérica*. Mexico City: Fondo de Cultura Económica, 1974.

Benedetti, Mario. "Martí y el Uruguay." *Brecha* (Montevideo), February 7, 1986, p. 31.

Benvenuto, Sergio. "El retorno del Che." *Brecha* (Montevideo), December 12, 1986, p. 22.

Boime, Albert. *The Academy & French Painting in the Nineteenth Century*. New Haven: Yale University Press, 1986.

Borges Pérez, Octavio. "Through Telarte People Get to Know Their Painters Better." *Granma Weekly Review,* June 5, 1988, p. 12.

Braudel, Fernand. *The Structures of Everyday Life.* New York: Harper and Row, 1979.

Brecha (Montevideo). "Cuba prohibe la entrada de dos publicaciones soviéticas." August 11, 1989, p. 31.

Brunner, J. J. "Seis Preguntas." *Revista de Crítica Cultural* (Chile), no. 1 (May 1990): 20–25.

———. *Universidad y sociedad en América Latina.* Azcapotzalvo, Mexico: Universidad Autónoma, 1987.

Buchloh, Benjamin. "Cold War Constructivism." New York, 1987. Photostat.

———. "Interview with José Bedia, Flavio Garciandía, and Ricardo Rodríguez Brey." In *New Art from Cuba,* pp. 7–36. Catalogue for the exhibit, SUNY, College at Old Westbury, New York, 1985.

Bueno, Salvador. "The Creative Facets of Marcelo Pogolotti." *Granma Weekly Review,* September 18, 1988, p. 6.

Cabrera, Carlos. "Rectification: Renewal in Cuban Socialism." *Granma Weekly Review,* September 18, 1988, p. 6.

Camnitzer, Luis. "Ana Mendieta." *Arte en Colombia,* no. 38 (December 1988): 44–49.

———. "Ana Mendieta." *Third Text* (London), no. 7 (Summer 1989): 47–52.

———. "Art Education in Latin America Bypasses Cultural Identity Problem." *New Art Examiner,* September 1986, pp. 30–33.

———. "An Art of Secular Mysticism: The Legacy of Juan Francisco Elso Padilla." *New Art Examiner,* November 1990, pp. 28–30.

———. "Between Nationalism and Internationalism." In *Signs of Transition: 80's Art from Cuba.* Catalogue for the exhibit, Museum of Contemporary Hispanic Art and the Center for Cuban Studies, New York City, 1988.

———. "The Eclecticism of Survival: Cuban Art Today." In *The Nearest Edge of the World: Art in Cuba Now,* pp. 18–23. Catalogue for an exhibit of contemporary Cuban art, Massachusetts College of Art, Boston, November, 1990. Boston: Polarities, Inc., 1990.

———. Introduction to *Convergences.* Catalogue for the exhibit, Lehman College Art Gallery, New York City, 1988.

———. *Latin American Spirituality: The Sculpture of Juan Francisco Elso, 1984–1988.* Catalogue for the exhibit, MIT List Visual Arts Center, Cambridge, Massachusetts, February 23–April 14, 1991.

———. "The Politics of Marginalization." *New Art Examiner,* Summer 1988, pp. 13–14.

———. *Telarte: Fabrics by Cuban Artists.* Catalogue for the exhibit, SUNY College at Old Westbury, New York, March 1990.

Campos, Magdalena. *Acoplamientos.* Catalogue for the exhibit, Galería L, Havana, May–June 1985.

Cannon, Terence. *Revolutionary Cuba.* Havana: Editorial José Martí, 1983.

Cardona Peña, Alfredo. *Conversaciones con Diego Rivera.* Mexico City: Editorial Diana, 1980.

Cardoza y Aragón, Luis. *Orozco*. Mexico City: Fondo de Cultura Económica, 1983.

Carol, Alberto Jorge. "Cuadrodebate," *Revolución y Cultura* (August 1974): 24–29.

Carreras, Julio Angel. *Esclavitud, abolición y racismo*. Havana: Editorial de Ciencias Sociales, 1985.

Casa de las Américas. *Claves del arte de nuestra América*. Vol. 1. Havana: Casa de las Américas, 1986.

Casaus, Victor. "El género testimonio y el cine cubano." In *Cine, literatura, sociedad*, edited by Ambrosio Fornet, pp. 85–108. Havana: Editorial Letras Cubanas, 1982.

Castañeda, Consuelo, Humberto Castro, and Gory. Catalogue for a three-person traveling exhibit, Havana, 1988.

Castañeda, Mireya. "Artistic Freedom in Cuba." Interview with Nuria Nuiry. *Granma Weekly Review,* March 16, 1986, p. 7.

———. "Commonality and Diversity in Third World Art." *Granma Weekly Review,* December 17, 1989.

———. "A Cuban Style in the Latest of Fashion." *Granma Weekly Review,* April 12, 1987, p. 12.

———. "Freedom for the Arts in Cuba." *Granma Weekly Review,* April 3, 1988, p. 5.

———. "Telarte: Happy Symbiosis between Art and Industry." *Granma Weekly Review,* September 4, 1988, p. 7.

Castro, Fidel. *Appearance of Major Fidel Castro Analyzing Events in Czechoslovakia.* Havana: Radio Habana, 1968.

———. *Apply Theory to the Particular Conditions of Each Country.* Havana: Ministry of Foreign Relations, Dept. of Information, 1965.

———. "Communism Will Be Abundance without Egoism: On Intellectual Property." In *Communications and Class Struggle,* edited by Armand Mattelart and Seth Siegelaub, pp. 288–295. New York: International General, 1983.

———. "Message to Gorbachev for His Election as USSR President." *Granma Weekly Review,* April 1, 1990, p. 8.

———. "Palabras a los intelectuales." In *Revolución, letras, arte,* edited by Víctor López Lemus, pp. 7–33. Havana: Editorial Letras Cubanas, 1980.

———. *La primera revolución socialista en América.* Mexico City: Siglo XXI, 1976.

———. Speeches published in *Granma Weekly Review:* April 21, 1986, supplement, 8 pp.; December 13, 1987, pp. 8–11; January 10, 1988, pp. 3, 6; February 7, 1988, pp. 1, 9; February 21, 1988, p. 3; July 24, 1988; August 7, 1988, pp. 2–5; September 25, 1988, p. 4, pp. 9–16; December 18, 1988, pp. 2–5; January 1, 1989, p. 6; January 15, 1989, pp. 1–6; January 22, 1989, supplement; January 29, 1989, pp. 3–5; July 23, 1989, pp. 7–12; February 11, 1990, pp. 1–4; March 4, 1990, pp. 2–3; March 18, 1990, supplement; October 14, 1990, pp. 2–5.

Center for Cuban Studies. "Interview: Lisandro Otero." *Cuba Update* 8, no. 5–6 (Winter 1987): 11–14.

———. *Cuba Update* 10, no. 4–5 (Fall 1989).

Centro Wifredo Lam. "Acosta, Gustavo." Press dossier. Havana: Centro Wifredo Lam, 1989.

——. "Bedia, José." Press dossier. Havana: Centro Wifredo Lam, 1989.

——. "Castro, Humberto." Press dossier. Havana: Centro Wifredo Lam, 1989.

——. "Finalé, Moisés." Press dossier. Havana: Centro Wifredo Lam, 1989.

——. "Franco, José." Press dossier. Havana: Centro Wifredo Lam, 1989.

——. "Proyecto metodológico para la investigación ramal del arte en Cuba." Havana: Centro Wifredo Lam, 1987.

——. "Sánchez, Tomás." Press dossier. Havana: Centro Wifredo Lam, 1989.

Chago. *El humor otro*. Introduction by Lisandro Otero. Havana: Ediciones Revolución, 1963.

Cobas Amate, Roberto. "Exploración de una sonrisa." In *Humor con risa, humor sonrisa*. Catalogue for the exhibit of Jesús González de Armas, Galería Centro Wifredo Lam, Havana, November 1988.

Cockroft, Eva. "Cuban Poster Art." In *Cuban Poster Art: A Retrospective, 1961–1982*, pp. 3–7. Catalogue for the exhibit, Westbeth Gallery, Center for Cuban Studies, New York, January 1983.

——. "Kitsch in Cuba." *Artforum* (Summer 1985): 72–73.

Colectivo de autores. *La sociedad neocolonial cubana: Corrientes ideológicas y partidos políticos*. Havana: Editorial de Ciencias Cubanas, 1984.

Colina, Cino. "Abakuás: African-based Societies in Cuba." *Granma Weekly Review*, March 19, 1989, p. 12.

——. "Cuban Women: Speaking from the Heart." *Granma Weekly Review*, October 22, 1989, p. 3.

Collins, Georgia. "Masculine Bias and the Relationship between Art and Democracy." In *Art and Democracy*, edited by Doug Blandy and Kristin Congdon, pp. 30–31. New York and London: Teachers College Press, 1987.

Comité Central del Partido Comunista de Cuba. *Sobre la cultura artística y literaria: Tesis y resolución*. Havana: Departamento de Orientación Revolucionaria, 1976.

Consejo Nacional de Cultura. *Manual: Desarrollo de las artes*. Havana: Consejo Nacional de Cultura, n.d. (ca. 1966).

Constitución de la República de Cuba. Havana: Ministerio de Justicia, Departamento de Divulgación, 1988.

Contrera, Nelio. *Julio Antonio Mella: El joven precursor*. Havana: Editora Política, 1987.

Cruz, Soledad. "Información inconclusa sobre coloquio crítico." *Juventud Rebelde*, May 29, 1988, p. 11.

——. "Tienen la palabra los filósofos." *Juventud Rebelde*, June 19, 1988.

Cuenca, Arturo. "Un artista pide la palabra: Response to Soledad Cruz." *Juventud Rebelde*, June 1988.

——. *Ciencia e ideología*. Catalogue for the exhibit, Castillo de la Real Fuerza, Havana, 1989.

——. *Espectador*. Catalogue for the exhibit. Museo Nacional de Bellas Artes, Havana, July 1983.

———. *Estética práctica.* Catalogue for the exhibit, Centro Provincial de Artes Plásticas y Diseño, Havana, April, 1987.

Cúneo, Dardo, ed. *La reforma universitaria.* Caracas: Biblioteca Ayacucho, 1988.

de Andrade, Oswald. "Manifiesto antropófago." In *Claves del arte de nuestra América,* compiled by Lesbia Vent Dumois, Hugo Rivera, and Lourdes Benigni, vol. 1, document no. 8. Havana: Casa de las Américas, 1986.

de Juan, Adelaida. "Arte y difusión gráfica de la Revolución Cubana." In *Revolución, letras, arte,* edited by Víctor López Lemus, pp. 536–556. Havana: Ediciones Letras Cubanas, 1980.

———. "Las artes plásticas en Cuba socialista." In *La cultura en Cuba socialista,* pp. 35–62. Havana: Editorial Letras Cubanas, 1982.

———. "Las paradojas de Rafael Blanco." In *Rafael Blanco: Homenaje en el 100 aniversario de su nacimiento.* Catalogue for the exhibit, Museo Nacional de Bellas Artes, Havana, 1985.

———. "Pintura cubana: Temas y variaciones." In *Panorama de la cultura cubana,* edited by Marilú Moré de Castro, pp. 171–196. Havana: Editora Política, 1983.

———. "Sobre lo afrocubano en nuestra pintura." *Bohemia,* May 20, 1983, pp. 16–19.

de la Fuente, Jorge. "Praxis, ideología y arte en Adolfo Sánchez Vázquez." *La Revista del Sur,* (Malmö, Sweden), no. 13 (1987): 17–22.

del Sol, Dania. "Ad infinitum." Master's thesis, ISA, Havana, 1990.

Departamento de Orientación Revolucionaria del Comité Central del Partido Comunista de Cuba. *Sobre la cultura artística, literaria: tésis, resolución.* Proceedings of the First Congress of the Cuban Communist Party. Havana, 1975.

Desnoes, Edmundo. *Cuban Posters.* Amsterdam: Stedelijk Museum, 1971.

———. "1952–62 en la pintura cubana." In *Pintores Cubanos,* pp. 39–48. Havana: Editorial Revolución, 1962.

Echevarría Echerri, Lesbia. "Hiperrealismo y necesidad estética." *Bohemia,* January 26, 1979, pp. 10–13.

Eligio (Tonel), Antonio. "Antonia Eiriz en la pintura cubana." *Revolución y Cultura* (March 1987): 39–45.

———. "Arte para llevar puesto." Review of Alvarez, Castillo, Moreno, Somoza, and Vizcaíno. *El Caimán Barbudo,* August 1988, pp. 4–5.

———. "Humor en una agenda." Review of Leandro Soto. *Revolución y Cultura,* (October 1986): 63–65.

———. "A mano alzada: Chago." *Unión,* no. 1 (January–March 1988): 93–95.

———. "Notas sobre la exposición 'A tarro partido II' de Tomás Esson." Havana, January 1988. Typescript.

———. "Pasó Rauschenberg sobre el mar." *Revolución y Cultura,* no. 5 (May 1988): 39–47.

———. "Tomás Esson Reid." In *Jóvenes artistas de R.D.A. y Cuba,* pp. 11–12. Havana: Museo Nacional de Bellas Artes; Berlin: Neue Berliner Galerie im Alten Museum, 1988.

———. "Trece que fueron uno." *Revolución y Cultura*, no. 7 (July 1987): 49–55.

———. "Umberto Peña expone." *Revolución y Cultura*, no. 9 (September 1988): 26–31.

Espinosa García, Manuel. *La política económica de los Estados Unidos hacia América Latina entre 1945 y 1961*. Havana: Departamento de Orientación Revolucionaria del Comité Central del Partido Comunista de Cuba, 1975.

Esson, Tomás. "Sinopsis para la futura realización de un animado titulado TALISMAN." Havana, January 1989. Typescript.

Esson, Tomás, Glexis Novoa, and Carlos Rodríguez Cárdenas. *Patria o muerte*. Catalogue for the exhibit, Castillo de la Real Fuerza, Ministerio de Cultura, Havana, March–April 1989.

Fals Borda, Orlando. *Conocimiento y poder popular*. Mexico City: Siglo XXI, 1985.

FAR, Dirección Política de las. *Historia de Cuba*. Havana: Editorial de Ciencias Sociales, 1985.

Feijoo, Samuel. *Mitología cubana*. Havana: Editorial Letras Cubanas, 1986.

Fernández, Pilar, Luz Merino, and Roberto Segre. "El Art-Deco en la Habana: La dimensión ambiental del sistema decorativo en la década del 30." Havana, 1987. Typescript.

Ferrán Oliva, Juan. "Education in Cuba: The Figures Are Eloquent." *Granma Weekly Review*, September 24, 1989.

Fisher, Louis. *The Life of Lenin*. New York: Harper and Row, 1964.

Foner, Philip. *Historia de Cuba y sus relaciones con EEUU*. Havana: Editorial de Ciencias Sociales, 1973.

Fornet, Ambrosio, ed. *Cine, literatura y sociedad*. Havana: Editorial Letras Cubanas, 1982.

Friedlaender, Heinrich. *Historia económica de Cuba*. Havana: Editorial de Ciencias Sociales, 1978.

Fusco, Coco. "Signs of Transition: 80's Art from Cuba, an Introduction." In *Signs of Transition: 80's Art from Cuba*. Catalogue for the exhibit, Center for Cuban Studies and Museum of Contemporary Hispanic Art, New York, January 1988.

Fusco, Coco, and Robert Knafo. "Interviews with Cuban Artists." *Social Text* (Fall 1986): 41–53.

García Canclini, Néstor. "¿De qué estamos hablando cuando hablamos de lo popular?" In *Comunicación y culturas populares en Latinoamérica*, edited by José Martin Barbero, pp. 21–37. Mexico City: Ediciones Gili, 1987.

———. "Escenas sin territorio." *Revista de Crítica Cultural* (Chile), no. 1 (May 1990): 9–12.

———. "Para una teoría de la socialización del arte latinoamericano." *Casa de las Américas*, no. 89 (March–April 1975): 99–119.

———. *Políticas culturales en América Latina*. Mexico City: Grijalbo, 1987.

———. *La producción simbólica*. Mexico City: Siglo XXI, 1986.

García Márquez, Gabriel. "The Cubans and the Blockade." *Cuba Update* 11, no. 1–2 (April 1990): 9–12.

Garciandía, Flavio. "Art Education in Cuba." Paper presented at the Encuentro

Regional sobre Formación y Promoción de las Artes Plásticas en América Latina y el Caribe, Caracas, Venezuela, 1990.

Goldman, Shifra. *The Critical Decade of the Cuban Avant-Garde.* Paper presented at the meeting of the Latin American Studies Association, Washington, D.C., April 1991.

———. "The Cuban Poster: Raúl Martínez, Alfredo Rostgaard, René Azcuy." *Icographic* 2, no. 4 (February 1984): 11–13.

———. "Homogenizing Hispanic Art in Houston." *New Art Examiner,* September 1987, pp. 30–33.

———. "Painters into Poster Makers: Two Views Concerning the History, Aesthetics and Ideology of the Cuban Poster Movement." *Studies in Latin American Popular Culture* 3 (1984): 162–173.

———. "A Return to Natal Earth." Review of Ana Mendieta. *Artweek* 20, no. 15 (April 15, 1989): 1.

González, Reynaldo. *Ponencias: I encuentro de intelectuales por la soberanía de los pueblos de nuestra América.* Havana: Casa de las Américas, 1985.

González Bermejo, Ernesto. "La segunda vida del Che Guevara." *Brecha* (Montevideo), February 3, 1989, supplement "La Lupa."

González Casanova, Pablo. *Imperialismo y liberación.* Mexico City: Siglo XXI, 1986.

Granma. "Al pueblo no se baja, se asciende." March 10, 1988.

Granma Weekly Review. "Che in Santa Clara." January 8, 1989, p. 12.

———. "Conversation with Carlos Aldana." November 26, 1989, p. 8.

———. "Council of State Meeting on Case No. 1 of 1989." July 23, 1989, pp. 2–6.

———. "Cuba Must Be Treated as the Socialist and Sovereign Country It Is." August 13, 1989, pp. 1, 9.

———. "Four Former High-ranking Officers Sentenced to Death for Drug Trafficking and Other Crimes." July 16, 1989, pp. 1–12.

———. "Ricardo Bofill Pagés: Ronald Reagan's Man." April 3, 1988, supplement.

———. "An Unavoidable Decision Consistent with Our Principles." August 13, 1989, p. 9.

———. "We Will Take Exemplary Measures to Eradicate Outrages Such as This." July 2, 1989, pp. 3–4.

González, Reynaldo, ed. *Ponencias: I encuentro de intelectuales por la soberanía de los pueblos de nuestra América.* Havana: Casa de las Américas, 1985.

Guanche, Jesús. *Procesos etnoculturales de Cuba.* Havana: Editorial Letras Cubanas, 1983.

Guanche Pérez, José, and Carmen Saénz Coopaat. "El programa de desarrollo cultural en las áreas rurales de Cuba." *Temas* no. 17 (1989): 119–133.

Guevara, Alfredo. "Autenticidad cultural y cultura artística en los medios de comunicación." *Brecha* (Montevideo), June 5, 1987, p. 28.

Guevara, Ernesto (Che). "La planificación socialista: Su significado." *Cuadernos de Marcha* (Montevideo), no. 3 (July 1967): 107–112.

———. "El socialismo y el hombre en Cuba." *Marcha* (Montevideo), March 12, 1965.

Gutiérrez, Carlos María. "Fidel Castro fija su relación con la URSS de Gorbachov." *Brecha* (Montevideo), January 13, 1989, p. 31.

Halperin, Maurice. *The Taming of Fidel Castro.* Berkeley, Los Angeles, and London: University of California Press, 1981.

Hart Dávalos, Armando. *Changing the Rules of the Game.* Havana: Letras Cubanas Publishers, 1983.

———. "Culture and Identity." *Granma Weekly Review,* Part 1, February 12, 1989, p. 2; Part 2, February 19, 1989, p. 2; Part 3, February 19, 1989, p. 2.

———. "Culture Expresses Itself in Defense of Identity." *Granma Weekly Review,* February 14, 1988, p. 9.

———. *Félix Varela: El que nos enseñó a pensar.* Havana: Ministerio de Cultura, 1988.

———. Speech delivered at the opening ceremony of the Second Biennial of Havana, November 1986. Manuscript.

———. "La Unión de Educadores, Escritores y Artistas, ha sido una constante en la historia de Cuba." *Revolución y Cultura* (December 1980): 36–51.

Harten, Jürgen, and Antonio Eligio (Tonel), eds. *Kuba o.k.* Catalogue for the exhibit, Städtische Kunsthalle, Düsseldorf, 1990.

Haya, María Eugenia (Marucha). "Autorretratos?" Introduction to *Martu Pérez Bravo.* Catalogue for an exhibit, Havana, 1989.

———. "Cuban Photography since the Revolution." In *Cuban Photography, 1959–1982,* pp. 2–7. Catalogue for the exhibit, Center for Cuban Studies, New York, 1983.

Hernández, Erena. Interview with Flavio Garciandía. In *Vereda Tropical.* Catalogue for the exhibit, Fondo Cubano de Bienes Culturales, Havana, November 1982.

———. "Un joven en el Salón." Interview with Gustavo Pérez Monzón. *Cartelera,* August 5–11, 1982, p. 3.

———. "El único sitio posible." Interview with Rodríguez Brey. *Revolución y Cultura,* no. 9 (September 1988): 73–74.

———. "Telarte: Tela por donde cortar." *Revolución y Cultura,* no. 5 (May 1984): 8–13.

Hernández, Orlando. *Oscuridad de Roberto Diago.* Catalogue for the exhibit, Fondo Cubano de Bienes Culturales, Havana, November 1989.

———. *Tres visiones del héroe.* Catalogue for the exhibit, Castillo de la Real Fuerza, Havana, April 1987.

———. "Viajes de Brey." *Jóvenes artistas de la R.D.A. y de Cuba,* p. 53. Havana: Museo Nacional de Bellas Artes; and Berlin: Neue Berliner Galerie im Alten Museum, 1988.

Hernández San Juan, Abdel. "Un esquimal que sabe dialéctica." In the catalogue for the exhibit "Hacer Arte a lo Cubano" by Ciro Quintana, Centro Provincial de Artes Plásticas y Diseño, Havana, March 1989.

———. "Magie oder Post-Kunst." In *Kuba o.k.,* edited by Jürgen Harten and Antonio Eligio (Tonel), p. 94. Catalogue for the exhibit. Städtische Kunsthalle, Düsseldorf, 1990.

———. "Sobre la crítica de arte y de cómo Elso Padilla, Rubén Torres, José Bedia y Arturo Cuenca parecen estar de acuerdo por telepatía." Havana, 1987. Typescript.

Herrera Ysla, Nelson. "Palabras (sin título)." In *Umberto Peña*. Catalogue for the exhibit, Museo Nacional de Bellas Artes, Havana, 1988.

Hess, Elizabeth. "Capture the Flag." *The Village Voice*, April 4, 1989, pp. 25–31.

Hexágono, (Grupo). Collective text and documentation for the catalogue of the exhibit, Galería Habana, Havana, June 1983.

Hurtado, Oscar. "Introducción a nuestra pintura." In *Pintores Cubanos*, pp. 7–38. Havana: Ediciones Revolución, 1962.

Instituto Superior de Arte. "Modelo del especialista." ISA, Havana, 1985. Mimeo publications on curricula for printmaking, painting, and sculpture.

Izaguirre Vichot, Julio. Untitled Ph.D. diss., Universidad de la Habana, Havana, 1987.

Jameson, Frederic. "Postmodernism and Consumer Society." In *Antiaesthetic: Essays on Postmodernism*, edited by Hal Foster, pp. 111–125. Washington: Bay Press, 1983.

Jiménez Pastrana, Juan. *Los chinos en la historia de Cuba, 1847–1930*. Havana: Editorial de Ciencias Sociales, 1983.

Kohen, Helen. "Heritage Keeps Art Alive inside Cuba." *Miami Herald*, March 13, 1988, pp. 1K, 5K.

Kramer, Margia. "Cracking the Concrete: Interventionist Posters." *Upfront*, no. 12–13 (1986): iii–vi.

Kunzle, David. "Public Graphics in Cuba: A Very Cuban Form of Internationalist Art." *Latin American Perspectives* 2, no. 4 (1975): 89–110.

Lippard, Lucy. "Made in U.S.A.: Art from Cuba." *Art in America*, April 1986, pp. 27–35.

Llanes, Llilian. "Cultural Policies in the Area of Professional Formation in the Visual Arts." Paper given at the UNESCO meeting, Caracas, November 1990.

Loeschner, Renate. "La presentación artística de Latinoamérica en el Siglo 19 bajo la influencia de Alexander von Humboldt." In *Artistas alemanes en Latinoamérica*, edited by Renate Loeschner, pp. 21–32. Berlin: Instituto Ibero-Americano Patrimonio Cultural Prusiano, 1978.

López Civeira, Francisca. *Historia de las relaciones de E.E.U.U. con Cuba: Selección de lecturas*. Havana: Ministerio de Educación Superior, 1985.

López Lemus, Víctor, ed. *Revolución, letras, arte*. Havana: Editorial Cubana, 1980.

López Núñez, Olga. *Asociación de grabadores de Cuba, 1949–1968*. Catalogue for an exhibit, Museo Nacional de Bellas Artes, Havana, March 1989.

López Oliva, Manuel. "Las artes plásticas de la Cuba de hoy." In *L'Arte con il Sorriso: Trenta artisti cubani di oggi*, edited by Giorgio Seveso and Manuel López Oliva, pp. 18–20. Milano: Vangelista Editori, 1986.

———. *Cuban Art: A Retrospective, 1930–1980*. Catalogue for an exhibit, the Signs Gallery, New York, January 1982.

López Ramos, Rafael. "La conciencia, el espíritu, el corazón del hombre." In catalogue of an exhibit of Rubén Torres Llorca, Galería Alberto Elía and Centro Cultural Recoleta, Buenos Aires, October–November 1990.

———. "Los más jóvenes exponen." Review of "1, 2, 3, . . . 11 y 12." *Revolución y Cultura*, no. 5, (May 1988): 74–75.

López Valdés, Rafael. *Componentes africanos en el etnos cubano.* Havana: Editorial de Ciencias Sociales, 1985.

Lucie-Smith, Edward. "A Background to Latin American Art." In *Art of the Fantastic: Latin America 1920–1987,* edited by Holiday T. Day and Hollister Sturges, pp. 19–24. Indianapolis: Indianapolis Museum of Art, 1987.

Marina, Sandra. "Pactos de la memoria." Review of Jesús de Armas. *Revolución y Cultura,* no. 7 (July 1987): 58–60.

Marques Ravelo, Bernardo. "I Have Been and Still Am a Dreamer." Review of Marcelo Pogolotti. *Granma Weekly Review,* June 21, 1987, p. 6.

Martí, José. *Cuba, nuestra América, los Estados Unidos.* Mexico City: Siglo XXI, 1973.

Martínez Arango, Felipe. *Cronología crítica de la guerra hispano cubanoamericana.* Havana: Editorial de Ciencias Sociales, 1973.

Matamoros Tuma, Corina. *De lo contemporáneo.* Catalogue for the exhibit (Bedia, Fors, Paciel, Pérez Monzón, Rodríguez Brey), Museo Nacional de Bellas Artes, Havana, August, 1985.

Medina, Alvaro. "Lam y Changó." Paper presented at the International Conference on Wifredo Lam, Havana, May 1984.

Memmi, Albert. *Retrato del colonizado.* Buenos Aires: Ediciones de la Flor, 1983.

Mena, Abelardo. "El objeto esculptorizado: reflexiones sobre la escultura de Alexis Somoza." Havana, 1989. Typescript.

Menéndez, Aldito. "La Revolución del arte y no el arte de la Revolución." Havana, 1988. Typescript.

———. "S.O.S. revolucionario." Havana, 1989. Typescript.

Menéndez, Aldo. Introduction to *Hacer arte a lo cubano.* Catalogue for an exhibit of Ciro Quintana, Centro Provincial de Artes Plásticas y Diseño, Havana, March 1989.

———. "Tonel Nacional." Introduction to *Clásicos de Tonel.* Catalogue for the exhibit, Galería L, Havana, March 1986; and Galería de Arte Minas de Matahambre, Pinar del Río, August 1986.

Merewether, Charles. *Made in Havana.* Catalogue for the exhibit, Art Gallery of New South Wales, New South Wales, Australia, October 1988.

Merino, Luz, Pilar Fernández, and Roberto Segre. "El Art-Deco en la Habana." Havana, 1987. Typescript.

Ministerio de Cultura, República de Cuba. *Documentos normativos para las Casas de Cultura.* Havana: Editorial Orbe, 1980.

———. *Instrucciones metodológicas, objetivos, funciones y funcionamientos y requisitos físico-ambientales de las galerías de arte.* 2 vol. Havana, 1988.

Miranda, Olivia. *Felix Varela: Su pensamiento político y su época.* Havana: Editorial de Ciencias Sociales, 1984.

Morais, Frederico. *4 artistas cubanos.* Rio de Janeiro: Realidade Galeria de Arte, 1987.

Moré de Castro, Marilú. *Panorama de la cultura cubana.* Havana: Editora Política, 1983.

Morejón, Nancy. "Manuel Mendive y el azoro." In *Para el ojo que mira de Manuel Mendive.* Catalogue for the exhibit, Museo Nacional de Bellas Artes, Havana, May 1987.

Mosquera, Gerardo. "Adriano Buergo." In *Roto*. Catalogue for the exhibit, Castillo de la Real Fuerza, Havana, June–July 1989.

———. "Africa en la plástica." *Cuba Internacional*, no. 10 (October 1986): 40–45.

———. "Art and Anthropology." *Granma Weekly Review*, April 15, 1984, p. 7.

———. "Arte con antropología." Review of José Bedia. *Revolución y Cultura*, no. 5 (May 1984): 80–81.

———. "Arte y filosofía en Arturo Cuenca." *Catalogue for the exhibition of Arturo Cuenca*, Galería de Arte Mexicano, Mexico City, 1990.

———. "Artista melodramático." In catalogue for an exhibit of Eduardo Ponjuán and René Francisco Rodríguez, Castillo de la Real Fuerza, Havana, September 1989.

———. "Bad Taste in Good Form." *Social Text* (Fall 1986): 54–64.

———. "Bedia: Tercer mundo y cultura occidental." *Brecha* (Montevideo), April 3, 1987, p. 28.

———. "La buena forma de las formas malas." In *Vereda Tropical*. Catalogue for the exhibit of Flavio Garciandía, Fondo Cubano de Bienes Culturales, Havana, November 1982.

———. "Carlos Rodríguez Cárdenas." In *Artista de Calidad*. Catalogue for the exhibit, Galería Habana, Havana, October 1988.

———. "Un cheo cultivado." Review of "Tonel." *Revolución y Cultura*, no. 4 (April 1986): 82–83.

———. "Los chistes pesados de Tonel." *Revolución y Cultura*, no. 8 (August 1989): 52–55.

———. *Cine del hogar*. Catalogue for an exhibit of Rubén Torres Llorca, Galería Habana, Havana, April 1983.

———. "The Conflict of Being Updated." In *New Art from Cuba*, pp. 44–46. Catalogue of an exhibit, Amelie Wallace Gallery, State University of New York, 1985.

———. "Crítica social en la plástica cubana." *Brecha* (Montevideo), December 9, 1988, p. 25.

———. *Crónicas Americanas III*. Catalogue for an exhibit of José Bedia, Centro Wifredo Lam, Havana, 1987.

———. *Cuatro*. Catalogue for the exhibit of Bedia, Pérez Monzón, Rodríguez Brey, and Torres Llorca, Fondo Cubano de Bienes Culturales, Havana, July 1982.

———. "Cuatro que van bien." *La Nueva Gaceta* (Havana), 1983, p. 6.

———. "Cuba: Young Painting." Poster/brochure. Havana: Dirección de Artes Plásticas y Diseño, Ministerio de Cultura, 1981.

———. *El diseño se definió en octubre*. Havana: Editorial Arte y Literatura, 1989.

———. *Ensayo sobre América*. Catalogue for an exhibit of Elso Padilla, Casa Cultura Plaza, Havana, March 1986.

———. "Essay on Raúl Martínez." In *Nosotros*. Catalogue for the exhibit of Martínez, Museo Nacional de Bellas Artes, Havana, July–September 1988.

———. *Esson*. Catalogue for the exhibit "A tarro partido," Museo Provincial de Villa Clara, Santa Clara, February 1987.

———. "Etica, kitsch, sexo y fantasía." *Imagen* (Caracas), November 1987.

———. *Exploraciones en la plástica cubana.* Havana: Editorial Letras Cubanas, 1983.

———. "The 14 Sons of William Tell." In *No Man Is an Island: Young Cuban Art,* edited by Marketta Seppälä, pp. 42–49. Catalogue for the exhibit, Pori Art Museum, Pori, Finland: May 1990.

———. "La fuerza de Elso." *Revolución y Cultura,* no. 4, (April 1986): 58–61.

———. "Función social de nuestra plástica." *El Caimán Barbudo,* July 1985, pp. 11–12.

———. "Identidad y cultura popular en el nuevo arte cubano." Typescript. Havana, 1987.

———. "Una irrupción revitalizadora." *Cuba Internacional,* no. 6 (June 1985): 42–49.

———. "Kubas bildende Kunst in einem neuen Jahrhundert." In *Kuba o.k.,* edited by Jürgen Harten and Antonio Eligio (Tonel), pp. 12–17. Catalogue for the exhibit, Städtische Kunsthalle, Düsseldorf, 1990.

———. "Una manito que le falta un dedo." *Revolución y Cultura,* no. 10 (October 1986).

———. "Mito, concepto y poesía en Brey." *Brecha* (Montevideo), January 29, 1988, p. 24.

———. "El mito por dentro." Review of Manuel Mendive. *Revolución y Cultura,* no. 8 (August 1987): 47–48.

———. "Mitología y vulgaridad." *Revolución y Cultura,* no. 9 (September 1986): 77–78.

———. "Nueva visión del paisaje cubano. *Brecha* (Montevideo), July 24, 1987, p. 28.

———. "Panfletos de Moya." *Revolución y Cultura,* no. 5 (May 1988): 16–19.

———. "La persistencia del uso." Text for catalogue for the exhibit of José Bedia, Museo Nacional de Bellas Artes, Havana, March 1984.

———. *Pinturas, dibujos, fotografías e instalaciones de: Rubén Torres Llorca, Katia García Fayad, Luis Gómez Armenteros, Abdel Hernández San Juan.* Catalogue for the exhibit, Museo Provincial de Villa Clara, October 1986.

———. "Sánchez Vázquez: Marxismo y abstracción." *Temas,* no. 9 (1986): 23–37.

———. "Sano y sabroso." Flyer for the exhibit, Centro de Arte 23 y 12, Havana, August 1981.

———. "Seis nuevos pintores." Text for catalogue of the exhibit by Bedia, Elso, Fors, Pérez Monzón, Rodríguez Brey, and Torres Llorca, Havana, 1978.

———. "Six New Cuban Artists." In *Contemporary Art from Cuba.* Catalogue for the exhibit of Bedia, Campos, Castañeda, Esson, Franco, and Garciandía, Riverside Studios, London; and Museo de Arte Contemporáneo, Sevilla, 1989–1990.

———. "Tendencias metropolitanas y arte en Cuba." *Brecha* (Montevideo), January 8, 1988, p. 25.

———. "Tierra, maíz, vida." Text for catalogue of the exhibit of Juan Francisco Elso, Casa Cultura Plaza, Havana, 1982.

———. "Tomás Esson: Mitología y vulgaridad." *Brecha* (Montevideo), May 29, 1987, p. 28.

————. "Tonel." Introduction to *Yo lo que quiero es ser feliz*. Catalogue for the exhibit, Castillo de la Real Fuerza, Havana, July 1989.

————. *Trece artistas jóvenes*. Havana: Departamento de Cultura, Universidad de la Habana, 1981.

————. "Trece criterios sobre el nuevo arte cubano." *La Gaceta de Cuba*, June 1989, p. 24.

————. "Tres visiones del héroe." *Granma Weekly Review*, May 14, 1987, p. 5.

————. "Visiones posmodernas de 2º Planes." *Huella* (Santa Clara), August 1987, p. 3.

————. "*Volumen Uno*." Text for catalogue for the exhibit, Centro de Arte Internacional, Havana, 1981.

Moya, Ramón. *Moya antimperialista*. Text for catalogue for the exhibit, Galería Centro Wifredo Lam, Havana, December 1987.

Moya, Rogerio. "The Reality and Dreams of Arturo Cuenca." *Granma Weekly Review*, September 23, 1984, p. 9.

Muller, Marion. "Chinese Paper Gems." *Upper & Lower Case*, February 1988, p. 32.

Murray, James. "How the Leopard Gets Its Spots." *Scientific American*, March 1988, pp. 80–87.

The Nation. Learning to Deal with Cuba. Special issue, October 24, 1988.

Navarrete, José Antonio, and Ramón Vázquez Díaz. "En torno al surgimiento del arte moderno en Cuba." In *La vanguardia: Surgimiento del arte moderno en Cuba*. Catalogue for the exhibit, Museo Nacional de Bellas Artes, Havana, December 1988–January 1989.

Navarro, Desiderio. *Cultura y Marxismo: Problemas y polémicas*. Havana: Editorial de Letras Cubanas, 1986.

————. "La retroabstracción geométrica: Un arte sin problemas: Es sólo lo que ves." *La Gaceta de Cuba*, June 1989, pp. 22–23.

Navarro Padrón, Raúl. "La investigación y la producción artística y sus relaciones con las necesidades culturales del país. Experiencias de la Facultad de Artes Plásticas del Instituto Superior de Arte." Paper presented at the First Latin American Meeting on the Teaching of Plastic Arts, Universidad Autónoma de Mexico, Mexico City, November 1981.

Nepomuceno, Eric. "La caza del dólar en Cuba." *Brecha* (Montevideo), September 22, 1989, p. 31.

The News (Mexico City). "Cuban Unemployment at 6 %." January 6, 1989, p. 35.

Nordheimer, John. "Arts Exhibit Dispute Splits Miami Cubans." *New York Times*, May 18, 1988, p. A14.

Novoa, Glexis. *To Be or Not to Be*. Text for catalogue for the exhibit, Galería Habana, Havana, November 1988.

Nuñez Oliva, Alexis. "Jóvenes creadores en 23 y G." *Juventud Rebelde*, April 6, 1988.

Nussa, Ele. "De la vulgaridad." *Bohemia*, April 29, 1983, p. 25.

Oliva, Milagros, and Cino Colina. "The Yoruba Religion in Cuba." *Granma Weekly Review*, May 1, 1988, pp. 2–3.

Padilla, Heberto. "Autocrítica." *Cuba: Nueva política cultural, el caso Padilla*. Cuadernos de Marcha (Montevideo), no. 49 (May 1971): 11–18.

Palmer, Rodney. "Aspects of René Portocarrero's Work." *Granma Weekly Review*, February 1988, p. 8.

———. "The Magic of Mendive Takes London's Fancy." *Granma Weekly Review*, March 13, 1988, p. 6.

Papanek, Victor. *Design for the Real World*. Toronto: Bantam Books, 1973.

Patiño, Adolfo. *Remedio para el mal de ojo*. Catalogue for an exhibit of Rubén Torres Llorca, Galería Diego Leño, Xalapa, July 1985.

Pensamiento Crítico (Havana), no. 39 (April 1970). Issue with Cuban documents from 1923 to 1935.

Perez-Stable, Marifeli. "Castro Takes the Economy in Hand." *The Nation*, September 26, 1987, pp. 298–300.

Petras, James. "Amigos distanciados." *Brecha* (Montevideo), January 17, 1991.

———. "Las transformaciones globales y el futuro del socialismo en América Latina." *Brecha* (Montevideo), April 20, 1990, pp. 15–18.

Pichardo Viñals, Hortensia. *La actitud estudiantil en Cuba durante el siglo XIX*. Havana: Editorial de Ciencias Sociales, 1983.

———. *Documentos para la historia de Cuba*. 4 vols. Havana: Editorial Pueblo y Educación, 1984–1986.

Piñera, Toni. "In Black and White." Interview with Humberto Castro. *Granma Weekly Review*, October 14, 1984.

Pisani, Francis. "La rectificación cubana." *Nexos* (Mexico), no. 119, (November 1987): 51–59.

Pogolotti, Graziella. "Raúl Martínez: El arte como exploración sentimental." In *Oficio de leer*, edited by Virgilio López Lemus, pp. 56–59. Havana: Editorial Letras Cubanas, 1983.

Política Actual, Equipo editor de. *Vindicación de Cuba*. Havana: Editora Política, 1989.

Portuondo, José Antonio. *Ensayos de estética y de teoría literaria*. Havana: Editorial Letras Cubanas, 1986.

———. "Itinerario estético de la revolución cubana." In *Revolución, letras, arte*, edited by Víctor López Lemus, pp. 160–187. Havana: Editorial Letras Cubanas, 1980.

Rama, Angel. *La ciudad letrada*. Hanover, New Hampshire: Ediciones del Norte, 1984.

———. "Una nueva política cultural en Cuba." *Cuba: Nueva política cultural, el caso Padilla*. Cuadernos de Marcha (Montevideo), no. 49 (May 1971): 47–68.

Ribeiro, Darcy. *La universidad latinoamericana*. Montevideo: Universidad de la República, 1968.

Ricardo, José. *La imprenta en Cuba*. Havana: Editorial Letras Cubanas, 1989.

Richmond, Mark. "Education and Revolution in Socialist Cuba: The Problem of Democratization." In *Education in Latin America*, edited by Colin Brook and Hugh Lawlor, pp. 9–49. London: Croom Helm, 1985.

Rigol, Jorge. "La Academia de San Alejandro." In *Revolución, letras, arte*, edited by Víctor López Lemus, pp. 506–526. Havana: Editorial Letras Cubanas, 1980.

———. "*Apuntes sobre el grabado y la pintura en Cuba.*" In *Panorama de la cultura cubana*, edited by Marilú Moré de Castro, pp. 111–156. Havana: Editora Política, 1983.

———. *Apuntes sobre la pintura y el grabado en Cuba*. Havana: Editorial Letras Cubanas, 1982.

Rodríguez, Carlos Rafael. *Cuba en el tránsito al socialismo (1959–1963)*. Mexico City: Siglo XXI, 1978.

———. "Félix Varela." *Granma Weekly Review*, April 10, 1988, p. 2.

———. *Letras con filo*. Havana: Editorial de Ciencias Sociales, 1983–1987.

———. "Problemas del arte en la Revolución." In *Revolución, letras, arte*, edited by Víctor López Lemus, pp. 49–85. Havana: Ediciones Letras Cubanas, 1980.

———. "Toward Culture through the Revolution." *Granma Weekly Review*, February 14, 1988, p. 7.

Rodríguez, Robaldo. Untitled Master's thesis, ISA, Havana, 1988.

Rodríguez Cárdenas, Carlos. *Artista de calidad*. Catalogue for the exhibit, Galería Habana, Havana, 1988.

———. "Pero se mueve." In *To Be or Not to Be*. Catalogue for an exhibit of Glexis Novoa, Galería Habana, Havana, November 1988.

Rodríguez de Armas, José Luis. "Un intento de desacralización." *Vanguardia* (Havana), November 1, 1987.

Rojas, Rafael. "La metáfora del conocimiento." In *Ciencia e ideología*. Catalogue for an exhibit of Arturo Cuenca, Castillo de la Real Fuerza, Havana, 1989.

Roque, Adalberto. "Mirar y ver más allá." *El Caimán Barbudo*, July 1988, pp. 4–7, and August 1988, pp. 2–4.

Rubio, Vladia. "Nuestra plástica joven: Diálogo o monólogo?" *Granma Weekly Review*, April 14, 1988.

Ruiz, Albor, and Rodolfo Quebleen. "Entrevista con Carlos Aldana." *El Diario–La Prensa* (New York), Part 1, January 1, 1989; Part 2, January 8, 1989.

Salcedo, Benjamin. "Humor." *Revolución y Cultura*, no. 9 (September 1988): 61–63.

Sánchez, Juan. "Escudo ideológico y moral." Interview with Armando Hart. *Bohemia*, October 20, 1989, pp. 4–10.

Sánchez, Osvaldo. "Children of Utopia." In *No Man Is an Island: Young Cuban Art*, edited by Marketta Seppälä, pp. 57–59. Catalogue for the exhibit, Museum of Pori, Pori, Finland, May 1990.

———. "Elogio de Poncio Pilato." *El Caimán Barbudo*, June 1988, pp. 16–17.

———. *El Espectador*. Catalogue for an exhibit of Arturo Cuenca, Museo Nacional de Bellas Artes, Havana, July 1983.

———. "La llama de la parodia." *El Caimán Barbudo*, April 1988, pp. 2–4.

———. *Programa de segundo año, especialidad de pintura*. Havana: Instituto Superior de Arte, 1990.

———. "Synkretismus, Postmodernismus und Kultur des Widerstandes." In *Kuba o.k.*, edited by Jürgen Harten and Antonio Eligio (Tonel), pp. 18–26.

Catalogue for the exhibit, Städtische Kunsthalle, Düsseldorf, April 1990.

Sánchez Vázquez, Adolfo. *Art and Society: Essays in Marxist Aesthetics.* New York: Monthly Review Press, 1973.

———. *Estética y Marxismo.* Mexico City: Ediciones Era, 1970.

Sarusky, Jaime. "Un gran reto, que nos conozcan internacionalmente." Interview with Roberto Fabelo. *Revolución y Cultura,* no. 5 (May 1984): 51–55.

———. "I Believe in the Will to Create." Interview with René Portocarrero. *Granma Weekly Review,* April 21, 1985, p. 12.

———. "La magia y los sueños." Interview with Manuel Mendive. *Revolución y Cultura,* no. 8 (August 1987): 40–46.

Segre, Roberto. "El significado de Cuba en la cultura arquitectónica contemporánea." *Cuadernos Summa-Nueva Visión: Arquitectura Cubana,* no. 46/47 (March 1970): 3–18.

———. "6 preguntas a José Joaquín Brunner." *Revista de Crítica Cultural,* no. 1 (May 1990): 21.

Seoane Gallo, José. *Eduardo Abela cerca del cerco.* Havana: Editorial Letras Cubanas, 1986.

———. *Palmas reales en el Sena.* Havana: Editorial Letras Cubanas, 1987.

Seppälä, Marketta, ed. *No Man Is an Island: Young Cuban Art.* Catalogue for the exhibit, Pori Art Museum, Pori, Finland, May 1990.

Shiskova, Albena. "Jesús de Armas: La conciencia de un continente." In *Humor con risa, humor sonrisa.* Catalogue for the exhibit, Galería Centro Wifredo Lam, Havana, November 1987.

Shorris, Earl. "Confiscating Cuban Art." *The Nation,* July 3, 1989, pp. 14–18.

Shriver, Maria. "Interview with Fidel Castro." *Granma Weekly Review,* supplement, March 13, 1988, pp. 1–12.

"Sinkendes Kulturgut." *Der Spiegel,* no. 4 (1988): 199–201.

Smorkaloff, Pamela María. *Literatura y edición de libros.* Havana: Editorial Letras Cubanas, 1987.

Somoza, Alexis. "Creo que toda actitud tiene sentido." Havana, August 1987. Typescript.

———. *Formas bajo la luz.* Catalogue for an exhibit, Havana, 1987.

———. "La individualidad artística en la sociedad socialista." Havana, 1987. Typescript.

———. "La materia con que pensamos es el lenguaje." Havana, n.d. Manuscript.

Soto, Leandro. "Así es como es." Text for catalogue for the exhibit, Galería Habana, Havana, July 1986.

———. "La historia como material artístico." In *Retablo Familiar.* Catalogue for the exhibit. Casa de la Cultura de Plaza, Havana, April 1984.

Stavrianos, L. S. *Global Rift: The Third World Comes of Age.* New York: William Morrow and Co., 1981.

Stermer, Dugald. "The Agit Pop Art of Cuba." *Ramparts* 7, no. 9 (December 14–27, 1968): 30–36.

Stubbs, Jeane. *Cuba: The Test of Time.* London: Latin America Bureau, 1989.

Suárez Suárez, Orlando. "Características de las enseñanzas de las artes plásticas en el nivel superior de Cuba." Paper presented at the Primer Encuentro Latinoamericano sobre la Enseñanza de las Artes Plásticas, UNAM, Mexico City, November 1981.

———. *La Jaula Invisible*. Havana: Editorial de Ciencias Sociales, 1986.

Szulc, Tad. *Fidel: A Critical Portrait*. New York: Avon Books, 1987.

Tamargo González, Jorge. "De la arquitectura en el Caribe hacia la arquitectura del Caribe." Paper presented at the International Conference on Visual Arts of the Caribbean, Havana, November 1986.

Tasalov, V. "Diez años del problema de 'lo estético,' (1956–1966)." In *Problemas de la teoría del arte*, edited by Victor Ivanov, vol. 2, pp. 306–384. Havana: Editorial Arte y Literatura, 1980.

Tercer Forum Nacional, "Fabricación y recuperación de piezas de repuesto. *Memorias*, pp. 30–33. Havana: Tercer Forum Nacional, March 23–25, 1986.

Tiscornia, Ana. "Que no se pierda ningún talento." Interview with Gerardo Mosquera. *Brecha* (Montevideo), January 16, 1987, p. 24.

———. "Sonrisas en la selva." Interview with José Franco. *Brecha* (Montevideo), June 3, 1988, p. 24.

Toirac, José Angel. "Grabado sobre grabado." Havana, 1987. Typescript.

———. *Scènes pittoresques*. Program for a concert. Havana, 1988.

Tomás, Angel. "Almuerzo para U. Peña." *Juventud Rebelde*, June 15, 1988.

———. "Desafío en San Rafael." *El Caimán Barbudo*, March 1981, pp. 7, 27.

———. "Ni sano ni sabroso." *El Caimán Barbudo*, November 1981, pp. 6–7, 26–27.

———. "Paisaje del peligro." Interview with Tomás Sánchez. *Juventud Rebelde*, 1988, p. 11.

Torres-Cuevas, Eduardo, and Eusebio Reyes. *Esclavitud y sociedad*. Havana: Editorial de Ciencias Sociales, 1986.

Torres Llorca, Rubén. *Estrictamente personal*. Flyer for the exhibit, Fototeca de Cuba, Havana, 1987.

———. *Una mirada retrospectiva*. Flyer for an exhibit with Lázaro Saavedra, Fototeca de Cuba, Havana, 1989.

———. "Ojos para ver." In *Dentro del labio*. Catalogue for the exhibit with Ana Albertina Delgado, Castillo de la Real Fuerza, Havana, June–July 1989.

———. "Qué importa una raya más en el tigre?" In *Hacer Arte a lo Cubano*. Catalogue for the exhibit of Ciro Quintana, Centro Provincial de Artes Plásticas y Diseño, Havana, March 1989.

Tronche, Anne. "Jesús de Armas" *Opus International* (Paris), no. 101 (Spring–Summer 1986): 32–35.

UNEAC. "Declaración conjunta de la UNEAC y la Asociación Hermanos Saíz." *Juventud Rebelde*, November 10, 1988.

———. *Informe central*. Havana: IV Congreso, 1988.

Van Aken, Mark. *Los militantes*. Montevideo: Fundación de Cultura Universitaria, 1990.

Veigas, José. *Crónicas Americanas II*. Catalogue for an exhibit of José Bedia, Havana, n.d.

———. "Estas láminas dicen mucho." *Revolución y Cultura* (August 1974): 30–35.

———. "La mujer en la plástica cubana." *Revolución y Cultura*, no. 10 (October 1974): 21–31.

———. "Nuestra pintura joven." *El Caimán Barbudo*, September 1979.

———. "La realidad y el recuerdo." Interview with Raúl Martínez. *Revolución y Cultura*, no. 10 (October 1978): 36–40.

Vindicación de Cuba. Havana: Editora Política, 1989.

Vitier, Cintio. "Apuntes para el encuentro de intelectuales por la soberanía de los pueblos de nuestra América." In *Ponencias: I encuentro de intelectuales por la soberanía de los pueblos de nuestra América*, edited by Reynaldo González, pp. 286–289. Havana: Casa de las Américas, 1985.

Wadler, Joyce. "A Death in Art." *New York*, December 16, 1985, pp. 38–46.

Wilkerson, Isabel. "Veterans Protest Flag Exhibit at Art Institute." *New York Times*, March 2, 1989, p. A19.

Williams, Eric. *Capitalism and Slavery*. London: Andre Deutsch, 1964.

Wood, Yolanda. *De la plástica cubana y caribeña*. Havana: Editorial de Letras Cubanas, 1990.

Zis, Avner. "Los caminos para la investigación de la naturaleza del arte." In *Problemas de la teoría del arte*, edited by Victor Ivanov, vol. 1, pp. 154–173. Havana: Editorial Arte y Literatura, 1980.

———. "Los epígonos de la estética burguesa." In *La lucha de las ideas en la estética*, edited by Luis Toledo Sande, pp. 512–547. Havana: Editorial Arte y Literatura, 1983.

———. *Fundamentos de estética Marxista*. Moscow: Editorial Raduga, 1976.

INDEX

Abakuá, 302, 362n.5
Abela, Eduardo, 69, 103, 133, 339nn.5,
6; and Estudio Libre, 154–155
Abstract expressionism, 108
ABTV, 188, 190, 251–255, 322; and
Raúl Martínez, 194, 252, 360n.39;
and burning of piece by Mendive,
254; and José Angel Toirac, 282; and
censorship, 328
Academia de San Alejandro, 101, 153,
155, 167, 198, 238; women in, 161;
resentment against, 187
Acosta Pérez, Gustavo, 264–266
Acuña, Rodolfo, 338n.19
Aesthetics theory in Cuba, 125–127;
as a discipline, 135–136
Afro-Cubanism, 122, 307; in Cuban
art, 17, 35–60, 302; and Ana Mendieta, 94; and Magdalena Campos,
211–215; Cuban government policy
regarding, 357n.9
Aguilera, Alejandro, 201, 274, 323; and
organization of exhibits, 196, 264;
and nationalism in Cuban art,
260–264; Christian symbolism in,
260–261
Aguirre, Mirta, 343n.43
Ahuehuete tree, 56

AIR (Artists in Residence Coopera-
tive, New York), 91
Alcántara, Pedro, 163
Aldana, Carlos: on the role of the
Communist Party in art, 130; on
"rectification," 165; and UNEAC,
193; on artistic responsibility, 322
Alfonso, Carlos José: exhibition of, 2
Alonso, Alejandro G., 3
Alonso, José Luis, 221
Alvarez, Santiago, and testimonial
art, 9
American Academy Fellowship in
Rome, 92
Americanism, in Cuban art, 17, 51
Amerindians, 18, 35; influences in
work of José Bedia, 44; influences in
work of Elso Padilla, 55–56
Andre, Carl, 93
Angulo, Tanya, 177, 188, 282; and
Pérez Monzón, 67; and ABTV, 251,
255
ANIR (National Association of Inno-
vators and Rationalizers), 303–304,
306; purpose of, xxv; and postmod-
ernism, 314–315
Annexationists, 146
Arciaga, Romero, 155

387

Arenas, Néstor, 290
Arias, Constantino, 315
Armada, Santiago. *See* Chago
Art education in Cuba, xxx, 138–171
Arte Calle (Street Art), 30, 129, 178,
  171–184, 186, 198; and UNEAC,
  177; and Grupo Provisional, 178,
  180
Arte en la Fábrica (Art in the Factory),
  116; and Grupo Hexágono, 175
Arte Povera, 271
Artex, 164, 331 n.7
Asociación Brigadas Hermanos Saiz,
  188, 355 n.18
Asociación de Pintores y Escultores,
  153
Aulet, Beatriz, 331, 361 n.55

Balla, Giacomo, 14
Ballester, Juan Pablo, 176–177, 188;
  and ABTV, 251, 255
Balthus, 308
Barnet, Miguel, and testimonial litera-
  ture, 9
Batista, Fulgencio, 90, 108, 253; impact
  of regime in Cuban design, xxv
Bauhaus, 150, 151, 156
Bedia, José, 15, 16, 99, 172, 330 n.5; and
  "Six New Painters" 1–2; and "Volumen I," 3; and Afro-Cubanism,
  17, 41–46; exhibitions of, 41, 44, 46;
  and issues of audience, 118; on Cuban art, 135; and hyperrealism, 168;
  and the ISA, 173
Beuys, Joseph, 44; influence of, on Cuban art, 29; in work of Rubén Torres
  Llorca and Lázaro Saavedra, 194
Bienal Hispano-Americana, 108
Biennial of Havana, 88, 136, 286; organization of, 120; and art education,
  163; and Rodríguez Cárdenas, 239;
  aims and functions of, 317, 319; and
  censorship, 328
—First (1984), 19, 20, 32, 44, 56, 118,
  120

—Second (1986), 22, 24, 46, 56, 115,
  118, 120, 182, 206, 264, 267, 338 n.22
—Third (1989), 35, 46, 50, 120, 121,
  209, 235, 296, 317, 347 n.63
—Fourth (1991), 221, 325, 327
Blanco, Rafael, 69, 101
Blockade, of cuba by U.S., xxx, 298,
  314, 351 n.54
Boán, Marianela, 314
Bogdanov, Vassilij I., 169
Bolívar, Simón, 142; in the work of
  Elso Padilla, 59
Borges, Jacobo, 266
Borofsky, Jonathan, 187; and Grupo
  Puré, 186; and Segundo Planes, 276
Borrero, Juana, 161
Bourgeois: humanism, 11; aesthetics,
  100
Breder, Hans, and Ana Mendieta, 90,
  94
Breton, André, 343 n.43; on Mexican
  art, 270–271
Bruguera, Tania, 194, 326
Buchloh, Benjamin, 135
Buergo, Adriano, 185, 194, 293, 296,
  305; and kitsch, 296
Buses project, 197–198

Cabrera Infante, Guillermo, 108
Cabrera Moreno, Servando, 156, 309
Cage, John, 282
Caibarién, 81
Camelot Program, 142
Campos, Magdalena, 173, 215, 323;
  exhibitions of, 211; and Afro-
  Cubanism, 211–215
Capelán, Carlos, 163, 286
CAPS (Creative Arts Program Ser-
  vices, New York), 92
Cardoza y Aragón, Luis, 149
Carnicer, Ramón, 141
Carol, Alberto Jorge, 156, 159,
  350 n.50. *See also* Grupo Escambray
Carpentier, Alejo, 104
Casa de las Américas, 82, 88, 127–128,

133, 258; events sponsored by, 6; and testimonial literature, 9; and Umberto Peña, 85; and poster art, 109; and Telarte, 115; and alternative art education, 161; and Heberto Padilla, 344 n.47; and UMAP, 345 n.48

Casa del Joven Creador (House of the Young Creator), 186

Casas de Cultura (Houses of Culture), 167, 168, 170

Castañeda, Consuelo, 173, 179, 270–274, 322; as a teacher, 188; influence on other artists, 193, 222, 273; and ABTV, 194, 251

Castillo, Marcos, 327

Castillo, Nilo, 194; and Proyecto Pilón, 196

Castillo de la Real Fuerza (Castle of the Royal Force), 133, 188, 196, 231, 254, 279, 322; exhibitions in, xxix; and Arturo Cuenca, 207; and ABTV, 252, 255; and Ponjuán and Rodríguez, 258

Castro, Fidel, 76, 146, 261, 346 n.54, 347 n.65, 351–352 n.58; on artistic freedom and individualism, xxviii, 108, 125, 129–130, 336 n.57; images of, in Cuban art, 35, 250, 253, 258, 289; on property, 60; on "rectification" campaign, 125; influence of, on Cuban art, 125–126, 137; and Heberto Padilla, 126; and education, 161, 166, 352 n.63; criticism of, in *Moscow News*, 321; on art and profits, 343 n.42; and UMAP, 345 n.48; and *P.M.*, 346 n.57; on Soviet issues, 347 n.62, 365 n.3; on copyright, 351 n.54; on bureaucracy, 352 n.61

Castro, Humberto, 173, 266–270

Catasú, Lirca, 198

CDR (Comité de Defensa de la Revolución): and Antonia Eiriz, 68; and Cuban art, 73, 76, 77

Censorship, 2, 14, 171, 195, 327–328; and self-censorship, xxix, 127, 132; and Cuban art, 129–133, 317–318; and Ponjuán and Rodríguez, 258

Center for the Development of the Visual Arts (Centro de Desarrollo de las Artes Visuales), 361 n.55

Centro Wifredo Lam, 49, 121, 161–162, 331 n.7

Chago (Santiago Armada), 69, 70, 222, 309

Che Guevara, 76, 79, 113, 127, 137, 138, 337 n.8, 342 n.39, 350 n.52; and testimonial literature, 9; images of, in Cuban art, 76, 207, 226, 230–231, 251, 254, 261, 270, 289, 337 n.6; on dogmatism in art, 123–124; and moral incentive theory, 165, 351 n.55; uses of portrait of, 177, 184, 187, 188; and fetishism in Cuban art, 192; in the writing of Aldito Menéndez, 199; public events and works in honor of, 221, 330 n.6; and the origins of the ANIR, 305

Chinese labor, 36

Christianity: and Cuban slaves, 36–37; symbols of, in Cuban art, 260–261, 302

Ciboney, 35

Cienfuegos, Camilo, 350 n.43

Close, Chuck, 14

Coca-Cola bottles, 303

College at Old Westbury (SUNY), 330 n.5, 341 n.38

College at Purchase (SUNY), 330 n.5

Colonialism and art, 140–141

Columbus, 35, 46

Comisión de Orientación Revolucionaria (COR), 87, 337 n.15

Comité de Defensa de la Revolución (Committee for the Defense of the Revolution). *See* CDR

Commerce, in Cuban art, 253–255, 298, 327

Commission for Revolutionary Orientation. *See* Comisión de Orientación Revolucionaria

Communist Party of Cuba, 108, 114, 235, 345–346 n.50, 351 n.57; position on art of the First Congress of, 10; challenged by newer artists of the 1980s, 177; and Glexis Novoa, 235; logo of, 253; First Congress of, 305

Conceptualism (in art), 5, 271, 274, 279–280, 282

Congress for Education and Culture, First National, 343 n.46, 344 n.47

Congress of Students in Cuba, First National, 143, 146–147

Consejo Nacional de Cultura (National Council of Culture), 128

Consejo Nacional de Desarrollo de la Escultura (National Council for the Development of Sculpture), 164

Convention of Innovators and Inventors, 305

Copyright, 163, 351 n.54

COR. *See* Comisión de Orientación Revolucionaria

Córdoba, Reform of, 142–144, 146, 147; impact on education in Cuba, 144

Crespo, Jorge, 187

Criterios magazine, 123

Cuadrodebate, 350 n.50. *See also* Carol; García Miló; Grupo Escambray

Cuban art: generations in, xxviii, xxx, 27, 172–176, 190; and Western modernism, 4; influences on, 10; content orientation in , 17; poster tradition in, 73, 88; function of, 81; criticism, 122; quality of, in international exhibitions, 136–137; and art market, 160; women in, 161; impact of urbanization on, 167; and socialism, 169; commerce and, 254–255, 341–342 n.29; production of, 298–299; as art "on the periphery," 299–300;

and the absence of Soviet socialist realism, 301–302; eclecticism in, 305–307; and functionalism, 310–311; as alternative to the capitalist model, 318; and individualism and collective responsibility, 318

Cubanía (Cubanism), 219, 255

Cuban Institute for Cinematographic Art and Industry. *See* ICAIC

Cuban Revolution, and art, 190

Cuenca, Arturo, 16–17, 132, 202–203, 274, 357 nn.2, 4; on art and revolution, 135; influence on younger artists, 179, 193; and kitsch, 202–208; and nationalism, 204; exhibits of, 204, 207; on fashion, 205; and Biennial of Havana, 206

Cuyas, Francisco Camilo, 153

de Andrade, Oswald, 361 n.3

de Arango y Gómez del Castillo, José, 146

de Armas, Jesús, 70

De Chirico, Giorgio, 308

Deira, Ernesto, 266

de Juan, Adelaida, 101

de la Cal, Fransisco (creation of Fernando Rodríguez), 289

de la Fuente, Jorge, 131

de la Guardia, Tony, 365 n.20

de Landa y Escandón, William, 141

Delarra, José, 330 n.6

del Cioppo, Atahualpa, 141

Delgado, Ana Albertina, 185, 293

del Río, Zaida, 161

del Sol, Dania, 282–286, 323, 361 n.56

Desnoes, Edmundo, 108

Diago, Roberto, 107

Díaz de Espada y Landa, Juan José, 37, 145, 153, 350 n.38

Díaz Gutiérrez, Alberto (Korda), 188, 254

Diego, Eliseo, 107

Dubuffet, Jean, 16

Duchamp, Marcel, 280, 282, 312
Durham, Jimmy, 335n.42

Eclecticism, 326, 364–365n.17; in art "on the periphery," 301; in Cuban art, 305–307, 314; in the West, 307
Eco, Umberto, 312
Education, development of, before the Revolution, 144–148
Eiriz, Antonia, 77, 161, 168, 169, 309; government restrictions on 10; influence on younger artists, 68; and the ENA, 156
El Caimán Barbudo, 4, 131
Elemental de 23 y C (School), 159–160
Elizondo, Sebastián, 173
Elpidio Valdés, 22
Elso Padilla, Juan Francisco, 17, 50, 99, 336nn.48, 53, 54, 56; and "Six New Painters," 1–2; in "Volumen I," 9; exhibitions of, 15, 51, 55, 56, 58; evolution of, 16; on aesthetic issues, 50–52; and Ricardo Rodríguez Brey, 50, 56; and José Martí, 52, 56, 58, 60; and *Santería*, 52, 56–58, 336n.55; and Ana Mendieta, 52; Amerindian influences on, 56
Embargo of Cuba by the United States, 126, 327
ENA (Escuela Nacional de Arte), 68, 81, 155, 167, 342–343n.39; Soviet influence on, 159, 168; graduates of, 255
Enríquez, Carlos, 105
Equipo Crónica, 255
Escalante, Aníbal, 130
Escobar, Vicente, 334n.36
Escuela de San Alejandro. *See* Academia de San Alejandro
Escuela Nacional de Arte. *See* ENA
Espada y Landa. *See* Díaz de Espada y Landa
Esson, Tomás, 131, 226, 229, 230, 236, 322, 323, 328; work of, with Ponjuán and Rodríguez, 190; and censorship, 196, 227, 231, 264, 359n.29; and nationalism, 225–231; exhibits of, 231, 359–360n.29
Estudio Libre (Free Studio), 154–155, 156
Europe, Cuban artists in, 105
Exhibitions, of Cuban art in Cuba: "Volumen I," xxviii, 15, 16, 32, 35, 41, 103, 279, 290, 321, 327, 342n.35; semiprivate, in Fors' house, 2; "Pintura Fresca" (1979), 2–3; "Salón Paisaje," 175. *See also* Biennial of Havana; individual artists
Exhibitions, of Cuban art outside Cuba, 121, 255, 286, 323, 330n.5. *See also* individual artists
Exposición de Arte Nuevo (1927), 3, 4, 103, 153
Expressionism, 266. *See also* Abstract Expressionism

Fahlstrom, Ovynd, 360n.34
FCBC. *See* Fondo Cubano de Bienes Culturales
Feltrinelli, Giangiacomo, 188, 254
Fernández, Antonio Eligio (Tonel), 173, 222, 241; on Umberto Peña, 86; and nationalism, 222; and Carlos Rodríguez Cárdenas, 240; on Tomás Esson's painting of Che, 359n.27
Fernández Retamar, Roberto, 85, 345n.48
"Festival of the Short Piece" (1980), 15
Finalé, Moisés de los Santos, 173
Fischel, Eric, 327
Fisher, Ernst, 127, 277
Fondo Cubano de Bienes Culturales (Cuban Cultural Goods Fund), 117, 119, 164, 234, 360n.39; and ABTV, 252
Fong, Flora, 161
Ford Foundation, 330n.5
Fornet, Ambrosio, 108
Fors, José Manuel, 1–3

France, influence of, on Latin American culture, 149
Franco, Francisco, 108
Franco Codinach, José, 173, 208–209; on younger artists in the 1980s, 175
Franqui, Carlos, 108
French Academy, 149, 151, 153
Frómeta, Alejandro, 196
Functionalism, and Cuban art, 310–311

Galleries, in Cuba, 120, 327
Garaudy, Roger, 127
García, Abigail, 175
García, Carlos Alberto, 173
García, Lázaro, 286–287
García, Víctor Manuel, and Cuban modernism, 101
García Buchaca, Edith, 128, 130, 346n.54
García Canclini, Néstor, 136, 341–342n.29, 363n.13
García Espinosa, Julio, 342n.34
García Joya, Mario (Mayito), 77
García Maroto, Gabriel, 154
García Miló, Juan, 156, 159. See also Carol; Grupo Escambray
Garciandía, Flavio, 4, 8, 16, 17, 19–24, 179, 229, 290, 323, 330n.5, 341n.24; exhibitions of, 2, 15, 19–21; in "Volumen I," 3; and "Volumen I" artists' group, 7; influences in , 14; evolution of, 16; and aesthetic issues, 19–21; and kitsch, 22, 24, 202; influences of, on other artists, 70, 193, 194; and Arte en la Fábrica, 116; and hyperrealism, 168; and the ISA, 173; and Grupo Provisional, 180; on Aldito Menéndez, 182; and Marta Pérez Bravo, 216; and Robaldo Rodríguez, 247–248, 249; and ABTV, 251; satirization of, by Adriano Buergo, 296
Goldman, Shifra, on Ana Mendieta, 94, 338n.28

Gómez, Erik, 194
Gómez, Luis, 194, 290
González, Carmelo, 10
González, Juan Enrique (Juan-si), 187
González Litvinov, Eryk, 293
Gorky, Maxim, 169
Gory. See López Marín, Rogelio
Government: policy on the arts, xxvii, xxix, 10, 100, 109, 125–128, 306, 343n.41; and the First National Congress of Education and Culture, 126, 127, 128–133; support of art in Cuba, 136, 171; and the Biennial of Havana, 319–320. See also Art Education; Censorship; Ministry of Culture
Goya, Francisco, 282
Graduate Institute of Art. See ISA
Graffiti, 182
Granma, 131
Gropius, Walter, 150, 151, 316
Group Material, 252
Group Zero, 16
Grupo de Teatro Escambray, 156, 159
Grupo Escambray, 112. See also Carol; García Miló
Grupo Hexágono, 173, 175; and Tonel, 222
Grupo Imán (Magnet Group), 177, 184, 187–188
Grupo Minorista, 102
Grupo Provisional, 129, 177, 178, 183, 236; happenings organized by, 179–181
Grupo Puré, 184–187, 247, 293; and Robaldo Rodríguez, 247
Grupo Reunión, 177, 187. See also Grupo Imán
Grupo "1.2.3 . . . 12," 177, 186–187
Guanahatabey, 35
Guevara, Alfredo, 128
Guevara, Ernesto (Che). See Che Guevara
Guggenheim Fellowship, 92
Guillén, Nicolás, 282

Haacke, Hans, "Homage to" by
   ABTV, 252, 254
Habermas, Jürgen, 317
Happenings, in Cuban art, 173, 177
Hart, Armando, 109, 116, 128, 132,
   347 n.63, 355 n.18; position on art is-
   sues, xxviii, 128, 130, 227; on art
   education, 138–139; and UNEAC,
   193; on art and patriotic symbols,
   359 n.28
Havana Biennial. See Biennial of
   Havana
Haya, María Eugenia (Marucha), 216
Haya de la Torre, Víctor, 143, 147
Hein, Hilde, 311–312
Heredia, José María, 146
Hermanos Ameijeiras Hospital, xxv
Hernández, Abdel, 193, 194; on Rubén
   Torres Llorca, 30; and Proyecto Pi-
   lón, 196
Herrera Ysla, Nelson, 85
Hispaniola, 35
Homophobia, in Cuban policy,
   345 n.48
House of the Young Creator, 186
Houses of Culture, 113, 119. See also
   Casas de cultura
Humboldt, Alexander von, 46
Hyperrealism, 9, 62–63, 168–169

ICAIC (Cuban Institute for Cinematographic Art and Industry), 332–
   333 n.15, 340 n.19; and poster art,
   109–110; art policy of, 127–128
Individualism: in Cuban art, 60, 122;
   and collective responsibility in Cuban art, 318
Iñigo, Angel, 335 n.1
Internationalism, 105, 107, 109, 179;
   and "Volumen I" exhibition, 14. See
   also Abstract expressionism; Bourgeois: aesthetics
ISA (Instituto Superior de Arte), 119,
   167, 168, 169, 171, 175, 186, 187, 222,
   227, 280, 286, 289, 322, 326; and

Marxism-Leninism, 124; origins of,
   159; definition of talent by, 160; economic constraints on, 161, 170, 327;
   approach to art techniques in, 169;
   curricular changes in, 170; graduates of, 173, 211, 215, 247, 255, 276;
   and younger artists of the 1980s,
   179; students of, in Grupo Puré,
   185; José Bedia teaching in, 193; and
   sculpture, 201; and censorship of
   Tomás Esson, 228; entrance require-
   ment, 354 n.9
Itten, Johannes, 151

Jameson, Fredric, 307
Jaruco, 95, 98
Jefferson, Thomas, 146
Jehova's Witnesses, 159
Jiménez, Luis, 14
Juan-si (Juan Enrique González), 187
Juara, José, and opposition to the Cu-
   ban Revolution, 253

Kagan, Mosei, 122, 123, 127, 136
Kahlo, Frida, 94, 213
Kandinsky, Wassily, 151
Kcho (Alexis Leiva), 293
Kepes, Giorgy, 150
Kitsch: in Cuban culture, xxiv–xxv; in
   Cuban art, 15, 17–18, 81; and colo-
   nialism, 17; and Flavio Garciandía,
   22, 24; and Rubén Torres Llorca, 29;
   and Arturo Cuenca, 202–208; and
   Ponjuán and Rodríguez, 255; and
   Adriano Buergo, 296
Klee, Paul, 151
Komar and Melamid, 190, 255
Korda (Alberto Díaz Gutiérrez), 188, 254
Kramer, Margia, 340–341 n.20
Kruger, Barbara, 282
"Kuba O.K." exhibit, 255, 286, 342 n.33

Lam, Wifredo, 70, 153; and Santería, 37;
   early exhibition of, 153; and the ENA,
   156

Lansky, Meyer, xxiv
Lara, Magali, 57, 336n.56
La Rampa, 79
Larson, Kay, on Ana Mendieta, 92
Lastra, Francisco, 180
Lawler, Louise, 255
Leal, César, 12; and Cuban art of the 1970s, 9; artistic devices of, 14; censorship of, 14
Leiseca, Marcia, 133, 258, 331n.7, 347n.63, 361n.55
Leiva, Alexis (Kcho), 293
Lenin, V. I., 11; art theory of, 127
León, Israel, in "Volumen I" exhibit, 3
LeParc, Julio, 163
Levine, Sherrie, 252
Lewitt, Sol, 277
Liberation Theology, 303
Lima, Lezama, 107, 108
Lippard, Lucy, 90, 335n.42
Literacy campaigns, 112, 113, 114
Llanes, Lillian, on the effects of the U.S. blockade of Cuba, 358n.22
López, Alejandro, and Proyecto Pilón, 196
López, Nélida, 9, 161
López Marín, Rogelio (Gory), 5, 9; exhibitions of, 2, 15, 62; in "Volumen I," 3; and "Volumen I" artists' group, 7; censorship of, 14; evolution of and influences on, 60, 62–64; and hyperrealism, 62–63
López Serrano, 141
Los Once, 3, 6, 71, 108, 340n.11; boycott by, 253
Los Papines, 323
Lothe, André, 149
Ludwig, Peter, 342n.33
Lunacharsky, Anatole, 11, 169
Lunes de Revolución magazine, 107, 108, 130

McCarran-Walter Act, 357n.4
Macció, Rómulo, 266
Maceo, Antonio, image of, in the work of Ponjuán and Rodríguez, 256

Machado, Gerardo, 105, 147, 349n.28
Magritte, René, 14, 225, 290; influence of, on Grupo "1.2.3 . . . 12," 187
Mahler, Gustav, 362n.11
Marielitos, 168
Marinello, Felio, 147
Marisol, 261
Markov, Dimitri, 122
Martí, José, 146, 168, 222, 329n.1, 350n.43; and "Testimonial Literature," 9; images of, in Cuban art, 52, 73, 234–235, 337n.6
Martínez, Jose, 365n.20
Martínez, Raúl, 81, 108, 112, 116, 156, 168, 340n.11; influence of, on "Volumen I," 9; career and work of, 70–81; exhibits of, 70–71, 77, 81; and aesthetic issues, 71–72, 108; and Cuban poster art, 73; and U.S. pop art, 76; and interdisciplinary work, 77; as teacher, 81–82; on abstract art and revolution, 125; contact with younger artists, 194; and ABTV, 251, 360n.39
Martínez Estrada, Ezequiel, 117
Marucha (María Eugenia Haya), 216
Marxism, 211, 253–254
Marxism-Leninism: aesthetics, 2, 123; and art criticism in Cuba, 122; and art education in Cuba, 156; and the ISA, 169
Masonry, 146
Massachusetts College of Art, 330n.5, 361n.56
Matta, Roberto Sebastián, 70, 156
Mayito (Mario García Joya), 77
Mederos, René, 250
Meeting of Young Latin American Artists, 6
Melamid, 190, 255
Melero, Alejandro, 153, 350n.42
Mella, Julio Antonio, 349n.28; on education, 147
Memmi, Albert, 141
Mendieta, Ana, 68, 326; career and work of, 89–99; education of and

Mendieta, Ana, 68, 326; career and work of, 89–99; education of and influences on, 90–91, 98–99; and the AIR, 91; politics of, 93; and aesthetic issues, 93–94; sculpture of, 95, 97–98; and Ricardo Rodríguez Brey, 97; and "Volumen I," 98

Mendieta, Carlos, 90

Mendive, Manuel: and *Santería*, 40–41; and ABTV, 253–254

Menéndez, Aldito, 132, 181, 194, 346n.60; on government policy on art, 184; on criticism in art, 198; and censorship, 231; on "young art" and revolution, 354n.7

Menéndez, Aldo, 180, 225, 358n.19; and Cuban art of the 1970s, 9; censorship of, 14; and Grupo Provisional, 180

Mestizaje, 307

Mexican Revolution, 154

Mexican School, in art, 156

Mexico: Cuban artists in, xxvii, 67, 123, 208, 323; influence on Cuban art, 10, 29, 107, 133; and Cuban artists, 58, 82, 94–95; and surrealism in art, 270–271

Microbrigades, 166

Military Units of Production Support (UMAP), 252, 345n.48

Ministry of Culture of Cuba, 114, 360n.42; and organization of exhibits, xxix, 196; promotional effects of, 7; compromises of, 7; role in Cuban art, 128–129; and censorship, 195; and Proyecto Pilón, 197; and Proyecto de las Guaguas, 198

Ministry of the Interior in Cuba, 316

Miranda, Ibrahim, 286

Modernism, and Cuban art, 101–109

Modotti, Tina, 349n.28

Moholy-Nagy, Lazlo, 150

Montserrat School of Visual Arts, 330n.5

Montessori, Maria, 150

Moreno, Hubert, and Proyecto Pilón, 196

Morera, María Elena, 175

Mosquera, Gerardo, 3, 16, 196, 323, 330n.1, 331n.7, 333n.4; influence of, xxv–xxvii, 193; and "Volumen I," 1; and "Six New Painters," 1; on Flavio Garciandía, 20; on José Bedia, 44; on Raúl Martínez, 81, 337n.11; on art and literacy campaigns, 117; on commercialization, 120; on radicalism in art, 124, 168; and Grupo Provisional, 180; on younger artists and the Revolution, 195; on Marta Pérez Bravo, 218; on Tomás Esson, 229; and ABTV, 252; on Segundo Planes, 274; on nationalism and art, 314; on utopianism, 317; on national identity, 331n.6; on prolekult, 353n.65

Movimiento de Aficionados (Amateur Movement), 113, 161, 167

Movimiento 26 de Julio, 130

Moya, Ramón, 355n.1, 357n.1

Mujica Lainez, Manuel, 141

Museum of Fine Arts (Havana), 201, 202

Napoleon, influence of, on education in Latin America, 148

National Association of Innovators and Rationalizers. *See* ANIR

National Council for the Development of Sculpture, 164

National Endowment for the Arts (U.S.A.), 92

Nationalism, 105, 107; in Cuban art, 4, 192; in "Volumen I," 14, 17; and identity in Cuba, 101, 219, 221; and avant-gardism, 104; and official ideology, 109; and ideological dogmatism in art, 126; as espoused by Félix Varela, 146; and Arturo Cuenca, 204; and Tomás Esson, 225–231; and Glexis Novoa, 231–

National Methodology Center, 160
National Museum of Fine Arts (Havana), 201, 202
Navarro, Desiderio, 123, 195
Navarro Padrón, Raúl, 169
Neel, Alice, 103
Neofiguration, 85, 169, 266–267; in Cuban art, 168
"New Art Show." *See* Exposición de Arte Nuevo
New York Council for the Arts, 92
Nicholás, Antonio, 305. *See also* ANIR
Noé, Luis Felipe, 266, 362 n.8
Novoa, Glexis, 178, 179, 196, 231, 233–234, 238, 247, 308, 323; and abstract expressionism, 17; and nationalism, 231–235; art philosophy of, 232; exhibitions of, 235–236; and Carlos Rodríguez Cárdenas, 236; and ABTV, 254. *See also* Grupo Provisional

OAS (Organization of American States), 113
Ocaña, Ernesto, 187
Ochoa, Arnaldo, 316, 321, 365 n.20
Orígenes magazine, 107, 108, 340 n.10
OSPAAAL (Organization of Solidarity with the Peoples of Asia, Africa, and Latin America), 110, 120

Padilla, Heberto, 126, 128, 344 n.47
Padrón, Amado, 365 n.20
Palo, 334 n.39
Palo Monte, 41, 302
Palau, Marta, 163
Panamerican Union, 108
Papanek, Victor, 303
Partido Comunista Cubano. *See* Communist Party of Cuba
Parts Committee, as antecedent to the ANIR, 305
Pavón, Luis, 128

Paz, Octavio, 282
Peláez, Amelia, 107, 153, 315, 358 n.20; impact on art in Cuba, 161; and nationalism, 219; Wifredo Lam on, 358 n.20
Peña, Umberto, 116, 309; government restrictions on, 10; career and work of, 82–89; education of and influences on, 82, 85; and neofiguration, 85; exhibits of 85, 88; contact with other artists, 87–88, 194; and printing aesthetics, 88
Pensamiento Crítico magazine, 127
Pérez Bravo, María Marta, 173, 323; and Afro-Cubanism, 215–219; and Flavio Garciandía, 216; on her art, 218
Pérez Jiménez, Marcos, 108
Pérez Monzón, Gustavo, 15, 64, 282, 323; and "Six New Painters," 1–2; in "Volumen I," 3; evolution of, 16; exhibitions of, 64, 66, 67
Pestalozzi, Johann, 145
Photo-realism, 4, 5, 9, 12, 14
Picabia, Francis, 308
Picúo, and popular kitsch, 18
Pilón, 197
Planes, Segundo, 178, 179, 185, 274–277, 323; work with Ponjuán and Rodríguez, 190; and Jonathan Borofsky's work, 276. *See also* Grupo Provisional
P.M. (film), 108, 125, 130, 340 n.19
Pogolotti, Marcelo, 105
Ponjuán, Eduardo, 133, 178, 190; and René Francisco Rodríguez, 190, 199, 255–260, 322
Pop art, 109, 271
Portinari, Cándido, 10
Portocarrero, René, 107, 153, 155
Portocarrero, Taller, 180, 322
Portuondo, José Antonio, on culture and the Revolution, 344–345 n.47
Poster art: in Cuba, 73, 88, 110, 365 n.19; and the Cuban Revolution, 109–111

Postmodernism: and Cuban art, 298–301; in Latin American art, 309–310; and "appropriation" and poverty, 312–313. *See also* Pseudo-postmodernism

"Prints-trouvés," and José Angel Toirac, 280

Prolekult: ideas of, 169; Gerardo Mosquera on, 353 n.65

Provisional Group. *See* Grupo Provisional

Proyecto de las Guaguas (The Buses Project), 197–198

Proyecto Pilón, 114, 196–197, 355 n.18, 360 n.42; and Lázaro Saavedra, 241

Pseudo-postmodernism, 308–309

Puebla, Carlos, and "testimonial art," 9

Quintana, Ciro, 185, 186, 244, 322, 323; and nationalism, 242–247. *See also* Grupo Puré

Race: in Cuba, 145; Spanish colonial policy regarding, 35; relations, 333–334 n.30

Radio Martí, 321

Rauschenberg, Robert, 114; influence of, on Cuban art, 33, 72; and Arte Calle, 182

Read, Herbert, 156

Reagan, Ronald, 362 n.11

Real Colegio Seminario de San Carlos y San Ambrosio, 145

Realism, as precedent of "Volumen I," 8, 12. *See also* Photo-realism; Socialist realism

Rectification, 129, 164, 316–317, 327; origin and significance of, 165; impact on the arts, xxviii, 166, 175, 192, 322; and vernacular art, 219; and the work of Alexis Somoza, 277, 279

Recycling, in Cuban culture, xxx

Reflection theory, in Marxist-Leninist aesthetics, 2

Reform of Córdoba. *See* Córdoba, Reform of

Regla de Conga. See *Palo Monte*

Regla de Ocha. See *Santería*

"Retrospectiva de Jóvenes Artistas" exhibit, 16

Revista de Avance magazine, 103, 107, 154, 179

Rivera, Diego, 133, 141

Rodríguez, Carlos Rafael, 138, 346 n.54, 351 n.55, 354 n.14; on culture, 81; on dogmatism in art, 130; and UNEAC, 193; on socialist realism, 342–343 n.39

Rodríguez, Emilio, 2

Rodríguez, Fernando, 289–290

Rodríguez, Jorge, 196

Rodríguez, Mariano, 107, 155

Rodríguez, René Francisco, 133, 178, 190; and Eduardo Ponjuán, 190, 199, 255–260, 322

Rodríguez, Robaldo: and nationalism, 247–250; and Grupo Puré, 247; education of, 247–248; artistic devices of, 248–249

Rodríguez, Simón, 142

Rodríguez Brey, Ricardo, 99, 323, 330 n.5; and "Six New Painters," 1–2; in "Volumen I," 3; exhibitions of, 15, 16, 48, 49, 50, 121; and Afro-Cubanism, 46–50; and Alexander von Humboldt, 46–49; artistic devices and aesthetic issues of, 47–50; and *Santería*, 49–50; and Elso Padilla, 50, 56; and Ana Mendieta; 97; and issues of audience, 119

Rodríguez Cárdenas, Carlos, 178, 179, 196, 231, 236, 238, 322, 323; and testimonial art, 9; and nationalism, 236–240; and Glexis Novoa, 236; and censorship, 236, 237; exhibition of, 239–240; influence of Antonio Eligio Fernández on, 240; aesthetic

philosophy of, 240; and ABTV, 255.
See also Grupo Provisional
Rojas, Heber, 160
Rose, Barbara, on Ana Mendieta, 92–93
Rostgaard, Alfredo, on poster art in Cuba, 109

Saavedra, Lázaro, 185, 186, 187, 194, 199, 241–242; exhibition of, 29; and artistic freedom, 132–133; and Rubén Torres Llorca, 194; and Proyecto Pilón, 196, 197, 241; and nationalism, 241–242; and censorship, 328
"Salón Nacional," 108
"Salón Paisaje '82" exhibit, 175
Sánchez, Oswaldo, 173; on bureaucracy, 132; on sex "happening" at UNEAC, 177; on the work of Consuelo Castañeda, 270; on "recontextualization," 307; on art and identity, 309
Sánchez, Tomás, 14; exhibitions of, 2, 4; in "Volumen I," 3; and "Volumen I" artists' group, 7; evolution of and influences on, 10; and hyperrealism, 168
Sánchez Vázquez, Adolfo, 123, 127, 136, 331–332 n.12; aesthetic theories of, 123
"Sano y Sabroso" exhibit (1981), 15, 62
Santamaría, Haydée, 128
Santería, 41, 302, 334 n.39, 336 n.53, 56; and Cuban kitsch, xxv; and Wifredo Lam, 37–40; and Ricardo Rodríguez Brey, 49–50; and Elso Padilla, 52, 56–58, 336 n.55; and Ana Mendieta, 99; in Pilón, 197; and Magdalena Campos, 211–212; and Yemaya, 215; and Marta Pérez Bravo, 217, 218; and Ramón Moya, 357 n.1.
See also Afro-Cubanism
Saura, Antonio, 156
Schnabel, Julian, 308, 362 n.11

School of San Alejandro. *See* Academia de San Alejandro
"School of Mexico," 107
"Six New Painters" exhibit (1977), 1, 14, 24, 64
Slavery: in Cuba under Spanish colonialism, 35; and the arts in Cuba, 37; in Cuba, 146. *See also* race relations
Smithson, Robert, 327
Socialism: relationship of, with art in Cuba, 10, 126, 325; and individualism, 60; in the writings of Aldito Menéndez, 199; and culture, 343–344 n.46; in Cuba, 359 n.28
Socialist humanism, 11
Socialist realism, 9, 168, 250, 331 n.12; influence on Cuban photo-realism, 10; and differences between Cuba and the Soviet Union, 10, 301
Social magazine, 102
Somoza, Alexis, 192, 196, 201, 277, 279; and organization of exhibits, 196, 279; exhibitions of, 264; as an "individualist" artist, 277–279; critique of "Volumen I," 277, 361 n.53
Soto, Leandro, 17, 31, 32, 35, 112, 323; in "Volumen I," 3; and "testimonial art," 9; and kitsch, 34; exhibition of, 35
Soutine, Chaim, 82
Soviet Union: influence on Cuban art, 9, 10, 100, 169, 250; and art education in Cuba, 10, 168, 170; and OSPAAAL, 110; relations of, with Cuba, 126–127, 165, 321; artists of, 190, 255; in the work of Glexis Novoa, 235; images of, in Cuban art, 256; and socialist realism in art, 301; and Russian constructivism, 323
Spanglish, in art, 91, 99
Stolovich, L. I., 122
Street Art. *See* Arte Calle
Student Confederation of Cuba, 147. *See also* Congress of Students in Cuba, First National

Suárez, Amauri, 187
Suárez, Carlos, 168
Suárez, Orlando, 10, 156
Suazo, Félix: and organization of exhibits, 196; exhibitions of, 264
Suter, Gerardo, 163
"Swan Lake": installation by Flavio Garciandía, 20, 249; satirization of, by Adriano Buergo, 296

Taíno, 35
Taller Portocarrero, 180, 322
Tamargo González, Jorge, 329–330 n.2
Taño Carrillo, Ermy, 185
Telarte, 114, 115
Testimonial literature, 9
Third World, issues addressed in Cuban art, 44, 46, 121
Third World Exhibition, 79, 88
Tishenko, Anatole, 168
Toirac, José Angel, 178, 188, 279–282, 312; and Pérez Monzón, 67; and ABTV, 251, 255
Tomás, Angel, 4, 5, 7; review of "Sano y Sabroso" exhibit, 15
Tonel. See Fernández, Antonio Eligio
Torres Llorca, Rubén, 24–30, 247, 323; and "Six New Painters," 1–2; in "Volumen I," 3; exhibitions of, 15, 24, 27, 29; evolution of, 17, 26; and aesthetic issues, 24–25, 30; and artists, 27, 193; and kitsch, 29; and Umberto Peña, 87–88; and the ISA, 173; and Lázaro Saavedra, 194, 241
Trapices, and Umberto Peña, 87
"Trece Artistas Jóvenes" exhibit (1981), 16
Turing, Alan, and theory of fur patterns, 208

UJC (Unión de la Juventud Comunista), 322
UMAP (Military Units of Production Support), 252, 345 n.48
UNEAC (Union of Cuban Writers and Artists), 128, 165, 227, 258; function of, xxviii; 1988 meeting (Fourth Congress), xxviii, 81, 125–126, 130, 135, 138–139, 161, 167, 184, 267, 314, 347 n.65, 354 n.14; and censorship, 131; sex happening at, 173; and Arte Calle happening (1987), 177, 179; and Arte Calle, 184; and younger artists, 192; exhibition at Fourth Congress, 193; membership of, 193, 254 n.14
Unemployment, 163
UNESCO, 358–359 n.22
Unidades Militares de Apoyo a la Producción, 252, 345 n.48
Union of Cuban Writers and Artists. See UNEAC
United States, blockade of Cuba by, xxviii, 298, 314, 351 n.54
University of Massachusetts at Amherst, 330 n.5
University of Puerto Rico at Río Piedras, Museum of, 330 n.5
University of San Jerónimo, 145
Urbanization, and culture in Cuba, 166

Valdés, Elpidio, 22
Valdez, Eliseo, 187
Varela, Carlos, 365 n.21
Varela, Félix, 145, 349 n.24
Vautier, Ben, 362 n.10
Verde Olivo magazine, 128
Vermay, Juan Bautista, 153
Vernacular art in Cuba, 102, 109, 135, 219, 300–301, 330 n.2
Villazón, Ileana, 178, 188; and ABTV, 251
Vitier, Cintio, 107, 134
Vizcaíno, Pedro, 186
"Volumen I" exhibit (1981), 1–3, 60, 161, 172, 188, 201, 325; impact of, xxviii, 3, 4, 5, 15, 16, 100, 173; criticism of, 4; and artists' promotional strategies, 7; antecedents of and influences on, 8–9, 14, 15, 68, 69, 70, 87; art issues

in, 17; and Ana Mendieta, 98; and art education, 138; and Grupo Hexágono, 175; and Grupo Provisional, 178, 179; and younger artists, 192, 277, 361 n.53; and ABTV, 251–252

Warhol, Andy, 63

Yanes, Orlando, 253
Yemaya, 212, 215. See also *Santería*
Yoruba, 362 n.4
Young Communist League, 322
Yunkers, Adja, 103, 339 n.5

Zis, Avner, 127, 346 n.51